Necessary American Fictions

Necessary American Fictions
Popular Literature of the 1950s

William Darby

Bowling Green State University Popular Press
Bowling Green, Ohio 43403

Kodak P.M.T. half tones furnished by Riverhill Publications & Printing, Inc.

Cover design by Gary Dumm

Copyright © 1987 by Bowling Green State University Popular Press
Library of Congress Catalogue Card No.: 86-73250
ISBN: 0-87972-389-0 cb
        0-87972-390-4 pb

Contents

95025

95025

95c

DESIGNED BY GAIL RAGS

POCKET
BOOKS

ALLEN DRURY

ADVISE
& CONSENT

ADVISE AND CONSENT · Allen Drury

Pulitzer Prize novel
smash Broadway
play now filmed by
Otto Preminger

Advise and Consent
Taking the lid off politics (Pocket Books)

Acknowledgements

Without various kinds of assistance the present effort, no matter how worthy or unworthy, would not now be seeing the light.

Professor Finley Hooper, of the Wayne State University History Department, encouraged the project when it was little more than idle scholarly discontent on my part. Professor Hooper challenged me to put thoughts on paper and commented insightfully and exhaustively on these initial drafts. The book and its author owe him a great deal for being not only a teacher and a mentor but also a colleague and a friend.

The late Professors Richard C. Bedford and Philip Traci offered inspiration and pedagogy which undoubtedly helped to shape my approach to this work. Professor John Beard, formerly of Michigan State University and Wayne State University, wisely suggested that I contact my present publisher.

James Monnig, a used bookseller extraordinaire, got me texts when other, more established sources fell short. James R. Panzenhagen graciously assisted in the preparation of the photographs which accompany this text. Ms. Pat Browne and the staff of the Popular Press were consistently helpful and a pleasure to work with.

William L. Darby, my father, helped immeasurably with the least glamorous but most essential task of proofreading. My son David willingly checked footnote references against original sources. I thank them both for their enthusiasm, willingness and care.

Finally, my wife Carolyn needs to be congratulated for putting up with my many moods during the various stages of preparation of this work. Since she still cheerfully speaks to me, and for many other obvious reasons, the book is dedicated to her.

None of these good people is responsible for any of the book's errors in interpretation of judgment which, naturally, belong solely to the author.

A PRIVATE'S MISADVENTURES IN THE
ARMY . . . THE HILARIOUS BEST SELLER
AMERICA LOVES

NO TIME FOR SERGEANTS

BY **MAC HYMAN**

PROFUSELY ILLUSTRATED including scenes
from the Broadway hit, and the great motion picture which stars Andy Griffith, and is a Mervyn
LeRoy Production, presented by Warner Bros.

A SIGNET BOOK COMPLETE AND UNABRIDGED

No Time for Sergeants
The triumph of innocence (Signet)

Chapter 1

Introduction

The 1950s are frequently described as either an inert, an idealistic or a paranoid time in our history; and such views invariably center on Dwight Eisenhower or Joseph McCarthy as representatives of these dominant tendencies. This decade remains the subject of anecdote and reminiscence because scholarship has not yet agreed on a "standard" view of the time. Textbook political history decrees a hiatus for this period so that significant activity seems to cease shortly after the dismissal of Douglas MacArthur by Harry Truman in April, 1951, and only resumes with the inauguration of John F. Kennedy in January, 1961. This distortion is paralleled by a nostalgic perception epitomized in such television fare as *Happy Days* or the cult status accorded to certain rock-and-roll performers. Still other critics and historians, eager to decry the Cold War excesses of the period, find it dominated by the Senator from Wisconsin and John Foster Dulles. The reality, of course, is more and less than any single interpretation would make it. The 1950s contained a fair share of perplexing incidents and individuals, so that any rigidly systematic reading goes beyond usefulness.

I will delineate certain popular beliefs of the 1950s by examining its bestselling novels. Such works are generally dismissed as opportunistic flatterings of vulgar taste or reduced to reflections of sociological truths better established elsewhere. While I shall treat fifty popular novels from the 1950s as evidence of that period's cultural values, I would hope, in part, to extend a greater respectability to an area that criticism and scholarship too easily dismiss. The movies loom large in my treatment, for most of these novels have come down to us through their cinematic versions; thus, Fred Zinneman's 1953 film rendering of *From Here to Eternity* is probably fresher than James Jones' 1951 novel for most readers. While the relationships between films and novels would require a separate book, common values color both media so that invoking well-known films to discuss the decade's novels becomes essential.

While I am not concerned with the personal or commercial motives which might underlie the creation and distribution of popular fiction, I am convinced that bestselling fiction serves as an intellectual barometer for a culture. Such novels are "necessary" because they reaffirm and often "sanctify" pre-existing values, especially for an audience which often attributes unquestioned authority to the printed word. Whether bestsellers reflect, follow or create popular taste is an issue that I shall try to avoid, for delineating the values surrounding politics, war, sex, the home, adolescence and work in these novels is a more than sufficient task. I believe that presenting popular values, while relying of necessity on the discrimination of the individual observer, represents a necessary step to a more sophisticated understanding of America in the 1950s.

Bestselling novels embody familiar generic and plot structures which often constitute their immediate attraction to the audience. Such familiar formula pieces as the hard-boiled detective story, the melodramatic western, the grandiose historical novel and the sentimental woman's fiction abound in 1950s bestseller lists. Indeed, Mickey Spillane follows in the tracks of Dashiell Hammett, Raymond Chandler and James M. Cain; Louis L'Amour succeeds Zane Grey and Max Brand; Frank Yerby follows Lew Wallace and Margaret Mitchell; and Frances Parkinson Keyes succeeds Fanny Hurst.

Critical interest in such formula productions generally centers on the variations that individual writers invoke on such familiar material. Thus, one could argue that the different sentiments and values of Lloyd Douglas' *Magnificent Obsession* (1929) and Morton Thompson's *Not As a Stranger* (1954) are more significant than their similarities of plot and characterization. It is, finally, the very familiarity of generic productions which enables one to see the period in which they are created reflected so strongly — a process that the movies most readily exhibit. In five films that deal with Wyatt Earp, Doc Holliday and the gunfight at O.K. Corral, made over thirty-five year period, neither Tombstone nor the historical West but contemporary moods are the real subjects. *Frontier Marshall* (1939), *My Darling Clementine* (1946),*The Gunfight at the O.K. Corral* (1957), *Hour of the Gun* (1968) and *Doc* (1971) reflect their own times' preoccupations in the guise of a familiar tale. Thus, the melodrama of the first film (with Randolph Scott as Earp), which accords with a need for moral certainty in a pre-war world, gives way to the nostalgia of the second (with Henry Fonda), the sense of Cold War duty in the third (with Burt Lancaster), the revolutionary cynicism of the fourth (with James Garner) and the post-Vietnam sense of despair in the fifth (with Stacy Keach now portraying Holliday as the leading character). These variations suggest that popular media serve as weathervanes recording shifts in value and mood in the culture at large.

Bestselling novels often contain rambling plots which follow the dynamics of soap opera so that each installment (or chapter) presents a physical or emotional crisis. The characters overcome one difficulty (always by actions rather than thought) only to fall into another and, because these incidents generally do not produce wisdom in the characters, it is not unusual to have bestselling novels run to enormous lengths. The very nature of such narrative implies that such reading is escapist; however, it is perhaps too easy to dismiss such "entertainment" as artistically worthless. Books often please us on a visceral level that cannot readily be explained so that expecting every work of fiction to resemble *War and Peace* or *Ulysses* asks too much. If anything, elaborate plots often wear better in novels that did not receive critical praise or even notice (e.g. *Mandingo*) than in more heralded efforts (e.g. *Hawaii* or *Exodus*).

For the most part, 1950s' bestsellers extoll middle-class and melodramatic manners and morals through plot, character, incident and symbol. An initial common thread in them is the primacy of emotion over reason: the reader is constantly urged to follow his or her heart rather than his or her head in important matters. While such an equation has long been a staple of popular thinking, America in the 1950s, with its outbreak of anti-intellectual fervor during Senator McCarthy's heyday, was extremely fertile soil for such views. Even characters like J.D. Salinger's Holden Caulfield and Sloan Wilson's Tom Rath ultimately trust their emotions rather than their ideas because they are convinced that feeling leads to happiness.

Closely allied to this notion is the belief that life imposes problems rather than conditions on the individual. This attitude, reflective of the optimism and prosperity of the mid-fifties, posits that troubles invariably have solutions which the individual can discover (usually by looking within himself). Even the extreme condition of death is overcome when Elaine Schuyler, the widowed heroine of Harold Robbins' *Never Leave Me* (1954), commits suicide to resolve her romantic dilemma and so choose between the living hero and her dead husband and family. This middle-class outlook is further reflected by the frequent implication that moral matters are questions of degree and not of kind. Thus, although the sexual drives of Frances Parkinson Keyes' and Grace Metalious' female characters are stylistically opposed, more sobering possibilities—simple disinterest in romance or satiation with sex—are never considered. These fictional heroines either get married or gladly suffer the proverbial fate worse than death.

A final recurrent value is that the ordinary man can become a hero, or at least exhibit extraordinary capacity in a crisis. America's long infatuation with individualism (a paradox given the country's increasingly bureaucratic and impersonal social arrangements) is reaffirmed by James Michener's Lieutenant Brubaker (in *The Bridges at Toko-ri*), Evan Hunter's Richard Dadier (in *The Blackboard Jungle*) and Louis L'Amour's Hondo Lane (in *Hondo*). These common men endure lasting tension and perform momentary acts of bravery; indeed, because of the static nature of the Cold War, such heroes had to embody both kinds of courage in struggling with North Koreans, juvenile delinquents and the Apache.

We should approach the vexing question of an individual book's enormous (and often unjustified in terms of literary merits) popularity by realizing that the creativity of a Grace Metalious is as inimitable as that of a William Faulkner. The popular success of a *Peyton Place* (1956), when compared to contemporary efforts with equal doses of prurience without comparable commercial acclaim, ultimately rests on the mystery of creativity. Metalious' narrative is not merely more "daring" but it also conveys a sense of total artistic and intellectual engagement. An imagination operating at its full stretch, even over such unsophisticated material, is an engaging situation for even cycnical specatators. One may come away from *Peyton Place,* Harold Robbins' *79 Park Avenue* (1955) or Leon Uris' *Battle Cry* (1953) without having gained great insights into human nature, yet the reader has been caught up in the fictional situations of these works.

The problem of selection for this undertaking was solved, as most difficulties are, through compromise. Finding a reasonable number of novels represented the major obstacle. To discuss every work that appeared on established bestseller lists for the 1950s would have been an admirable exercise in scholarly thoroughness; however, as Andrew Marvell noted, the pressures of "world and time" quickly curb such zeal. A discussion of more than two hundred novels would cause most readers to be quickly awash (if not drowning) in a sea of detail. While the number of novels selected for this survey may sound gimmicky ("fifty from the Fifties"), my sample is large enough and popular enough to substantiate the generalizations underlying the bulk of the book. Thirty-seven of these novels are listed in Alice Payne Hackett's *80 Years of Bestsellers* as the leading sellers in total copies, while the remaining thirteen titles were chosen for their continuing popular association with the 1950s.[1] Six of these thirteen were on Hackett's yearly bestseller lists,[2] while the remaining seven represent a more personal selection based on their prominence as films,[3] ideological stances,[4] or success with later audiences.[5]

Two other principles governed the selection of the novels: (1) they had to have been originally published between 1950 and 1959, thus some bestsellers which were published prior to that time—Lloyd Douglas' *The Robe* (1942), Thomas Costain's *The Silver Chalice* (1948) and Jack Schaefer's *Shane* (1949)—were omitted; (2) the authors had to be Americans, so that Daphne Du Maurier's *My Cousin Rachel* (1952), Annemarie Selenko's *Desirée*, (1953), Boris Pasternak's *Doctor Zhivago* (1958) and, perhaps most regrettably, Vladimir Nabokov's *Lolita* (1958) were excluded. Since my aim is to present the leading popular ideas expressed in bestselling fiction, total sales rather than yearly popularity have taken precedence. Seventeen of the first thirty-seven titles do not appear on any yearly list in Hackett; indeed, only two of the top ten bestsellers of the decade, *Peyton Place* and *Exodus*, appear on such compilations. This disparity suggests that sales longevity is not always sustained, while literary taste often governs bestseller lists through discreetly removing works like *My Gun is Quick* (1950) or *Mandingo*. While total sales figures may distort the contemporary popularity of a given book, the relaxing of censorship standards in the late 1950s suggests that the earlier novels of Spillane, Robbins and Huie enjoyed larger sales than the "official" lists would reflect.

The sales of J.D. Salinger's *The Catcher in the Rye* (1951), on the other hand, have been considerably augmented by later readers so that one may question its lofty status within the 1950s. However, the continuing popularity of this novel, which still gets regularly removed from high school library shelves, implies its warm initial reception. One needs to realize that in the 1950s the compiling of bestseller lists was guided by a public morality more guarded than today's. The censoring of bestseller lists represents an attempt to comply with the social and intellectual standards of decorum (always a prominent concern in a business, like publishing, which must placate public opinion) rather than to satisfy the subsequent interests of historians or critics. Thus, there was a literary underground in which Spillane, Robbins and their imitators (Richard Prather, John Farris, Brett Halliday) existed comfortably alongside the official literary world.

Since I was seventeen when the 1950s ended, I was no doubt influenced by the ideas of that period, albeit, my perspectives on life and literature have hopefully changed, although perhaps not improved, with the passage of time. Thus, on one level this book attempts to see how my memories of certain 1950s' novels stack up against the actual works. In what follows I have tried to balance a natural affection for the fictions of my youth (hallowed by memory) with the more critical insights that later training has bred. My primary critical allegiance must be to E. M. Forster's *Aspects of the Novel* which supplies a broad enough basis so that even bestsellers can be judged without blushing.

Although tone may reveal individual bias more powerfully than any direct statement, I would forewarn the reader that the woman's novel— the works of Anya Seton, Frances Parkinson Keyes and Irving Stone—has probably been given short shrift. I do so because there remains an indelible gap between the ways in which men and women perceive the world; and I would be foolhardy (in this age of women's lib) to claim that the female psyche was an open book to me. Like Michener's sailors in *Tales of the South Pacific* (1947) who looked at every bit of naked female flesh because no man can ever learn enough about women, I must continue to struggle with the elucidation of what is, I fear, a permanent mystery. The same reservation might have accompanied my readings of Grace Metalious and Rona Jaffe, but I find myself more comfortable with their cynical views of human nature. The traditional woman's novel, with its emphases on marriage and social conduct, exhibits values that I find less amiable; yet I do not wish to dismiss Seton, Keyes and Stone as outdated, for their idealism undoubtedly spoke to many in the 1950s and still strikes responsive chords today.

Compulsion, Hondo, The Man in the Gray Flannel Suit, The View From Pompey's Head, The Revolt of Mamie Stover, The Best of Everything and *Anatomy of a Murder* surprised or delighted me. I found myself disenchanted with *The Caine Mutiny, East of Eden, Advise and Consent, The Cardinal* and *Hawaii* because they seemed unconscionably long in an effort to be "profound." I found Mickey Spillane infinitely more intriguing than I had been led to believe, Harold Robbins to possess a genuine talent for narrative (i.e. he reads "easily") and Grace Metalious to be absorbing because of her sincerity. I am also convinced that James Jones' *From Here to Eternity* should share equal status with *The Catcher in the Rye* and *Invisible Man* among contemporary readers and critics. Indeed, Jones' masterpiece has only one flaw—it does not fit the traditional college syllabus because of its length.

The organization of the twelve chapters which follow is undoubtedly less schematic than academic scholarship would approve. The chapters on Mickey Spillane (2) and James Jones (13) are designed to counterpoint each other with the melodramatic certainties of the former's fictional world standing in sharp contrast to the tragic perplexities portrayed in *From Here to Eternity*. Chapters 3 and 4 take up novels concerned with war— World War II as a collective expression of American idealism and the Cold War as a ubiquitous phenomenon going beyond any recognizable battlefield. Closely allied to these subjects are the "epic" novels of chapter 5 which delineate man in history. Sex and love, often coupled in popular 1950s' thought, are the subjects of the next two chapters (6 and 7), while the struggles of adolescence and the need for domesticity are central to chapters 8 and 9. Two popular phobias—psychology and racism—are treated in chapters 10 and 11, while work, the pressures of having a career or finding a "calling," is the subject of chapter 12.

The reader will quickly realize that this scheme is a convenient way of organizing perceptions rather than a profoundly rigorous delineation of the subject matter of these novels. While these chapters focus on what appear to be the primary interests of the various novels they contain, certain other emphases spill over so that sex, love, work and adolescence may be discussed in the treatment of a single novel. In addition, I have attempted to present the novels within a single chapter in terms of their allegiance to customary middle-class ways of seeing the world. I have therefore tried to juxtapose traditional efforts (e.g. *The Bridges at Toko-ri*) to more skeptical and critical treatments (e.g. *The Manchurian Candidate*) in terms of the primary emphasis being treated. Once again, this scheme is more suggestive than rigorous, for my primary effort throughout has been to let these novelists speak in their own words and so reveal some of the intellectual complexity that was America in the 1950s.

Chapter 2

"Why couldn't they act like men and fight with me?"

If pornography's real subject matter is violence rather than sex, Mickey Spillane's novels have no redeeming value. Since his initial work (*I, the Jury*, 1947), critics have dismissed Spillane's writings as lamentable proofs that one can never underestimate mass taste. Spillane has been consistently treated as a fortunate hack whose formulas were "low" enough to titillate popular subconscious and prurient fantasies. Thus, his hard-boiled 1950s' detective novels, five of which feature Mike Hammer, are regarded as destructive wish fulfillments, bastions of reactionary political values, or pornographic daydreams of sex and violence. Commentators also deplore Spillane's style with its clichéd expressions and character types. Yet, despite such objections, these works retain a freshness that many more celebrated 1950s' novels have long since lost. The Mike Hammer stories epitomize facets of popular American thinking, especially its need for melodramatic certainties to offset disturbing political pressures, while containing more artistry than critics have allowed.

Melodrama demands stereotypical characters and ritualized situations, and can easily be seen in a film like *Shane* (1953) where good guys are always pure and bad guys are always sullied. Should Shane (Alan Ladd) openly express his love for Mrs. Starrett (Jean Arthur), or the hired killer (Jack Palance) display any sympathetic traits, the entire fabric would collapse for then the climax, in which Palance's violent death is obligatory, becomes an occasion for doubt and dismay rather than cheering. The killing of one compromised character by another would force the audience to confront the moral dilemma of tragedy, a much more perplexing problem than any found in melodrama. Since we do not cheer if an ostensible hero proves to be a cad (John Wayne as a rapist) or laugh if buffoons turn into thinkers (Laurel and Hardy as Hamlet and Claudius), any suggestion of contradictory levels in stereotyped characters must be dealt with judiciously by a formula writer like Spillane. However, much of our enduring pleasure in such standardized productions arises nor merely from seeing a familiar ritual but from noticing how the individual creator plays with the generic conventions. As we shall see, Spillane maneuvers his melodramatic material to modify and enhance an otherwise standardized product.

7

His repetitive plots reflect Spillane's disinterest in detection per se; for him, as for Dashiell Hammett and Raymond Chandler, hard-boiled detective fiction centers on personality and locale. Spillane has insisted that a "book isn't plot, a book is characterization"[1]; and the Hammer novels do not develop character so much as, in accepted melodramatic fashion, reveal it. The typical Spillane plot uses its all-too-familiar characters in a five-stop ritual.

1. Exposition
Hammer meets the victim who immediately elicits his sympathy and dies violently shortly thereafter. The protagonist decides to seek revenge for the victim and then searches unceasingly for the causes of the latter's death (the quest).
2. The Respectable Partner
Hammer soon meets a "pillar of society" (a philanthropist, a banker, a would-be United States Senator) who offers to help but turns out to be the cause of the initial murder. Three of these figures are (apparently) women who approach Mike on both seductive and business levels.
3. Complication
A lengthy search for the immediate cause of the crime follows. In this process Mike is aided by Velda, his faithful secretary, and Pat Chambers, a homicide detective. Other helpers, usually women so smitten by Hammer's animal magnetism that they gladly do his bidding, often die because of the dangers in which the detective unwittingly places them. This section centers on looking for what Alfred Hitchcock calls the "MacGuffin"—the apparent reason for the crime (e.g. incriminating photographs, narcotics, scientific secrets).
4. The False Climax
Hammer sadistically annihilates those who seem to control the organizations (e.g. the Mafia, the Communist Party, a blackmail ring) responsible for the initial killing. These characters sometimes die before Hammer can administer his own brutal justice.
5. The Real Climax
Mike realizes that a character who has gained his trust has been responsible for the initial murder. These final, explicitly graphic confrontations are the scenes toward which Spillane has pointed his entire narrative. The master criminals are destroyed violently (two are burned, one is shot by a playful infant, one is stripped and then shot, one is strangled) in situations which uncloud the mysteries (which are always logically opaque, if not outright inexplicable). Hammer delivers a sadistic diatribe that adds emotional release as well in these sections.

Spillane's standard cast, in addition to the impervious detective, the resourceful secretary and the accommodating policeman, includes: (1) Mr. Big, a crime czar who hides behind an elaborate social front and voluntarily consorts with Mike (often even hiring the hero to investigate the very murder he had brought about); (2) the Dame whose sexual appetite causes her to help Mike in perilous circumstances; (3) the Hoodlum who runs the day-to-day racket and proves a coward when confronted by Spillane's hero.

Gore Vidal, reviewing the ten best-selling novels of 1973, offers a useful interpretive key to popular works when he insists that the "novels under review...reflect to some degree the films each author saw in his formative years."[2] Certainly the Hammer novels of the 1950s are marked by the same ambience that movie critics have discerned in film noir. Many of the motifs, settings and characters Spillane uses would fit comfortably into such films as *Double Indemnity* (1944), *Mildred Pierce* (1945), *Dark Passage* (1947) and *The Lady from Shanghai* (1948). These films which consistently avoid natural light and locations imply that man inhabits a sinister and incomprehensible world. Moving through these arenas of night and death are insurance agents, ex-soldiers, private eyes and escaped convicts who appear outwardly cynical about the the personal and social corruption that engulfs them. The emasculating female, Joan Crawford as Mildred Pierce or Rita Hayworth as Mrs. Bannister in *The Lady from Shangai,* combines sexual promise with the threat of death.

The protagonist in film noir, for personal or professional reasons, must discover who is responsible for a crime, usually murder. Humphrey Bogart as an escaped, but innocent, convict seeks the truth about his wife's death in *Dark Passage* so that he can be free both personally and psychologically, while Edward G. Robinson, as an insurance investigator in *Double Indemnity,* pursues the truth as an obligation to his craft. These searchers inhabit a world where character emerges against a background of roadhouses, office buildings and apartments barely lit by auto headlights or neon signs, and they are driven because "understanding the dark past and making some sense of it are essential to the film noir hero."[3] Nobility attaches to these cynical urban knights errant for whom discovering personal identity or the cause of society's ills takes precedence over conformity or compromise.

Mike Hammer inhabits the same urban setting and, like the heroes of film noir, seeks the truth, even though his quest inevitably leads to danger and compulsive behavior. In a universe dominated by bars, apartments and offices in sinister shadow, Hammer must often sleep until noon to recuperate from the physical and emotional batterings he endures in the night world—breakfast is only prominently treated once in these novels. Spillane's hero constantly meets compulsive women whose sexual appetites threaten to divert the protagonist from his goal. Hammer naturally refrains from excessive involvements with these oh-so-willing ladies and, in so doing, creates a sadistic diversion for the audience. Hammer denies the call of the flesh because he implicitly believes sexual energy must not be "spent" recklessly. Mike must withstand master criminals, beautiful models, willing secretaries and the accommodating Velda, all of whom want him as a stud. While he occasionally obliges, Hammer ultimately remains true to his higher calling and to Velda, who represents love *and* marriage.

My Gun is Quick (1950) compares the inhabitants of the modern nightmare city to the ancient Romans and their Colosseum with lions assaulting unarmed men serving as the appropriate metaphor for surrounding society. Mike, while discussing an investigation with Pat Chambers, declares: " 'They talk about the Romans. They only threw human beings into a pit with lions. At least then the lions had a wall around them so they couldn't get out. Here they hang out in bars and on street corners looking for a meal.' "[4] This comparison lends a literary respectability to Spillane's undertaking (a weakness he shares with more celebrated American novelists like Herman Melville and Jack London.) In urging that the environment is parasitic, the hard-boiled protagonist obscures the possibility that life is surrounded by existential absurdities involving choice and conduct. Hammer's proclamation that the world may be desolate is compromised by his ruthless efficiency in his quest. The audience perceives that success in the hero's world of darkness and hoodlums depends on physical prowess, a devil-may-care bravado and the right questions. Despite the gloomy atmosphere, Hammer shows that rugged individualism inevitably triumphs over impersonal corporate power and organized crime.

My Gun is Quick opens with a long aside in which the Colosseum, the arch symbol of human depravity, leads Hammer to speak of the joys of voyeurism. Spillane's hero painstakingly distinguishes between the second-hand life in books and the real existence of the city's streets. Mike chides the reader for wanting to escape from daily trivialities. "Fun isn't it? You read about life on the outside thinking of how maybe you'd like it to happen to you, or at least how you'd like to watch it.... Oh it's great to watch all right. Life through a keyhole."[5] Hammer thus mocks the audience's voyeurism, while suggesting that we, like spectators in a darkened theatre, are seeing life through a keyhole. This contradictory process distinguishes the reading audience from society-at-large (i.e. those who don't understand the ethical implications that Hammer puts forth) so that the hero's initial abuse quickly focuses on a larger target. The detective's aside rapidly turns into a plea that the fiction which follows portrays reality: "But remember this: there are things happening out there. They go on every day and night making Roman holidays look like school picnics."[6] Hammer ends by asserting his own prowess in dealing with this nightmare. Like the searchers in film noir, Mike must seek for answers because he cannot live with himself until he finds the truth and exacts retribution. Unlike the reader, Mike deals with people as they really are and, given his brand of violent justice, rights the situation. Thus, the hero possesses a power to act that the reader conspicuously lacks. There is also a subtle prurient note here, for we are being forewarned about knowledge that is apt to be harmful. Like Eve, we can be tempted into acting against our best (i.e. "ignorant") interests; and, by implication, Spillane's view of man as an inherently obstinate rebel emerges for the first time.

Given their clawing, predatory state, the city's streets are naturally crowded with hoodlums and punks to whom Hammer (like the more contemporary Dirty Harry) represents a "tin god" because he carries a gun.[7] In *The Long Wait* (1951) respectable society, which Hammer spoke of as "out there" in the beginning of *My Gun is Quick*, takes on the aura of a prison. The amnesiac protagonist, Johnny McBride, visits a bank run by Gardiner (this novel's Mr. Big) and recognizes why the man he has sworn to revenge fled such an environment.

Now it was easy to see why he took to the outdoors. You got dirty, rained on, cursed at and worked to death, but at least you were free. There was plenty of air around you.

Gardiner took me to the door, unlocked it, passed me through the grillwork outside and walked across the hall to the front door beside me. The animals in their cages stopped talking and tried to make like they were very busy.[8]

This contrast between natural outdoor freedom and unnatural indoor confinement accentuates the grim, urban environment in all these novels. Gardiner surrounds himself with timeservers for whom he is the symbolic jailer. *Kiss Me, Deadly* (1952) extends this motif by portraying the city as a "sprawling octopus whose mouth was hidden under a horribly clawed beak."[9] When seen as a ravenous mouth, the city, like the numerous femme fatales, becomes an obstruction to Hammer's realizing his quest.

The conflict between surroundings and hero inevitably works in Hammer's favor. The detective can see that Manhattan reeks of death.

> The river was gray in color, not the rich blue it should have been, and the foam that followed the wake of the ships passing by was too thick. Almost like blood. In close to shore it changed to a dirty brown trying to wash the filth up on the banks. It was pretty if you only stopped to look at it, but when you look too close and thought enough it made you sick.[10]

In keeping with Hammer's personality, this passage reflects the same dichotomous, melodramatic thinking which introduced *My Gun is Quick*: the detective is separated from the audience because he sees deeper into things. Hammer can withstand, and so vicariously present, reality. This portrayal of death and destruction as wet, clammy water should sicken the average reader, but Mike obviously has greater strength. For him, the city can be maneuvered and, at last, overcome. Its sidewalks reflect the heartlessness and parasitical nature of society, but Spillane's hero never doubts that he is master of the scene. "The city. The monster. It laughed at me, but it was the kind of a laugh that didn't sound too sure of itself any more."[11] In animating the sinister city, Hammer makes it psychologically manageable; since it embodies human attributes like laughter, the environment can be dominated just as criminals can be. Hammer's retort thus becomes an intellectual scheme to render terror subject to the same chance which governs men.

A closely allied motif presents the underworld as a coherent network from which valuable information can be gathered, as opposed to public and police officials who fail to act or fall foul of their own red tape. Hammer searches the underworld because only there can identities be established and contacts made with the proper people. In *Kiss Me, Deadly*, for example, two hired killers trail Mike through Manhattan and Hammer, eager to tangle with these assailants, goes from bar to bar proclaiming his availability to the stool pigeons who are the underworld's grapevine. The message here echoes that of the celebrated film *The Godfather* (1972)—if you want something done efficiently deal with criminals. Hammer, of course, also preys on this outlaw society because its haunts are places where "nobody smart went even on a slumming party, but...where people who knew people could be found and gotten drunk enough to spill over a little excess information if the questions were put right."[12] While such sources being available to the lone investigator represents a familiar element in the private eye genre, the larger implication is that the world is more rational than it seems. The underworld operates not simply to account for and smooth over coincidences and plot lapses but, more important, as a reassurance to the reader that society is made up exclusively of good and evil, rather than nebulously gray, individuals.

Because Hammer's world contains only moral absolutes, he can describe his opponents in derogatory terms; and, thus, like many World War II vintage films with their stereotyped Nazi and Japanese sadists and cowards, Spillane's novels present evil as so personally inferior as to detract unwittingly from the efforts of the hero. If Hammer's enemies are really the morons he describes, why does crime exist at all? If the communists are such puerile antagonists, why does America allow their threat to continue? Spillane does not pursue the logical implications of such character drawing; indeed, if he did, he might lose much of his audience which wants to be reassured about the melodramatic certainties of their world. In providing his customers with what they want, Spillane has a would-be killer faint in *My Gun is Quick* when Hammer merely leans over and shows that he too is armed.[13] In *Kiss Me, Deadly*, Mike delights in imagining how his bloody justice will bring down the opposition: "I was dreaming of a slimy foreign secret army that held a parade of terror under the Mafia label and laughed at us with our laws and regulations and how fast their damned smug expressions would change when they saw the fresh corpses of their own kind day after day."[14] Hammer preaches a holy war on this organization and urges that its members, like all the other criminals he has encountered, cannot face a day-in, day-out struggle. Thus, in the long run, the good guys (the Americans) will outlast all the bad guys (including the communists) because the latter lack the guts for total war.

The enigma of such cowards being in control leads Hammer to appeal to the magical power of money, a talisman whose possession allows even perverted people to have their way. Capitalistically-generated wealth should ordinarily insure its owners against the critical temptations of the world, yet the bad guys are often rich and unredeemed. For Hammer this shortcoming has, at least in part, been caused by so many of the villains coming from outside the pale of American society. "The Mafia. The stinking slimy Mafia. An oversized mob of ignorant, lunk-headed jerks who ruled with fear and got away with it because they had the money to back themselves up."[15] The equation of his enemies with "slime" is an obvious verbal device; however, such insults make Hammer's enemies seem childish, if not unreal, to anyone who finds melodrama an inadequate perception of the world.

In reflecting the conspiratorial mentality of political life in the early 1950s, Spillane's hero becomes most rabid when he struggles with the communists in *One Lonely Night* (1951). As he infiltrates this group—an act requiring only a minimum of daring, given the myopia of the Reds—Hammer constantly notes the personal and emotional defects of these would-be world conquerors. When he sees them indoctrinating the unwary he refers to the communists as "lumps" of "vomit" and "Judas sheep" who are wolves in other clothing. The all-seeing protagonist remarks that these villains "had a jackal look of discontent and cowardice, a hungry look that said you kill while we loot, then all will be well with the world."[16] Like many a more critically respected novelist (Joseph Conrad, Henry James, Ayn Rand), Spillane caricatures revolutionary ideology by presenting its exponents as malicious hypocrites or gullible ignoramuses. While it might be comforting to believe in such simplistic villainy, it is difficult to take such naive character drawing seriously, for Korea and Viet Nam suggest that even communists have motives other than greed or stupidity.

Spillane's style occasionally shows the vitality of street argot. In expressions such as "bug mills" (whorehouses) and "squat box" (electric chair) the novelist adds a flourish to the mundane tone with which he normally surrounds his characters. Unfortunately, the Hammer novels, unlike those of Raymond Chandler, do not abound with such ingenious expressions, so that such gaucheries as the villains' names become too noticeable. Spillane gives his gangsters names that reduce them to comic status; indeed, only the most naive reader can seriously question how Mike (the) Hammer will fare against such opponents as Feeny Last, Dinky Williams, Ed Teen, Lou Grindle and Toady Link. In each instance melodrama triumphs, for the individual character embodies a cowardly, weak or malevolent image before his initial appearance. Feeny Last suggests fiendishness and extinction, Dinky Williams implies impotence, Ed Teen connotes immaturity, while Lou Grindle exudes witchcraft and children's fairy tales. Toady Link best epitomizes this pattern, for his name shows both his connection with the underworld (link) and his basic nature (toady). While one is reminded of the comic strips by such devices, the theme of the subservient nature of men in organizations also emerges. Spillane's names thus underpin one of the more serious value judgments contained within the Hammer novels.

These works further abound with examples of bureaucratic inefficiency and corruption and, once again, Mike, in telling off such incompetents, provides a vicarious satisfaction for the audience. This psychological one-upmanship most clearly surfaces in the detective's dealing with the District Attorney, a figure who lacks a personal name and so remains the embodiment of an office rather than emerging as an individual. The District Attorney always insists that Hammer's presence at the scene of a murder should lead to the revocation of the hero's professional license. Their confrontations reveal the public official to be a vindictive, tongue-tied sycophant whom Mike has no compunction about insulting. The flunkies who surround him further signal the District Attorney's incompetence: "It was quite a gathering. The D.A straddled his throne with two assistant D.A.'s flanking him, a pair of plainclothesmen in the background and two more over the the window huddled together for mutual protection apparently."[17] Clearly, the beleaguered official needs all the support he can get when talking to Hammer because the detective is too dynamic to be faced alone. Mike's description, with its emphases on sycophancy and trappings (the "throne"), flatters the popular notion that bureaucrats need to hold each others' hands constantly. Such a view implies that Hammer's one-man crusade is directed against both criminal and governmental institutions. Bureaucratic wastefulness once more becomes apparent when the hero receives an official letter revoking his license in *Kiss Me Deadly*. The detective notes that the "letterhead was all very official and I was willing to bet that for the one sheet they sent me a hundred more made up the details of why the thing should be sent."[18] Thus, public officials are parasites and idlers who indulge in wasteful red tape to prove their own power.

Bureaucrats are also stupid, as one sees time after time when Hammer confronts the police. Unless Pat Chambers is present, such meetings reveal sadism and stupidity to be the cops' standard operational procedures. While Pat remains exempt because he and Mike used to work together and still share a genuine concern for justice (although even Pat occasionally moves too slowly for the zealous protagonist), the other police are shortsighted bullies and timeservers who, when facing Hammer, run away like dogs with their tails between their legs. In *Vengeance is Mine* (1950) three policemen search Mike's apartment and one of them tries roughing up the hero; however they (unbelievably!) lack a search warrant and so the protagonist orders them out and indulges his passion for verbal rage. Just as one sadistic cop is about to smash his face, Mike's quick and sour tongue comes to the rescue.

> "Where's your warrant?" I demanded easily. "Show me your warrant to come in my house and do that, then I'll talk, you yellow-bellied little bastard. I'm going to meet you in the street not long from now and carve that sissified pasty face of yours into ribbons. Get out of here and kiss yourself some fat behinds like you're used to doing. I'll be all right in a few minutes and you better be gone by then and your stooges with you. They're not cops. They're like you...political behind-kissers with the guts of a bug and that's not a lot of guts. Go on, get out, you crummy turd."[19]

Such bureaucratic fumblers epitomize a government that is often corrupt and compromised. Like the hoodlums who run the criminal organizations Hammer takes on, these officials and their subordinates lack the courage and quick wits to fight man-to-man.

Elected officials who maneuver the system to loot it are a greater evil. Hammer views the democratic electoral process as a means by which the little man is robbed by protected legions of crooks in Washington. Spillane's hero shares this paranoid view of government with the other good characters he encounters. Thus, one finds Marty Kooperman, a reporter who offers to help Hammer in *One Lonely Night*, giving his support because, " 'I'm just another little guy who's sick of being booted around the block by the bastards who get themselves elected to public office and use that office to push their own wild ideas and line their pockets.' "[20] Why such "bastards" get elected in the first place is never addressed; at best, Hammer urges that the public does not understand politics and that newspapers pursue headlines rather than information. Spillane's protagonist once more reassures for he, like the majority of the audience, openly resents government red tape and bureaucrats who don't function.

Hammer's vigilante outlook allows him to defy and rant about a world whose custodians are bumbling fools. When he undertakes a personal vendetta against the Mafia, Mike insists that a resourceful individual brings chance into any situation and can tip the odds in his favor merely by risking his life. Hammer stands in marked contrast to Gary Cooper's famous besieged sheriff in *High Noon* (1952), for Spillane's hero eagerly embraces his uneven duels with crime while Will Kane went stolidly, if regrettably, into his shoot-out with the returning outlaws. In a passage echoing conventional American beliefs in self-reliance and self-determination, Hammer argues:

> Someplace in the city were people with names and some without names. They were organized. They had big money in back of them. They had political connections. They had everything they had to stay where they were, except one thing and that was me with my own slab in a morgue. They know what to expect from the cops and what to expect from the vast machine that squatted on the Potomac but they didn't know what to expect from me.[21]

The detective thus assures his audience that individuals have genuine significance within a society seemingly controlled by a larger institutional conspiracy.

In simultaneously defending and rebelling against the social system, Mike invariably falls foul of procedures—due process and legal safeguards—which place individual rights above efficiency. The detective's consistent anger at bureaucratic rules obscures a crucial paradox for, by dismissing the rights of others, the zealous Hammer subverts the very process he is supposedly defending. By meting out justice as he sees fit, Mike loses the larger ideological struggle upon which the Cold War centers. The hero's ruthless tactics, which imitate the vigilante proceedings of Senator Joseph McCarthy on the national scene, present a good man using the methods of supposedly bad men to root out the latter. In a democratic society which believes that means and ends inevitably condition each other, the adoption of totalitarian tactics can hardly lead to desirable goals.

In *One Lonely Night* Hammer delivers a sermon against communism and the servile tactics and traits which identify its adherents. Posing as a member of Russian Intelligence, and not being seriously challenged by anyone in the clandestine group he infiltrates, Mike lights a cigarette and blows smoke in the face of a new-found "comrade" who, naturally, relishes such attention.[22] While the smoke dramatizes Hammer's ability to deceive the Reds, the larger intention is to emphasize the enemy's servility. As the scene progresses, Mike takes a cup of coffee and, after noting his dismay at being in a "pigsty," sips it only to discover that the "crumbs couldn't even make good coffee."[23] Hammer's complaint sounds unwittingly funny now, however in the 1950s neither Spillane nor his audience would have been as amused. The detective's diatribe ultimately builds to the comparison Hammer makes when he urges that the communists and their followers "were dumb as horse manure."[24]

Madness also identifies the villains in these novels; indeed, insanity explains criminal conduct. While the power of money remains the ostensible motive for those who control gambling, prostitution and blackmail, Spillane's master criminals go a step beyond to pursue a total control of their surroundings. This ambition, in turn, leads to the murders which bring Hammer down upon them. Such extreme evildoers act like bogeymen in a nightmare: pure malevolence causes their insanity. For Hammer, if an individual commits certain acts or espouses particular ideas, then that character is mentally imbalanced; and so, to the protagonist, one is mad if one is a criminal, and one is a criminal if one is mad. This tautology is spelled out in Oscar Deamer, the master criminal and communist psychopath in *One Lonely Night*. Oscar has escaped from a mental asylum and killed his upstanding twin brother, Lee. Assuming Lee's identity, Oscar becomes a candidate for the United States Senate and, in a bit of hypocrisy worthy of the characters in Richard Condon's *The Manchurian Candidate* (1959), becomes America's leading anti-communist voice. Mike's customary explanation-diatribe which ends the novel equates being a communist with being insane. In explaining the murder of a nurse who could have identified Oscar and revealed his having taken Lee's place, Hammer lets his rage boil over.

> *"Whatever happened she recognized you as Oscar and all her illusions were shattered. She knew you were Oscar Deamer and demented as hell."*
>
> "That's why you were a Commie, Oscar, because you were batty. It was the only philosophy that would appeal to your crazy mind. It justified everything you did and you saw a chance of getting back at the world."[25]

This tirade, the verbal vengeance the detective imposes on evildoers, paradoxically shows the hero behaving in the same excessive manner for which he stigmatizes Oscar.

Many commentators feel Spillane's sole talent lies in catering to the wish-fulfillments such derogatory speeches and polarized thinking satisfy. Thus, Hammer would seem to embody that mentality of the early 1950s which saw the world through the melodramatic prism of Cold War; however, there are some difficulties with such a reading. In *One Lonely Night*, the most conspicuously political of these novels, the identity switch of Oscar Deamer suggests that good guys can be fooled; and even the smash ending, in which Hammer strangles Oscar slowly, provides no satisfying resolution since the narrative simply ends at this point. Oscar represents a warning (in the overblown style of J. Edgar Hoover) that one can never be sure who is an enemy and who is not. However, such an unsettling possibility hardly accords with the audience's desire to be reassured, since this is a disturbing message to contemplate seriously. Spillane may be pandering to popular taste much of the time, yet here his artistry (the desire for "smash endings") takes precedence over melodramatic certainty.

Hammer's Americanism often clashes with the "respectable" views held by the compromised society in which he lives. The timid public never supports the detective's single-minded crusades so that the hero must often proclaim his love of country while realizing that such devotion will not be appreciated. In *The Long Wait* Johnny McBride returns to Lyncastle to untangle a murder and a robbery in which he was implicated years before. McBride, who believes that he is really George Wilson, an exact double of Johnny and an Army buddy who only wants to clear his dead friend's name, speaks for himself (and for Hammer) when he attacks society's hypocritical reception of veterans after war.

> So a guy is yellow because he gets his belly full of killing. He gets so that he doesn't want any part of killing or the things that cause it and they call him yellow. A typical civilian attitude. *Here's a gun, go get them, feller. Attaboy, Johnny, good job. Here's some more bullets. What? You've had enough of it? Why, you yellow-bellied bastard, get away from me.* [26]

Killing for one's country is laudable, while killing to revenge social wrongs or to right the past is criminal. Yet McBride, like Hammer, must be a scourging agent that purges society and so enables it to continue.

Throughout the Hammer novels weather provides a symbolic atmosphere. In four of the books rain is the predominant condition, while drizzle and snow are prominent in the others. Bright or clearing weather invariably gives way to wet or damp conditions. In one instance the sun's dominance only confirms what the protagonist already thinks of his surrounding, a sin city "hot as hell."[27] The weather symbolizes Hammer's progress in his cases because, while the muddled atmosphere of snow and rain suggests his inner confusions, clearing patterns become more pronounced as Mike gets closer to cornering Mr. Big. Thus, the snow in *Vengeance is Mine,* which impedes Hammer's movements around the city and draws his wrath on several occasions, finally represents the hero's growing mastery. When Hammer discovers who is responsible he can relax and realize that the snow "wasn't something to be fought any longer."[28] This unity between man and nature goes even further in *Kiss Me, Deadly* when, at a similar moment of discovery, the hero finds: "I was glad of the rain. It...bathed me in its coolness."[29] Hammer's movement toward harmony as he approaches the final extermination of his unnatural criminal enemies becomes even more overt when the detective anticipates killing Oscar Deamer in *One Lonely Night.* The rain here has finally become a cleansing agent restoring the earth and the man-made structures upon it. At the same time, Hammer, who has temporarily doubted the validity of his quest, regains his sense of identity. Since the destruction of the enemy can restore the detective to himself, the rain takes on the ritualistic properties of baptism and rebirth. Hammer emphasizes these Christian associations when he reflects: "The rain came down steadily. It was clear and pure. It swept by the curb carrying filth into the sewer. *We know now, don't we, Judge? We know the answer.*"[30]

Spillane uses fog and dusk to shroud the action and to impose ambivalent and confusing elements on the atmosphere. Often, early in the narrative, as Hammer plunges into his quest for retribution, the coming of dusk accentuates the hero's descent into the maelstrom of nightclubs, apartments and bars that comprises underworld life. Snow covers the acts of man and so restores order by concealment. When he finishes strangling Oscar Deamer, Hammer points to the obliterating power of the snow and to the spring thaw which must follow: "The snow was coming down harder now. Soon that dark mass over there would be just a mound. And when the sun shone again the thaw would provide the deluge that would sweep everything into the sewer where it belonged."[31] Nature's restorative powers augment the violent justice Hammer metes out as society's agent. In ridding the world of a communist madman Spillane's hero has enabled the sun to shine figuratively for its inhabitants. Mike's reference to the spring washing away Oscar's body implies that justice is cosmic. Once again, upon completion of his quest, Hammer has found that nature verifies his own zeal. He is just and so is the weather.

The few children who appear in these novels are either off-stage plot devices or infants lacking personalities. An illegitimate granddaughter, who dies before the story begins, adds to the psychological agonies of the villain Berin-Groton in the real climax of *My Gun is Quick*. In his harangue to this figure, Hammer torments the dying villain with the knowledge that he murdered his own pregnant granddaughter and so destroyed his family name. Since Berin-Groton has built an elaborate mausoleum, and since Mike has ended the aged villain's dream of enjoying that memorial, this news about his dead granddaughter represents a final sadistic nail in his coffin. However, such a revelation pales beside the physical sadism of the scene, for it is doubtful that this psychological contrivance distracts from the spectacle of Berin-Groton being in flames as Hammer presents such information. Another child looms much larger in *The Big Kill* (1951) when the infant son of a murdered safecracker becomes the agent of retribution. Hammer, who naturally seeks revenge after the killing, takes this orphan home with him. In the real climax, after Mike has discovered that Marsha Lee, a seductive model with whom he has dallied, masterminded the original murder, Hammer finds himself trapped by the murderess in his own apartment. Marsha plans to kill Mike and one of her accomplices to create an alibi when cosmic justice rears its head. The nameless infant, who has been prevented from playing with Hammer's pistol in earlier bits of foreshadowing, pulls the trigger on Mike's unattended gun and kills Marsha. This ending epitomizes Spillane's avowed strategy of building to an abrupt, shattering finale, for "the tongue of flame that blasted from the muzzle seemed to lick out across the room with a horrible vengeance that ripped all the evil from her face, turning it into a ghastly wet mask that was really no face at all."[32] Justice takes on the most appropriate forms, for in revenging his father the child destroys the feminine allure of the villainess. This system of "just deserts" in which the master criminal is both destroyed and degraded conditions each closing scene. Mike can never be content merely with the death of his antagonist; so far as possible his enemy's personality must be eradicated from human memory.

Spillane frequently uses fire to destroy these master villains. Thus, Berlin-Groton momentarily has the drop on Hammer but, since the environment aids the just, a support beam of the old warehouse fortuitously breaks away then "and just like a giant falling pine tree, crashed into the room and nailed the goddamn killer to the floor under it."[33] The falling beam suggests a perverse crucifixion in which the villain cannot lift the cross which pins him to the floor. The trapped Berin-Groton, appropriately rendered harmless by the arch symbol of Christianity, burns as Hammer flagellates him with an avalanche of words. During Mike's tirade the master criminal is reduced to quivering flesh, no better than any other man's. This sadistic exorcism proceeds as Berin-Groton's leonine gray hair slowly burns off and as the hero stresses that no one will every recognize the charred remains of the criminal's body. Hammer revels that the killer's hair smoked, puffed up in a ball of flame and he screamed again. He looked like a killer being bald like that."[34] While baldness and being a killer might be a connection that Dick Tracy rather than logic would make, the flames reduce the criminal to anonymity.

Fire exhibits more traditional symbolic patterns in *One Lonely Night* and *Kiss Me, Deadly* for it not only destroys but also purifies. After Mike rescues Velda from being whipped by the lust-crazed communists and kills all those who witnessed her physical nakedness under the lash, he burns the abandoned building where his fiancée has suffered. This ritual conceals the bodies of Hammer's enemies and re-establishes the purity of both Velda and the society Mike is pledged to protect. Lily Carver, the wily master criminal of *Kiss Me, Deadly* comes to Mike as an ostensible fugitive from hired killers but really just wants to spy on the hero's activities after gaining his confidence. Mike finds himself drawn to Lily, who shares his apartment, but he never consummates their relationship and so remains symbolically pure. Spillane foreshadows the real climax by continuously referring to the smell of rubbing alcohol surrounding Lily. It is only just that she be hideously scarred because of an earlier fire, and that her physical disfigurement be accompanied by a psychological crippling which made her refuse Mike's amorous advances (although not without second thoughts). In the novel's final scene Lily has the obligatory drop on Mike, but the detective remembers her penchant for rubbing alcohol (which she uses to ease her withered flesh) and asks for one last cigarette. As he lights up and watches the naked Lily taunt him, the wounded hero:

...thumbed the lighter and in the moment of time before the scream blossoms into the wild cry of terror she was a mass of flame tumbling on the floor with the blue flames of alcohol turning the white of her hair into black char and her body convulsing under the agony of it. The flames were teeth that ate, ripping and tearing, into scars of other flames and her voice the shrill sound of death on the loose.

I looked, looked away. The door was closed and maybe I had enough left to make it.[35]

This shattering ending (literally the novel's final words) incorporates many symbolic and psychological preoccupations found elsewhere in Spillane's works; and such interweaving suggests the novelist's dexterity, if artistry is too strong a word. The use of "blossoms" combines with the villainess's names to suggest floral imagery, while the flames as "teeth" impose an appropriate death on a potentially castrating female. Like so many other situations, these closing scenes stress the acute test Hammer has passed and reassure the audience that moral goodness invariably triumphs and lives into the future.

The hero's masculine rhetoric surfaces time and again. Hammer questions a building supervisor and is confronted by the man's wife who talks for him. Mike silences her and makes the man answer for himself. As he leaves them, the detective confidently asserts that he has restored the browbeaten husband's self-respect and declares that when "men learn to be men maybe they can handle dames."[36] The need to "handle dames" arises, of course, from their supposedly natural vulnerability; however, such feminine weakness identifies a real woman because it is absent in the perverted females who have become criminals and, thus, intruders on customary male traits. The most passionate charge Hammer directs against the communists in *One Lonely Night* is that, by kidnapping Velda, they don't fight fair (i.e. like men). Mike feels trapped because his opponents have taken advantage of his personal code about women, and his rage is also directed against himself for assuming any shred of masculine honor in such foes.

I thought I was clever. I thought they'd try for me. But they *were* clever when the chips were down and now they had something they could trade. That's what they'd say...trade. Ha, that was a laugh. They'd take the documents and when I asked them to give her back I'd get a belly full of slugs. Nice trade. A stupid ass like me ought to get shot anyway.

Goddam'em anyway. Why couldn't they act like men and fight with me? Why did they have to pick on women? The dirty yellow bastards were afraid to tangle with me so they decided to do it the easy way. They knew the score and they knew I had to play ball.[37]

While the standard macho value of fighting man-to-man without bringing women into the contest emerges, Spillane also reassures his audience once more by presenting a protagonist who, like most of them, is neither foolproof nor aloof—like more sagacious fictional private eyes such as Sherlock Holmes, Hercule Poirot or even Philip Marlowe.

The most obvious variation Spillane plays on the conventions of the hard-boiled detective story arises from his protagonist's flawed nature. Hammer not only lacks the cleverness of more cerebral sleuths but also fails to be calm and insightful like Sam Spade or Lew Archer. Unlike such cool cynics who really trust no one, Mike continuously overlooks characters who are unworthy and dangerous and so, unwittingly, brings suffering and death to others. He is easily persuaded by Berin-Groton that they share a concern for a dead girl and should work together to bring the real culprits to justice. This arrangement eventually leads to Lola's death because Berin-Groton, who has hired Mike, knows of any progress and steps in to murder her when she discovers incriminating evidence. Hammer thus contributes to the death of a woman he loves, conduct hardly worthy of a character the mass audience fantasizes as the surrogate hero of its violent daydreams. Juno Reeves deceives Hammer for much of *Vengeance is Mine* (indeed, until the real climax when the transvestite is stripped and shot by the protagonist) and Connie Wales dies because of this trust. While Mike's shortsightedness causes the deaths of women who would have been too possessive in the long run, his inabilities raise the issue of stupidity. How can the audience identify with this obviously flawed figure when hard-boiled detective fiction seems to demand that a hero at least be shrewd? This apparently logical dilemma is resolved by the violent tactics of the central character which finally serve as a vicarious catharsis for the audience.

Another characteristic feature is that ennui and despair mark Hammer's initial appearances in these novels as a chronic, hostile loner whose wrath arises from a general disgust with humanity. Hammer's initial dismay suggests a natural letdown from the horrors he endured in a previous adventure, as though his hopeful statements, made as he dragged himself away from a previous traumatic final scene, had withered in quieter moments. A typical opening sequence has the detective in a bar where a prostitute approaches him, hustles him for a drink, and tries to engage him in conversation.

> I said, "Scram."
> This time she scowled a little bit. "Say, what the hell's eatin' you? I never...."
> "I don't like people. I don't like any kind of people. When you get them together in a big lump they all get nasty and dirty and full of trouble. So I don't like people including you. That's what a misanthropist is."[38]

This initial despair quickly disappears when Hammer witnesses a wanton killing. If anything, Mike's misanthropy breaks down too rapidly into its diametric opposite, as though the hero embodied a manic-depressive outlook which accords with the nature of melodrama and so consistently forces his thoughts into rigorous either/or patterns. Since his psychological economy centers on rage, the hero must be initially depressed and violently aroused to anger. Consistent with his later extreme deeds, Mike acts out of frustration and, in so doing, touches the deepest nerve in his audience: Hammer's crusades are therapeutic vendettas waged against the traditional enemies thought to exploit the mass audience—business and its impersonalities, government and its diplomatic compromises, intellectuals and their complexities.

Again, in keeping with convention, Spillane's hero has symbolic dreams which loosely incorporate Freudian devices. These nightmares consistently emphasize the detective's helplessness and thus offer subconscious fuel for his conscious undertakings. Hammer's dreams are populated by mysterious females, images of his own impotence, and Velda as the redeeming love of his life. A typical instance in *One Lonely Night* opens with a symbolic rehash of the mystery insofar as Mike has unravelled it, moves on to his attempt to rescue a woman in distress and then graphically records the detective's feelings of inadequacy: "I...tried to run to catch her, only to have my feet turn into stumps that grew from the very soil."[39] In *The*

Big Kill the same arrangement, albeit with a mystery woman as the dream's central figure, leads to another picture of impotence: "She was a woman in black hovering behind me. I called to her and received no answer. I tried to walk to her, but she was always the same distance away without seeming to move at all. I ran on leaden feet without getting any closer...."[40] Mike's frustration at being unable to solve the murder receives the primary emphasis here; indeed, since "gumshoe" and "leg work" call attention to obvious facets of his profession, the detective's immobile feet symbolize his inabilities. The dreams thus not only pay slight homage to the traditional difficulties of sleuthing found in whodunits but also, and more important, present Hammer suffering from a guilty conscience.

Instead of exhibiting remorse when his trust has brought death to an infatuated, female, would-be helper, Hammer's defenses only slip in dreams so that his nightmares dramatize his inability to save these innocent victims. Mike's dream in *Kiss Me, Deadly* illustrates his guilt-ridden inner workings, while developing thematic concerns and artistic devices found in the whole series.

I thought I heard voices and one was Velda's. She kept calling to me and I couldn't answer back. Somebody was hurting her and I mouthed silent curses while I fought invisible bonds that held me tied to the ground. She was screaming, her voice tortured, screaming for me and I couldn't help her. I strained and kicked and fought but the ropes held until I was breathless and I had to lie there and listen to her die.[41]

Hammer is remembering Velda's whipping in *One Lonely Night;* however, some clever alterations have taken place. In the dream it is Hammer who is tied and cannot make a sound, while in that actual scene it was Velda who was bound and speechless because of pain. The protagonist's guilt at allowing even this much to happen to his beloved has not been assuaged by the rescue and bloody retaliation, for the fear of losing Velda haunts his sleep and awakens him to violent trembling, sweating and a parched throat. In his dream Hammer has again been rendered impotent (his futile wrestling with the ropes) and degraded further by being on the floor, grovelling.

Another staple convention in hard-boiled detective fiction and film noir concerns the protagonist's struggle with memory. Usually the film noir hero tries to forget a lost or corrupt love whose memory continually distresses him. Orson Welles as Michael, the lovelorn sailor victimized by Rita Hayworth in *The Lady from Shanghai,* speaks for all these tormented males when he concludes: "Everybody is somebody's fool. The only way to stay out of trouble is to grow old. So I guess I'll concentrate on that. Maybe I'll live so long that I'll forget her. Maybe I'll die trying."[42] Jack Nicholson, as Jake Gittes in *Chinatown* (1974), suffers from the same kind of memory, so that when Faye Dunaway's Mrs. Mulwray (his new love) dies he must realize he is caught in a world where events figuratively, if not quite literally, repeat themselves, and where emotional wounds can never be healed. Mike Hammer suffers from the memory of a dead beloved, Charlotte, the femme fatale and master criminal he killed in *I, the Jury*

(1947). Her image haunts him repeatedly in *Vengeance is Mine* until he finally rids himself of this possession. Mike initially achieves freedom in a dream where the image of Charlotte gives way to that of Velda. The throb of a drum, a signal of the hero's anguish over present difficulties, precedes Charlotte's memory and the detective, although momentarily wishing to have her back, reaffirms his earlier act.

> "Charlotte, Charlotte...I'll kill you again if I have to! I'll kill you again, Charlotte!"
> And the music increased in tempo and volume, pounding and beating and vibrating with
> such insistence that I began to fall before it. The face with the gold hair laughed anew
> and urged the music on. Then there was another face...with clean beauty and a strength
> to face even the dead.... "Velda, thank God! Velda, Velda, Velda."[43]

This triumph of life over death in the dream carries over when Hammer finally confronts Juno Reeves and hesitates about shooting this criminal because "I was seeing Charlotte's face instead of hers."[44] This moment of indecision ends abruptly when Juno jumps Mike and almost overpowers him. Their grappling exposes the villain as a transvestite and the justice of Hammer's killing of Charlotte is reaffirmed. Mike cannot compromise with evil and hope to live so that, no matter how personally painful its eradication, such emotional cost is always appropriate.

Memory also defines identity when Hammer recalls killing a Japanese soldier during World War II. Mike recognizes that he has always enjoyed killing those who needed it in *One Lonely Night* and, in casting off any doubts that respectable society has created in his mind, the hero recollects: "I cut down that Jap with his own machete and laughed like hell when I made slices of his scrawny body then went on to do the same thing again because it got to be fun."[45] Hammer's belief that he embodies cosmic justice clearly shapes this memory, for Mike uses the enemy's own weapon against him (as he uses guns and "kill lust" to destroy the criminals who run the city) and tries to obliterate his foe physically. Thus, Hammer only finds peace of mind and a secure identity through violence. After beating two hoodlums into bloody pulps, and smashing one's hand just for the hell of it, Mike can declare: "I got out of there feeling like myself again."[46] When he is only a few tantalizing clues away from uncovering the master criminal in the *The Big Kill,* the hero again discovers that peace of mind results from his crusades: "I'll know all that and I'll be able to live with myself again."[47] The detective values self-contentment above reputation; and, while his view supports the traditional American values of self-reliance and initiative, Hammer only experiences this transformation through seemingly cathartic violence.

Mike's crusades against crime, while ostensibly undertaken to bring about justice, have the private purpose of defining the protagonist's identity. Once again, Spillane parts company with his literary predecessors, Dashiell Hammett and Raymond Chandler, whose characters' personalities are revealed through their adventures. Hammer articulates this deeper quest most overtly in *One Lonely Night* when, after briefly talking of quitting his profession and going into real estate (!), he tells his faithful secretary:

" 'I want to find out about myself, Velda.' "[48] The search for identity figures most extensively in *The Long Wait* where, because of the protagonist's amnesia, establishing one's real self solves the mystery. Johnny McBride meets a local reporter, Logan, who offers to help and, more ominously, to search for the hero's lost past.

> "Maybe you have a history I can run down."
> "Go to it, pal. I tried and didn't get very far."
> "You might not like what I dig up."
> I tossed the cigarette and watched it sizzle out in the water. "Maybe not, but it's better than not knowing," I told him finally.[49]

McBride will have the truth no matter what the personal cost, for a man must discover himself first even if such discovery brings down the wrath of God or, in McBride's case, the wrath of police, criminals and society. This quest for self-knowledge (a major theme in tragedy) represents an extremely literary theme, and Spillane's incorporation of such an interest suggests another point at which he is playing with the conventional melodramatic context of the genre.

More familiar and comforting cliches make up Hammer's views on women. For the hero, females, in keeping with the "less enlightened" 1950s, fall into only two categories: (1) sex objects to be used or (2) love objects to be guided. The world is clearly divided between men, who fight and do society's serious tasks, and women, who can aid their superiors but must never aspire to independent careers. While nearly every female character throws herself at Mike, truly aggressive women are punished because their zeal to possess the detective either leads them to their deaths or reveals them to be master criminals. Only Ellen Scobie, an aide to the District Attorney in *The Big Kill*, falls slightly outside of this pattern. Ellen gives up Mike after lusting for him enough to have stolen confidential records: her parting speech testifies to Hammer's magnetism and demonstrates that Ellen is consciously choosing a second-rate romantic life.

> "You're the kind I dreamed of and the kind I want and the kind I'll never have, because your kind are never around long enough. They have to go out and play with guns and hurt people and get themselves killed.
> "...I dreamed too hard, I guess.
> "...I'm going to forget all about you and stop looking for a dream...I'll get all these foolish romanticisms out of my head and live a bored and relatively normal life."[50]

The girl's resignation does not prevent her from throwing open her robe and seducing Mike just once more so that she will have memories to sustain her in a dreary, domesticated future. Thus, while she doesn't die, Ellen accepts "death-in-life" because she cannot possess her hero.

The stylistic equation of women with cats is more disconcerting. While such an association reflects a familiar masculine arrogance about women (i.e. they're just "pussies"), Spillane's comparisons serve to further reveal the sexual ambiguity within Hammer. The feline female represents woman as a sexual hunter and, of course, the detective consistently meets such nymphomaniacs, but there is a still darker side. Since the city as a jungle is virtually a stylistic cliche in hardboiled fiction, references to lionnesses and hunting naturally bring more sinister urban associations into play. On two occasions Mike confronts cat-seductresses, and the outcomes of these meetings reinforce the basic sexual dualism noted earlier. Ann Minor, a hostess in Murry Candid's Zero-Zero Club, a front for prostitution and blackmail in *My Gun is Quick*, takes Mike to her apartment to show him incriminating evidence. Once there, Ann changes into the proverbial "something more comfortable" and assaults the detective with drinks and soft lights. As she settles into a chair and begins to eyeball him, Hammer notes that the "way she sat there reminded me of a cat, completely at ease, yet hiding the tension of a coiled spring."[51] While such a description seems patently obvious, particularly after Hammer says he needs an ice pick or a chisel to open the robe Ann is wearing, this sequence also reflects melodramatic principles. Ann and Mike make love but, in keeping with the purity of Hammer's quest, the girl dies five pages later! Apparently no woman who has known the hero can remain alive for long; and so sexual proximity becomes a measure of character and vulnerability. Ann Minor, whose name suggests her status, represents only an interlude in Hammer's life: if she became a permanent fixture, his purity and freedom would be compromised by inhibiting domestic concerns.

The most elaborate values in the Mike Hammer novels of the 1950s center on sexuality. This is hardly surprising for, as Russel Nye explains, the "most obvious ingredient added to popular fiction after 1920 was sex, treated openly and aggressively."[52] Much of Spillane's immediate appeal undoubtedly resided in the sexual scenes his works embody, yet the complexity of Hammer's sexual ethics belie such an all-encompassing, commercial view. The hero arouses lust wherever he goes in spite of, or perhaps because of, his ugly face. Women are drawn to him since they recognize that Mike will dominate them; in essence, Spillane's hero represents an antidote to the demanding females and, thus, a reassurance to male readers. Mike also attracts homosexuals, as in *Vengeance is Mine* where the master criminal tries to seduce the hero for both personal and professional reasons. The sinister transvestite Juno succumbs to the same feelings that "real" women experience in Mike's animal presence. Wendy, who proves to be the missing link between Johnny McBride's past and present in *The Long Wait*, speaks for all these beleaguered ladies when she tells the protagonist: ' "I was doing fine until you came along. There's a hundred men out there who'd love to make love to me and the only one I want is you.' "[53]

Hammer's chauvinism surfaces most clearly with Velda, the love of his life. Naturally, their relationship embodies a sexual double standard for Mike can (and does) sleep around while Velda, despite continuously being a sexual decoy, is never violated either for pleasure or in the line of duty. Once they have become engaged (in *One Lonely Night*) much voyeurism and teasing takes place between Mike and Velda, but they agree to wait for the sanctity of marriage and the imagined beauties of "some day." Although Mike believes Velda is shrewd enough to be his partner (albeit cleaning the office and typing remain exclusively her preserves), the hero draws a line when it comes to deciding a course of action: ' "What you think makes a lot of difference, kitten, but when it comes to making the decisions I'll make them on what I think. I'm a man.' "[54] Later, when Velda gets ready to do some investigating on her own, Mike insists: " 'No dame can take care of herself, including you. Be careful, will you?' " The accuracy of Mike's sentiments is proved when Velda must be rescued from a sadistic gambler (in *Vengeance is Mine*) and a sadistic whipping (in *One Lonely Night*). In both instances Velda falls into traps to show she can't take care of herself and to allow Mike to effect bloody rescues that release her. The lovers seal their faith when they struggle with Clyde, a petty criminal Hammer tracked down and wounded even before the opening of *Vengeance is Mine* and who subsequently became the apparent boss of a fashionable gambling den. Even though the lovers are not able to capture Clyde immediately, Mike and Velda pause in their pursuit to enjoy a respite in which the detective's head rests in the secretary's lap.

While a flirtation scene between Mike and Velda develops the sinister cat-woman stylistic ploy, we can be certain that there will be no physical consummation to compromise the secretary and put her on the execution block. Velda momentarily becomes a tigress seeking fulfillment (and so embodying the demon of the male audience—the lusty, independent female) against a background of jungle imagery. Her description links the worlds of sexuality and crime and makes one of Spillane's murkier obsessions overt; indeed, Freud's "vagina with teeth" looms close to the surface in this passage.

> Velda was watching me with the tip of her tongue clenched between her teeth. There wasn't any kitten softness about her now.... The lush fullness of her lips had tightened into the faintest kind of snarl and her eyes were the carnivorous eyes you could expect to see in the jungle watching you from behind a clump of bushes.[55]

Velda has been transformed from a controllable woman (a kitten-pussy) into a potential maneater as symbolized by the tongue to which her teeth are fastened. However, the faithful assistant redeems herself in the very next paragraph when she willingly sets out to find clues for a case. Thus, Mike's fiancee only indulges vicariously in the conduct that brings Ann Minor and a host of other smitten women to their deaths.

Velda does provide a voyeuristic display in a hospital in *Kiss Me, Deadly* since she and the hero are engaged by then. Mike has been battered during the killing of the initial victim and, needing to rest for a few days, believes that a little diversity will help him endure his confinement. The detective's fiancee willingly lifts her skirts, seductively posing all the while, and, after a glowing description of her legs, Mike uses a humorous classical allusion to demonstrate their special relationship.

> Before I could say anything else she laughed down deep, threw me a kiss and grinned, "Now you know how Ulysses felt."

Now I knew. The guy was a sucker. He should have jumped ship.[56]

This teasing by-play reveals a different facet of Hammer, for in previous love scenes the mood has always been serious; here, in one of the few funny passages in these novels, the erstwhile man of iron momentarily becomes a comic buffoon plagued by being in the wrong place at the wrong time. The irreverent reference to Homer sustains Hammer's anti-intellectual bias and tone; indeed, to speak reverently of "literature" would be to risk being thought a sissy. Yet, paradoxically, Hammer knows the allusion.

Much of the sexual tension in the protagonist dissolves through voyeuristic episodes in which naked female bodies and mildly obscene double-entendres replace graphic sexual intimacy. The ladies Hammer meets are living wish-fulfillments, the hourglass-shaped daydreams of an adolescent who imagines that woman are constantly preoccupied with sex and with him in particular. While their delight in satisfying the hero's whims represents an all-too-familiar anti-feminine view, Spillane uses this character trait to sort out good girls from bad ones. In nearly every instance a voyeuristic episode indicates that the woman will only enjoy a transient relationship with Hammer (and often with life itself). Only Velda remains exempt because Mike has explained his chauvinistic philosophy to her, while the other exhibitionists play for control of the detective because they are unaware that he cannot be manipulated. Ellen Scobie initially appears fixing her stockings in an office in *The Big Kill* and the suave Hammer, seeing one her legs, urges her to show the other.

So she stood there in one of those magazine poses and pulled the dress up slowly without stopping until it couldn't go any further and showed me. And she was right. The other was just as pretty if you wasted a sight like that trying to compare them.[57]

Ellen, of course, is infatuated from the moment she sees Mike, so her behavior is hardly surprising; however, much of the sensuality of the scene arises from its locale. Hammer's mere presence causes this woman to forget her workaday surroundings and start acting like a burlesque queen. As is often customary in pornography, Spillane combines a deeply ambiguous feeling about female sexuality with the strangeness of the setting. Sex in the bedroom is one thing, but sex in the office is something special; of course, a special man creates special conditions.

Voyeuristic sex takes on a more sinister overtone in *The Big Kill* when Marsha Lee, the master criminal, taunts Mike with her body. Although she has seduced Hammer, her jealousy flares when the hero ogles other models working on the same set; and, while such feminine pique seems only normal to the detective's macho psyche, a more symbolic and psychological note underscores this scene.

And there she was leaning on the stack of stairs like a nymph under a waterfall with her own toga wide open down the middle and impish little grin playing with her mouth. . .the toga came shut slowly before I could move and she was out of reach.
"You don't have to be jealous of anybody," I said.

She smiled again, and in the darkness her hand touched mine briefly and the cigarette fell out of my fingers to the floor where it lay like a hot red eye. Then she was gone and all I could think about was tonight.[58]

While the sadistic tone of the Hammer world finds reinforcement here in the postponement of sexual gratification, it is more significant that Marsha, and not Mike, brings about the delay. The villainess clearly usurps the hero's prerogative and aspires to a role she must never play. The scene incorporates other symbolic touches that emphasize Marcha's unnatural character. Her toga recalls the images of the Colosseum and so links her with the violent world Mike customarily confronts. The fallen cigarette suggests that the femme fatale wants to castrate Hammer, a bit of symbolism that reinforces the demonic view of women in these works. The cigarette's burning tip reinvokes the image of fire and associates this temptress with that force which often cleanses the world of evil.

Spillane operates less subtly when Hammer describes the female anatomy. In keeping with the "mammary madness" that beset popular culture in the 1950s, female bosoms are given veritable lives of their own. While their breasts are often exposed to get Mike's attention, the lust-inflamed females who approach the hero usually have both prepossessing and willful endowments. A typical confrontation has Mike eyeballing a photographer's model who, in turn, does everything possible to demonstrate that she is well built.

When she was set just right he stepped back behind the camera, muttered a cue and the girl threw her bosoms (?) toward the lens and let a ghost of a smile play with her mouth. There was a barely audible click and the model turned human again, stretching her arms so far over her head that her bra filled up and began overflowing.[59]

The photographer, Anton Lipsek, is a homosexual ally of Juno Reeves so that the model's strained pose further establishes who is really evil here. Naturally, when the girl returns to a "normal" posture, her cup all but literally runs over. While Mike and Velda's various postponements embody delaying tactics more acceptable to courtly love then to twentieth-entury mores, the secretary's true feelings are captured by awesome breasts that are constantly "rising and falling faster than they should, fighting the wispy thinness of the dress.[60] Emotions are thus rendered graphic and the dichotomy of desire and duty is underscored by a male wish-fulfillment.

Sexual intercourse in these novels reminds one more of Hollywood's visual euphemisms than of D. H. Lawrence for, although Spillane never resorts to pounding waves or screaming horses, physical contact is never explicitly described. Instead, women become embodiments of passion and bliss that mysteriously please and, more important, are satiated by Hammer. Since waves and fire describe such aroused moments, Spillane remains closer to Frances Parkinson Keyes than to Grace Metalious at such times. Hammer occasionally indulges in sex to escape the pressures of his larger quest; thus, the "blonde had a brunette base, but it only made her more intriguing, enough to make me forget about the...killings and beatings that left you too sore to move."[61] While the daring quality here lies in his reference to the girl's pubic hair, on a symbolic level this small duplicity links her with the predatory world that Hammer is fighting. As a further device to thwart sympathy for Ann Minor, the willing body here, Spillane has Mike and the girl kiss after they have revived from a delirium of ecstasy. During this embrace Ann breathes into Hammer's mouth and bites him on the neck. Such aggression obviously precludes a lasting relationship since it challenges Hammer's virility.

Intercourse thus identifies affairs that must come to an end. Lola, a former call girl, becomes another "lost love" in Hammer's life in *My Gun is Quick*; and the scene of passion between the hero and this woman reiterates many of the novels' sexual ambiguities. After Lola has taunted the protagonist by urging that her negligee is only to be worn once, Mike confides:

> A devil was making love to me.
>
> My fingers closed over the silk and I ripped it away with a hissing, tearing sound and she was standing in front of me naked and inviting.
>
> Her voice had angels in it, though. "I love you, Mike," she said again.
>
> She was my kind of woman, one that you didn't have to speak to, for words weren't that necessary. She was...capable of loving a man with all her heart had to give, and she was giving it to me.
>
> Her mouth was cool but her body was hot with an inner fire that could only be smothered out.
>
> It was a night she thought she'd never have.
>
> It was a night I'd never forget.[62]

Hammer's sexual values are clearly integrated in this scene and, while such an ethic may be dismissed as unenlightened, such compression implies a craft commentators do not normally attribute to Spillane. The references to angels and devils suggest an abiding dualism in Lola, yet another melodramatic scheme. Hammer's physical assault upon the woman, with its implication of a female wish to be sexually dominated, flatters an abiding male fantasy about therapeutic rape. This wish-fulfillment aspect is further enhanced because the characters do not talk: Mike's actions (rather than his personality) in bed are enough to bind this woman to him. In keeping with the euphemistic sexual descriptions of 1950s' novels, Spillane refers to Lola's "heart" and the "fire" of her passion; however the latter reference and the use of "smothered" carry more sinister overtones. The concluding lines suggest that subconsciously Hammer has already prepared for Lola's death, and so his use of the past tense jars by foreshadowing so blatantly.

Sexual relations dramatically counterpoint the plot in *The Long Wait*. Johnny McBride must find Vera West, an old love who fled from the robbery-frame-up of years ago. Shortly after arriving in Lyncaster, and being recognized by a friendly old man and the local police, Johnny meets Wendy who agrees to shelter him during his search. Since McBride embodies a sexual dynamism similar to Hammer's, he and Wendy soon become lovers; however Spillane deliberately stages their initial lovemaking in complete darkness. The supposedly modest girl insists on this "lights out" policy, but Johnny breaks down her resistance enough to gain a fleeting glance at her body in their second encounter and a full-fledged, all-the-lights-on tumble in the third. Wendy, of course, is Vera West and was briefly married to Johnny before the bank robbery and the hero's disappearance and amnesia. While such coincidences tax a reader's patience (if only because the townspeople and the villains seem unable to perceive what is in front of their faces), the increasing light in these sexual encounters symbolizes the novel's major action. As McBride comes to know more, he sees more of Wendy's body so that as the secrets of the past come to light and as McBride's amnesia dissipates, the reality of the woman's physique also gets clearer.

In the final scene between Johnny and Vera, Spillane toys with his readers' expectations. Since we are accustomed to shattering conclusions, we accept McBride's rage at Vera as but another prelude to the exposure of another master criminal. Johnny forces Vera to strip so that he can beat her with his belt because he is convinced she has used him to destroy the real thieves and to gain the stolen money. Johnny still does not know that he is Johnny, and it remains for Vera to provide the final clue to his identity. She does not do this in a pleading (i.e. feminine) way; instead, she pulls out a gun and forces McBride to strip before she tells him about himself and her idealistic motives for helping him. McBride is symbolically reduced to infancy and reborn through the ministrations of his similarly naked woman-wife. The weakness of the protagonist, which is more muted in the Hammer novels, emerges strikingly here; indeed, only love and marriage, as embodied by the patient Vera, can save McBride. On the other hand, the device of the increasing light contradicts some of the supposedly idealistic values of the 1950s. While Vera has not forced Johnny to face the truth too rapidly, the romantic idealism associated with the one and only has been severely compromised by the hero's inability to recognize his beloved on first sight or at first touch.

Vera West epitomizes the "fallen angel" for her descent into the underworld and her disappearance after McBride's flight from Lyncastle cry out to be redeemed by the love of one man. Such redemption occurs frequently in Spillane's other novels; indeed, Mike Hammer has the capacity to create sexual ecstasy and a total change of heart for many a compromised female who shares his bed. Lola, after a single night with the detective, returns to legitimate modelling and gladly earns less than she did as a call girl. A more crude reversal occurs in *One Lonely Night* when Mike seduces Ethel Brighton, a millionaire's estranged granddaughter whose ennui has caused her to embrace communism. Initially, Hammer cannot comprehend why Ethel, who has been exposed to the talismanic power of capitalistic profits, can follow such demented doctrines; however, after he has met the perverts and dregs who make up the communist movement, the hero decides that all Ethel really needs is a virile man. After he has performed this harrowing duty for democracy, and after the sexually awakened Ethel has regrettably left Hammer's apartment, the detective fixes himself a drink and feels guilty, but then "it occurred to me that now that she had a taste of life maybe she'd go out and seek some different company for a change."[63] In such a scene the ideological attractions of communism are reduced to bodily maladjustments: good (i.e. American) sex will entice the misguided back to democracy.

In postponing physical pleasures Mike and Velda remain aware that their romantic goal (love and marriage) can never be attained by compromising the values (doing one's duty and waiting for a better time) which define their identities. More overt sexual conduct reveals that a character is too flawed to be a permanent part of the hero's life. Thus, Connie Wales shows her limitations when aroused by Mike in *Vengeance is Mine*. Not only does Connie rip off her own clothes (and thus assume a male prerogative) but she also hits the hero in the mouth. Connie threatens to usurp the violent tactics which make up Mike's identity, and he must win them back as quickly as possible.

> Her teeth were clamped together. Her eyes were vicious.
> "Make me," she said.
> Another trickle of blood ran down my chin, reminding me what had happened. I reached up and smacked her across the mouth as hard as I could. Her head rocked, but she still stood there, and now her eyes were more vicious then ever.
> "Still want me to make you
> "Make me," she said.[64]

This battle is resolved in the next chapter when, as Connie and Mike eat dinner, she does not speak. In her ecstatic silence Connie epitomizes the male daydream that sex can cure all female ills. We also know that, because of her earlier rebellion against male dominance, Connie must die because she was not perfect enough to be Hammer's lifemate.

Johnny McBride's relationship with Venus, a gangster's moll in *The Long Wait*, represents a further exploration of sexual sadism. Because her criminal lover is extremely jealous, Venus never wears clothes so that, like her mythological namesake, she appears as pure woman at all times. When McBride barges in on Venus to get information, he is stunned by her beauty, but her compromised nature quickly causes her to attempt to beguile him. She lies on a couch, challenging Johnny with her eyes, and when the hero comes over to kiss her Venus burns his hand with a cigarette. The moll later kisses McBride but her kiss calls up images of betrayal.

> She didn't kiss me. Her fingers grabbed my arms and she bit my lip then took the sting out of the bite with her tongue.
> All so damn fast it was like being struck by a snake whose venom was a vicious, poisonous pleasure that left you rigid and trembling in your shoes.[65]

Clearly, Venus is an emasculatrix par excellence and her sadistic traits are simply Spillane's shorthand method for judging her. Venus' death at the hands of her gangster boyfriend is foreordained because such a predatory nature could not fit into the restored, normal society brought about by McBride's actions.

Sadistic whipping scenes highlight *One Lonely Night* and again demonstrate the physical prowess and moral fitness of Hammer. In the first of these encounters Mike is about to whip Ethel Brighton because he believes (falsely, as it turns out) that, despite his earlier sexual therapy, she has remained faithful to the communists. Hammer has stripped Ethel in order to flagellate her all-too-bounteous flesh (described in abundant detail) when fate steps in. At the same moment that Mike's belt falls across the socialite's thighs, a shot rings out and Ethel slumps forward. Fortuitously, Ethel, though badly wounded, survives because, as Hammer notes, his blow forced her to twist slightly so that the bullet did not strike a fatal place. Velda, stripped and beaten later in the same novel, is rescued when Hammer fights his way into the communists' midst and kills everyone in sight. While his bloody trail rids the world of human vermin, Mike's hysteria at seeing his beloved tied and raised off the ground reveals more about the hero's identity. The protagonist must reassure himself that his quest for justice remains a proper pursuit.

> She was stark naked.
> ...The guy in the pork-pie hat waited until she turned to face him then brought the knotted rope around with all the strength of his arm and I heard it bite into her flesh with a sickening sound that brought her head up long enough for me to see that even the pain was dulling under the evil of this thing.
> ...Then there was only beauty to the nakedness of her body... There was the beauty of the flesh that was the beauty of the soul....
> And in that moment of eternity...I knew why my rottenness was tolerated and kept alive...
> *I lived only to kill the scum and lice that wanted to kill themselves. I lived to kill so that others could live... I was the evil that opposed other evil, leaving the good and the meek in the middle to live and inherit the earth.*[66]

This outburst defines Hammer as an avenging angel because violent action has again effected a therapeutic release while providing Spillane's protagonist with a reason for being. Hammer's view of women is also epitomized here, for he sees no body-soul dichotomy in Velda: physical beauty is spiritual in the weaker sex and, thus, human life has a strictly materialistic basis. In implying that men are only what they appear to be on the surface, Hammer reinforces the melodramatic wishes of the mass audience which wants to believe that existence can be managed through such absolute dicta.

Spillane supplies qualities to his protagonists that, while not altering the basic melodramatic tenor of his novels, suggest compromised and equivocal levels in these characters. In keeping with the conventions of hard-boiled detective fiction and film noir, the Hammer novels portray an obsessed protagonist moving against the murk and gloom of a predatory setting that is out to trap and, if possible, destroy him. The insanity of the city, symbolized by the madmen and perverts who are its criminal masters, finds a mirror image in the obsession of the detective so that a paradox arises. Hammer's crusade against evil threatens to come apart if the contradiction of his using his enemies' methods becomes too apparent.

Yet, in spite of all the stylistic and narrative predictabilities which critics have noted since the appearance of these novels, Spillane remains an acute barometer of popular thinking in the 1950s and a more consistent artist than his detractors allow.

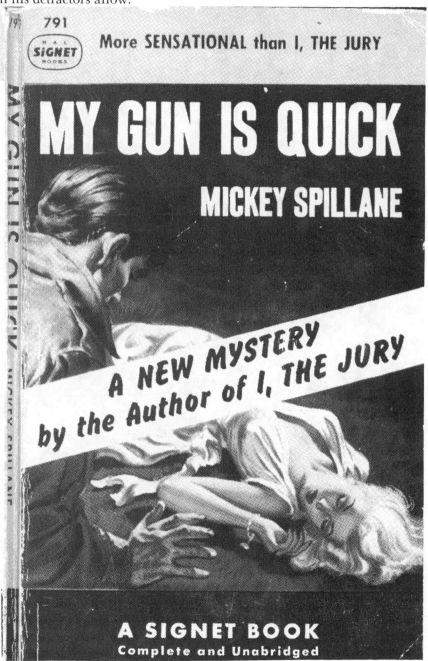

My Gun is Quick
Revenging the victim in a schematized plot (Signet)

959   959

The Astounding Story of an Amazing Woman

The Revolt Of
Mamie Stover

William Bradford Huie

A SIGNET BOOK
Complete and Unabridged

(spine) The REVOLT of MAMIE STOVER   William Bradford Huie

The Revolt of Mamie Stover
Decorum is the Goal (Signet Books)

Chapter 3

"I can't leave my outfit."

The popular view of World War II, which saw that conflict as a necessary struggle against a discernible evil, was questioned during the 1950s but only gave way to a more cynical view in the 1960s. While such novels as Harry Brown's *A Walk in the Sun* (1945), Irwin Shaw's *The Young Lions* (1948) and Norman Mailer's *The Naked and the Dead* (1948) had attacked the idealism which surrounded the war, the majority of 1950s' treatments remained in tune with the spirit and values of such wartime films as *Desperate Journey* (1942), *Air Force* (1943) and *Back to Bataan* (1945). A typical example, which was filmed, was Francis Irby Gwaltney's *Between Heaven and Hell* (1955) with its stress on idealism and sacrifice; while another Broadway and Hollywood success, Donald Bevan and Edmund Trzinski's *Stalag 17*, demonstrated in witty style the necessity for the individual to abandon personal aims for the greater good of the group, a lesson which underlies the familiar classic film *Casablanca* (1942). American reverence for World War II was, perhaps, even more noticeable in the stature that its leaders — MacArthur, Bradley, Marshall and, of course, Eisenhower—continued to enjoy during the decade. While the 1960s were dominated politically by World War II's "junior officers" (Kennedy and Nixon) the earlier decade belonged to their commanders.

The three novels discussed in this chapter do not exhibit the degree of difference found in those which center on the Cold War. Leon Uris' *Battle Cry* (1953) epitomizes traditional reverence toward the world conflict. Herman Wouk's *The Caine Mutiny* (1951) renders the personal doubts and organizational dismays of the war's participants while emphasizing the moral necessity for the struggle. William Bradford Huie's *The Revolt of Mamie Stover* (1951), largely seen by contemporaries as a "daring" sexual novel, embodies a more skeptical view of the war's domestic scene while urging compromise with that amoral social order as the individual's only practical course of action. Clearly, these bestsellers do not echo the more biting sentiments of Brown, Shaw or Mailer nor do they seriously anticipate the more satirical view found in Joseph Heller's *Catch-22* (1961).

* * *

Battle Cry uses the characters, cliches and dialog one finds in World War II propaganda films. *The Sands of Iwo Jima* (1949) exhibits the standard techniques of such fare. In it, a tough sergeant (John Wayne of course) trains raw recruits to perform like seasoned United States Marines. The group initially includes diverse ethnics so that its emergence as a fighting unit symbolically reaffirms America's "melting pot" status. Certain individuals require special attention because of romantic involvements or momentary cowardliness that interfere with their allegiance to the Corps. However, the devoted sergeant, a mother hen with fists, straightens out these momentary lapses so that Mount Suribachi can be stormed; and, when the Wayne character is killed (shot in the back while lighting a cigarette) there isn't any doubt that the platoon will go on because of his example. *Battle Cry* does not follow this plot in exact detail; however Uris' Marine Corps, its veterans and recruits, their love affairs and social values all seem taken from Hollywood. The commercial success of *Battle Cry* (as both a book and a movie) suggests the reassuring nature of the values being presented.

The spirit of the marines is uppermost in the novel, particularly since so much space is devoted to the basic training of the recruits. The purpose behind all the drills and marches becomes apparent when the "gyrenes" defeat the Japanese. Indeed, the radio platoon in *Battle Cry* endures because its members possess "something extra" that sets them apart as fighting men. While the grizzled veterans responsible for training the newcomers continuously lament that the Corps isn't what it used to be (i.e. before December 7, 1941), the stature the new recruits achieve belies such nostalgia before the book is done. In effect, the new crop is as good if not better than the old one; and, in any event, the Marine Corps transforms its recruits into superior fighting men just by its very nature. Mac, the narrator and platoon sergeant, outlines the difference between a Marine and other servicemen.

> I always got that good feeling when I passed a Marine in town. He had that sharp shine and gait, like he was something special and knew it. Lots of times I felt sick looking at some of the dogfaces. There is a certain dignity, I think, that comes with a uniform and it must be rotten to belong to an outfit that doesn't have enough pride to keep that dignity up...maybe, it was because the price of Marine greens came so high to a man that he never let himself get that way.[1]

Mac's outlook suggests that shiny shoes make fighting men, an attitude that would set well with Herman Wouk's Captain Queeg. While one questions if courage and a spit shine are synonymous, Mac's attitude reflects inter-service rivalry, a beloved device in Hollywood films.

Other stock situations include the familiar scene in which an exhausted Marine, after reluctantly accepting aid from a medic, insists he must get back to his outfit.

> He grabbed the corpsman, tears streaming down his cheeks. "I can't leave my outfit," he cried. "You can't send me back...I don't care if I die but you aren't turning me in. We're working our asses off up there. If I go it means more load for them to carry..."[2]

Such devotion, which Mac later celebrates as more exalted than the love between men and women, results from Marine training and discipline. Those who endure this protracted, difficult process establish a symbiotic relationship with those who command them. In order to keep his outfit in fighting trim, Major Sam Huxley orders his men out on a thirty-mile hike during maneuvers in Australia. The resultant tension between the Marines and their commander produces a contest in which pride keeps everyone going: the individual Marines pit themselves against Huxley and suffer blisters and fatigue to prove they are as good as the "old man." Since the men's grumbling disguises affection for their commanding officer, they are clearly making it as a team.

Lieutenant Bryce, who breaks down under fire after being efficient as a desk jockey, cannot be a Marine or, by implication, a man. In order to make Bryce a better soldier, Huxley gives him command of a rifle company but, in the mopping-up operations in the Gilbert Islands which constitute the novel's climax, Bryce must be led away from the battlefield. The Lieutenant is pronounced insane (for wanting to get out of combat!) and the stereotype of the gung-ho Marine is reinforced.

> "Don't kill me...God, don't kill me!"
> He rolled over into the mud, emitting little laughs. For several moments Huxley stood over him and stared down. He shook his head and gritted his teeth.
> "He is completely insane, Kyser said.
> "Poor devil," Huxley said. "I am to blame."
> "Not any more than you are to blame for the war."[3]

While the rapidity of such a total diagnosis seems highly suspect, Kyser's verdict fits the tenor of the novel. Bryce is, in the eyes of real Marines, a madman because he cannot endure what every fighting man must.

In contrast to Bryce, real Marines act like Mac, Sam Huxley and Captain Max Shapiro. Mac watches over his boys, guards their interests when women or gambling threaten, and cries when they get bad news or are wounded. Mac lives and breathes for his charges so that, at the end of the novel, he spends his furlough consoling the families of the dead boys in his outfit. Like Mac, Major Huxley is a "lifer" who constantly works his troops and seeks more dangerous assignments for them. In yet another cinematic cliche[1], Huxley breaks down when his orderly is killed by a grenade. The battalion is under murderous fire (because of an assignment Huxley begged to get) and the Major suddenly realizes that many of his men have been killed. As he loses control, Mac brings him back to his duty.

> Huxley began screaming. "He threw himself on a grenade: Mac, they're killing my boys: They're killing my boys."
> He was berserk. I straightened him up and belted him in the mouth. The punch knocked him down. He struggled up to a sitting position and sat there shaking his head and blinking. A Jap screaming-meemie whistled down. I threw myself over him and pinned him flat till it passed over.
> "Thanks, Mac."[4]

All that remains is the obligatory "I needed that" which most readers will unwittingly supply. Captain Shapiro is impervious to danger but has troubles getting along with the brass; as a result, he is available when Huxley needs a replacement. Shapiro represents a fantasy—the good field officer whose courage offends the desk soldiers and whose survival defeats the system. One can hardly believe in such a figure who refuses to observe military decorum and yet remains an officer; indeed, such a creative misfit contradicts the rigid discipline that Mac has praised earlier. While it may be comforting to believe that nonconformists can be creative within institutions, such an idea represents a popular hope rather than a reality in twentieth-century America.

Mac, Huxley and Shapiro remain at the periphery of *Battle Cry,* for most of the novel concerns the young men they train and command. Since these characters represent a cross-section of America, their resolution of personal animosities in order to become a fighting unit turns them into a microcosmic projection of what American society wanted to believe about itself during and after World War II. It is the power of the group and the institution that are celebrated in *Battle Cry.* Milt Norton, an older recruit who counsels the younger men, makes this point when he tells Danny Forrester, the protagonist: " 'Funny, Danny, how people from different worlds, different lives, people who wouldn't bother to talk to each other before the war, are drawn together in such fine friendships in such a short time.' "[5] Here one sees a nostalgia for the military experience, a stress on the crisis psychology that bound divergent personalities together and made a virtue of a necessity. It is only natural that such times are remembered fondly as having more "direction" or "meaning" than those periods of peace in which individual egotism can have greater play. The members of Mac's squad work diligently to draw together so that Marion Hodgkiss, a would-be novelist, beats up the braggart Indian Joe and then becomes the latter's best friend in order to look out for him.

Danny Forrester, who lives through the battles to return home, exemplifies the one-hundred-percent, All-American boy. He enlists after a distinguished high-school football career (inevitably, he is wounded in the leg and must abandon the game) even giving up an athletic scholarship to do so, for his conscience tells him he must sacrifice for his country. As such a heroic American youth, Danny also has ideal parents who do not question his decisions; indeed, Mr. Forrester constitutes every adolescent's ideal father for, in true 1950s' fashion, he feels his son is a better person than he is. One can almost see poor Jim Backus as James Dean's father in *Rebel without a Cause* (1955) when the elder Forrester tells Danny:

"I've envied you, son. You've turned out to be all the things I wished I could have been...Ever since you were a little bugger you haven't needed me...You'd be bloodied up from the big boys...But you always went back and slugged it out.

"...You've had the guts to stand up to (Mother). I never have.

"...I wanted you to play ball. But I took her side—I always have. Still, I guess inside me, I'm the proudest man alive that you want to join the Marine Corps."[6]

While this speech hints at some darker psychological possibilities—Danny's being a potential Mama's boy—it essentially flatters that revolt of youth which occurs in nearly every culture and time. Even though Mom may be a possessive demon out of Philip Wylie and Dad a eunuch, the child— be he James Dean or Danny Forrester—is tough enough to grow up in spite of his surroundings. There is no doubt some comfort for adolescents in believing that they create themselves; however a more suspicious mind recalls Mark Twain's advice about his father seeming a fool when the son was seventeen and having acquired so much more knowledge by the time his offspring has reached twenty-one.

Constantine Zvonski, or more appropriately Ski, is the most prominent ethnic character in *Battle Cry*. He plays the "Dear John" role so that, after parting from his beloved, a girl whose father habitually drinks and beats her, Ski tries to save enough money to bring his girl to him. After Ski does dirty jobs (such as others' laundry) in order to earn that extra money, he learns that his girl is married and pregnant. This news naturally pushes him into cynicism, which means he gets drunk, nearly falls into a prostitute's clutches (a fate from which Mac and the others save him) and talks bitterly to his comrades. Ski naturally dies early, but his willingness to stay behind after being severely wounded and fight a rearguard action against the Japanese shows that, despite his romantic melancholy, he is still a real Marine.

Jake Levin and Pedro suffer because of their ethnic backgrounds. Levin, a replacement, is initially resented because he has not endured what the others have faced; however, this New York Jew works feverishly to prove he is as good as anyone else. Although there is an unintended irony in Mac's always calling him Levin (and never Jake), the Jewish character becomes a respected team member. Pedro, a medic, only wants to return to Texas and care for his underprivileged Mexican-American family and friends. Racial hostility finds its spokesman in Speedy, a southerner who despises "kikes" and "spics"; however the teamwork mystique of the Marine Corps finally touches even this reprobate. When Levin is seriously wounded, Speedy gladly takes him on his back to an aid station (in a scene that recalls Lew Ayres' carrying Louis Wolheim in *All Quiet on the Western Front* 1930) only to discover that he has been lugging a dead man. Later, Speedy naturally offers to take the deceased Pedro's personal effects back to Texas.

> "But he was a Mexican and you're back home now, Speedy."
> "He was my buddy," Speedy whispered.[7]

Marion Hodgkiss, the squad intellectual, writes constantly of his experiences in an effort to produce the "great" American novel. As an "egghead" Marion inevitably lacks experience in the real world, so that his comrades only respect him after he proves himself in war. Initially, Marion is not taken seriously; thus, his most interesting speech—in which he criticizes the dichotomous thinking in American reactions to communism and the Cold War—is compromised by his naivete . He cautions that total extermination of the Japanese would make the United States as morally reprehensible as its enemies for if " 'we used your method we'd be the same as the people we're fighting.' "[8] Marion is the most reasonable and intelligent member of the squad; however, he dies because as an idealist he cannot finally exist in the world.

Battle Cry clearly urges that romantic passion centered on one other person represents the only sane choice. The women, who remain faithful and offer homes to their beleaguered warriors, loom as the stronger figures in such relationships. Danny loves Kathy, but he suffers because even though "he thought of how wonderful it would be to sleep with her," he knows "if a fellow felt the way he did about a girl—that wasn't right."[9] While such sexual postponement characterizes middle-class American values about love and marriage in the 1950s, a distinctly bourgeois time, Danny experiences a romantic crisis when he meets the attractive and willing Elaine Yarborough whose husband is overseas.

They quickly become lovers and in a moment of passion Elaine demonstrates the reverence accorded intimacy during the 1950s. In this period sex took on a literary air of being an ecstatic because imprecise mystery. Uris' lovers cohabit in the rapid-fire, impressionistic manner that Hollywood championed; and their comments throw light on contemporary mores.

> "You're strong, darling."
> "Don't talk."
> They exchanged fiery kisses.... He lifted her into his arms and held her, and she became faint with passion. "Danny.... Danny," she sobbed.
> He walked to the bedroom door and kicked it open.... Their bodies seemed to melt together; she sunk her fingernails into his flesh. "Oh God...God...God..." she said in a dull, interminable rhythm.[10]

Sobbing and fainting express the bliss which Elaine experiences, while Danny, who knows that words cannot express the intensity of his feelings, utters the traditional masculine remark about being quiet. Elaine's references to God show the value she places on Danny's performance and its "interminable" sensations. In essence, Uris presents intercourse as an act that can be experienced but not described, exactly what the mass audience wants to believe anyway. After being warned by Mac that he might wash out of radio school, Danny is saved when Mac has Kathy call to make the young Marine realize the error of his ways and repent. Later, on leave, Danny and Kathy become lovers in a motel, an event that Danny laments because such surroundings are inappropriate (there should have been flowers and a wedding first). Kathy reassures him, however, that she doesn't really mind either the decor or that he slept with another woman first because she's got him now. Such understanding does not go unrewarded for Danny and Kathy marry on the following day and, when confronted later by another willing female in Australia, Danny refuses to cheat.

An even more idealized woman is Pat Rogers, an Australian whose first husband has been killed. She falls in love with Andy Hookans, the product of a broken home and a prostitute mother, who hates all women. Pat brings Andy out of his misanthropy rather easily and thus humanizes him; however this accomplishment becomes secondary to persuading him to remain with the Marines instead of with her. After they have been lovers for a short time, Pat and Andy play a scene that even Hollywood might have found hoary by 1953.

> "You mean...we're going to have a baby?"
> She nodded.
> "Why didn't you tell me, honey?"
> "I didn't want to use that to hold you, Andy."
> He took her hand.... "You...you'd send me away? Oh, Pat, you'd have done that for me."
> "I've loved you for a long time, darling," she whispered.[11]

Pat is the all-forgiving female found in adolescent daydreams rather than a character who shares significant ground with real women. Her willingness to let Andy leave if he doesn't love her enough to stay accords with romantic idealism. After they marry, Andy wants to go A.W.O.L. to see their child born; however, by gentle insinuation, Pat makes Andy realize he belongs with his buddies. Uris symbolizes the propriety of this choice when, after Andy leaves to rejoin his outfit, Pat feels the first kick of life from their child. This moment occurs in the morning so that the rising sun underscores the beginnings of life within Pat and reaffirms Andy's decision. Before he ships out to the battle that will cost him his lower legs, Andy sees Pat briefly and, in a passage that verbally echoes the climax of *Casablanca*, tells her: " 'I know that sometimes there is something more important than just two people.' "[12] (The final scene in the movie between Rick (Humphrey Bogart) and Ilsa (Ingrid Bergman) has the nightclub owner turned patriot urge: " 'I'm no good at being noble, but it doesn't take much to see that the problems of three little people don't amount to a hill of beans in this world.' "[13] Obviously, the patriotic assumptions of *Casablanca* still operate for Uris.

Major Huxley and his waiting wife are the model couple because of their trust and devotion. In the letters they exchange she never mentions the discomforts of being married to the Marine Corps but instead dwells on how being near him "overpowers any reason I might master."[14] Her apologetic husband urges that he has not provided a comfortable life and so reflects that sense of obligation toward the "good" woman a man is expected to show. In essence, Danny's conduct and the Major's words reflect that every man needs a decent woman and that, paradoxically, in acquiring such love the man somehow brings the woman down to a lower level. Although Uris' Marines are ostensibly magnificent fighting men, they become tongue-tied and guilt-ridden in the presence of women, and so reflect yet another celebrated movie cliche which presents the cowboy hero as too shy to be even coherent in a woman's presence. The Major also adamantly pleads that Mrs. Huxley not try to see him because, even though rank has its privileges, such a meeting would weaken his troops' morale.

> *Lord knows I'm not punishing myself for their sake, but what kind of love would it be if I had to face them knowing I'd stolen something that is denied them? Could we cheat? I must see it through with them, Jean. I am their skipper. Darling, you must understand.*[15]

This convoluted logic, particularly when one asks what the troops would feel Huxley had stolen in embracing his wife, accords with the commander's personality and the "gung ho" spirit of the Marines. When Major Huxley dies, the sentimental pathos becomes even more accentuated for, like any good showman, Uris tries to make his audience laugh, cry and wait.

The novel's attempts at humor are elementary appeals to the audience. There certainly is nothing witty about a character who constantly needs to urinate after he's bundled up for the night and must postpone this function or suffer the cold night air. While the character's remark that his back teeth are "floating" may be momentarily amusing,[16] such material reveals the novel's rudimentary comic sense. Another example of a vintage comic cliche is the presentation of Andy and Pat's wedding. Even a casual reader can predict that Andy's buddies will get roaringly drunk and cry over his fate, and that the groom will be:

> . . .trembling so badly he couldn't light up his cigarette. The sweat was rolling over his face and he could hardly talk. . . .
> "Hey, Andy, you look awful," L.Q. said.
> "I feel awful," he moaned. "The whole church is filled up."
> "Buck up, old buddy. We're with you."
> "What you scared for, cousin?"
> "I. . .dunno. . .I'd rather be hitting a beach."[17]

Few in the audience would be able to compare a military landing with a wedding, so that Andy's reaction reflects melodramatic exaggeration rather than artistic verisimilitude.

A more extensive set of clichés surrounds Marion and the girl with whom he falls in love. In an early conversation with Mac, the young aspiring novelist tells of his ambition.

> "Mac, someday I'm going to be a writer. I guess you think it's kind of silly."
> "Hell no. No ambition is silly. Have you got talent?"
> "I don't know, Mac. . . . You might say nothing has ever happened to me," he fumbled.[18]

Mac sees that Marion is confused for the younger man cannot write but merely dreams about doing so. Marion lacks experience, not having been bloodied by life sufficiently so as to have something to say. Popular notions of aesthetics underlie this passage, for it urges that only an individual who has experienced a great deal can be a significant writer. Such an argument equates quantity with quality and is in thoroughly American fashion; unfortunately, its appealing hypothesis ignores that experience by itself never creates a work of art. If that were the case, Polly Adler would have been a much more significant literary craftsman than Henry James. Marion, of course, receives appropriately therapeutic experiences, ones that turn him into a short story writing demon as the novel proceeds.

The key encounter for Marion is meeting Rae, a San Diego prostitute who responds to his gentleness and decorum. After they have fallen in love and he has learned of her past, another conversation takes place between Marion and Mac.

"Mac," he said, "I don't understand about these women."

"Whores...I mean prostitutes?" He nodded. "I don't know, Marion, it's hard to say.... I know a couple of the guys who married them. They seemed happy enough."

"Can one of them...I mean, Mac, well...I never asked her much about herself...I always thought they were rough and hard, like the books make them."

"They're women just like any other women. You'll find all kinds, same as they're all kinds of Marines."

"...They've got a tenderness that maybe all of us want but few guys are lucky enough to find. But you've got to pay a price for it, you've got to be pretty big and erase a lot of ugly pictures from your mind...." I fumbled and floundered.[19]

Marion suffers because he only knows prostitutes from books and Mac, operating as a Father Confessor, reassures the young man. The old bromide about whores having hearts of gold because they've been exposed to life's tribulations accords with the notion that Marion can only become a writer through experience.

In *Battle Cry*'s climax, a bloody mopping-up operation, most of the squad is killed and Major Huxley dies. Uris' novel comes closest to breaking away from melodrama when the Marines move from small island to small island. Danny's treatment of a captured enemy soldier reflects that the prisoner is "just another poor guy doing what he was ordered to do."[19] While Forrester's insight is similar to Marion's realization that the atolls have not been "raped clean" by the Japanese, these characters never seriously pursue such implications. *Battle Cry* thus remains true to its primary aim of reasserting that World War II was a "just" struggle whose sacrifices were painful but necessary. When Danny momentarily doubts, Marion assures him that their suffering is worthwhile.

"This much I can say, Danny: don't let anybody tell you that you were a sucker. Something better has got to come from it all, it has to. Sure, we're going to get kicked around and they'll tell you it was all for nothing. But it can't be for nothing. Think of the guys like Levin. For him, the issues were pretty clear cut. I wish ours were."[20]

It is this post-war note—that doubters will call World War II a futile gesture in which the United States replaced fascist enemies with communist ones— that makes *Battle Cry* so distinctly a work of the 1950s. Uris recreates the predominant atmosphere of sacrifice and glory-seeking one associates with World War II vintage films; however, for a moment, his characters are commenting on later events. While Marion's advice can be dismissed as a speech on readjustment, his emphasis on "clear-cut" issues and answers certainly reflects the period in which *Battle Cry* appeared. Like Senator McCarthy and Mike Hammer, Uris' Marines only want a society where all issues are black and white.

*   *   *

Over the years Herman Wouk has become a "profound" writer. *The Caine Mutiny* (1951), his first major bestseller, while not as lengthy as his later productions, disenchants because of its pomposity and special pleading. Although the novel has action at sea and a trial, its moral position is so forced that melodrama replaces profundity. Wouk's concern with the nature of command, a question that haunted the 1950s, is central to the plot; yet the resolution of this problem, on which the work turns as a serious intellectual exercise, muddles rather than enlightens. Wouk's smug values, however attractive to a generation living in World War II's aftermath, date the novel markedly. In overemphasizing the weaknesses of artists and intellectuals *The Caine Mutiny* reflects a time when Senator McCarthy dominated the political landscape. Wouk's story is told in a style that never slows; however, his symbolic heavy-handedness, in which characters become merely good and bad, vitiates the overall effect.

Willie Keith, a spoiled Princeton graduate who still lives with his parents and plays the piano in a nightclub to have something to do, is Wouk's protagonist. In familiar literary fashion Willie learns about other men and himself during the narrative, for he is present at the actual mutiny and at Barney Greenwald's post-trial confrontation with Tom Keefer. Moreover, when the reader meets the *Caine* and its crew, Willie, as the typical American who doesn't want to fight and is initially horrified by the grubbiness of the military life, represents the common experiences of the novel's readers; and, as he adjusts to being aboard the old ship, his transformation becomes a subtle flattery of that audience. Willie's mistakes and successes reflect Wouk's belief that, given a crisis, democracy produces men who, however reluctantly, do what is necessary for victory. In *The Caine Mutiny* Willie (directly) and the audience (by inference) are confronted with ideas about romantic love, the difficulties of command, the strength of a volunteer force, and the character failings of those who think too much.

By the novel's midpoint the disparity between what historians will write about past events and what Willie is experiencing is commented on:

> Willie didn't have a historian's respect for the victories at Guadalcanal, Stalingrad, and Midway. The stream of news as it burbled by his mind left only a confused impression that our side was a bit ahead in the game, but making painful slow work of it. He had often wondered in his boyhood what it must have been like to live in the stirring days of Gettysburg and Waterloo; now he knew, but he didn't know that he knew. This war seemed to him different from all the others: diffuse, slogging, and empty of drama.[21]

Willie hasn't grasped that all wars are similar for those who fight them; indeed, Wouk's protagonist has to discover a theme contained in Thomas Heggens' bestselling *Mr. Roberts* (1947)—that war is drudgery. While Willie Keith may finally have seen the real nature of war, his slow learning underscores his personal shortsightedness. It is not until the novel's final page that the reader can be certain Willie has begun to act on the reflections which have arisen from his experiences on the *Caine*.

The main lessons Willie must learn relate to duty. When in Hawaii waiting for his ship, Willie reads a letter from his father which he has been instructed not to look at until actually aboard the *Caine*. This missive initially announces that Willie's parent is terminally ill; thus, the letter contains advice and reflection from father to son. The elder Keith stresses that his son is tougher than his mother wants him to believe. In the midst of lamenting that his own life never provided him with a test to prove his own manhood, Willie's father notes, so that Wouk's intention will be patent:

It seems to me that you're very much like our whole country—young naive, spoiled and softened by abundance and good luck, but with an interior hardness that comes from your sound stock...And I think you're going to make a good naval officer—after a while. After a great while, perhaps.[22]

Given such a passage, it is only natural that Wouk will transform Willie Keith from spoiled, naive child to responsible and reasonable adult.

The letter also introduces a religious note for Willie's father advises him to consult the Bible for emotional sustenance. After Willie has failed to relay a message to Captain DeVriess, his first commander on the *Caine*, the young man receives a parcel from his father, as the letter had promised. At the end of day when his youth and arrogance have led him to breach naval regulations, Willie finds a Bible with a section specially marked out.

Whatsoever thy hand findeth to do, do it with thy might; for there is no work, nor device, nor knowledge, nor wisdom, in the grave, whither thou goest.

The words were underlined with wavering ink lines. Beside them Dr. Keith had written in the broad margin: "He's talking about your job on the *Caine*, Willie. Good luck."[23]

Thus, Willie's initial reactions—that the *Caine* is part of the "garbage" Navy and that DeVriess is a martinet—are reduced to arrogance and shortsightedness. Willie must stick to his work to realize that the Navy's methods embody the wisdom of collective generations wiser in the aggregate than any individual can ever hope to be.

Initially, Willie is influenced by Tom Keefer, an added handicap to the protagonist's realizing that the Navy's way is right. Keith bridles against the commands of both DeVriess and Queeg because he fails to think for himself, but gradually he disengages himself from Keefer and comes to see that things must be done in "official" ways. When he replaces Keefer as radio officer Willie notices how slovenly his predecessor's code books have been kept and realizes that following the prescribed routine about filing additions and deletions (rather than being "brilliant" and carrying such information in one's head) is best. By the time Willie becomes the final commander of the *Caine*, his assimilation of this lesson resembles the fond feelings a child has toward a kindly parent. After reading about proposed demobilization schemes and realizing that, according to them, he will be in the Navy until 1949, the protagonist remains calm because he knows that the Navy is more efficient than that.

He was not disturbed...he was certain that it would be superseded in a couple of weeks, as soon as the wave of anguished screeching had traveled back up the chain of command and splashed over into the press. He could picture clearly what had happened. This point system had been drawn up in wartime and filed away for a remote future...[24]

His certainty derives from a realization that of the three captains he served under the one he most admired as an individual (Keefer) proved to be the poorest commander. Willie has achieved independence because the world has upset his preconceived notions about it.

As a further reflection of maturity, Keith acts reticent about his war experience at home; indeed, while awaiting the court marital, Willie experiences "an obscure shame" whenever he considers boasting about what he has been through. While he makes the most of "taciturnity" as a "subtler and quite respectable form of boasting,"[25] Willie understands that war isn't something to glory in and that a man is judged by what he does rather than by what he says. The Biblical passage has not been lost on him for he recognizes that the quickness of death means that only a fool will waste his life boasting instead of doing. The protagonist's gradual awakening is accompanied by authorial asides that force the reader to see that Willie still has a way to go; thus, the audience knows more about Keith's eventual fate than the character does himself. Wouk's juxtaposing of a shortsighted protagonist and a better informed audience finally becomes cloying, for one encounters too many passages like the following.

> Since then he had seen the toys in action, settling the issues of life and death, and freedom and slavery, for his time; and he had swung so far away from his undergraduate wisdom that he now regarded the Navy's big ships with reverent awe.
>
> And in so regarding them, he was still only an older sort of sophomore; because what was Ulithi, after all? A tiny enclosure of coral in the empty, empty ocean...and all the great Third Fleet, sinking at once, would not have raised the level of the sea by a thousandth of the breadth of a hair. The world's arena remains, to this hour somewhat too big for the most ambitious human contrivances.[26]

No matter how rhetorically impressive one finds this description, reflecting on the insignificance of life hardly seems consonant with wanting to grow up to be a better person. The recognition of one's minuteness should prod the individual to action, and Willie hardly needs to brood further over his youth.

As if merely surviving the *Caine* weren't trouble enough, Wouk's main character falls in love with May Wynn (whose name emphasizes the groping to maturity theme of the novel for Willie "may win" her if he grows up) and agonizes over whether he can marry someone who lacks a comparable education. Willie meets May during an audition at the nightclub where he works and their relationship quickly blossoms. While he remains a proper gentleman for the most part, the protagonist initially sees May as a convenience. On his first leave, after Queeg has replaced DeVriess and alienated the crew by his petty tyrannies, Willie meets May at Yosemite. The surroundings and the moonlight cause the inevitable to occur.

> ...it happened the more easily because they had both read lots of books which dismissed the rules as pretty primitive taboos and asserted that all morals were relative to time and place. Willie, floating in a daze of well-being, was certain at this moment that the books contained true wisdom. May, for some reason, wasn't so sure.[27]

Sexual intimacy thus provides an opportunity for Wouk to condemn intellectuals, for his lovers appear less motivated by physical drives than by psychological rationalizations. Again, Willie errs by trusting his initial feelings: May is obviously more adult because of her resultant unease. The ethical dilemma of the young lovers is clearly conceived in either/or terms and rebounds finally on Wouk. How can an author reduce romantic passion to an excuse for whipping permissive writers?

A deeper crisis occurs between the lovers when, on his second leave, feeling he should end their engagement, Willie tries to seduce May and is rebuffed. May, who has been going to college while supporting herself as a singer, thus again shows her deeper moral sense. Her refusal leads to a serious discussion in which she tells Willie she genuinely loves him but that he is either too immature or too tied to his mother to appreciate what that means. In reaffirming monogamy May thanks Willie for giving her someone to be true to while he's been at sea. Wouk's protagonist is dumbfounded because May has taken the initiative away from him; and his dismay is described in a familiar refrain on his immaturity: "He still had not the slightest understanding of why he had really come; he blamed himself for a late flare of desire crudely masked as a need for advice. He had no way of recognizing the very common impulse of a husband to talk things over with his wife."[28] When Willie can redefine his feelings toward May—a process that requires the trial, his being Keefer's second-in-command aboard the *Caine*, and his own stint as Captain—he returns and proposes to her.

This final scene occurs in another nightclub in which May works and is the mistress of the band leader (although they have not consummated the relationship because he is waiting for a divorce and May is, well, May). Willie accepts this and still insists they can be happy; indeed, the protagonist now appreciates what his capacities are (he wants to teach English in a never-never land small rural college in the Midwest) and knows that emotional fulfillment will require effort. He does not totally convince May, although she is weakening; however, given values that have been established elsewhere in the text, the reader can be certain that Wouk's lovers will be reunited. When Willie meets Walter Feather (as in "light as a") the band leader who is his competition, he becomes completely confident.

> They faced each other for a moment, and there was something in the bandleader's face that unaccountably reminded Willie of Tom Keefer—the mocking condescension perhaps, or perhaps a softness under the brightness. He felt encouraged. He had matched Keefer.[29]

This is the thematic climax of *The Caine Mutiny* because Willie can now deal with the world. Although he wants to pursue a supposedly intellectual profession, Willie still dismisses creative people as too "soft" to endure what life sends their way. Being able to "match" someone (a macho distinction, if there ever was one) culminates Willie's quest which has been prompted by the personal exhortations of his father.

More fundamental issues in *The Caine Mutiny* concern the good commander, his personal qualities and how far his subordinates must follow him in a crisis. Willie's three captains are distinctly different: DeVriess, who appears slovenly and unconcerned (Willie first sees him seated naked behind a desk), focuses on preparedness rather than rigid adherence to regulations; Queeg, who epitomizes the "book" sailor, lacks capacity as a commander or a fighting man and makes inarticulate attempts to enlist greater support from his contemptuous subordinates; Keefer, who disdains regulations as the products of small minds, proves cowardly during a fire and, since he fomented the mutiny which displaced Queeg, comes off as heinous. Time enables Willie to see that DeVriess, whom he despised, was the best of the three—a decision that is therapeutic because it forces Keith to change his thinking.

When Willie visits Ensign Keggs, a former buddy in basic training, the latter's ship appears neat and palatial by comparison with the *Caine*; however Keith learns that its commander is a martinet who makes life hell. When he returns to his own ship, Willie questions his views of DeVriess and the old mine sweeper.

> In the first place, he had considered DeVriess a tyrant; but compared to Iron Duke Sammis his captain was lazily benevolent. Then, the *Moulton* was a model of naval order and efficiency, the *Caine* a wretched Chinese junk by comparison. Yet the smart ship had dropped a paravane; the rusty tramp had led all the ships in mindsweeping performance. How did these facts fit together?[30]

Finding the answers takes up most of *The Caine Mutiny*. Ensign Harding poses the issue of a commander's competence most clearly when, after Queeg has dropped a dye marker and abandoned some landing craft during an invasion, he suggests:

> "The purpose of a captain is to get us out of jams, Willie, not to check off due dates on reports and assignments...if it helps the *Caine* for a professional CPA to audit the nickel-and-dime ship's service, why, I'll audit it. But in return the Navy's supposed to give me a ship that goes, and a captain that fights—That's what all this muck is for, isn't it?"[31]

Willie naturally answers that they must endure a bad commander and "see" things through in spite of him; however, such philosophizing sounds hollow when Queeg is relieved and Willie, as Officer of the Deck, concurs with the decision of Steve Maryk, the second-in-command, to take charge.

Harding's complaint about having to audit the ship's store of O'Henry bars echoes Keefer's more cynical arguments which simply dismiss the service as a moribund institution run by and for idiots. As Captain, Keefer deserts the *Caine* (during a fire which Willie puts out) only to return in a forlorn and repentant mood. Wouk's dissident artist-intellectual disowns his previous views and admits that the Navy has been right all along. Keefer realizes that his judgment of Queeg was hasty and grossly unfair; however, only the actual physical experience of command brings this insight home. While he now sees his hypocrisy, Keefer argues that a commander's role partially excuses such conduct.

"I feel more sympathy for Queeg than you ever will, unless you get a command. You can't understand command till you've had it. It's the loneliest, most oppressive job in the whole world. It's a nightmare, unless you're an ox. You're forever teetering along a tiny path of correct decisions and good luck that meanders through an infinite gloom of possible mistakes.... An ox like DeVriess doesn't see that or he doesn't have the imagination to be bothered by it—and more, he has a dumb oxlike sure-footedness for the right path. Queeg had no brains, but he had nerves and ambition, and it's no wonder he went ga-ga."[32]

Keefer's argument reduces itself to a belief that being responsible is hard on sensitive people. Thus, instead of facing the issue of the nature of command, Wouk focuses instead on Tom Keefer, who now gets his just deserts. Because Willie stays aboard while Tom jumps ship clutching his manuscript (which is, of course, a searing attack on the Navy) he has "matched" Keefer.

DeVriess quickly comes to view Willie skeptically. Although he feels Keith will eventually make a good officer (and it is later revealed that he argued his point to Keefer who naturally doubted that Willie would ever make it), DeVriess submits a report that downgrades Willie for failing to bring him a decoded message promptly. This submission reflects DeVriess' concerns about combat readiness and taking responsibility seriously so that, while Willie cannot see that DeVriess is a good leader under a gruff and demanding exterior, the reader discerns such qualities readily. In launching paravanes, which serve as targets for larger ships, the *Caine* outperforms the other mindsweepers in the exercise; yet DeVriess bawls out Maryk and insists that the launching must be done more rapidly next time. Then, in an ironic aside to Keith, who has applauded Captain Queeg's imminent arrival as his replacement, DeVriess adds: " 'The book calls for one hour.... The standard on this ship is thirty minutes. I've never been able to make these stumblebums do it. Maybe Queeg will have better luck.' "[33] DeVries' insistence on beating the regulations shows how he prizes efficiency above formalities.

Although he drives the men hard, DeVriess can express deep feelings for them. When Queeg comes aboard earlier than his orders indicated, DeVriess takes the new commander on an inspection tour which quickly becomes a formality rather than an exchange of information. Queeg lacks command experience and tries to bluff the more experienced DeVriess, but Wouk uses their conversation to emphasize what DeVreiss truly thinks of his ostensibly ragged crew: " 'It's the hooligan navy, to look at them. But give them half a chance and they deliver. They've backed me in some bad spots.' "[34] DeVriess' affection for his men comes through when he leaves the *Caine* and receives a watch from the crew, a gesture which echoes Mr. Roberts' receiving a "medal" when he transfers off the supply ship. DeVriess initially scorns the gift because regulations forbid his accepting it, yet, after ruminating that he's been in the "hooligan navy" too long and will have to start observing discipline, the departing Captain eyes the watch and exclaims:

"Whaddya know,...Some silly bastard left a watch lying around." He picked it out of the box and strapped it on. "Might as well steal myself a souvenir of this old bucket. Not a bad watch, at that," he said, glancing at it critically. "What time is it, Mister Keith?"

"Four o'clock, sir," said Willie.

"Three-thirty," grunted DeVriess, adjusting the hands. "I'll always keep it half an hour slow," he said to the sailors, "to remind me of the fouled-up crew of the *Caine*. Somebody toss down my gear."[35]

DeVriess combines military necessity with a personal style that places him above, but not remotely above, the men he commands. Significantly, Maryk, the best sailor on the *Caine*, praises DeVriess while Keefer dismisses him. Willie's recognition of DeVriess only comes belatedly and subconsciously to him for, in complaining of Queeg, Willie prompts May to ask if all commanders are as difficult: " 'Oh, no. The skipper before Queeg was a grand guy, and damned capable too.' The words were out of his mouth before it occurred to him to smile at his change of heart about DeVriess."[36]

Captain Queeg is a classic instance of a man trying to do a job for which he is unfit; while later generations could dismiss such individuals with the Peter Principle (and thus accept incompetence as an inevitable accompaniment of institutionalized society), inefficiency looms as more serious and complex in *The Caine Mutiny*. The subordinate officers prove incapable of protecting Queeg from his own cowardice and lack of judgment, and their open contempt for him represents a failure to "adjust." Only Maryk resists this tide of feeling and, finally, even he is sucked into it. Naturally, Queeg's errors are rendered worse because he refuses to accept responsibility for them. Trapped within a vicious circle, Queeg lies to cover up his immediate tracks, and then changes his version of what happened to accord with later, paranoid feelings of hostility toward those whom he imagines are responsible. When he runs the ship aground (after having refused to let DeVriess show him how the *Caine* maneuvered) Queeg tries to evade submitting the required report. He later insists that all shirt tails must be tucked into trousers and makes Willie the "morale" officer responsible for reforming a veteran crew. The *Caine* subsequently steams over a tow line and cuts loose a target because Queeg is busy reprimanding a sailor about his shirt tail and forgets that the ship is turning. The crew's hostility toward their Captain is reflected in no one's mentioning the 360 degree revolution until it is too late to avoid the mishap.

Queeg reprimands his second-in-command when he learns the incident must be explained at headquarters; however, such lashing out constitutes Queeg's way of asking for help. The mutiny results from collective shortsightedness because no one, least of all the creative Keefer, puts himself in Queeg's shoes and tries to understand that his anger is a way to save face. When he chews out Gorton, his initial second-in-command, for example, Queeg is trying to make things run smoothly and, at the same time, to retain his own personality. Unfortunately, the Captain's plea sounds like hollow snobbery.

"I readily grant you...that it called for a little intelligence on your part to understand your duty in this matter and give all the dope. But it was definitely your responsibility.

Hereafter, of course, if you want to be treated as if you don't have the professional background which I respect in you, that can easily be arranged."[37]

Thus, Queeg's initial reaction to the cut cable, a fiasco he magnifies by refusing to retrieve the floating target despite Maryk's advice, displaces responsibility to a subordinate. However, as tension increases aboard the *Caine*, Queeg's version of the incident changes. Since he has personal trouble with Stillwell, the helmsman on that occasion, Queeg gradually comes to blame that sailor for the entire incident. After refusing to grant Stillwell a furlough and discovering that Maryk has countermanded this order, Queeg launches into a tirade that reveals his emotional weakness.

"...it was Stilwell's fault. Imagine a helmsman not warning the commanding officer that the ship was in such danger: I know why he kept his mouth shut, of course. I'd bawled him out in the morning for being too goddamn fresh and making his own decisions at the helm, and he was just playing it real smart, see, letting me get myself in trouble. Kay. I know his kind. These vindictive little troublemakers that bear grudges are just my meat. I'm gunning for that little squirt and I'm going to get him, believe you me."[38]

Queeg's incompetence thus boils over into paranoia, and his desire to get even with Stillwell reflects his retreat into a safer existence; since he subconsciously recognizes his own incompetence, Queeg reverts to dealing with routine matters that a subordinate officer (such as he had been for years) must treat.

The same flight into more comfortable circumstances colors Queeg's concern about the stolen strawberries later. He awakens his officers and holds a full-scale investigation, replete with cups of sand measured to approximate the strawberries served at dinner, a strip search of every man aboard and a testing of all keys in their possession. This grandiose waste of time and energy over a quart of strawberries (which the departing Harding reveals were stolen by the mess boys) reenacts Queeg's greatest professional accomplishment—discovering who pilfered rations on a ship in which he previously served. The epithet "old yellow stain" attaches to Queeg because of his absence from the bridge during actual fighting when he attempts to position himself as far as possible from that side of the ship closest to action. This fear resurfaces during a typhoon in which Queeg rigidly adheres to sailing with the prevailing wind rather than sailing against the wind for greater balance. At this point Maryk relieves Queeg and precipitates the mutiny, an action that requires the acquiescence, if not the enthusiastic support, of the ship's other officers. While the subsequent trial reveals how that agreement becomes lukewarm when confronted with official penalties, the issue of Queeg's competence still remains.

Was it in the best interests of the *Caine* and its crew (and, by implication, the United States and its war effort) to allow Queeg to continue? While Wouk urges that the officers owed Queeg loyalty as their commander and as a member of the regular Navy which guarded their well-being, the harsher reality that an entire crew could have been lost is dismissed. Even if one feels that the officers of the *Caine* behaved abominably, does their lapse justify following an incompetent leader to death? Ironically, the *Caine*'s survival makes the issue of Queeg's removal moot, for the only way the mutineers could have proved their case was by letting the ship sink.

The mutiny trial reaches its climax when, after lengthy repetition of much of the rest of the novel, Queeg condemns himself by revealing his paranoid personality. Although psychological issues have been looked on as improper by the court, in Queeg's case personality speaks louder than facts. Queeg is skillfully manipulated until he breaks and denounces his "betrayers" in a muddled syntax which shows his state of mind.

> "Now, you take that strawberry business—why, if that wasn't a case of outright conspiracy to protect a malefactor from justice—Maryk carefully leaves out the little fact that I had conclusively proved by a process of elimination that someone had a key to the icebox. He says it was the steward's mates who ate the strawberries but if I wanted to take the trouble I could prove to this court geometrically that they couldn't have.... Mr. Maryk the hero of the crew wanted to go right on mollycoddling them and—or you take the coffee business—no, well, the strawberry thing first—it all hinged on a thorough search for the key and that was where Mr. Maryk as usual with the help of Mr. Keith fudged it."[39]

Queeg runs on nervous energy by this time, so that his groping testimony (which becomes more rapid and tangled) counterpoints the incessant clicking of the metal balls he holds to calm himself. Our last image of him suggests that, unlike Willie who learns, however haltingly, from experience, Queeg remains trapped in a permanently deluded world where mistakes are always occurring because of others who envy him.

Tom Keefer's intellectual and cynical outlook masks his own shortcomings. He emerges as a hypocrite and a villain, yet Wouk's treatment is so heavy-handed that he creates sympathy for the beleaguered Keefer. When first seen, Tom insists that everything in the Navy is confused, for his brother, Roland, who wants safe duty has been assigned to a carrier, while he, who knows that the significant actions will be fought on larger ships, is stuck on the *Caine*. Keefer's desire to be in the thick of combat arises from his being a novelist always looking for material. His dismissal of the function he currently performs comes across drastically when he tells Willie: " 'War is ninety-nine per cent routine—routine that trained monkeys could perform.... But the one per cent of change and creative action on which the history of the world is hanging right now you'll find on carriers. That's what I want to be part of.' "[40] Ironically, Roland dies in combat while Tom proves a coward when commanding the *Caine*; thus Keefer performs the right job for what he is. His pride is only one blind spot that this aspirant novelist possesses; indeed, the more one reads of Keefer, the less likely a writer he becomes, even though Willie endorses his novel enthusiastically. Keefer's outlook opposes the advice Dr. Keith gave his son and so Tom serves quite literally as a temptation to the younger Keith. He all but seduces Willie by insisting that the Navy represents 'a third-rate career for third-rate people, offering a sort of skimpy security in return for twenty or thirty years of polite penal servitude. What self-respecting American of even average gifts, let alone superior ones, will enter such a life?' "[41]

Since he insists that the Navy resents the abilities of those who have been drafted into it, one expects that Captain Queeg, the epitome of the mediocre "lifer", will hardly fare well in Keefer's eyes. To make the character even more obviously hypocritical, Wouk has Keefer enthusiastically welcome Queeg as " 'just what the doctor ordered' " and then dismiss the new commander as a " 'joke' " within twenty-three pages. Keefer quickly finds fault with the new Captain so that he can continue to nurse his own personal grudge, however his cowardice precludes him from any open show of defiance so that, after coming to despise Queeg, Keefer tries to impress others with the Captain's mental weaknesses. He nearly convinces Maryk that Queeg is a psychopath; however, when they go to the Admiral's flag ship to air their suspicions, Keefer characteristically backs out at the last minute. He is just as equivocal at the mutiny trial where he denies any complicity in Queeg's removal to keep his own record clean. His comeuppance occurs later when, after jumping ship even though he is its commander, a member of the *Caine*'s crew who stayed aboard and helped Willie in putting out the blazing Kamikaze, says the last word on Keefer: " 'Hope the captain enjoyed his dip....He's got Queeg beat a mile for fast footwork.' "[42] Since Keefer has already had a drink thrown in his face by Barney Greenwald after the trial, such repetition works in reverse, for the character is so consistently embarrassed that he becomes a martyr.

Barney Greenwald, a Jewish attorney from Phoenix who specialized in "Indian" cases before the war and had acquired a substantial practice in Washington, defends Maryk and the other mutineers. Greenwald's record with underdogs makes him an acceptable defense counsel, and he stuns the Judge Advocate by insisting the defendants will be acquitted. The prosecution has momentary worries over Greenwald's being a draftee (the trial must not pit "reserves" against "regulars") and a possible "pinko" (because of Greenwald's interest in civil rights—a connection that would have been more appropriate in 1951). Although Greenwald wins the case by goading Queeg into revealing himself, he is not primarily important as a legal technician but rather as yet another warning against Keefer's heinousness. Greenwald forms a mental picture of Maryk before meeting him and, when they actually sit together, the lawyer realizes that the man before him cannot be solely responsible for the mutiny. Greenwald trusts his "clear picture" of the instigator ("slight, thin, nervous, dark, and with the self-satisfied expression of a petty intellectual"[43]) and knows that Maryk, whose physique is nearly the opposite, must be innocent.

The lawyer's clairvoyance is borne out, of course, by Keefer; yet such anti-intellectualism is overdrawn. While denouncing Keefer's actions, Greenwald consistently suggests that only an egghead could do such things. Thus, what Wouk intends to be a reasonable critique runs amok and becomes a general attack on artists and intellectuals that accords only too well with the climate of opinion created by Senator McCarthy. When he learns that Keefer has written a novel while on board the *Caine*, Greenwald becomes even more bitter and ironic.

"I'd like to read it. I'm sure that it exposes this war in all its grim futility and waste, and shows up the military men for the stupid, Fascist-minded sadists they are. Bitching, humorous, lovable citizen-soldiers.... Well, I'll tell you, Maryk. Your sensitive novelist friend is the villain of this foul-up, all right, but it doesn't do us any good—"

"...The fact that he's running for cover now—well, he warned you on the *New Jersey*, didn't he? He had all the insight of a sensitive novelist."[44]

Keefer has become an archetypal bogeyman, one whose very interests render him reprehensible and suspicious.

While Keefer may be one in a long line of American intellectual ogres, Wouk lapses into melodrama by having Greenwald tongue-lash Keefer so that no reader will forget who is right and who is wrong. After the trial, at a dinner where Maryk and the others celebrate their acquittal, the drunken Greenwald makes a late entrance and castigates Keefer as the real culprit who should have been on trial. After insisting that he would like to write a war novel to " 'make a hero' " of Queeg, Greenwald goes on to argue that the Navy was the only force that stood between American innocence and Hitler's barbarism. He praises Queeg for doing a dirty and boring job which, ultimately, saved Greenwald's mother's life. While her son was unsuccessfully trying to be a pilot:

"...who was keeping Mama out of the soap dish? Captain Queeg.

"Yes, even Queeg, poor sad guy, yes, and most of them not sad at all, fellows, a lot of them sharper boys than any of us, don't kid yourself, best men I've ever seen, you can't be good in the Army or Navy unless you're goddamn good. Though maybe not up on Proust 'n' *Finnegan's Wake* and all."[45]

What begins as a defense of Queeg and the regular Navy thus turns back to Keefer; and the resultant argument implies that one's interests (be they Proust or Joyce) are infallible guides to one's conduct. Certainly the mentality of such McCarthy assistants as Roy Cohn and G. David Schine, who checked the contents of overseas Army libraries to be certain they contained no "subversive" literature, would applaud such a diatribe. Greenwald eases his guilt over destroying Queeg by throwing champagne in Keefer's face; unfortunately, Wouk must accompany this moment of high drama with the symbolic note that the wine is yellow.

The Caine Mutiny alludes to anti-Semitism and, while such references never become dominant, a theme of accommodation gradually emerges. Willie must overcome his own ethnic prejudice, which briefly flares up when he sees May with her agent, Marty Rubin; however, since Rubin likes the young man, such adjustment constitutes a sort of noblesse oblige. Greenwald, the novel's intellectual hero, tells Maryk at a lull in the trial that the presiding officer doesn't like Jews, yet: " 'It won't make any difference. You're not supposed to love Jews necessarily, just to give them a fair shake. I've always had a fair shake in the Navy and I'll get it from Blakely, too, despite the eyebrows.' "[46] Greenwald knows the Navy to be above prejudice or pettiness; indeed, he loves the service as a situation in which his instincts for self-sacrifice and duty can have free rein. His trust in the integrity of the court martial board underscores the absence of that quality in Keefer. In speaking of the death of Keefer's brother, a survivor tells Tom and Willie: " 'Roland passed out and they took him down to sick bay. But by that time he had all the guys back to doing everything they always did at drills, and of course that's what counts.' "[47] This emphasis on duty's arising from a set of instructions so familiar as to be second-nature represents yet another moral rebuke to Tom and an affirmation of Captain DeVriess. There is, finally, very little that does not add to *The Caine Mutiny*'s didactic purpose; and Wouk's strident novel benumbs rather than enlightens.

* * *

No novel dates so rapidly as the sexually "daring" or "explicit" work of a bygone era; indeed, what one age considers shocking often appears quaint or whimsical to later eyes. Since book censorship operated in the United States until 1960, novels before that time either observed some obvious ground rules in treating sex or sought out underground or foreign markets. Such culturally conditioned reticence makes William Bradford Huie's *The Revolt of Mamie Stover* seem particularly tame when compared to later works in film (e.g. *Deep Throat*, 1972) and fiction (*Fear of Flying*, 1973; *The Betsy* 1971). Huie's novel, which probably would not have been purchased by respectable sources (i.e. libraries) on its initial appearance, has become a somewhat rare item today for a permissive age will hardly demand such old-fashioned titillation. Indeed, present-day readers will more likely be impressed by the political and social attitudes in *The Revolt of Mamie Stover* than by its glimpses of brothel life. Huie's cynicism about America's future (which seems less pronounced in *The Americanization of Emily*, 1958) controls his tale of a southern belle turned hooker ascending the ladder of social respectability in Honolulu. James Monroe Madison, the narrator, befriends Mamie on the boat trip from the United States and their shipboard romance becomes a permanent friendship so that Madison can record the girl's success in revolting against the laws and manners regulating prostitution in the Islands. The narrator's feelings toward Mamie remain ambivalent for, while he admires her drive, he loathes her profession and hates the changes that Mamie's revolt make inevitable in Hawaiian society.

Huie portrays some of the domestic consequences of World War II through Mamie Stover who, like many a more respectable citizen, uses shortages and dislocations to accumulate wealth and respectability; indeed, Mamie simply represents an extreme example of a predatory temper that was everywhere.

A six-foot-tall, yellow-haired whore from Mississippi was the most successful revolutionary of the Second War.... The war wasn't a disaster for her; it was an opportunity.... It made her a partner, then a pensioner, of government. It offered her a chance to revolt against onerous old restraints, to rise in the world, to acquire property, to feel important. And, more skillfully than any of her competitors, Mamie Stover used the opportunities of war to make herself rich and comfortable.[48]

Thus, Huie's novel initially appears to be a tale of a more calculating Sister Carrie; however this emphasis eventually competes for space with the narrator's own sense of loss and dislocation. In every successful revolution there are aristocrats who must fall or readjust. Mamie wants to succeed because, as a beauty queen who left Leesburg, Mississippi, to seek her fortune in Hollywood, she can only go home as a has-been or as a resounding success. When Madison meets her, she has just been run out of Hollywood by a producer-boyfriend. The girl suffers because of her exposure to the luxuries that money can buy and, as she says, having been so close to the good life has given her an unquenchable taste for it. Thus, she arrives in Honolulu determined to rise above her present status.

Once Mamie has achieved financial independence and social acceptance, she exhibits typically nouveau riche attitudes about decorum and propriety. In a bit of pointed irony, the former prostitute who has retired into marriage because the war is winding down, finds her guests' behavior unbecoming and lewd. She tells Madison that she had to throw people out whom she invited to her new home because:

> "I couldn't believe they'd act like they did...those women...were messier and louder and dirtier. They tore up everything. They strewed powder and lipstick and ashes and whiskey and food from my front door to my back. They'd lie in a bedroom with some guy and not even close the door. They'd get out in the yard and holler 'Roll me over, lay me down, and do it again' until everybody in Pacific Heights must know that song."[49]

While these supposedly respectable citizens behave in ways no whore would, the larger irony is that Mamie wants the very respectability that her revolt has destroyed. Human nature, whether embodied by the son of an old-line aristocratic family or a whore from Mississippi, remains the same in similar circumstances; wealth brings a desire for tranquility and for a life style to demonstrate one's position within the community. Man, Huie is arguing, is a profoundly conservative animal once his basic needs are satisfied, and woman is even more so.

World War II's social levelling is bemoaned throughout *The Revolt of Mamie Stover*. In the narrator's eyes the disruptions brought to Hawaii by the influx of thousands of military personnel far outweigh the economic or defensive advantages that derive from their presence. Madison even suggests that this particular war spawned a different corruption than had previous conflicts.

> In previous wars a nefarious few—the International Bankers, the Merchants of Death, or the Big Manipulators have been accused of profiteering at the nation's expense. But in the Second War it was the American people—the humble along with the arrogant—who spurned sacrifice and insisted upon enriching themselves while the nation bled.[50]

While his argument is not consistent (one wonders at whose expense, if not their own, these profiteering souls were enriched) Huie's emphasis on the role of the common man seems insightful since the Second World War had Adolf Hitler—a common man, if ever there was one—as a major precipitator. By stressing corruption on the home front, Madison criticizes the century of the common man, an era the Spanish philosopher Ortega Y Gasset characterized by the title of his most famous book, *The Revolt of the Masses* (1929). Interestingly, Madison carries this book with him on his wartime travels.

Mamie's covert earnings represent a very small percentage of the "black market" dollars afloat as a result of the momentary prosperity and economic dislocations of wartime. Thus, Mamie's prostitution metaphorically represents a wide spectrum of criminal activities which normal citizens pursue during this hectic period.

These were...the dollars which passed under the tables; the dollars which bought the three-hundred-dollar neckties in Miami...the dollars which increased the great inflationary pressures; the dollars which cheapened all other dollars;...the dollars which were kept off the record and in the safe deposit boxes of banks and hotels; the dollars which identified an American as a cash-carrying whore who was enriching himself by defrauding his country while other men were dying for it.[51]

This bitter assessment, lamenting the lack of idealism and the unwillingness to sacrifice, might well have come from the pen of a Roman grieving over the end of the Republic, for Huie's narrator certainly embodies the same hard-line conservatism one associates with a figure like Cato the Younger.

Madison finally sees Mamie's rise as neither unusual nor particularly praiseworthy; indeed, her means of acquiring wealth are more honest than those of other war profiteers couched in supposed respectability. The narrator's admiration for Mamie grows because of the way she uses her money: he invests sums for her and offers her advice about such transactions. In a conversation with Annalee Johnson, a respectable girl with whom he carries on a desultory love affair, Madison implies the popular equation of riches and intelligence by defending Mamie because of her net worth.

"Is she intelligent?"

"No, I wouldn't call her intelligent. But she isn't stupid. She's about twenty-four now, and she's worth at least one hundred and fifty thousand dollars. Whatever that indicates, it isn't stupidity."[52]

In a society dominated by the principle of caveat emptor Mamie's acquisition and retention of a fortune demonstrates her superiority. Madison thus compliments her for winning the game, even though he finds the game ultimately loathsome.

Sexuality in *The Revolt of Mamie Stover* exhibits a more mechanical air than one might expect. Mamie's physical antics are conditioned by her drive for money: eroticism is awash in efficiency so that Mamie's indecencies serve as a means to excoriate the federal government and the wartime American mentality rather than as occasions for "steamy" sexual passages. While the same euphemistic impressionism that marks most sexual descriptions in 1950's novels is here, Huie assumes his readers know what goes on in the clinches, so that sex becomes more matter-of-fact. Life within a whorehouse is treated almost sociologically, for far more attention is given to the Thirteen Articles, a municipal code regulating brothel operations in Honolulu (and an inevitable war casualty) than to physical couplings. The novel's most erotic passage takes place aboard ship between the narrator and Mamie; for, even though Madison regards the girl as a pickup, the possibility of marriage momentarily lingers between them. For the most part, however, Mamie is treated like a piece of merchandise whose height, blonde hair, long legs and breasts (whose generous size is mentioned sixteen times in the first eighteen pages) set her apart. Mamie also possesses a sexual capacity that is strong, to say the least.

> In my bunk she became so desperately hungry that for a moment I feared I'd be unequal to her. She wasn't passive and yielding; she was fierce and wild and strong.... She moaned, then screamed so that I had to hold my hand over her mouth lest she rouse the ship.... At last, after a third, hot convulsive release, she went limp and collapsed into sleep.[53]

Mamie foreshadows Grace Metalious' hot-blooded wenches in possessing the same sexual aggressiveness, albeit without the verbal candor that marks those later creations. Mamie's capacity is implied by the use of "limp" (a term that makes her appear as the male in bed). While Madison doubts he may possess the capacity to stay on "top" of Mamie in this contest, American manhood is reaffirmed when the girl is driven into ecstasy by his physical skills and stamina.

The heroine's sexuality conditions her profession (it will be a measure of the difference in mores that Metalious' nymphs are just country folks); and, to be efficient as a prostitute, Mamie indulges in activities that are, for the time, perverse. Because the lines of servicemen grow ever longer before each brothel, Mamie develops an assembly line which allows her to turn anywhere from fifty to two hundred "tricks" a day. Her production line underscores the assumption that more is better, and Mamie grows rich operating what the narrator calls the Bull Ring. As an efficient entrepreneur, Mamie enters a room as a doctor might visit a patient, pleasures the client, and then moves on to another room while her assistants clean up, provide fresh towels, and bring in another customer. After she retires, Madison ships the Bull Ring to the Smithsonian Institute because he believes it reveals the inventiveness of the American character.

> It seems to me that the Bull Ring is an impressive example of that ingenuity which has contributed so much to American Progress...that ingenuity on which we now must depend for world supremacy. The Bull Ring...is proof that we can still build the better mousetrap; it is evidence that our youth can still open New Frontiers, that Fame and Fortune still await the ingenious young American who Has What It Takes.[54]

Madison's irony reinforces his dismay over America's moral decline; in effect, the war has revealed that Americans are as corrupt as the rest of mankind and, since prostitution is the world's "oldest" profession, Mamie's inventiveness hardly represents "progress." Madison, implying that the United States no longer leads by example but by technological supremacy (the Atomic Bomb), finds such a prospect disheartening because he believes nations have moral as well as physical lives.

The narrator's conservatism clashes mightily with the modern world, for he is an elitist in an age of egalitarianism. Madison sets forth his vision about society in a discussion with Mamie. The girl feels that her wealth entitles her to the same respect granted to others, but Madison insists that society is unfair for good reason.

"I believe that men may properly seek exclusiveness. I believe that segregation and stratification are proper, though they are cruel. There is nothing more pathetic than the little girl who has been rejected by the sorority, but the cruelty doesn't make sororities improper. Society is cruel, but life is cruel—it's cruel for one person to have more brains or money or virtue than another. So I respect society and I wish that Waikiki (a beach Mamie has openly visited in defiance of the Thirteen Articles) could have been kept exclusive."[55]

Given the novel's advocacy of such a view, there is little likelihood that *The Revolt of Mamie Stover* will enjoy renewed popularity today. Madison's diatribe implicitly attacks such later movements as civil rights and women's liberation; thus, he is a voice from the past, one urging excellence in a society that only wants to be comfortable and "fair."

In keeping with his outlook on men's inherent differences, Huie's narrator insists on degrees of suffering that contradict the egalitarian levelling of this phenomenon. For Madison, tragedy presupposes individuals sensitive enough to experience it; and, while the melodramatically-minded refer to any calamity as a "tragedy," he is more guarded in his use of the term. The little girl's dismay at being rejected is "pathetic" and not "tragic" because there are situations which cannot be perceived in heroic terms. Madison sees Mamie as a tough individual who is not sensitive enough to feel tragedy.

"...there are individuals who dream and struggle and yearn and aspire, and there are others who don't give a damn. I believe that physical suffering in a dolt is regrettable, but is not to be compared with anguish in a sensitive, aspiring man, which is tragic. I believe that there is an aristocracy among men—an aristocracy of will, work, intelligence, and character."[56]

Madison's definition establishes his own alienated position: he remains "in" but not "of" American society. While Huie's plot never turns his protagonist's ire into anything more than verbal dismay (a quality Ayn Rand presents more heroically in *The Fountainhead*, 1943, and *Atlas Shrugged*, 1957), further comments on wartime corruption make Madison's desire to escape seem reasonable.

In her drive for respectability Mamie decides that she should pay taxes, but Madison argues that even a country must have a moral character.

"...I believe that for the whores not to pay makes more sense than for the whores to pay.... For I believe that the United States as a nation has to stand for something. When it errs it must always err in the direction of the ideal.... If the American government ever ceases to be grand and noble in the eyes of its people, if it ever becomes just an ordinary government, the nation will have lost its reason for being.... And a government that demands support from whorehouses, I can't see how such a government can appear grand and noble to its people."⁵⁷

Huie's narrator thus argues that nations are collective acts of faith in which the citizens must believe in the ideal aims of their rulers: to reduce government to a matter of mere accommodation and maximum tax-collecting efficiency would be to destroy this trust. After Watergate and two decades of eroding faith in the federal government, Huie's words seem prophetic. Although modern politicians and commentators often talk of an individual's "charisma," this self-centered quality pales in the light of the faith that Madison describes. Such idealism founders because of the effects of the war on the domestic front. Madison understands that all armies wreak devastation on the civilian population and so the military influx spells an end to Hawaii as a retreat for unique individuals. Madison joins other property owners in feeling that social changes, such as Mamie's moving to an exclusive neighborhood, have destroyed their way of life.

Madison's dislike of the military results from his own experiences, for as a soldier he comes to believe that the tendencies he saw as an outsider are similar when viewed from the inside. The narrator tells Annalee that military rootlessness breeds the same intransigence that caused Mamie to move onto Waikiki with a horde of attending officers.

"The officers she is with," Annalee said. "I suppose they are Southern Californians."

"I guess so. They are of our new homeless, traveling man culture. They don't give a damn."

Before we left I asked one more question. "Annalee," I said, "do you resent Mamie Stover's being at Waikiki?" She reflected a moment, then answered, "Yes, I like the way Hawaii has been and Mamie Stover and her officers are going to cheapen and ruin us."⁵⁸

This feeling of unavoidable loss, which Huie's narrator angrily describes at one point as turning the beach into a "dirty, tropical nigger-infested Coney Island,"⁵⁹ finally becomes dominant. Even the aged Chinese proprietor of Hawaii's best restaurant tells Madison he can no longer take pride in preparing fine food because " 'the pigs has come. Pigs and whores. Slop is for pigs. And who can have pride in serving slop to pigs. Fine food is for fine people; but fine people is being run over by pigs.' "⁶⁰ Chong's diagnosis seems quaint in the age of the Big Mac; however, he echoes the narrator's (and the author's) view of modern America. In the novel's final irony, Huie juxtaposes the old landowners talking of escape to an uncluttered island paradise in the western Pacific with Mamie's ongoing resilience and ambition. While Hollywood and southern California have come in for some knocks from Madison, he is last seen listening to Mamie's proposition that he help her write a book about her life. She now has all the luxuries ('not even Zanuck could give me more'⁶¹) and intends to live in style in the United States; moreover, she wants to produce an autobiography that will make her even more "respectable." Huie's protagonist, despite all his conservative and nostalgic values, epitomizes the typical American by being more attracted by Mamie's energy than by the escapism of his defeated neighbors.

Chapter 4

"Perhaps we'd stabilize at the Mississippi?"

Cold War tension dominated American politics through the 1950s. The euphoria that marked the end of World War II soon gave away to anxiety over the prospect of another war. The Truman Doctrine, the Soviet dominance of Eastern Europe, the Berlin Airlift, and the emergence of Communist China all created a tense international atmosphere which quickly spilled over into domestic life. By 1950 the continuing investigations of the House Un-American Activities Committee and the sensational espionage trials of Alger Hiss and the Rosenbergs had created a public opinion which readily accepted the anti-communist zeal of Senator Joseph McCarthy of Wisconsin. In the ensuing decade popular fears of communism experienced a lengthy "paranoid" phase, a mild interruption, and then a renewed sense of urgency.

The conflict in Korea (1950-1953) was bewildering to Americans for stalemate rather than victory—a psychology of containment which implied the communists could not or should not be obliterated as the Nazis and Japanese had been—was the avowed goal of our participation. The struggle unsettled because the United States, while thinking of itself as the lone embattled gunfighter (Will Kane of *High Noon* or television's Matt Dillon), did not triumph over the outlaws; if we couldn't defeat the supposedly backward North Koreans and Chinese, how could we hope to beat the Russians? Popular distress was epitomized by the firing of General MacArthur (April 11, 1951), a leader who had sought total victory, been forced to retreat when the Chinese struck from Manchuria, and interfered in the subsequent negotiations which eventually ended the war. MacArthur's dismissal, popularly seen in the United States as an assault on the reputation of a hero by a petty and jealous president,[1] marked the end of that sense of American military superiority which had attended the conclusion of World War II. In this atmosphere of suspicion and recrimination, Joseph McCarthy became, for a brief time, the country's most influential politician. While this earlier Asian struggle has generally been ignored in fiction or film, novels like *M.A.S.H.* (1968) and movies like *Pork Chop Hill* (1959) represent standard reactions.

The United States greeted the launching of the first Sputnik (October 4, 1957) with shock and dismay. This Russian scientific coup led to a national outcry that American education had failed to train the engineers necessary to keep the United States ahead in the "space race." Thus, the relative tranquility which followed Senator McCarthy's eclipse after the televised

61

Army hearings of 1954 came to an end. Once again, Cold War tensions, which had been forgotten in the "Eisenhower Equilibrium" of 1954-1957, dominated American politics. Sputnik ended a brief idyll in which Americans supposedly enjoyed unmatched prosperity and political tranquility (an image of the 1950s which later generations have sentimentalized). The U-2 incident and the subsequent collapse of the Big Four Conference in Paris (May, 1960) ushered in a new decade in which the Cold War again loomed large. Clearly no dramatic or permanent answers existed, and the American public had reluctantly learned by 1960 that the Cold War would be a test of endurance.

Four best-selling novels reflect the 1950s' fears of communism. During a decade in which J. Edgar Hoover's *Masters of Deceit* (1957) became a bestseller widely regarded as an accurate analysis of Marxism, it is not surprising to find novelists emphasizing that America could lose the Cold War. The conflict with the Soviet Union would be decided by an act of national will, whether directed to armed conflict (James Michener's *The Bridges at Toko-ri*, 1953), foreign aid (William Lederer and Eugene Burdick's *The Ugly American*, 1958), diplomacy (Allan Drury's *Advise and Consent*, 1958) or espionage (Richard Condon's *The Manchurian Candidate*, 1959). In any case, the United States could fail only through overconfidence or lack of vigilance. Thus, the Cold War was to be a contest in which individuality—a characteristically American value—would be decisive. In dramatizing this wish-fulfillment about international relations, these novels increasingly emphasize the struggle within the domestic scene. The threat of communism moves from Asia's wars and diplomacy to presidential and congressional politics.

In addition to this symbolic geographical movement, these novels also chronicle a transformation of American heroism. The familiar courage of the characters in *The Bridges at Toko-ri,* which easily accords with popular beliefs about World War II, gives way to the more limited possibilities facing Condon's cast in *The Manchurian Candidate.* Admiral Tarant and the reluctant Brubaker performed halfway around the world in fighting communism in Michener's work. Condon's characters, on the other hand, struggle within the United States to resist a Soviet subversion that has already penetrated American society. The relative impotence of American resistance emerges dramatically when Tarant's didactic stoicism, which constitutes a fighting faith, is juxtaposed to General Jorgenson's suicide, which implies the lack of options available to men of good will in *The Manchurian Candidate.*

The same disappointed hopes can be seen in *The Ugly American* and *Advise and Consent,* novels which plead that problem-solving will bring America through the crisis. While these works imply that good men can resurrect the system, their emphases on the personal greed and congressional double-dealing that maintain the State Department and the Senate compromise their optimism. The prevalence of second-rate bureaucrats and drumbeating press agents contrasts sharply with the removal of Gilbert MacWhite in *The Ugly American,* while Brigham Anderson's suicide seems more decisive than the ongoing patriotic reveries that close *Advise and Consent*. Indeed, these four novels stand as warnings to America for they suggest that apathy has become standard operating procedure. The uncaring crowds that Michener chastises in *The Bridges at Toko-ri* are replaced by fumbling diplomats, like Ambassador Sears in *The Ugly American*, and amoral opportunists, such as Fred Van Ackerman in *Advise and Consent* and the Iselins in *The Manchurian Candidate*.

*   *   *

Fear underlies *The Bridges at Toko-ri*, a defense of the American cause in Korea. Michener, eager to demonstrate that the sacrifices of American fighting men are truly in the best interests of the United States, uses a simple plot fleshed out with speeches about patriotism and the necessity for the Cold War. The novel urges a philosophy of history which insists that the individual willingly lay down his life for his society. Michener, who turned to a more epic style with *Hawaii* (1958), a vein he has diligently mined since, is succinct in this novel; however, he indulges a recurrent tendency to sound like the voice of God in passages that supposedly persuade the way a "voice over" in a movie does. When Brubaker, the protagonist, attempts to get his disabled jet out of Korea and into the sea to have a greater chance of being rescued, Michener describes this struggle in cosmic terms: "So they fought to the sea. As if caught in the grip of some atavistic urge that called them back to the safety of the sea after millions of years during which men had risen from this element, these two pilots nursed their jets away from inhospitable land and out toward the open sea."[2] This invocation of the origins of mankind suggests an affinity between the stricken pilot and all men in history. However Michener's universal rhetoric runs contrary to his political partisanship so that *The Bridges at Toko-ri* becomes another all-too-familiar melodrama of good guys against bad guys.

Admiral George Tarant, Brubaker's hard-bitten but not insensitive commander, voices Michener's patriotic concerns. As a career sailor whose professional skill is genuinely admired by subordinates, Tarant personifies benevolent authority. The Admiral, who has lost two sons in World War II and seen his wife retreat into depression, "adopts" the protagonist. Brubaker, recalled to active duty, constantly wonders why he and his family have suffered while millions of other Americans have not been inconvenienced. His distress, which never becomes open defiance, is soothed by Tarant who places Brubaker's sufferings in a larger context. Like the younger man, the Admiral has a disagreeable assignment and, since Tarant's outspokenness has alienated his superiors in Washington, there is no lure of promotion to make him stick to the task. The Admiral has accordingly become a stoic: " 'I know I'll never get promoted again. But you're here and you do the job.' "[3]

The Admiral knows Korea is not the ideal place to fight, but he remains equally convinced that struggles always occur in unsuitable terrains. While Tarant can endure the deprivations of Korea, just as he bore those of

Guadalcanal, he is dismayed over the lackluster response of the American public to the war. While acknowledging Brubaker's lament that he was drafted into a war which nobody in America seems to care about, Tarant argues that the Cold War struggle must be willingly undertaken.

> He felt that his nation did not realize that it was engaged in an unending war of many generations against resolute foes who were determined to pull it down. Some of the phases of this war would no doubt be fought without military battles. Whole decades might pass in some kind of peace but more likely the desultory battles would stagger on and from each community some young men would be summoned to do the fighting.[4]

Tarant envisions the United States fighting an endless war, one of attrition in which a dramatic victory becomes secondary to the will to endure. This grim prospect, which contradicts the outlook of General MacArthur, turns Korea into a moral test by which the worthy prove themselves through struggle. The United States will only survive if it achieves the same kind of cohesiveness that the sailors and pilots aboard Tarant's aircraft carrier, the *Savo*, show. Since Tarant's flag ship is named for an ignominious defeat it, further symbolizes America's need for eternal vigilance and awareness.

Tarant believes that Asiatic communism can only be contained through systematic bombing. He wants to destroy the bridges at Toko-ri because they serve as a supply line from China to North Korea; but he is even more concerned with maintaining the willingness to destroy this and all other significant targets. The United States must keep fighting, keep bombing, and keep coming back for more, if it is to succeed and to survive. In what sounds like a Delphic foreshadowing of military thinking about Vietnam, Tarant insists, " 'If we keep enough planes over them enough hours somebody's got to get hurt. And when they get hurt bad enough, they'll quit.' "[5] The Admiral's faith in such tactics reflects an American desire to fight on modern (i.e. technological) terms and echoes popular views about both American wars in Asia.

After Brubaker's death in a drainage ditch in North Korea, Tarant momentarily despairs about where America's new fighting men will come from, but then he takes heart from the ever-efficient pilots already back in the air wreaking havoc on the enemy.

> "Why is America lucky enough to have such men? They leave this tiny ship and fly against the enemy. . . . Where do we get such men?"
> . . .Admiral Tarant watched them go, two by two from the lashing catapult, planes of immortal beauty whipping into the air. . . . They did not waste fuel orbiting but screamed to the west, seeking new bridges in Korea.[6]

Tarant's watching these American fighting men supplies the final image in *The Bridges at Toko-ri* and makes the novel end on a note of defiant optimism. Despite the loss of Brubaker, Mike Forney and Nestor Gamidge, a helicopter rescue team comprised of other self-sacrificing individuals, dedicated Americans still embrace the war's purpose.

Admiral Tarant's elitist philosophy of history is hedged by democratic principles. Although he cannot explain why Brubaker has been called upon and others have not, the old sailor argues that all societies require the sacrifices of a select few in order to survive. In the present situation this chosen group fights a war to insure that an ungrateful society can enjoy creature comforts. When Brubaker complains that he had to give up job, home and children, while others sacrificed nothing, Tarant retorts:

"Rubbish.... Burdens always fall on a few. You know that. Look at this ship. Every man aboard thinks he's a hero because he's in Korea. But only a few of you ever really bomb the bridges."

"But why my wife and me?"

"Nobody ever knows why he gets the dirty job. But any society is held together by the efforts...yes, and the sacrifices of only a few."

Brubaker couldn't accept this.[7]

The plot crisis of *The Bridges of Toko-Ri* comes when Brubaker finally realizes that his commander is right. The younger man dies knowing his sacrifice has been made in the right place, at the right time, and for the right reasons; indeed, in death Brubaker sees that society's demands are integral to his own well-being.

The novel's central section shows the American pilot realizing his duty when exposed to the things he wants to preserve. On a furlough in Japan, Brubaker meets his wife and children; and, while Admiral Tarant tries to persuade Mrs. Brubaker, it remains for the protagonist to convince himself and his wife that flying over Korea represents a moral obligation for both of them. When the Admiral meets Brubaker's family, he muses that civilization is "composed mainly of the things women and children want."[8] In their presence Brubaker longs for the peace he knew as a civilian in Denver but gradually sees that protecting that sanctuary is also essential. Although Nancy still feels that fate has been unjust, she is ameliorated by Brubaker who begins to sound like Tarant. Michener's linking of the two characters prepares us to accept their intellectual fusing; thus, the older man's conversation with Nancy foreshadows what Brubaker will argue. The Admiral tries to explain why Nancy's husband must make a sacrifice; and, after she deplores America's apathy about Korea, Tarant presents his code of the "voluntary men."

"Your husband bombed a bridge. Because he's one of the best pilots in the navy he knocked out two spans. He didn't have to do it. He could have veered away from the bridge and no one would have known. But some men don't veer away. They hammer on in, even though the weight of war has fallen unfairly on them. I always think of such men as the voluntary men."

Nancy fought back her tears and asked, "So until the last bridge is knocked out a few men have to do the fighting? The voluntary men."

"That's right. The world has always depended upon the voluntary men."[9]

Since history's designs are executed by those who sacrifice themselves, Brubaker must offer his life to insure that the group will survive. Michener never suggests that the communist opposition may operate under the same premises and so his novel becomes a sermon on American patriotism based on the argument that elitist individuals are the real "stuff" of history. In effect, Michener combines Tarant's view, which reflects an aristocratic outlook, and a reluctant democratic American protagonist, Brubaker, so that a small band of men can be exalted while the egalitarian principles of the United States are preserved.

Teamwork distinguishes the pilots and crew in *The Bridges at Toko-ri*; indeed, Michener repeatedly presents situations which stress the collective cohesion aboard the *Savo*. The crew's maneuverings of grounded planes insure incoming pilots the very best chance to land on the treacherously rolling deck. Each man dedicates himself to the collective enterprise and some, like Mike Forney who rescues downed airmen, and Beer Barrel, who guides jets onto the pitching air strip, become special because their particular skills augment the larger undertaking. The collective pride which arises is epitomized by Cag, Brubaker's squadron commander, who gladly flies a difficult reconnaissance mission over Toko-ri. After viewing two previous attempts to get photographic information, Cag growls (as do so many Michener characters): " 'What's the matter? They afraid to go low? We'll show 'em how to take pictures.' and he assigned himself the dangerous mission, choosing Brubaker to fly protective cover."[10] Michener's Navy, unlike Herman Wouk's, possesses commanding officers who don't dodge perilous assignments as well as subordinates who believe that each man can depend on his fellows to see him through. While this optimistic view of military life was a cultural commonplace, novels such as *The Naked and the Dead* (1948) and *The Young Lions* (1948), as well as the 1955 manuscript that would become *Catch-22* (1961) were presenting an antimilitary outlook.

Michener's emphases on teamwork, unique individuals, and the strengths needed for command, color the meetings between Cag and Tarant. While the Admiral initially doubts that Cag has the capacity for command, their second meeting, after Brubaker has been lost, proves to the older man that the squadron leader possesses these qualities, for Cag now talks back. The subordinate reminds his commander that when a pilot is downed over hostile territory, only volunteer helicopter crews can be assigned; and, in keeping with Tarant's elitist views, there are never enough volunteers like Mike Forney. Cag finally blows up at the Admiral for moping over Brubaker's loss.

"Admiral, everybody in the air group knows that you selected Brubaker as your special charge.... So today I led your boy to death. But it was a good mission. We did everything just right. And it was your boy who helped destroy the bridges. Admiral, if my eyes are red it's for that kid. Because he was mine too. And I lost him."

"...I don't care any longer what kind of fitness report you turn in on me because this was a good mission. It was a good mission." Without saluting he stormed from flag country, his fiery steps echoing as he stamped away.[11]

While the bereaved commanding officers resemble those in films like *Command Decision* (1948) and *Twelve O'Clock High* (1949), Cag's insubordination points up his loyalty to the group. He can grieve over

Brubaker, but he does not forget the larger purpose and so brings the Admiral back to his proper role. Michener ignores the obvious irony that Cag impresses Tarant by becoming a younger copy of him, a note that would have sounded natural in contemporary sociological works like *The Lonely Crowd* (1950) and *The Organization Man* (1956) but which can hardly be expected in a novel that extolls patriotic sacrifice.

Brubaker's conversion, the central event in *The Bridges over Toko-ri*, finds the technically competent American pilot learning to believe personally in the struggle for Korea. Brubaker does not become a melodramatic caricature because Michener never allows the character to lose his fear of being killed. Thus, group solidarity and technical expertise only take the individual so far before he has to rely on his own convictions, as one sees in the novel's intellectual climax. On the photographic mission with Cag, Brubaker observes a courage greater than his own and tries to equal it. After he returns to the *Savo* the protagonist worries about surviving another attack on Toko-ri; but as he considers how easy it would be to back out, Brubaker:

> ...stood alone, sweating, in his dark room and recalled the Cag's flight into the valley, and almost without knowing it he uttered the tricky words that bind a man to duty, those simple words that send men in jet planes against overwhelmingly protected bridges: "If Cag can fly that flak, so can I." ...You could weasel out any time, but within the essence of your conscience lived the memory of other men no less afraid than you who were willing to tackle the dirty jobs. So you stuck.[12]

At this point Michener emerges as a moralist whose central character dramatizes the birth of a conscience because in an amoral world man must enact that morality which best accords with his solitary disposition. After his final crash Brubaker fights to the end, even though he knows such resistance will not save him. The protagonist has become as adamantly opposed to communism as Mike Forney, who dies beside him; however, while the helicopter pilot draws on religion for assurance, Brubaker's faith comes from his struggle to overcome social considerations and personal grievances. Even though Brubaker's death serves a necessary plot function in a novel designed to affect public opinion, the central character dies contented.

In *The Bridges at Toko-ri* political ideology lurks beneath a fictional surface. Michener wants to warn Americans of the long-range dangers in Asia. When Brubaker is about to die, the author notes:

> In his home town at that moment the University of Colorado was playing Denver in their traditional basketball game. The stands were crowded with more than 8,000 people and not one of them gave a damn about Korea.... And in New York thousands of Americans were crowding into the night clubs where the food was good and the wine expensive, but hardly anywhere in the city except in a few homes whose men were overseas was there even an echo of Korea.[13]

The novelist diminishes his argument by such absolute language for, while one would concede that apathy attended America's involvement in Korea (as it did in Vietnam), to believe that "no one gave a damn" is to lapse into melodramatic overstatement. Even fictional artistry founders on such overblown rhetoric and *The Bridges at Toko-ri* finally becomes a thinly plotted contrivance presenting a one-sided argument.

Given Michener's characters and their outlooks, Admiral Tarant's advocacy of the "domino theory" hardly comes as a surprise. Since he doubts whether American will power will be sufficient to outlast the communists in Asia, Tarant hopes that destroying the bridges at Toko-ri will have a devastating effect on the "commissars" who run China, Russia and the Panmunjom negotiations. The Admiral's larger fear is that America's self-generated doubts will bring the enemy to our shores.

> "What would they have us abandon to the enemy?" he asked. "Korea? Then Japan and the Philippines? Sooner or later Hawaii?" He walked back and forth pondering this problem of where abandonment would end, and as the sleet howled upon him he could not fix that line: "Maybe California, Colorado. Perhaps we'd stabilize at the Mississippi." He could not say.[14]

While subsequent events have shown this theory to be a working premise among diplomats and governments on both sides of the Iron Curtain, the ideological unity Tarant attributes to communism has been shredded by internal developments in China, Vietnam and elsewhere. Michener's novel dramatizes the temperament of the early 1950s which saw communism as a "bloc" moving inexorably to swallow up "free" people everywhere; and, although it falters as fiction, *The Bridges at Toko-ri* does reflect the anguish which accompanied America's new political rule as guardian of the "free" world.

*　　*　　*

In *The Ugly American* William Lederer and Eugene Burdick record the misdeeds of the American foreign service rather than present a tightly plotted or symbolically suggestive novel. As a result, their work emerges as a series of vignettes dealing with how Americans should conduct themselves overseas. Lederer and Burdick offer answers to a public distressed by Sputnik. In their novel diplomacy supersedes war and American bad manners consistently lose to Soviet efficiency. The struggle between communism and democracy will be decided among the neutral and third-world nations, a contest in which salesmanship and appearance loom larger than physical might. The authors are concerned with presenting a "winning" diplomatic strategy and with demonstrating why current practices fail. They tacitly assume that men are controlled by interpersonal relationships so that commitments to ideology or to material gain cannot overcome the right "image." While their novel takes place in the fictional

Asian nation of Sarkhan, Lederer and Burdick's arguments embrace United States' diplomatic dealings with any neutral or friendly third-world nation.

John Colvin, an idealistic American who wants to mechanize the Sarkhanese dairy industry, becomes the first victim of diplomatic inefficiency in *The Ugly American.* Colvin receives little help or encouragement from the American ambassador and his staff, especially after being beaten and shot by local communists who claim Colvin's technology will poison the Sarkhanese. The American ambassador accepts a fraudulent cover story about Colvin's injuries because neither he nor his staff has the ability to find out what really happened. The Sarkhanese nationalist Deong, who believes communism represents the only hope for genuine social change, tells Colvin: " 'You've done nothing but lose since the end of the war. And for a simple little reason: you don't know the power of an idea. The clerks you send over try to buy us like cattle. You people are like the fable of the rich man who was an idiot.' "[15] Deong thus reduces the international struggle to a matter of respect: American diplomats fail because they impose their materialistic ethos on every situation. This argument turns foreign relations into a matter of empathy and ignores that power often determines events without consulting as to which side has been most polite or humane. Lederer and Burdick's optimism about diplomatic understanding seems overdrawn for, if nothing else, the negotiations which preceded World War I and World War II demonstrate that the best wills do not always prevent catastrophe. Moreover, understanding another culture is not simply a matter of the application of intelligence. Learning to speak French does not make one a Frenchman; and, while steeping oneself in another nation's history and customs may increase understanding, world politics are not always susceptible to control by rational expertise.

Deong's pessimistic forecast recurs throughout the novel in the mouths of more friendly characters. U Maung Swe, a Burmese journalist with an impressive American academic background, believes the United States has lost more prestige in Asia in ten years than the British did in one hundred. When pressed by the new American ambassador to Sarkhan, Gilbert MacWhite, as to the reasons for this decline, the reporter suggests: " 'For some reason, however, the Americans I meet in my country are not the same as the ones I knew in the United States. A mysterious change seems to come over Americans when they go to a foreign land. They isolate themselves socially. They live pretentiously. They are loud and ostentatious.' "[16] Once again, personal rudeness becomes the key to deteriorating relations: Deong's "idea" can thus be paraphrased as "when in Rome, do as the Romans do." Such a solution, however, presupposes an established society into which an individual can fit himself; but how, for example, would one decide which element of Vietnamese society to cultivate in 1958? in 1963? in 1968? Lederer and Burdick express a hope—that foreign people are just like us, if we will only take the time to appreciate their customs— rather than acknowledge the inherent difficulties in understanding others as they are. In effect, American diplomats must perform the tourist feat of going to another country "to see the people rather than the sights."

It seems doubtful that such sentiments have any serious validity in foreign affairs where countries seek "allies" rather than "friends." By reassuring readers that success in the Cold War depends on being friendly, Lederer and Burdick reduce diplomacy to the level of a Dale Carnegie self-help course.

American diplomats fumble time and again in *The Ugly American*; indeed even the best intentioned become myopic bureaucrats inside the American embassy. This establishment occupies an impressive mansion in Sarkhan and is surrounded by a picket fence which symbolically separates it from the natives. In avoiding contact with the Sarkhanese, the Americans have created a compound similar to the British walled city in E.M. Forester's *A Passage to India* (1927). Since the foreign service is staffed by time-servers and incompetents, it is hardly surprising to find Soviet agents stenciling "This rice is a gift from Russia" on supplies sent from the United States, and have the authors note that none of the Americans present is sufficiently fluent in Sarkhanese to notice the message.[17] Ambassador Sears, MacWhite's predecessor, commits a series of blunders because he cannot abandon his materialistic American mentality in dealing with the natives. When the local newspaper runs a demeaning cartoon, Sears pressures Sarkhanese officials to insure more satisfactory future notices; thus, this ugly American denies that very freedom of the press embodied in the Constitution while interfering in the domestic affairs of his hosts. The Sarkhanese officials fear an American loan will be denied unless Sears is mollified and, in keeping with his temperament, Sears sends a case of whiskey to the editor of the local paper after the cartoon has been squelched.

The insidiousness of the diplomatic establishment becomes even more apparent during the visit of Senator Jonathan Brown. Initially determined to find out what is really going on in French Indochina and elsewhere, Brown allows himself to be guided by local "experts" through a frantic itinerary which provides him with everything except time to think. The Senator is briefed on innumerable matters but reaches the end of his tour only to realize that "in all of the time in both Saigon and Hanoi, he had talked to only two natives, and to only three military officers below the rank of general—two of them had been drunk."[18] Senator Brown is probably our earliest fictional prefigurement of the tactics used in official reporting of the Vietnamese War to the American public for the Senator, like Robert MacNamara, Dean Rusk and Lyndon Johnson, goes home to present a glowing account of the situation.

The Ugly American concentrates on solutions to the diplomatic impasse that America and her allies face in southeast Asia. Knowledge and expertise are keys to the new tactics that Lederer and Burdick advocate; and, since one can infer the Peace Corps in their thinking, personal contacts loom as *the* means by which Americans can stop being ugly. Gilbert MacWhite understands Sarkhan and Sarkhanese (he served there in World War II and is fluent in the language) and recognizes the importance of the entire area to American security. On a visit to Indochina, MacWhite observes French officers reprimanding a subordinate for using guerrilla tactics against the

Viet Minh. The clear-thinking MacWhite asks if anybody, save the junior officer, has read Mao Tse-Tung's military writings. While his logic temporarily wins the day, the independent MacWhite constitutes the threat of efficiency to his lethargic subordinates and colleagues so that his removal becomes inevitable. In a system where "snafu" is standard operating procedure MacWhite is a liability. While the ambassador got his position after undergoing a Senate confirmation, the clerks and officials who do the embassy's everyday tasks were not so rigorously chosen. Lederer and Burdick insist time and again that long-term commitments from foreign service applicants are essential for any continuity to exist between the United States and other nations.

While they make several specific proposals about upgrading the training and the backgrounds of subordinate diplomatic employees, Lederer and Burdick's criticism remains more striking. They devote a long section to how Joe Bing, a press agent assigned to the embassy, goes about recruiting new members for the Sarkhanese post. Joe preaches material advantages, of course, and the would-be recruits are alerted to the pleasures of houseboys and reduced prices. Later, one of the author's spokesmen, a career diplomat named Upton, uneasily sees that greed insures second-rate diplomatic personnel: " 'You know...there's something wrong with our recruiting system. With the exception of Atkins, that engineer, every applicant will be making more money with the government than he does in the job he has now. Frankly, I think we're getting slobs.' "[19] Diplomacy should represent a full-time career (if not a calling) rather than an occupation an individual can pick up because the money is good; however such an argument contradicts the oft-heard proposition that larger salaries attract better people into government work. While Upton suggests the style of diplomacy embodied by Dean Acheson and the Eastern "establishment" (an implication that would not have sat well with public opinion in the early 1950s), one wonders if his prescription is worthwhile. American diplomacy has generally been controlled by career types, and the sort of brain trust Lederer and Burdick advocate most closely resembles the advisers around John Kennedy who moved so precipitately on Vietnam.[20]

Functioning Americans also appear in *The Ugly American*; however their deeds are either misunderstood or fatally compromised by the diplomatic establishment. Ruth Jyoti, an Asian editor and publisher on tour in the United States, describes one in Bob Maile of the United States Information Service. Ms. Jyoti urges: " 'Bob never brags about what his office does. He doesn't have to. In my country good deeds are publicized all over by the bamboo telegraph. Bob Maile is the best known American in the country.... I wish the other Americans were all like him. If they were, the Communists couldn't last long in Asia.' "[21] The appeal here is once more to personality and individual diplomacy; and one again wonders if being a good samaritan represents a viable policy or simply a wish-fulfillment that reduces the real world to an exercise in personal (and manageable) proportions. In their insistence that diplomacy utilize emotional channels, the authors of *The Ugly American* imply that foreign relations are simpler than they are. Such later phenomena as the Peace Corps and the radical criticism of the Vietnam War pinned their hopes and arguments to a similar premise that one had to be a "good guy" to reach the "good guys" on the other side. Such trust in personality ultimately fails because there are only "compromised guys" on both sides.

Lederer and Burdick believe that entrepreneurial capitalism constitutes the West's ultimate weapon against communism. The elderly Martins came to Burma to help the natives become economically self-sufficient. This couple, both of whom learned Burmese before leaving America, earns high marks because:

> They came to Burma to help us, not to improve their own standard of living.
> You don't need publicity if the results of what you are doing are visible and are valuable to the people.[22]

Homer Atkins, another enterprising American, comes to Sarkhan with his wife to help the natives and, eventually, enables some villagers to reconstruct a better water pump by means of bicycle gears. In the course of this undertaking Homer meets Jeepo, a mechanic in the hamlet of Haidho who shares the American's fascination with machinery. Jeepo proves that men of different cultures can unite to achieve a common technical goal for he aids Atkins in contriving the best means for pumping water up to the town. In the course of their tinkering Atkins realizes that he and Jeepo share a common humanity. After several fruitless negotiations with the reactionary elders of Haidho who, because of their dilatory ways resemble the diplomats Atkins encountered at Phnom Penh, the American finally finds a kindred spirit, someone who acts decisively to correct technical problems: "He was quite sure that Jeepo had an answer...and he was also sure that it was not a political or a personal answer, but technical."[23] The American's faith is not misplaced, and he and Jeepo soon become partners in the water pumping operation. Atkins, unlike Westerners who have exploited the natives in the past, insists on this arrangement because he recognizes that pride in ownership will turn the Sarkhanese into useful friends of the United States.

After Atkins and his wife leave Haidho, they receive a letter from its inhabitants which makes the point even more patent. The Sarkhanese compliment Mrs. Atkins for showing them how to use long-handled brooms, an improvement that enables the elderly to work comfortably at sweeping. The introduction of this simple but significant change epitomizes how the solutions of common people are more fruitful than the elaborate plans of a diplomatic bureaucracy. Mr. and Mrs. Atkins won friends because they scaled their efforts down so that common people could benefit. Upon receiving this letter of praise, which refers to her use of local reeds for broom handles as fortuitous, Mrs. Atkins exclaims: " 'What does he mean "lucky accident"?... Why I looked all over for three months before I found those long reeds. That was no accident.' "[24] By implication, American diplomacy does not have to be accidental either, for more enlightened administration of foreign embassies and more practical aid programs can restore the United States' prestige in Asia.

* * *

While it was considered "daring" and "discriminating" in 1958 because of its portrayal of the sometimes sordid details behind the workings of the United States Senate, *Advise and Consent* has been outdistanced by political realities since. Its rapacious and amoral characters pale beside the real people who guided the United States through Vietnam and Watergate. If anything, the pragmatic immorality of Drury's President now appears the requisite for any politician. Manipulation of the press, a constant emphasis on getting re-elected, and the need to create a favorable image have also become familiar perceptions of working politicians. On the other hand, Drury's belief that the Senate represents a collective deliberative body whose members eventually do the right thing seems quaint, if not ludicrous, today.

When Robert Leffingwell's name is initially sent up for confirmation as Secretary of State, a veteran colleague calms Senator Bob Munson, the majority leader, who is angry about not having been consulted. Stanley Danta reminds Munson that Senators stay on while presidents come and go: "well, take it easy... we were here before he came and we'll be here after he's gone.' "[25] This sense of time underlines Munson's own reflection that: "Dealing with prickly John Adams was probably no different from reasoning with prickly Orrin Knox, and certainly Arly Richardson in a pet could be no more difficult than Edmund Randolph."[26] Thus, his position as a power broker convinces Munson that men remain temperamentally the same, even though their social or technological surroundings may change. The majority leader further believes that the Senate's historical continuity derives from its rules of admission and standards of behavior. Drury's description of the Senate chamber also emphasizes this sense of security: "It was ten minutes to noon on the day of the Leffingwell nomination and the Senate, with the exception of minor changes here and there, looked exactly as it had at ten minutes to noon in 1820, 1890, 1910, 1935, 1943, or any other time."[27] Given this quality, the Senate, a conservative group representing propertied and professional interests in America, has the time and the skill to decide what is really best for a nation that too often gets carried away by enthusiasm and demagoguery.

Within the Senate's chamber disparate individuals are transformed into a government capable of functioning, if only during times of crisis, dispassionately. While individual Senators may never attain such capabilities by themselves, Drury notes that in a floor debate the members were "losing their identities to become imperceptibly, inexorably, for a subtle second, institutions instead of people."[28] The Senate thus becomes the place where necessary political deals are made to protect the people from learning how sordid their rulers can be. Brigham Anderson, hopelessly compromised by a homosexual liaison during World War II, and being blackmailed by the President and Leffingwell's more zealous supporters, reflects that politics in Washington are politics in the smallest town.

> There was a sort of necessary workaday hypocrisy, as inescapable here as it was back home on a thousand Main Streets, that imposed its own adjustments on a society caught in the overriding need to keep things going. More often than the country suspected this enforced a combination of frontdoor idealism and back-door acceptance of human realities that worked its own imperatives upon such situations. The government went on, people who knew the most startling things about one another met with bright unblinking urbanity at Georgetown cocktail parties...and few echoes, or none, reached the country.[29]

While such a conspiracy of silence based on gentlemanly decorum has operated in the Senate, Anderson's hope that the "establishment" will keep his scandal quiet is short-lived. In the hysterical atmosphere of Cold War, nuclear holocaust and space race, ends have become so important that any means to attain them can be utilized. Drury does, however, show the Senate still adhering to its gentlemanly code in the censure it moves against Fred Van Ackerman. The final defeat of Leffingwell, a foregone conclusion after the reason for Brigham Anderson's suicide becomes known, follows a reporter's remark which encapsulates Drury's view of the Senate: " 'There comes a time for most clever men in this town when they get too clever, particularly when they deal with the Senate.... The Senate doesn't like it.' "[30] While this opinion reinforces the suspicion surrounding intellectuals throughout *Advise and Consent,* the larger emphasis is on the Senate's inherent sagacity. Leffingwell loses not simply because he is an evasive egghead but because his supporters treat the legislators condescendingly.

Drury urges that America is slipping from being a world leader to being merely a contender for such a role because of self-inflicted doubts and shortsightedness. Bob Munson intuits that America's troubles derive from a clash between excessive self-preoccupation and the accomplishment of Sputnik.

> In his lifetime he had seen America rise and rise and rise, some sort of golden legend to her own people...and then, in the sudden burst of Soviet science in the later fifties, the golden legend crumbled, overnight the fall began, the heart went out ot it, a too complacent and uncaring people awoke to find themselves naked with the winds of the world howling around their ears, the impossible merry-go-round slowed down.
>   ...A universal guilt enshrouded the middle years of the twentieth century in America; and it attached to all who participated in those times. It attached to the fatuous, empty-headed liberals...the embittered conservatives...the military, who had been too jealous of one another and too slow, and...the scientists, who had been too self—righteous and irresponsible and smug...and on the press, which had been too lazy and too compliant...and on the politicians, who had been too self-interested...and not least upon the ordinary citizen and his wife, who somehow didn't give quite enough of a damn about their country...[31]

This lengthy indictment of apathy accords with the World War II mentality which colors most of these characters' thinking about foreign relations; for, while history never works in rigidly repeatable patterns, the errors of Munich and Pearl Harbor are considered axiomatic principles which only the most foolhardy would ignore. Munson cannot concede superiority to the communists but must explain defeat away through internal weakness.

World affairs thus again become a contest in which sincerity and will power can overcome physical and technical advantages. Such an argument flatters the melodramatic taste of the audience but contradicts history; indeed, one needs only to look at the Civil War to realize that a willingness to make personal sacrifices hardly guarantees success or even survival, for the Confederacy's will could not overcome the Union's industrial advantages. Thus, Drury makes the same—individual initiative superior to material force—argument that colors *The Ugly American.*

In doing so, Drury lapses into dogmatism and rhetoric which is appallingly simplistic. The President, constantly aware of the "mindless evil" of communism, echoes Munson in damning public apathy: he believes the country to be experiencing an "Age of the Shoddy" and "of the Shrug" when a "dry rot affected America...and every sensitive American knew it."[32] Such pronouncements constitute having one's cake and wanting to eat it too. No government official would argue that citizens should be supplied with a complete knowledge of diplomatic relations; yet, despite such an obvious lack, the same citizens are damned for not being enthusiastic over what the government tells them.

Appeasement and apathy are linked by the leading figures in *Advise and Consent* who believe that a dispirited people will make concessions simply to avoid their duty. The argument over Leffingwell constantly reveals that appeasement is a bete noire in many characters' minds. Lafe Smith, a playboy bachelor friend of Brigham Anderson who becomes a tower of strength after the latter's suicide, believes that in choosing a Secretary of State: " 'We can't have somebody in there who would sell all those little countries down the river just to appease the Russians, you know.' "[33] Even a dissolute young legislator (possibly modelled on John F. Kennedy?) advocates outright resistance to communist aggression. The President, in defending Leffingwell's evasiveness during the confirmation hearings, argues: " 'Is it not possible that a mind that self-protective, a mind that strong—yes, if you like, a mind that arrogant and unyielding —may be just exactly what we need in dealing with the Russians?' "[34] This opinion runs against the democratic grain because it implies a government by experts who are so egocentric that they cannot be held responsible for their actions. Such a prescription points out the ends-means paradox of the Cold War: the communists can only be resisted by individuals who are as amoral as they. The President's defense of his nominee stresses social preservation at any cost, but there comes a point at which mere survival must yield to principle. Munson worries because: "People don't understand a war unless there's a gun going off someplace; they still don't see the other kind that doesn't make any noise but just goes on eating the guts and heart out of you until you collapse."[35] Drury's majority leader fails to understand that human beings cannot live without hope, so that the prospect of an endless Cold War will hardly gladden their hearts.

Drury uses Seab Cooley, a cantankerous old Senator from South Carolina, to probe contemporary liberalism, which is equated throughout with cowardice in the face of the Russian threat. While he has personal reasons for disliking Leffingwell, Cooley's ire is more than just pique: "For he saw Bob Leffingwell, with all his graceful flirtings with this cause and that over the years, with all his clever skatings along the outskirts of the flabbily-principled and dangerously over-liberal fads of the era, as that perfect symbol of mid-twentieth-century America, the Equivocal Man."[36] Drury has Leffingwell preach appeasement when he confronts the Foreign Relations Committee. The nominee answers questions with questions, a tactic which infuriates his interrogators and makes him appear vacuous. When Leffingwell is asked where he would draw a line with the communists, he can only question whether his interrogator wants war and, in doing such special pleading, discredit liberalism.

During his confrontation with Herbert Gelman, a former student who claims Leffingwell was once a communist (Chambers and Hiss revisited?), the nominee, in cross-examining this hostile witness, falls into a trap of his own making. After suggesting that Gelman has only presented hearsay, Leffingwell naively asks:

"Then why was it so important? . . . . What would it matter now? Why would it be significant of anything, if it all happened so long ago and meant so little?"

"The only reason it would be important or significant now," the witness said, and the room quieted down completely to hear him, "would be the way in which we react to it now. If we tell the truth about it, the way I am, that is one thing. If we lie about it, as— if we lie about it, then it casts a reflection on everything we have done and raises serious questions about what we may do in the future. That is why it is important, Bob."[37]

In having Leffingwell's questions submerged in Gelman's argument about small lies being the forerunner of larger ones, Drury has clearly stacked the cards against the President's liberal nominee. Although he compromises Gelman's testimony so that a "draw" results, Leffingwell comes off badly because he can only operate negatively. His ability to muddle Gelman's testimony and to show that the witness may be psychologically unreliable smacks too much of a lawyer working to raise "reasonable doubt." The designated Secretary of State cannot establish his own innocence, even though he can compromise others'; thus, Leffingwell seems capable only of criticizing in the manner of the stereotypical intellectual.

Fred Van Ackerman, another exponent of liberalism who lacks moral convictions and merely espouses causes that are politically advantageous, staunchly advocates Leffingwell because of an enthusiastic response at a Madison Square Garden rally. Like Joseph McCarthy who found communism was an issue that would "play" in 1950, Van Ackerman strikes a nerve and discerns the possibilities: " 'Well, I tell you...you've no idea how hot people are for this idea of getting together with the Russians. I didn't realize it myself, really, until I began making these speeches a couple of months ago. It's taken hold like nobody's business.' "[38] Van Ackerman sounds like a huckster describing a hot item to another drummer rather than a legislator concerned with national issues on their own merits. Drury makes the comparison between his fictional creation and the Wisconsin Senator even more obvious when Van Ackerman claims a "point of personal privilege" in tones that echo McCarthy's famous nasal refrain about a "point of order."

The author's favorable view of the Senate is reinforced when Van Ackerman is censured two days after Senator Anderson's death. Even allowing that every novel must be extended some suspension of disbelief, one can more readily believe in blackmail, suicide, late night rendezvous between Munson and a prominent Washington hostess, and even an amoral President, than in the United States Senate acting this swiftly. Of course, the censure motion symbolizes Drury's conservative values; in effect, his Senators realize that such a heinous breach must not go unpunished. Van Ackerman appropriately misses the roll calls on his censure and Leffingwell's nomination and so symbolically proves that liberals are cowards at heart. Van Ackerman's methods finally condemn him because, in the words of yet another anonymous reporter: " 'It isn't quite slander, it isn't quite libel, it's just enough to murder a man. He doesn't come right out with anything, he never does; he just skirts the edge of absolute evil, destroying people as he goes.' "[39] This vague formulation almost, but never quite, succeeds in defining a "half-truth." Perhaps, since such verbal equivocations are endemic to American Senators, Drury should have taken more time to establish why Van Ackerman's conduct was different in kind (rather than in degree) from his colleagues'.

The most enlightening political personalities in *Advise and Consent* belong to Brigham Anderson and the President. When the senior Senator from Utah, the chairman of the sub-committee before which Leffingwell appears, becomes convinced that Gelman is telling the truth, he comes into direct conflict with the leader of his party. Their confrontation marks the climax of the novel, for after this meeting the deaths of Anderson and the President and the rejection of Leffingwell become virtually inevitable. Even though he becomes a martyr, Senator Anderson exhibits many of the more dispiriting aspects of a political personality. While he has been a good "mixer" since childhood, Brigham lacks enduring friendships or close ties to anyone. His relations with his wife are distant since he refuses to confide in her, even though he can rationalize such conduct as protecting a woman who is overmatched in Washington society. The Senator's suicide dramatizes his self-infatuation for he dies because he is too proud of his "image" and cannot contemplate a future in which he could be limited to a less-exalted position. Brigham Anderson unwittingly portrays the popular middle-class belief that doing the right thing naturally leads to more and more prestige so that his suicide becomes an act of narcissism.

Of course, Anderson's homosexuality would have been regarded more harshly in 1958 than today (indeed, Drury's choice of this "crime" acutely reflects the moral standards of the period); yet one is dismayed by the well-adjusted young Brigham who "found himself able to cope with the mercurial tides of liking and disliking, playing together and not playing together, being in a group or out of the group at a moment's notice...without much jolt to his nervous or emotional systems."[40] While this absence of deep feeling seems admirable to Drury, his creation emerges as a zombie rather than a man. Brigham survives nicely because he never becomes deeply involved; indeed, the only times he becomes really concerned are when he worries about his career. Thus, the adaptable child cracks not under the ire of a president but from the anxiety of being seen as a fallible human being. Brigham Anderson's egotism also appears in his concern over the Leffingwell nomination: "And would the Lord give him some sign, in a dancing sunlight and the perfect day, that he was still all right, that he was still a worth-while human being who had something of value to contribute to his country, his family and his people?"[41] While most individuals would seriously question if God ever passed on their lives in one way or another, Brigham merely asks for a reconfirmation. He has only temporary doubts as to his own worth in a scheme of things; and so he emerges as a victim of excessive pride rather than the martyr Drury intends.

The President does what he must and hurts whom he must to do things in accord with his own gloomy sense of the weakness of the American people. He is, as his old friend Senator Munson notes, basically amoral. When the majority leader realizes that the President will use any means to achieve an immediate goal (even Brigham Anderson's past indiscretion to get Leffingwell nominated), Munson fights down an impulse to run, dutifully tells all he knows, and then feels: "that he was close to the absolute essence of the American Presidency, in the presence of a dedication so severe, so lonely, and so terrible, so utterly removed from the normal morality that holds society together, that he should flee from it before the revelation proved too shattering."[42] In Munson's reaction Drury captures some of the essence of the Presidency under Kennedy, Johnson and Nixon. Indeed, his cutthroat approach to power makes the President the least dated character in *Advise and Consent,* for Drury's chief of state rules by indirect wish and does not allow himself to know too many sordid details. The President chooses Van Ackerman to pressure Senator Anderson as a means of conveying political prestige (although in such a way that the connection can be disowned when Brigham kills himself). When confronted by an angry Senator Anderson (who has been misled into believing that time was needed to make the dismissal of Leffingwell look "better" to the press), the President indulges in sophistries worthy of any lawyer. After correctly denying that he ever called Senator Van Ackerman, the President reluctantly admits that the junior Senator from Wyoming had telephoned him: " 'But he didn't tell me what he had been doing to you, if anything. And I didn't ask him.' "[43] Such a technically correct admission hardly personifies a man citizens should unquestioningly follow.

The sick President reveals another unpleasant personality trait when he contemplates dying in office. While this event would elevate Harley Hudson (a man of whom he is mildly contemptuous) to the Oval Office, or even worse, find the President himself an invalid unable to run the government's day-to-day business, the beneficial aspect of this possibility suggests a more sinister level in the character.

He does not mind the thought of dying in office, for there is no surer guarantee of martyred greatness in the history books than to die at just the right moment when people will remember the good deeds and forget the bad ones...so in that sense he rather welcomes the idea of a dramatic demise with his hand on the helm, a great man sacrificing his life in the cause of peace....[44]

Drury's President is, perhaps, too sanguine about how the future will view him and his administration. Hardly anyone remembers Garfield and McKinley as martyrs, while the apotheosis of Lincoln suggests that a man can, indeed, be turned into a monument because of dying in office. The death of John F. Kennedy would support Drury's view, except that that stalwart's erotic activities have replaced his picture's being next to Christ's in popular consciousness.

For a former reporter Drury comes down very heavily on the news media. There is little intelligent or investigative journalism in his Washington press corps; indeed, for the most part, these Capitol Hill reporters spend their time waiting for some legislator to take pity and throw them a quotable crumb. At one point the suggestion that an active press conspiracy works to get Leffingwell nominated is made; and it is even urged that these opinion makers do not have to consult each other to get such a media blitz functioning. When a story breaks about a private meeting between Senatorial leaders and the British and French ambassadors, Drury describes how guesswork replaces evidence in the erroneous report that all the participants had given ringing endorsements to Leffingwell. Drury's irony comes through when he proclaims "The author of the story...by keeping his eyes open and his intuition untrammeled, by mixing a scrap of information with a hunk of conjecture and building twenty bricks with two pieces of straw...had managed to come up with a good, sound, typical piece of informed Washington correspondence."[45] This passage almost relieves the ponderous tone of the novel, however Drury remains so uncertain of his audience that he must refer to "bricks: and "straw" so that no one can miss his intention. A more serious charge against the press comes from an irate Senator who, tired of the evasions and posturings of Leffingwell before the sub-committee, argues that journalists have coddled the nominee.

"...if you were a Nazi, say, or a die-hard reactionary, or a labor-baiter or somebody else like that whom the press doesn't like and doesn't play up all over the country with a lot of hero worship the way it does you, you'd be charged with evasion and duplicity and double talk and every other kind of nasty thing that could be thought of to say about you."[46]

While many a newspaper has practiced advocacy journalism (e.g. The Los Angeles *Times* in its treatment of Richard Nixon[47]). Drury's fictional spokesmen fail to convince because they consistently forget that some newspapers and some reporters and not all newspapers and all reporters.

Hal Knox and Crystal Danta, the engaged children of Senators, reflect on their fathers' occupation and decide that, on balance, most things turn out for the best in the Senate.

"I know lots of people I don't think are dirty politicians. Don't you?"

"I suppose so," she said..."but they never seem to win out."

"They don't seem to win out as often as you'd like, that's what you mean," Hal said. "They win a good deal of the time. It seems to balance out in the long run."[48]

Hal's reassurance reveals a moderate who, in good democratic fashion, sees the necessity for conflict about issues and why one side cannot always win. Thus, while those most immediately involved in deciding issues see them in black-and-white terms, the young man introduces a more balanced perspective in which the struggle between good and evil becomes one of ends and means. For Brigham Anderson, individual conscience counts for more in the Senate than careful planning; indeed, its members are sufficiently independent so that one can never be certain of a roll call. The best preparation (means) does not always lead to a foreseeable result (end), for:

> ...sometimes a thoroughly righteous cause can win in ways that are completely unforeseen by those who think in terms of votes pledged and favors conferred. Just when things seem at their most cynical, something comes along that appeals to idealism and fair play, and the forces of deceit go down before it like tenpins.[49]

These fortuitous possibilities sustain those who work for the good of the nation; indeed, the genuinely talented and dedicated senators move their less than inspired and more craven colleagues to keep things on the right track.

The struggle between means and ends surfaces again when Senator Anderson rejects an early vote on the Leffingwell nomination. Even though such a polling would serve his immediate interests, Senator Munson so respects his younger colleague simply because Brigham is a senator that he silences any objections and agrees to the delay. The majority leader's speech rhapsodizes about his belief that the Senate calmly and reasonably considers issues on their merits.

> "But it might hurt us all most grievously if it should become the habit here that the safeguards of our liberties, of which the regular show and patient procedures of the Senate, for all their faults, are among the most supremely important, are to be tossed away whenever it suits us in the heat and passion of the passing moment."[50]

Munson obviously embodies enlightened conservatism as sanctified in the "checks and balances" principle so beloved by political scientists. In his mind how one travels is at least as important as where one is going.

Drury's rhetorical outbursts work most effectively at the end of the novel when they counteract the death of Senator Anderson and relieve the sense of gloom. Bob Munson carries the burden of having informed the President about the secret in Brigham's past. While this revelation was made without any awareness of how the President would use the information, Munson blames himself for his younger colleague's death; and, in doing so, he transcends "not wanting to know" what others are doing, as the President failed to do with Van Ackerman. After enduring his time of trial:

...the senior Senator from Michigan could not find it in his heart to be so concerned about his country, when all was said and done. The system had its problems, and it wasn't exactly perfect, and there was at times much to be desired, and yet—on balance, admitting all its bad points and assessing all the good, there was a vigor and a vitality and a strength that nothing, he suspected, could ever quite overcome, however evil and crafty it might be.[51]

Drury's style creates an unintended verisimilitude here, for his sentence sounds "pondered" (if not ponderous) and suggests how real United States Senators speak (and alas) think.

On the concluding pages of *Advise and Consent* Orrin Knox, the "prickly" Senator from Illinois, becomes the principal focus; and after he has accepted Harley Hudson's offer to be Secretary of State, been confirmed in record time, and joined the new President on a flight to a summit meeting with the Russians, Knox engages in a blatantly patriotic reverie. While he hopes that grounds for accommodation can be found, Orrin realizes that he and his colleagues are:

...not necessarily carrying the wealth of the Indies with them, but only a few scraps of things, the memory of a meeting in Philadelphia, a speech at Gettysburg, a few fragments of valor still echoing down the American wind from distant battles and far-off things, Chancellorsville and The Wilderness, the Alamo and San Juan Hill, Belleau Wood and the Argonne, Bataan and Corregidor....[52]

This catalog of American history serves as the proper fadeout for the novel; indeed, it reads like many a Hollywood film ending in which a plane flies into the horizon and a thunderous voice rises over stirring music. Such a conventional, bravura ending is consistent with *Advise and Consent*'s being a cleverly plotted reaffirmation of traditional American political beliefs. The novel's enormous popularity significantly measures the distance between that time and surrounding periods: its essential optimism differs markedly from the tone of both *All the King's Men* (1946) and *The Armies of the Night*(1968), for the corruption and agony in those novels contrast starkly with the problem-solving mentality that characterizes Drury's fictional world.

* * *

The Manchurian Candidate contains characters who symbolize brainwashing, mommism, female aggressiveness, and political opportunism a la Senator McCarthy. The cast also includes an ideal soldier, Ben Marco, his adoring girlfriend, Rosie, and a General who commits suicide (after performing political dirty tricks) to retain his own ideal vision of America. The novel fluctuates between being a thriller and a symbolic nightmare ridiculing the United States. Condon possesses a sharp comic eye for political foibles, and there are moments when *The Manchurian Candidate* resembles Vladimir Nobokov's *Lolita* (1958) in its portrayal of a morally and culturally desolate nation. Condon takes certain popular fears and pushes them to extremes so that a programmed killer can ultimately decide the next President by assassination. Mind manipulation by sinister Chinese and Russian agents suggests a world-wide conspiracy whose members have a singleness of purpose that far surpasses America's capacity to resist. Yet Condon implies that constant vigilance leads to excesses that are worse than the initial diseases.

Raymond Shaw, the programmed assassin who has returned to the United States as a supposed war hero and become a newspaper columnist, must listen to his mother, the wife of Senator Johnny Iselin and Raymond's "control," recite familiar sentiments about the Cold War. Her diatribe illustrates how means become ends in themselves in the charged anti-communist atmosphere.

> "I have to be a fraud.... And I have to be the truth, too. And a shield and the courage for all the men I have ever known, yourself included, excepting my father. There is so much fraud in this world and it needs to be turned away with fraud, the way steel is turned with steel and the way a soft answer does not turneth away wrath."[53]

Mrs. Iselin's outburst implies her incestuous relationship with her father while, at the same time, underscoring her contempt for those weaker than herself. She masterminds Johnny's political career and uses the Cold War to gain her ends. While Senator Iselin hurls public accusations, Mrs. Iselin remains the puppeteer whose machinations suggest Joseph McCarthy run amok.

The psychological tenor of *The Manchurian Candidate* is established in its opening pages when Raymond, enroute to Washington to receive the Medal of Honor for bravery in Korea, stops in St. Louis to visit the family of a dead army buddy. During this condolence call, Raymond keeps wondering why he bothered to stop since he is deeply offended by the parents' grief. His nausea, brought on by the excesses of Mrs. Malvole which remind Raymond of how cold his own mother would be in similar circumstances, does not match his outward melancholy. This division in feeling also characterizes some of the other surviving members of the patrol on which Raymond won the nation's "highest honor." The Medal, of course, has been awarded under false pretenses for Raymond and his cohorts were led into a trap behind enemy lines, whisked away to a psychological laboratory in Manchuria, and individually programmed to believe that Sergeant Shaw had rescued everyone in a manner "above and beyond the call of duty." This elaborate scheme provides a "cover" for Raymond who has been trained to carry out orders unquestioningly when presented with the proper "keys." Choosing her only child to be the means by which Johnny will gain the Presidency is not lost on Mrs. Iselin who swears murderous revenge on the Chinese and Russians when she gets control of the White House.

Yen Lo, the Chinese clinician who trains Raymond, demonstrates how the young American has been turned into a machine. In making this presentation before a group of communist officials and secret dignitaries, Yen Lo stresses that mental instability helps men of action, for: " 'Although the paranoiacs make the great leaders, it is the resenters who make the best instruments because the resenters, those men with cancer of the psyche, make the great assassins.' ''[54] Raymond's deprived childhood and young adulthood, in which his emotions were forced underground by his mother's hasty marriage to Johnny Iselin and his own father's subsequent suicide, make him an ideal killer. After Raymond has strangled Ed Malvole and shot Bobby Lembeck in front of the other patrol members, who believe they are waiting for a bus after a weekend in New Orleans and are sharing a hotel lobby with a local garden club, he is rewarded by Yen Lo. The Chinese "wizard" decides to unlock Raymond's repressed sexual drive (" 'More than that no man can do for you, Raymond' " the Chinese psychologist amusingly notes[55].)

Condon underscores the relationship between creator and creation further when, as the programmed Americans are removed to be flown back to the south, he shows Yen Lo on the lawn surrounded by disciples: "He would hold up a sheet of paper, move his hands swiftly as he paid out the gentle and delicious jokes, and lo!—wonderment dropped from his fingers, the paper had come to life, and magic was everywhere in the gentling evening air."[56] Yen Lo's dexterity with paper echoes his success with Raymond; indeed, his ability to shape a mind (which can be regarded as a blank sheet—a la Locke) is epitomized by the shapeless paper on which he exerts his skill. The stories of Pygmalion and Galatea and, perhaps more appropriately, GePetto and Pinocchio, in which the creation does not always accede to its creator's wishes, serve as background here. Such fairly tale motifs give Condon another way of manipulating his readers into accepting the paranoid atmosphere of *The Manchurian Candidate*. Yen Lo, who reappears later to "recheck" Raymond, also embodies the mysterious Orient—a racial aspect of the Cold War that is often neglected.

Raymond Shaw's personality is unlikely to win anyone's affection, let alone those of men who have to endure it in close quarters under conditions of life and death. Given Raymond's hypersensitiveness and misogyny, Yen Lo had to strenuously program the other patrol members into believing that Shaw was their best buddy. Later Raymond's communist masters decree that he murder Senator Jordan, a strident foe of the Iselins. Unfortunately, this assignment leads to the death of Raymond's wife, Jocie, Senator Jordan's daughter, who had been staying with her father while Raymond was out of town. Their marriage, which reaffirms the power of first love for Raymond, represents a further irony. When Mrs. Iselin manages to get her son alone at a costume party to give him instructions, she is interrupted by a call. Jocie Jordan then enters the room dressed as the Queen of Spades, the decisive psychological "key" for manipulating Raymond. This series of coincidences, which drives Mrs. Iselin to distraction and reveals her dependence on drugs, causes Raymond's immediate proposal and subsequent elopement with Jocie, a woman he had loved years before. After he has murdered Senator Jordan and instinctively shot Jocie when she intruded, Shaw must undergo a double grief when Marco proves to him that he killed the only person he ever loved. At this moment Raymond stops feeling superior to the rest of mankind, so that his subsequent reversal of the assassination plan—in which he kills his mother and Johnny Iselin instead of the Presidential nominee—seems more probable.

Until this point Raymond's arrogance implies that self-sacrifice was not in his makeup. As a newspaperman, he was convinced of the artificiality of social life and cynical about politicians and entertainers whose numbers include so many phonies. When being interviewed himself during his visit to St. Louis, Raymond remembers his own disgust at his first meeting with an actor: "It was hard to believe that man's face had been so pocked and welted as a waffle, yet he was one of the biggest names in the business which gives an idea what those swine will do to kid the jerky public."[57] Raymond's disgust when confronted with the truth about his brainwashing reveals the emotional walls that Shaw has erected against the rest of the world. He is dismayed, even though he does not completely believe Marco, by the tampering that has been done, or even considered. He feels violated and thinks: "What kind of a world of fondlers has this become?"[58] Raymond's nausea poignantly catches contemporary fears about brainwashing and mental conditioning. His question also reduces such psychological tactics to the sexual terms of rape and masturbation: his privacy has been violated by those who have turned him against himself.

The major figure in this process is, of course, his mother; and her seduction of Raymond (an attempt to soothe his anguish over Jocie and to fulfill her own wish to be with a "real" man—one who murders) only accentuates her demonic character. Mrs. Iselin unsettles Raymond in scene after scene, for she is both despised by and yet attractive to him. Raymond's discomfort surfaces with her when, after noticing that he always "loses" discussions with her, Condon's befuddled assassin asks himself some hard questions.

> Oh, what a woman! What a beauty she is and what a dirty fighter. She is where the world should spit when they seek to spit upon Johnny Iselin. How can I forget that? How can I look upon those serenely lovely eyes, how can I be so deeply thrilled by the carriage of her exquisitely wholesome body and grow so faint at the set, the royal set of that beautiful head and not remember, not always and always and always remember that it encases a cesspool of betrayal, a poisoned well of love, and a city of deadly snakes? Why am I here? Why did I come here?[59]

Raymond's ambivalence catches the psychological dynamics in their relationship. His mother is associated with snakes and, thus, with a temptress like Eve, while the future intimacy between them is foreshadowed in the references to her physical charms. If nothing else, then, the Iselin family stands in sharpest contrast to the sugary groups one often finds on television (*Father Knows Best*) and in fiction (*The Cardinal*) during the 1950s.

When Raymond receives the Medal of Honor at the White house, he "wanted to put his head on the President's chest and cry because he hadn't seen very many sane people since he had left Ben Marco."[60] This wish is fraught with irony for Marco is all but insane with worry through most of the novel. When he initially visits Raymond, who by now has a New York apartment and a job with a syndicated columnist, Marco spends his furlough bringing home girls that he and his host share. This idyllic interlude, in which Raymond responds to Marco's friendliness, ends when the career soldier begins to experience nightmares about Korea. Another member of the patrol, Al Melvin, has experienced similar dreams and, since he believes that Raymond Shaw was his best army buddy, has written to Condon's brainwashed robot for help. Thus, when Ben breaks down, Raymond ironically suggests that he get in touch with Melvin and sets in motion his own discovery and destruction. Marco's initial anguish leads to his being all but dismissed from the Army that is his life; however, his devotion to duty, and the stabilizing influence of Rosie, enable Ben to uncover Raymond and so to protect the higher interests of the service and the nation. Since Marco hates the Iselins because of their having gotten him promoted to prevent his asking embarrassing questions about Raymond's Medal, he programs Raymond to wreak vengeance on them.

In the novel's abrupt ending, as Marco and some F.B.I. agents rush to the small booth from which Raymond has assassinated the Iselins, Ben reaches Shaw first for a few moments of private conversation. Marco then reappears and a third shot is fired inside the booth. Ben defends Raymond's suicide as an act that preserves the dignity of all Medal of Honor winners. In keeping with this love of Army life, Marco even urges that there must be: "'No electric chair for a Medal of Honor man.' "[61] This dramatic ending (Ben's words are in the novel's final paragraph) implies that Raymond truly deserved the nation's highest award for, in ridding his country of powerful enemies, he acted "above and beyond the call of duty."

On a train to New York after he has begun suffering from his recurrent nightmare, Ben meets Rosie, a theatrical agent's Girl Friday. Marco is so nervous he cannot stay inside the club car, yet the love-struck Rosie gladly follows him outside and spontaneously comforts him. Clearly, she has been looking for someone like him for years and Marco, suffering from insomnia and loss of appetite, eagerly surrenders to her love: "He was so tired. He was so tired. She took his hand gently away from his mouth. 'I want you to put your head on my shoulders.' The train lurched and he almost fell, but she caught and held him, then she led the way into the other car where there were plenty of seats."[62] Rosie represents a dream female—a woman who sacrifices everything (including her ego) to take care of her man's every whim. Marco literally does nothing to win her, for she breaks her previous engagement as soon as they arrive in New York, even though he has said nothing about marriage, or even another date. Rosie gives Ben her phone number (a plot contrivance that becomes useful when Marco assaults Raymond's houseboy, Chunjin, who led the patrol into the trap in Korea and who now guards Shaw), but his illness distracts him from courting her. Rosie's dismissal of her fiancee is another plot device for this fellow, an F.B.I. agent, helps Marco unravel the mystery of Raymond Shaw. Rosie, who remains content with Ben's promises that they will marry, stands in the starkest contrast to the emasculating Mrs. Iselin.

Another figure who throws that sinister character into relief, while reaffirming the Army's code of duty before self, is General Jorgenson who must bribe Marco with higher rank in order to stall the investigation of what happened in Korea. Jorgenson acts for Senator Iselin and, when Ben balks, commands Marco to accept the bribe because that is the General's duty. However, after the orders have been signed and Ben dismissed: "Marco left the office at four twenty-one in the afternoon. General Jorgenson shot himself to death at four fifty-five."[63] Jorgenson epitomizes the good soldier, the man who acts for personal reasons only after his orders have been carried out. While doing Johnny Iselin's political dirty work obviously revolted Jorgenson, he let his conduct say what would have sounded petty if spoken. Thus, the morality of the Army, with its emphasis on action speaking louder than words, is upheld by the suicides of Jorgenson and Raymond.

Johnny Iselin enjoys power for the privileges and pleasures it brings and, throughout the novel, he remains nearly as much a robot as Raymond. Like the younger man, Johnny is chained to Mrs. Iselin, albeit, his enslavement has a more obvious basis than Shaw's. The Senator's wife dominates him so completely that he is impotent whenever they attempt lovemaking; while he was virile enough when she was anxious to divorce Raymond's father (who lacked the ambition and the greed necessary to seek elective office and be guided by her), Johnny goes from a backseat Romeo to a wet blanket with their marriage vows. As a politician, Iselin is clearly modelled on Joseph McCarthy, even to the extend of having a similarly spurious World War II service record. Like the Wisconsin Senator, Johnny has been a desk soldier anxious to get press attention to aid his future political career. When there is no genuine news, a journalist drinking buddy of Johnny's allows Iselin to create a story about supposed wartime heroics. Thus, just as McCarthy became "Tail Gunner Joe" because of his picture in the cockpit of a plane in which he never flew, so Johnny Iselin becomes the "one man battleship" when he tests some Navy guns on harmless targets.

As a Senator, Johnny accuses the Defense Department of harboring communists, offers various numbers (even arguing with Mrs. Iselin for one figure, saying he's too dumb to remember all the different numbers), and emerges as a dominant force in the paranoid atmosphere he helps to create. By using blackmail, Iselin makes the government respond to him.

He would sidle up to a fellow senator or another member of the government placed as high and mention the name and habits of some young lady for whom the senator might be paying the necessities, or perhaps an abortion here, or a folly-of-youth police record there. It worked wonders. He had only to drop this kind of talk upon five or six of them and at once they became his missionaries to intimidate others who might seek to block his ways in government.[64]

Gradually, Johnny becomes the best hope of the radical right, and Condon ridicules those who customarily compose such groups. In a description of the guests at the Iselins' costume ball, one reads that such reactionaries constitute a clan that "had turned out from ten thousand yesterdays in the Middle West and neolithic Texas." Condon then reports that their clothes were "encasing various sizes of fleshy prejudice which exchanged opinions they rented that week from Mr. Sokolsky, Mr. Lawrence, Mr. Pegler, and that fascinating younger fellow who had written about men and God at Yale."[65] This dismissal represents a prejudice rather than an argument; and so, however amusing as caricature, it is intellectually undercut by its pejorative tone.

If Condon errs by eschewing facts for satire, Senator Iselin embodies more serious shortcomings by dealing in half-truths and manipulating events into media "happenings." The mentality necessary for creating half-truths (a capacity to avoid asking which half of a statement is true) is embodied by the reporter buddy who makes Johnny a war hero. Ramen, in explaining what really happened, is hardly apologetic: " 'You know. It was filler copy. Not strictly a lie, you understand. Every fact was strictly factual all by itself...' " [66] Thus, one sees an early version of what has come to be labelled media hype. Paradoxically, Ramen's arrangement created something greater than these same facts made up separately. Good politician that she is, Mrs. Iselin knew that any press coverage would help to win votes, so that what struck Ramen as frivolous was deadly serious to her. The Iselins later gave the reporter a case of gin, a bribe he readily accepted.

The news media are consistently presented in *The Manchurian Candidate* as panderers to bad taste, devoted to soothing the mass with trivia and overemphasizing national figures who make a lot of noise. When Raymond accompanies his mother to Paris, he steadfastly refuses to report on the accusations she hurls at various embassy heads until his editors insist that he clarify his position on "subversives" in government. Once again, Raymond feels violated; however his reaction also derives from the nature of the news-consuming audience.

The Daily Press, his employer in New York, was said to have had to resort to threats to force Raymond into writing and publishing a statement regarding his own position. This was the sheerest nonsense: the kind stimulated by the need of metropolitan people who feel that they simply must be seen as having inside information on everything.[67]

Shaw's distaste centers on the public's desire to be informed not merely of events but of what might happen. In such an atmosphere, knowledge yields to appearance and "sincerity" so that success resides in projecting an "honest" image. This world of playacting, epitomized by Mrs. Iselin's remark that people only read headlines anyway, runs counter to the ethics of Condon's good characters; indeed, when challenged by the Iselins over his personal opposition to Johnny's vice-presidential ambitions, Senator Jordan responds too concretely to a reportorial question: "'How long will you let this man use you and trick you?' " [68] The Senator, however right he may be, fails to "play" the media so that the Iselins will be hurt by creating a headline. Senator Jordan as the representative of an older tradition—which places substance above style—has become anachronistic in the contemporary political arena. The Iselins are more "relevant" in their awareness of staging and drama to catch the nation's attention. Johnny gains the media's attention when he hurls unconfirmed charges at the Secretary of Defense because the very act is so fraught with tension that spectators are invariably drawn to it. Indeed, the Iselins know that loud voices and startling accusations attract attention and make one's opposition look foolish.

The capstone of the Iselins' orchestrated drive for power is set to take place at the national convention in New York where, after being nominated for the vice-presidency, Johnny is to be elevated to the top spot by Raymond's sniper fire and his own rehearsed response to the crisis. As Raymond explains it to Marco, after the latter has learned his "keys":

> "I am ordered to shoot the nominee through the head and to shoot Johnny...through the left shoulder, and when the bullet hits Johnny it will shatter a crystal compound...which will make him look all soggy with blood.... Mother said this was the part Johnny was actually born to play because he overacts so much...he will get to his feet gallantly amid the chaos that will have broken out at that time, and the way she wants him to do it for the best effect for the television cameras and still photographers is to lift the nominee's body in his arms and stand in front of the microphone like that because that picture will symbolize more than anything else that it is Johnny's party...."[69]

Johnny has been supplied with a rousing speech to deliver while holding the dead nominee in his arms to stampede the convention and the nation into accepting him as the next president. The Iselins count heavily on the audience's subconscious belief that if something happens on television it must be more real than if it happened in the house next door. Johnny will appear as a national savior binding up the wounds of emotional shock through a fighting image and, thus, play upon the immediate visceral reactions of the viewers. The plan obviously has been designed as a media "happening," one that includes perhaps the most important element—the audience can enjoy a "happy ending" without having to endure the agony of confusion (and dead air time) while having a resolution before its attention span lapses.

Mrs. Iselin sacrifices nearly all human feelings (save hatred) to attain the presidency for herself and Johnny. When she first appears, she has been called by Raymond, who has just returned from Korea and is enraged at the press coverage being given to his Medal of Honor. To symbolize her hypocrisy, Mrs. Iselin pretends to be having another conversation with Johnny as she answers Raymond's charges; since her husband has already left, her little game establishes her supremacy over both men. When she feels threatened, Mrs. Iselin resorts to drugs, so that her character foreshadows some of the tumult of the 1960s, as does the entire novel. After preparing Raymond for orders only to be interrupted and return to find an empty room, Mrs. Iselin needs a "fix so badly that she nearly scrambled up the back stairs to get heroin and an arm banger."[70]

Her sexual drives are also perverse, for after finding her ideal lover in her father and having him die, Mrs. Iselin simply manipulates others' feelings for her. While her physical presence renders Johnny impotent, she, being the dutiful wife every politician must have, refuses to divorce him (ironically, he performs lustily with less threatening females). Mrs.

Iselin turns predatory and passionate with Raymond for whom she feels pity and desire after learning that he is to be the instrument of her ultimate political coup. At lunch, she orders a carpet-bag steak stuffed with oysters and proceeds to devour it as Raymond watches in fascinated horror. Suffering as he always does in her presence from Oedipal longings, her son insists that this dish must have been discovered by Johnny because: "in the world's literature of food there couldn't be a dish which expresses his vulgarity better than a thick, contemptuously expensive piece of meat pregnant with viscous, slippery, sensual oysters."[71] Raymond fails to notice that his mother's psychological appetite craves such a dish; thus, she devours a "piece of meat" and so reverses the customary sex roles at the same time that she eats oysters, a food associated with male sexual potency.

Mrs. Iselin finally becomes so excessively symbolic that she ceases to be sinister and becomes a caricature of the bitch-mother whom Philip Wylie vilified in *Generation of Vipers* (1942). She seems most exaggerated when ranting about the coming right-wing takeover of the United States, for she is convinced that only a tremendous bloodletting can return the nation to its original "purity." Her tirades, while consistent with the image she is trying to create, point up the irony of her alliance with the communists. In effect, Mrs. Iselin and her Soviet and Chinese allies agree on the necessity for a politics of vengeance, one in which violent action supersedes philosophy or ideology. Her ultimate ego satisfaction emerges clearly when she tells Raymond:

"This country is going to go through a fire like it has never seen...until it becomes a country purged and purified back to original purity.... And when that day comes.... Johnny, and only Johnny is going to save us... (and) you will kneel beside me and thank me and kiss my hands and my skirt and give only me your love as will the rest of the great people of this confused and blinded land."[72]

Mrs. Iselin's grandiose vision has her as the savior of America, the nurturing mother who cannot console Raymond in real life.

On another level, Mrs. Iselin feels contempt for the very public she wants to save. When Johnny fears initial public reactions to her divorce of Raymond's father (a matter adjudicated in record time by Johnny to, again, make the connection with McCarthy who was famous for dispensing quick justice in Wisconsin) she reassures him that their hasty marriage will be popularly accepted.

"And we'll get married right away. At the split second that it becomes legal under the great American flag, see, lover? We'll be as respectable as anybody else right at that instant, except just like everybody else, underneath. You know what I mean, lover? They're all tramps in their hearts and we'll want them to identify with us when the time comes to line up at the polls. Right, sweetheart?"[73]

Her view of the public as harried and resentful automatons who easily forgive those who resemble them is never seriously questioned in *The Manchurian Candidate*. When one remembers the popular 1930s' and 1940s' films of Frank Capra, with their emphases on the Lincolnesque sentiment that no one can fool "all the people all the time," it becomes apparent that the 1950s were becoming increasingly cynical about the common man's capacities.

Early in the novel Condon makes the point that official accounts of events and the actual events are often at odds; thus, Raymond rejects the Army's report of Ed Malvole's death in the line of duty and ponders more brutal possibilities such as a bayonet in the rectum . Of course, this invoking of the difference between appearance and reality takes on additional irony when we learn that Raymond strangled Malvole. Shaw's subsequent refusal to be photographed brings out the importance of publicity in American life, particularly when Condon notes that only "sex criminals and dope peddlers tried to refuse to have their pictures taken by the press."[74] While such a reflection implies the values of the Iselins (and the connections to sex and dope especially suggest Raymond's mother), Mrs. Iselin catches an unhappy reality about contemporary American politics when she instructs Johnny not to worry about what he is saying but to concentrate only on how he is saying it. She lauds her husband's skill as a television performer, someone whose outward appearance conveys sincerity and, thus, disarms criticism; in effect, Johnny Iselin possesses the ideology of Senator McCarthy and the looks of John F. Kennedy. He projects honesty so well that even Mrs. Iselin compliments his "delivery" of old, stale charges by noting: " 'I was beginning to feel real deep indignation myself.' " [75] The Iselins have learned that television unlocks the hearts and minds of the American people more effectively than the truth.

The Iselins are flawed only by degree for, in spite of their excessive ambition and disgusting means, their drive for success is a trait shared by other characters and never seriously questioned in the novel. Ben Marco's anxiety about his Army career represents a permissible ambition, one founded on patriotism and a recognition that others have abilities. In worrying about the promotion he must accept from General Jorgenson, Marco exhibits admirable ambition. His fear that such a promotion will prejudice his superiors and preclude further advancement reveals two crucial contemporary attitudes. On the one hand, Marco wants to succeed on his own terms and for his own worth, while, on the other, he recognizes that success will only come if he conforms to the institutional demands placed on him. The dilemma of individuality and conformity was, of course, a favorite topic during the 1950s; and, in his turmoil, Marco reflects insights found in William Whyte's *The Organization Man* (1956), David Reisman's *The Lonely Crowd* (1950) and Robert Lindner's *Must You Conform* (1956).

Condon's satirical tone emerges to better advantage when he describes a song, played on a juke box where Marco is meeting with F.B.I. agents, as containing, "the rhyme of the proper name Betty Lou and the plural noun *shoes* repeated, in a Kallikakian couplet, over and over again."[76] Anyone even slightly familiar with darkened barrooms, neon-lit juke boxes and country music will recognize the description; indeed, when viewed against a society of disproportionate noise and size, Condon's suspense-thriller almost becomes a spoof. The same comic tone sounds when Condon briefly describes General Francis "Fightin' Frank" Bollinger, a retired Army officer and enthusiastic supporter of Johnny Iselin. Bollinger suspiciously resembles Douglas MacArthur, especially when we learn that he became a business executive after leaving the service. The General had taken up:

> ...the helm of the largest dog-food company the world had ever known. He had often said, in one of the infrequent jokes he made... "I'd sure as hell like to see the Commies try to match Musclepal, but if they ever did try it they'd probably call it Moscowpal. Get it?"... He had been a patriot, himself, for many years.[77]

This slow-witted extremist is too heavy a caricature to be taken seriously; indeed, if Condon only presented such cretinous types as the General and Johnny Iselin, his novel would have possessed the same comic exaggeration one finds in *Catch 22*.

What makes *The Manchurian Candidate* more unsettling is its portrayal of the government team set up to unlock the mystery of Raymond Shaw. This expensive operation not only includes full-time surveillance of Raymond (which breaks down to allow him to elope with Jocie, to murder her and his father-in-law and, finally, to assassinate the Iselins) but also involves elaborate wire-tapping operations. Once Marco discovers how to manipulate Raymond, this official group searches high and low for the would-be assassin; however, in yet another bit of irony, these agents are frustrated because they cannot divest themselves of rational considerations. Thus, they overlook the Iselin house (where Raymond has gone) because they feel certain that the political hostility between the Iselins and Senator Jordan precludes Raymond's going there. Such an obvious oversight implies that rational men cannot deal with irrational ones; since the government's agents are incapable of understanding Raymond, they cannot find him. All the expertise that is marshalled against Shaw can only react to his movements, so that, like many another profession or supposed science, this intelligence operation can only prognosticate from hindsight. It remains for Marco, the amateur, to find Raymond and program him for the final assassinations. Like Chief Brody, the local sheriff who lacks expertise but who finally conquers the Killer shark in *Jaws* (1974), Ben Marco overcomes the powers of evil and makes society safe once more.

Hawaii
Epic scope for a tranquil time (Bantam Books)

Chapter 5

"The on-going thing that she had started...was now more powerful than she."

World War II was not the only inspiration that prompted American novelists to treat relationships between the individual and the group. Two of the more celebrated bestsellers from the late 1950s—Leon Uris' *Exodus* (1958) and James Michener's *Hawaii* (1959)—urge that the individual derives meaning and identity primarily from his social setting which, in turn, is an amalgam of historical experiences grounded in religion and geography. The leading characters in *Exodus* only find romantic happiness when they understand that they must conjoin nationalistic, religious and personal aims. *Hawaii* consistently promotes the same theme of reciprocity, albeit its characters are concerned about family and status over a period of generations. Hamilton Basso's *The View from Pompey's Head* (1954) explores the individual's need to reconcile his present with his past by bringing the two times (and their often conflicting wishes and choices) into an ironic equilibrium. In Basso's novel a man comes to realize that his own regional history goes with him all the days of his life.

Max Shulman's *Rally Round the Flag, Boys!* (1957) and Mac Hyman's *No Time for Sergeants* (1954) are comic reflections of the 1950s' concern with conformity. In a decade which saw the publication of David Riesman's *The Lonely Crowd* (1950) and William H. Whyte's *The Organization Man* (1956), Shulman and Hyman present comic views of the degree to which an individual must tailor himself in the group's image. Shulman's commuting males bridle against a suburban life style dominated by women and children, but these beleaguered breadwinners ultimately endorse community rituals once they establish emotional rapport at home. Through bending, but never breaking, the rules of the Army, Hyman's naive protagonist triumphs over an institution that would remake him in its image. Like such traditionally American heroes as the gunfighter and the private eye, Will Stockdale shows that individualism underlies success and identity. John D. MacDonald's *The Damned* (1952) presents a group brought together by accident rather than any larger social or historical purpose. MacDonald's characters achieve personal meaning and identity through private action and thus, like the more acclaimed existential figures of Camus and Sartre, literally make themselves.

* * *

Exodus, Leon Uris' most celebrated novel, illustrates the tendency of popular writers in the late 1950s to turn out "epic" tomes. *Atlas Shrugged* (1957), *Some Came Running* (1958), *Hawaii, Advise and Consent* and *Exodus* all reflect the sense of tranquility and well-being that accompanied Eisenhower's second term. Indeed, these loosely plotted and often digressionary works are, perhaps, the best evidence of the financial and political calm that marked the middle years of the decade. While they demonstrate a recurrent native penchant for sheer size (i.e. "more is better"), these bestsellers are so loosely crafted that they constitute ideal "casual" reading. *Exodus,* for example, contains so much historical and political data that it becomes a chronicle of contemporary Judaism rather than a mere fiction. Uris uses his characters to show how Israel emerged during the late 1940s; and, to accomplish this aim, he also explores such anti-Semitic hotbeds as Tsarist Russia and Nazi Germany. All of this background and reports of the events of 1946-1948 that concern the settlement of Palestine make *Exodus* a means by which the casual reader can assimilate major contemporary world affairs, an everyman's guide to the Arab-Israeli struggle as it were. Given this aim, Uris' novel must be judged on both literary and factual merits; and, as fiction and history, *Exodus* is neither skillful nor unbiased.

The novel's main theme is that Israel serves as a spiritual entity to its inhabitants. The land symbolizes the larger issues of what it means to be a Jew and why men must suffer to remain true to this faith. Both of Uris' principal Gentile characters, Brigadier Bruce Sutherland, a British officer whose Jewish ancestry causes him to overlook the sailing of immigration fleets for the Holy Land from Cyprus, and Kitty Fremont, a war widow and nurse, learn the spiritual superiority of Judaism. When Sutherland's mother is dying, she regrets abandoning her ancestors' faith and instills a similar longing within her son: " 'I wanted so much...so very much to be the mistress of Sutherland Heights. I did a terrible thing Bruce. I denied my people. I denied them in life. I want to be with them now. Bruce... Bruce, promise that I shall be buried near my father and my mother....' "[1] Her deathbed example finally causes her son to give up his commission and go to Israel. By the novel's end, Sutherland, now a convert to Judaism, has become an elderly bachelor uncle in the Ben Canaan family. His mother's mystical sense of community drives Sutherland to seek his birthright; like the exiled Moses who sought his Jewish (i.e. "real") identity after being raised as an Egyptian, Sutherland personifies the questing and outcast motifs that are integral to Jewish history.

The permanence of being Jewish is further dramatized by Dov Landau, a potential anarchist softened by love upon emigrating to Israel, who recollects the teachings of his persecuted father: "What Mendel Landau gave his children was an idea. It was remote and it was a dream and it was unrealistic. He gave his children the idea that the Jews must someday return to Palestine and reestablish their ancient state. Only as a nation could they ever find equality."[2] Thus, Israel insures justice and status and becomes the place where the individual finds coherence and trust in society.

Elsewhere the Jews remain intruders living on the edge of suspicion even in the best times. Israel represents the fulfillment of a dream for those who reach it; indeed, as an elderly social worker tells Kitty, most Jewish orphans do better if they remain in the Holy Land, even though staying there is fraught with peril. Harriet Saltzman, who is later killed by an Arab bomb, insists that Jewish patriotism is so powerful that children who have experienced it first-hand, and are then relocated, " 'never become adjusted to living away from Palestine.' "[3] The struggle to create and maintain this spiritual community breeds an idealism among the Jews; and Uris stresses that such constant pressure also creates heroism in them. Ari Ben Canaan, a leader of the Jewish revolt, is born in circumstances that symbolize his people's quest, for Ari's mother, Sarah, is tortured by Palestinian Arabs shortly before she gives birth. She endures her torments without crying out so that, because they are shamed by her courage, the Arabs let her return home where bearing Ari all but kills her. Despite weeks between life and death, Sarah survives and prospers, although showing signs of the struggle. For the rest of her life Ari's mother walks with a limp—an injury that symbolizes the price she and all Jews, must pay to survive.

Unfortunately, this idealistic theme is soon awash in Uris' melodramatizing of history; in effect, his narrative presents only heroic Jews and cowardly and ignorant Arabs, so that any possibility of seeing both sides as possessing legitimate rights and being composed of recognizable human beings is lost. Since so much of *Exodus* is devoted to the history of Palestine in the twentieth century, Uris' pleading and pejorative tone reveals a less than dispassionate observer. No historian is, of course, completely neutral about any subject he treats; however there are limits of decorum which even the more zealous try to observe. When Uris describes an Arab leader, Haj Amin el Husseini, as "the most vile underhanded schemer in a part of the world known for vile, underhanded schemers," and as "backed by a clan of devils,"[4] those limits of historical decorum have been breached. Such diatribes may flatter the audience, since the Arab-Israeli conflict, like all partisan struggles, engenders extremist rhetoric and thinking; however, presenting such figures in this light only diminishes Uris' credibility. Indeed, if the enemy consists only of lunatics and cutthroats, where is the glory in resisting such evil? Uris lapses once more into the melodramatic excesses of war movies that *Battle Cry* echoed in making the Japanese enemy so heinous as to be unbelievable. Presenting one's foe in such colors (the one Marine can handle three Japs syndrome) causes one constantly to ask why it took so long for the good guys to defeat the inept bad guys.

Later, we read of an Iraqi officer named Kawukji who was "so obsessed with himself...his egomania knew no bounds" and his gang of "thieves, dope runners, white slavers and the like" who were "as vicious, degenerate and brutal a gang as had ever been assembled."[5] In contrast, the freedom the Jews gain in Israel "fired them with a drive and purpose without parallel in man's history,"[6] an inspiration which, in turn, meant that Israel was to become "an epic in the history of man."[7] While such imprecise claims can never be proved or disproved, Confucius' dictum that right thinking is right naming has to be applied even to a popular novel.

Uris' most serious historical pronouncements concern Arab society and augment his portrayal of these licentious villains. In his eyes the Arabs are an exhausted culture whose men gamble and become freebooters and whose women serve as docile beasts of burden. While such a perception would likely render the Arabs damned in the eyes of the largely female audience for American bestsellers, Uris' appeal to basic American values surfaces more clearly when he casually mentions:

> The Arabs were experts in building on other people's civilizations and had, in fact, constructed only one wholly new city in all of Palestine in a thousand years. Some of the magnificent Roman statuary and columns had been dragged off with Caesarea and could be found in Arab homes throughout the Samarian and Sharon districts.[8]

Since he never asks whether wholly new cities were necessary, Uris simply portrays the Arabs as looters who lacked any ability to construct; however, the history of Islam belies such a verdict. That the Arabs built on the foundations of a previous civilization is hardly unusual, for nearly every people has utilized the technological accomplishments of its predecessors. Uris flatters American pride in inventiveness and new beginnings—the belief that the United States was the land of opportunity—to excoriate, rather than to understand, another society. The novelist's zeal thus trips him because, in his eagerness to make a case from the past, he does not deal with common historical knowledge.

Uris' aim is, of course, to justify the Jewish capture of Palestine, an act that ultimately cannot be sanctioned or condemned. While possession represents at least "nine-tenths" of the law in such instances, such a cynical explanation is not likely to satisfy average men who, in order to act, must believe in the righteousness of their cause. Barak Ban Canaan, Ari's father and an early immigrant to Palestine who subsequently procures land for later Jewish refugees, writes a lengthy report on the Arabs displaced by the war of 1947-1948. He concludes by urging: "Israel today stands as the single greatest instrument for bringing the Arab people out of the Dark Ages."[9] Barak's optimism coincides with the novel's political biases, for it equates technological expertise with progress and dismisses the entire medieval culture of Islam. Uris' view of history is finally jarring for he seems to have forgotten that the Dark Ages ended, in part, because of knowledge that the Arabs protected, nurtured and transmitted.

Dov Landau and Karen Clement come to Israel as orphans of World War II, meet and fall in love as a further testimony to Israel's healing powers. This romance is reminiscent of *Battle Cry* for, once again, the woman rescues the man from his baser self. Dov, who developed a talent for forgery in the Warsaw ghetto, initially refuses to participate in the activities that are turning Palestine into the Jewish homeland. He spends his days so submerged in self-pity that he refuses to forge passports so that Ari can get more refugees into the Promised Land. Dov's introversion ends when he meets Karen who was separated from her family and adopted by a Dutch couple, discovered her need to preserve her Jewish faith, and came to Israel to establish her own identity. As a teenager adept in handling younger children, Karen attracts the attention of Kitty Fremont who, in time, wants to rescue the girl from the war in Israel. Karen redeems the irascible Dov by showing him that others have suffered fully as much as he has. When she learns her father is alive and in Israel, Karen rushes to him only to discover that he no longer recognizes her. When he sees Karen break down in Kitty's arms, Dov feels compassion and so escapes from his self-created prison. "For the first time since his brother Mundek had held him in his arms in a bunker beneath the Warsaw ghetto, Dov Landau was able to feel compassion for someone other than himself. His sorrow for Karen Clement was, at last, the ray of light that illuminated his black world."[10] Dov soon joins the Jewish guerrilla forces and resumes his forgeries.

At the novel's conclusion, Karen lives on a distant kibbutz and the other characters are awaiting her arrival for the Seder festival. When word comes that Karen has been killed by Arab marauders, Kitty is temporarily crushed but Dov reacts like a Jew. The American nurse rushes to Dov's side because she fears he will act rashly and bring about his own death; however Dov reaffirms that Israel is more important than any individual and that those who are alive must live for those who have died.

> "I'll stay with you, Dov...I'll take care of you," Kitty said. "We will get through this, Dov."
>
> The young man stood up shakily. "I will be all right, Kitty," he said. "I'm going on. I'll make her proud of me."
>
> "I beg you, Dov. Don't go back to the way you were because of this."
>
> "No," he said. "I thought about it. I cannot hate them, because Karen could not hate them. She could not hate a living thing. We...she said we can never win by hating them...."[11]

Dov thus sees the necessity for compassion in dealing with enemies and so becomes the fulfillment of Barak's vision of the future relations between Jews and Arabs.

The plot of *Exodus* loosely centers on the love between Ari Ben Canaan and Kitty Fremont. This on-again, off-again relationship enables Uris to sustain the novel's enormous length by having his readers wait upon the outcome of a "she loves me, she loves me not" situation. These two characters find their values consistently at odds, and Kitty's attempt to rescue Karen brings her into open hostility with Ari. While the Israeli patriot wants the American nurse to serve aboard the ship (the "Exodus") taking the exiles back to Palestine, Ari cannot understand Kitty's need of Karen nor allow the American woman's desires to endanger the well-being of the group. He rejects her pleading for special favors for Karen by reminding Kitty that the greater morality is to act for the good of the greater number.

> "Is this humanity of yours so great that it cries out for all these children or does it appeal for the life of one child?"
>
> "You have no right to ask that."

"You are begging for the life of one girl. I am begging for the lives of a quarter of a million people."[12]

The last line epitomizes Ari's character for his entire life, which has seen him arrange escapes from Hitler's Germany and expedite passages to Palestine, has been dedicated to helping others. The bitter loss of his first love, Dafna, who was raped and killed by Arabs, enables Ari to subordinate his feelings to the causes of people and homeland. However, Ari's unnatural calm is emphasized by the way in which he repressed his feelings when Dafna died. He is clearly waiting for someone to unlock the natural passions that his concerns and duties have obscured.

Kitty Fremont, who lost her husband on Guadalcanal and became a nurse to forget, embodies the same emotional deprivation; however, as the product of a more affluent and softer American society, she must learn that suffering and sacrifice outweigh creature comforts. Mark Parker, a long-time journalist friend, meets Kitty on Cyprus and his reaction immediately establishes her as the novel's heroine: "How lovely she is, Mark thought. Kitty Fremont was the one woman in his world who was different. He had no desire to make love to her. Mark Parker honored little in the world. He wanted to honor Kitty."[13] Thus, Mrs. Fremont is special and her conversion to Judaism constitutes the principal thematic action of the plot. She has to learn that being feminine does not mean being weak; however, in keeping with Uris' emphases on sacrifice and pain as essential to the formation of character, these lessons do not come easily to Kitty. She must prove herself, especially to Ari's sister, Jordanna, who mistrusts her as an adventuress trying to lure her brother away from Israel. Kitty's conversion to Judaism is intermingled with her acceptance of Ari as a lover; however, when she asks " 'Whoever this God is who watches Israel, keep Ari alive...please, let him be alive.' "[14] she is well on her way.

The relationship between Ari and Kitty moves through three distinct stages. After their initial hostilities aboard the "Exodus," they become travelling companions in Palestine with Ari serving as a tourist-host. However, after a day together, they begin to make love in a hotel room only to discover that personal pride prevents them from consummating anything. Ari refuses to expose his emotions to Kitty, and she is unable to accept his physical advances, even though he is obviously deeply in love with her.

"Ari," she whispered, "please kiss me."

All that had smoldered for months burst into flames of ecstasy, engulfing them, in the first embrace.

How good he feels. How strong he is. Kitty had never known a moment like this with any man—not even Tom Fremont.

"...I want you," Ari said.

She ran into his arms...with an abandonment she had never known...Kitty felt faint. She gripped the sheets and sobbed and writhed.

Ari lowered the shoulder strap of her nightgown and caressed her breast.

With violent abruptness Kitty spun out of his grasp and staggered from the bed. "No," she gasped.[15]

This rupture cools things between them and forces the reader to wonder when, if and how the lovers will get back together. Later Ari confesses he's obsessed with Kitty, but she refuses him because she still fears the lack of emotional contact she felt in him earlier. Kitty, who remains blind to her lover's reticence, scorns Ari as too zealous for real feelings and, in her anger, demonstrates that she has not been completely converted to Jewish life. She insists," 'I don't live my life as a noble mission. It is very simple with me, Ari. I have to be needed by the man I love.' "[16] Kitty wants to be regarded as an individual and not merely as a member of a group; however Uris never allows her to become a spokesman for female liberation because Ari retains the power to move (and thus subordinate) Kitty emotionally.

Before these lovers can be finally united, they must be taught by other characters. Ari learns from his dying father that emotion is life's most important element and not to be denied or repressed. Barak recognizes that love for Kitty is destroying Ari and urges his son to "crawl" to the woman he loves because:

"...I would have crawled to your mother a million times. I would crawl to her because I need her in order to live. She is my strength. God help me, Ari, I have been a party to the creation of a breed of men and women so hard they refuse to know the meaning of tears and humility.

"...You have mistaken tenderness for weakness."[17]

After Barak's death, Ari realizes that his advice must be acted on; in effect, the community has spoken and the son must reaffirm the essential faith of the father. In the same way, Kitty is transformed when Karen Clement finally forces her to see what being a Jew means. While quarreling with Karen about staying with Dov, Kitty suddenly sees the light.

"Israel stands with its back to the wall," Kitty cried. "It has always stood that way and it always will...with savages trying to destroy you."

"Oh no, Kitty, no". Israel is the bridge between darkness and light."

And suddenly Kitty saw it all, so clearly...so beautifully clear. This then was the answer. Israel, the bridge between darkness and light.[18]

Karen insists that Israel's existence proves evil can be purged from the world and that everyone must join this struggle. Kitty has been a pessimist in wanting to escape to America and its creature comforts, instead of facing what she really had to do—become a Jew and marry Ari.

The chastened protagonists are thus ready for the climax in which they reconcile. In this extended "education" process the audience's wish that the fated lovers be together has been created and satisfied. Uris' final pages celebrate romantic love's awesome power by portraying Ari and Kitty as better human beings because of their affection. Ari can now weep and show the depths of his suffering and, in so revealing himself, win Kitty. She is initially afraid that in the morning he will revert to being the cold, unemotional Ari; however, the sentimentally reborn hero finally convinces Kitty that he knows their love is the "home" both of them must have.

> "Before we go in, Kitty, I must tell you something. I must tell you I never loved Dafna as I love you. You know what kind of a life you must share with me."
> "I know, Ari."
> "I am not like other men...it may be years...it may be forever before I can ever again say that my need for you comes first, before all things...before the needs of this country. Will you be able to understand that?"
> "I will understand, always."[19]

Thus *Exodus* closes in triumph: struggle has turned two characters into better human beings in keeping with the ethnic and nationalistic biases of the book. As a reflection of American society in the later 1950s, *Exodus* implies that romantic, happy endings were still customary and flattering. In the popular mind love was not simply the *only* thing but *everything*.

* * *

With the publication of *Hawaii* the relative economies of plot and character in James Michener's *The Bridges at Toko-ri* give way to geographical and historical description run riot. *Hawaii* details the successive waves of immigration to the Islands in a plot that gradually interweaves these different groups into a society. Thus, an opening section in which the geological emergence of Hawaii is chronicled gives way to successive accounts of the Polynesian, American, Japanese and Chinese arrivals, and a final melding of these groups against the social and political conflicts that follow World War II. Michener's epic again reflects the "Eisenhower equilibrium" because its very bulk shows the novelist's solemn view of the importance of his craft. While lengthy novels (e.g. *Anthony Adverse*) frequently become bestsellers because their very bulk satisfies their audience's desires, Michener's new format implies a more tranquil view of the world than that found in *The Bridges at Toko-ri*. Since Hawaii became the fiftieth state on August 21, 1959, initial readers naturally saw Michener's novel as a means of keeping abreast of history (a perception that probably also conditioned the popularity of Edna Ferber's *Ice Palace*, 1958, which chronicled the "taming" of Alaska at a time when that region was becoming the forty-ninth state).

Michener's themes are so didactically pointed they strain, if not rupture, his artistry. Although *Hawaii* is delivered as a first-person narrative by Hoxworth Hale, a conservative ancestor of American and Hawaiian lineage, strict adherence to his single point of view soon disappears in the multitude of characters and situations. Michener's narrator becomes clumsy because he not only possesses too much information but vacillates in tone between compassion and bias. While Hoxworth may represent Michener's political and social views, the narrative scope of *Hawaii* is too broad to sustain the illusion of a single teller or Michener's primary aim of preaching a lesson about human nature in history. Whip Hoxworth, a second-generation

American immigrant, discovers how to irrigate heretofore arid land and possesses the energy to make his scheme a reality. His drive causes the narrator to philosophize over a recurrent historical process: "In the traditional pattern of Hawaii, the intelligence and dedication of one man had transformed a potential good into a realized."[20] This view, according to which unusual men create progress, reaffirms a traditional democratic belief in individual power. It is also an assumption which challenges the institutional organization of American society, for Michener, like John Steinbeck,[21] contrasts the creative powers of the individual with the primitive instincts of the group. Thus, the history of Hawaii shows unusual individuals impressing their wills to shape the seemingly anonymous tides of events. Given this view, history can be manipulated, although not controlled, by human energy.

Women, the emotional centers of family life, provide the continuity that ultimately tames male extremism so that civilized society results when patience tempers passion; as a result, the deeply-rooted middle-class belief in marriage is reaffirmed time and again in *Hawaii*. The austere Abner Hale, who never loses his cultural biases in a land of "permissiveness," is only tolerated by the natives because of his compassionate wife, Jerusha. Among the original Polynesian settlers, Teroro cannot rest until he has returned to Bora Bora and abducted Marama who represents the other half of his soul. Nyuk Tsin, kidnapped from her highland village to be a prostitute for the hordes of Chinese laborers being brought to Hawaii in the later nineteenth century, pleases Kee Mun Ki, a lowland Chinese worker, and so they live together in the Islands even though he is already married. In time, Nyuk Tsin, always referred to as "Auntie" (even by her own children), becomes the spiritual and economic head of the Kee family and a dominant force in business and politics. The sacrifices she makes for her family dramatize the correlation of bourgeois culture and civilization. Nyuk Tsin's constant planning reveals an entrepreneurial drive one associates with Carnegies and Rockefellers; yet all of her conniving leads to an emotionally satisfying end: "It was a curious thing for an old woman of ninety-six to be worrying about the future, but she was, and it was not her future that concerned her, but that of her great family, the on-going thing that she had started but which was now powerful than she."[22] Nyuk Tsin epitomizes the United States as the land of "possibility," for she benefits from the capitalist ethos which ensures riches to those who gamble shrewdly for them. This character is the ugly duckling who wins through patience and energy what she cannot gain through beauty and charm. Finally, the future of Hawaii is assured when Noelani Hale, Hoxworth's divorced daughter, helps Shigeo Sakagawa, the son of Japanese parents running for office as a Democrat in a Republican district. Noelani, like Nyuk Tsin, breaks with tradition and her class because: " 'For the time being, they're worn out...I've been living for a long time with worn-out people, so I'm ready to accept new ideas.' "[23] This young woman represents the same, forward-looking mentality of the novel's other strong female characters; thus, her engagement to Shigeo embodies an ongoing historical tide.

Their imminent marriage symbolizes the final breaking of racial stereotypes in *Hawaii*. As each successive immigrant wave shatters on the rocks of prejudice that its predecessors have set in its path, the novel's dominant motif—to take one's place as a responsible and respected member of society—is reaffirmed. While the Polynesians and the Americans come as colonists and missionaries, the Chinese and the Japanese arrive only after a society, with prejudices and mores, has been established. Thus, the later arrivals must struggle against the ethnic stereotypes which always attach to newcomers; in the financial and political rise of the Kees and the Sakagawas Michener dramatizes this struggle for acceptance and respectability. While such a process is gradual and painful (it takes three generations for the Kees to gain wealth, and the Sakagawas must lose sons in a World War fought against their homeland), its implementation symbolizes American social mobility. *Hawaii* implies that the individual can rise (if not as dramatically as Horatio Alger's newsboys did) so that the traditional American dream of success through hard work is celebrated. In Michener's fictional world respectability is attained when the family embodies the individual's aspirations, so that the Kees, for example, rise through the guidance Nyuk Tsin.

This struggle for status reveals Michener's qualified belief in brotherhood, for his characters continuously think about the commonality of men. In detailing the ethnic origins of the settlers who populate Hawaii, Michener ruefully notes: "In truth, all men are brothers, but as generations pass, it is differences that matter and not similarities."[24] Thus, history shows men continuously denying the larger truth of brotherhood and opting for personal prejudice, only to be convinced that their private visions have been shortsighted. Kelly Kanakoa, a beachboy and a gigolo, has a brief affair with Elinor Henderson, the descendant of missionaries who left Hawaii in the nineteenth century. While Kelly has survived by catering to female tourists (one of whom wistfully notes that her own marriage wouldn't have ended in divorce if she had wedded such a physical specimen), he becomes unsettled when, after he tells Elinor she must learn to take life as it comes, she replies:

"...The biography of one man is the biography of all men.... In the passage of time, Kelly, we become one person."

"Do you honestly think a kanaka like me is as good as a haole like you?" he asked.

"I was once taught that if a pebble falls in the Arabian desert, it affects me in Massachusetts. I believe that, Kelly. We are forever interlocked with the rest of the world."[25]

The girl's idealism reaffirms a popular belief that all actions have meaning—a hypothesis which engenders humility since the individual can never know which of his actions will produce fruitful results. Unfortunately, such providentialism contradicts Michener's view of the creative individual for, if any action is potentially fruitful, how can the creative personality ever be shrewd enough to analyze the bewildering maze of human activities and so sort them out? Such logical inconsistency, of course, does not vex the popular audience which, if nothing else, can simultaneously entertain contradictory ideas.

The most immediate obstacle in *Hawaii* is Michener's portentous style. The novel's opening section, in which the lava eruptions that produced the Islands are described as though God were speaking, epitomizes Michener's penchant for sounding cosmic. Written entirely in italics and entitled *"From the Boundless Deep,"* this section sets forth the novel's principal themes; however, a recitation of geological occurrences for pages on end, instead of the presentation of more animate entities, finally unsettles. Through the repetition of certain words, and because he is describing creation, Michener naturally sounds Biblical:*"The chance emergence of the island was nothing. Remember this. Its emergence was nothing. But its persistence and patient accumulation of stature were everything. Only by relentless effort did it establish its right to exist."*[26] The imperative mood, in which the reader is ordered to remember, aids such an effect, however the very baldness of the presentation of theme is dismaying. Clearly, Michener wants to suggest that the endurance of nature comes to be embodied by humans; yet his method tells rather than shows the reader by dramatic means about such a value. This overt didacticism goes on unabated through the opening section and reading it becomes comparable to trying to run in sand. After comparing Hawaii to a woman patiently waiting for her lover, Michener's narrator concludes:

> *All that would be accomplished in these islands, as in these women, would be generated solely by the will and puissance of some man. I think the islands always knew this.*
>
> *Therefore, men of Polynesia and Boston and China and Mount Fuji...if you come with growing things, and food and better ideas, if you come with gods that will sustain you, and if you are willing to work until the swimming head and the aching arms can stand no more, then you can gain entrance to this miraculous crucible where the units of nature are free to develop according to their own capacities and desires.*
>
> *On these harsh terms the islands waited.*[27]

Fortunately, the reader is eventually removed from this sea of pleading prose and thrown upon the shores of more traditional fictional material. After such an opening, even the stilted dialogue of the Bora Borans, who speak like Hollywood Indians mixing illiteracy, anachronistic diction and wisdom in roughly equal amounts, sounds welcome.

Michener recognizes the human tendency to create a "mythic" grandeur around one's predecessors. The Polynesian settlers, religious and political exiles from Bora Bora who find Hawaii through despair and luck, become encased in a legend that stresses their heroism and ignores their practicality.

> Later ages would depict these men as all-wise and heroic, great venturers seeking bright new lands; but such myths would be in error, for no man leaves where he is and seeks a distant place unless he is in some respect a failure; but having failed in one location and having been ejected, it is possible that in the next he will be a little wiser.[28]

This perception takes much of the gloss off these early settlers, and says something to Americans about one of their favorite myths—that the West was settled by adventurous pioneers fired by boldness and curiosity. In Michener's eyes, men do not make dramatic qualitative changes since misfortunes only prepare them to be slightly more insightful when confronted by a new opportunity.

This capacity for small adjustments enables the human race to endure because men can only change by degree and not in kind. When Micah Hale, the son of Abner and Jerusha, comes of age he begins to question his father's account of the voyage from America to Hawaii; in so doing, the son learns of Abner's biases because past events quickly turn into legends among those who lived through them.

One night Micah whispered to his mother, "Father tells us that all men are brothers, but the ones who sailed on the *Thetis* are a little better than the others, aren't they?" And to the boy's surprise his mother said, "Your father is correct. The world holds no finer people than those who sailed aboard the *Thetis*." But Micah noticed that year by year, in his father's stories of that fateful voyage, the waves got higher and the space in the little stateroom more cramped.[29]

The Hales' voyage is celebrated as a "rite of passage" in which human beings controlled by such immediate problems as seasickness and personal prejudices, are transformed into heroes handling the gravest physical crises with equanimity. Abner's story presents the actual events (which the reader has already seen in all their vomit-stained naturalness) as a myth comparable to the poetic accounts of the Bora Borans' arrival. By creating a useable past, Abner exhibits the same mental habits as the heathens whom he has come to convert to Christianity. This human desire for an elevated past remains constant, for as *Hawaii* draws to its close the families which are commercial forces and "leaders of the community" delight in their (often fictitious) connections with the nobility of their homelands. Thus, the Hales, who came from lower middle-class surroundings in New Hampshire, brag of their "knightly" English ancestry, and the Sakagawas claim a connection with the ruler of Hiroshima in 1703.

Michener insists throughout that any individual man's value ultimately derives from a group. Status is valued even above life itself in the struggles of the Japanese and the Chinese immigrants because, while the individual may satisfy certain primary needs within his family, drives for religious and legal order can only be met within the larger society. When the exiles from Bora Bora arrive in Hawaii, Teroro, their king, and his high priest decide that restraint is essential to community.

Teroro...argued: "We had too many restraints in Havaiki-of-Red-Oro (their homeland in Bora Bora). Here we ought to be free. I like our life the way it is."

"For a few months, perhaps," the priest argued. "But as the years pass, unless a community has fixed laws, and patterns which bind people into their appointed place, life is no good."

"But this is a new land," Teroro reasoned.

"It is in a new land that customs are most necessary," the priest warned....[30]

Thus, the libertarian Teroro sees that fixed rules are essential; and, since religious societies favor hierarchical status arrangements, the static views of Michener's Polynesian characters hardly come as a surprise. Later, however, these religious views conflict with the more dynamic ideas of American democracy and competitive capitalism. The Chinese and Japanese immigrants who follow thus find themselves caught between the natural conservatism of propertied (Polynesian and American) classes and a popular rhetoric which teaches that everyone can be president.

Hawaii symbolizes the United States as a land where successive waves of immigrants are assimilated and, ultimately, given participation in decision-making (the "melting pot"). Island society incorporates such diverse groups as Polynesians, Caucasians and Orientals to prove that democracy represents a workable organization. Michener's newcomers quickly learn that assimilation is essential for spiritual happiness; indeed, because the Sakagawas "had paid a terrible price to prove their loyalty...it had been worth it."[31] For this Japanese family the lure of the old country (which remains sacrosanct until the father actually returns there and flees gratefully back to Hawaii) cannot measure up to the possibilities of the new land. The Sakagawa sons gladly risk their lives to insure the family's future in Hawaii, so that, after 1945, Shigeo, the nominal head of the family, can move into the forefront of society as a lawyer and a politician.

Hong Kong Kee, the rich merchant head of the Kee family, offers Shigeo a prestigious position on a bank's board of directors as the ultimate sign that the Sakagawas have arrived. In persuading the somewhat reluctant young attorney to work with the established "old money" families who are Hawaii's genuine rulers, Hong Kong Kee voices the conventional wisdom learned by a minority which has to prove itself. For the older man breaking into the corporate chambers where important decisions are made represents the final goal.

"So I work hard and show them I can run real estate better than they can, and they make me a partner.... If you smart young Japanese don't pretty soon start joining up in the real running of Hawaii, it only means you aren't clever enough for anybody to want you. Getting elected is the easy part, Shigeo, because you can rely upon stupid people to do that for you, but getting onto the boards, and running the schools, and directing the trusts is the real test. Because there you have to be selected by the smartest people in Hawaii."[32]

As a reflection of the serenity of American society in the later 1950s, this admonition clearly implies that power in society belongs to just men. According to Hong Kong Kee, politics is a simple matter of manipulators controlling the unthinking mass; thus a man only proves his real worth when other successful men pass judgment on him.

In keeping with this conservative social philosophy, Michener presents work and property as the values which best delineate character. Nyuk Tsin buries her emotions after Kee Mun Ki's death and lives only to create economic prosperity for her family. After she acquires property by patient industry (growing pineapples and hawking them in Honolulu), Nyuk Tsin comes to equate ownership with citizenship and with her very identity.

Nyuk Tsin's years fell into an almost sacred routine. On the first of March she went to the land office and paid her taxes on her two properties, and her most valued physical possession became a box in which she kept her receipts. For her they were a kind of citizenship, a proof that she had a right to stay in the Fragrant Tree Country.[33]

Such acquisitiveness makes Nyuk Tsin an entrepreneur who, in true capitalist fashion, continuously looks for the main chance. After a fire guts Honolulu's Chinatown, Nyuk Tsin hatches a plan whereby the family's fortune is made. The old woman realizes that many of her neighbors will sell their damaged properties cheap; thus, through prudent planning (i.e. sending the entire family out to work) the Kees can acquire vast holdings. Nyuk Tsin further convinces her sons to find uses for the burned buildings they acquire. By turning every acquisition into grist for the family mill, and after convincing one of her sons to lobby for government relief, Nyuk Tsin shows that the successful entrepreneur has luck and timing as well as character.

Abner Hale, the religious fanatic whose descendants eschew the missionary for the mercantile life, dramatizes the most well-known confrontation in Hawaii's history—the struggle between Christian ministers and polytheistic natives. While the missionaries and their middle-class proprieties have come to be seen as the causes which destroyed a beautiful primitive culture, Michener's Reverend Hale is ultimately as great a victim as those he tyrannizes. Abner suffers from sexual repression and his marriage to Jerusha abounds with ironies beginning with his reluctant suit for her hand because he needs a wife to do missionary service. As the newlyweds are about to embark on the *Thetis*, the smug Abner "could not believe that the levity, the profane music, the novels and the deficiency in grace that marked the Bromley home were in any sense blessings. In fact, he rather felt that in bringing Jerusha onto the *Thetis* he was somehow saving her from herself."[34] Hale's excessive pride only underscores the subsequent irony when Jerusha proves attractive to the natives while Abner remains isolated because of his stern demeanor. Jerusha realizes that the new ways the missionaries and the merchants have brought to Hawaii require that the natives be instructed in more than Christian worship. Mrs. Hale symbolizes the wise, adaptive female while her husband remains confined in the frenzied religion he preaches and practices.

Reverend Hale can only condemn and never appreciate the natives' natural qualities: "these Hawaiians...were clean, free from repulsive tropical diseases, had fine teeth, good manners, a wild joy in living; and they had devised a well-organized society; but to Abner they were vile."[35] Thus, he becomes a pitiful figure for he loses Jerusha (who is worked to death), receives a beating from the man who truly loved her (Rafer Hoxworth), is replaced in his parish, and lives as a veritable derelict. In his final years Abner becomes a curious eccentric asking each newly-arrived captain if he has seen an ex-parishioner (a girl who ran away and became a whore). Abner's Christianity belies the very charity of the Gospel message, for his God is one of fire and brimstone. Even Jerusha, who subordinates her better sense to Abner's supposedly more inspired morality, knows that her husband lacks any sense of Christian love: " 'In these crucial times you ought to be calmer than usual, quieter and more forceful. You've...told them...."God will destroy you!" But you haven't told me or shown me how with Christ's gentle love you have tried to guide the people in these confusing times.' "[36] Abner's eclipse implies that religion is no longer central in popular consciousness; indeed, his later life coincides with Hawaii's emerging commercial importance—a process marked by the intellectual and material inroads that business makes upon the missionaries' descendants.

The increasingly secular concerns of Michener's characters lead them to battle for civil rights in the twentieth century. Thus, in the novel's final section Hawaii becomes a microcosm in which the course of American history is foreshadowed. Kee Mun Ki, who works as a pimp in a Chinese brothel, discusses his future with his uncle, Chun Fat. The older man has returned after making a fortune in America and admonishes his nephew to go get rich too. Uncle Chun advises Kee Mun Ki how a second-class citizen must deal with his first-class masters.

"It's ridiculously easy to make a fortune in America if you remember two things. Americans understand absolutely nothing about Chinese, yet they have remarkably firm convictions about us, and to prosper you must never disappoint them. Unfortunately, their convictions are contrary, so that it is not always easy to be a Chinese."[37]

Like many another second-class group, Michener's Chinese learn to disguise their intelligence and to conform to popular ignorance.

Michener finally argues that such misunderstanding marks all human history which presents an unending record of man's inability to attribute equal feelings to his fellow man. The individual cannot or will not assume the same depths of thought or emotion in others; and, while experience blurs such shortsightedness, there remains an unreachable place in men harboring at exclusiveness.

Even when each had the full vocabulary of the other, this basic fact of brotherhood— that all have known misery—could not be shared, for just as Abner Hale had refused to believe that the Polynesians had suffered heroic privation in getting to Hawaii, so the Chinese of the *Carthaginian* (who have suffered the rigors of an ocean crossing to be laborers in Hawaii) would never accept the fact that the wealthy white man had known tribulation too.[38]

Since man retains an inviolable need for individuality, a competitive ethos, like that of the United States, is more in tune with human nature than a collective one. At the end of the 1950s, when Martin Luther King was emerging and Congress was becoming aware of the plight of Blacks (the Civil Rights Act of 1957), Michener has civil rights be the next issue his evolving Hawaiians confront. Despite such prescience, *Hawaii* reads as a lengthy paean to conventional wisdom in an overdrawn and imprecise style designed, like the sea working on the shore, to gradually erode critical resistance.

* * *

The View from Pompey's Head embodies the historical and nostalgic themes one associates with William Faulkner and Thomas Wolfe. In returning to his hometown Anson Page, the central character, must come to terms with his own past. While such an excursion would customarily lead to bemused feelings over the discrepancy between what was and what is, Basso's protagonist discovers that the past remains inextricably alive in the present. In spite of his best efforts to escape from the memories of his earlier years, Anson's feelings about Pompey's Head reawaken and he realizes that a man remains emotionally vulnerable all his life. The plot of Basso's novel, which brings Anson back to his former hometown to resolve a legal difficulty, is decidedly secondary to the protagonist's reactions upon returning. Indeed, the threat of a suit concludes so rapidly that it constitutes a sop to probability rather than an integral part of the novel. Lucie Wales, who wants to sue a New York publisher and one of its deceased editors, Philip Greene, for the supposed misappropriation of her husband's royalties, becomes a paper tiger when she learns that the money has been sent to her husband's Negro mother. The compassion Lucie then shows to the drunk and blind Garvin, who paid so that his wife would never know about his racial taint, belies the horror stories Anson has heard about Mrs. Wales in New York. Indeed, Lucie Wales' conversion to compassion emphasizes a major theme of *The View from Pompey's Head* for she adjusts to the past within the present. As a dyed-in-the-wool Southern lady, Lucie can see that her husband's clandestine payments grew from the depth of his love for her and were an attempt by Garvin to protect Lucie's own sense of herself.

The problem of identity also impinges on Anson who, unlike Lucie, must survive in professional and family circumstances that constantly challenge his values. Meg, Anson's wife, reminds him of the inescapable changes time brings when she mentions marrying him on the rebound; and, while she believes her earlier love affair would not have worked out, Meg's pragmatism hardly accords with Anson's sense of nostalgia. For her, saying " 'That was then, not now,' "[39] dismisses a subject completely. Meg's entire background (working on a national news weekly and coming from the urbanized north) puts her in opposition to Anson, so that their conversations take on a frequent edge. Meg remains adamant that New York's energy, bustle and atmosphere of success are a tonic; and so, while she would like to move to Connecticut, she refuses to go to a farm in North Carolina which Anson has inherited. For him, the city with its constantly changing architectural skyline, unsettles.

He would then tell himself, along with thinking that New York was like a blacksnake that was always shedding its skin, that if he were back in Pompey's Head he could walk in the same shadow or the same trees and houses that his father and grandfather had walked in, but that was pure nostalgia, of course. Nobody had roots any more, as Meg said, and she could argue convincingly that any person who was really adjusted, able to stand on his own two feet, didn't need an inherited background to support him like a crutch.[40]

Meg is convinced that moving, a rather prominent aspect of a society in which twenty percent of the population relocates in any given year, represents a desirable goal. For her, going to a new house signals the success of her marriage, while moving to North Carolina, with its slower, more traditional life, would represent a step backward.

Anson is deeply in love with Meg (he experienced love-at-first-sight upon their initial meeting) and so he finds himself caught between sympathies for past and present. Thus, although *The View from Pompey's Head* cannot be called a historical novel, Basso's work does deal with historical experience—the perception of the past and the knowledge that such awareness brings to the individual. Anson must learn that the past shapes the present (historical consciousness) to become human in the fullest sense—a lesson that repeats the experiences of such literary forebears as Walter Scott's Waverley, Leo Tolstoy's Pierre, and Margaret Mitchell's Scarlett in celebrated historical novels. The main character is predisposed to such a lesson for, in telling Meg of the suit his father brought against another white man on behalf of a Negro, Anson dismisses her liberal reaction. When his wife recoils at what she regards as callous prejudice on the part of Pompey's Head's natives, the protagonist tries to suggest that there are human concerns which go deeper than legal rights.

"Identity—the question of identity. On the one-hand you have the white man trying to protect his identity—or so he imagines—and on the other you have the Negro trying to establish his. That's what it's all about. That's what it has been about for years—for generations, ever since the first boatload of slaves arrived."[41]

In keeping with such historical awareness, Anson eschews easy judgments on human conduct: he knows that society's affairs involve loss for every gain, and that, no matter how just a cause may seem, its opponents nearly always have comprehensible and justifiable motives for resisting it. Anson perceives that history comes closer to tragedy, in which balanced rights struggle for survival, than to melodrama, in which the "right" side inevitably displaces the "wrong" one.

This sense of balance enables Anson to be the best observer of Pompey's Head; indeed, because he loves the old town, he sees its blemishes as well as its beauty marks. His allegiance is ultimately based not on ancestor worship (a subject Anson wrote about in a book published under Philip Greene's guidance) but an affection based on his own need for identity. Because he doubts either/or arguments, Anson never becomes a prisoner of his own conclusions: he could write about a blind reverence toward the past and never lose his own sense of wonder that such excesses exist. He recalls the snobbery of Pompey's Head when he remembers Kit Robbins, his first love whose rejection drove him to New York, and the agonies her family endured when they restored the old house they had brought;

while acquiring a more prestigious home could be dismissed and forgiven as a natural desire:

> It was what came after—the carpenters, the plasterers, the painters, the electricians; the Negroes spading in the gardens and the other Negroes unloading antiques; the elaborate act of restoration that turned the old house into one of the show places that the tourists went out of their way to see.
>
> But only the tourists. The tight, hard core of the inner circle, taking one look, decided to look the other way. It was done too expensively and too soon.[42]

Because of this faux pas, Kit Robbins never fully becomes part of Pompey's Head; and, in falling in love with her, Anson psychologically cuts some of his ties. Appropriately, years later, after he has fallen in love with Meg, Anson meets Kit on a busy New York street and discovers that she also has fled Pompey's Head.

An even more damning prejudice of the old town is its popular attitude toward Negroes. Shortly after his return to Pompey's Head, Anson hears a taxi driver casually wonder:

> "Now what do you reckon that old nigger is out this early in the morning for?" he asked
>
> Anson felt himself begin to stiffen. Here it was again, that loathsome word. Here, conjured out of nowhere by an ignorant countryman, were all the things that had caused him to leave Pompey's Head. And out the past...two shadowy figures—a small, anxious, fearful boy and a tall, irate, white-haired man, himself and his grandfather. "Young sir, you ever let me hear you use that word again, just once, and I'll thrash you so that you'll still be feeling it when Gabriel blows his horn."[43]

While Anson's grandfather argued from noblesse oblige, the old man's emphasis on each individual's integrity reinforces the novel's principal theme. Anson discovers, over and over, that people, in doing the unexpected, provide a variety to life that goes beyond preconceptions and stereotypes. Thus, while he can be dismayed by the changes in his old house, Anson can also be moved when Lucie Wales buries her pride and lies to save Garvin's. The protagonist's childhood interest in history, fired by legends of the town, develops into a perception that human beings are complex and interconnected. The past is "a bundle of fishhooks; pick up one and all the others were caught in it."[44] Basso adheres to this image for, as with the cab driver's remark, incidents in Anson's present are inevitably associated with memories of his past; thus, by implication, no man can divest himself of his own history.

The central character finds himself mildly at odds with contemporary society and its emphases on material success and equalitarian politics. While Meg sees misappropriated refrigerators as symbols for the failure of a particular president, Anson can agree that such crimes indicate small minds but still view these bribes as signs of a more general breakdown.

> He agreed with Meg that it was hick, that even graft ought to have style, but he was surprised that she didn't see that there had been a falling off in style all along the line.

It was his belief that style was one of the most important things in the world.

"It's all of a piece," he said. "It's what you have to expect."

"What must I expect?"

"The iceboxes. They're part of the new order."

"All right, I'll bite. What new order?"

"The century of the common man."[45]

Meg, of course, remains impervious to such an argument because she doubts the premises—nostalgia, history, and human irrationality—on which it rests. Anson avoids becoming a reactionary because he recognizes intuitively, and after his trip even more consciously, that the "fishhooks" are constantly in one's brain. Thus, to postulate that things had to be better in the past simply because they were in the past (and not in the present where a man finds himself closer to death) is foolhardy. Anson's conservative outlook makes him aware of the present so that his views shift because of what he experiences. In arguing that ours is the "century of the common man" he is saying that certain motives—the need for identity, fear, greed—remain the same for all men in all times.

When Anson finishes telling Meg about the trial of his father's Negro employee who was injured by one of the town's leading citizens, his reaction is significantly more muted than hers. Meg, who has been dismayed by the jury's obvious bias, believes that the lesson to be drawn is that people should always be "frank and open with each other." Anson politely agrees with this hope but inwardly he doubts that complete candor is either possible or even desirable. When Meg asks if the story is finished, Anson thinks:

In one sense it was and in another it wasn't. It could be taken as an illustration of the truism that nothing ever ended and that what sometimes appeared to be an ending was actually a new beginning. Anson wondered how it would be if he told what happened next. That thought was impossible...he did not think she would want him to be as frank and open as that.[46]

Paradoxically, the future remains more real for Anson than it does for Meg because he attributes an open-ended quality to the past: in perceiving life to be conditional rather than problematic, Anson allows for the impingement of the future.

As *The View from Pompey's Head* reaches its climax and resolution, scenes in which he unravels the Wales' problem and realizes his love for Dinah Blackford, Anson experiences the pains that go with being ethical in an amoral world. Anson realizes that the past, which possesses its own intrinsic conditions, cannot be done over "correctly" in the present; thus, although he loves Dinah more than Meg, being an adult (with spouse and children) precludes any commitment. The novel's last lines suggest the bittersweet irony of this situation. Anson and Dinah part realizing that nothing can change their immediate situations: they are too mature to elope and breaking ties with respectability would ultimately be more destructive than any romantic solace they might find. The two characters demonstrate that life does not always turn out well, yet they resolve to carry on because personal happiness must be subordinated to the greater social good. When

Anson boards the train bound for New York, he still trembles at their parting, yet he allows a porter to light his cigarette and to ask:

> "Well, sir,...how did you find things in Old Pompey? Just the same?"
> "Yes," Anson said. "Just the same."[47]

While his remark sounds like idle chatter, Anson recognizes that, for him, life in Pompey's Head will always retain the same quality. By visiting the old town, the protagonist has been drawn back into his childhood and early manhood, and by falling in love with Dinah he has come to realize that an indelible part of his spirit remains in those times and that place.

Anson associates Pompey's Head with two women—Midge Higgins and Dinah Blackford Higgins. Midge, the daughter of lower-class parents, lives on "the wrong side of the tracks." As an outspoken "Channel girl" Midge attracts Anson against his better judgment (and the warnings of his family) so that he seeks her out and they have some dates. In keeping with the linkage of past and present, Anson and Midge's dates establish the basis for the subsequent marriage of Mico Higgins and Dinah Blackford. While Anson indulges in a romantic interlude with Midge, he learns about Mico who, even as a teenager, has an unyielding ambition to possess Dinah. Since Anson has seen the crafty Mico up close in a poker game, he is not surprised when Dinah later describes her loveless marriage; indeed, a boy who prized ownership and profits could only turn into a grasping adult. Midge is open (and totally different from her brother) about love and passion in ways that unsettle the central character's chivalry. When they first kiss Anson experiences a revelation.

> ...he kissed her, not gently as before, feeling the shiver that swept over her as she came into his arms, and then he was in stunned, trembling possession of all that the night had promised in the moon-struck darkness of its deepest folds—he had never kissed anyone, nor been kissed like that, before; he had never imagined; he had not once dreamed.[48]

Anson does not remain euphoric however for, being the descendant of an established family, he cannot allow himself to feel as the girl does. Basso's protagonist doubts, even at this impressionable age, that romantic feeling constitutes the most important human activity: Anson either lacks courage or has an old head on his young shoulders. In either case, part of him remains content to observe so that he never experiences the intensity of feeling for Midge that she does for him.

Anson's values are strained even further when, in another petting scene with Midge, he lodges the eternal male request to go further and is not completely rebuffed.

> They had not, since Midge had finally and completely established that she was not that kind of a girl, and yet they did not have to go unsatisfied. There was something in Midge's management of the situation that he did not like to think about. He was willing to accept...that Midge must have kissed many men...but it troubled him to think what had just happened

must have happened before. It simply must have. How else could Midge have known so well how to manage? It was his fault, he told himself, more his fault than hers, but she need not have let it happen.[49]

Anson obviously suffers from the double standard: he is still young enough to equate innocence with a lack of experience rather than perceiving it as a frame of mind. He judges Midge rather than face the contradiction of wanting her to be both passionate and virginal, exciting and inexperienced. While conforming would account for much of Anson's tone, his discontent suggests that psychologically Midge is not the girl of his dreams. When he meets her again in the present, there are no romantic sparks; indeed, their brief conversation in a drugstore stresses their dissimilarities.

> "How are you, Sonny?"
> "I'm fine Midge. And you?"
> "I can't complain," she said. "You look like the world's been treating you all right. You haven't changed a bit."
> "Neither have you, Midge."
> "Shinola!" she said. "I'm getting big as a house. It seems to agree with me, though."[50]

Midge remains one of life's survivors, a woman with ordinary goals—house, husband, children—who doesn't think too much about life's ways. In meeting her again, Anson discovers that the past means more to him than it does to others. Yet, in Midge's bland reaction the mystery of human individuality is again celebrated, for she remains a product of her own wishes rather than an extension of Anson's nostalgia. The Midge of the drugstore and the Midge of the front porch swing are but aspects of a continuum that can be observed but never predicted.

Change also colors Anson's initial encounter with Dinah Blackford, who visits his hotel when he fails to call. Because he has only just learned of her marriage to Mico shortly before, Anson makes a polite excuse about his neglect upon meeting her. However, the protagonist also notices that Dinah, the youngster who always chased him out of what he thought was "playfulness" years before, has become a beautiful woman. Of course, "Anson had always known that she would turn into a beauty—she was already a beauty before he went away—but now that it had happened, now that he could see the proof before him, it was not easy to take it in. He had not expected the promise to be so abundantly fulfilled."[51] Dinah symbolizes life in which things never work out exactly as the individual wishes. Anson soon finds himself infatuated when Dinah invites him to lunch and arranges a meeting with Lucie Wales.

Dinah has married Mico because of her desire to remain within the town's upper class, a prospect that was diminishing rapidly as her father and happy-go-lucky brother spent her family's accumulated wealth foolishly. In becoming Mrs. Higgins, Dinah enjoys the enterprising Mico's wealth (generated by a patent medicine that sounds like a con man's cure-all) and restores her family home, Mulberry, to its former glory. Dinah has to be a good hostess, care for two children, and put up with a husband whose real love is business, to gain these benefits; and her life of quiet anguish is visible only to Anson who knows both her and Mico.

> If there were times when her eyes seemed sad, he thought he knew why. A will to humiliate left no room for love, and Dinah was one of those people who needed love. But you could not love anyone whom you believed you had bought, especially if in the act of buying you managed also to satisfy the need to humiliate, and Dinah must have been made to understand—in some way or other, even though he might regard her as his prize possession, Mico Higgins would have brought it home.[52]

Anson rejects Mico, who envied him when they were young, when the latter offers a lucrative retainer to see how greedy the protagonist is. Mico is taken aback when Anson suggests that his law firm lacks the expertise to properly advise in such a situation; and so these characters, who had instinctively disliked each other when they first met, part as still wary adversaries.

Dinah and Anson, however, slowly fall in love during their afternoons together and, as seems appropriate, the moving force is the woman who knows now (and knew then) her real feelings about the protagonist. Anson, in trying to remain decorous and proper, and thus not to surrender rational control of himself, argues that their infatuation arises from the surroundings: they are both in love with their past and are simply using each other as symbols for that time of hope and promise.

> "There's always that, the man and woman thing. But even that is colored by the unreality, the moonlight-and-magnolia dream—for that's what it is, you know. And life isn't. It can't afford to be. It never could, except down here in this one place for that one short time. It's over now, dead and gone forever, but Mulberry betrays you into thinking that it isn't. And that's our trouble, I repeat. Because of Mulberry, we're sort of anachronisms, you and I."[53]

It remains for Dinah to show the difference between a generalized abstraction and a personalized experience to the main character. As she draws him closer, and he willingly gives in, one sees dramatized the notion that life is a set of fishhooks in which people are inextricably caught by past events operating like waves to precipitate new happenings. When Anson and Dinah finally make love, in the old brass bed where he used to sleep when he visited Wyeth (Dinah's older brother), Anson has come home on several levels. Not only is he restored (if only for a night) to his place in the Blackford home but he is also brought back to the poignant realization that one never leaves the past completely behind. Anson can finally appreciate that he carries different selves within himself, so that he can simultaneously love Dinah and Meg and yet be unable to "solve" this situation. When he leaves Pompey's Head, Anson remains true to his conditional view of existence: he must endure separation from Dinah, the only person who understands his nostalgic self, because life presents dilemmas to be borne rather than problems to be solved. *The View from Pompey's Head*, while reaffirming the power of romantic love, implies the more melancholy notion that an individual's emotional attachments cannot be thrown off like a snake's skin. The price of remaining human (as Anson and Dinah do, while Mico and, to a lesser extent, Meg do not) is to suffer consciously over the shortsighted emotional decisions that one must make.

* * *

Max Shulman's *Rally Round the Flag, Boys!* combines topical satire and an allegiance to middle-class values. His comic intentions require viewing society as an institution needing reform and reorganization. Thus, Shulman illustrates the satisfied tone of American life in the middle 1950s, for his characters want only to restore or reimpose values that have been momentarily under attack. *Rally Around the Flag, Boys!* catalogs suburban phobias and lifestyles so that excesses can be held up to ridicule: the momentary disequilibria—brought on by women and the Army — are ultimately righted by endurance and example. Shulman's theme is that while middle-class, suburban existence has temporary irritations and momentary dilemmas, in the long run it represents the best life that America can offer.

Survival is the dominant motif in the novel's most obvious relationship between Guido di Maggio and Maggie Larkin. While Guido has come to Putnam's Landing as a public relations spokesman for the Army which wants to build a guided missile launching base there, Maggie has arrived to be an elementary school teacher. Guido, in keeping with the less heroic characters one finds in comedy, sought this assignment to avoid overseas duty, while Maggie suffers from the myopia of the well-intentioned but inexperienced novice. She has simply never dealt with the "real" world (as Guido has, if only by virtue of his desire for easy duty). Maggie has partially digested Freudian psychology so that she can prattle about "emotional insecurity" and a teacher's duty to undo the "traumas" home life inevitably breeds. While she gets her comeuppance for being too radical for Putnam's Landing, her psychological determinism would be outlandish (and a lot more painful) in a different setting.

Maggie and Guido separate when he learns she has delivered a sex (and it is always to be thought of as S-E-X in this fictional context) lecture to her second graders. While they are reunited in keeping with the novel's comic tone, their tiff is highlighted by Guido's initial support and eventual dismay at learning how specifically Maggie has attempted to alleviate repression and trauma. After telling him she intends to fight for reinstatement, and having Guido reluctantly agree, Maggie asks:

> "Do you think I'm going to let Mr. Vandenburg get away with this?"
>
> "Who?
>
> "Mr. Vandenburg—the principal. He's the one who found out about my sex lecture."
>
> "Oh, grand! What'd he do—walk in while you were talking?"
>
> "No. As a matter of fact, he didn't come in till after the class. But, of course, the pictures were still on the board."
>
> "YOU DREW PICTURES?" screamed Guido.
>
> "How else do you explain anything to seven year old children?" answered Maggie hotly.[54]

Maggie's transgression is one of degree in Guido's eyes; indeed, she has committed a faux pas in being explicit and, thus, showing she does not understand the proprieties the community expects in its members.

Maggie is a kook whose enthusiasms must be bridled by the community's sense of decorum. In a happy suburbia she raises the unsettling issue of ignorance and its relation to bliss; appropriately enough, she only re-emerges after acknowledging that she has overstepped herself. The foolish Maggie must be saved by a man, a situation that would not appear as frequently in comic works in later, more feminist times.

> Guido banged the horn of his car, stopping Maggie in mid-sentence. "Damn it, Maggie," he said sternly, "didn't you just finish telling me you were all through with your crazy theories about child psychology?"
>
> "But—"
>
> "But nothing! You're starting all over again, aren't you?"
>
> Maggie fell silent. She nodded sheepishly. "I guess I am," she said in a tiny voice. "I'm sorry, sweetheart."
>
> "Okay.... But let's don't let it happen again, huh?"
>
> "Yes, dear."[55]

While Maggie sells out for a man, her treatment indicates the traditional American aversion to ideas and intellectuals. It is the common isolated man—Frank Capra's John Doe or Sheriff Will Kane in *High Noon* (both played by Gary Cooper, to be sure)—who is the traditional American hero; however, in the more settled world of comic fiction, the community often embodies such heroic traits. In being saved from herself, Maggie Larkin learns that life in Putnam's Landing supersedes any set of ideas and so returns to the safety of the American fold.

The suburban world which Maggie accepts is dominated by hypocrisy rather than maliciousness. Wives may crave sexual adventures because their own husbands ignore them but never because of real dismay over the quality of their home lives. Angela Wexler can calculate the advantages and disadvantages of her marriage to television producer Oscar Wexler, but she also knows that at thirty-eight she cannot ensnare another man so easily. Her vague sexual ennui, which eventually leads her to pursue Harry Bannerman who seems the most likely neighboring prospect, reflects customary American preoccupations with desirability and never growing old. Their liaison is never serious because they both prefer security to passion. Harry's wandering occurs because his wife, Grace, seems to have forgotten that sex is part of married life, and because suburbia has become a never-ending series of repetitive actions to him.

> Or it was amateur theatricals. Or ringing doorbells for worthy causes. Or umpiring Little League games. Or setting tulip bulbs. Or sticking decals on cribs. Or trimming hedges. Or reading Dr. Spock. Or barbecuing hamburgers. Or increasing your life insurance. Or doing anything in the whole wide world except sitting on a pouf with a soft and loving girl and listening to Rodgers and Hart.[56]

Harry's lament catalogs the insularity of Putnam's Landing, in which everyone is young, married and has children. Grace, who dismisses his constant references to a vacation that they will take alone, errs by repressing Harry's passion; and the questions she asks herself when thinking of her husband's dissatisfaction reveal this flaw: "How can anything be wrong which is so solid, so basic, so full or real, lasting values? Can good, healthy, happy children be wrong? Can a fine, well-kept house be wrong? Can an alert, enlightened community be wrong?"[57] She has dichotomized the issue so that Harry's requests are seen as attempts to destroy what she values when they are really only cries for attention. Grace needs to abandon her either/or thinking and, as one would expect, after a requisite period of disagreement and hostility, the married lovers are reunited. Once again, the female must be guided by the male whose long-suffering patience embodies rationality.

The society around the Bannermans is a consumer-oriented group whose commuter husbands are victimized by distracted wives, supposedly innocent rural types, and land developers. The stratifications in Putnam's landing emphasize the new arrivals' role.

(As any journeyman sociologist can tell you, the commuting villages of Connecticut's Fairfield County...show three distinct social categories, vertically divided. First, there are the Yankees, descendants of the original settlers and still the wielders of power. Second, there are the Italians...who initially came...as track layers for the New Haven Railroad and remained to become the storekeepers, artisans, mechanics, gardeners, police and fire departments. Third there are the New York commuters also called the lambs, or the pigeons, or the patsies.)[58]

This parody of sociological method, with its underlying note of cynicism, is compromised by the novel's plot; for, if men like Harry Bannerman are "pigeons," they are happy victims of their families and the system. The excesses of suburban living are thus held up to mild rather than stern ridicule. The commuters come off as the most affected, for one sees them talking "animatedly of topics that occupy the commuter mind: Neilsen ratings, sheep manure, penis envy, vermouth, and the like."[59] Shulman's list captures the transitory and fashionable nature of middle-class small talk, for it recognizes that one day's fads always sound silly because they are ephemeral. However, the very diversity of these topics implies the "smorgasbord: minds that take them up. Shulman's commuters obviously equate having glanced through *Time* magazine with intellectual sophistication.

The quality of suburban life is best captured by the amateur theatrical performed on July 4th. This awkwardly staged pageant has local high school youths, more interested in their own pubescent and nubile problems than in American history, conducted by domineering adults. Thus, official (i.e. parental) notions about American patriotism are humorously imposed on sex-obsessed teenagers; and the reenactment of the Battle of Yorktown leads to a brawl between the local teenage boys and the Army's enlisted men who are supposedly placating public opinion about the missile base. These groups have naturally divided over the small supply of unmarried girls, and the resultant chaos epitomizes the uneasy feelings that exist between the community and the military over the installation. However, even before this outbreak, Shulman implies the contrived nature of the event in lines that smack of double entendre. Responding to a speech about the prowess of the British soldiers with their long rifles, a male character declaims: " 'I fear not.... If my blood contribute to the seed-time of this new nation of free men, I count it well spent, hey.' "[60] Clearly, "spending well" may have applications beyond mere patriotism.

Shulman's other satirical targets include teenagers, television and the Army. Comfort Goodpasture, the immediate cause of the July 4th brawl, spends most of her time daydreaming about Elvis Presley. Her fan letters abound in teenage argot and celebrate the hostility youngsters are supposed to feel toward their parents. The physically endowed but sexually naive Comfort even composes a poem about James Dean—the ultimate image of teenage rebellion.

> I dreamt I saw James Dean last night
> A-sitting lonely on a cloud,
> And I said, 'What are you doing?'
> And he said, 'I watch the crowd.'

> 'When I see them digging Elvis,
> When I hear that rocking strain,
> When I feel that rolling rhythm,
> I know my life was not in vain.'[61]

Comfort's doggerel reveals how suburban society has assimilated (and watered down) the original serious implications behind the rebellious characters portrayed by Dean. Grady Metcalf, who is enamored of Comfort and wants to project an image of alienated youth, is the "leading juvenile delinquent of Putnam's Landing"; however:

(The term "juvenile delinquent" is here used loosely. Grady was not the lean, hard, Sal Mineo type. He was more on the well-fed, spongy side. The tenement that spawned him was a $40,000 ranch house on two well-kept acres and the sight of a switchblade would have put him in shock. Grady was a member of the new school of juvenile delinquency.... A boy was no longer excluded from the glamorous ranks of the delinquents simply because he had the rotten luck not to be born in a slum.... If he would wear his hair in a duck-tail cut and his sideburns at nostril level, forsake grammar, dress in black khaki trousers with the cuffs narrowed to fourteen inches, never do his homework, and spit a lot, his origins, no matter how respectable, would not be held against him.[62]

Grady again symbolizes a suburban society in which form displaces content; like his elders, who are always concerned with doing the right thing, the young man substitutes style for substance. While his mannerisms display an unwitting hypocrisy, Grady's muddleheadedness can be gently corrected by society in time.

Oscar Wexler embodies the worlds of television and advertising. His corporate milieu, in which Biblical heroes are utilized to sell breakfast foods, is governed by ratings and sponsors; and Oscar, who has no pretenses about quality programming, is a conspicuous leader in the "industry." He sneers at the idea that serious literature can be presented on television when he tells a would-be reformer:

"Important writers. Remember when NBC tried to beef up their Sunday nights with important writers? Plays by Robert Sherwood—Thornton Wilder—Ferenc Molnar. Important enough for you?...So what happened? I'll tell you what: forty million people nearly broke off their dials turning back to Ed Sullivan to watch a dog fart *The Star-Spangled Banner*."[63]

Oscar's cynicism is perspicacious: he may be deficient as a husband because he spends too much time at the office, however his shortcoming coincides with the comic tone of *Rally Round the Flag, Boys!* Oscar must divorce Angela so that her threat to the Bannermans can be neutralized. Putnam's Landing is, if nothing else, a solidly monogamous society where only an occasional flirtation and the constant female concern with physical appearance are allowed to intrude.

A more dangerous individual is Captain Walker Hoxie, a career soldier assigned to command the Nike station at Putnam's Landing. Hoxie despises civilians and sees communists behind every bush. In a town meeting, when the suggestion that the Army seek another site is made, he launches into a tirade.

"We see the point, all right. The point is that Putnam's Landing is full of yellow-livered, money-grubbing, fat-bellied feather merchants, and if I had my way, I'd line 'em up against the wall and shoot the whole sickening lot of 'em'.

"...Your country is in danger. The *United States of America* is in danger. Are you an American? Or are you some kind of commie rat bastard?"[64]

Hoxie reflects the either/or mentality of caricature; and he remains true to rigid militarism. While he receives an appropriate reward (in the form of a nagging Angela Wexler), his type of military idiot strikingly confirms a shift in values in the mid-1950s. Such a fictional type would have not been welcome in the America of Joseph McCarthy in which military preparedness was too serious a business to be ridiculed. Americans might accept comic soldiers, such as the inmates of *Stalag 17*, GIs who joked to endure a terrible time, but never an excess like Captain Hoxie, who would fit comfortably into the paranoid worlds of *Catch-22* and *Dr. Strangelove*. Naturally, in keeping with the secure sense of Shulman's novel, even this radical Cold Warrior is assimilated into the soothing society of Putnam's Landing.

Indeed, the conclusion of *Rally Around the Flag, Boys!*, in which Grace Bannerman is blissfully pregnant and Harry has become a lion at PTA meetings, Grady Metcalf has been sent to a military academy, and the Army has bribed its way into the community's heart by donating land for a garbage disposal plant, represents a restoration of order consistent with comic traditions. One leaves this novel satisfied that the good people have survived and will prosper while, in true therapeutic fashion, the excessive characters have either been redeemed or restrained. Middle-class suburban' society has surmounted a series of pseudo-crises and is girding its loins for the inevitably solvable problems which will follow. Certainly Shulman's world, in which difficulties can be overcome through goodwill, reflects what the historians have labelled the "Eisenhower equilibrium." This uncluttered society in which attaining status in the proper suburban community is the primary goal suggests an America in which being the character that Ozzie Nelson played on television represents the highest achievement. Such a sentiment further implies that happiness results from an incapacity to see difficulties, so that the society of Putnam's Landing is blissfully happy because procreation and satisfying creature comforts are its major interests.

* * *

Comedy is often better appreciated than described. Yet one can safely say that one decade's humor often becomes stale because imitation and repetition render it a cliché. Moreover, given the popular media's needs for ever-new material, fresh comic ideas and situations are quickly rendered commonplace. *Catch-22*, for example, gives birth to *M.A.S.H* which, in turn, spawns a television series whose intellectual bite is further dissipated because of the need to be "appropriate" viewing for the family. An original comic situation becomes a consumable commodity whose very repetitiveness turns the original characters and their insights into stable entities no longer threatening to the banalities of the front room. This kind of dilution surrounds Mac Hyman's *No Time for Sergeants,* a novel that became a stage play and a film in the 1950s. Its "over-exposure" was continued indirectly by various sitcoms about military life (e.g *McHale's Navy*) while Andy Griffith, as the stage and film Will Stockdale, as well as in his subsequent television role as a southern sheriff in *Mayberry R.F.D.*' helped to render the protagonist far too familiar. In essence, Hyman's country innocent whose naivete thwarts and then overturns Army regulations became Gomer Pyle; thus, when reading *No Time for Sergeants* one must fight an almost overwhelming sense of having been surrounded by its characters for years and years.

Hyman pits his unsophisticated country boy against the supposedly more worldly atmosphere of barracks' life. The disproportion between Will and his environment represents a stock comic device (e.g. the Marx Brothers in *Duck Soup*) in which the individual's capacities and responsibilities are at odds. The audience, whether seeing Chico Marx as a cabinet minister or Will Stockdale as an Army private, immediately recognizes the incongruity and roots for the underdog. The mismatched individual usually wins (by succeeding or simply surviving) and, in so doing, proves that the barriers erected against him are not nearly as awesome as officials or professionals would like him (and us) to believe. The cathartic nature of such comedy derives from its undermining the fixed values of the audience's society: it satisfies a popular fantasy by stressing that individuality can overcome institutionalism. Will Stockdale ultimately survives and triumphs because he is determined to be the person he is. While he adjusts to Army life, Will's success lies in being "true" to himself, so that getting ahead hinges on being authentic in the deepest sense. In such a comic world, survival on one's own terms is the goal; and, since all the characters are flawed either intellectually or emotionally, conflict occurs between degrees of incompetence and shortsightedness rather than between ethical absolutes. The audience cheers for Will Stockdale in his struggle against bureaucratized Army minds because his flaw (naiveté) derives from ignorance while theirs (close-mindedness) results from cynicism.

No Time for Sergeants shows its protagonist being inducted, enduring the rigors of basic training and, finally, being placed in an appropriate section of the Army. For a time, Hyman's country boy endures the practical jokes of his peers, but he is eventually roused, like a bear from hibernation, and beats some sense into his tormentors. Hyman juxtaposes Will's desire to get along and his lack of sophistication to the antics of another recruit, Irvin, who has had R.O.T.C. and to whom Will attaches enormous respect. When Hyman's protagonist turns on the tormentors whom Irvin has led, the basic design of the novel is revealed. Will's triumph, which arises from his natural strength, foreshadows his subsequent victories in more sedate situations. When Will must be assigned, the harried Sergeant King, "about the saddest-looking man I ever looked at,"[65] emerges as the exasperated comic foil who must endure the protagonist's actions while trying to preserve his own sense of Army life. The Sergeant, who wants things to run as effortlessly as possible, initially "hides" Will by making him permanent latrine orderly. This scheme, which would preserve the status quo and the Sergeant's "lifer" mentality, is discovered by some horrified brass who decree that Will must be tested and placed.

An examination of the protagonist's manual dexterity and problem-solving capabilities brings the comic clash of recruit and organization to its heights. Will clearly does not understand the instructions, when presented with two metal rings and told to join them through manual manipulation.

> So I got to fitting mine too, but it didn't work out at first, so then I reached down and got a right good grip on one of the pieces and straightened it out and slipped back inside the other one and tied them back up together, which was a right good way of doing it because I was the first one finished.[66]

Will's taking matters into his own hands confounds the closed mentality of the tester who has been taught to react in only one way and cannot deal with any variation. This individual cannot cope with Will's breaking the rules and destruction of government property, while the audience is delighted because authority has been defeated by common sense. The same satisfaction arises from Will's dealings with an Army psychiatrist who tries desperately to raise the protagonist's ire by insulting his home state.

> "Where you from, Stockdale?"
> I told him Georgia, and he come back with: "That's not much of a state, is it ?" which

didn't sound very polite to me.

But I said, "Well, I don't live all over the state. I just live in one little place in it."

Then he kept staring and said, "That's where they have the tobacco roads and things, isn't it?"

"Maybe so, but not around my section," I said. "I never seen no tobacco planted in a road. Maybe you from some other part than me."[67]

Will cannot be insulted because he lacks the literary associations to recognize the intended abuse; he pits innocence against experience and, through treating the psychiatrist's language literally, renders his more learned adversary impotent.

Their conversation escalates when the psychiatrist suggests that Will probably hated his parents. Such analytical theory is, of course, ridiculed when Hyman's protagonist, vexed at what he considers stupid questions, reassures his interrogator.

"Sir, I don't hate my pa and I don't guess I hated my ma either, and if that's all you want to know, you can write down there on that air paper that I didn't hate neither one of them, and not my grandpa or my grandma either, because I like all my folks 'ceptin this one uncle I got that I ain't too partial to because every time he comes out to the house, he's always wanting to rassle with our mule, and I just think he ain't got very good sense because every time he comes out there he heads back for the barn and keeps the mule all wore out and tired...."[68]

It is, of course, a well-known paradox that psychological definitions of normal human conduct (i.e. the individual is normal if he makes an adequate adjustment to his surroundings) substitute the description of a process for the formulation of a logical category. Normalcy consists of doing what is necessary to get along rather than creating precepts by which the individual gains a more reasonable state of being. Moreover, as Hyman's protagonist shows, the patient's willingness to accept the analyst's exalted status is *the* necessary correlative in the psychiatric process. Because Will does not speak the same language, or at least not the same connotative language, there can be no communication between these characters; and, to deepen their incompatibility, the psychiatrist attempts to probe into the background (Will's mother is dead) he has either not studied or simply ignored. Their conversation presents a masterful dismissal of the disciple who, in his zealotry, besmirches the ideas of his master; hopefully, Freud, had he observed this contemporary scene, would not have been a Freudian.

The comic resolution of *No Time for Sergeants* occurs when Will and his best friend, Ben, who have been assigned to aircraft duty and are presumed dead because their plane crashed, return to the post just after they have been awarded "posthumous" medals. In order to save face, their commanding General has Will and Ben transferred to the infantry so that their return will not be a continuous blot on his record. It is, however, at this point that Will exerts his personality once more by insisting that Ben, who always wanted to be in the infantry despite his puny physique, and he still receive their medals. Will manipulates the exasperated General into performing a symbolic ceremony, with other officers at rigid attention in front of jeep headlights, that punctures official pomposity. In order to assuage his pride in some small measure, the General not only sends Will and Ben to the infantry but also orders Sergeant King, now reduced to a private, to accompany them. Thus, *No Time for Sergeants* ends with the protagonist not merely having survived but having permanently reduced a small part of the Army to his own genuinely human level.

* * *

John D. MacDonald, who attained greater popularity and more critical prestige in the 1960s and 1970s with his Travis McGee stories, consistently produced entertaining novels in the 1950s. Writing paperback originals, an innovation in publishing then, MacDonald created fairly sophisticated tales of suspense and murder. *The Damned*, MacDonald's most popular work from the 1950s, concerns characters who must wait out a delay at a ferry crossing. Waiting to go from Mexico to the United States these figures experience severe changes in their inter-personal relationships; however, such plotting, which would ordinarily tax the reader's patience, is kept in bounds by the ironic scenes which begin and end the novel. In effect, MacDonald creates tension and suspense while simultaneously suggesting that existence is highly repetitive. This scene of deja vu is illustrated by the multiple viewpoints *The Damned* provides. We move from character to character so that melodrama never becomes intrusive; in effect, the reader takes each character's side "one at a time" and, thus, avoids seeing any single figure as the embodiment of simplistic moral characteristics.

Its rapid plot prevents *The Damned* from becoming overly serious for the characters never move beyond the needs for love, safety or a career. Moreover, while they can verbalize the ethics or wishes that drive them, none of these characters has an involved mental life; so that overt physical action predominates and none of these figures stays in mind once the book is finished. The rapidity of the plot enables the novelist to be momentarily philosophic (or "deep") but then quickly to subsume such reflections in more story. When Linda Gerrold realizes her marriage to Carter must end and then confronts Bill Danton, a Texan who sweeps her off her feet, she verbalizes the anti-melodramatic tone of MacDonald's writing.

"Pat endings are from O. Henry and Metro-Goldwyn-Mayer and Edgar Guest. I can't have my marriage blow up in my face and give a big contented sigh and fall into your arms and we walk away into the sunset with violin music. No, Bill. Life doesn't work that way."[69]

It is this realistic tone which enables MacDonald to create, even in this conventional situation, characters whose personalities are more than stereotypes. Even though Linda has fallen in love with Danton at first sight, she does not need a man to justify her existence. Instead, she will go to New York and sort out her feelings; and, in holding Danton off as a test to discover if her feelings are "real," she emerges as a more credible character than many another bestseller's passion-swept females. The plot, which moves from situation to situation, is also described when Linda says: " 'This is a crazy day. As if the world had stopped. I feel as though I were dreaming it.' "[70] MacDonald's concern about numerous individuals prevents melodrama from looming too large because any single character's emotions are never sufficiently treated so as to seem central.

The Damned can be enjoyed as a smoothly crafted and succinctly executed entertainment which, in presenting the problems of three sets of characters, sustains a hectic pace. The most striking of these sets comprises Carter Gerrold, Linda and Bill Danton. Carter and Linda first appear as conventionally happy newlyweds whose bliss has been only slightly marred by his mother's joining them at the end of their honeymoon. After they arrive at the crossing and join the line of cars, Carter and Linda go into the brush and make love. However, as they wander off, Carter feels ashamed of the earlier scenes of their marriage; and, after they have made love, he is distraught because Linda enjoys sexual relations.

> She seemed to enjoy it too much, and that didn't seem right, somehow.
> He wished she would hate it. And then he could feel that almost pleasant guilt afterward, and apologize to her abjectly, and beg her forgiveness for dirtying her.[71]

This unsettling psychological note, which implies Carter's masochism, causes Linda to question her husband's character. She fears Carter will be content to remain a supernumerary in his uncle's business and a companion to his mother. Linda wants to exorcise her husband's sexual prudery by getting the "real" reasons for it into the open; in effect, she wishes to play Freud to his mother fixation. Unfortunately, Carter's troubles are more deep-seated than Linda realizes; and when she brings up the fact that Carter's father ran away with the woman he truly loved as an example of what real intimacy should be, her neurotic husband flares up. While Linda understands romantic love, Carter remains psychologically fixed in childhood. After Mrs. Gerrold's death, Carter slaps Linda and chides her for taking him away from his proper station: he insists that her lust has caused his mother's loss (an infantile associative pattern, if there ever was one) and refuses to have anything more to do with his bride. Linda thus realizes that she has placed too much faith in sexual attraction and been as shortsighted as Carter: "It no longer seemed important to think of her marriage as a dilemma. She would go on...or she wouldn't. She had been tricked. She had given her body to the white knight who had never been. Given it with a high eagerness."[72] Linda becomes self-critical and gains wisdom by seeing that the situation deteriorated in part because of her.

If Linda's indictment of such romantic love serves as a mild critique of popular values, Carter's emotional repression stands as a warning against homosexual self-indulgence. After his fumbling attempts to prevent the local embalmers from making his mother look garish, Carter decides to annul his marriage. He then thinks it would be a good idea to retain his mother's house and ask an old friend, Tommy Gill, to come and live with him. While Carter's tendencies are latent, MacDonald imposes a symbolic scheme on the young man's thoughts to assure that the reader will "get" Carter's homosexuality. In reflecting about a statue of Diana that adorned his parents' garden, Carter reveals the masturbatory and masochistic furtiveness with which he surrounds sex.

> ...his hands atremble against the marble loins, and there, in the dewy night, with the crazy thickening, and then ignoring the cold eyes of God staring down the slant of moonlight, and forgetting the white milk eyes of the carven Diana, the secret and shameful act, the thing like a heat and a sickness, with the statue seeming to tilt as though it would fall, fall and smash him utterly.[73]

This initial memory takes place before his mother's death; however, after he has decided to leave Linda, Carter becomes more tranquil about the statue. As Danton drives Carter's automobile onto the ferry (and thus proves more practical and worthy of Linda) Gerrold dozes off and has an obviously symbolic dream in which:

> ...he could see the statue across the years.... He walked up to it, and it seemed as though he had never really looked at it before. Uncle was silly calling it Diana, and calling it a girl. Anybody could see it was the marble statue of a young, clean-limbed boy...it was Tommy, as he had known it would be.[74]

Carter realizes his sexual nature in this dream; and, while his dependency on his mother caused him to treat Linda badly even before their arrival at the Rio Conchos crossing (e.g. he started turning out the lights on their lovemaking *after* Mama joined them), Carter's final lapse into the gay life relieves the reader from feeling anything for him. Carter Gerrold has passed a personal crossroads and can no longer elicit either wrath or compassion from the audience.

Linda also arrives at a moment of crisis; however, unlike her childish husband, she is conscious that a crossroads has been reached. Moreover, she is honest enough to realize her folly in choosing Carter, for not only may she have "confused weakness with sensitivity" but she probably erred in marrying a person who had no sense of humor about himself. Thus, while Carter regresses, Linda learns from her mistakes so as to build character. This difficult process culminates when she realizes that she "had grown older on this day, and that John Carter Gerrold would never grow older."[75] Bill Danton, a young American rancher whose father lives in Mexico, offers Linda a way out by restoring the girl's faith in herself. Because Danton recognizes that "here was that rare and lovely thing, a woman with beauty but also loyalty, sensitivity, and the funny humor which is at once lusty and pixie,"[76] he can share an adult love with Linda in one day. Danton knows that happiness is being with *the* woman you love, so that, if he must sacrifice like his father, who gave up his American citizenship to live with a special woman, he will do so. When Linda turns to Danton for advice about her ruptured marriage, the young rancher raises questions that force Linda to decide for herself. Linda finally presents her father's philosophy of human nature and, in so doing, realizes that Danton should be her husband.

> She spread her arms wide.... She was holding up her two index fingers. She waggled the one on the left hand. "Now here is what you think you are, see?" She waggled the index finger on the right hand. And here is what you actually are. If the two things are way apart like this, you get a bore, somebody who can't see himself as others see him. The closer together you bring the two hands, the better sort of person you represent. If you actually are what you think you are, with the fingers right together like this, then the chances are that you're a pretty decent human being. A nice guy."[77]

Linda's pronouncement can serve as an epitaph on MacDonald's fictional world. In effect, his characters are trying to break through to their real selves; and while society may impose barriers to such self-realization, nearly all his individuals consistently espouse this broader purpose.

A second group in *The Damned* centers on the vague and promiscuous Betty Mooney, a sometime secretary who has gone off on an extended weekend with Darby Garron, a businessman experiencing middle-age sexual pangs. During their stay in Mexico this odd couple has come to dislike each other intensely: the man is guilty and depressed about deserting home and family, while Betty is dismayed at the brevity of the "fling." Garron abandons the woman and the other cars to seek a deserted spot where he can sit and meditate. Ironically, while communing with himself, he is shot and killed by a stray bullet fired by a Mexican official's bodyguard. Garron cannot initially understand what has happened, and his shortsightedness leads to his death for he doesn't even cry for help.

> Suddenly his attention was ripped away from the distant scene when one of the children playing in the road hit him in the belly with a stone hurled so hard that it felt like a blow from a hammer.
> ...The blow had given him an oddly hollow feelings.... He opened his shirt and looked at where the stone had hit him. There was a small hole, and blood ran slowly out of the hole and down under his belt.[78]

In keeping with MacDonald's ironic and underplaying tendencies, Garron blunders because such a reaction is consistent with the ordinary experiences of common men. His collapse into death reflects the all-too-human faith that each individual has in his own indestructibility.

Betty Mooney's personal dilemmas can only be resolved by others, for she is a laconic tramp whose only motive is the fear of death. Betty wants to survive as easily as possible, and that is why she accompanied Garron to Mexico, where he discovered: "In conversation she repeated herself interminably, expressing childish infatuation with movie actors, TV stars, disc jockeys. Her love-making was an unimaginative compound of all the movies she had seen, all the confession stories she had read."[79] Betty's artificiality is underscored by this catalog, for she is clearly so dull that she makes Garron's teeth ache. Her playacting nature reflects the mores of the 1950s and later, for she is obviously in tune with a consumer society. Betty's sources—TV, films, radio—are in keeping with the emphasis that media hype has assumed in American society. Her amorphous nature—

she is guided seemingly by the last striking image she has encountered—causes her to be maneuvered by those who possess more will power.

Del Bennicke (alias Benson), a con man on the run from killing a prominent Mexican matador over a prostitute, quickly sees that Betty is an opportunity for escape and brief prosperity. After noticing that she thrusts her breasts unnaturally forward, and reflecting that she "could be broken down and put on the road,"[80] Del decides to take charge of Betty's life for a while. His desire to live off her is aided when Betty falls in love with him, even though she realizes he is a bum. Their relationship culminates as they hide Garron's body and Del spells out the master-victim status that each will enjoy in the days ahead. He beats this truth into Betty, and after hitting her a few times, tortures her even more dramatically.

"From now on you do everything I tell you to do, and you do it exactly the way I want it done." He reached out and his hand closed on her breast.

"Don't Del. My God!"

"We got to keep straight."

"Let go of me. You'll give me a cancer. You're crazy or something. Ow!"

...She knew that she would go with him, and that he would hurt her again, out of irritation, or anger, or indifference, or just to amuse himself. And she would take it, and stay around for more. She wept for herself, and for the lost years.[81]

Betty has found a master; and her acquiescence in and her foresight about their relationship suggest that she is, finally, a victim of fate.

Another threesome that alters during *The Damned* includes Phil Decker, a veteran nightclub comedian, and the twins Riki and Niki, he has groomed as a novelty act. While Decker constantly utters gag lines and sees the possibility of new material in every situation, the girls are tired of the vagabond life to which he has exposed them. They are dismayed because they believed show business would be something more glamorous than a strip tease act in which each sits on one side of a false mirror. Their illusions are further shattered when they are asked to perform for some producers in a hotel room. After their refusal, the twins are given serious advice by a press agent who tells them to "unlearn" what Decker has taught them. Thus, they have become resigned to being floor walkers for old men to gawk at and, when they arrive in Rio Conchos, realize they must tell Phil the bad news. While Decker accepts their resignation with outward good grace (nothing is going to get under his skin), his real feelings are more desperate. The aging comic ruminates about his wasted years in show business. The collapse of his partner, Manny, and the dissolution of his marriage have stripped him of friendship and finances and so, at forty-nine, Phil Decker faces being a third-rate comic for the rest of his life. He reflects that it's "damn hard to be a comic, to think of the punch lines, to dress up the routines, when way down in your mind you kept thinking of death."[82] After they cross the Rio Conchos, Phil and the twins set out on definite roads for they have realized their limits and more honestly face the future.

A more sinister figure, the Mexican tyrant Atahualpa, enables

MacDonald to comment on politics. Bill Danton, who knows Mexicans, instinctively brands Atahualpa a blind nationalist whose politics are little more than fascism. This obvious appeal to force can be checked because Atahualpa is a coward and a bully; however, the political cauldron, which produces such a leader, can continually spew forth such individuals. In keeping with the temper of the early 1950s, Danton believes that communism poses the real danger, for Mexico, despite great material progress, suffers from grinding poverty: "Truly it was a race against time. The *communistas* bred in discontent, like flies in offal. *Turista* arrogance created no love for the powerful neighbor to the north."[83] Here, in brief, is the major concern of *The Ugly American* for again one sees native unrest and American myopia creating a breeding ground for communism. While the Marxist outlook being equated to flies and dung hills accords with the rhetorical sentiments of Joseph McCarthy and Mickey Spillane's Mike Hammer, Danton never lapses into such simplified views. He urges Linda that one must fight against being stereotyped, for such labels promote misunderstanding and violence. After explaining that he grew tired of defending his Mexican citizenship against American boys in school, and how relieved he felt when he stopped responding, Danton casually remarks that the world " 'is full of people objecting to labels. Washington is full of people calling each other communists!' "[84] Thus, according to Danton, one must avoid confusing ideological generalizations with actual individuals.

Manual Forno and his wife, Rosalita, the central figures in the novel's prologue and epilogue, serve as an ironic chorus in *The Damned*. Because the Americans are waiting to get across a river by means of a ferry, the classical myth of Charon and the river Styx comes to mind; and, since MacDonald's characters experience significant personal changes, allusion to the river of death may not be entirely accidental. While he does not want to impose so much symbolic weight that *The Damned* becomes a literary trophy for symbol hunters, MacDonald does operate at more than one level. Manual and Rosalita establish the irony that MacDonald wants the reader to feel as the book's final impression. As Manual stumbles through dinner and collapses into bed after an exhausting day, and as Rosalita convinces him that he has enough energy to make love with her, their exchanges establish MacDonald's larger theme.

Thus *The Damned* offers irony as resolution. Its characters have changed, but the world, as symbolized by these Mexican peasants, has hardly noticed. MacDonald implies that life is simultaneously vicious and humorous—a prescription that satisfies a popular audience while providing "levels" to intrigue more analytical readers.

Chapter 6

"He felt her body arch crazily against him and saw red lights behind his eyes."

Novelists have treated sexual relations more explicitly since 1960 with extended descriptions of the physical dynamics of romantic couplings. Such graphic detail has been accompanied by an increase in the types of human sexuality portrayed: oral, anal and group sex have become standard fare in contemporary bestsellers in contrast to the 1950s when heterosexual intimacy was the general limit of authorial "daring." While homosexual activities occur in the newer works, 1950s' bestsellers exhibit a consistent distaste for "fairies" and "queers," while lesbians are rarely even alluded to. The euphemistic style which, wittingly or unwittingly, parodies Hollywood's visual portrayals of sexual release through shots of pounding surf and "throbbing" crescendi in music scores, governs such popular presentations of sex. Indeed, no writer from the 1950s describes intercourse so as to suggest to the inexperienced how human beings actually accomplish the act. While some might applaud the passing of such imprecision, more recent efforts introduce ennui by their very explicitness; at best, sexual love has never been a spectator sport.

Physical romantic bliss was never seriously questioned in the bestsellers of the 1950s. While sexual activities figure prominently in the plots of nearly all of the novels treated in this study,[1] Harold Robbins, Charles Mergendahl, Frank Yerby and Grace Metalious present fictional environments—business, medicine, plantation society, small town— essentially as backdrops for portraying the sexual preoccupations of their characters. For these novelists life's sexual aspects take precedence over any occupational or social relationships the characters might have. Robbins' *Never Leave Me* (1954) presents an extended defense and elaboration of the sexual double standard: his protagonist is free to seduce any woman because of his awesome sexual powers and technique (so often an attribute of males in hard-core pornography). Mergendahl's *The Bramble Bush* (1958) uses its vicious, gossipy small town as a background for the therapeutic transformation of its characters who are psychologically or physically thwarted in love. Yerby's *Floodtide* (1950) delineates an antebellum Mississippi plantation society whose violent ethos is manipulated by a sadistic nymphomaniac who challenges some of the male dominance so prevalent in popular thinking. Metalious' *Peyton Place* (1956) and *Return to Peyton Place* (1959) present more domesticated versions of this same type of woman—one who seeks her own sexual gratifications because, like the male characters, she is driven by physical needs.

* * *

Harold Robbins is a literary gold mine whose every novel reveals veins of popular feeling. His characters are slightly more libidinous (i.e. "daring") than the general public and are always involved in exotic or exciting occupations. During the 1950s Robbins' novels concentrated on emotions and sexual mores rather than professional ethos. Thus, although the central character in *Never Leave Me*, Brad Rowan, heads an advertising agency, the novel's business sections are decidedly secondary to its romantic ones. Although he nearly loses his business because of a client he offends and an envious subordinate, Brad's affair with Elaine Schuyler constitutes the novel's major interest. Brad, a family man of forty-three, finds himself caught between his love for Elaine and the responsibilities of home and family. The novel ultimately preaches self-sacrifice and surely reflects basic American beliefs in doing so. *Never Leave Me*, a typical Robbins' effort, presents characters doing things society would allegedly frown on (e.g. adultery) but having these transgressions sanitized by the novel's moralistic plot denouement. The audience thus enjoys both the titillation of an extra-marital affair and the satisfaction of seeing standard middle-class values (marriage, children, home) reaffirmed by the very characters who have transgressed. There is, ultimately, no dissonance in this fictional world, for characters who "sin" can always be redeemed; thus, Brad Rowan undergoes the private agonies of losing an illicit love to become a better man.

Never Leave Me starts with its final events so that one reads to see how the characters got to these initial pages. Paul Remy, a friend and business associate, calls from Washington D.C. to inform the protagonist that Elaine has committed suicide. The distraught Brad keeps asking why his beloved would take her own life; and, even though he trusts Elaine never revealed their affair, he wants to know:

> "Did she leave a note?"
> "No note. Nothing. Nobody knows why."
> A small sigh of relief escaped my lips. The kid had played it straight right down to the wire.... "It's a terrible shock, Paul."
> "To all of us, Brad.... Just a few weeks ago Edith was saying how happy Elaine seemed, now that you were helping on that infantile drive. She said Elaine had found herself again, doing something for others."
> ...I had to stop talking like that, or he'd kill me.[2]

While this opening passage establishes the connection between Brad and Elaine (without divulging its intimate details), the value attached to self-sacrifice looms large even here. Elaine "found" herself, after the death of her husband and children, in doing volunteer work, and such self-sacrifice carried over to her relationship with Brad. It is only a matter of time, however, until Brad receives the note Elaine did not want the world to see. She has committed suicide because of her faith in love and marriage. She could not destroy the Rowans' marriage because her own emotions remained so deeply entwined with her deceased husband. Her suicide represents the strongest fictional reaffirmation from the 1950s of the family, the traditional foundation of American middle-class values.

In his struggle with Matt Brady, who wants to buy his business, Brad seeks an emotional secret to stop his rival. When Rowan learns that Brady's receptionist, Sandra, is really the old man's illegitimate daughter, he confronts his rival only to find himself unable to use such knowledge. All is not lost, however, for Brady so admires Rowan's tact and spirit that, as the seemingly defeated protagonist starts to leave, the old tycoon makes him his ad agent once more. And, when Sandra enters the office, even though Matt Brady says nothing and Rowan does not reveal her paternity, the emotional significance of family life is again apparent. Sandra, who has tried unsuccessfully to find work elsewhere and always returned to Brady, accepts the old man's offer to go to New York and work with Brad on a new ad campaign; however, instead of dashing out with the protagonist with whom she has already made love, Sandra:

> . . . smiled at the old man. "If it's all right with you, Mr. Brady," she said quickly. "I'd rather stay here with you for a while."
>
> The old man couldn't hide his pleasure. The radiant smile on his face was bright enough to light up the whole room.[3]

Family pride, even in an unknowing illegitimate child, proves stronger than any desire for revenge, so that, in effect, there are no thoroughly bad people simply those whose family lives have gone wrong in some way.

Elaine Schuyler's final letter to Brad makes these values even more apparent, for by the time it is written Robbins' main character has been reunited with his wife because one of their children has suffered a serious illness and been hospitalized. In explaining why she has killed herself, Elaine urges how a cemetery visit made her realize that, by choosing to be with Brad, she would be denied being with David and her children in the next world.

> It was then it came to me that if I were to be with you, I could never be with him and the children. We could never be together again; we who meant so much to each other.
>
> That is how I found that I did not love you less, but that I loved David and my children more.[4]

Even though Brad reminded Elaine of her dead husband (in his treatment of wife and family, naturally!), she could literally never leave her loved one. Such a bravura climax reveals another of Robbins' secrets for he, like most popular novelists, writes for a feminine audience and tailors his characters' emotions so as not to jar such sensibilities. Thus, the more decorous emotions associated in popular thinking with women are reaffirmed dramatically in *Never Leave Me*.

In Robbins' patently fictional business world personality clashes are uppermost and work becomes a further testing ground for a man's sentimental nature. In waxing philosophic over his profession, Brad sounds like a successful Willie Loman: " 'I sell intangibles. You can't hold what I give you in your hands, you can't put it on a scale and weigh it, you can't count it and put it into inventory.' "[5] Since he offers this paean before a group of businessmen, Robbins' protagonist indulges popular ignorance by rehashing a stereotype (the ad man as Svengali) instead of presenting what such an individual might really discuss before such a group. Brad's argument reflects central aspects of the twentieth-century American Dream, particularly his belief that success results from individual personality and talent, and his insistence on being hired for what he is rather than for what he does. One could easily dismiss such a scene as simply authorial laziness, however a deeper impulse gets reflected by the protagonist's emphasis that personality is more important than ability. While earlier versions of the American Dream cited work (Horatio Alger), money (*The Great Gatsby*) or popularity (*Death of a Salesman*) as the particular keys to success, Robbins' Brad Rowan is the defiant businessman who prospers by selling his own personality ("doing his own thing"). The protagonist embodies the same talk-back-to-the-boss attitude one finds celebrated in Rod Serling's *Patterns* (1955). At an early meeting Rowan challenges Matt Brady and receives praise from the older man: "He held up a magnanimous hand, interrupting me. 'Say no more. I admit I gave you sufficient provocation. But what you said impressed me. You were the only one there who had the nerve to call a spade a spade.' "[6] The successful businessman thus asserts his will rather than merely accommodating himself to the wishes of the group.

Moreover, the dynamic individual solves corporate crises by finding the emotional key to checkmate his opposition. In such a corporate community, balance sheets and human egos, not to mention profit, have vanished to be replaced by individual will. Being successful only requires assertiveness in presenting one's personality. Rowan espouses a deep-seated cynicism about other businessmen, so that playing on human weakness becomes his modus operandi. When lacking time to prepare a smooth presentation Brad doesn't worry because his audience is: " 'Human ain't they? The same as us. They like money, dames, liquor. They wear clothes, not wings. We'll get to them the same way as we get to anybody else. Everybody can be reached once you know what they're looking for. And when we find out, we'll get the job. It's as easy as that.' "[7] While Robbins' protagonist contradicts himself by hedging his bet on personal dynamism with blackmail, his outlook reduces business once more to personality. The audience enjoys seeing that rich businessmen are just plain folks manipulated by wine, women, and laundered cash, for few ideas are more consoling than to believe a successful man is controlled by the same lusts as oneself. Robbins' view of business reaches its crescendo when Brad laments the cost of his success. Since Elaine helped him with Brady, her death initially seems to have been caused by Brad's needs for money and prestige.

As he looks down on Madison Avenue, after hearing of Elaine's suicide, Rowan pontificates:

> This was a part of the big time and the big time was a part of me.
> This was what I had wanted ever since I was old enough to know anything. Now I knew what it was worth. Nothing. Absolutely nothing. One tiny little person on the street was worth more than all the city put together.[8]

Robbins' characters suffer from the overstatements and the either/or conclusions so familiar to melodrama; however, such elementary logical errors flatter the audience's desire to believe that every situation can be reduced to black-and-white simplicities.

Never Leave Me's central character is, at last, sufficiently humbled so as to atone for his indiscretions. While Paul Remy (and thus, by implication, the world) doesn't know about Brad and Elaine, Remy's emphasis on her capacity to face trouble takes on a deeper meaning because Brad is his listener.

> "We all wondered where she got so much courage from, the strength to face all the things she had to. Now I guess we'll never know."
> I closed my eyes. They'll never know, but I knew.[9]

Elaine's courage derived from Brad's love; and, while one might question the equation of facing troubles with a woman who has just committed suicide, Elaine's death has preserved the social order. In effect, she acted to reaffirm her belief in romantic love, a faith which Brad's attentions restored. When they first meet, Elaine is trying to bury her sorrows in charity work and wants Brad to supply advertising expertise. The protagonist senses Mrs. Schuyler's emptiness and, since he is smitten, kisses her on their second meeting. When he asks Elaine if she still loves her husband, she retorts:

> "That's not a fair question. David is dead."
> "But you're not," I pointed out cruelly. "You're a grown woman now, not a child any longer. You have needs—"
> "Men? she asked, interrupting me. "Sex?" She laughed thinly. "You think that's important?"
> "Love is important," I answered. "Loving and being loved is necessary to everyone."[10]

Brad's final remark is the novel's thematic key, for love is so essential to these characters that Elaine finally decides she cannot destroy the love Brad has created and received within his family because the love she created with David would be desecrated. Even Brad ultimately subordinates sex to love and, in so doing, flatters the audience's belief that the spiritual side of romance should dominate its physical aspects.

Popular mores are further reaffirmed by Brad's reunion with his wife and family. Marge, who could tolerate the publicity of Brad's romance with Elaine as long as it was business, revolts when her woman's sixth sense tells her that things have gone beyond merely trying to upset Matt Brady. Yet, she only appeals to Brad when their son, Junior, is stricken with polio. Since Elaine has lost her husband and children to the same disease (a dreaded illness in 1954 and yet another way Robbins taps audience interest), she sees Junior's sickness as a form of divine judgment. Brad's regeneration is foreshadowed by his son's recovery; indeed, as the protagonist's family triumphs, Elaine, in a bit of mawkish juxtaposition, decides to rejoin those she has lost to the disease. After the Rowans are ordered out of Junior's room so that the doctors can "do everything humanly possible," Marge goes to the hospital chapel and the repentant Brad joins her.

> Slowly I walked down the aisle and knelt beside Marge.
> I looked at her. Her hands were clasped on the rail before her and her forehead touched her fingers. Her lips were moving and her eyes were closed, but she knew I was beside her. She moved slightly closer to me.[11]

This scene renews the Rowans' marriage for symbolically they are placed in a setting that recalls their wedding vows. The marriage service emphasizes the phrase "until death do us part" and *Never Leave Me* seems to take that pledge a step further with Elaine Schuyler's literal rendering of it.

As a sexual athlete, Brad Rowan is as dynamic in bed as in board room. Women seek him out and gladly trade the agony of never possessing his love for the ecstasy he can provide. Sandra throws herself at him, even though she knows his heart is elsewhere. Brady's secretary-receptionist intuits that Rowan's love belongs to another (at this point Elaine, in striving to do the right thing, will not see Brad), yet she doesn't care. Sandra thus fulfills a dual role; on the one hand, she is the fantasy female who can't get enough sex fast enough while, on the other, she is the victim female subject to the romantic unfairness of a male world. Sandra, like Marge and Elaine, accepts woman's traditionally passive emotional role and gears her life to pleasing men. She loves well but not wisely, and her dependent nature makes it impossible for her to do otherwise with Rowan. Sandra goes to New York to seduce Brad and gladly takes him on the rebound: her maneuvering includes the familiar, take-off the blouse and flash-the-breasts tactic so beloved by 1950s authors and readers, and elicits a customary response.

> I reached out a hand and touched a snap. The brassiere came off in my fingers. Her nipples were like rosebuds bursting open in the summer sun.
> "When you look at me like that, Brad, I could die," she whispered. "If you could love me as you do her, there is nothing I wouldn't do for you."[12]

Sandra's willingness to sacrifice her own ego dramatizes a necessary fiction about male sexual vanity and female passivity. At this point Sandra turns more resistant and Brad overpowers her (on friendly terms, of course) on the floor. In effect, Sandra wants to be dominated and the ensuing scene reinforces a popular male superstition (women want to be raped) while simultaneously flattering a similar female preconception (men are such beasts).

In keeping with this spirit of male dominance, Brad describes their lovemaking as a contest between primordial drives.

Ten thousand years ago we had been together and it had been the same way then. Always she had been afraid. I bent over her and tore the last of her clothing from her.

. . . We embraced on the ground, our bodies interlocked in fierce combat. Her heavy sobbing was a pleasing sound to my ears, proof that I was superior to her, as I was superior to all women. Without me she was nothing—empty and fit only for menial labor. I was the instrument of her pleasure and the reason for her existence.[13]

Male sexual chauvinism has rarely been presented as directly and, in the 1950s, Brad's egotism merely reflected popular thinking. The protagonist's insistence on his sexual power—the thrust that binds, as it were—finds further confirmation in another encounter with Sandra. The girl, who has gone back to Brady and caused trouble for Brad, is now repentant about her jealousy. Although she wants to ask Rowan for a job, she quickly forgets this purpose in his presence.

She was very close to me now and I could sense the urgency in her body, the purely animal sexuality she had for me. I fought the drag and waited.

"You may have nothing for me, but I have a feeling about you. I've known enough men to know what I'm saying. No one ever made me feel the way you do; no one ever can."[14]

Although Brad dismisses Sandra's words as excesses she will forget when "Mr. Right" comes along, his ego has received the ultimate flattery—a woman who knows he has no deep feelings for her will be ecstatic if she can simply receive an occasional sample of his sexual technique. Even though operating in second gear, Brad has enraptured Sandra because a real man's sexual prowess is always more than a woman can stand.

With Elaine, Robbins' protagonist must bring a reluctant female out of her shell. Brad's prowess is even more masterful finally because he devotes full attention to Elaine; and, as one would expect, the passion he creates in Mrs. Schuyler is even more pronounced. The psychological dynamics between Brad and Elaine establish the mores deemed appropriate; indeed, when Brad's father consoles him about Elaine's death, Robbins' protagonist fervently argues that his own heinous conduct has caused her death: " 'I made love to her and lied to her and made promises that I knew I'd never keep; because she believed me and loved me and trusted me and never thought I'd leave her. When I did there was nothing left in this world for her because I had become her world.' "[15] Brad's grief leads him to overestimate his importance to Elaine; however, the protagonist's feelings reemphasize the second-class emotional existence attributed to women in the 1950s. A man can exist simply in work while a woman must live for romance. After falling in love with Elaine, Brad decides to ask Marge for a divorce (an action he abandons when he fortuitously learns of Junior's illness). At this point even Elaine feels sympathy for Marge who is going to hear the words that every woman most fears: " 'You're going to say what every woman faces in her secret heart, in her most terrible nightmares. We live in dread that one day he will come and say that he no longer cares.' "[16] Such a comment dramatizes the lack of reciprocity accepted by contemporary readers, for Elaine never considers that a love affair might consist of a man's desperate need of a woman, or that a woman might announce the end of a relationship to a fearful male.

In courting Elaine, Brad exercises that prerogative which urges that only a man can recognize when a woman needs physical attention (indeed, Sandra's aggressiveness blatantly signals that she will not ultimately satisfy Brad). When they first meet Brad even contemplates making love to Elaine as an act of charity: "Then there was nothing but her eyes and I was lost in the dark blue pain of them. I fought an impulse to take her in my arms and wash the pain away. No one should know such pain."[17] Thus, sexual intimacy can guarantee the individual against the agonies the world throws in his path and bring ecstatic happiness as well. Once he has discovered that his feelings cannot be soothed in Sandra's arms, Brad must pursue Elaine until they have consummated their love, for their happiness and, presumably, their sanity depend on on it. Robbins' description of the love scene between Brad and Elaine becomes a veritable lexicon of the euphemisms of the time, for its imprecision (which allows the underaged and the immature to imagine what they will) derives from imagery one associates with Hollywood's visual "double talk." During a night of passion:

> The love that we made was like music we had known all our lives. Its sounds, its motions, its passions, and agonies were as one, each into the other. It was ever new and fresh and when at last we perished in its flames, we fought it not by ourselves, but together.
>
> The warning cry, the beginning shudder, the tightening grip and rocketing thrust. The bomb would burst and we would spill our passions far into the endless world where there was no world, then float gently on its tide back to this earth.[18]

While the images of music, death, fire, war, outer space and the sea constitute an extreme hodge podge, their very familiarity and the piling up of standard sentiments epitomizes Robbins' guile. *Never Leave Me* succeeds because it never surprises: one can simply sit back and enjoy its characters falling from and then resuming the path of virtue without ever encountering an idea or an image that questions conventional American values.

*   *   *

There are times when nothing succeeds like excess; and in popular fiction a workable formula inevitably spawns imitations. The runaway sales of *Peyton Place* naturally caused New England and small towns in particular to seem like fictionally workable hot beds in which the lusts of the flesh could be catalogued. Charles Mergendahl's *The Bramble Bush* presents the prurient secrets of East Norton in which everyone's closet has a skeleton. Mergendahl's novel also shows that to attract readers such a derivative work must incorporate ever more sensational elements. The same situation arises with pornographic movies in which ever new ways of highlighting old activities must be sought to fight off the audience's ennui. Thus, Mergendahl, while employing the basic situation of Metalious' novel, and assuring himself of a "carry over" effect with the buying audience, adds some machinations to enhance his soap opera. In addition to the gossipy ambience in which the townspeople are nosy but unsympathetic (traits that make one wonder why decent characters feel any loyalty to such a place), Mergendahl works in medical and ethical problems—euthanasia, abortion— that force the protagonist, Dr. Guy Montford, to return to religion. In combining prurience with medicine and faith, *The Bramble Bush* misses hardly any sure bet.

Nearly every prominent character undergoes a personal change for the better. Like a Cecil B. DeMille epic in which the glamor of sin makes more of an impression than the picture of goodness, Mergendahl's novel presents figures whose transgressions and redemptions are so sensational that the reader is tititlated and uplifted at the same time. Salvation results from personal relations so that the world exhibits a moral scheme in which no action, however trivial, lacks potential value. Typically, Guy Montford, who performs euthanasia on his dying best friend, Larry McFie, seduces and impregnates Larry's wife, Margreth, and then wishes to marry her, elicits compassion. Since Margreth's conscience troubles her after Larry's death, she decides to get away and think, and only the Treleavens, a minister and his wife, know her hiding place. When Guy asks them to reveal where Margreth is, they oblige and, within a few pages, John Treleaven pronounces the lovers man and wife.

After several drinks, Frances Treleaven decides it's time that she and John started behaving like lovers instead of old married folks. Fired by the obviously passionate Guy and Margreth, Frances sets about seducing her husband by lying in bed and acting wanton (apparently she never— or hardly ever—has appeared naked in front of him). Frances is profoundly bored by propriety.

> Now suddenly she was tired. She had never had any real *fun*. Other people had real fun, but not she. Other people, like Guy and Margreth, lived exciting, romantic lives. Immoral lives, shoddy lives, disgusting lives, yet romantic all the same. And why was it that good people found nothing to be thankful for but their own goodness?[19]

Thus, the minister's wife turns over a new leaf because of Guy and Margreth. Later, when he asks John's advice about Margreth, whose pregnancy is complicated by pneumonia and her stubborn refusal to submit to an abortion, Guy notices the marked change in Frances, who:

> ...looked different somehow, as though in the past weeks she'd become more of a woman and less of a wife. Guy had seen this same quick blossoming in many girls during the month or so after their marriage. Suddenly, with all their frustrations gone, they gained weight, and relaxed into an entirely different being.[20]

Sexual abandon has cured Frances of the repressions ("tensions") she felt with her overly proper spouse. After his initial chagrin at her commanding him to kiss her "dusky" breasts, John (whose immediate reaction was that they never had sex on Fridays) turns into a sexual tiger.

The same redemptive pattern is repeated with Parker Welk, the editor of the local newspaper who delights in blackmail and voyeurism. His wife, Polly, whom he raped and had to marry as a result, refuses to divorce him and goes merrily along the road to obesity while Parker, after some furtive affairs, settles for intimate photography. Parker's neurosis has led him to hate "the town and Polly...and himself and God. Eventually he learned to hate sex too, so that he lived completely without it except in his own half-romantic, half-perverted way."[21] When he discovers that Fran Walker, the chief nurse at a local hospital, was clandestinely registered at a motel where there was a fire, Parker blackmails her into posing for him. Unfortunately, Bert Mosely, Fran's lover, follows her to this assignation and beats Parker senseless. Later, when Guy Montford tells the prostrate Welk that the photographs of Fran have been destroyed, Parker is incredulous that the protagonist isn't a voyeur like himself. While Guy protects Fran, Welk believes the world consists only of victims and victimizers. When Guy goes on trial for Larry's death, Parker prints an enraged editorial against euthanasia for the older man cannot forgive the destruction of the photographs.

> His mind stayed on the pictures—gone, lost, never to be seen again. He had others at home, but none so exciting as those of Fran Walker. And it was a shame, even though he'd been relieved at first to know they'd been destroyed—now their loss was a dirty shame, an horrendous tragedy. And walking on in the cold, he dimly understood one particular reason why he hated Guy Montford. Guy had destroyed the pictures.[22]

Welk's voyeurism symbolizes his desire for power and shows how he has perverted the newspaperman's calling—the collection of facts—into a means to indulge his sexual inadequacies.

Parker's self-reinforcing delusion comes crashing down when he persuades Nancy Messner, his naive young assistant, to pose. During their photographic session, the idealistic Nancy is shocked by what Parker is doing behind the camera (one can't be certain if it's a look or something more overt) and flees. Disconsolate, Parker broods while ignoring a fire in the town (an obvious news story) and appropriately burns his collection because "there were none of Fran Walker and none of Nancy Messner— only that old saggy waitress Betty from the Lincoln, only a couple of skinny school-teachers from summers past, all yellow now, so familiar as to be repulsive."[23] At this point Polly informs Parker that their daughter will soon be visiting, and the erstwhile voyeur looks at "voluptuous" Alice in a snapshot and ponders inveigling her into posing, only to break down completely and ask Polly's forgiveness. Parker has been saved by an internal process in which evil thoughts have led to good deeds; he has finally understood that Fran and Nancy are somebody's daughters too, an observation which leads him to compassion and regret.

Bert Mosley, an aspiring lawyer who wants to get away from East Norton, possesses a sexually passive nature which needs to be flattered and challenged. While he and Fran are weekend lovers, their relationship fails because she is too "normal" in assuming the lead in their encounters since something "prevented him from enjoying sex in an absolutely free and unashamed way."[24] Bert's physical salvation establishes his reprehensible personality. When Guy is arrested, Bert intuits the relationship between the Doctor and Margreth and forces Montford to hire him. Bert believes that the case's notoriety will lead him to future financial rewards, so that he conveniently forgets that Guy suppressed his name at the motel fire and after Parker's beating. Bert's sexual trauma dates back to childhood, the constant warnings he received about masturbation, and the physical tauntings of a younger sister. He needs a woman to taunt him into dominating her; and Fran simply will not play this game. During the trial, however, Bert meets Sylvia Stein, a Boston journalist who precisely fits the bill by demeaning him and promising him that he won't be able to handle her in bed. When Bert and Sylvia finally make love the scene naturally resembles rape.

> She fought him furiously. Her fingernails raked at his face and her knee dug hard at his groin. He ripped the jacket from her shoulders, tore off the blouse and the bra beneath... And then finally, when her body arched suddenly like a quick steel spring beneath him, when she gave a little cry of sudden pain, then Joanie (his sister) flashed crazily through his mind... And yet there was no guilt now. There was only the greatest relief and pride in the certain knowledge that he, Bertram Mosley, had finally taken charge.[25]

Such psychological exorcism is underscored by Sylvia's being a virgin; thus her fast-talking demeanor proves false and her lack of knowledge matches Bert's own "virginity." After Guy's trial, Bert plans to go to Boston, marry Sylvia, and set up a new practice; however, he must still suffer losing Fran (who guesses at his two-timing and sends him packing) and being thrown out of a local bar by some patrons who dislike Bert's opportunism.

Fran Walker feels no pride with a man she loves. She is enraptured by Guy but never strikes a reciprocal chord; however, by the novel's end, when the protagonist has been widowed for a second time (with the added burden of an infant son), Fran finally persuades him to let her care for him and the child. Although she brought the charge of euthanasia against Guy out of jealousy, Fran quickly repents when she sees Bert cashing in on the case's publicity. She eavesdrops as Bert makes love with Sylvia and, after Miss Stein has gone, she then confronts him with some bad news.

> She smiled and opened her coat and the blouse beneath. "See me, Bert.... Do you want me, Bert?" He only stared and she knelt before him the same as last time. She touched him and smiled and said, "What's the matter, Bert? Don't I excite you, Bert?"
> "For God's sake!
> "You had her, didn't you? So now you're completely helpless."
> Bert glared at her in anger and embarrassment.
> She laughed. "I'm *glad*, Bert. You *used* me, Bert. I almost *hate* you, Bert." She bent forward, exposing both naked breasts to his temporarily indifferent eyes, said "Take a good look, Bert, because you'll never see them again, and I'll never touch you again."[26]

Such punishment seems thoroughly appropriate for baring her breasts is a tremendous physical advance by 1950s' standards. When she first offers herself to Guy, Fran gets her hands under his shirt and bares herself to the waist without any help (!), so maneuvering Bert represents a snap, as it were.

Mergendahl's emphasis on mammary glands accords with contemporary sexual tastes so that female breasts are nearly always prominent in any romantic scene. When embracing Sylvia, Bert notices that "her breasts were firm beneath, and . . . wondered if she wore falsies."[27] While the lawyer is gentleman enough to doubt such deception, his interest is reflected even in Margreth's imagination, for on their wedding night she gushes to Guy:

> "You remember, I promised you a surprise," and he said, "Yes," and she said, "Undress me, darling," and he did, and saw her white breasts, full and round, and she said, "Do you like the surprise? I mean my bosoms (?) have grown, you see what with our baby, and I'm so very proud of them, you see."
>
> He said they were beautiful.[28]

Since Guy is a doctor, one questions whether such a "surprise" can be news to him: presumably love does strange things, even to men of medicine. Margreth's rapture at her swollen breasts, while addedly poignant because of the sanctity popularly associated with childbearing, epitomizes a mental framework in which a bursting bustline constituted the acme of feminine allure.

In such a culture, Fran Walker naturally exhibits her "assets" to move Guy emotionally. Even though she pleads to be used as an emotional doormat, her offer is too overt for the decorous protagonist.

> "If you ever need anything—comfort, understanding—if you want to cry—if it would help for you to sleep with somebody—you see, I love you, so I have no shame, and if it would help—if you want me—"
>
> . . .he heard her crying softly, and he put an arm around her shoulder and held her close against him. She cried into his chest. . .until her hands groped beneath his shirt, and. . .he. . .watched her unbutton. . .her bra and drop that too, until she was naked to the waist. . . .
>
> "Fran," he said. . .and could not keep his eyes from her body, could not stop his hands from reaching out to caress the wonderfully firm breasts. . . . . "Oh, Jesus God, Fran!. . .No Fran!. . .No Fran!" And he pulled back, breathing heavily, and laughed and lit a cigarette and forced himself under control once more.[29]

The barking of Guy's dog, Caesar, who has been in the car's backseat during this tryst, restores the protagonist to the insular loneliness he has cultivated since his first wife's death. For Guy, Fran remains a victim of circumstances and other people, so he cannot feel compassion for her. After Fran has cast Bert aside, and after Guy experiences his shortlived idyll with Margreth, they are both capable of more genuine feelings toward each other. Since Guy also experiences a religious conversion because of Margreth's death, he now sees the selflessness of Fran's offer to care for him and his son (named of course for Margreth's first husband). *The Bramble Bush* ends with Guy and Fran dedicating their lives to bringing up little Larry as an atonement for the excesses that their passions have produced. Fran even convinces Guy that East Norton will forgive and forget if he will be patient and, in so doing, she finally gains a place at his side.

Guy Montford must learn the limits of human knowledge to become capable of feeling. Through much of the novel Guy stands alone; and even after Larry McFie's death, which he causes by a drug overdose, he accepts the possible consequences without any explanation. The protagonist's desire to be a solitary, noble man belies the connections that society makes inevitable; of course, Guy's sense of profession aids his individualistic excess by making him an authority figure. Paradoxically, "the more he'd seen of death, the more he'd lost that awe of medicine; though in a strange way, he'd gained even more respect for the men who practiced it."[30] Guy's awareness of the shortcomings of doctors must be extended to all men, including himself. He must abandon the cynicism which colors his early discussion with Margreth about Larry: " 'If God had any understanding, he'd have let him die months ago, saved him all this pain — saved you this horrible waiting, with no way out for anyone.' "[31] Such an argument ignores the view that God may cause what seems like senseless injustices to man in order to bring about larger goods. Since serious pessimism hardly satisfies the appetites of bestselling novel readers, Guy's philosophy must be exposed as merely excessive pride for which he will naturally be rebuked by circumstances. As Guy debates whether or not to kill Larry, his arguments underscore his unique position; indeed, the main character's sin is pride for, in deciding who will live and die, he is usurping God's prerogative.

Guy's shortsightedness is underscored by his urging that there is a purely human law sanctioned by what seems reasonable to sane men.

> Perhaps, if he could confess, he would be forgiven, except that he was not prepared to be forgiven for an act which he did not honestly believe to be a sin at all. In the eyes of the church—a sin; in the eyes of the courts—a crime. In the heart of Guy Montford—sober, clear-thinking again—a merciful act which transcended the laws of both.[32]

Such pride must be beaten down by events so that Guy can learn that the human heart cannot guide unless directed by someone or something larger than the individual. Thus, in jail, he discovers that Stewart Schaeffer, an old man whom he once found in his mother's bed (an affair that drove Guy's supposed father to suicide) is his real father; and Guy appears reconciled to this fact when he accepts Schaeffer's support in the novel's concluding pages (a gift more verbal than material since Schaeffer is the town drunk). The discovery of his parentage causes Guy to become more compassionate since he now has a skeleton in his closet. In a similar fashion, Margreth's death reconciles Guy with the ways of God for she chooses to risk her life to have their child. Margreth feels abortion is wrong and, as a necessary corollary that, no matter what its cause, euthanasia is also a sin. She proves her faith through conduct; and her death makes Guy return to the Catholic faith he fled as a youth, as signalled by his ultimate confession.

> "Father Serrano," Guy said. "Father... I am not God after all."
> "Made in His image," the old man said, and touched his arm.[33]

This theological epiphany, in which Guy surrenders his egotistic will to the priest's ministrations, dramatizes the sentimental optimism that colors the entire novel.

Mergendahl taps another popular vein in the relationship between Guy and Margreth for their lovemaking emphasizes the male's power to reduce the female to dependence. Their first encounter, which occurs on Guy's docked boat under a flickering lamp, shows two emotionally overwrought people sharing their anguish at the impending death of a loved one (Larry).

> "Please, Guy—help me, Guy—
> "Away, Mar. Somewhere, Mar..."
> ...he looked down into her eyes...until finally something exploded in himself, too, and his mouth crushed down on hers, and he felt her body arch crazily against him and saw red lights behind his eyes...she was crying again, but like a child now, huddled close in his arms with her naked body smooth under his comforting hands and her face in his shoulder and the world outside.
> "I'm sorry," he said finally..."You were hysterical, you see, and I—only planned to slap your face."[34]

Although Guy's closing remark sounds unwittingly funny, his assumption of command enables Margreth temporarily to forget her dying husband.

Their second interlude takes place in the house of Larry's father because Guy is compelled to possess Margreth. Since Sam McFie blames Guy's father for the death of Larry's mother years before (another abort-the-child or kill-the-mother dilemma), Guy's seduction represents violation on several levels. Although Margreth has to be carried upstairs (Rhett Butler ascending with Scarlett in *Gone with the Wind*), she is engulfed by her own responsiveness when things get more serious.

> She said, "Please, Guy, please, Guy," as her body sank into the feather bed. And then his hands again, caressing now, undressing her gently, gently, and then the wet tears in her own eyes and that terrible wonderful sinking—that hated wanted drifting away—until she was gone from this house and the world, and somehow now—in some strange way—she was almost a little child again.[35]

Margreth's sexual bliss leads to her death and brings the protagonist back to the church and tranquility. After hearing that Guy realizes he cannot allow her to take the witness stand in his defense, Margreth urges that nothing which happens is without some benefit to someone. Guy even understands that Schaeffer "did serve some purpose,"[36] and, in seeing the possible usefulness of a man he had despised, the protagonist implicitly agrees that good deeds can come from ostensibly bad sources. It is then only a small step to the belief that God moves in mysterious ways, and that transition occurs when Guy must deal with his son's birth and Margreth's death. Doctor Kelsey, the attending physician, summarizes the novel's principal theme when he urges, " 'everything seems reversed—it gives me a weird feeling, Guy, as though—well, as though you, myself, medicine—nothing has any control over this at all.' "[37] Guy would have agreed, but by now he knows that God rather than "nothing" is in charge.

* * *

In Frank Yerby's *Floodtide* scenes of promiscuity and sadism all but swallow up the historical background. The same antebellum South that distinguishes *Mandingo* (1957), one in which decadent planters and their hot-blooded wives indulge in excesses designed to destroy any rational social order, marks *Floodtide*. Except for the compromised but melodramatically pure Ross Pary and the real love of his life, Conchita, a virgin where it really counts—the mind, Yerby's characters are an unpleasant collection of emotional excessives lacking wit or ideas. Since none of these figures possesses emotions or perceptions that suggest human complexity, it is difficult to sympathize with them or the troubles they bring upon themselves. Yerby's sense of history subordinates rational, economic or idealistic motives to those of love and lust; and, since his characters' impulses can be swayed at a moment's notice, their conduct is presented rather than elaborated. At one point, Ross Pary even becomes an outspoken abolitionist, a change, especially in Mississippi in the 1850s, that needs a more plausible explanation than his merely wanting to shock society and his nagging and unfaithful wife, both staunch defenders of the peculiar institution.

Yerby's plantation society combines violence and amorality in a sexual madhouse atmosphere: everyone continually indulges his senses and this spirit breeds endless quarrels over love and cards. This group's basic moral tone is established when Morgan, the new bride of Lance Brittany, a local planter, throws herself at Ross. Her forwardness leads to some reluctant embracing by the protagonist (who's only a man, after all); yet, just as Morgan's hands arrive where they can create real problems, Tom Pary, Ross' uninhibited and dissolute brother, comes upon the scene. His reaction epitomizes the basic amorality of the characters in *Floodtide*: " 'Mighty pretty!... Yes sir, mighty pretty! Congrats, Ross—didn't know you had it in you.' "[38] Tom's remark also reveals the pervading emphasis on dominance, for he delights in embarrassing his brother rather than retiring quietly. It is, perhaps, inevitable, given Yerby's tangled plot, that Tom will turn up in Morgan's arms later, for she can never get enough. Morgan's frivolities naturally produce jealousy and violence since she delights in having men fight over her. In conversation Ross poses the hardly hypothetical question as to what action Lance would take if Morgan turned to another man for emotional comforts. Lance's apocalyptic response underscores the psychology of revenge that permeates the entire narrative.

"I'd kill him...and afterwards I'd kill her. Because Morgan could never be forced or persuaded. It would be her idea, Ross—conceived entirely by her long before."

"But—if she inherited her father's weakness...."

"How do I know? All I know is she's mine. And she's going to stay mine, if I have to kill every man in the State of Mississippi. Night, Ross."[39]

Since this outburst follows a lengthy account of Morgan's father, who wasted a fortune in twenty years because of cruelty and madness, Lance's inability to offer compassion dispels any sympathy which might have attached to his character.

Floodtide's reason for being is the gratuitous violence of its characters, so consistencies of motivation or transitions of plot are not well-handled. While Lance doesn't have to challenge the entire male population of Mississippi, he does end up defending Morgan's "honor" more than she ever does (to paraphrase Groucho Marx). Morgan's emotional ambivalence and instability, while supposedly due to genetics, enable Yerby to present "daring" situations. At one point Morgan, eager to spoil Ross' marriage to Cathy, arranges for a friend to rape Mrs. Pary. Morgan entices Cathy to pay her a visit and then to come up to her bedroom. Once Cathy has arrived in Morgan's boudoir, Mrs. Brittany immediately makes an excuse and leaves; then:

> . . .the door opened again, and Cathy looked up. But it was not Morgan who stood there. It was a man. A tall man—Henry Montcliffe.
> ". . .What do you want?" Cathy said.
> "You," Henry Montcliffe said."
> Then. . .Cathy felt herself being borne over backward, then lifted, and thrown down across the bed, hard. His big hand was among her skirts, hot upon the flesh of her thigh. And it came to Cathy that she had been tricked. . . .
> She brought her knees up until they crowded against her small breasts and kicked out with both feet. They caught Henry Montcliffe full in the belly and sent him over backward. . . . She lifted (the lamp) in both hands and brought it down upon his head. It broke. . .and the blood and the kerosene mingled in curious streams on his face.
> Morgan. . .began to laugh.
> "That Cathy!" she said. "A girl after my own heart."[40]

Paradoxically, Morgan, despite her scheme's failure, delights in the bloody Montcliffe as an amusing example of what a woman can (and seemingly should) do to a man. Morgan and Tom Pary are outstanding examples of temperaments that gawk at an accident or cheer on drunks in a fight. Their idle maliciousness implies that existence can be no more than a passing spectacle in which human misery and desire provide episodes to momentarily divert jaded onlookers.

Yerby juxtaposes the amorality of Morgan and Tom to Ross' ethical growth, for the protagonist learns, through love of course, that cynicism and self-absorption are but disguises for weaknesses that more normal (i.e. compassionate) individuals lack. The protagonist reaches a nadir when he argues that coarse personalities create historical change while softer types, like himself, are but excess baggage.

> Maybe, Ross thought, kindness is itself a sickness—part of the effeteness of civilization. Certainly people afflicted with it, like me, don't stand much of chance when they're confronted with these dawn-age ones, these absolutely certain ones, people like Morgan who are very clear and direct and terrible. While I'm thinking about the why's, people like Morgan act.[41]

Thus, those who lack any capacity for kindness or for worrying over ethical distinctions are the only people who can act, so that, in Morgan Brittany one sees Social Darwinism ("survival of the fittest") combined with Fascism (the belief that violence is the *only* ideology). Ross Pary, who must win the love of his life and then (seemingly) lose her, is symbolically tempted by Morgan; however, when the protagonist discovers that Mrs. Brittany is an insatiable sadist, he is freed. In the novel's climax, the Brittanys' mansion goes up in flames and Morgan dies, but not before Ross discovers the torture chambers she has constructed to torment her slaves. In freeing himself, Ross emerges with a different view of man: his dismissal of Morgan and his setting his own slaves free suggest that an individual can improve his circumstances.

Ross' new-found faith is rewarded when Conchita, the beloved he thought lost in the maelstrom of a Cuban revolution, re-emerges as the dancing toast of Europe. After years as a courtesan and entertainer, Conchita returns to New York and, in a letter to a mutual friend, confides that Ross, whom she thought dead, remains the only man she has ever loved. Because of this double misunderstanding, Ross and Conchita can be reunited in appropriately symbolic terms. Ross also survives because he possesses foresight, a quality no other Yerby character has in any substantial degree. This attribute first emerges in a scene that, again, harkens back to *Gone with the Wind.* Just as Rhett Butler deflated the assembled guests at Twelve Oaks by arguing that the "Yankees" had more ships and railroads with which to fight and win a war, so Ross predicts how Southern hopes are likely to fare in any armed conflict. Governor Quitman believes hostilities would bring English support because of Britain's need for cotton; however, the more insightful Ross cautions:

"England would be divided.... The upper classes, particularly the mill owners, would be for us. But there's tremendous anti-slavery sentiment among the masses.... In the end, I think, she'd remain neutral. You must not forget, gentlemen, that England is a limited constitutional monarchy, and the people, after all, hold the balance of power."[42]

Quitman's umbrage at such a lack of enthusiasm reveals that the Governor, like most other plantation owners, has never accepted the principle of popular rule which forms the basis of democracy. Ross' insistence on the will of the people separates him from his society and supports the view of history his later conduct implies.

Morgan Brittany resembles the emasculating female who appeared in the novels of Mickey Spillane, a woman whose sexuality reduces men to impotence and enslavement. Yerby's femme fatale combines sexual insatiability with a penchant for torture; albeit, her sadism is definitely "bizarre" and not "liberated." Indeed, Morgan's engulfing sexuality disguises madness, a trait which comes to the forefront when Ross, in one of their encounters:

...in spite of himself...kissed her in return with real enthusiasm, and at the last, as he tried to draw his head back and away from her...was conscious suddenly, of a blindingly sharp pain. He freed himself and raised his hand to his mouth. It came away dark with his own blood, where Morgan had caught his underlip in her white teeth and bitten it through.[43]

The reader is supposed to cringe (and yet be delighted) at the perversity of all this; however, Yerby's characters are so slow-witted (Cathy only realizes, when a man's hand is up her dress, that she's in a trap and Ross only discovers his lip has been severed when he touches it) that this intention is sorely dissipated. When Ross rejects Morgan, she shoots him to express her love (a motif that figures strikingly in the 1946 film *Duel in the Sun*) and then keeps asking to see the wound. Later, the protagonist's imprisonment in Cuba only elicits Morgan's interest when Ross mentions being tortured.

> Morgan stared at him in breathless fascination.
> "And tortured you too?" she whispered.
> "Yes."
> Morgan came up to him, and let her fingers stray over the rugged contours of his battered face.
> "What did they do, Ross?" she moaned. "Tell me, what?"
> Ross stared at her. The tone was—ecstasy.[44]

While the protagonist's reticence is ironically sadistic, Yerby's hero tells Morgan what she longs to hear. Her "orgasm" over the prospect of Ross' being changed from, say, Leslie Howard to Humphrey Bogart, would have seemed extremely daring and explicit in the 1950s, rather than amusing and overwrought as it must in our time.

Naturally, Morgan enjoys being raped (or "ravished" as she puts it) by any overheated male she has goaded into such urgency; indeed, her first sexual encounter at fifteen, in a home where her father was openly unfaithful, took place with a stable boy who tried to assault her. Morgan beat the boy (of course!) for that affront and then went back and raped him. By assuming the dominant role Morgan emerges as a contemporary demon, the woman who has saddled the man, as it were, and turned him into a "pussy-whipped" creature with no will. While a night with her might be interesting, a lifetime with such a creature (e.g. playing Emil Jannings Professor to Marlene Dietrich's Lola in *The Blue Angel*) would be a nightmare, for such a woman combines sexual and emotional instability sufficient to guarantee that no man could satisfy her. In keeping with the tone of *Floodtide*, Morgan praises Ross' lovemaking when it is brutal and thus lacking in those feelings that nurture civilization. " 'You're my lover, Ross. Such a wonderful lover, too! So strong and so tireless—so brutal, too—when I goad you into it. I like you best then. You should always be brutal. Tenderness is a kind of weakness.' "[45] By redirecting the protagonist's energies, Morgan reveals the parasitic relationship she truly seeks; her instincts, symbolized by Ross' bitten lip, represent a quest for emotional possession. Morgan wants to enslave Ross as surely as Count Dracula did his victims, and the protagonist is only saved when he sees Morgan's private torture chambers: "On the wall were hung whips as cruel as the ones he'd felt in Cuba. Ross put out his hand to take one of them, but he drew it back.''[46] Once again, Yerby uses symbolism—Ross' refusal to touch the whip—to point up the meaning of a scene: the protagonist nearly touches the instrument, which represents Cuba and the loss of Conchita, because he has become so embroiled with Morgan, yet his better instincts prevail. Ross remembers the pains of Cuba on his back and in his heart, and decides he owes a greater loyalty to memory than to pleasure. In his refusal Ross becomes a historical man, one for whom there exists an indelible past which serves as a moral guide to the present. Unlike Santayana's shortsighted figure who had to relive history because he did not know it, Ross Pary learns that the man who has suffered must not make the infliction of pain a way of life.

Floodtide presents familiar dichotomies in its romantic triangle which has Ross at its apex, for while Morgan symbolizes sexual passion, Conchita represents love's spiritual mysticism by which bodies mingle so that souls can know each other. When Ross meets Conchita, the daughter of wealthy Cuban expatriates, he is dismayed by her aloofness even though they have obviously fallen in love at first sight. The girl insists they can never marry because she is not a virgin; however, within twenty pages, we learn that Conchita was assaulted because her family was dispossessed by a revolution, a situation that allows Yerby to describe vividly what was done. Conchita, who doesn't want Ross to see her scarred physique, still manages to get in bed with the protagonist (so that her foresight seems as limited as the rest of Yerby's cast's). While Conchita may have hoped a gentleman wouldn't notice what's under the covers in the dark she is mistaken about Ross.

> ...he put his hand on the coverlet and drew it down and looked at her, seeing her slim, soft-curving, utterly lovely except the hard, white circle of scars, that started upon the perfect, soft golden hillock of her left breast and traveled at intervals across her body, and down to a little below her waist. They were, he saw, the type of scars that a saber would make, or a broad-bladed dagger.[47]

Conchita's ravished body demonstrates the counter argument to Morgan's sadism, for the girl's sufferings show that those who inflict pain are inevitably "villains." Unfortunately, although Yerby's equation of myopic brutality with decadent societies about to fall before popular assault seems apparent, his sense of realism slips again. Ross examines Conchita after they have made love and, while one can allow that their both being so overcome by passion might have operated for a time, scars in critical places cause tactile stimuli. Of course, for Yerby's fans, such inconsistencies are not disturbing and, in the starved-for-prurience 1950s, his daring (rather than his logic) was all. Conchita's love for Ross leads the girl to offer herself to their Cuban captors so that the hero may live—in following her the protagonist has become a revolutionary sympathizer and fallen into the hands of the "establishment." Conchita, fearing that she and Ross will be captured, frantically urges her lover to " 'kiss me with all the kisses of your life of yesterday and today and tomorrow that I do not die of too much feeling oh Ross, Ross, Ross!' ''[48] Dying from love always looms as a larger possibility in the consciousness of young lovers than in the eyes of the world, so that Conchita's outburst illustrates an all-too-familiar tradition.

The spiritual and intellectual struggle for Ross Pary colors the lovemaking scenes between the main character and Conchita and Morgan that Yerby presents. Tranquility results when Ross makes love with Conchita, for their passion leads to a sharing of hopes and dreams. Sexual intimacy is simply better between them than it is (or has been) with others, as Conchita reveals.

> "I have much wickedness, no? But I have dreamed of this. Before that time when you were hurt I did not know it could be like this...."
> "But now that you know?" Ross prompted.
> "It must be like this forever—all our lives, until we are tired and old and one day dead."[49]

This blissful mood embodies a vision of the future, so that intimacy leads these lovers into rationality—they have a past (symbolized by Conchita's scars and, later, by Ross' battered face) and a future which raises them above the cloying present controlled by Morgan and decadent Southern society. Conchita becomes so physically sensitive that when Ross comes to her, after fighting off Morgan's advances, she knows he has been tempted, if only momentarily. After Ross and Conchita make love in the oblique style similar to many a 1950s' fictional tryst, he wants to indulge again but she slaps his face because: " 'That...is for coming to me from her— filled up with the ugly passion she gave you! I feel bruised—and unclean. I have the desire to go and wash myself! That you could come to me with your mouth still sticky with kisses—oh Ross, Ross—....' ''[50] Conchita's action suggests that Ross has psychologically raped and injured her, always a favorite sexual motif which flatters the male ego by stressing strength and size. On the other hand, Conchita's awareness of the other woman represents an elevation of female "instinct" to a degree of omniscience that only a foolhardy male would dare to challenge.

When he returns from Cuba believing that Conchita is dead, Ross drifts into an affair with Morgan, a coupling that reflects despair rather than passion on his part. The protagonist allows Morgan to dominate him, even though he continues to feel guilty about cuckolding (the appropriately named) Lance.

> But...she whirled against him and her hands ripped at the dressing robe and then at the remainder of her own clothing. He tried to draw back, but she locked her arms about his neck and hurled herself down backward and away from him, still holding on so that he was drawn down too and lost his balance at the last and fell heavily with her.[51]

The very violence of Morgan's act (are they falling into bed or onto the floor?) demonstrates her excessiveness: she inflicts pain at every opportunity and, in attacking Ross, reverses customary sex roles to once more prove her insatiability. While a host of sexually aggressive females would emerge in later 1950s' novels, Morgan Brittany represents perversity rather than liberated womanhood. Her madness contrasts with Conchita's devotion, so that when the Cuban girl tells the hero she must return to fight in her native land, Morgan, who just happens to be visiting Ross and is momentarily offstage, returns clad only in one of his robes. Morgan's possessiveness causes such behavior, even though she rationalizes about having saved Ross from death. After Morgan maliciously calls for a towel, Ross:

> ...felt Conchita stiffen in his arms.
>
> "That perfume!" she whispered: "that scent I smelled when I came into the room! Her! Oh. Ross!"
>
> Then Morgan was coming through the door, clad in Ross' green silk robe, and under the robe was only Morgan. She had tied it carelessly, so that the long sweep of her thigh showed each time she moved, and her black hair, under the turban she had made of the towel, dripped water.
>
> Conchita stared at her wordlessly.
>
> "How cozy!" Morgan said. "The minute my back was turned. Oh, darling, how could you!"[52]

Morgan's insouciance sustains the irony of her last remark; indeed, her fledgling wit makes Mrs. Brittany finally the most engaging character in *Floodtide*.

Her desire for Ross ultimately has nothing to do with love, for Morgan would never understand that such a feeling embraces the possibility of mutual freedom in which each lover best realizes himself. Morgan feels jealousy toward Conchita (even when Ross believes her dead) for Yerby's sadist resents even those memories which threaten her physical mastery. She chides Ross for being squeamish about making love in a bed where he formerly enjoyed Conchita.

> "Not here," Ross said thickly. "Not here, Morgan."
>
> Morgan looked at his eyes and traced their line of vision past her to the little bed. Her hands came away from her clothing and anger flared up in her.
>
> "Not here," she said very quietly, "Not here—not upon her bed. That would dishonor her memory, wouldn't it, Ross. Damn your soul to hell, I told you I wouldn't play second fiddle to a ghost!"[53]

Morgan Brittany exemplifies the vibrance of fictional evil, for her outspokenly malicious energy suggests some depth of response. Her madness is finally unalloyed with any propriety or decorum, and she emerges as less illogical then Yerby's other characters who constantly defend the decadent outrages of a moribund society (Lance) or priggishly attempt to introduce virtue into a cesspool (Ross).

*　*　*

Grace Metalious' "sensational" novels "lift the lid" on "respectable" New England towns and demonstrate that all their inhabitants are obsessed by sex and death. While Metalious sounds like a neighborhood gossip telling

all the local dirt, her novels were the most popular and sexually explicit
fictions of the 1950s. What *Forever Amber* and *The Amboy Dukes* may
have been to the 1940s, and what *Valley of the Dolls* and *Portnoy's Complaint*
may have been to the 1960s, *Peyton Place* and *Return to Peyton Place*
were to their contemporaries. Metalious' fictions suggested to many a teenage
mind that being an adult was more exciting and more bitter than they
imagined. The rampant sexual concerns of the characters in *Peyton Place*
hardly disguise a facile cynicism about the very society which fosters such
goings-on. However, just as James Dean's film rebel could never adjust
because of personal nobility, so Metalious' readers were flattered into
believing that somehow they too could remain untouched by the adult
world's hypocrisies. Despite their predictabilities, however, Metalious' works
incorporate an energy in the telling that stands as her particular artistic
gift.

These novels incorporate alcoholism, homosexuality, incest,
menopause, menstruation, masochism, masturbation, murder, rape, sadism,
suicide and deflowering as crucial plot elements. In the 1950s this list would
represent as wide a fictional gamut as one would encounter and it suggests
how "erotic" Metalious was considered. Of course, the novelist did not
present anything totally unknown (none of her characters has three of
anything), but for an age marked by *Ozzie and Harriet* and Kinsey's studies
on sexual behavior, Metalious was advanced. By present standards, sexuality
was muted in the 1950s[54] and, as even a perfunctory survey of that decade's
popular music lyrics will show, fused with marriage in popular thinking.
At a time when at least one hundred novels were still banned (although
such standards would be reversed after the publication of the uncensored
version of *Lady Chatterley's Lover* in 1959), Metalious looked indeed like
a libertine. Her characters, avowing prurient interests and discussing bodily
functions, convey a sexually deterministic view of man and society. Their
open talk enables them (and the reader vicariously) to get even with society's
demands for conformity and decorum. Metalious' women talk like men
about sex and, thus, imply that the female's psychological and sexual drives
are similar to the male's. While Frances Parkinson Keyes flatters the female
psyche by urging its sentimentality is a mirror image of the male psyche,[55]
Metalious implies that male horniness is shared by females. Either position
reassures by a simpler view of the genetic differences between the sexes
than is warranted; in effect, all the individual has to do is look within
to understand the psychology of the opposite sex.

Metalious draws on familiar sources for her ideas and so kindles pleasant
memories among her more knowledgeable readers. Her borrowings suggest
the notion of cultural lag, the belief that the general public remains thirty
to fifty years behind avant garde accomplishments in science and the arts.
Sherwood Anderson's *Winesburg, Ohio* and Sinclair Lewis' *Main Street*,
both written in the early 1920s, debunk the propriety of outwardly decorous
small towns. However, while these works have become respectable college
texts, *Peyton Place*'s popularity shows that the general public, which resisted

the Freudian and anti-bourgeois approaches of Anderson and Lewis earlier, had accepted such assumptions by the mid-1950s. Metalious' reductionism, in which people become "by sex possessed," makes the acceptance of such unpopular ideas more palatable by couching them in either/or finality.

Other literary echoes are even more in tune with the American psyche. The argument between the doctors and the town council in *Peyton Place* over the threat of a typhoid epidemic, which runs counter to an industrialist's wish for continued profits, raises the same situation as Henrik Ibsen's *An Enemy of the People*. This lone honest man against grasping, hypocritical society situation is a well-known formula in American films and fiction. In the classic *High Noon* Will Kane must face four gunmen after exposing the cowardly indifference of the town's citizens, while in *Jaws* the town council resists Chief Brody because closing the beaches will be bad for business. This recurrent type of conflict reflects a traditional American faith in individualism, and a dissatisfaction with those forces—towns, businesses—that make for society. Popular taste still clings to the possibility of a frontier, a place where one can escape respectable communal life. In *Peyton Place* no member of the town council assumes the role which devolved on Doctor Stockmann in Ibsen's play, Will Kane or Chief Brody for, at best, Metalious' characters are too weak and compromised for heroism.

Since she lacks stylistic finesse, Metalious must create prurient and hypocritical characters who whet readers' appetites without lapsing into caricature. *Peyton Place* finally succeeds through sincerity. The rapidity of the telling and the involvement with numerous characters force the reader to suspend disbelief and give over to uncritical enjoyment. If read at a suggestive age, *Peyton Place* becomes a comforting way station on the road to maturity; and, in such a light, even its clichés can be forgiven: "Looking at her, small, gentle-voiced and rather fluttery, Jess said he thought he knew now what the women of the South must have been like when they gave their wedding rings to the Confederacy to be made into weapons of war."[56] Obviously, Metalious remembers Melanie Wilkes gladly giving up her wedding ring to a Confederate collection plate in *Gone with the Wind*.

The principal character in these novels is the town as a corporate spirit speaking as "public opinion" through numerous tangential characters to reveal society's hypocrisy and wisdom. Such characters' concerns with each other's affairs parody the reader who, in order to enjoy Metalious' novels, must delight in being a snoop. As a figure in *Peyton Place* notes: " 'Gossip's just like amoebas.... Multiply, divide and multiply.' "[57] In other scenes different characters comment on the malicious effects of rumors, yet exchanging confidences remains their preoccupation. Like Brer Rabbit, who didn't want to be thrown into a briar patch, Metalious' good citizens hide their real wishes in persiflage. Everybody has something to conceal and, as members of a duplicitous society, they constantly try to focus attention on others' shortcomings. While life seems outwardly tranquil and uneventful in her fictional community, "the closets of small-town folk are filled with such a number of skeletons that if all the bony remains of small-town shame were to begin rattling at once they would cause a commotion that could be heard on the moon.''[58] The implication here is that heroes do not exist and, perhaps more significantly, that the possibility for heroic action has also vanished, for the flawed community in *Peyton Place* denies any individual a chance for significant social action.

The themes that run through Metalious' novels are essentially bromides that, precisely because they lack verifiable bases, appeal to uncritical minds. The most obvious and one that accords well with traditional American mores insists that the individual contains his own perfection. When Allison Mackenzie becomes an author-celebrity in *Return to Peyton Place*, her publisher and lover, Lewis Jackman, reassures her: " 'Nothing very bad can happen to you, Allison, as long as *you* don't forget who you really are.' ''[59] As a vague wish about life this may be passable advice, however as philosophy it borders on solipsistic insanity. Such a pronouncement raises the spectre of Charles Manson legitimately listening to his "heart"; and, while one might have excused this outburst from the youthful Allison, such advice from a middle-aged business tycoon sounds sophomoric indeed. Jackman comes across as a windbag and a stuffed shirt, traits that make his subsequent death quite bearable despite Allison's grief.

The benevolence of work is another theme developed in these novels. After Allison writes her bestseller about the original (Negro) founder of Peyton Place, and becomes a consultant on her book's screenplay, she confronts the dilemma of being creative or well-liked. She must learn that people are inconstant while work is not. Rita Moore, an aging Hollywood star who used to have a "body," informs Allison about success being an either/or proposition. One must be dedicated to its pursuit and not to achieving personal happiness at the same time. Since Allison is in love with Jackman, a married man who will not get a divorce, she cannot initially accept Rita's pronouncement. Indeed, Allison has significantly compromised her art by coming to Hollywood and promoting the film version of her novel. David Noyes, a serious (i.e. non-selling) novelist who is in love with Allison, chides her for becoming a celebrity.

"You're not in this business to sell books! You're supposed to be a writer, not some clown on a radio or television program. Not some idiot running off at the mouth to some fifth-rate lush of a reporter.

"...People discover good books for themselves.... And *Samuel's Castle* is a good book. People would have realized that in time without every paper in the country touting it as a work of pornography."[60]

Noyes' hectoring again stresses that life is an either/or matter with no intermediate possibilities. David believes that sincerity is the keynote to creativity, an outlook characteristically American in its emphasis on individual personality rather than actual accomplishment.

Naturally, Allison soon feels corrupted by Hollywood and demonstrates that, in Metalious' fictional world, characters are ambivalent about the emotional costs of riches and fame as well as being often incapable of "playing the game" without losing their souls in the process. Typically, after several weeks of promotion, Allison "wanted to break every window and rip to shreds the royal purple curtains. She wanted to do something so wild and destructive that it would shake her back into sanity, into a realization of her true self which she now felt was lost."[61] Clearly, Metalious' heroine wants a unitary personality which melds her private and public selves; however, in an institutionalized society, such a wish cannot be granted. After Jackman dies in a car accident caused by Allison, the heroine experiences some doldrums that make her angst over being a celebrity seem petty. At this point, like a fairy godmother, Rita Moore visits Peyton Place (on New Year's Eve) to cheer up Allison. Their conversation leads to a hymn of praise for work as the ultimate consolation and therapy. According to Rita, work is all that remains when the individual inevitably finds herself alone.

> "This is the final lesson, Allison. This is what success means for people like us—that when everything else is gone, friends and lovers and husbands, we have got our work. It's the only constant thing in our lives. And when we betray our talent, then we might as well give up and return to the original chaos."[52]

Thus, success means doing the work one wishes to perform and giving oneself completely over to it. In effect, work enables Metalious' women to endure the emotional devastations that men constantly and inevitably bring into their lives.

There can never be any question of existing without men or love; indeed, the popular aesthetic judgment that art comes from experience underlies this conventional value. Throughout the novels physical intimacy sparks artistic creativity. Allison becomes a writer because she indulges in sexual daydreams as a teenager; however, she cannot undertake a major work (her novel) until she has become sexually knowledgeable. Her talent enables her to sell short stories but it remains insufficient to make her into a serious novelist. Constance, her mother, and Mike, her stepfather, make this distinction clear when they discuss Allison's career.

> Constance removed a cake from the oven. "Maybe she gave up the idea of writing a novel. The magazines pay very well, you know. I always thought that novelists had to be middle-aged."
> "Not if they have as much talent as Allison. On the other hand, I've always understood that authors have to have some experience with life before they can sit down and write about it successfully." Mike chuckled.[63]

This outlook, articulated by the most intelligent character in *Peyton Place*, becomes even more overt when Allison, after losing her virginity to her married agent, Bradley Holmes, completes the first draft of her novel.

Since Holmes has taken precautions to insure that Allison will not become pregnant (and thus have any control over his future), the manuscript still lacks something—presumably, because Allison needs a permanent lover. Such a figure appears in *Return to Peyton Place* when Lewis Jackman guides Allison through the throes of revision. He also subscribes to the experience school of aesthetics for, when he first meets Allison, he urges: " 'There's youthful energy and curiosity in your novel, but there is also a lifetime of lived experience. Now that I see you, all I can say is that I'm amazed.' "[64] In the subsequent emotional turmoil of her life, in which she is still partly in love with Bradley, falling in love with Lewis, and being courted by David, Allison creates a bestseller; indeed, such sentimental upheaval, in which a former small-town ugly duckling becomes a romantic prize, insures Allison's artistic maturation. As she settles down with Jackman, Allison exhibits a monogamy the popular audience would applaud; however, the connection between aesthetic capacity and physical experience also remains valid. In an argument over merchandising herself and the novel, Allison asks Bradley Holmes why he's been avoiding her. His response, which shows she was only a "fling" for him, clearly articulates the "good sex makes for good art" theory.

> "I'll tell you what happened. You lost your virginity and became an adult. You lost your pretty illusions about sex and became a writer. You stopped thinking of love twenty-four hours a day and began to dwell on reality. What the hell are you complaining about? I think you gained far more than you lost."[65]

Holmes' argument once more underscores Metalious' correlation of art and physical experience.

The characters in *Peyton Place* and *Return to Peyton Place* are either predictable or one-dimensional. In the latter category, while none of these figures is so schematized as to resemble a medieval "humor," Metalious does present people who can be reduced to single dominant traits. Leslie Harrington, the avaricious industrialist whose son is a spoiled brat, zealously grasps for riches and power. As a teenager he learned that success "meant money, the biggest house in town and the best car. But most of all it meant...'being the boss.' "[66] The elder Harrington must endure his son's accidental death and the subsequent tribulations of persuading Betty Anderson, the mother of his illegitimate grandson who was driven out of town through Leslie's machinations, to return to Peyton Place. Although Betty and Mike Rossi, whom Harrington originally brings to town to teach in the high school, succeed in defying Leslie, such encounters with humility do not seriously change his character. Kenny Stearns, the town drunk, is another character who remains incapable of real change. Kenny, who spends weeks in a cellar with other alcoholics during the winter, only to come close to killing himself by cutting his foot with an axe, behaves in a manic-depressive style throughout. His wife, Ginny, has cheated on him and her conduct supposedly causes Kenny's alcoholism; however, after recuperating from his self-inflicted wound, Kenny becomes a religious zealot. In keeping with the novel's either/or tenor, he gives up drinking entirely and becomes a preacher. Thus, while his outward circumstances have drastically changed, Kenny's basic personality, with its refuge in extreme conduct, remains unaltered. He has replaced an alcoholic "high" with a spiritual one; and, in being incapable of any real change, he stands for common men who rarely abandon emotional for reflective lives.

Metalious' melodramatic tenor is further exemplified by her heroes. Mike Rossi, whose appearance leads to the emotional rejuvenation of Constance, epitomizes masculine toughness and wisdom. Upon his arrival, for an interview to be high school principal, Mike surveys the town for himself rather than being escorted through it by Leslie Harrington because the hero knows that welcoming committees are "a pain in the ass." Like many another solitary figure in fiction or film, Rossi only slowly, reluctantly and partially conforms to the community's wishes. His desire to be a teacher results from an education he personally earned, and his integrity has been tested because of a dismissal for presenting controversial (though necessary) material as well as by his subsequent working in a steel mill until he got another offer. Mike's dual nature underscores Metalious' initially overblown description.

> Michael Rossi was a handsome man, in a dark-skinned black-haired, obviously sexual way, and both men and women were apt to credit him more with attractiveness than intellect. This was a mistake, for Rossi had a mind as analytical as a mathematician's and as curious as a philosopher's.[67]

Surprisingly, Rossi's outspokenness does not get him into trouble with the powers-that-be.

Indeed, his capacity for direct speaking controls his relationship with Constance. She symbolizes the hypocrisy of Peyton Place and Rossi must bring her real self to the surface. In transforming Constance both sexually and intellectually, Mike frees her from those inhibitions which have prevented her from being happy. When Constance fears Allison may have sexual feelings and wishes, Rossi presents insights that anyone familiar with Freud would already know. This process upsets Constance, who bore Allison illegitimately and fears that her daughter will repeat that mistake; but such distress necessarily accompanies the process by which Rossi remakes her.

> One of the few things about Mike which annoyed Constance was his habit of questioning every questionable word in her arguments. More often than not, she had discovered , he could render her opinions utterly senseless and baseless by making her say exactly what she meant, word for word....
>
> Mike raised an eyebrow. "What the hell have you got against the word intercourse?" he asked. "It's a good, serviceable word. Yet you'd rather rack your brain for fifteen minutes to find a substitute rather than use it."[68]

Rossi destroys the euphemistic temperament Constance has acquired in Peyton Place; and, just as he initiates her into genuine sexual pleasure, he also shows her that honest language leads to honest thinking.

Ted Carter plays the hero with feet of clay for, although he makes a good beginning at growing up in *Peyton Place*, he lapses into being dominated by the end of that novel and is even more thoroughly so in *Return to Peyton Place*. Once again, Metalious describes an All-American type.

Ted Carter's was the kind of body that older people look upon with satisfaction. Things can't be so bad, they said, when this country can produce young men like that.... Ted Carter's body...was the envy of every adolescent in Peyton Place. Because of it, and also because of his outstanding talent at sports, other, less fortunate, sixteen-year-olds forgave him his good marks, his charm, his easy way of making friends, and the good manners which many mothers flung constantly into the faces of sloppy-talking, often discourteous sons.[69]

Ted is also a sober and serious ("beyond his years") individual who loves work and is highly attractive to girls. All these traits attach to a conventional hero, yet Ted lacks critical intelligence and events also show he lacks character. When Selena Cross is tried for her father's murder, Ted deserts her for the grasping and mercantile aspirations of Harmon and Roberta, his parents, who earlier connived to get "established" in Peyton Place. The seduction of old Doc Quimby, a rich, local physician, by Roberta and her subsequent adultery with Harmon which drove her elderly first husband to despondency and death, delineate the Carters' viciousness. Roberta, who only wants the best for Ted, convinces her son to abandon Selena and, thus, to lose his one true love. In *Return to Peyton Place* Ted, now married to the demanding Jennifer, can only fight against his emotions about Selena. He externalizes such feelings by blaming them on an impersonal fate: "In his heart he knew that salvation for him lay with Selena, but it could not be. It could not be. He soothed himself with this thought. It could not be! It was Fate at fault, not Ted Carter."[70] Ted's weakness repeats the flaws of his parents; in effect, he cannot transcend the sins that have been visited on the children.

Metalious does better with her heroines who are vivid, if not more realistic. Constance Mackenzie, the most interesting and revelatory of these creations, dramatizes Peyton Place's smugness until she meets Mike and comes to terms with her own libido. As the owner of a local dress shop and a "proper" (i.e. celibate and frigid) widow, Constance suffers from vague symptoms of unrest that are, of course, sexual. Since she is trying to adhere to the town's mores, Constance denies her feelings with such vehemence that the reader knows the exact opposite must be true: "If at times she felt a vague restlessness within herself, she told herself sharply that this was *not* sex, but perhaps a touch of indigestion."[71] Metalious flatters her audience by such obvious dramatic irony: the reader can confidently predict that Constance will ultimately have to answer the call of the flesh.

Mike Rossi breaks down Constance's propriety when he insists that she accompany him on a midnight swim. Although she is surprised that she obeys him (a dominance motif essential to their relationship), Constance goes along. At the beach, they begin one of the great seduction scenes of the 1950s when Rossi insists: " 'Untie the top of your bathing suit...I want to feel your breasts against me when I kiss you.' " Constance's immediate reaction is shock and she stands like a statue until:

...he stepped in front of her and untied the top strap of her bathing suit...he pulled her against him without even looking at her. He kissed her brutally, tortuously, as if he had hoped to awaken a response in her with pain that gentleness could not arouse... When he lifted his bruising, hurtful mouth at last, he picked her up, carried her to the car and slammed the door behind her.... Without a word he...dropped her onto the chintz-covered couch.

"The lights," she gasped finally. "Turn off the lights.... I'll have you arrested...for...rape—"

He stood her on the floor beside the bed and slapped her a stunning blow across the mouth with the back of his hand.

"Don't open your mouth again," he said quietly. "Just keep your mouth shut."

He bent over her and ripped the still wet bathing suit from her body, and in the dark, she heard the sound of his zipper opening as he took off his trunks.

"Now," he said. "Now."

It was like a nightmare...until...she felt the first red gush of shamed pleasure that lifted her, lifted her, lifted her and then dropped her down into unconsciousness.[72]

Constance has been raped for her own good and the waves of pleasure (suggested by the repetitive diction) transform her from a New England prig into a human being. Rossi's violence is an essential cathartic, for the town and her own past have turned Constance into a shrew. The popular idea that orgasmic sex is all anyone needs to be happy is, of course, implicit, as is the equally doubtful notion that women must be coerced into relations for their own good. Constance's struggle with outward conformity and inward need is resolved when she urges that the lights be turned off.

The heroine's liberation remains incomplete however, for she still remains hypocritical about her daughter's sexuality; and Rossi must break down these ideas before they can wed. Constance's hypocrisy is underscored by her reluctance to recall her initial lovemaking with Rossi; and, when she tyrannizes over Allison's brief flirtation with Norman Page, Mike finally takes action. He argues that her fears about Allison's possible promiscuities are really just projections of Constance's own past onto the present. At this moment of supreme crisis, as Mike is about to drive away and (presumably) out of her life, Constance breaks down and begs his aid, thus lowering herself from an imaginary pedestal. After Rossi tells her, " 'I cannot stand to look at you and know you lie every time you find the truth too disagreeable to be faced,' "[73] they engage in a lengthy therapeutic session in which Constance reveals her past to him. Throughout this recitation Rossi unerringly interrupts whenever she equivocates so that Constance's soul is genuinely bared.

When her confession is finished, Constance possesses the same confidence that characterizes Mike: "In the weeks that followed it was as if she were a new and different person who walked freely and unafraid for the first time. It was never again necessary for her to take refuge in lies and pretenses."[73] Constance's transformation becomes apparent in another seduction scene with Rossi when she takes the lead and, significantly, leaves the lights on.

For the first time in their relationship she undressed herself and let him watch her, and still there was this joy of giving in her. She could not lie still under his hands.

"Anything," she said. "Anything. Anything."

"I love this fire in you. I love it when you have to move."

"Don't stop."

"Here? And here? And here?"

"Yes. Oh, yes. Yes..."

"Am I good for you, darling?"

"Good! Christ!"

"Do it to me then."[74]

Constance has become a willing collaborator in their mutual gratifications. Metalious, like the director of an effective suspense film, intrigues by imprecision; in effect, each reader supplies the locations when Rossi asks Constance where his hands (?) feel especially good. *Peyton Place*'s seduction scenes, which comprised much of the novel's initial attraction, illustrate that, in addition to making an audience laugh, cry and wait, the good entertainer also makes it imagine.

Selena Cross is more frequently victimized than Metalious' other women. As the daughter of lower-class inebriates, Selena only wants to find love, marriage and a middle-class existence. She endures rape at the hands of her father, Lucas; and the resultant unwanted pregnancy leads the girl to kindly old Doctor Matthew Swain, who compromises his principles by performing an abortion. In time, Lucas, forced out of town by Doctor Swain, returns to the house where Selena and her younger brother, Joey, live. His forced entrance causes Selena to kill him and precipitates a trial that brings Peyton Place into national headlines. During her ordeal, Selena is deserted by Ted Carter, the Mr. Right on whom she had built her bourgeois dreams; however, her lawyer, Peter Drake, the man who will eventually marry her, comes along as a replacement. Unfortunately, Drake is neither exciting nor aggressive, so Selena finds herself restless for physical intimacy; indeed, the girl "had to admit that she was quite often what Corey called 'touchy' and what she referred to as 'cranky.' "[75] Within two pages Selena has experienced love at first sight for an actor named Tim Randlett. Their infatuation quickly builds to the obligatory love scene in which the patient male primes the female so that: "It was as if a dam had burst within her, as if she were fighting a tidal wave of feeling. Until, finally, she let go and gave in to the strength that claimed her, that took everything from her in one shuddering, screaming, ecstatic moment."[76] While this description utilizes imagery associated with Hollywood (euphemistic dams and waves), the characters' sexual roles conform to the acceptable mores of the time.

Selena's emotional odyssey continues, however, for Tim proves more interested in his own ego than in her well-being. Indeed, in yet another "daring" sequence, the actor insists on extended graphic descriptions of Lucas' rape of Selena so that he can play at being "psychological." While Selena finds such disclosures embarrassing, she finally yields, lashes out at Tim and, in so doing, loses him. Hoping that he will quit asking her about the past, Selena elaborates on what Lucas did to her.

"...he grabbed and tied me to the bed and then did it to me. Then I'd be awake and aware of every second and I'd feel him hurting me and smell his sweat and his breath and hear him grunting like a rooting pig...He was big, Tim. Bigger than you. And most of the time I'd bleed before he got through with me. Lucas didn't bleed though. He got me pregnant and I had an abortion."[76]

Tim's desire to know such details, and his later insistence that Selena enjoyed being raped, separates him from the novel's more normal characters. It comes as no surprise when Tim deserts Selena, for his curiosity indicates his depravity. Selena is thus forced back to Peter Drake; and, while such a rebound is not accomplished rapidly (for the girl is too sensitive to hop from bed to bed), their love leads to her spiritual rebirth. As Peter slowly eases Selena into sexual intimacy, the girl realizes that this will really be her "first" time, for Peter is the only man who has truly loved her and Selena can still consider herself a virgin on those terms.[77] The urgency with which she embraces Peter reinforces a standard pattern for, like Constance, Selena now enjoys an open and honest relationship.

Metalious' villains and weaklings suffer from the same sexual determinism. Jennifer Burbank, the respectable Radcliffe girl Ted Carter marries, is the most calculating of such figures in these novels. Moreover, her villainy is rendered more heinous by her youth; for given the 1950s' fondness for innocent youth beset by hypocritical age (e.g. James Dean suffering at the hands of Raymond Massey in *East of Eden*), she is young enough to know better. Her struggle with Roberta Carter, who still wants to dominate Ted's life, sets off much of the emotional fireworks in *Return to Peyton Place*. While the older woman spies on Jennifer and her son when they go to bed, her voyeurism is offset by the girl's delight in knowing her mother-in-law can overhear. Jennifer also reveals herself to have been a lesbian and retains ambiguous feelings about her sexual role with Ted so that she alternates between frigidity and nymphomania. Knowing that Roberta is listening, Jennifer makes passionate love and then chides Ted for being unable to satisfy her.

> She had heard them make love, had heard Jennifer torture Ted and tease him into doing all sorts of perverse and evil things. She had writhed in anguish for poor Ted.
> Then she had heard Jennifer's salacious whisper.
> Ted said, "You're insatiable, darling."
> "More," Jennifer said. "I want more. Oh goddamn men, anyway!"[78]

This shock soon fades when Roberta overhears her daughter-in-law threaten to cheat on Ted (who is, after all, pining for Selena) and decides her son will have no peace until Jennifer is dead.

Roberta thus begins to plan her daughter-in-law's murder but foolishly sets down her plans in a diary that Jennifer reads. The two women have a confrontation in which their words are meant to stun the audience. After she tells Roberta that she knows about her murder scheme, Jennifer utters some "deeper" Freudian truths.

> "You're jealous of me," she said softly. "Every time Ted and I go to bed, you're huddled in the little room next door to us and you listen to your son make love to me and you're so jealous you can't stand it."
> Roberta staggered back toward the desk as if she had been struck.

"You're jealous," said Jennifer. "So jealous you can't stand it. You wish it was you in bed with Ted."[79]

When Roberta gets pushed down the stairs on the very next page, she is the only one who is surprised.

Norman Page, a sensitive boy who loves Allison briefly in *Peyton Place*, further illustrates the smothering power of mother love. Norman, a "sissy," indulges his mother with emotional scenes that inevitably end with him saying " 'I love you, mother.' " Their relationship also includes masochism and sadism, for whenever Norman returns home with a flushed face his mother insists on physicking him. At one point Metalious notes that the boy's mother "might even give him an enema, and while Norman always got a bittersweet sort of pleasure from that, he had to stay in bed afterward."[80] When Norman spies on Mr. and Mrs. Card making love in their backyard, he is sickened and flees in horror. Norman, who has always been frightened yet attracted by an elderly crone named Miss Hester, trespasses on her property before watching the Cards. When Miss Hester unexpectedly comes out on her porch, Norman scrambles to avoid confronting her; and, while he is underneath her porch listening to her rocking chair and her cat, he sees the Cards. In order to make this situation additionally lurid, Metalious has Mrs. Card in the advanced stages of pregnancy so that her bloated abdomen can be a source of juvenile awe (what can she do in that shape?). Mr. Card's passion consists of hiding his face in his wife's flesh, a description that once more releases the reader's imagination. As if all this weren't enough, during this scene Miss Hester, who is also presumably enjoying the "show," dies (from excitement?) when her chair stops rocking.

Norman's trauma later leads to a Freudian mishmash of a dream. By now, Page has gone into the Army and been discharged as unfit; and, to prepare himself for the rigors of Peyton Place, he meets his mother in New York to rehearse a story for public consumption. While such machinations suggest that public opinion in the town is worse than boot camp, Norman's symbolic dream reassures him about returning to Mama.

> He still dreamed the old, recurrent dream about Miss Hester Goodale and her tomcat. In his dream, Miss Hester always wore the face of his mother, while the two people whom she watched through the gap in the hedge were no longer Mr. and Mrs. Card, but Allison Mackenzie and Norman. In his dream, when he stroked Allison's abdomen he would feel a tight excitement in his genitals, but always, just at the moment of release, Allison's abdomen would burst open and spew forth millions of slimy blue worms.... Sometimes he woke up at this point...but most of the time he succeeded in reaching the arms of his mother before he awoke. It was always at that moment, when he reached his mother, that Norman reached a climax in the excitement engendered by Allison. At such times, Norman awoke to warmth and wetness and a sense that his mother had saved him from a terrible danger.[81]

One hardly needs an advanced degree in psychology to recognize that the character's wet dream is being utilized for shock value. Norman is repelled by the birth process—the blue worms replace the blue veins of Mrs. Card's stomach—and in fleeing from Allison he shows his willingness for sexual abstinence. However, Norman only escapes biology's claims at the price of a recurrent nightmare that underscores his neurotic personality. After returning to Peyton Place, he spends the rest of his life bringing home his uncashed checks to his mother.

Allison Mackenzie, the erstwhile novelist, also naturally grows up worrying about sex and, like the town's less enlightened members, being outer-directed and voyeuristic. As a youngster, she tries on a padded bra to get the attention of the wastrel Rodney Harrington who has kissed her in an exciting way. This concern with the bosom in a decade of Marilyn Monroe, Jane Russell and Janye Mansfield, is hardly atypical; however, by later turning Allison into a peeping tom, Metalious reemphasizes her belief that sex drives everyone. Allison, Selena's best friend, comes to visit the Cross home; however, she meets the terrified Joey and then sees Lucas assault Selena. During this scene Allison's reactions center on a clinical concern with Selena as a peer and do not lead to any pity for what Lucas is doing. After Selena's blouse has been ripped away, Allison notes: "the ends of hers are *brown*.... And she does not wear a brassiere all the time, like she told me."[82] While such observations may represent a valid view of adolescent self-preoccupation, they certainly imply that being a spectator beats being a participant. Ultimately, such voyeurism presents a dilemma for, if certain characters can judge others (e.g. Mike Rossi can dismiss Leslie Harrington), and yet everyone is tainted with sexual obsessions, then such distinctions are hard to sustain. Melodrama simply cannot function in a world of degrees as well as it does in a world of kinds.

Metalious' female characters often talk and think like males. Such aggressiveness is demonstrated when Betty Anderson and Rodney Harrington make love in *Peyton Place*. While they have enjoyed an on-again, off-again relationship since adolescence, this consummation scene is full of ironies. When Rodney was forced by his parents into seeing other girls, Betty started to play the field with abandon; and, at this later juncture, the boastful Rodney lacks Betty's expertise and must become her pupil. Rodney, who doesn't seem to know about birth control, relishes Betty's responsiveness and the ease with which she loses her supposed virginity to him: Betty, after guiding Rodney, fears she may be pregnant. While her fertilization is a necessary plot element, why didn't Betty, as being supposedly more experienced, notice Rodney's lack of foresight? Such a logical objection probably denies the popular values that operated for Metalious' audience. Birth control would have been seen as a man's problem, particularly one like Rodney who constantly boasted of his sexual exploits; and, once physical intimacy had reached a certain plateau, nobody could be rational enough to think about the consequences anyway.

Another set of popular values and clichés surrounds Allison's deflowering by Bradley Holmes. After that sophisticate has persuaded her that being "nude" is infinitely more exciting than being "naked" (which connotes what's under a rock, he urges, in providing a great "make out" line), Allison must endure losing her maidenhead. This process is described in dialog which again makes the reader do the imagining; and this passage ends with a sentiment worthy of every adolescent male's fondest sexual daydream.

> "Don't," he commanded, when she tried to twist away from him at the first thrust of pain. "Help me," he said. "Don't pull away."
> "I can't," she cried. "I can't."
> "Yes, you can. Press your heels against the mattress and raise your hips. Help me. Quickly."
> . . .and then she had cried out the odd, mingled cry of pain and pleasure.
> Later, after they had smoked and talked, he turned to her again.
> "It is never as good as it should be for a woman, the first time," he said. "This one will be for you."[83]

The experienced older man knows that such largesse is essential and, of course, he can supply the necessary balm (Allison had avoided sex with David Noyes presumably because he lacked such knowledge and/or capacity). The loss of virginity is played to the hilt here for it becomes a trial in which the intrusive male forces his way into the female and brings pleasure out of pain. Sexual ecstasy also brings on Bradley's admonition to hurry, for he, too, is about to involuntarily lose his control of things.

Return to Peyton Place spells out more clearly that sexually-drenched atmosphere that sustains Metalious' commercial success, for such standard fare as therapeutic rape, incest and physical love's being tied to spiritual intimacy are trotted out to re-establish the characters from the earlier novel. When we first glimpse the happily married Rossis, who will suffer because of the publication of Allison's novel, they are still indulging in civilized rape.

> "Ask me for it," he demanded, his voice harsh.
> "Go to hell. I'll never ask you!"
> "Yes, you will," he said, "oh yes, you will."
> "Make me," she cried. "Make me, darling, make me." And then, quickly, "Now, darling. Now."
> ". . .Say it, damn you. Say it to me now!"
> The words tore from her throat, anguished, as if they were the last words she would ever utter.[84]

It is reassuring that Mike and Constance continue to play the dominant male and the coy female, even though they have been married for some time. In effect, rape is now being enacted at the verbal and fantasy levels, so that physical consummation represents the end of an involved, almost masturbatory process. Once again, the familiar romantic association of love and death is dusted off as a capstone to Constance's bliss.

Peyton Place and *Return to Peyton Place* still entertain because Metalious deals in such detail with her characters' problems that her essentially melodramatic ideas are obscured. Her fictional world, however second-rate, causes one to suspend disbelief while reading so that her novels' bestseller status is, finally, dependent not on their salacious subject matter or the plain speaking of their characters but rather on their sincerity and creativity. Metalious is fully engaged in her novels and, since her subject matter accords with the interests of large numbers of readers, she creates runaway hits. The very fervor of her writing gives an energy to her work missing in more derivative efforts. Thus, one can disagree with the psychology illustrated in these novels, yet the very pervasiveness with which their outlook is presented is disarming.

During her affair with Lewis Jackman, Allison Mackenzie articulates the ultimate theme in Metalious' fiction. After a lengthy description of their lovemaking replete with "buffetings" and "tidal waves," Allison, as a willful (i.e. mature) female, finally draws his "throbbing body down to hers" and philosophizes that: "This is the only truth there is...this expression of love. The rest is acting out a part."[85] In this conjunction of physical intimacy and reality itself one finds a bedrock popular value of the 1950s. In spite of its being a less sexually tolerant time than our own, that decade exhibited stereotypical certainties while our period indulges in incessant role-playing. To paraphrase Metalious, we live in an endless succession of the "rest," a time when each individual must act to please, or at least not to displease, those around him. Thus, although *Peyton Place* and its author consistently elicit condescending smiles and belittling remarks among many, the problems Allison Mackenzie touches on in her philosophic reverie are very much with us. Indeed, in spite of all their stylistic and intellectual drawbacks, Metalious' novels remain acute cultural barometers of their time and, although not so widely recognized or acknowledged, of ours as well.

The explosive best seller
that lifts the lid off a
respectable New England town

PEYTON PLACE

by Grace Metalious

Peyton Place
A skeleton in every closet (Dell)

Chapter 7

"But you care in another way and it's a good way."

The woman's novel (or "weepy") centers on a heroine's finding a happy marriage. These often lengthy and leisurely narratives allow for romantic vicissitudes; thus, the heroine rarely finds true love at the first opportunity but must, instead, go through the emotional sufferings that inevitably accompany trial and error. The heroine searches for her "one and only" (just as the less inhibited characters of Robbins and Metalious do) but the qualifications that Mr. Right must possess are decidedly different than those of the "stud." In women's novels love is so fulfilling and so necessary that it surpasses sex, social problems or, indeed, any other human activity. The cinematic archetype for such narratives is *Daisy Kenyon*, a 1947 Joan Crawford vehicle, in which the heroine must choose between two eager suitors—one whom she finds "exciting" (even though married) and one whom she finds "worthwhile" (and to whom is she is eventually married). It is crucial that such a romantic choice devolve on the woman so that she can become the center of a fictional universe with willing males revolving around her. Women's novels are inhabited by "denatured" males whose virtues lie in being decorous, patient and gentle, and " intuitive" females whose feelings alert them to everything their men experience. Deep feelings are clearly more valuable than being reasonable or pragmatic so that the world comes to be controlled by the heart and never by the mind or the loins.

Frances Parkinson Keyes' *Joy Street* (1950) and *Steamboat Gothic* (1952) examine the dilemmas in choosing between a "safe" and an "exciting" love within the confines of married life. Irving Stone's *Love is Eternal* (1954) utilizes Abraham and Mary Todd Lincoln's married life to develop the conflicts between romance and career against a historical background. History also serves in *The Winthrop Woman* (1958) by Anya Seton, a chronicle of romantic agonies and religious redemption in seventeenth-century America. Rona Jaffe's *The Best of Everything* (1958) presents characters who, while anxious to marry, have initially opted for "careers" and so begun to assert themselves. Thus, these novels move from an absolute dependence on the appearance of Mr. Right to a dawning realization that such a male may not be destined to arrive in every girl's future.

* * *

Joy Street, a characteristic woman's novel, considers the traits of a happy marriage from the perspective of the drawing room rather than the bedroom. The novel unfolds at an excruciating pace, so that didactic scenes between Emily Thayer Field, the protagonist, and her grandmother, Mrs. Forbes, record even slight fluctuations in emotional states. For Keyes, passivity and reflection replace tight plotting. While the self-confident patience of Emily may, indeed, accurately reflect contemporary mores, one hates to believe that even in the conformist 1950s women's lives were so dull. Although it alludes to historical events to provide a rough chronology, *Joy Street* focuses on love and marriage, human activities Keyes regards as synonymous. Emily initially realizes she can be comfortable without necessarily being happy because of marriage; and, while never unfaithful, Keyes' heroine must experience an unrequited love to recognize the man who can provide her with a truly blissful union.

The story begins with Emily's marriage to Roger Field, a rising Boston attorney. In a reversal of the customary romantic pattern in which the female is in ill or questionable health, the male character plays this role in *Joy Street*. When he is rejected by the Army at the beginning of World War II and then throws himself into a gruelling home front schedule, Roger places himself in "plausible jeopardy." Later, as Emily becomes increasingly restless and offended by some of the legal cronies Roger brings home, he conveniently contracts pneumonia and dies. Thus, the heroine is left to struggle alone with her emotional and social feelings toward Irish, Italians and Jews.

David Salmont emerges as the most exciting character in *Joy Street*, at least for readers who associate activity with being alive. This suave Jewish lawyer even attempts to seduce Emily while she is married to Roger before he becomes a zealot seeking revenge for the Jewish people at the expense of the Nazis. His mercurial personality, thus, hardly accords with the staid tradition of Boston which Emily represents; yet, while she can hold him off initially, she falls in love with Salmont once she is a widow. To spare Emily from the social pressures of a mixed religious marriage (as well as any personal guilt attached to a man who tried to compromise her), Keyes provides another love for Salmont. When David returns from the war he announces his impending marriage to the disappointed but outwardly imperturbable Emily. Thus, the protagonist must soothe her emotions elsewhere, a task she accomplishes by the novel's final page. In keeping with Keyes' sense of decorum, Emily and David indulge in none of the physical gropings found in sexually-oriented 1950s bestsellers. Salmont, in fact, exhibits an almost feminine conscience when he apologizes to Emily for what he thought (not what he did!) during their first encounter. That meeting occurs because Roger, pleading fatigue, unwittingly persuades David to escort Emily to a dance. David subsequently becomes a regular visitor in the Fields' home and one evening, when Roger is out, inveigles Emily into dancing. The heroine is drawn closer and closer to the charming Salmont, and then:

As the music rose to a crescendo, David bent his head and pressing his face against hers, kissed her on the mouth.

Instantly she wrenched herself free and confronted him trembling and incoherent with rage....

"I'm sorry you feel that I insulted you. I certainly didn't mean to.I felt as if a kiss were a suitable climax to our dance, that's all."[1]

While Emily doubts she can ever face Roger again, David vows to make "serious" love to her in the future, thus refusing to recognize the sanctity of marriage.

In the rest of his appearances in *Joy Street,* however, the Jewish lawyer does little besides apologize and urge that kissing Emily was only a momentary lapse (the closest any Keyes' character ever gets to being carried away). At their next meeting David repeats his promise-threat only to heighten his profuse apology.

"I did mean what I said when I told you that someday I'd make love to you, I did think perhaps that I could get away with it, once anyway, perhaps often. I won't go into all the reasons why I thought so—probably you can make a pretty fair guess, when it comes to that. I don't think it's necessary for me to explain what I meant by 'love- making' either. That's beyond the point anyway. The point is, I was mistaken in what I said. I found I couldn't."[2]

Keyes deals in euphemism and rectitude so that Salmont's ideas, however licentious or fanciful, remain distinctly veiled and Emily does not hear anything indecorous. The ironic possibility that Salmont's reasons may be unflattering to the protagonist never comes to the surface and only the most skeptical reader would supply such a motive to Keyes' character.

Salmont's excessive concern with his conduct reflects a common feature in women's novels, namely, that their male characters act like surrogate females rather than men. The same psychological simplification structures both hard-core pornography and soap opera—one sex unquestioningly submits to the other. Thus, Salmont, in expressing feminine concerns, caters to Emily as befits her rank as the central figure of the novel. In a later scene between David and Priscilla, the young woman he eventually marries, Salmont presents himself as a victim of ethnic prejudice and so wins back some reader sympathy.

"Priscilla... you're a perfectly grand kid and I'm very fond of you, but I'm not in love with you. There's not the slightest chance that I ever will be."

"... Why not?"

"Because I'm a Jew... (and) I wouldn't think it was fair to subject a girl like you to running the risk of having the kind of treatment she might get if she were married to a Jew."[3]

In *Joy Street* chivalrousness supplants social outrage, so that Salmont places Priscilla's future comfort above any attempt to get even with a society that treats him like a second-class citizen. The war releases Salmont's pent-up anger and, after returning from Europe, he reflects: " 'that was when I began to know I was doing what I'd been waiting for, what I'd been living for —years and years and years! The only thing I regret is that we couldn't do more damage and more killing, because there wasn't time.' "[4] Salmont's rage (which might have led him to attack the very Boston society to which Emily belongs) is finally assuaged by love. David finds a safe harbor in Priscilla who, besides not feeling compromised as Emily was by David's "lustful" kiss, can listen to the harsher realities the heroine wants to ignore.

Since she remains far too decorous and self-conscious ever to show her real feelings to a man, Emily cannot openly urge that she, and not Priscilla, should become Mrs. Salmont. Keyes' heroine believes that love and marriage constitute a sacred obligation and she is so steadfast that even Roger, who has become slightly jealous or David, can think: "Thank God, Emily was loyalty itself, steadfastness itself. On that score he had no anxiety. The anxiety was all for his own inadequacy."[5] Keyes again reverses customary psychology for Roger feels inadequate and jealous: he must win Emily over and over, though she is "steadfastness itself." Mrs. Forbes consoles the protagonist after Roger's death, the subsequent miscarriage Emily suffers, and the dispiriting news that David plans to marry another. Because of Salmont, Emily learns that a torrential passion for a man is just another common part of a woman's life. Even Mrs. Forbes, a member of Parisian cafe society before 1914, lives with the memory of a Russian Duke who perished in the 1917 Revolution. Although Feodor was the true love of her life, Mrs. Forbes found happiness in others when she lost Prince Charming; indeed, her grief has bred compassion and wisdom which she passes on to Emily when the heroine urges:

> "...I've felt for a long while there must have been a David in your life. I mean, someone you cared for in the same way I've cared for him. If there hadn't been, I don't see how you could have been so—so understanding."
> "There's someone like David in a good many women's lives, Emily."[6]

In steering Emily through this emotional crisis, Mrs. Forbes justifies her existence as a link between past and future. Her views imply that each woman must wait and let experience (i.e. men) seek her out, and so she offers solace to Emily and to generations of fellow feminine sufferers.

Mrs. Forbes' greatest gift to her granddaughter is the distinction she makes between a "safe" love and an "exciting" one. Although she does not disapprove of Roger Field as a husband for Emily, Mrs. Forbes questions whether he is exciting enough. In a bit of obvious foreshadowing Keyes even has the older woman hoping Emily never meets a more dynamic man. Mrs. Forbes knows Roger is not the real thing because:

> "My dear, if you had been (in love), in the sense that I mean it, you never would have voluntarily gone off to Kentucky and postponed your marriage for over a year, to prove your point. You'd have eloped, in the face of family opposition, within a week after Roger's proposal of marriage. You may not care for the comparison, but falling in love is something like having labor pains. You can have 'false pains' and you can imagine you're in love. But when the real labor begins, you know the difference right away; you don't see how you ever could have thought you were suffering before."[7]

Mrs. Forbes flatters the audience by her insistence that the recognition of love is an intuitive process as purely feminine as giving birth; thus feeling is again celebrated as the primary means of organizing experience, and readers are encouraged simply to trust their emotions.

Joy Street's heroine finds a new life with Brian Collins, another old friend of Roger's who successfully runs for Congress (as Irish lawyers from South Boston are wont to do) and escapes into the hectic world of Washington. Brian understands the emotional traumas Emily has experienced and, more important, doesn't overvalue his allure to her. In urging her to share his life, Collins argues that the heroine doesn't belong on staid, old Joy Street because Emily has outgrown its prejudices and snobberies. He then wisely adds:

> "I know you don't care for me the way you cared for Roger, much less the way you cared for David. *I know you* never will. But you care in another way and it's a good way.... And you know I love you with all my heart and soul. Will you marry me whether I win or lose?"[8]

Brian is a veritable mirror image of Harold Robbins' Sandra Brady who offered herself to the protagonist in *Never Leave Me*, even though knowing she would never be his "one and only." In the same way, the Irish lawyer-politician compromises his ego to gain someone he cherishes. The psychological motivation of a character whose feelings are subordinated to another's will represents the underlying wish-fulfillments assuaged by soap opera and pornography. There is finally no difference between a female character who devotes her conscious life to the sexual gratification of a male character and a male character who constantly worries about the sentimental satisfactions of a female character. *Joy Street* naturally ends on an upbeat note, for Brian, in sweeping Emily away to Washington, enables the heroine to "elope"—at least from her past.

*   *   *

Steamboat Gothic finds Keyes working familiar territory in a novel that spans three generations of the Batchelor family of Louisiana. This tale is, as John Cawalti suggests,[9] prototypically melodramatic in its rambling plot which tests the characters in order to reaffirm their belief that romantic love forms the basis of society. *Steamboat Gothic* ends with a new Batchelor generation happily contemplating their future wedded bliss—more money and more children, hopefully in that order. The power of married life is symbolized when, as a youngster, Cary Page, Clyde Batchelor's adoptive daughter, delights in digging for supposed buried treasure in the most worthless ground at Cindy Lou, the Batchelor estate. The girl's faith in the secret treasure foreshadows the future importance of this land; indeed, after being used as an asphalt quarry, it becomes the source of oil and makes Larry Vincent, Clyde's grandson, rich and self-sufficient when confronted by the possible loss of the entire property. This faith in the beneficence of land, so powerfully engrained in Margaret

Mitchell's *Gone with the Wind*, represents a bedrock value for Clyde and his descendants. When Cary confronts Clyde whom she regards as her real (i.e. emotional) father with her belief in the buried treasure, the sentimental protagonist decides:

> It was evident that she still clung to her childlike belief, which he had been the first to encourage. Well, after all, her unquestioning faith in the buried treasure had as much foundation as her unquestioning faith in him. Since he would have gone to any lengths to prevent shaking the one, why should he shake the other?[10]

Clyde's concern reflects the inherent magic of the seemingly worthless land (a fairy tale motif, if ever there was one) and his extreme deference toward women.

Naturally, Clyde is devoted to his wife, Lucy, because of having been so smitten on their first meeting. While his fortune derives from being a gambler on the antebellum Mississippi and investments in the "Yankee" North, Clyde's true sympathies lie with domestic life in a Southern environment. He must, therefore, hide his past from Lucy, the descendant of a prominent Virginia family whose first husband, a Confederate colonel, dies shortly after their first meeting. Clyde subsequently falls into a trap set by Dorothée Labouisse, the widowed owner of Cindy Lou from whom he buys the plantation as a wedding gift. In the novel's conclusion, Keyes has Louise Vincent, Larry's French-born bride, discover through reading a long-lost diary that Lucy had known about Clyde's indiscretion all along. Thus, *Steamboat Gothic* reaffirms the double standard by suggesting that men must be forgiven their indiscretions by women who recognize their animality. Even though Clyde is haunted by his indulgence, and even though Cary suffers social ostracism for falling in love with a French Count (Dorothée's son, of course!) and dancing with him in public, Keyes emphasizes that a woman's lot is to suffer patiently the wandering foolishnesses of men. Life's real meaning, as epitomized by the lazy opulence of Cindy Lou twenty-five years after Clyde and Lucy have moved there, lies in the contentment produced by married love's duration and never in the flesh's momentary pleasures.

Since *Steamboat Gothic* spans generations, the replacement of one set of characters by another represents its major technical problem. Clyde, who founds the family's establishment in Louisiana, links the generations; for, after the deaths of Lucy, Cary and Savoie Vincent, her husband, in a fire, Clyde becomes the sole parent to Larry Vincent and works zealously to insure his grandson's future by acquiring additional property. In keeping with the beliefs that age produces character while youth needs direction (a motif that still worked in the 1950s, the age of the last presidents who seemed like grandfathers—Truman and Eisenhower), the wise and dignified Clyde consistently outmaneuvers younger men. His stepson, Bushrod Page, whom Clyde instinctively disliked and only endured because Lucy was his mother, emerges as the typical "cad" of melodrama; but the older man outfoxes Bushrod by beating him in poker because of his skill from the riverboat days.

Armande de Chanet marries Pierre, the Frenchman with whom Cary is infatuated, experiences a difficult wedded life, and returns to Louisiana to separate from her husband. Armande, who cultivates the aged Clyde as a sort of uncle, tells the protagonist: " 'An old man or an old woman who's really fine is about the finest creature there is, just as one that's handsome or beautiful at eighty is about five times as remarkable as one who's handsome or beautiful at eighteen.' "[11] Her praise establishes a moral scheme by which truly good people retain their beauty because they are happy in living while those who connive become ugly. Armande's own mother has failed on these grounds, for she became more hypocritical the longer she lived in France with the de Chanets and their relatives. Even Clyde's early indiscretion with Dorothée is partially excused by later developments for, unlike the elder Mrs. Vincent, Clyde was not corrupted by his contacts with Madame de Chanet.

The protagonist at least had the good sense to abandon Dorothée as an incurable wanton (after two turns in her bed), a decision that underlines his good sense and moral judgment. Clyde's reward for such conduct is his sweetly melancholy life after Lucy's death for, in caring for Larry (and the future), the main character earns the tranquil death which Keyes bestows on him. After writing three letters (to Larry, to Louise, his grandson's intended, and to Pierre De Chanet who has sponsored Larry's suit for Louise's hand with her haughty French family) the patriarch gently passes on.

Nappy (a servant). . .did not find his master under the great shady tree, so he went on to the enclosure which was Lucy's resting place. As he expected, Clyde was seated beside her grave, sleeping quietly. It was still warm and sunny, so Nappy made no effort to waken him. It was a long time before the faithful servant realized that this was the deepest and most tranquil sleep of all.[12]

It is surely appropriate that Clyde expires near Lucy's grave, for their love transcends even death; indeed, just as Lucy died trying to save Cary and Savoie (after she removed Larry from the burning house), so Clyde has sacrificed himself for the larger good of the family.

Cary Page experiences the trials one expects in a generational melodrama like *Steamboat Gothic* for her life as Clyde's spoiled stepchild leads to a convenient marriage and a subsequent meeting with a man she passionately loves. In a requisite bit of plotting, Cary must put aside Pierre de Chanet because society expects her to be faithful to Savoie and because she is pregnant. Cary only bemoans her fate with Clyde who, because of his experience with Dorothée, intuitively recognizes the guilt of illicit love. Clyde's insistence that she do her duty does not sit well with Cary; however, the impending blessed event and the news that Pierre will marry Armande bring the girl back to her senses (in much the same way that Emily absorbed David's loss in *Joy Street*). After returning from her honeymoon in France, during which she met and flirted with Pierre because he was willing to go riding while Savoie declined, Cary exhibits a new restlessness. Her preference for staying in New Orleans, rather than in the house which Clyde has built for the newlyweds, leads to a round of parties in which: "Cary herself revealed no unseemly degree of satisfaction over the furor she was causing; indeed, she seemed almost indifferent to it, as far as any special participation in it was concerned, eagerly as she craved constant excitement."[13] Clyde knows that Cary is distraught when he subsequently meets her riding alone at Cindy Lou, a desperation symbolized by her disinterest when he says that the land on which the "buried treasure" was secreted may be sold. After eliciting a confession about her infatuation with Pierre, Clyde's admonitory tone about duty causes Cary to rebuke him. When she later experiences terrible morning sickness, a psychosomatic reaction to the news that Pierre is about to visit New Orleans and to her unwanted pregnancy, Cary symbolizes the malaise which inevitably accompanies a denial of proper values. Cary suffers because of her transgression against the emotional monogamy a woman must possess to be able to guide the naturally philandering male.

When Cary realizes that her proper place is with Savoie as the mother of their child, she overcomes her symptoms and begs for Clyde's forgiveness. She wants her stepfather's love because he guessed her secret and did not reveal it; thus, Cary finally tells Clyde: " 'Savoie hasn't guessed and we mustn't let him—ever.... I think Mother may have, but I can't risk telling her, in case she hasn't.... But you *know*. You *understand*. Oh, Father, I need you so much. You won't fail me, will you?' "[14] Society's basic structure, the family, thus represents its most important value; indeed, Clyde and Lucy symbolize the perfect married unit, one whose blissful example creates happiness for those of their offspring wise enough to imitate it. After Lucy and Savoie are burned to death, Cary lingers and Keyes plays on the pathos of Clyde's losses. Once she has made him promise to care for Larry (even though Savoie's parents have a stronger legal claim), Cary dies and Clyde must arrange her funeral. In a scene that emphasizes the melancholy tone so essential to a woman's novel, Clyde decorates the dead Cary with flowers culled from Lucy's garden.

> With the tenderest care, he placed the flowers around the quiet form, laying a cluster of buds on the still breast and putting a single perfect blossom between the hands which he folded himself. Then, long and lovingly, he looked down on his daughter. Never, in her most radiant moments, had she seemed so beautiful to him.[15]

While such a scene echoes other turgid sequences like the death of Little Eva in *Uncle Tom's Cabin* or the demise of Lucy Butler in *Gone with the Wind*, Cary's beauty in death dramatizes that she found the right moral path in life.

Cary's dissolute brother, Bushrod, marries an ugly rich heiress, then allows her father to pension him off, and then tries to cheat Clyde out of Cindy Lou after Lucy's death. Finally appearing as Larry Vincent's commanding officer who refuses to allow the young man to marry Louise, Bushrod is last seen living on the profits from his first wife's estate. Keyes uses Bushrod as a test of Clyde's essentially Christian goodness for the protagonist consistently tries to return good for the evils Bushrod brings. The Batchelors' marriage becomes strained however when Bushrod blackmails Clyde. This exchange of $20,000 for the younger man's promise to remain silent about his stepfather's past occurs because Clyde does not want to disillusion Cary or Lucy. To further elevate Bushrod's dastardliness, his blackmail scheme nearly bankrupts Clyde because it follows the expenses of Cary's wedding and the building of the house for the young couple. Even though he has been rescued years earlier by Clyde from a number of gambling debts in Richmond (an act the protagonist naturally keeps from Lucy), Bushrod uses his newly-found knowledge.

"If Cary took my Richmond peccadilloes as seriously as you claim she did, how do you think she'd feel about your prolonged—and highly successful—prewar activities on the Mississippi steamboats?"

"If you say anything to Cary that will shatter her faith in me, I'll kill you! And you'd better believe that, because I mean it!"

Clyde had sprung up, the suppressed hatred of years suddenly unleashed.[16]

Clyde's histrionic response underlines the fantasy aspects of the character and the situation. Clyde is the answer to every woman's prayers since he keeps any sordid truths about the world from reaching the ears of those he loves.

Clyde's financial problems are finally solved by Lucy, who has saved the funds her husband gave her to spend frivolously in the past. Just as she knew Clyde would inevitably wander off the narrow path of monogamy, Lucy also intuited that her husband would need the "mad money" he had lavished on her. Bushrod's later attempt to secure the title to Cindy Lou, which turns in part on his misunderstanding of local tax law, leads to a showdown between him and his stepfather. When Bushrod offers to play poker on a winner-take-all basis for the plantation, Clyde wisely examines the decks of cards so that Bushrod is hoisted on his own petard and forced to steal away in the night (but not before he has choked the flamingoes whose cries disturbed him). Keyes offers a less than subtle portrait of Bushrod, as a veteran of the Spanish-American War concealing his real nature beneath a suave exterior.

His unimpaired figure set off his uniform to immense advantage; pallor gave a Bryonic touch to his fine features; and the dark circles under his eyes, far from suggesting dissipation, only added to this air of romanticism; in every way he embodied the popular conception of a patriot who had suffered in a noble cause, and who was still suffering from the results of its hardships and its dangers, but who was making a valiant effort to conceal his pain under a cloak of buoyancy. And this was the dissembler who was accepting hero worship from a generous and cordial people at the same time that he was preparing to abuse their hospitality, so prodigally offered, with practices as adroit as they were dishonorable.[17]

Thus, Bushrod serves as a warning that evil and hypocrisy can never be completely eradicated, even if the villainy of the character leads to his isolation.

The same sequence by which moral depravity leads to frustration and loneliness is exemplified by Dorothée Labouisse who becomes the Marquise de Chanet, an embittered old woman whose only pleasure lies in temporarily thwarting Larry Vincent's marriage to Louise. Her sour old age arises from Dorothée's affair with Clyde in Louisiana. As the widowed owner of Cindy Lou, Dorothée finds herself penniless and eager to return to France when Clyde offers to purchase her plantation. The protagonist initially even finds himself torn between his long-term commitment to Lucy and the momentary allure of Dorothée.

His admiration for Lucy increased every time he appraised her attributes; but this did not keep him from making other appraisals. He hardly took his eyes off the revealing black bodice as he and Dorothée Labouisse went out on the gallery and down the branching staircase.[18]

In the decorous seduction which follows, Keyes presents Clyde's conduct as a kind of simple reflex action. Life has taught the protagonist to accept good breaks that come his way, and so Clyde thinks that Madame Labouisse gives herself as a form of gratitude. In keeping with the sexual double standard (and as a clumsy foreshadowing of his eventual dismissal of Dorothée) Clyde believes things would have been entirely different if Lucy had been in Madame Labouisse's place, for no gentleman wantonly seduces a true love.

Several hundred pages later we learn that Dorothée was more seriously affected and schemed successfully (through buying a wardrobe that revealed more of what the black bodice hid, and then inviting Clyde to dinner) to renew their romance. However, on this second occasion, although he again gives in, Clyde's disgust with himself and the woman comes to the surface.

"...you planned and plotted for this. You laid a trap for me. I saw it and I walked into it just the same."

"If I hadn't thought you really loved me, at least that you would—"

He laughed harshly. "You didn't think anything of the kind. You're not in love. You're in heat. And God! What a beast I've been myself!"[19]

Once again, the male character voices the sensibilities and values traditionally associated with female views of love and passion. As a character beloved by soap opera audiences, Clyde's every waking moment centers on pleasing Lucy by anticipating her wishes. Clyde's sense of guilt is so strong after he rejects Dorothée that he never errs again.

Years later, when Pierre de Chanet brings his mother back to the United States, Madame de Chanet, who remains committed to the shallow values of power and sexual manipulation, rages inwardly at the happy spectacle of Clyde and Lucy's life at Cindy Lou.

The consciousness of that placid, uneventful domesticity was what rankled most. If once— just once—she could have troubled its tranquility, the marquise would have not asked for more: that would have been enough to shatter Lucy's security, to test Clyde's susceptibility and to prove her own diminishing, but still dangerous powers.[20]

This malevolent woman schemes to make the Batchelors' life as miserable as her own, a design she fosters by encouraging Pierre to pursue the married Cary. Her shortsighted aims clearly reflect her unwillingness to grow up and accept the limits and responsibilities of age. The futility of Dorothée's quest for revenge becomes most dramatically evident when Pierre, in helping Larry Vincent, dismisses his mother as a haughty and vengeful woman. Thus, in accord with the novel's moral scheme, the repentant Clyde receives the love of the younger generation (in Cary and Larry) while his one-time lover reaps only its polite scorn.

Keyes' principal positive values reside in Lucy Page, the faithful wife who epitomizes true wedded love. Although she is infatuated with Clyde on their first meeting, when he inquires if he can aid her and her destitute family, Lucy is enough of a lady not to throw herself at him. She remains true to her position as a Southern lady with two children and a husband slowly dying from war wounds; indeed, Lucy is so genteel that when Colonel Page dies, she retreats to her family's plantation without notifying Clyde that she has left Richmond. The protagonist must seek Lucy and go through the rituals of courtship to win her hand—a process that enables Keyes to illustrate the compromised nature of both characters. While Clyde suffers from his past as a gambler and his indiscretion with Dorothée, Lucy's flaw is that she can have no more children. Thus, Clyde must be content as an adoptive father to her children and with her alone; and, of course, the smitten protagonist sees the absence of more children as a small price to pay, while his acceptance of her inability makes Lucy even more compassionate toward his missteps. When Louise Vincent discovers that Lucy knew about Clyde's indiscretion with Madame Labouisse (an intuition that arises when Lucy hears about the revealing wardrobe Dorothée purchased from a New Orleans dressmaker), the reader realizes the depth of Lucy's devotion. In living so happily, Clyde and Lucy transcend the earthly duration of their lives to become indispensable parts of the present and the future.

Clyde and Lucy's compatibility surfaces early in their marriage when the protagonist (who fusses excessively over Lucy's being tired during their honeymoon travels, and so seems more of a parent than a lover) declares that their passion must spring from a mutual source.

> "I want you to get over the idea that it's shameful for a woman—and again, I mean a woman like you—to feel passion and to show that she does. It's normal for men and women to share the full experience of love, and they can't do it, if the desire for it is one-sided. *It's got to be mutual.* And it will be for us, if you'll just believe me, if you'll just trust yourself to me."[21]

While such a speech sounds incongruous considering Lucy's two children, it caters to deeper expectations in the audience. Clyde reaffirms the conventional notions of male knowledge and female innocence so essential to the double standard while drawing a line between women who are wanton and those, like Lucy, who only allow their feelings to emerge after marriage, as is "proper." Keyes' readers are thus supported in their customary assumption that a woman only finds herself in marriage; indeed, true love as embodied by Clyde represents a second virginity for Lucy. Since she was coerced by social pressure into her first marriage, the heroine remains emotionally innocent until she weds Clyde whose speech "liberates" her. His sensitive coaxing brings Lucy into the full joys of requited bliss for, "the opulent bridal suite had become the scene of repeated raptures, for, as Clyde had promised Lucy, their marriage quickly became one of shared desires and shared delights; but he was also insistent on her need for repose and refreshment...."[22] Thus, in the midst of physical ecstasies, Clyde never forgets to pamper his bride.

This example of true love, in which male attentiveness creates feminine emotional rapport, initially guides Cary's conduct. Her engagement to Savoie Vincent, which comes about only after he has courted her for ten years and because she fears becoming an old maid, surprises Clyde and Lucy who wonder (like Mrs. Forbes in *Joy Street*) if their daughter is choosing this marriage for the right reasons. The wise Lucy urges that a romantic bond, the feeling that compels one to choose another, must underlie any enduring happiness and reveals her own sentimental and romantic soul in their discussion.

> "I cannot help thinking that, if you were deeply in love with Savoie, it wouldn't have taken you ten years to find this out."
> "But you kept Father waiting a long time, too!"
> "Not ten years. And not because it took me a long time to find out whether I loved him. I found that out inside of ten minutes."[23]

Such parental doubts prove prophetic when Cary returns from France restlessly pining for Pierre; indeed, the girl only finds her way back to married (i.e. normal) love through the birth of Larry which establishes a greater bond.

Cary signals her new maturity in conversation with Madame de Chanet at Cindy Lou when she shows Pierre's mother around her former home and points out changes that infuriate the already envious Dorothée. To assuage her pride, Madame de Chanet nearly reveals her clandestine affair with Clyde, while Cary not only infers the relationship but goes on calmly to insist:

> "There's one thing you're right about though.... That's the part about forgiving and forgetting. Of course Mother wouldn't *forgive* Father for something that happened more than twenty-five years ago. You don't forgive people you love. You just love them. And you don't have to force yourself to forget something that doesn't matter anyway."[24]

Cary thus defines true love in a passage that anticipates Erich Segal's celebrated bromide about "never having to say you're sorry" in *Love Story*. Married love precludes taking advantage of one's spouse. Those with "unequal" marriages—in which one member is more loved than loving— are doomed to unhappiness like Pierre de Chanet, who tried to redeem his own marital failure by helping Larry and Louise, and Bushrod, who turns to gambling and debauchery to make up for the void he cannot recognize.

The morality of true love is best expressed by Larry and Louise when the young people, although already smitten, behave decorously because Pierre has allowed them to go into a garden without a chaperon. Larry, who has seen extensive combat in Pershing's force, recognizes that Louise is a special woman, comparable to Lucy.

> Finally Larry, looking into Louise's eyes, knew that he wanted to kiss her—more than he had ever wanted to do anything else in his life; knew, too, that she wanted to have him do so. But because she was what she was and what he wanted her to be, and not merely because Pierre had trusted her to him, he also knew that he must not do that until he had told Pierre, before he told Louise, what she meant to him and had asked for permission to marry her.[25]

Larry embodies Clyde's gentility and these characters, who have survived the Civil War and World War I, testify to love's continuing validity. When Larry returns to Cindy Lou with Louise, he becomes the planter-patriach of the community; and, as his interests expand into shipping and oil, Larry becomes ever more mindful of being a social pillar.

In the final section of *Steamboat Gothic*, as further evidence of his humanity, Larry donates his grandfather's old house at Cindy Lou as a recreation center for the numerous workers that new business has brought to the area. Thus, Larry Vincent recognizes that middle-class workers deserve their own place rather then simply noblesse oblige from the master of the land. Such generosity is appropriately rewarded when an oil company buys the mineral rights to Cindy Lou and Larry gets a contract to ship their production upriver. This arrangement makes Larry a shipping entrepreneur on the Mississippi just as Clyde had been; and, just as Clyde named one of his steamboats the Lucy Batchelor, so Larry perpetuates Clyde's name when he hears of a diesel barge for sale: "Larry rose abruptly and turning, looked out of the low window nearest him toward the truncated terraces. The Clyde Batchelor! The return of that beloved name to the river!"[26] *Steamboat Gothic* ends with Larry and Louise confidently facing their future, a rosy prospect they have earned by reaffirming the best parts of the past.

* * *

Love is Eternal explores the life of Abraham Lincoln through the eyes of his wife, Mary Todd Lincoln. In writing of such familiar figures, Irving Stone enjoys a ready-made plot so that, even though much of the action centers on domestic life, various historical events—the Freeport Debate with Frederick Douglas, the bombing of Fort Sumter, the drafting of the Gettysburg Address—are treated at length. *Love is Eternal* also illustrates the difficulties which beset a novelist writing of historical personages; indeed, for anyone familiar with Lincoln or his times, the novel's "lessons" will seem elementary. It is, therefore, in its supplying of his characters with needs and desires that Stone's novel should be judged. Unfortunately, the choice of Lincoln, probably the most revered of American presidents and a figure close to sainthood in popular thought, induces a tone of respect that turns *Love is Eternal* into sentimental bathos.

Since it is a melodramatic romance fleshed out in historical garb, Stone's novel has the Lincolns' married life as its fulcrum. Mary's feelings about love and marriage are expressed early and subsequently tested by the emotional and political conflicts that surround Abraham. In her youth Mary listens to the advice of John Ward, a teacher who never discourages her attempts to be as well-educated as her male peers. The kindly Ward believes life offers compensations, even though it seems to be denying the individual's fondest desires; and, when Mary asks what she can do as a woman in a society dominated by men, the wise old man urges: " 'Perhaps you will have to create your place in the world through a husband, or a son. Do not despise this approach...if it is all that is open to you.' ''[27] While such a speech represents obvious foreshadowing, the Doctor's prophetic words raise a major stumbling block in historical fiction: since the audience already knows what the characters' fates are to be, such prescience supplies the fictional narrative with a foreordained future that life seemingly never exhibits. Mrs. Lincoln, because of Abraham's selfless example, can return good for evil some of the time. This ability surfaces during the Civil War when, under scrutiny because of her Southern relations, she does volunteer work in local Washington Army hospitals. Mary's ministrations also come on the heels of her son William's death and at a time when she is being accused of burying herself in grief. A veteran doctor ironically notes: " 'So this is the woman the papers say shows excessive grief! Mrs. President, I wish more of our Washington ladies understood the nature of grief, these homesick boys would get well sooner.' ''[28]

It is Mary's lot in life, like that of her husband, to be misunderstood; and, while the dead leader becomes a martyr, his wife's better nature is seen only by a few, a critical impression that eventually causes Mrs. Lincoln to cave in emotionally. The death of William, the rumors about Abraham having loved another (the story of Ann Rutledge which appears, ironically, in a laudatory campaign biography), the pressures of the war, and her own jealous nature all conspire to push Mrs. Lincoln into depression and open hostility. After hearing of her dream that William has returned and stood at her bedside, Abraham gently urges that such a will to believe represents the first step to being institutionalized (significantly *Love is Eternal* ends in 1865 so that Mrs. Lincoln's mental breakdown is not presented). In a scene that foreshadows her later existence, the President's wife angrily berates a Mrs. Ord, who had ridden on an inspection tour before Richmond with the President when Mrs. Lincoln had been delayed. This ceremonial slight leads Mary to brush aside Mrs. Ord's solicitations: " 'You take my place! May I inform you, Mrs. Ord, that no one takes my place. In the future I'll thank you not to impersonate the wife of the President.' ''[29] Mrs. Lincoln's emotional problems underline a terrible irony—she is destroyed by the same elevated life she actively sought, while her husband, not goaded initially by such ambition, grows because of the same catastrophes.

Another aspect of Mary Lincoln is her conscious rationalizing about the type of man she must marry. Her desire for a man of intelligence who will be a fighter like Andrew Jackson or Henry Clay seems more than sufficient foreshadowing, yet Stone must add, "conventional good looks had never had any importance for her."[30] While Mary Todd Lincoln may have married a homely man, one doubts that she looked forward to the prospect, even as implicitly as Stone suggests. The predestined nature of the main characters crops up later when Lincoln gains the Republican Presidential nomination and returns to their Springfield home with the good news. He embraces Mary:

> And she relived their first embrace almost twenty years before. She had known then what she knew now, nor had it taken a hundred cannon or a hundred ringing bells to tell her. No one else had known about Abraham because no one else had loved him. Love had told her everything, with the end implicit in the beginning. She had fallen in love with the last man that any other woman wanted, for she had known him to be the first and finest of them all.[31]

Mary knows all this because she loves, so that that emotion is not only eternal but also prophetic.

Mary's foresight about Abraham fires her ambition to succeed in national politics. Mrs. Lincoln energetically serves as advisor and secretary to her husband for, as she realizes more clearly in time, Abraham must be in politics. Their marriage runs smoothest during crises when the pressure of work and consultation fuses them into a dynamic partnership. Mary even outreasons her lawyer husband occasionally at such times, as when she argues that they need a more respectable (i.e. more expensive) house in Springfield.

> "In twenty years we'll be living in a much finer house, in fact the finest in the land, and we'll not have to buy or even rent it: people will pay us to live in it!"
>
> Puzzled, he asked, "What house could that be?"
>
> She broke into a radiant smile.
>
> "The White House."
>
> He joined her laughter.
>
> "I assure you, Molly, my ambitions don't reach that high."
>
> "Really? Didn't you aspire to the United States Senate at the age of thirty? Being the debt-ridden, black-futured tyro you have portrayed yourself, why should you not aspire to the presidency as well? The White House over the Senate is a difference of degree rather than kind."
>
> He was amused but also flattered by her logic.[32]

While Mary's arithmetic is slightly conservative (the Lincolns make it to the White House in less than twenty years), her ambition clearly underscores the idea of marriage implied by the novel. She "completes" her husband by spurring his deepest ambitions and reassuring him that his goals are viable.

The melodramatic tenor of *Love is Eternal* is further served when Mary becomes First Lady only to discover that life at the top can be lonely and harrowing. Hannah Shearer, a long-time friend, comes to visit but, when Mrs. Lincoln asks her to live there permanently as a confidante, Mrs. Shearer wisely counsels:

"...Washington would resent you moving a whole family into the Executive Mansion. Only the president's family is supposed to live there. That's part of your job, Mary, to live alone amidst the crowds."

Mary stared out over the sea, her lips quivering.[33]

Stone's final line insures that no one will misunderstand how lonely his protagonist has become; however, since she accepts that she must live vicariously through and for her husband, Mary accepts her loneliness. She even endures a flood of critical press notices and vituperative letters because she submits to being guided by Abraham's sense of compassion.

Since Lincoln represents a legend as well as a historical figure, in presenting him a popular artist must use some of the familiar guises that folk memory has created around the sixteenth president. While he possessed a verbal style and wit that made him more cogent and humorous than other politicians, the circumstances of his death have caused hagiographers and lovers of tall stories to transform Lincoln into the spokesman for the common man and for democracy that he has become to succeeding generations. From Walt Whitman's poem, *When Lilacs Last in the Dooryard Bloom'd,* to John Ford's *Young Mr. Lincoln* (1939), American artists have celebrated Lincoln as the most monumental national leader. When a young James Stewart finds himself perplexed in *Mr. Smith Goes to Washington* (1938), Frank Capra's cinematic tribute to the power of individual decency and political idealism, he naturally gravitates to the Lincoln Memorial where the statue reduces him to awestruck silence and inspires him to go on fighting. It is this monumental image of Lincoln which Americans revere, and Stone does nothing to transform the sixteenth president into a more human figure. One is constantly beset in *Love is Eternal* with the sense that Lincoln "belongs to all the ages." In keeping with such reverence, Mary first sees Abraham when he drops out of the ceiling into a public meeting to quiet the objections of one political faction so that another may be heard; already in character as the protector of free speech, Lincoln takes on a symbolic heavenly cast through such a "descent." His personality as the spinner of tales and the "man of sorrow" emerges when John Logan, a cousin of Mary's, describes the future leader as: " 'a strange kind of fellow, gets under your skin. Just when you think he's in the grip of a hopeless melancholy and about to go into the woods and shoot himself, his face lights up and he'll tell you a yarn with such tremendous gusto that you just have to throw back your head and howl.' "[34] This verbal picture establishes the poles at which Lincoln operates for he becomes more interesting when depressed or telling a story.

Humorous anecdotes of Lincoln, which constitute a veritable cottage industry among Lincolnophiles, flesh out Stone's narrative. When, after asking her to dance by stating that he wishes to do so in a the "worst way," and then proceeding to step on her feet repeatedly, Mary retorts, " 'Mr. Lincoln, you have achieved your ambition.' "[35] When Lincoln attends an opponent's rally, he is nonplused to find it has become a religious meeting in which doubt is being cast on his personal faith. When Peter Cartwright solemnly asks Lincoln where he is going in terms of Heaven and Hell, Abraham convulses the audience by declaring, " 'I am going to Congress.' "[36] In presenting Lincoln as a lover, Stone becomes awkward because, as a monument and a dichotomous personality, the future president appears, like the all-too-familiar Hollywood cowboy, befuddled by passion. While the Lincolns are never shown in more than an affectionate embrace, Stone resorts to symbolism to express Abraham's burgeoning love. He wins a local contest, in which an individual must lift two axes and hold them steadily at arm's length. This exhibition of muscle and discipline causes Mary to feel appropriately faint, but that is as close to a sex scene as the novel ever comes. The interests of the audience are more cogently served when Stone treats of the year-and-a-half separation of Mary and Abraham. This term of trial, which arises because Mary is so anxious for marriage that she rushes Lincoln into a premature engagement party on New Year's Eve in 1841, begins when he fails to appear at that celebration and then goes on because of Abraham's guilt. During her ordeal, in which she must exhibit the characteristic feminine ethic and wait patiently until her man returns, Mary suffers from numerous psychosomatic illnesses. Of course, her agonies are not in vain for Lincoln returns, and so the audience's desire to believe that a good woman gains her ends through private suffering and public patience is reaffirmed.

As troubles mount within the nation and his family, Lincoln becomes ever more magnanimous toward enemies and critics. He embodies Christian idealism, constantly turning the other cheek as it were, and preaching that one must ignore his opponents. While one wonders how such a pacific portrait can be reconciled with the politician who directed two national campaigns and the war manager who put large areas of the Union under martial law, Stone does nothing to moderate this familiar iconography. When Mary complains that the newspapers write about her undue influence, Abraham sagely counsels:

"Mary, if we were to try to read, much less answer, all the attacks made on us, this shop might as well close for any other business. Let's do the very best we know how, the very best we can; and keep doing so until the end. If the end brings us out all right. what is said against us won't amount to anything. If the end brings us out wrong, ten angels swearing we were right will make no difference."[37]

Lincoln, the philosopher in office, shrugs off critics by appealing to history for ultimate vindication. The character's apotheosis takes place shortly before the fatal evening in Ford's Theatre, so that the familiar thesis that Lincoln could have bound up the nation's wounds had he lived can be suggested. It is at such a juncture, where legend and history meet, that *Love is Eternal* takes the conventional turning, for what might intrigue the student of history would probably disconcert the popular audience. Lincoln's saintliness looms larger and larger until Mary, who has been gloating over her husband's re-election, recognizes it openly.

"Perhaps I have too little personal resentment, but I never thought it paid. A man has no time to spend half his life in quarrels. If any man cease to attack me I never remember the past against him. The same goes for the south: we must give them a friendly and helpful peace, so that they can get back on their feet as quickly as possible."

Mary reached up her arms to him in a jubilant victory embrace.

"It's all clear to me now, Abraham: you be the saint in the family, I'll be the prophet."[38]

In an America which had experienced the most deeply destructive war of modern times (before the twentieth century) Lincoln's magnanimity seems wishful thinking for a work-a-day politician.

Criticizing Stone's work on historical and political grounds obscures its central intention of presenting the pathos of Mary Todd Lincoln's life. Mrs. Lincoln suffers the same emotional disappointments and trials in love that one associates with other melancholy ladies from Samuel Richardson's Pamela to the latest heroine of Harold Robbins. Mary's ethical fiber emerges early when, after turning down Sandy McDonald's marriage proposal, she disagrees with her stepmother about this rejection.

"Frankly, I'm disappointed. Sandy comes from such a fine family."

"You wouldn't have me marry a man I didn't love?"

"There is such a thing as closing your mind to love."

"How does one do that?"

"By insisting upon remaining a schoolgirl. Are you sure you're not waiting for a knight in shining armor?"

"I don't think I'm a foolish romantic. It's just that I'm in no hurry. Need I be?"[39]

Mary's refusal dramatizes her innate dislike of slavery, since Sandy is the son of Mississippi plantation owners. Mary lives for the right man rather than for the first likeable one who comes along. Her faith is rewarded by Abraham who ultimately proves true to the inscription—"love is eternal"—that he has engraved on her wedding ring. Mary's feelings occupy considerable space, particularly her bouts of jealousy which imply that she must worry while her husband can safely ignore the possibility of wandering on her part. Naturally, Mary is relieved when Abraham, after considering himself washed up politically, rises in ire at Stephen Douglas' assault on the Missouri Compromise in 1854, for she knows that her husband's drive will bring them closer together.

Their love blossomed, deep and strong on understanding. Their loves had been compounded of a common faith in accomplishment; without it their relationship had lacked spiritual succor. Now that she was again a full participant he shared with her the slow painful process of his growth.[40]

The bourgeois emphasis on accomplishment drives them both; unhappily, while such ambition makes them less legendary and more human, Stone only implies and never develops this aspect of the Lincolns.

Lincoln's death only re-emphasizes the emotionally sacrificial nature of Mary's personality; indeed, the nadir of her romantic life occurs in the early 1850s when Abraham, depressed by his all-too-brief career in the House of Representatives and seemingly resigned to being a circuit-riding lawyer, grows distant.

> She cried to herself, Why? Our failure has not been that great! Our end in not in sight! We have committed no unpardonable crime!
>
> She ached as she had during the twenty months after Abraham had abandoned her. Now she had a husband, two children, a home, but her suffering was more intense, the failure cut deeper, the impending tragedy loomed greater. Then she had been a young girl, in danger of losing her love. Now she was committed. Should she lose the love of her husband she was doomed to a fragmentary existence.[41]

Since melodrama requires its characters to suffer continuously "deeper" torments, each crisis is the "greatest" until its inevitable replacement by another. For the logically minded such extreme situations and overstated diction become tiresome; yet these techniques remain essential for any author trying to satisfy a large audience in this mode. Mary's crisis can only be solved when Abraham admits he has lacked affection, a confession that justifies Mary's being uxorious. Of course, Abraham's remorse really signals a call for love: " 'Try to understand me, Mary: it's only when I come home that I realize I've been a failure. That's when I feel I would rather be any place in the world than here.' "[42] This potentially devastating remark is quickly subsumed by a rising tide of feeling in a reaffirmation scene between the united lovers.

Stone uses the Lincoln children to deepen the pathos; indeed, Tad, who remains childish, becomes a prominent source of consolation in the novel's closing pages. When Mary loses a son while in the White House, her grief makes Abraham doubt his course in regard to the South.

> "It's not only Willie, it's all those other boys on the battlefields...Bull Run, Ball's Bluff, others to come...dying so senselessly, so needlessly. Mary, do you think if we had stayed home in Springfield, if Stephen Douglas had moved into the White House, there would be none of us parents losing our sons...?"[43]

Lincoln recalls Mary to herself by his remark, for he obviously needs consolation as much as she does. The status that children hold in middle-class thinking also underscores Lincoln's despair, for he must justify the deaths of thousands of children in the name of a higher cause to parents as morose as Mary. When she is about to break down completely after Abraham's assassination—a scene in which her sobbing is interrupted by Secretary Stanton's assuming control of the funeral arrangements—Tad pathetically urges: " 'Don't cry, Mama, or you will break my heart.' "[44]

Mary thus finds reason to go on and, despite several weeks of disorientation (a "trial" that becomes a cause for gossip since Andrew

Johnson and his wife want to occupy the White House), emerges with a melancholy triumph. There is a further poignance in Tad's reaction to an interview between Mary and the guard who neglected the Lincolns' box on the night of the shooting. When Mary dismisses this browbeaten figure by urging: " 'It's not you I can't forgive, it's the assassin,' " Tad reminds everyone of the legendary figure who has been lost: " 'If Pa had lived...he would have forgiven the man who shot him. Pa forgave everybody.' "[45] In his childish way Tad discerns Lincoln's real importance (he is the first convert to the legend, as it were) and so understands what has been lost. The elder son, Robert, in being critical of his mother's grief, does not comfort or support Mary. He is moved by decorum rather than pity and accompanies Abraham's body to Springfield because the emotional Mary cannot.

Tad, on the other hand, illustrates the popular belief that wisdom comes out of the mouths of, if not babes, at least slightly retarded children. He unwittingly characterizes Lincoln as the ideal Christian, a religion which seeks converts who are "as children." Love is Eternal's melodramatic conclusion shows Mary and Tad going off into the sunset as the custodians of the Lincoln legend.

> She raised her left hand, slipped the wedding ring off her finger. Slowly out of the blindness and the unseeing, the well-worn words of the inscription came forth to her, standing clear and strong, the living and ultimate truth:

> LOVE IS ETERNAL

> This, then, was what she had left: her love for Abraham. His love for her.
> She took Tad's hand in hers. Together, they went down the steps.[46]

Mary has found a reason to live; indeed, her feelings for Abraham symbolize a bond that goes beyond the grave. Love has provided her with a past, a present and a future.

* * *

The Winthrop Woman utilizes journey and generational motifs while presenting the life of Elizabeth Fones Winthrop Hallet. Anya Seton's central character must endure the death of her first husband, the mental breakdown of her second and the disgrace of her third, as well as a rejection by the first man she loves. And, if such romantic vicissitudes were not enough, Elizabeth must also suffer the censure of a Puritan community, the trials of life in an unsettled new world, and the deaths of friends. The principal character remains "in" but not "of" the society in which she finds herself, and her transitional personality enables Seton to show past conflicts more dramatically than history does. By incorporating a plot in which characters grow up, replenish the population, and die in their turn, The Winthrop Woman justifies its leisurely pace. Elizabeth's quest for true love occurs against a panoply of supporting characters and pages of historical narrative which summarize events and trends to enable readers to feel somewhat familiar with the novel's era. Seton also uses real people as characters (e.g. John Winthrop); fortunately, *The Winthrop Woman* treats a remote enough period so that the author can be fairly inventive in such characterizations.

In a period marked by the Thirty Years War, the flight of the Pilgrims to the New World, and the beheading of Charles I, Elizabeth's religious skepticism seems improbable. At the Winthrop family prayer: "Even to Jack she dared not admit how prayers and sermons bored her, and that in the fastness of her heart there was a void of disbelief, or rather a secret certainty that there was nothing in the world or out of it to sustain her but herself."[47] Although Seton is providing a basis for Elizabeth's later dramatic reawakening, and while the protagonist's disenchantment has an immediate cause in a beating she receives from her uncle, John Winthrop, the main character seems to have wandered out of the historical context here. One might accept Elizabeth sounding like a forerunner of Franklin and Voltaire, but not of Nietzsche and Camus. Her loss of faith, at a time when religious affiliation virtually defined an individual's political and social status, becomes too extreme when it lapses into "boredom" for in such circumstances fear would seem a more likely reaction. Thus, Elizabeth's feelings are too radical and too close to the surface: to exist even in the alienated way she does, Elizabeth would have to sublimate her religious instincts more than she does.

The courtesan Mirabelle, whom Elizabeth meets while crossing the Atlantic, presents another case of twentieth-century feelings parading in seventeenth-century dress. While her libertine attitudes about lovemaking might accord with her profession (although one wonders, given the birth control and sanitation measures that existed in the first half of the seventeenth century), Mirabelle's openly sensuous nature, especially in a ship full of Puritans, seems improbable: " 'My father was a marquis, and considered chastity vulgar. True, I was born on the wrong side of the blanket, as you say, but no matter. I inherit the trait. Love-making is agreeable. Why not enjoy it?' "[48] Mirabelle sounds like a character from the 1920s rather than the 1620s. Even Cousin Jack, who never gets beyond flirting with Elizabeth because of being John Winthrop's son, emerges as anachronistic later. When he learns that Elizabeth and Will Hallet, her last husband and the man she truly loves, are not legally married, Jack offers the judgment of a historian rather than the opinion of a Puritan. He tells his own critical wife: " 'I must remind you that there are many societies and periods of history when the Hallets' conduct would not be shameful, when indeed their fretted love and loyalty to each other might rather be thought brave and praiseworthy.' "[49] The character's words sound reasonable, yet such dispassionate relativism belies his religious background. Since one doubts both the character's verisimilitude and his intelligence, the entire fabric of the novel is tattered as a result.

The Winthrop Woman portrays the Pilgrims as harsh individuals whose religious austerity created a living Hell for those who doubted even slightly. Elizabeth suffers because she thinks for herself, and subconsciously seeks for a more merciful Jesus than her Puritan relatives are willing to recognize.

When John Winthrop whips Elizabeth because she appears lax at prayers, the sadistic impulse behind such treatment comes dramatically to the surface. Elizabeth is constantly restored by a feather (tickling) and wine so that she will be conscious of her punishment; when she is forced to kiss the rod that flayed her, she vomits and Winthrop appears content to let her wallow in her own filth. This lack of compassion causes Adam, John's father, to enunciate the novel's religious theme by urging: " 'Before God I liked the old ways best when there was more talk of love and merriment and less of the Devil and groanings of sin.' "[50] The repressive outlook of these Puritans extends to sex so that John Winthrop's desire to beat and humiliate Elizabeth suggests that subconsciously he lusts for her. When the marriage between Harry Winthrop and Elizabeth is agreed to by John Winthrop, the older man remembers his sister, Elizabeth's mother: "He glanced once at Elizabeth, seeing there briefly the image of her mother and not the flaunting carnal beauty which always infuriated him."[51] Thus, Winthrop represses his natural instincts, always a dangerous thing to do according to psychologists. Meeting Anne Hutchinson in Massachusetts reinforces Elizabeth's more compassionate perception of God and her fellow men; indeed, the older woman's conduct when exiled by the Puritan leadership inspires the protagonist and her second husband, Robert Feake, when things become too repressive for them in Massachusetts.

In a bit of obvious symbolism, Feake feels guilty because of a crime he committed in England, but then finds himself emotionally and physically healthy after he and Elizabeth flee from the Bay Colony: "He was no longer seasick, and indeed felt better than he had in years. As each day brought them further west, he took more interest in their journey and the coastline that they glimpsed at intervals."[52] In going to Connecticut with Feake, Elizabeth enters the second stage in her emotional journey away from the Puritans and their repression. By going west and subsequently south with Will Hallet to New Netherland, the protagonist moves literally and figuratively away from a God of judgment to a God of love and forgiveness. Her life constitutes an odyssey in which she moves from England, where her father was a failure and she became the unwanted ward of the Winthrops, to Massachusetts and Connecticut, where she is a transient, and finally to New York, where she feels genuinely at home. When the Hallets lose their property in New Netherland because their marriage is not legal in the eyes of the new English rulers, Seton's heroine understands that "home" is a state of mind only attained when the individual makes peace with God. Despite their personal losses, the Hallets remain optimistic because Elizabeth can say: " 'I've found at last that Religion is not melancholy. The Spirit of God is not a dampe.' "[53] Her articulation of this gentle vision of God represents the intellectual climax of *The Winthrop Woman*; significantly, this passage occurs after Elizabeth has found true love so that the spiritual life is given primacy over the romantic one.

As the central character in a woman's novel, Elizabeth spends considerable time and energy on affairs of the heart. She must adjust to indifference from Jack, the sudden death of Harry, the physical and mental weakness of Feake (who finally deserts her), and the bigamy of her union with Hallet. Elizabeth ultimately triumphs because her faith in love's redemptive power never abates. Her first marriage with Harry Winthrop initiates Elizabeth into physical intimacy rather than any genuine bonding of souls; indeed, her young husband prefers bravado to making her the be-all of existence. This distinction between love and passion underlines an intimate encounter between them. If anything, Seton is more discrete and oblique (although every bit as euphemistic) as her bestselling colleagues in such a scene: " 'Harry, Harry —she whispered falling back on the pillows. 'When we are like this, together, and I forget everything but you—' He laughed low in his throat, and she shut her eyes, abandoning herself to pleasure so keen that it was indistinguishable from love."[54] Even though Harry has fondled her breasts before this outburst, there is no sense of sexual duration such as Metalious implies in *Peyton Place*: indeed, a thoroughly Hollywood treatment, in which the lovers are roused (after an indefinite interval) from their encounter in the next paragraph, predominates. Thus, with her lusty husband Elizabeth discovers that physical passion alone does not constitute love—a "lesson" women have been trying to teach men at least since recorded times, and presumably a value that most readers of *The Winthrop Woman* would endorse.

The ideal lover must be more solicitous; indeed, Will Hallet feels torn between his physical desires and his wish to see Elizabeth happy: "He did want Elizabeth, without discovering any logic in it. More remarkably, however, he also wanted her happiness above his own, which seemed to produce a painful state of deadlock quite contrary to all pious teaching."[55] Hallet's quandary epitomizes a feminine notion of love, for he will gladly sacrifice himself for a beloved who, in turn, will do the same; in such a blissful scheme, the happy couple always possesses more emotional capital than they can expend. Elizabeth manifests her bliss by reflecting, after she has married Will, that daydreams no longer attract her: "Her garden and her children—and Will's arms at night-sufficed. She wanted to think of nothing else."[56] As an expression of feminine psychology, Elizabeth's contentment reflects a desire to lose oneself: she has reached a romantic haven in which life has contracted to the limits of home, children and husband. Will Hallet remains the essential daydream hero of women's fiction and soap opera, governed by the same self-obliterating temperament one finds in hard-core pornography. When Elizabeth achieves her final peace with God, Will embraces her yet refrains from going further: "He felt a stirring of passion, and the desire to kiss her, but he did not. The closeness between them was too sweet for interruption."[57] Will conveniently feels awestruck before her spiritual conversion. Such soaring emotion dwarfs physical passion and, by being passive, Hallet recognizes Elizabeth's individual rights and feelings as comparable to his own.

In keeping with the novel's length, the main character not only survives but prospers because she endures anything that man can do. When Martha, John Winthrop's second wife who was borne the rigors of Massachusetts and numerous pregnancies, lies dying, she draws the distinction between her personality and Elizabeth's: " 'I am made of cobweb that tears at a touch. But you, Bess, have fiber like the great seines that seldom break no matter their burden, if they do they can be mended again and again.' "[58]

By such imagery, Seton establishes that endurance leads to growth of character and the discovery of happiness, an association of values beguiling to the popular audience which wants desperately to believe that life's vagaries contain a meaning. In her struggles Elizabeth demonstrates the familiar American drive to better oneself through individual effort. As the Hallets face the loss of their home, Will dismisses Elizabeth's suggestion that she lacks the courage to start over: " 'Oh yes, you have.' He took her by the shoulders and looked at her searchingly. 'You've got endurance and courage beyond the reach of most, as who knows better than I' "[59] Thus, Elizabeth's staying power is more life-enhancing than the qualities of many figures whom history regards as notable. By being a better person than John Winthrop, who judged her, Elizabeth demonstrates that domestic life is civilization's real achievement. Seton implies that public events are what men do to protect their homes and families, the places where truly significant actions take place.

Will Hallet foreshadows the future because he constantly struggles to be a free man on his own land; and in his willingness to start over, Hallet echoes the celebrated American desire to seek new frontiers. This urge to be free from the constricting rules of society is evident in Hallet even when he initially comes to America as an indentured servant. Seton provides Will with a yeoman's social standing and an aristocrat's education, a situation which reflects a loss in prestige due to shifting fortune; however, Hallet uses this normally debilitating reversal to become a better judge of himself and others: "The inborn shrewdness of the English yeoman had in Will Hallet, through the accident of his aristocratic rearing, ripened to a sophistication which his recent years of total independence had matured. People's foibles and motives often amused him, and for his age he was an acute observer."[60] On the voyage to Massachusetts, Hallet rescues a drowning girl and earns Elizabeth's gratitude. The protagonist is stunned when Hallet refuses a reward and corrects Elizabeth by deriding her reaction: " 'I wouldn't take money for a thing like that.' He spoke with anger. 'You're like all the gentry, think you can buy a man body and soul for silver. I'll make my own way and work for what I earn.' "[61] As a foreshadowing of American virtues, Hallet stresses hard work and implies the necessity for abandoning the older society of rank and privilege.

The protagonist's desire to be free of any obligations to John Winthrop, a situation that worsens in Massachusetts because of Harry's death, makes her spiritually akin to Hallet long before they become lovers. They move willingly into new and dangerous circumstances because they have each other and value individual freedom above security. In their persecution and wanderings Will and Elizabeth come to embody that idealism which motivated the original Pilgrims and, by implication, the later colonists turned rebels who would launch the United States. In New Netherland, Hallet voices their belief in freedom when he philosophizes: " 'But in any case, of this I'm certain, Bess: Every human being should have the liberty to worship—or not—exactly how he pleases, which has always been the virtue of the Dutch.' "[62] Thus, Seton's happy couple arrive at the temperament which forged the Declaration of Independence and the Constitution approximately one hundred and fifty years later. Ironically, Hallet exhibits a better understanding of democratic principles than many in the popular audience normally do, for he recognizes that freedom includes the right not to participate. The various societies through which he and Elizabeth journey cannot assimilate them because such bodies exhibit an eternal human reluctance to accept anyone who insists on being different.

* * *

The Best of Everything chronicles the successful and unsuccessful love affairs of five New York career girls. Rona Jaffe's characters run the gamut from wide-eyed country girl seeking a permanent position at Fabian Publications to a plain Jane city type saving to get married in style and settle into a permanent domesticity. While Mary Agnes, whose only worry is gathering a trousseau and seeing that her wedding comes off smoothly, is the least interesting character, Jaffe's other principals undergo the dilemma of "he loves me, he loves me not" pretty steadily. Caroline Bender, who wants to be an editor, gets her career wish but loses the man she loves not once but twice; April Morrison loves a rich cad not wisely but too well only to wind up blissfully married to an old beau; Gregg Adams, an aspiring actress, becomes the mistress of a famous producer and commits suicide when he abandons her; Barbara Lemont, a bitter divorcee, finally meets Mr. Right and experiences the ecstasy of reciprocated love. These situations allow Jaffe to expose the "man problem" and to suggest what the good girl must do to survive in the emotional battleground between the sexes. While Helen Gurley Brown would standardize such information in *Sex and the Single Girl* (1962), Jaffe's novel characteristically expresses how such a subject was perceived in the later 1950s when sexual advice had to be sugarcoated by a fictional framework which kept the emphasis on love rather than sex. A persistent belief in the search for the "one and only" marks Jaffe's heroines; for them physical intimacy cannot be separated from this quest which, it is assumed, invariably brings happiness.

Only Caroline questions the equation of marriage with happiness, and even her doubts never leave a rhetorical level, for her conduct supports the premise to the nth degree. At the end of the novel, after she has refused to be Eddie Harris' mistress (and thus "lost" him for the second time), Caroline flies to Las Vegas with a gambler-playboy, Johnnie Cassaro, a client who doesn't bore her quite as much as the other men in her life. Jaffe concludes *The Best of Everything* by having a picture of Caroline and Cassaro appear on the front pages of America's newspapers so that the hypocritical Eddie, on his way back to his wife, can ironically feel lucky because he has been jilted by such a "loose" woman. Jaffe's final scene reaffirms that men are in control, and that women, who only want

monogamy, will never be understood by their "masters." Mary Agnes, who
knows the sordid details about everyone in the office, tells Caroline about
Mike Rice, an editor with whom Miss Bender has a brief, all-but-
consummated affair. When Caroline cannot believe that Mike has a ten-
year-old, Mary Agnes asks:

> "How old d'you think he is?"
> "About forty-eight, I would guess."
> "He's *thirty-eight*. He looks that way because he leads such an unhealthy life.... If
> he was married and lived with his wife and children he wouldn't look that way."
> "Marriage solves everything?" Caroline asked.
> "What a funny thing to say."
> "Why it it funny?"
> "Well..." Mary Agnes said, "there are only two ways to live, the right way and the
> wrong way... If you get married it doesn't mean positively you're going to be happy, but
> if you get married and walk out on it then you *can't* be happy."[63]

Mike Rice, a divorcee, must lead an unhappy life because he has deserted
his responsibilities. While Caroline doubts Mary Agnes' either/or vision,
she comes to learn that Mike prefers being a spectator to being a participant,
a tendency that accords with his heavy drinking and his editorial cynicism.

Caroline is the only female character who doesn't unquestioningly
subscribe to the marriage equals children equals contentment complex of
values; she even tells another girl who wants to fix her up with a blind
date that she will work after marriage because she wants a career and not
simply a job. Mary Agnes consistently symbolizes the opposite extreme,
for her work has been a means to obtain a big wedding and its psychological
benefits. Because her goals are clear-cut (and because she is homely), Mary
Agnes finally experiences that one day when:

> ...there would be one star and many admirers, even if it was only for a few hours...
> Caroline remembered an ad she had read in a newspaper one night with a picture of a bride
> in it and the headline: "GIVE HER A WEDDING SHE'LL REMEMBER ALL HER LIFE."
> That's what Mary Agnes had been given display and applause and all.... For twenty-two
> years Mary Agnes had been a plain, thin, flat-chested little girl, and for this one evening,
> the culmination of all her dreams and plans, she had been a radiant beauty. She would
> remember it all the rest of her life.[64]

The wedding represents the perfect day for the bride, the time at which
her real life begins; and, while still held in awe by most, this rite of passage
is probably no longer a woman's only goal.

Barbara Lemont, barely surviving emotionally with a young child and
an aging mother, makes the most thorough plunge into love, for as someone
who has been "burned" she can judge what is "real" and what is not.
Barbara takes solace from parent-child love yet knows, "None of them is
the same in any way as love for a man who loves you too."[65] Barbara
is clearly looking for a soulmate whose passion will equal hers. Such a
quest, which implies star-crossed lovers like Tristan and Isolde or the Flying
Dutchman and Senta, guides millions of lives, although it seems patently
illogical. While such an illusion may sustain civilized society, Jaffe's

characters only demonstrate their values at the more mundane level of immediate emotional comfort. When Barbara falls in love with Sidney Carter even sex takes on a more vibrant quality because it has been amalgamated with romance: she "had never felt this physical pleasure before, to such a degree, and she realized that it was love that made the difference."[66] Thus, although Barbara enjoyed sex with her first husband, all barriers come tumbling down with Sidney for whom her feelings are deeper. Clearly, romantic passion and physical satisfaction are equated so that waiting for the right man not only sustains one's idealistic views but also leads to concrete sexual gains as well.

Gregg Adams, who precedes Caroline as secretary to the tyrannical Amanda Farrow, is the saddest of Jaffe's girls. Gregg wants to be an actress until she meets David Wilder Savage (whose very name should put her on guard), a Broadway producer. When he makes love to her, Gregg assumes that marriage is around the corner; however David, who has apparently enjoyed a homosexual liaison with a dead playwright and produced his friend's last work to "flop" notices, is on the rebound and soon tires of the girl. Gregg's possessiveness leads him to dismiss her love as ownership. He refuses to be Gregg's master-husband and to provide meaning for her life: " 'You ask me if I love you and what you really mean is will I devour you, envelope you, obliterate life for you and worse, will I allow you to do that to me. That's why I never answer you, because I do love you, but not in the way you want, and I never will.' "[67] Savage's steadfast refusal to provide an identify for Gregg drives her to insanity and death. The thwarted girl even searches through her lover's bureaus to satisfy her curiosity; and, when he catches her, David empties the drawers and then orders her out of his life. Gregg then begins haunting the stairwells of Savage's apartment building and rummaging through garbage cans for clues about what he is doing. Finally, she is confronted in the hall by a drunken neighbor and, in a panic, backs out of an open window to her death. Gregg epitomizes the lovestruck girl who must make life conform to her preconceptions.

Clothes are a veritable obsession with Jaffe's characters, for in the sexual arena apparel reveals social status and taste. Buying a new outfit can provide a therapy to overcome life's traumas, and constant attention to personal appearance necessarily precedes impressing the right people and getting the man of one's dreams. All of this emphasis may disconcert anyone who feels clothes are less important than personality, however as a social observer, Jaffe is perspicacious. Indeed, she catches the flavor of her characters' lives by showing their concern about outward appearance. In a typical situation, Caroline avoids embarrassment by convincing April not to go to Sardi's, even though Caroline has asked April to pick a restaurant.

Caroline looked at April. She was wearing that shiny baby-blue gabardine suit again, and tonight because she was going out she was wearing a hat, a dreadful little white felt hat that made her look like Sunday Morning in East Cozyville. Caroline felt a pang of self-consciousness at the thought of being seen with her at a good restaurant. It was bad enough to go there without dates, but with April in that outfit, with that hair... "Hey," Caroline said, "I'll bet you've never been to the Automat."[68]

Clothes are a necessary burden, a badge of propriety, until one finds the right man; then, getting dressed becomes an act of love transfigured by a desire to please. Caroline experiences such rapture when Eddie, who broke their engagement when he went to Europe after his senior year, visits New York. Their reignited passion, which leads (at last!) to Caroline's losing her virginity, features all the excesses—nightly dates, unending bouquets, idealistic talks—that are popularly associated with romance; and Caroline naturally discovers "how different it was to try to make herself look beautiful for someone she loved, it was more fun than almost anything."[69] Such impressionistic language accords with the character's age and background. She uses "fun" and "almost anything" because to think in more precise terms would be to spend time and concentration on something besides Eddie.

Jaffe's girls gravitate to first loves for, although they may be involved with men they do not love (in order to go to Sardi's, if nothing else), the "one and only" is always special. April falls in love with Dexter Key, the reprehensible son of a rich and doting mother, and suffers because he promises marriage only to slowly back out after impregnating her and forcing her to have an abortion. Dexter is more heinous than Savage, who could plead the theatre and homosexuality—popularly linked entities— as causes for his treatment of Gregg. Dexter uses April and then discards her for, in *The Best of Everything*, the possibility that a woman might use a man for physical gratification is sternly eschewed. April recovers and gets engaged to Ronnie (whom Caroline notes is "normal"); indeed, as she prepares to leave New York for a life "back home" with him, April confesses to Caroline (a) that she and Ronnie have not been intimate— a sure sign that he is cut from different cloth than Dexter—and (b) that she met Dexter recently (appropriately enough looking for ties in Brooks Brothers) and, while he could probably still get her back, April realizes that what she has with Ronnie is different and better. Her confession prompts April to reflect on the power of first love.

> "It's funny, I was thinking on Saturday how unfair it is that every girl's first love can't be the one who'll turn out to be right for her. Sometimes he's the worst person in the world. But there's always something about your first love—if you're old enough, I don't mean sixteen— that you can't forget. It's like suddenly, for the first time, everthing's important because you're doing it for him."[70]

Ironically, Caroline, who always appears sophisticated and "mature," lacks April's insight so that their earlier scene about going to Sardi's is balanced.

When Eddie returns, Caroline goes through the same trials that April does with Dexter; however, her situation is complicated because her lover is a husband and a father. The malevolent dream world Caroline and Eddie inhabit is implied by their conversation about erasing the past and starting over.

"Let's run away," he murmured. "Let's run away somewhere. I don't know where."
"Where?"
"Back to four years ago. Do you think we can do that? Make everything else disappear?"
"If we really try...."[71]

This daydream, which attempts to obliterate time, represents a refusal to face one's own maturity: Jaffe's lovers are hopelessly naive in wishing to undo what cannot be undone. It comes as no surprise that Eddie, in flight from reality, should want Caroline gives as a mistress rather than a wife. After Caroline gives herself to him as the ultimate expression of her love, she is awestruck because she seems to be succeeding in making her first love permanent.

I'm glad I waited for Eddie, Caroline thought... Eddie was my only lover, and he always will be. With Eddie it was different, there was no thought of pain or of fear, but only love and closeness. She could never have believed that something so important as sleeping with someone could be so natural. There was no word to described it except Love, "sleeping with" sounded so foolish.[72]

Her final semantic distinction unwittingly reveals what has happened and, when she spurns Eddie to flee with Cassaro, one sees that Caroline's loss of idealism will be similar to April's, who "slept around" after Dexter left her. Thus, although love and sexuality are linked, three of Jaffe's heroines suffer in relationships in which they offer physical consolations before marriage: the right man, it would seem, will wait until the knot is tied.

Men are accorded sexual expertise because of their gender, and the double standard is implicit in the characters' speech and actions. In an early conversation, Caroline and April voice their own sexual innocence and their belief in male expertise.

"I guess this sounds awfully naive.... But when I try to picture going to bed with somebody I can never figure out where the sheet and blankets go. Do you do it underneath the blanket, or do you take the blanket off?"
Caroline couldn't help laughing. "Didn't you ever neck on a bed with somebody?"
"My heavens, no. Not on a bed."
"Well, when the time comes, whoever he is, *he'll* know what to do about the blanket."[73]

Such flattering of the male psyche by attributing wisdom where it often did not exist (if one is to believe Kinsey), makes Jaffe's women more approachable than the sexually demanding females of Spillane and Metalious. Mary Agnes is uneasy about her wedding night, but only for a moment since she is convinced that her husband will naturally guide her in the mysteries of the bedroom. For Mary Agnes sex, after a while, will get "to be just as ordinary as going to sleep at night."[74] While readers may not envy her husband, Mary Agnes diffuses the anxieties of sex as best she can. The plain girl shares the double standard mentality of the other characters; indeed, Mary Agnes would echo Caroline's early perception of Eddie. When they are engaged at college, she "was quite sure that she loved him more than he loved her, but he was a man, after all, and men had other things to worry about."[75] Although Caroline is unhappy at the

novel's end—life on the rebound, by definition, doesn't bring happiness—
her refusal of Eddie represents a fledgling attempt to break out of a male-
dominated world. She no longer excuses Eddie's conduct because men have
some natural right to be less attentive: as a career woman, Caroline has
learned some of those supposed distractions and now seeks a man who
can reciprocate her feelings.

Virginity represents the female corollary of the double standard
mentality: in the minds of the main characters it is the treasure to be bestowed
on the first (hopefully true) love. This anxiety over innocence reflects
concerns that seem dated now when "serial monogamy" has supposedly
replaced "true love." Caroline and April continuously speak for what is
proper, and in a late night coffee klatsch they feel intimate so Caroline
confesses:

> "Boys are funny. They seem to think that girls who have been married before can't live
> without sex. I wonder if it's true. Do you think so?"
> "I wonder too..." April said... "Are you a virgin?"
> "I must admit I am. Are you?"
> "Oh sure. What do you mean 'admit'? None of the girls back home will admit they
> aren't—if they aren't, which I don't know."[76]

For Caroline virginity constitutes the last symbol of idealism about love
and life rather than a prize to be hoarded and protected; thus, she is, again,
just slightly ahead of her time. During her brief liaison with Mike Rice,
Caroline hears a more sobering view of female sexuality; indeed, she is
compromised both physically and intellectually by the older man. Their
attempt at lovemaking fails because Mike, in effect, prefers a half-drunken,
guilt-ridden existence to starting over with someone new. Although he does
slightly penetrate Caroline, so that her virginity (on which she later
congratulates herself when thinking about Eddie) is slightly battered if
not broken, Rice plants a more important seed when he offers Caroline
his own interpretation of women. When the girl mentions meeting David
Wilder Savage, Rice asks:

> "Would you like to sleep with him?" Mike asked calmly and curiously.
> "Mike! I don't think about men I meet *that* way."
> "Why not?"
> "Well, girls don't."
> "Of course they do," Mike said, finishing what was his eighth or ninth drink. "Women
> have exactly the same feelings as men do, if they'd only admit it to themselves."[77]

While Mike's capacity for alcohol seems staggering, his plain speaking
represents an honesty which Caroline starts to practice at the novel's end.

The same candor marks Rice's references to another unmentionable
subject—masturbation. He persuades Caroline that their affair should be
conducted in their minds (and not in their bedrooms) and the girl finally
takes comfort in conjuring up his image as she goes to sleep. However,
Caroline realizes that Mike probably has more physical feelings and asks
him how he assuages these stronger impulses.

When he told her what he did about it she was appalled.

"Why?" he asked.

"But that's so...that's for children. Little boys. Adolescents..."

"Caroline, when will you learn that nothing two people do when they love each other is wrong?"

"That's just it; it isn't two people, it's you by yourself. It's dreadful. It's so isolated."[78]

While Mike offers an elaborate defense of such conduct, his Achilles heel has been displayed and his subsequent failure at the real thing with Caroline foreshadowed. Mike has created a dream world that no living woman could inhabit, so it is perhaps only natural that he prefer that ideal place. If nothing else, the character demonstrates that masturbation, while no longer connected with madness and hairy palms, was still behavior for peculiar people.

Other sexual activities that are exploited in *The Best of Everything* include voyeurism and breast size. Gregg, in her frenzy to possess Savage even after he has acquired a new mistress, longs for a means to see his apartment.

She would forgive him anything, as long as he was only using that girl's body and did not love her. She wondered whether there was a way to find out these things as well, whether there would be a way to see what went on inside that apartment instead of only to hear.[79]

Gregg satisfies her masochism by listening to muffled noises coming from Savage's apartment and bedroom; however, what is wish with her had become act in the more "daring" *Peyton Place*. Another characteristic sexual anxiety particularly prevalent in the 1950s emerges when Caroline and Mike begin their attempt at lovemaking. Before she experiences his shortcomings at entry, Caroline disrobes and asks a touchy questions: " 'You don't think I'm flat chested?' " Rice suavely assures " 'You have just enough.' "[80] Thus, while Caroline's fears are soothed, no real compliment has been paid and Mike remains something of a wit. Although his response is a "make out" line every young man should possess, Mike's detachment shows he is not convulsively in love with Caroline.

Jaffe's principal characters believe that intercourse represents the acme of love, for it is that time a woman experiences enormous new physical sensations, provided she is with the right man. Caroline revels in her intimacy with Eddie not simply because it brings them emotionally close but also because "there was another pleasure, the physical one, almost unbearable because her heart was so full of love for him."[81] While Caroline's ecstasy proves transitory, Barbara Lemont finds a more permanent rapture in the arms of Sidney Carter.

She had not been to bed with any man since her husband, and it had been two years, a long time, so that at first Sidney hurt her, but only for a second. Then she welcomes him. She had not known such skill existed, and yet she was not surprised because she had known that Sidney Carter would do everything well... The only thing that surprised her was her own reaction; she was suddenly a creature without shame, all made of sensations and motion without any consciousness of what was happening outside of herself and him. She heard herself screaming in her throat as at a great distance, and felt him very gently putting the corner of the pillow between her teeth.[82]

Barbara has found Mr. Right, a man expert enough to bring her to orgasm and yet decorous enough to "gently" gag her so the neighbors won't hear. Love frees Barbara from the surface frigidity of work-a-day existence and makes her come alive in Carter's arms. The passion born of love thus turns out to be the best of everything, and such a condition only occurs when a woman feels a man's reciprocal love. Given such an emotional-sexual scheme, Caroline can open herself to Eddie but not to Mike, for her subconscious feels love from one man and self-absorption in the other. Thus, Caroline Bender, the girl who has the ability to pursue a successful career, continues to search for, even though her lovers have proved inadequate, the larger romantic- idealistic vision, in which woman are guided by men, which still remains the best of everything.

Chapter 8

"A man without a woman, without a home, and without a child was no man at all."

The family as the benevolent embodiment of civilized values is celebrated in three 1950s' bestsellers. Louis L'Amour's *Hondo* (1953) uses Arizona in the 1880s, John Steinbeck's *East of Eden* (1952) uses California in the early 1900s, and James Gould Cozzens *By Love Possessed* (1957) uses the contemporary East to demonstrate man's recurrent need for domestic life. These novels imply that middle-class values—children as the future, parents as guides, homes as security—are the bases of individual happiness. In addition, these novels stress that compassion rather than pity enables man to find his spiritual home through recognizing personal weakness in himself and others as the basis of a common humanity. If a man is bound to a family, he must realize that his love is both a strength and a weakness, for to be without such feeling is to be inhuman, while to possess it is to be vulnerable to oneself and those one loves.

John O'Hara's *Ten North Frederick* (1957) and Jack Kerouac's *On the Road* (1958) present darker views of American domesticity. O'Hara's central character is devoured by the possessiveness of his wife and shallowness of his neighbors; thus, he ceases to challenge life and accepts aging and death. Kerouac's protagonist only comes alive when wandering outside the framework of "home" and gathering new experiences through movement. While Kerouac's character substitutes quantity for quality in pursuing sensations, his flight from middle-class respectability marks him as the diametric opposite of L'Amour's Hondo. These five bestsellers demonstrate that, while popular culture still adhered to the vision of domesticity immortalized by *Ozzie and Harriet*, the flight from such a life style—as seen in rising divorce rates and novels like John Updike's *Rabbit Run* (1960)—had also begun.

* * *

Hondo Lane epitomizes the strong, silent hero of western movies and fiction. This resourceful and independent figure represents a tradition in which men are rugged and in control, and women are soft and in need of male protection. *Hondo* presents a more domesticated West than does Jack Schaefer's *Shane* (1949), for L'Amour's scout settles down while the angelic gunfighter of the earlier novel leaves his adoptive family because his very existence has become an anachronism. While western films and

197

novels often present nostalgic yearnings for the past, *Hondo* praises the sacrifices its characters make for the present and the future. As a result, although Shane and many of the protagonists of John Ford's films poignantly express the passing of an age and its mores, Hondo Lane tames his roving instincts to become husband, father, and useful (i.e. civilized) community member.

In protecting Angie Lowe from the Apache and her ne'er-do-well husband, in introducing order to the run-down Lowe ranch, and in guiding the life of young Johnny, Hondo overcomes evil whites (Ed Lowe) and indians (Silva) to restore order to an entire setting. While *Hondo*'s Apache are threats to civilized life, the conflict between Vittorio, their venerable chief, and the pioneers approaches tragedy since each side feels intrinsically justified in its actions. Vittorio's dignity marks him as Hondo's only moral equal, and when the Apache leader dies (offstage), the inevitable climax between Hondo and Silva, the cowardly and sadistic new Apache leader, can take place without any of the perplexing sentiments that tragic confrontation creates. While one may suffer in having to choose between Achilles and Hector, no such dilemma arises when the cavalry scout kills Silva whose malevolence has been established beyond any doubt by his murder of Sam, Hondo's dog, when the protagonist lay unconscious.

Hondo abounds in customary western motifs and characters. There is, for example, a constant emphasis on the value of land and on the need to struggle to maintain it in the face of debilitating odds. This pioneer spirit illuminates Angie Lowe who befriends Hondo and then falls in love with him. While she lies in saying her husband is looking for stray cattle when he has deserted his family for a poker table and the security of an Army fort, Angie remains too proper ever to throw herself at Hondo. After he leaves for the fort (knowing Mrs. Lowe's symptoms for what they are), Angie decides to put her daydream of life with the virile scout aside, because:

> It was enough to think of her son, enough to see that he grew tall and strong, that he became a citizen of his land, a father of children in his time, that he learned to build instead of destroy, that he learned to use the land and protect it, not waste the wealth it gave. This was her mission, her problem.[1]

Her concern about her son dramatizes a familiar middle-class devotion to children and ties her even closer to Hondo; indeed, their mutual concern about Johnny foreshadows their reunion. Mrs. Lowe's aim of adjusting to the land rather than living off it represents the stage of civilization she embodies. Her pastoral instinct clearly ranks higher than the parasitism of Ed, who lives as a thief and a gambler, the nomadism of the Apache, who want to return to when the prairies were a hunting ground, and the wanderlust and reserve of Hondo, who has closed himself off to the life of the heart.

Angie Lowe embodies the sacrifices of past generations, for she gladly works to insure a more settled future. From her father, the only other good man in her lonely life, Angie learned the virtues of work and home, and these values remain ideals she wishes to transmit to Johnny.

To live with honor and to pass on having left our mark, it is only essential that we do our part, that we leave our children strong.... The important thing is to do the best one can with what one has.

... This was her home.... Here was all she could give her son aside from the feeling that he was loved.... And she could give him this early belief in stability, in the rightness of belonging somewhere.[2]

In her insistence on roots, Angie Lowe completes the hero, for Hondo lacks a fixed loyalty to a place or a people. His isolation, best symbolized by his travelling companion Sam, a dog toward whom Hondo never shows affection, breaks down before Mrs. Lowe and the force of circumstances; thus, Sam's violent death represents a necessary passage in the hero's life. Since Angie could not leave her home to follow Hondo because the sacrifices of her ancestors to tame it constitute a moral obligation, her sense of duty between generations elevates her character.

If Angie supplies the kind of idealism needed to settle the land, Hondo possesses the adaptability to implement this vision. In the midst of arid ground L'Amour's protagonist finds: "a desert strangely alive. Not a dead land, but a land where all life is born with a fire, a thorn, a sting. yet a strong land, a rich land for the man who knows it. One cannot fight the desert and live. One lives with it, or one dies."[3] Thus, the love of L'Amour's couple roots itself in more settled values than romance (family, home) and enables them to bring civilized order to a frontier. When Angie learns that Hondo has killed her husband (Ed tried to bushwhack the scout after an argument about a horse Hondo borrowed), she easily forgives her beloved and describes why her former spouse was to be pitied. " 'Poor Ed. He wasn't the type of man to die well. I'm sorry now that I hated him so much... after I got to know how tawdry and weak he was. I guess he couldn't help being that way. He never saw the beauty of this country. Not the way my father and I saw it.' "[4] In his failure to see the potential of the land, Ed Lowe lacked the most basic value of the pioneer. His being out of place is further symbolized by the condition of the ranch and by the form of his death, when Hondo must kill him to prevent Lowe from stealing the only horse left after they have been ambushed by the Apache. In his last moments, when he realizes there is only one animal between himself and Hondo, Ed reverts to type and dies badly.

The Apache resemble the settlers for both groups include heroes and cowards. When he and his band come to the Lowe ranch after Hondo has left, Vittorio significantly worries about Johnny Lowe's upbringing. To prevent the boy's death, after Johnny has recklessly enraged Silva, Vittorio makes him a blood brother and then insists that Angie either produce a husband (who will teach Johnny the Apache ways) or marry one of the young bucks in his war party. After she persuades Vittorio that her husband will soon be home, Angie:

...clutched Johnny. Vittorio swung to the back of the palomino. "I knew you were a great warrior," she said "I hope someday someone befriends your sons."

The iron face turned bleakly savage. "My sons are dead—in a white man's prison."[5]

Vittorio shares Hondo's and Angie's faith in the future because of his concern with children; indeed, the Apache retains this concern despite his losses, so that he ironically possesses an even stronger faith.

The other type of Apache is Silva, who is made a laughing stock when Johnny fires a pistol at him. As the war party leaves their ranch, Angie knows that only Vittorio stands between her and Silva's wrath against her son. The Apache's malevolence is brought further to the fore when he contemplates torturing the captured Hondo to death. Having tied the wounded scout to a horse so that he can go to the Apache camp and "die slowly, over a fire, head down, or staked out on an ant hill, or bound in a green hide and laid out in the hot sun,"[6] Silva ignores Hondo's taunts, for:

> ... Silva was a patient as well as a vindictive man. There was no desire in him to give the white man quick death instead of the hours of torture he planned. And this one had courage. He was a strong man, with wiry, powerful muscles. He would die slowly, and when at the end he broke, it would be a triumph to be remembered.[7]

Silva, of course, never gains this triumph, for the vengeful Apache is thwarted when Vittorio discovers that Hondo carries a picture of Johnny and assumes the scout is Angie's long-lost husband. While this coincidence suggests Hondo has been symbolically saved by the family he craves to join, the protagonist's freedom still remains contingent on Silva's wishes for, according to tribal custom, a captor can challenge a captive to a duel. This fight between Hondo, nursing a wounded arm, and Silva ends when the scout overcomes the Indian and then, in a gesture which rankles his foe, refuses to take the Apache's life. Silva's excessive pride surfaces at the end of the novel when his band enjoys a numerical advantage over the fleeing cavalry patrol, the Lowes and Hondo, and can seemingly massacre the whites at leisure. At this point, Silva is foolishly drawn into another one-to-one combat with the scout, an action that leads to Silva's inevitable death and forces the Apache to retreat and lose their advantage (custom decrees they cannot fight without a chief).

L'Amour celebrates the United States Cavalry in terms familiar to moviegoers. Just as the mounted soldiers of John Ford's *Fort Apache* (1948), *She Wore a Yellow Ribbon* (1949) and *Rio Grande* (1950) personify unquestioning loyalty in trying and demeaning circumstances, so L'Amour's cavalrymen put duty before personal safety or gain. Lieutenant Creiton Davis, who has volunteered for a frontier assignment after the Civil War, dies well in resisting the Apache. Lieutenant McKay, a younger officer who comes to the Lowe ranch after Hondo has been returned there by Vittorio, represents a lack of experience. McKay is a "shave tail" leading his first patrol into enemy territory yet, though he must be guided and "wet nursed" by a veteran scout named Buffalo, McKay will inevitably come through such tests of manhood and become a soldier. Hondo, who refuses to tell McKay where the Apache have gone because of a promise made to Vittorio (in the fictional West a man is only as good as his word), immediately recognizes that the Lieutenant is a novice. When he tells Buffalo that McKay will get the entire patrol killed, the other scout doesn't disagree but simply shrugs in the realization that McKay "was not the first he had seen come to Indian country. Nor, with luck, would he be the last. Some of them had it, some of them did not. Some were only pretty, some were all spit and polish, and some of them sharpened down into first-class fighting men."[8] Buffalo knows a man's education isn't complete until he leaves teachers behind, so that, while there is truth in what Hondo says, the other scout is allowing McKay to grow up by making his own mistakes.

Buffalo understands that luck ultimately decides survival once certain limits of expertise have been reached, so he believes that every man must be prepared to die at any time. This is Hondo's code too and when he is a prisoner of the Apache, and knows the slow death that awaits him (particularly since he lived among the Mescalero and married one of them), he resolves:

> ...he must be strong, to show no fear, to show no pain. He must at all costs die well.
> And it was not easy to die well. He had seen other men die, and he had seen the remains of men who had died well. It had never seemed possible that what they had endured could be endured by any man. Could he do as well?[9]

Death as the final test of manhood represents an all-too-familiar motif of western films and fiction; however, this concern also colors the writings of Ernest Hemingway, whose characters, while perhaps not as obviously as Hondo, dwell on achieving "grace under pressure." Hondo must die well if his own identity is to remain inviolate: to die badly would be to reveal oneself as a hypocrite who killed out of fear rather than necessity.

As a teacher Hondo Lane offers advice based on the experience gained from staying alive on the frontier. His wisdom becomes immediately apparent to the Lowes after he arrives at their ranch needing a horse to carry dispatches to the fort. While Angie admiringly notes that Hondo carries himself with the grace of an indian, Johnny learns from the protagonist that one should always sink an axe blade into a log to prevent the tool's rusting. As he awaits his supposed death among the Apache, Hondo reflects on his essentially futile life and regrets being unable to pass his wisdom on to the future.

> He left behind him nothing. A few people who would remember for a day or an hour. A man needed something on which to build. A man without a woman, without a home, and without a child was no man at all.
> Johnny. If there had been no son of his own, he could at least have given Johnny what he had learned.[10]

This passage constitutes the novel's intellectual climax, the moment when the protagonist chooses domesticity over life in the wilderness. Hondo, unlike John Ford's heroes or the more literary but equally isolated Natty Bumpo of James Fenimore Cooper, decides not to ride into the sunset but to stay and watch it set from a front porch. Hondo wants to survive so that his code of ethics can be transmitted through Johnny; and, after he has returned to Angie (who acquiesces when Vittorio asks if Hondo is her husband), the scout begins to teach the boy the ways of the frontier.

When he discovers Johnny can't swim, Hondo simply throws the boy into a nearby creek and lets him struggle (the same technique for which he criticizes Buffalo with Lieutenant McKay) until he starts swimming. In this episode Hondo acts so that Johnny can become a man—a process that leads to total independence such as that of Sam, the dog of whom the protagonist said earlier: " 'Sam's independent. He doesn't need anybody. I want him to stay that way. It's a good way.' "[11] While Hondo realizes a man cannot live totally alone, his treatment of Johnny underlines the scout's fatherly role in the family he makes with Angie and the boy. After he has recovered from his first fight with Silva, Hondo asks how old Johnny is; and when Angie replies that the boy is six but still a baby, the hero declares: " 'Time there was a man around here. Treat him like a baby and he'll be one. Spoils a boy to be protected. How'll he ever learn to care for himself?' "[12] Hondo clearly believes Johnny must be challenged to do his best; and the importance of the son learning the father's wisdom is expressed by the novel's most obvious symbol—the tintype picture of Johnny that Hondo takes from Ed Lowe's body. In the course of the Apache ambush, even the nefarious Ed avoids death because the tintype deflects an indian bullet, so that, when Hondo kills Ed, the talismanic picture passes from Johnny's biological father to his emotional father. The power of the tintype, and thus the symbolic power of having a son, is shown again when Vittorio recognizes the picture and frees Hondo.

Familiar romantic clichés also find their way into *Hondo*, for while the protagonist never openly woos Angie (indeed, his brutal frankness about her husband's desertion and a chance remark about women " 'who always think every man that comes along wants 'em' "[13] establish Hondo's initial distrust), he thinks about her continuously. Both the protagonist and Buffalo act skitterish around Mrs. Lowe in a later scene, when Hondo insists that the other scout refrain from telling Angie any unpleasant details about the Apache. Thus, Hondo protects the woman from both physical elements (by taking charge of the ranch) and emotional ones (by shielding her from unpleasant news). While Angie, who has never experienced true love, prattles about the one special person for everybody, the previously reserved Hondo lapses into an elaborate poetic description of his Mescalero wife.

"I don't remember anything unhappy about Destarte."

"Destarte! How musical! What does it mean?"

"You can't say it except in Mescalero. It means Morning, but that isn't what it means, either. Indian words are more than just that. They also mean the feel and the sound of the name. It means like Crack of Dawn, the first bronze light that makes the buttes stand out against the gray desert. It means the first sound you hear of a brook curling over some rocks—some trout jumping and a beaver crooning. It means the sound a stallion makes when he whistles at some mares just as the first puff of wind kicks up at daybreak."[14]

This exposition, which goes on for another paragraph, is, of course, Hondo's longest and most modified speech; and, while it establishes the depth of his feeling, it also reveals Hondo's abiding love of the land in its images of buttes, brooks and horses. The scout loved Destarte because she was an integral part of the land and in Angie, who willingly endures for the sake of her property, he recognizes a similar spirit. After telling Angie that she reminds him of Destarte, Hondo pulls Mrs. Lowe to him and momentarily kisses her. At this point, L'Amour's protagonist experiences a dilemma between his feelings and his code of independent individualism. He can deplore the possibility of Angie's scalp adorning Vittorio's lodge pole but he will not cajole her into coming with him: " 'But a long time ago I made me a rule: I let people do what they want to do.' "[15]

This mood has changed after the trials Hondo endures in getting back to the ranch; indeed, the scout now willingly adopts a proprietary role toward Angie and Johnny. Unlike the heroes of John Ford, such as Wyatt Earp (Henry Fonda) who rides off despite his love for Clementine in *My Darling Clementine* (1946), Ethan Edwards (John Wayne) who cannot enter the family circle after restoring the lost Debbie to the hearth in *The Searchers* (1956), or Tom Doniphon (Wayne again) who drowns his sorrows in alcohol after killing the villain and losing his love to the new, Eastern-educated lawyer who symbolizes civilization in *The Man Who Shot Liberty Valance* (1962), Hondo Lane sacrifices for a settled domesticity. While Ford's protagonists and Jack Schaefer's Shane symbolize a heroic form of existence which is passing, L'Amour's hero refuses to become an anachronism by clinging to the life of a scout. Hondo ultimately refuses to accept the fatalism which the Apache have subconsciously adopted in fighting the settlers: "The Apache knew his hour was past. He knew the white men would take even his last land, but it was not in him to knuckle under. He would fight, sing his death song, and die."[16] Hondo Lane's transition from solitary wanderer to family man stamps him as a western hero for the 1950s— one who combines the classical virtues of that character type with a desire for domesticity and conformity that echoes such works as David Riesman's *The Lonely Crowd* and William H. Whyte's *The Organization Man* .

* * *

East of Eden, a leisurely paced generational novel, indulges a penchant for moral philosophy at the expense of narrative movement. Steinbeck writes in a "wise" authorial voice to demonstrate his mellowness about human nature and, while full of dramatic moments, reflection finally dominates *East of Eden.* Although youth's anguish is presented, its agonies are consistently viewed from the perspectives of middle and old age, times when desire has been banked by duty and impending death, and times which suggest that youthful agitations are not life's real business. *East of Eden* uses the tale of Cain and Abel to introduce an ethical problem which the characters solve in a predictably American way by abandoning the fatalism of the Old Testament for a belief in the possibility of individual action. Thus, the Trask family's conflicts are resolved when the bedridden Adam forgives his son Cal by uttering the Hebraic term "timshel," a word which has come to mean that each man defines himself through his actions. The stern God of Judgment, embodied in Adam's father Cyrus, has been overthrown because Adam has adopted a more compassionate and, ultimately, more human outlook

The earliest generation of the Trasks is dominated by Cyrus, who rises to the top of a bureaucratic organization which lobbies for Grand Old Army veterans. A conspicuous failure as a farmer and as a father, as well as a nondescript soldier who was wounded and mustered out after only a couple of months of service, Cyrus finds his calling and his fortune in Washington. When he dies, Cyrus' wealth comes to his sons, Adam and Charles, who are dumbfounded at their father's having grown rich. Until this point Cyrus had allowed Charles to farm the family land while Adam pursued a career in the Army (at his father's urging) and became a bum. In denying Charles' love while lavishing what affection he can on Adam (who doesn't want such attention), Cyrus turns the brothers against each other so that Charles beats Adam out of frustration. Cyrus calmly views the battered boy, then insists on knowing why Charles has done what he has.

"Tell me! I want to know. Tell me!... Goddam it, you're always protecting him! Don't you think I know that? Did you think you were fooling me? Now tell me, or by God I'll keep you standing there all night!"

Adam cast about for an answer. "He doesn't think you love him."

Cyrus released the arm and hobbled back to his chair and sat down. He rattled the pen in the ink bottle and looked blindly at his record book. "Alice," he said, "help Adam to bed. You'll have to cut his shirt off, I guess. Give him a hand."[17]

Cyrus symbolizes the stern God of the Old Testament who prefers truth to love: the father has prejudged his sons and Charles, despite his physical prowess, simply does not measure up, while Adam must be tested in order to become a man.

A terrible irony in Cyrus' prescription for Adam lies in the father's make-believe bravado about his own role in the Civil War; indeed, his limp from a war wound reflects his state of mind more than his physical condition. Cyrus makes a difficult situation worse for, as Steinbeck notes, every child experiences a diminution of his preconceived image of his parents with the passage of time.

When a child first catches adults out—when it first walks into his grave little head that adults do not have divine intelligence, that their judgments are not always wise, their thinking true, their sentences just—his world falls into panic desolation. The gods are fallen and all safety gone. And there is one sure thing about the fall of gods: they do not fall a little; they crash and shatter or sink deeply into green muck... And the child's world is never quite whole again. It is an aching kind of growing.[18]

Adam and Charles experience such a loss with a father who never shows them any sympathy and they grow up with permanent scars on their personalities. Cyrus so impresses his will upon them that neither son grows completely free of him until, after nearly fifty years, Adam relents with his only remaining son, Cal.

Charles never reconciles himself with his father's refusal to love him. While he makes a small success of the farm, Charles smolders inside because of such neglect. He even seeks relief from prostitutes but never gains any solace for his feelings. It is almost too ironic that Charles should feel guilt about accepting Cyrus' legacy, while Adam, who has freed himself psychologically from much of Cyrus' spell, gladly takes his share. Charles remains distraught over the possibility that Cyrus' name may be damaged for his wealth was illegally obtained; Adam, on the other hand, feels no concern about his parent's reputation or the source of his riches. When scheming to be first in his father's eyes becomes impossible with Cyrus' death, Charles determines to get even with Adam. He reenacts the jealous brother (Cain) seeking vengeance against the seemingly favored sibling; and when Cathy Ames stumbles into the Trask farm, herself the victim of a vicious beating by a man she tempted once too often, and is aided by Adam, Charles gets his opportunity. Adam, who falls in love with Cathy at first sight, nurses her back to health, proposes, and is accepted; however, on their wedding night, Cathy drugs Adam in order to seduce Charles. Later, in California Cathy gives birth to twins (Aaron and Cal) so that the dual legacy of Cyrus is reborn and Charles' envy is carried on by Cal.

Cathy Ames emerges as a "monster" from her first appearance in *East of Eden*. She hates her parents after her mother discovers her playing sexually with two neighbor boys at age ten. While her parents are distraught, their conventional child-rearing precludes facing this difficulty directly: "Nearly all parents are faced with the problem sooner or later, and then the child is lucky if the parent remembers his own childhood. In the time of Cathy's childhood, however, it was harder. The parents denying it in themselves, were horrified to find it in their children."[19] Cathy quickly gets over any idealistic feelings about love, or about sex as an expression of deeper feelings. She runs away after burning down the family home and murdering her parents and, eventually, comes to Boston in search of a more exciting life. There she meets Mr. Edwards, the owner of a chain of rural brothels constantly looking for new talent; however, the married proprietor, heretofore impervious to the charms of his employees, falls in love and makes Cathy his mistress, an arrangement that leads to his complete submission and degradation. Cathy keeps Edwards off balance by constantly implying that she is seeing other men when he is not around, and by her sexual cunning: "In their sexual relations she convinced him that the result was not quite satisfactory to her, that if he were a better man he could release a flood of unbelievable reaction in her."[20] The girl couples this calculating sadism with descriptions of the many men she has known and how she understands every nerve in a man's body and could drive Edwards wild if she chose. Ironically, Edwards cannot bear to hear such obscenities from her, and it is a measure of his frustration (comparable to Charles Trask's) that he nearly beats her to death on a road near the Trask farm.

The rehabilitated Cathy soon realizes she needs a fresh "stake" so she works on Adam, having recognized his affection as an exploitable weakness. She goes to Charles on her wedding night to prove she can exercise power over the brother who ignored her.

> He grunted and turned, trying to get comfortable, and then he opened his eyes. Cathy was standing by his bed. "What do you want?"
>
> "What do you think? Move over a little."
>
> ... He breathed harshly. "I already been with a whore."
>
> "You're a pretty strong boy. Move over a little."
>
> "How about your broken arm?"
>
> "I'll take care of that. It's not your worry."
>
> Suddenly Charles laughed. "The poor bastard," he said, and he threw back the blanket to receive her.[21]

In California, Cathy quickly tires of Adam and, after countless arguments, shoots him. While such an action epitomizes the calculating style with which Cathy approaches lovemaking, the wound shatters Adam's spirit and leaves him despondent for years. After deserting her family, Cathy moves into a Salinas brothel, ingratiates herself with its madame, and then poisons her to gain control of the entire operation. In the years that follow Cathy's house caters to the kinkiest clientele and she, ever desirous of more power, has her patrons photographed for blackmail purposes. Cathy dies from a drug overdose induced, in part, by Cal's introduction of Aaron to her in 1918. While Cal can live with the shame of his mother's being a prostitute (indeed, he is even clever enough to unsettle the normally imperturbable Cathy), Aaron, who wants to be a minister, goes to pieces because of this meeting.

Adam Trask, who believes California to be a land of opportunity, suffers from the injuries that Cathy heaps on him and from his remorse which renders him oblivious to his sons until they grow up. Adam's rational personality ultimately identifies him as the material from which civilizations are built. When Cyrus decides he should go into the Army, Adam argues Charles would make a better soldier.

> "Why don't you talk to my brother? Charles will be going. He'll be good at it, much better than I am."
>
> "Charles won't be going," Cyrus said. "There'd be no point in it."
>
> "But he would be a better soldier."
>
> "Only outside of his skin," said Cyrus. "Not inside. Charles is not afraid so he could never learn anything about courage. He does not know anything outside himself so he could never gain the things I've tried to explain to you. To put him in an army would be to let loose things which in Charles must be chained down, not let loose. I would not dare to let him go."[22]

Cyrus' speech echoes the Cain-Abel pattern by implying that Charles has murder naturally in his heart. Adam's career in the United States Cavalry as an indian fighter makes him aware of his pacifism (he only goes through the motions in battle) and, paradoxically, of his lack of direction (he re-enlists despite hating the entire operation).

After his traumatic marriage dissolves, Adam slowly emerges from depression because of Samuel Hamilton, a neighbor whose large family keeps him poor, and Lee, a Chinese servant who takes on the burdens of the household and the boys. When Samuel Hamilton dies and is buried in Salinas, Adam attends the funeral and, only recently having learned that Cathy is the town's leading madame, goes to see his former wife. At this charged interview, Adam finally frees himself by refusing to be shocked or tempted by Cathy. She is thwarted and becomes angry.

"You were such a fool," she said. "Like a child. You didn't know what things to do with yourself. I can teach you now. You seem to be a man."

"You have taught me," he said. "It was a pretty sharp lesson."[23]

Although Cathy has him beaten and thrown out because of his calm, Adam has thrown off one of his life's evil legacies by refusing to be involved again with her. In losing the son on whom he dotes and having to forgive the less-beloved child, Adam finally overcomes the legacy of Cyrus.

The central ethical dilemma of *East of Eden* emerges when Sam Hamilton, Lee and Adam discuss the story of Cain and Abel. Their interest eventually narrows to God's message to Cain when He sees that figure is distraught: " 'And if thou doest not well, sin lieth at the door. And unto thee shall be his desire, and thou shalt rule over him.' " (Genesis 4:7). Lee is so stirred by this passage that he becomes a Hebrew scholar and asks the area's leading Chinese wise men to aid him in an exegesis of this story. In his investigations Lee discovers that the Hebrew verb "timshel" can be translated conditionally, so that he can argue to Adam and Sam that God's message to Cain was not a rigid order to overcome sin but a presentation of that possibility to the wayward brother. It remains for Sam Hamilton, leaving his farm to visit his successful urbanized children in the certainty that he will never return to the land, to grasp Lee's argument.

" 'Thou mayest rule over sin,' Lee. That's it. I do not believe all men are destroyed. I can name you a dozen who were not, and they are the ones the world lives by. It is true of the spirit as it is true of battles—only the winners are remembered. Surely most men are destroyed, but there are others who like pillars of fire guide frightened men through the darkness. *'Thou mayest, Thou mayest!'* What glory!"[24]

Adam lacks Sam's insight for most of the novel, but he too slowly realizes that the central point of the story of Cain and Abel was not merely that all men are brothers who must look out for each other (as he tried to do with Charles) but that such concern must extend between generations.

In a conversation with Lee, when they have become old and settled, Adam remembers an earlier discussion.

"I said that word carried a man's greatness if he wanted to take advantage of it."

"I remember Sam Hamilton felt good about it."

"It set him free," said Lee. "It gave him the right to be a man."

"That's lonely."

"All great and precious things are lonely."

"What is that word again?"

"Timshel—thou mayest."[25]

Lee's translation introduces freedom and choice into a situation seemingly dominated by determinism. While Aaron and Abra Bacon have been betrothed in their own minds since childhood, they gradually grow apart so that, by 1918, the girl dislikes Aaron's increasing religiosity and pompousness. Cal, whose feeling for Abra only slowly emerges, decides to get rid of his brother, and so he introduces Aaron to Cathy—an event that precipitates Aaron's enlistment because of drunken disappointment. When news of Aaron's death reaches Salinas, Adam suffers a stroke and Cal finds himself, like Cain, fraught with guilt because he failed to be his brother's "keeper." In the novel's final scene Lee persuades Adam to forgive Cal and to bless the future union of his son and Abra; and, when the prostrate father utters "timshel" the characters of the novel are redeemed because the possibility of exoneration exists in the world. It is as though Adam Trask had undone the original sin which mankind had carried since the days of Eden. Thus, the actions of Cyrus, Charles and Cathy prove futile in the long run, for Adam demonstrates that man's legacy is freedom and not a fixed emotional and ethical inheritance.

Lee represents the novel's wise man, a position he gains quite early when he impresses Sam Hamilton with the dualism he uses to deal with white men. Lee has developed a conscious patois which makes him sound like any other uneducated Chinese murdering the English language in order to conform to the stereotype of the Oriental expected of him. When Sam breaks through this surface, Lee becomes quite articulate and quickly demonstrates his sagacity. In discussing his role in the Trask household, Lee tells why he became a servant: " 'I don't know where being a servant came into disrepute. It is the refuge of a philosopher, the food of the lazy, and properly carried out, it is a position of power, even love.' "[26] Lee indeed assumes these roles within Adam's household, for he becomes the best friend (and an opiate mother) to Aaron and Cal as well as an adviser to Adam.

As their friendship deepens, a closeness symbolized when the servant fails to become the proprietor of his own bookstore, Lee tells Adam of his parents and their flight from China. While they were brought to America as laborers for the railroad, Lee's mother was able to disguise herself as a man and work alongside his father. This romantic idyll was interrupted by Lee's birth in a railroad camp, an event that precipitated the multiple rape and death of his mother and his father's rescue of him from the dying woman's body. Despite the horror of these events, Lee tells Adam: " 'Before you hate those men you must know this. My father always told it at the last: No child ever had such care as I. The whole camp became my mother. It is a beauty—a dreadful kind of beauty. And now good night. I can't talk any more.' "[27] Lee's recognition of humanity's mixed nature, and of the necessity for forgiveness, enables him to guide Adam's final meeting with Cal: as one who has suffered the utmost cruelties and the most bountiful blessings at men's hands, Lee knows that life is a matter of "thou mayest" and not of "thou must." When Abra feels caught between a sense of duty toward Aaron and a burgeoning love for Cal, she turns to Lee for solace.

After her revelation that Aaron has become so pious she can hardly endure him, Lee comforts Abra by suggesting that living up to a role is often too difficult.

> "I'm always afraid he'll see something in me that isn't in the one he made up. I'll get mad or I'll smell bad—or something else. He'll find out."
> "Maybe not," said Lee. "But it must be hard living the Lily Maid, the Goddess-Virgin, and the other all at once. Humans just do smell bad sometimes."[28]

As a spokesman for human possibility, Lee recognizes the limits of being human, and so he can comfort Abra, in the same way that he consoles Adam, by stressing that her passions are simply human.

Steinbeck incorporates large sections of moral philosophy that turn *East of Eden* into a wonderful quarry for potential biographers, while dismaying those who appreciate tightly-knitted plots. In an aside about Cathy, long after she has been called a "monster," Steinbeck urges that compassion must be shown even to her because, like all humans, her motives remain mysterious: "The trouble is that since we cannot know what she wanted, we will never know whether or not she got it."[29] Just as Dostoyevsky insists in *Notes from the Underground* that individuals act irrationally simply to prove their freedom, and as Welles implies in *Citizen Kane* (1941) that the more one knows of a man's external life the more enigmatic his internal self remains, so Steinbeck urges that any human is bound to remain perplexing to his fellows. Such an observation accords with the moral lesson that Lee's translation affirms; indeed, Steinbeck goes on to argue that human creativity and individuality are indissoluble, so that, while the great majority of mankind never achieves real creativity (just as Sam Hamilton noted how "most men are destroyed" without gaining ethical insight), life's conditional nature allows an inspired few to emerge. In a passage that sounds remarkably like Ayn Rand's diatribes against group interests, Steinbeck presents creative activity as a "lonely" business, and then urges: "And this I would fight for: the freedom of the mind to take any direction it wishes, undirected. And this I must fight against: any idea, religion or government which limits or destroys the individual. This is what I am and what I am about."[30] The traditional American belief in individualism is reaffirmed by such sentiments; and when one contrasts this argument with the end of *The Grapes of Wrath* (1939), in which Tom Joad becomes the spokesman for the little people who have been victimized by the Depression, one sees a definite intellectual change in Steinbeck.

The novelist has adopted a more classical view of man and society; thus, while Tom Joad implied that the individual must act for the group's betterment, the authorial voice in *East of Eden* suggests that the individual needs to fortify himself against the group.

> Our species is the only creative species, and it has only one creative instrument, the individual mind and spirit of a man. Nothing was ever created by two men.... Once the miracle of creation has taken place, the group can build and extend it, but the group never invents anything. The preciousness lies in the lonely mind of a man.[31]

By arguing against the parasitic way in which society uses its creative people and for the primacy of the individual creator, Steinbeck reveals his differences with the twentieth century, an era marked by mass movements. Clearly, the novelist does not subscribe to the theory that technological change represents a quantum leap by which men transcend their human weaknesses: "Humans are caught—in their lives, in their thoughts, in their hungers and ambitions, and in their kindness and generosity—in a net of good and evil. I think this is the only story we have and that it occurs on all levels of feeling and intelligence."[32] Despite his all-too-human qualities, every man wants to be loved so that life takes on a tragic cast, if only because this common desire produces so much individual anguish. A man fails if he dies unloved, and even characters as vicious as Cathy and Cyrus yearn for emotional fulfillment; indeed, for Steinbeck, morality consists of living so that one's death "brings no pleasure to the world."

The essential tranquility of *East of Eden*, a quality which derives from its settled characters and the repeated avoidance of dramatic confrontations (we do not see Aaron confront Cathy, for example, even though the denouement hinges on this encounter) reinforces Steinbeck's view of good and evil. For him, evil can only be defined as the absence of good; indeed, evil always changes its exterior while good remains the same in all ages: "We have only one story. All novels, all poetry, are built on the never-ending contest in ourselves of good and evil. And it occurs to me that evil must constantly spawn, while good, while virtue, is immortal. Vice has always a fresh young face, while virtue, is venerable as nothing else in the world."[33] Growing old, or arriving at the age in which one has become venerable and virtuous, remains the central concern of *East of Eden*. The tone and the characters reaffirm that morality consists of doing ordinary things—loving one's children, establishing a home, being compassionate to one's friends—while vice delights in fashionable changes and pandering to ever-changing tastes—Cathy's exotic brothel. In the span of seventy years, the Trasks undergo bitter times to learn compassion, the quality that transcends any evil no matter how attractive.

* * *

Undoubtedly the most stylistically difficult bestseller of the 1950s, *By Love Possessed* includes some of the decade's most graphic fictional sex scenes and descriptions. Cozzens' novel reflects highly refined feelings and perceptions so that, given its characters' introspectiveness, its intimate scenes stand out. In recounting three days in the life of Arthur Winner, a lawyer whose surname prepares the novel's conclusion, Cozzens portrays a character who spends nearly every moment in counselling or consoling others. Arthur's sagacity keeps numerous dependents—his mother, his aunt, his wife, his clients—afloat; and, because of all this activity, Winner emerges as a snob so that his being driven to the conclusion that love rather than rationality must guide his conduct is welcome. At the novel's end Arthur realizes that everyone, even he, is controlled by love and not by ego.

This central theme is dramatized when Arthur represents Ralph

Detweiler, the brother of his firm's secretary-bookkeeper, Helen. Ralph has been charged with rape by Veronica Kovacs who, in turn, is trying to escape her mother's wrath for returning home late and disheveled. While Ralph and Veronica were backseat lovers, the situation is further complicated by Joanie Moore, Ralph's pregnant and desperate fiancée. Since he knows Helen dotes on Ralph, Arthur feels compelled to defend the boy; yet, as he comes to see that Ralph's actions were due to extenuating circumstances, Arthur assumes a moral obligation toward everyone involved. Winner does not want to shatter Helen's illusions about her brother, and yet the lawyer must deal with the Kovacs' and the Moores' feelings as well. In observing all these protective sentiments, Arthur comes to doubt the validity of love.

What did the cherishers in fact cherish? Must the "powerful instinct" and all its myriad shapes of earnest devotion and eager sacrifice be, to a psychologist, suspect? Subject of so much piety and praise, did this great paternal tenderness's every exercise boil down (alas, alas!) to: *I love me?*[34]

Arthur's dismay finds characteristic expression in Cozzens' syntax which slows the reader down by a series of questions that shift the burden of proof to him.

By Love Possessed would probably not have enjoyed such commercial success if it presented Arthur's doubts as valid in the long run, for such an argument would be intolerable to the sentimental audience of American bestsellers. The novel's opening paragraph, a description of a clock in his mother's home, sets the stage for Arthur to find love's power. While this objet d'art implies the Winners' social status and exhibits all the maudlin cupids and nymphs customary to such pieces, Arthur's "faint familiar amusement" ironically underscores the importance of the clock's inscription: "Love conquers all— *omnia vincit amor*, said the gold scroll in a curve beneath the dial of the old French gilt clock."[35] The protagonist's shortsightedness is again uppermost when, while listening to his aged mother's multiple petty complaints, Arthur reflects on the clock's cupid.

His victory was love—love's bliss of thoughtlessness. Love pushed aside the bitter findings of experience. Love knew for a fact what was not a fact; with ease, love believed the unbelievable; love wished and made it so. Moreover, here where love's weakness seemed to be, love's strength resided. Itself all unreality, love was assailed by reality in vain.[36]

At this point Arthur resembles his father, always referred to as the Man of Reason, in seeing love as a necessary illusion by which men protect themselves from the world; in Arthur's eyes, love sanctions lust and indulging one's ego by shutting out reality. Such cynicism requires a shattering experience to create a more compassionate perspective—Arthur must lose his confident sense of always being above more sordid human actors and actions. While he has experienced grief (the deaths of his first wife and a dissolute son), Arthur has never fully experienced his own humanity.

Cozzens signals the protagonist's transformation to a man of compassion in the opening and closing chapters of *By Love Possessed*. Initially, Arthur leaves his mother's home after arguing with Aunt Maud, who wants to invest in a speculative stock rather than be guided by Noah

Tuttle, who is the trustee for her estate. Noah, Arthur's aged law partner, steadfastly refuses to allow Maud to withdraw her money, and the protagonist, firmly convinced that Tuttle has better judgment, supports that position. By the end of the novel, Arthur has discovered that Noah is as fallible as his relative, and so the main character returns to his mother's house and symbolically closes off the action by speaking to Aunt Maud. After looking once more at the clock and reflecting that its figures embody the human condition, Arthur: "Raised to call back, to answer his Aunt Maud,... (and) heard his own grave voice. He said: 'I'm here.' "[37] While such words sound like a stock response to a stock situation, Cozzens has labored to establish that his protagonist has gained compassion in dealing with others. Arthur now appreciates that all men are weak (and wicked at times) so that no one of them can divorce himself from the human condition.

Cozzens' principal thus symbolizes a deep-seated optimism about human nature, for Arthur learns compassion when he is fifty, an age when most men settle into routine skepticism about the world. The protagonist hardly matches popular stereotypes of the leading man, since he is bald as well as middle-aged. Cozzens, who delights in irony, seems to be suggesting that, contrary to popular assumptions nurtured by countless films, a hero doesn't have to be either handsome or rugged. Arthur's malleability is emphasized quite early when he tells his mother, who constantly compares her son to his father as a lawyer: " 'The truth is I'm only now starting to see how well father knew his business. He and Noah Tuttle made quite a firm in the old days. Getting old myself, I can realize how good they were.' "[37] Even this statement has an ironic ring, for Arthur must still discover how well his father really knew life—a connection that is symbolized by the elder Winner's having purchased the clock. When he discovers that Noah has juggled numerous trust accounts because, being human, the older man wanted love from those who depended on him, Arthur's words resonate even more. The protagonist and Julius Penrose, the law firm's younger members, decide to deal with Noah compassionately so that the company can continue to be "quite a firm." Arthur's age is further exploited when he celebrates the joys and freedoms of middle age—another incongruous theme in a culture which generally equates an individual's years with physical decay rather than happiness. While popular thinking frequently equates youth, beauty and freedom, Arthur believes life offers permanent solace at any age: "What you knew at fifty—that a hundred years, far from being forever and ever, was not long; that all wonders in time will prove supposititious—left untouched the amazing thoughts you were at liberty to have at ten."[38] As a sensitive observer of the passage of time that has conditioned him, Winner only needs to learn that love provides the same sense of inviolability that time does.

Arthur devotes much energy to speculating on other people's motives and future actions, so that he offers opinions on the conduct of a new minister, the ambition of a local district attorney (who wants to be a judge), and the stubbornness of another man's wife (who wants to have a baby even though a pregnancy could endanger her life). Given such didacticism, it is hardly surprising that Arthur is continuously in conversation with figures who either seek his advice or use him as a listener. When he learns that Ralph Detweiler had relations with Veronica, as well as with Joanie, Arthur offers legal advice that represents a kind of practical bonus. Just as one might feel rewarded by the technical legal points presented in a Perry Mason novel, so can the reader conclude that Cozzens' protagonist offers sound advice on courtroom behavior here. As an officer of the court, Arthur consistently impresses upon Ralph the necessity for telling the whole truth; indeed, he argues that lies demand more lies to support them and, inevitably, are uncovered by the prosecution. When Ralph says attorneys always try to confuse witnesses, Arthur brings him up short: " 'That's not quite it... That's done only in stories, or motion pictures. What the district attorney will be doing is testing your statements where they're in conflict with those of his witness or witnesses. If your statements are nothing but the truth, what really happened, you're quite safe.' "[39] Such advice implies Arthur's contentment with his society; indeed, his optimism about the beneficence of the law and lawyers no doubt sound more questionable in our time. Arthur's faith that the institutions of the law embody justice also avoids the more serious issue implicit in his dismissal of Ralph's remark. Certainly Arthur must know that human beings, simply by being arrested for a crime, are already partially compromised. Juries are, alas, not always reasonable so that the protagonist's advice seems utopian when compared to, say, Paul Biegler's preparation of his client in Robert Travers's *Anatomy of a Murder*.

Arthur appears on safer ground when discussing the judicial ambitions of J. Jerome Brophy, the local district attorney, with Fred Dealey, a former member of his law firm and now himself a judge. Dealey is appalled that Brophy wants such a position, since he regards the latter as a political hack with decidedly second-rate legal abilities. While he agrees with some of Dealey's assessment, Arthur argues that social envy is pushing Brophy so that, rather than become a part of the establishment under false pretenses, the prosecutor feels compelled to prove that he is even better than those who snub him. " 'He doesn't want to join you; he wants to lick you. If it's the last thing he does, he's going to make you take back what you may not have said, but what he knows you think. That's why.' "[40]

Arthur recognizes there may be more to Jerome Brophy than mere ambition and, in so doing, he attributes some of the complexity he extends to himself and his immediate circle to the district attorney. The central character's conservatism is again apparent for, while there might be a reason to doubt that Brophy will master the law he failed to master as a district attorney simply because of a promotion (the Peter Principle), Arthur remains confident Brophy will grow because of the challenge.

The sexual explicitness of *By Love Possessed* traces Arthur's increasing sophistication about love. He moves from a reverential first marriage to a ferociously physical affair with Marjorie Penrose and, finally, to a mutually satisfying union with Clarissa, his younger second wife. In keeping with his highly literary style, Cozzens requires one to make these connections without being prompted; thus, the novel exhibits a surface prurience as well as a more extended thematic artistry. The first Mrs. Winner, whose very name, Hope, suggests how Arthur has approached their marriage, endures her husband's passionate lovemaking because that is a woman's lot. The mere thought of sexual relations offends Hope's sense of decorum, yet she equates marriage with growing up, so she prepares to allow Arthur to have his way after the wedding.

> If stirrings of curiosity sometimes troubled her; anxious wonderings about what *it* was *really* like; attempts of the mind, revulsively fascinated, to imagine how two people would look, what they could find to do and say, as they prepared to accomplish, and then (how could they!) went ahead and accomplished their joint obscenity, these speculations would be against her conscious wish and will... She did not like any of it.
>
> Nevertheless, what Hope did not like, Hope was going to do. Undeterred by chill or revulsion, Hope was going to agree, consent, submit. To help her, would be a girl's settled impression that marrying was what you did when you grew up.[41]

Hope cannot be dismissed as frigid for she does respond; however, her sense of herself never allows her to forget that she is a social being first and a loving one second. Their marriage, thus, epitomizes middle-class ambivalence in which jealousy and recalcitrance uneasily combine: Arthur, who never cheats on Hope, is allowed to take care of her—a process that means protecting Hope from life's grimmer realities.

The second stage in Arthur's sexual odyssey resembles Ralph Detweiler's one-night stand with Veronica Kovacs. In the same way that the young man turned to the waitress when frustrated, so Arthur Winner latches onto Marjorie Penrose after Hope's death. The same clinical exactitude Arthur demands of Ralph when cross-examining him characterizes the protagonist's own liaison with his partner's wife. In these meetings, one encounters inserted penises, premature ejaculation, and semen-stained mattresses, all of which details are presented in a mood of mild disgust and regret. Even the settings emphasize the sordidness and guilt that attaches, for Ralph mounts Veronica in the backseat of a car while Arthur enjoys Marjorie in a deserted summer home: "They are now arrived at the appointed place of execution. An old iron bedstead underpropped a worn mattress, terrain of their engagements."[42] While Ralph's tryst is marred by a girdle that sticks and his own impatience, Arthur and Marjorie's encounters suggest war rather than love. While Mrs. Penrose knows she loves the protagonist more than he loves her, Arthur rationalizes that he is driven solely by his physical needs. He fails to understand that Marjorie is moved by love and not physical passion, a distinction he cannot make because he does not love her. For Arthur, Marjorie, who consoled him when Hope died by letting him rest his head on her bared breasts, represents a convenience rather than a person. In their rendezvous Arthur sees sex as Hope did.

> Deaf as yesterday to all remonstrances of reason, he purposed to sell himself over again to buy venery's disappearing dross—some moments of transient dallying with eye or hand, to which untied impatience quickly set a term; some impassioned moments of the now

engendered beast of two backs, of that acting androgyne whose he-half was excitedly prodding and probing, whose she- half was excitingly prodded and probed. The little life span of the beast soon sped, its death was died.[43]

Arthur errs in projecting his values onto Marjorie and, thus, denying her any individuality.

It is, finally, with Clarissa that Arthur finds a rewarding love-and-sex relationship. Her personality emerges as a chattering and advice-seeking one that naturally flatters Arthur's desire to be a counsellor; indeed, their compatibility resonates in page after page of dialog devoted to the events of the day, and culminates in the middle of the night in bed. Arthur has risen to close the windows because of a sudden storm; and, upon returning to bed, one thing leads to another until the protagonist "mounted and made all one with him," a moment that soon leads to:

> ...the thoroughgoing, deepening, widening work of their connection, and his then no less than hers, the tempo slowed in concert to engineer a tremulous joint containment and continuance. Then...the pace unreined, raised, redoubled, all to pass, no sooner his the very article, his uttermost, the stand-and-deliver of the undone flesh, the tottered sense outgiving of astoundment, then...provoked by that sudden touch beyond any bearing—the deep muscle groups, come to their vertex, were in a flash convulsed; in spasms unstayably succeeding spasms, contracting on contraction on contraction—hers! Hers, too; hers, hers, hers![44]

This tour de force, in which Cozzens renders an overdone but more moving account of lovemaking than found in many a more clinical passage, provides *By Love Possessed* with the most "adult" love scene in a 1950s bestseller. The elaborate syntax should not obscure the difference in this relationship: Arthur has finally found a woman with whom he experiences mutual orgasm, and while male stereotypes never emerge in this novel, certainly this scene plays to popular audience beliefs. In effect, Arthur has found his true love because they simultaneously induce climax in each other, an accomplishment that represents a popular wish-fulfillment about "real" love.

In confronting the truth about Noah Tuttle, Arthur realizes love's pervasiveness by coming to see that the entire human community is governed by this feeling in nearly all its important actions. The central character must dismiss his preconception of his father as a rationalist who only bought antiques for their monetary value and realize that Arthur Winner, Senior, knew the deeper truth in the inscription— *"omnia vincit amor"*— on the clock. Because Arthur regards "the world of men, [as] mostly, in respect to reason, unlike him,"[45] he must learn compassion toward others and stop insulating himself from the world because, as he comes to see, he is as unreasonable as the next man. His partner, Julius Penrose, crippled by polio, teaches the protagonist this final lesson. His initial appearance finds Julius agitated and bemused by his wife's impending conversion to Catholicism, a situation that involves Arthur because Mrs. Pratt, Marjorie's friend who has brought about this religious fervor, insists upon discussing the protagonist's former love affair with him. During their interview in Arthur's garden, Mrs. Pratt, who has insisted that everyone must face his troubles and admit to "sin," is startled by a snake.[46] She, who has been so certain in discussing human evil, becomes so upset that she cannot continue the interview; and, once again, Cozzens uses irony to celebrate the mystery of human personality.

Julius Penrose's mind and character subtly color his remarks: he tells Arthur he has been studying Catholic doctrine but that, to his legal and logical intelligence, faith and dogma remain closed mysteries: " 'My final reflection, I'm afraid, was that if hypocrisy can be said to be the homage vice pays to virtue, theology could be said to be a homage nonsense tries to pay to sense.' "[47] The witty and paradoxical Julius sees more clearly than Arthur, and it is pleasant to find the central character confronting someone who doesn't need his advice. Only Cozzens' constant reference to Julius' leg braces and the awkward contortions he must undergo to get around suggest the mental anguish of the character. The second discussion between Arthur and Julius leads to the protagonist's finally accepting his own fallibility. Ralph Detweiler, unable to face the pressures of an impending hearing and a marriage of necessity, steals his sister's car and flees to New York—an effort that is easily thwarted by the local police. At the same time, Helen, still driven by unquestioning love for her brother, tries to bribe Veronica Kovacs and then, in despair, commits suicide. Arthur feels guilty for not telling Helen of Ralph's whereabouts: love has come crashing into his rational world and proved stronger than any reasons which his calculating mind could advance. Helen's death further precipitates a crisis in the law firm, since she has kept Noah's books for years and is the only one, save the aged attorney, who knows how they are arranged. Thus, a Sunday afternoon meeting between Arthur and Julius, who has only just returned from a conference with a client, becomes imperative.

Their discussion soon moves beyond the problems of the moment however, for Julius confronts Arthur with the fact that Noah has juggled his trust accounts for years. While the protagonist is thunderstruck, since he always attributed superhuman wisdom and character to his older colleague, Julius argues that Noah's motives are common enough.

> "But he'd have to be crazy," Arthur Winner said. "He'd have to see that in the end——"
>
> "Not necessarily, not necessarily!" Julius Penrose said. "Emotionally deranged was my preferred term. He would betray himself, sacrifice himself, before he let down, sacrificed, those who had put faith in him. An emotional idea. Ah, what a mess these possessions by feeling may make of lives!"[48]

Noah has been possessed by love and, in order to maintain what others extended to him because of his acumen, he undertook day-to-day maneuvers to avoid hurting those who trusted his sagacity. Arthur worries about the legal aspects of this revelation, but Julius urges that, even though he entered the firm long after Noah started his sleight-of-hand tricks (and so is not technically responsible), he will accept a full share of any court suit that might arise. Julius even insists that he will demand to be a party to any such suit; and Arthur, who initially sees such bravado as foolhardy, gradually understands that his partner is motivated by love. When Julius adds that the firm should strive to make all of Noah's accounts balance, Arthur wants no further involvement; however, Julius argues that protecting Noah, who erred from compassion, constitutes a moral obligation that outweighs any legalities. Julius does not simply urge that their firm's good name is at stake, but rather that as men—as beings who can and must feel love— they owe such an obligation to Noah and to the people he sought to protect.

Arthur finally agrees, but still wonders whether they shouldn't tell Noah of their plan. Julius, who believes that being "able to know and still say nothing often seems...the most creditable of human accomplishments,"[49] urges that even this amount of truth telling is unnecessary. His view of love, shown in his attitude toward Marjorie's religiosity, suggests that a wise man knows it cannot be a means of possessing another human being but only a way of allowing that other individual to be himself. In Julius Penrose's eyes men ignore each other's defects because love is ultimately more important than truth. He insists:

"If you knew of something that you believed I didn't know, and that you thought it better I should not know, I'm persuaded you'd do as much for me—try every way to keep it from me." He paused. "Let me be more explicit. I'm persuaded, Arthur, that you *have* done as much for me. And, if unknown to you, I've always thanked you for it."[50]

Being exposed to Julius' arguments, and to the implied fact that his affair with Marjorie was guessed at by his partner and forgiven, causes Arthur to become a changed man. He has experienced the compassion that love embodies and can now begin to extend that same concern, even to his Aunt Maud. The protagonist of *By Love Possessed* thus makes a most difficult passage from self-centered respectability to compassionate humanity and, in so doing, becomes himself a permanent member of the human family.

* * *

John O'Hara's *Ten North Frederick*, which won the National Book Award in 1958, surrounds its moving account of a man's life with voluminous details of his society. The novel works to satisfy those who seek sexual "realism," being "in the know," seeing generations respond to life's challenges, or contemplating the paradox that a man may still be alive even though his genuine life has ended. While one suspects O'Hara equated success and intelligence, his major faults are technical rather than ideological. As the chronicler of upper- and upper-middle class life in a small town (Gibbsville, Pa.), O'Hara indulges a penchant for verisimilitude that keeps one asking why particular details are included (i.e. what is their relation to Joe Chapin's life?), even though such social topography creates the sense of a stuffy, inbred dominant class and its mores. A more serious weakness concerns the central character whose relatively uneventful life seems pale when compared to the more vibrant beings around him. When

Joe realizes he has wasted his life and then finds his one true (brief and melancholy) love, everything proceeds so rapidly that a one-night stand seems to be foisted off as an emotional *volte face*. While O'Hara may have intended precisely that effect to show how little Joe attained, the lovers part so quickly that their motives become extremely clouded.

O'Hara is best when recording the mores and personalities of Gibbsville. He can illuminate the town's political organization, its official and private channels of power and the discrepancies between them, or the ancestry necessary for admission to a particular social club. The Chapins live in an older, long-established neighborhood which gently falls into decay as other families move to the suburbs; indeed, their house symbolizes Joe's conservatism and foreshadows the defeat of his fondest dreams. Like the house, the central character ultimately founders on the egalitarian realities which surround him. Joe Chapin believes in pride and decorum in an age when such values are anachronistic and self-defeating. He remains heroic because of his code, and Chapin's passing ultimately serves as a verdict on his society. O'Hara ends *Ten North Frederick* with a short section that chronicles Joe's last years and describes his death (the novel's opening sections deal with his funeral and its immediate aftermath). Chapin's passing leads to a reflection on the process by which he becomes a memory:

> Somewhere, finally, after his death, he was placed in the great past, where only what he is known to have said and done can contradict all that he did not say, did not do. And then, when that time was reached when he was placed in the great past, he went out of the lives of all the rest of us, who are awaiting our turn.[51]

Death causes the living to adjust from sadness to affection to forgetfulness: no man remains "alive" as he really was, at best he becomes a more idealized (i.e. legendary) version of himself with some traits heightened and others forgotten. The same point takes on additional poignance throughout *Ten North Frederick* because of the (largely implied) failure of the other characters to understand or appreciate Joe while he is alive. O'Hara thus suggests that individuals rarely do more then project their own wishes so that understanding others is subsumed by fears and hopes.

Surely such a sobering theme—that men simply imagine the world as the sum of their own projections—cannot account for the popularity of *Ten North Frederick*. Indeed, this serious perception is ameliorated by the "secrets" that every character in O'Hara's world possesses. In seeing how this "better half" really lives, we learn what folk wisdom has always suspected—that the rich have the same vices as the poor. This emphasis colors O'Hara's discussion of the formation of the Lantenago Country Club, a process which stresses the commonplace that boys will be boys. While he draws distinctions between those who will be admitted and those who won't to emphasize the town's social demarcations, O'Hara ultimately reduces rich men to whoremongers: "Almost any sufficiently solvent Christian man, who had made his money in a sanctioned enterprise and did not habitually leave his car parked in front of whorehouses, could be reasonably sure of election to the Gibbsville Club within two years of proposal and seconding."[52] This insular society is reminiscent of *Peyton Place*, albeit, with the reservations that skeletons remain private and sex is not the sole item of interest.

While the characters' social snobbery maintains class barriers, their aristocratic sentiments are obscured somewhat by their ordinary lives and sexual conduct. This group's stereotypical thinking carries over to outward appearances, for when Edith Chapin spends a day alone in Philadelphia, she emerges as the prototypically affluent Eastern woman: "She dressed like a Member, belonging exactly to her class, with a Yale husband in the background, tennis and swimming for exercise, Protestantism for her religion, extravagance nowhere in her character, and discontent never far from her contemplation."[53] This acidic portrait, at the expense of the novel's least likeable character, catches a type frequently seen but not generally described so articulately. By typing her, O'Hara shows Edith to be a bundle of prejudices, a woman so self-assured that she never anguishes over defining herself. Edith's aplomb stamps her as unfeeling, a trait that seems even more pronounced when, during the same visit to Philadelphia, she has a one-night stand with a Gibbsville acquaintance because she feels neglected.

Years later, when Joe tries to run for Lieutenant Governor, Lloyd Williams, Edith's one-time lover, discusses Chapin's foolish venture into politics. Williams knows that Mike Slattery, the wardheeling boss of Republican affairs in Gibbsville, is stringing Joe along for a big contribution. Mrs. Williams, however, does not share Lloyd's concern, for she wishes Edith to be taken down a peg.

> "There's the cold fish, that Edith Stokes."
> "No."
> "You bet she is."
> "No, I screwed her years ago," said Williams.
> "Yeah, that was when I was the Queen of England. I don't think she has a good screw in her, if you want to know what I think."
> "She has two children," said Williams.
> "That's just getting pregnant. You know darn well what I mean."[54]

O'Hara's dialog panders to what the popular audience sees as realism; in effect, people always talk candidly in private, and women, in spite of being public symbols of family and purity, have always been just as outspoken as Lottie Williams. *Ten North Frederick* thus reaffirms the shallow cynicism one might associate with veteran newspapermen—when you've "seen it all," there isn't anything new or unspoiled. The same skeptical note surfaces after Joe's funeral when some of the mourners, those who came from Gibbsville, decide to erect a memorial to him. Joe's local cronies soon begin arguing over how the memorial should be financed and, naturally, who will direct the subscription. O'Hara cynically notes: "Joseph B. Chapin was finally dead. They had started fighting over him."[55] Paradoxically, in a social circle where pedigree is given so much lip service, there is no genuine sense of loss.

The mourners at Joe's funeral embody the mores of Gibbsville, values which ultimately define the "in" group O'Hara is discussing, and one finds the same insularities embraced by other figures. In a pensive mood, these lesser denizens of polite society believe rich people have a special sense of themselves, so that when they congregate they are inevitably drawn to each other. W. Carl Johnson, Gibbsville's superintendent of schools who has been invited to the Chapin funeral as an honorary representative of the town, expresses this view when he tells his wife:

> "Do you know something? Most of those men would seem just as important among a bunch of teachers.... When you get a group like that together they take one look at each other and they know right away who belongs and who doesn't...there's an American type, or maybe fifty American types, and they're all used to having authority."[56]

This reverence for one's economic superiors flies in the face of popular egalitarianism; indeed, O'Hara surrounds the rich with a group mystique that gives them an innately talismanic power to identify each other without even being formally introduced.

Shortly after Johnson's effusion, the leading figures at the Chapin funeral discuss their departed friend, and one of these characters, a judge, urges: " 'My opinion of my fellow man is that the man that reaches fifty without every doing time—has been lucky.' "[57] The audience thus sees that Johnson's belief in inherent group superiority is shortsighted for, just as Lottie Williams showed us a real woman in her domestic abode, so these respectable citizens dramatize the real basis of society's "successes." While luck and larceny helped most of these individuals, Joe Chapin conspicuously lacked both qualities. In falling in love with Edith, Joe accepted a frame of mind at one with Gibbsville; indeed, their views as a couple stress such all-too-familiar thinking and upbringing.

> Their over-all belief, which was not unique at the time, was that friends who professed the other Protestant religions were likely to be overconcerned with matters of theology; that Catholics (Roman) were people who had lost control of the beauties of ritual; and that Jews were strange Biblical characters in modern dress.[58]

Joe Chapin's life seems even more pathetic because his marriage only strengthens his ill-formed prejudices. Indeed, it is only natural that Edith would strive to keep Joe "arrested" at a fairly simple (and controllable) level.

Mike Slattery provides O'Hara with an opportunity to delve into politics, an area where his journalistic experience can come into play. Like everyone else, Slattery fails to understand Joe Chapin for, while the politician can read the protagonist's ambitions as though they were an open book, he has no appreciation of Joe's private feelings. Slattery's life is defined and limited by the rough-and-tumble of party meetings and graft, a world in which survival takes precedence over winning or losing; thus, he feels relief when Joe's ambition to be nominated for Lieutenant Governor is squelched. Slattery can show equanimity since Chapin's contribution is already safely within the party's coffers; however, when he is wheedling the money from the main character, Mike cannot understand Joe's insistence that, should his nomination not go through, this contribution will be his sole commitment to the Republicans for the next ten years. Slattery's supposedly thick professional politician hide conceals the same pettinesses as other men's. O'Hara further establishes the tone of local politics when he mentions how a particular judge always parks in the same lot for free. This bit of "graft" epitomizes the mutually attractive arrangements by which society runs.

(It was not likely that the owners would ever ask the judge for a major favor, but if they did he would take his custom elsewhere, and if he were to do that the owners would lose prestige. And, of course, it was possible that a telephone call from the judge might remind the police department that the parking-lot owners illegally obstructed sidewalk and street traffic throughout the day and part of the night. A judge is the only official who can give them orders and even make fools of them with impunity, and at the same time remain vaguely on their side.)[59]

In providing an inside view of local politics, O'Hara appropriately dispenses information in parenthetical asides; thus, the reader feels he is being let in on a secret by someone "in the know." The power of Slattery, who relishes being a party hack and has no aspirations to a more prestigious role, first becomes apparent when Joe Chapin seeks a Washington appointment without first consulting Mike. Chapin unfortunately assumes class distinctions rather than professional ones truly matter and he cannot understand that any politician's first loyalty is to his cronies and not to members of his social class: Joe naively believes that government embodies the noblesse oblige of a ruling class rather than the beneficiaries of a ramshackle system of mutual obligations. Mike Slattery is the grease that keeps the wheels turning; and Joe Chapin, the pros uct of a Yale education and a successful law practice, never grasps that reality.

Chapin's views about Franklin Roosevelt further demonstrate his lack of political savvy. Joe would like to run for president because he believes F.D.R. has betrayed the legacy of his social class through popular demagoguery. Slattery eagerly fuels this illusion by encouraging Joe's quest for state office; however, Mike has decided long ago never to seriously help Chapin. When Joe returns from his earlier visit to the Senator in Washington, Slattery angrily confronts him.

"Do you have to go all the way to Washington D.C., to be a pillar-robber?"

"Who do you think you're talking to, Mike?"

"I'm talking to a man with political ambitions. I'm talking to man that goes behind my back to *further* his own political ambitions. I'm talking to a man that I could help, and that I offered to help. I'm talking to a man that goes out of his way to weaken the support of an organization that I built up.... Now what have you got to say?"

"I say you can get the hell out of my office." said Joe.

... And thus ended Joe Chapin's chance of a Federal appointment, even to the postmastership of the smallest village in Lantenango County.[60]

Only after he has pledged $100,000 to the Republican war chest and been rebuffed by its "king makers," does Joe realize how things stand. Being a consummate political animal, Mike Slattery never reveals his feelings; and, despite their quarrel, Joe continues to support the Republicans because such a loyalty is an integral part of his patrician self-image.

Sex is frequent in *Ten North Frederck*, yet little glamor attaches to it, except when Joe and Kate Drummond physically consummate their spiritual and emotional union. Although O'Hara never suggests sex is depressing, his characters exhibit a realism about it that titillates on a social rather than an emotional level. No character's activity is ever described to the extent one finds in 1960s' and 1970s' bestsellers, and often O'Hara's presentation of such scenes discourages prurience. Despite such a tone, however, *Ten North Frederick* contains stereotypical encounters that reaffirm popular preconceptions. Although Edith proves to be a tigress in intimate moments, before marriage she voices the familiar double standard: in a conversation with Joe in 1909, after they are engaged, Edith fumbles: " 'You will have to—I must learn everything from you. Men always know, don't they?' "; Joe appropriately responds, " 'Yes, we find out.' "[61] Such social observation is vitiated by Edith's desire to dominate her husband, her own lively sexuality when aroused (a trait she exhibits with Lloyd Williams in Philadelphia), and her lesbian experiences in a girls' boarding school. Edith feigns purity because she believes that her virginity will tie Joe to her.

Teenage petting is the subject of a scene between Joe and his daughter, Ann, who has been on a "joy ride" with another girl and an older boy. Ann circumspectly characterizes their mutual fondlings which turn out to be far less exciting or innovative than one hoped. The very details— falling bloomers, groping hands, male fatigue—catch the sense of curiosity which seems uppermost and, because of the girl's refusal to be ashamed before her father, establish the mundane banality of the whole affair. The same naturalness colors Edith's lesbian tryst with Barbara Danworth, a situation that crops up when Barbara and her present travelling companion (who shows an interest in Ann) visit a summer cottage where Edith stays while Joe remains in Gibbsville. Edith feels no moral qualms about her past, viewing the affair only in relation to Joe: she has confessed some mild youthful activities, and:

> Now, at this late date, to have to admit the totality of her schoolgirl affair and the year's time it lasted, would have been to give Joe some kind of advantage that she had resisted giving him all her life. He...would hold it over her even now, and she would be compelled to relinquish some of that ownership of him that she needed for her soul.[62]

O'Hara's characters live on a sexual battlefield where individual desires pair off in mutual incompatibility. While there is no hint of enjoyment in these activities, since curiosity and role-playing count for too much in these characters' minds, such figures do catch the duality of desire and duty which often attends lovemaking among middle-class Americans.

Edith Chapin's most damning weakness is to confuse love with ownership, and so to perceive her relationship with Joe as a contest of wills in which she must constantly strive to be dominant. While Joe has genuine feelings about her and remains, for most of the novel, solicitous, Edith always examines her actions to see if they help in dominating Joe. At moments when Edith's decorous exterior breaks down she becomes capable of genuine passion. On her wedding night, for example, she momentarily becomes aroused and aggressive, only to relapse into equating the sex act with owning Joe.

"Do you want me to stop?" he said.

"*No!*" she said.

He felt her breasts and she pulled up her nightgown.

"Do it to me, do it to me," she said, "Hurry." She made it difficult for him to find her; she was already in the rhythm of the act and could not stop. "For God's sake," she said. "For God's sake."

"I'm trying, dearest."

"*Do* it then," she said angrily.

The moment he entered her she had her climax, with a loud cry. His own climax followed and immediately she wanted him again, but when she realized it was impossible she lay calmer, while he stroked the hair on her head and kissed her cheek.

". . . Are you asleep, Joe?"

He did not answer, his breathing was an answer.

"I own you," she said. "At last." But he was asleep, and even in her glowing she wondered and doubted.[63]

Edith's desires reflect a popular male nightmare in which the female remains cold until she becomes an insatiable threat. To the astute 1950s' reader, Edith's demands inevitably underscore her malevolence, for she combines hypocrisy with sinister sexual urges.

Edith's desires become obvious to Ann and Joby, the Chapin children, for as the son notes: " 'She always gets credit for showing restraint, being ladylike, shy. But after all, what's restraint? If the hate is there or the bad temper, it's better for all concerned to get rid of it than store it up.' "[64] Edith resembles Mike Slattery in nursing grudges and patiently waiting for vengeance; and Joby, who has not made a success of his own life, sees that such repression is more insidious than open rage. The Chapin children have, thus, transcended part of their legacy—a revolt that Ann signals when she thanks Kate Drummond for being her father's lover and bringing some happiness into his life. It is appropriate that Joe should attain insight with Kate, his children's contemporary; indeed, O'Hara makes his main character receptive to children throughout to suggest that Chapin is always "young at heart." Edith is dead spiritually because she has dedicated her life to consuming one man and turned their relationship into a marriage between a jailer and a prisoner. Mrs. Chapin's fixation allows her to control her emotions so she can easily dismiss other men: "And suddenly she laughed at infidelity: what a foolish admission of inferiority to want to squander time with more than one man when the owning of one man was going to be such a fascinating passion! What did it matter if the owning were inevitably unachievable? She had a life with a plan."[65] In her final quarrel with Joe, who admits he has been with another woman (Kate), Edith delights in recounting her own adultery as a means of retaliation; thus, even her night with Lloyd Williams was only a means to gain an advantage over Joe.

The central character's growth can be measured by his lack of reaction to Edith's secret; in effect, even though he slowly drinks himself to death, Joe has defeated Edith. At Joe's funeral, Mike Slattery suggests Chapin may have led a more involved life than any of his acquaintance suspected. After noting that people attribute buried secrets to Edith because of her reserve, Slattery argues that Joe may have been more of a mystery: " 'I've always thought there was a great deal more. In fact, Joe was a much more interesting study than Edith. We think, we conceded that the woman had more because she showed practically nothing. We don't bother to think the same thing about the man. Because we think we've seen it all.' "[66] O'Hara's ward boss thus suggests the same theme as found in *Citizen Kane*—the more we know of an individual, the less certain we can be that we understand him; thus, just as one views the celluloid life of Charles Foster Kane to discover the answers to outward questions (i.e. what is Rosebud?) only to be finally perplexed by larger issues (why did Kane choose the life he did?), so does Joe Chapin emerge as a mystery. While O'Hara's protagonist lacks the dynamism of Kane because the novel overwhelms Joe Chapin in a sea of social and psychological observations, the same humanistic theme arises. Ironically, Joe, in sounding out his law partner and friend since childhood, Arthur McHenry, about one of them enlisting in World War I, says: " 'Edith has altogether different ideas about me. In fact, I don't think anyone really knows me. If they did—oh, well.' "[67] Certainly Joe Chapin marches in that legion Thoreau described as leading lives of quiet desperation.

His secret ambition to be president, the discovery of which causes much laughter between the Slatterys, marks Joe as an innocent who still believes that men of virtue can and should rule in an age when character has long since given way to image and connections. In striving to be another McKinley waiting at home for the call, Joe appropriately embraces a past when society still counted for more than money. His idealism emerges even more strikingly during the interview with the state committee when Joe is seeking to be Lieutenant Governor; after they have dismissed that ambition, Joe rebukes their offer to make a speech showing he's just a regular guy after all. Following an extended drinking bout, Joe returns home to Edith's nagging and, as she tries to placate him by urging that there is always another chance, remains honest enough to dismiss such a bromide.

"Edith, what do you mean I haven't lost? I've wasted dear knows how many years, how many miles of travel, a hundred thousand dollars—and my conceit."

"Those things, yes. But you still haven't lost an election."

"Small comfort that. I never lost the Harvard game either. But I never played. Never made the team. Never sat on the bench."

"They'll offer you something. If only because you gave them all that money. Are you

going to accept?"
"No."[68]

Joe Chapin remains true to his own vision of himself and his class by refusing to be gulled into thinking an irredeemable defeat is only a temporary setback; and, in keeping with his pride, he refuses to become part of the new order. For Chapin, the ends cannot be divorced from the means used to achieve them, and so being true to one's self ultimately means more than winning.

It is only after abandoning his political ambitions that Joe discovers his real self. In illustrating that we "grow too soon old and too late smart," Chapin finally meets a warm, human woman in Kate Drummond, Anne's New York roommate who, after an evening with Joe, falls in love with him. Although Kate is being kept by another married man, she breaks off this arrangement to belong exclusively to Joe. However, the lovers agree that Kate cannot be Joe's mistress (because he refuses to have her cooped up) and that they cannot marry (because she believes such an act would cut Joe off from his friends). Even though they bow to rational considerations, Kate and Joe enjoy one ecstatic night which makes up for all the lovelessness the protagonist has experienced: " 'We'll make love and sleep together, and we'll always have it.' "[69] Their special night takes on more meaning when Joe, in saying goodbye, answers Kate's remark that she will always be in love with him, by urging: " 'The unhappy middle-aged gentleman loves you, Kate, and is grateful to you for being all that you are. I have a soul now, and I never believed in it before.' "[70] The novel's emotional climax thus reaffirms the popular belief in the power of love; indeed, O'Hara's protagonist only gains a sense of identity through experiencing a genuine romantic relationship. In melding soiled realism and romantic sensibility, *Ten North Frederick* ends by reaffirming one of the 1950s' most cherished beliefs.

By following Joe Chapin further (in an admittedly desultory fashion) the novel reasserts O'Hara's pessimism, albeit one takes away an overriding impression that Joe's life has been redeemed from complete despair. When he leaves Kate for Gibbsville, Joe knows that his decision ends his real (i.e. emotional) life: " 'Practically nobody in the town will know I've been away, and won't know I've come back to what? To nothing. To death. To the end of life. To death. To life away from you.' "[71] Without Kate there is only a walking death for the protagonist yet, in keeping with his pride, tradition and sense of honor, Joe Chapin goes back to North Frederick Street and his loveless marriage. Joe never violates his farewell promise to Kate by experiencing deeply again; and, as the novel's short final section opens, O'Hara notes:

If it is foolish to say a man's life is over while there is life in him that will respond to new life...it is just as foolish to deny that in a man's life a time comes when he does not respond, because he is unwilling or unable. It is that time, that point, which now has been reached in the chronicle of Joe Chapin...the story became not Joe Chapin's but the stories of other people, and with Joe's part in the stories one of diminishing importance.[72]

Ten North Frederick finally shows its hero, a man who places old-fashioned values above self (a virtual Don Quixote), accepting the consequences his values demand. Joe Chapin, a man suited to an age less "liberated" than his own, slowly drinks himself to death because he remains true to his belief that life has defeats which are determinative and not merely problematic.

* * *

The picaresque novel, in which a central character's adventures constitute the plot, has an honorable history. As a literary motif, the journey, with inevitably symbolic overtones of an initiation into experience, is as old as *Gilgamesh* and the *Odyssey*, while modern fictional travelers include Cervantes' Don Quixote, Goethe's Faust and Conrad's Marlow. In American literature, Herman Melville (*Moby-Dick*), Mark Twain (*Huckleberry Finn*) and John Steinbeck (*The Grapes of Wrath*) have supplied stature for this motif. Jack Kerouac is the most obvious 1950s' exponent of the journey-into-experience convention, for *On the Road* describes a series of trips taken by its protagonist and his friends. Kerouac's characters move primarily in space rather than in time, and their frenetic journeys represent characteristically American ways of finding oneself. Sal Paradise, the novel's leading character, directs his keenest perceptions to spatial rather than temporal concerns. He also embodies a voraciousness for experience that reminds one of Walt Whitman ("I contain multitudes") or Thomas Wolfe; and, like these literary precursors, Kerouac's hero never finds a final resting place. As a portrayal of the Beatnik life style, *On the Road* celebrates an improvisational existence that embodies a gentle disdain for America's "establishment." Sal finds much of the country and many of its inhabitants ghastly, but his love of the open road prevents him from railing against an indifferent society. Thus, Kerouac's characters have more thoroughly "dropped out" than many of their hippie and yippie successors.

Kerouac's major theses seem fairly obvious. In a culture where physical movement, whether as the constant shifting of domicile or the love of the automobile and the "freedom" it supposedly brings, is prized, Kerouac's characters imply that life's meaning can only be found in travel. Late in the novel, when Sal and Dean Moriarty drive to Mexico, they come upon a three-year-old indian girl who has (presumably) never left a mountain ledge. After trying to talk to the girl, Dean laments: " 'Gee, I wish there was something I could give her! *Think of it*, being born and living on this ledge—this ledge representing all you know of life.... She'll never, never leave here and know anything about the outside world.' "[73] Dean urges that because the road brings a veneer of twentieth-century civilization to everyone exposed to it, such a tranquil and mindless life must be avoided. Old Bull Lee, who puts up Sal and his companions in New Orleans, represents the other end of the spectrum, for this old man, who still lusts after women, wine and drugs, has had enough experiences to be a sage.

...it may be said that he had every right to teach because he spent all his time learning; and the things he learned were what he considered to be and called "the facts of life," which he learned not only out of necessity but because he wanted to. He dragged his long, thin body around the entire United States and most of Europe and North Africa in his time, only to see what was going on....[74]

Although the life of a Mexican girl may be slightly above that of a swine, existence should be spend "seeing what was going on."

While Kerouac's characters are looking for themselves, Dean, Sal and the others appear naive in their emphasis on acquiring a broad range of experiences rather than contemplating the experiences they have. Their assumption that quantity of experience comprises quality of experience is a belief that links Kerouac to typical American middle-class thinking. Like many another popular writer, he forgets that experience only brings about wisdom when the individual applies intelligence and imagination to whatever he encounters. Since American culture constantly urges that more is better (whether in cars or sexual equipment), the illogicality of such an argument (how much caviar can one consume at a single sitting?) underscores *On the Road*. Whenever Sal Paradise leaves someone, he feels loss and a hint of his own mortality, yet his desire to keep moving quickly heals these wounds: "But we lean forward to the next crazy venture beneath the skies."[75] In his emphasis on movement and adventure, the protagonist echoes the melodramatic illusions about American pioneer life put forward by popular culture. Just as the Western hero moves on to clean up another town, so Sal Paradise looks forward to each new trip with its new highs.

Kerouac's protagonist travels constantly from east to west, for going back to his New York "home"—living with his aunt and going to Columbia on the G.I. Bill—is always mildly depressing. While many of the individuals he encounters—hoboes who speak like prophets, truck drivers who delight in highballing their rigs, and local con men with hearts of gold—reaffirm the varieties of human goodness, many places depress the narrator. When Sal arrives in Cheyenne, Wyoming, on his first trip to Denver and San Francisco, he ruminates: "The floors of bus stations are the same all over the country, always covered with butts and spit and they give a feeling of sadness that only bus stations have. For a moment it was no different from being in Newark, except for the hugeness outside that I loved so much."[76] The more public and crowded a place is, the more likely it will be to distress the narrator: genuine human feelings can only be exhibited in small or intimate surroundings, such as bars, apartments or bus seats. Unfortunately, as Old Bull Lee insists, even the neighborhood bar is in danger of becoming extinct.

"The ideal bar doesn't exist in America. An ideal bar is something that's gone beyond our ken. In nineteen ten a bar was place where men went.... Now all you get is chromium, drunken women, fags, hostile bartenders, anxious owners who hover around the door, worried about their leather seats and the law; just a lot of screaming at the wrong time and deadly silence when a stranger walks in."[77]

However, this sentiment reflects the romanticism of the entire novel, for the older man indulges a wish about human nature (that people be communicative instead of playing roles) rather than presenting any insight about bars.

On their trip to Mexico, Dean and Sal meet people who don't feel any need for role-playing. Thus, there arises an equation of honesty and truth with primitive people that would have warmed Rousseau's heart; Sal even finds enduring love (with whom he lives for a couple of months) with a Mexican girl named Terry. The contrast between the United States and Mexico is quickly established by Sal's description of Laredo, Texas, the jumping-off point for the south: "All kinds of cab-drivers and border rats wandered around, looking for opportunities. There weren't many; it was all too late. It was the bottom and dregs of America where all the heavy villains sink, where disoriented people have to go to be near a specific elsewhere they can slip into unnoticed."[78] This sordid scene is quickly replaced by the Mexican countryside, its excessive heat and its pleasant people—an idyll that reaches its crescendo when Dean and Sal indulge in an orgy of dance, drink, drugs and debauchery at a local whorehouse.

Their excessiveness pushes them on to more intense levels of feeling, and only their lack of funds prevents their attaining even greater "kicks." This promise of heights remaining to be scaled is, of course, a recurrent aspect of romantic thought: the possibility of a secular beatitude in which the individual reaches tranquility through emotional excess underlies this entire sequence. The sincere gentleness of the Mexicans finally prompts Dean to declare: " 'Dig all the foolish stories you read about Mexico and the sleeping gringo and all that crap—and crap about greasers and so on— and all it is, people here are straight and kind and don't put down any bull. I'm so amazed by this.' "[79] Dean thus reflects how his American pre-conditioning has been unsettled by the elaborate human realities of the Mexicans he meets. Despite his dismay at the "crap" and "bull" he has been taught, Dean has no wish to correct American ignorance; indeed, he and the other characters no longer feel that American society is worth their concern—a disinterest that separates Kerouac's radicals from their 1960s' and 1970s' counterparts.

References to movies abound in *On the Road*. When Sal works at a construction company barracks, he describes a local road as being, "like in *The Mark of Zorro* and like all the roads you see in Western B movies."[80] This description enables any reader familiar either with the Tyrone Power vehicle or any of the thousands of cheap cowboy features to supply his own picture of a path beset by boulders and occasional trees and illuminated by moonlight. The one thing Sal notices when climbing numerous hills near the barracks is this road—always the symbol of experience and of life itself. After his friend Remi, a con man who persuades Sal to write a movie script which he can peddle in Hollywood, fails to return to San Francisco, Sal goes to the movie capitol himself. On his trip there, the protagonist meets Terry on a bus and together they travel to Hollywood: upon arriving at the corner of Sunset and Vine, they experience a vision of humanity reminiscent of Nathanael West's premiere crowd in *The Day of the Locust* (1939).

> Great families off jalopies from the hinterlands stood around the sidewalk gaping for sight of some movie star, and the movie star never showed up. When a limousine passed they rushed eagerly to the curb and ducked to look: some character in dark glasses sat inside with a bejeweled blonde. "Don Ameche! Don Ameche!" "No, George Murphy! George Murphy!" They milled around, looking at one another. Handsome queer boys who had come to Hollywood to be cowboys walked around, wetting their eyebrows with hincty fingertips. The most beautiful little gone gals in the world cut by in slacks; they came to be starlets; they ended up in drive-ins.[81]

This motley scene enables Sal to dismiss Hollywood as a depressed area for those who, like himself, need money fast.

The most extended references to movies come in, of all places, Detroit where Dean and Sal flop in an all-night haunt for derelicts and watch a double feature among a crowd that if "you sifted all Detroit in a wire basket the better solid core of dregs couldn't be gathered."

> The picture was Singing Cowboy Eddie Dean and his gallant white horse Bloop, that was number one; number two double-feature film was George Raft, Sidney Greenstreet, and Peter Lorre in a picture about Istanbul. We saw both of these things six times each during the night. We saw them waking, we heard them sleeping, we sensed them dreaming, we were permeated completely with the strange Gray Myth of the West and the weird dark Myth of the East when morning came.[82]

American culture is again Kerouac's target, for Sal suggests that these formula pictures provide Americans with ready-made myths about areas of the world and past epochs. In the same way that popular opinion stereotypes Mexicans, so does it believe that the melodramatics of singing cowboys and the ham acting of Greenstreet, Lorre, et al., represents truth. As Kerouac's protagonist suggests, such cinematic fantasies are best observed in a somnolent state. When the theatre closes in the morning, Sal appropriately wakens beside a pile of garbage collected from the movie house floor.

On the Road has achieved a reputation for being sexually candid; however, such openness only becomes extreme with Dean who is unhappy unless he has two girls simultaneously on the string. Indeed, Dean develops a timetable by which he goes from one bedroom to another, only stopping to talk about the "meaning of life" with various male friends. Kerouac never describes sexual activity in anatomical detail, so that, for the uninitiated looking for knowledge, *On the Road* is about as useful as a novel by Frances Parkinson Keyes when it comes to understanding who does what to whom and how. Sal has love affairs but he remains more interested in women as minds and spirits than as "tails." On his first visit to Denver, Sal sleeps with Rita Bettencourt, a girl Dean has persuaded to be nice to the protagonist. Sal tries to prove the girl's sexual fears are unfounded but, even though she "let me prove it, I was too impatient and proved nothing."[83] It is, however, during the aftermath of their lovemaking that Sal more importantly asks Rita what she intends to do with the rest of her life: " 'I don't know... Just wait on tables and try to get along.' She yawned. I put my hand over her mouth and told her not to yawn. I tried to tell her how excited I was about life and the things we could do together... She turned away wearily."[84] Such ennui implies Rita's fate; ironically, when Sal says his final goodbye to Dean it is, in part, because Rita's brother Remi insists that Dean isn't good enough to ride in his cab. Rita suffers from what Kerouac's characters would label as "bad faith" in that she lacks any capacity for wonder and only wants to exist on an animal level.

For Sal, Rita epitomizes a peculiarly American weakness: "Boys and girls in America have such a sad time together; sophistication demands that they submit to sex immediately without proper preliminary talk. Not courting talk—real straight talk about souls, for life is holy and every moment is precious."[85] While such casualness about sex would have shocked many parents in 1958, Sal's argument seems even more apt now than it did then. The character suggests that, for those like himself, sex has more meaning than for more conventional people who ignore the communication essential to love. Thus, the characters in *On the Road* love not wisely but (especially in the case of Dean who has numerous offspring, legitimate and illegitimate) too well. On a bus from Chicago to Detroit, Sal sits next to a pretty, vapid girl who unsettles him because the beauty of her breast "tops" contradicts her lack of inner vitality.

> Her great dark eyes surveyed me with emptiness and a kind of chagrin that reached back generations and generations in her blood from not having done what was crying to be done—whatever it was, and everybody knows what it was. "What do you want out of life?" I wanted to take her and wring it out of her. She didn't have the slightest idea what she wanted. She mumbled of jobs, movies, going to her grandmother's for the summer, wishing she could go to New York and visit the Roxy....[86]

Sal momentarily rages over a world which nurtures and rewards dullness; and, although he grieves for this girl who only wants the clichés and surface values she has been taught, the additional point that he and Dean are not society's beloved children also emerges.

Dean Moriarty enjoys nothing more than "rapping" with a friend into the morning's wee hours. While his conversation consists of reminiscences about himself and his father (who lived together as hoboes) or of random outbursts of enthusiasm over some sight or person, Dean conveys his love for life in torrents of words. He finds sex "holy" and wants "so much to live and get involved with people who would otherwise pay no attention to him."[87] He is also the archetypal con man able to sweet talk women so that his two-timing hardly bothers them. At one point, Dean comes to New York and takes up with Inez who, in turn, engages in long phone conversations with Dean's San Francisco-based wife, Camille. Since Dean must pay child support to Camille, he constantly fast-talks his customers at a parking lot into not counting their change. This elementary scam enables Dean to stay afloat, and to remain with his beloved cars; indeed, his mastery behind a car wheel looms large in the novel, for Dean's superhuman driving abilities enable him and Sal to negotiate tremendous distances in relatively short times. Obviously, the more unsettling question that Thoreau posed about building a telegraph line—what's the point if no one at either terminal has anything to say?—never intrudes upon the consciousness of the characters in *On the Road*. For them, it is enough to move at ninety miles per hour and head for someplace different: or, as Marlon Brando's young motorcyclist puts it in *The Wild One* (1954), " 'We just go.' "

While Dean Moriarty seeks out (and impregnates) several women, and even leaves Sal sick in Mexico to go back to Inez and his "real" life (with yet another unborn child), his wanderlust has a private origin which no other individual can control or comprehend. He is at his best waxing enthusiastic over something he has seen or is watching. When he and Sal go to hear George Shearing play a "set," Dean's words reflect Ernest Hemingway's familiar emphasis on *aficion*, the appreciation which arises from understanding the limits and purposes of a performance. In the same way that Jake Barnes derives consolation from the bullfighter's grace in *The Sun Also Rises* (1926), Dean believes in the artistry of Shearing's performance. Sal records his friend's frenzied reaction and seconds Dean's notion that the pianist was a true artist when they saw him.

> "There he is! That's him! Old God! Old God Shearing! Yes! Yes! Yes!" And Shearing was conscious of the madman behind him, he could hear every one of Dean's gasps and imprecations, he could sense it though he couldn't see. " That's right!" Dean said. "Yes!" Shearing smiled; he rocked. Shearing rose from the piano, dripping with sweat; these were his great 1949 days before he became cool and commercial.[88]

The change which disfigures Shearing in Sal's eyes also foreshadows Dean's disappearance from his life. On each successive meeting (usually separated by the nine-month school year) Dean appears more harried; and in their second-to-last encounter he has a whole series of ailments (including an infected thumb with a mountain of bandage around it which gets more soiled as he travels) brought on by having to cope with wives and work.

Sal Paradise seeks experiences because he is a writer; and, even though he has been in the Marines and through a divorce, he still seeks the footloose life he associates with Dean and the road. Sal appears remarkably naive; yet, if certain assumptions about innocence and experience (i.e. that one can remain "pure" even though he has through the most sullying experiences) are accepted, he is not unbelievable. While he possesses a loveable nature and can be genuinely moved, Sal's search for fictional "grist" serves as the impetus to his travels. His initial empathy with Dean combines a sense of spiritual affinity with Sal's own aesthetic theories to justify his wandering.

> Yes, and it wasn't only because I was a writer and needed new experiences that I wanted to know Dean more, and because my life hanging around the campus had reached the completion of its cycle and was stultified, but because, somehow, in spite of our difference in character, he reminded me of some long-lost brother....[89]

While this identification builds to the novel's final moving paragraph, Sal's view of his art reflects the uncritical formula which urges that an artist must have numerous experiences to create moving works. The similarity between this idea and the broader popular notion that more is better in any activity seems all too obvious.

Sal is liberated enough to have a Mexican girlfriend and, at another point, to savor the prospect of picking up some "black chicks"; however, the narrator's affinity with "ethnics" does not derive from guilt, as did that of so many later radicals. Sal admires Blacks and Mexicans because he believes they embody a more natural life style than Wasps do. He wants to be a "brother" because he things his spirit would be happier in another skin.

> I wished I were a Denver Mexican, or even a poor overworked Jap, anything but what I was so drearily, a "white man" disillusioned. All my life I'd had white ambitions; that was why I'd abandoned a good woman like Terry in the San Joaquin Valley. I passed the dark porches of Mexican and Negro homes. . . . A gang of colored women came by, and one of the young ones detached herself from motherlike elders and came to me fast—"Hello Joe!"— and suddenly saw it wasn't Joe, and ran back, blushing. I wished I were Joe.[90]

To be white and middle-class, to be a writer and go to Columbia, are all qualities that foster disillusion; and Sal realizes too late that abandoning Terry—the natural woman—because of society's prejudices about race has been a serious mistake. Yet, his regret, born of an idealized view of minority groups, never leads to any restorative action: Terry remains a fond memory, not someone to be sought out anew, for there is always the road to assuage any deep loss.

The final paragraph of *On the Road* echoes Fitzgerald and Melville, for it combines the perception of a vanished character with the narrator's sense of his own permanent attachment to a way of life. Thus, in it one hears the voices of Nick Carraway, mourning the loss of Jay Gatsby in *The Great Gatsby* (1925), and of Ishmael, introducing himself as a man who must get away to the sea in *Moby-Dick*.

> So in America when the sun goes down and I sit on the old broken-down river pier watching the long, long skies over New Jersey and sense all that raw land that rolls in one unbelievable huge bulge over to the West Coast, and all that road going, all the people dreaming in the immensity of it. . . which is just before the coming of complete night that blesses the earth, darkens all rivers, cups the peaks and folds the final shore in, and nobody, nobody knows what's going to happen to anybody besides the forlorn rags of growing old, I think of Dean Moriarty, I even think of Old Dean Moriarty the father we never found, I think of Dean Moriarty.[91]

While Kerouac's attempt at sounding poetical is overwrought, those who would dismiss *On the Road* as, in the words of Truman Capote, mere "typing" are surely too harsh; while those who would praise the novel as the "Bible of the Beat generation" are surely too kind. At its best, Kerouac's novel offers some serious insights that might serve as starting points for an individual to begin to come to terms with American society. As an expression of a new and liberated life style, *On the Road* remains as incoherent as most of the women Sal meets on his travels; and, while it could be argued that Kerouac's characters feel in ways that cannot be put into words, such a defense only echoes Capote's charge. Ultimately, one comes away from *On the Road* not dismayed but nonplused by the intellectual naivete of the central character: Sal and, presumably, Kerouac need to understand that being human means being as intellectually rigorous with oneself as with others.

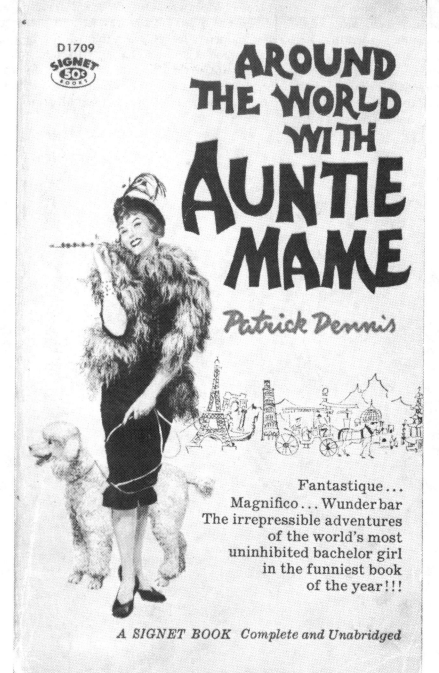

Around the World with Aunti Mame
Comedy as Correction
(Signet Books)

Chapter 9

"When in *hell* are you going to grow up?

The novel in which a youthful character is "educated" (i.e. "grows up") because of his experiences has been a popular literary commodity since the eighteenth century. Among others, Fielding's Tom Jones, Goethe's Wilhelm Meister, Dickens' David Copperfield and Maugham's Philip Carey illustrate the continuing popularity of such tales. In American literature the heroes of Thomas Wolfe and James T. Farrell's Studs Lonigan are contemporary protagonists who try to reconcile their wishes with the world's demands. This familiar pattern is a primary concern in Harold Robbins' *79 Park Avenue* (1955) and *A Stone for Danny Fisher* (1952), Patrick Dennis' *Around the World with Auntie Mame* (1958) and J. D. Salinger's *The Catcher in the Rye* (1951).

While Robbins' novels are "sensational" in dealing with a prostitute and an overly ambitious young man, they present a standard view of the difficulties of growing up. Their central characters believe maturity is achieved in sexual relations, but they quickly discover love is more important than physical sensation. They are also convinced that the individual's freedom of choice supersedes any group "conformity." Their trials finally make Robbins' protagonists aware that home and family (i.e. "roots") constitute the most important values; and, in true middle-class fashion, they place children on a pedestal. Yet, in keeping with an era in which the relationship between generations was symbolized by James Dean's tormented young characters in *Rebel without a Cause* and *East of Eden* (both 1955), Robbins' principals do not get along with their parents. In their initial disdain of and final reconciliation with the older generation's values, Maryann Flood and Danny Fisher exhibit intellectual contradictions in tune with popular beliefs: they easily shift from despising the timidities of their elders to espousing the same values because they lack any abiding sense of logic.

Patrick Dennis' comedy shows a young man growing up because of being liberated from his parents and roaming the world with his madcap aunt. Young Patrick matures because Mame treats him like an adult, and so the stifling influence of home (symbolized comically by Patrick's own wife who now worries over their son whom Mame has spirited away) is overcome. J. D. Salinger's Holden Caulfield exhibits a similar antipathy to his parents, but he is more consistent in realizing the implications of his attitude. Holden sees hypocrisy and "phonys" everywhere and, to preserve his innocence, decides he must be truly different from other people. In this choice, the character opts for an innocence based on experience—an attitude forged from the indignities and obscenities to which life exposes him—rather than for reconciliation with the older generation. Life remains full of possibilities for Salinger's teenager who believes that doing what the majority does is absurd. In the same way that Kerouac's Sal Paradise railed at the vapidities of popular aspirations, Holden questions the ceaseless repetition of banal deeds and remarks that distinguishes polite society. His resigned solution, a recognition that preserving his innocence will be a difficult task, causes Holden to choose to be isolated in the world—to be alone, though not lonely.

* * *

79 Park Avenue dramatizes the 1950s' popular perception of the prostitute, a traditional literary figure since Zola's *Nana* (1880) and Dreiser's *Sister Carrie* (1899)—and later in O'Hara's *Butterfield 8* (1935). Maryann (Marja) Flood's career centers less on the sexual details of a life of vice than on the emotional common ground connecting all human beings. Indeed, Robbins offers little salacious material, for his characters are largely caught up by the emotional traumas of love and children. Maryann becomes a prostitute because she's good at it and can feel a professionalism about her craft, a candor that separates her from her literary predecessors who were in it strictly for the money. Unfortunately, while Robbins suggests what might be an unpleasant truth (i.e. that whores enjoy their work), Maryann's honesty is quickly drowned in sentiment. Traditional middle-class allegiances to love and children overcome her cynicism so that Maryann embodies the hooker's proverbial heart of gold. While she eventually becomes a madame, Maryann's love for Mike Keyes represents her deepest ambition.

Robbins' plot hinges on a love triangle in which a hoodlum, Ross Drego, loves Maryann who, in turn, loves Mike; so that, when Drego exerts "muscle" (as only Mafia types can) Maryann sacrifices herself to save her beloved. In time, Ross is "rubbed out" by his cohorts and Maryann wends her way back to New York and a Park Avenue address. By now, Robbins' heroine has had Mike's child (a detail that did not bother the lovesick Ross) and Keyes has become an assistant district attorney. Their paths inevitably cross when a young prostitute dies from a botched abortion. Naturally, Keyes must prosecute the woman he loves; and, as in *Never Leave Me* and *A Stone for Danny Fisher*, Robbins uses a character as the first-person narrator operating retrospectively. This technique, which becomes awkward when events the narrator does not directly experience are presented, is fortunately not pressed consistently; indeed, Keyes' portion of the narrative often serves as little more than an interlude between third-person accounts of Maryann's career. Robbins feels more comfortable with a male point of view than the more appropriate female one (Maryann); perhaps this arrangement implies (wisely) that a male author cannot presume to be convincing about the female psyche.

79 Park Avenue abounds in situations and sentiments which echo Hollywood's all-too-familiar concoctions. Robbins uses such material because his novels are commodities comparable to a star's pictures, so that the same marketing techniques, in which the presentation of familiar values takes precedence over individual storylines, are applicable. Just as a Clint Eastwood or a Charles Bronson film must present its leading man as a macho figure, so Robbins must depict familiar scenes and sentiments in his novels. In both cases, if these artistic entrepreneurs were to modify their images too drastically, consumers might well become confused and not purchase the next production. The mass audience wants to be "entertained" through not having to think too much; and if Clint Eastwood appears as, say, a homosexual, this dependable relationship is shattered. The audience expects Robbins to be sexually "daring" (i.e. slightly ahead of popular daydreams) within a melodramatic framework; thus, his characters' vices only exist on the surface, since their hearts and minds are bastions of middle-class American morality. When Mike Keyes suffers the pangs of conscience in developing his case against Maryann, a colleague reassures him: " 'She had her chance, Mike. No matter what you say or what anyone did, she had the final say. She herself threw it away.' "[1] This defense of American society, in which the individual is never the victim of the group but only of his own decisions, means Maryann was free to choose because that is the American way; however, the girl's choices should have been apparent to her from the start. Thus, despite such emotional upheavals as being raped by a stepfather, there can be no appeal to mitigating circumstances.

This emphasis on individualism, so dear to American hearts, is accompanied (on the same page!) by a perception of parents that became a cultural cliché during the 1950s, even though it initially seemed shocking. In the same way that James Dean's "rebel without a cause" dismissed his folks as hopelessly out of touch, Mike Keyes remembers his parents' reaction when he asked for advice about Maryann. Their inability to see the depth of his love for the girl led Mike to reflect, after his father had walked away disinterestedly and his mother had gone into violent and brief hysterics: "I wondered if I would ever understand their point of view. I had long since given up hoping they would understand mine."[2] This alienation between generations, which other novelists would resolve through good will (*The Blackboard Jungle*) or maturation (*Not as a Stranger*) becomes a permanent condition in *79 Park Avenue*. Only Mike's boss, who has attained professional mastery and not merely age, is exempted from this dichotomous arrangement.

Probably Robbins most hoary (with no pun intended) cliché centers on Maryann's sacrifice for Mike. In the same way that many a saloon girl stepped in front of a bullet intended for the hero she loves (e.g. Marlene Dietrich in *Destry Rides Again*, 1939), Maryann, who is ultimately too impure to marry the good guy, offers herself to Ross Drego when the latter is beating Mike senseless. Although these men have been good friends, Drego, in revealing Maryann's career as a whore (a fact unknown to Mike who has been overseas) has unstrung Keyes. Mike's shock enables Ross to get the better in the scuffle which follows and, because he is a coward, Drego revels in his advantage.

> Ross stood over him, panting heavily. His eyes were glazed with hatred, the small billy still swinging in his hand. He slashed Mike viciously across the face. "I've owed you that for a long time." he said. Then a fever took hold of him and he began to swing wildly.
>
> "Stop, Ross, stop!" she screamed, clawing at him. "You'll kill him!"
>
> "That's just what I want to do," he said crazily. "For a long time now!" He raised his arm again.
>
> "I'll go with you if you stop!" she cried.[3]

True love saves Mike from having his brains beaten in; and, naturally, he never suspects Maryann's sacrifice, preferring instead, because of inevitable male shortsightedness, to believe the girl simply reverted to her whorish ways. Such an attitude reflects the double standard so prevalent during the 1950s, for Mike sees Maryann as tainted without perceiving himself as a contributor to her "defilement."

Keyes' outlook also suggests another refinement in this kind of thinking: a prostitute supposedly makes love without real feeling, thus Maryann has transgressed against romantic idealism at its deepest level. Mike's idealism surfaces when he remembers the dead girl in the morgue: " 'I keep remembering that poor kid in the hospital. The way she looked. That wasn't what she came to town for.' "[4] Keyes shows concern for the victim of a crime (a trait he shares with countless other fictional public defenders from Perry Mason to Columbo) and a belief that New York, which offers hopes and dreams to millions, must not be corrupted by prostitution, unwanted pregnancies and abortions. While Robbins' prosecutor seems contradictory (how can he judge Maryann as a victim of her own free choices and not apply the same standard to the dead girl?), Mike's duality reflects popular values. As the victim of an incompetent abortionist, the dead prostitute is forgiven because she has paid for her sin; yet Maryann, who has prospered because of her sins, must be punished, even though her success is a result of her own initiative. *79 Park Avenue* ends when Maryann goes to prison after revealing to Mike that her child is really their little girl. Keyes brings this three-handkerchief scene to an end by realizing that, although he has done what the law and morality demand, he must show mercy. Once again, Mike's boss, in presenting a necessary wisdom, reminds his assistant that justice must be tempered with mercy. This bromide leads Mike to reflect, after a moment of awestruck silence: "Mercy. It was a big word. The biggest. I wondered if I would ever be man enough to show it."[5] Fortunately, the audience can rest assured because the novel's last line finds Mike gently taking his daughter's hand and walking into a presumably brighter tomorrow.

Maryann Flood demonstrates that everyone needs love (and not just passion) to exist. Her character emerges early in the novel when, in another flashback, Mike's mother warns her son to stay away from the girl because: " 'She's been brought up without love and she has no understanding of it.' "[6] This pronouncement resounds ironically throughout the novel for, while Maryann has been raised in straitened emotional circumstances, she sacrifices enormously for Keyes' love. In marrying Drego and in her circumspect revelation of her daughter's parentage (so as not to destroy Mike's case against her!) Maryann shows a depth of feeling unmatched by any other character, until Keyes takes their child's hand and finally redeems himself. Of course, given the 1950s' distrustful views of parents, Mrs. Keyes' verdict can be dismissed because of its very source.

Robbins' protagonist grows up emotionally by thinking seriously about the relations between men and women. For Maryann, romantic situations are, for the most part, conflicts in which stronger individuals impose their wills. When she accompanies Drego to a beach house for excitement, Maryann allows the enraptured young man to lightly maul her and suffer the agonies of unconsummated passion before she finally brings things to a halt. In the midst of this groping, Maryann thinks: "This was what was so wonderful. What they would do for her, what she could make them do. This was what she liked about being a woman. Because, in the end, she was always the stronger."[7] Of course, her self-assurance reveals the character's immaturity, since the manipulation of physical impulses must never be confused with real love—a lesson Maryann learns through discovering how much she feels for Keyes. While Ross Drego is thwarted by a well-placed knee in the groin, Maryann does not tease him simply to enjoy an emasculating victory over all men (after all, this is 1955 and not 1975).

Maryann becomes smart about men early, so that when she is sixteen she already possesses "a sixth sense that most women spent all their lives without ever finding."[8] Her awareness of male sexuality reflects a consistent 1950s' literary emphasis on that facet of human experience. For the popular audience, sexual relations constitute life itself, so that physical intimacy takes on the same air which surrounds a religious mystery. Maryann knows how to play upon men's physiques and desires, a technique she has learned from innumerable couplings and a willingness to please. Given the girl's outlook, humanity is reduced to automatons motivated by a single desire; and the more unsettling view of men possessing disparate drives in innumerable combinations is concealed from the popular audience which wants reassurance and happy endings. Only the rare popular vehicle can succeed in making intellectually subversive suggestions, and in such instances mitigating circumstances usually account for the work's success. *Citizen Kane* (1941), for example, was not well received initially; however, even though time and critics have sanctified this film, its paradoxical theme—the more one learns about the central character's external life, the less certainty one can feel about his private self—has generally been obscured by enthusiasm over the film's techniques and performances. Thus, considerations of style prevent (or save) the audience from being unsettled by *Citizen Kane*,"[9] while melodramatic views of man (as sexually dependent and driven) prevent such issues from ever surfacing in *79 Park Avenue*.

Maryann Flood is most unsettling when she becomes a full-time whore, for she merely adds commercial and professional considerations to an already satisfying activity. While conventional wisdom urges that one should seek enjoyable work, Maryann's professional frankness tampers with values that are too sacrosanct. As an abandoned member of a nightclub act—a legitimate career she briefly pursues—Maryann sells her body to survive; thus, while the District Attorney insists on individual free will and responsibility, Robbins' heroine finds herself in circumstances where she must either compromise or starve. Maryann flaunts propriety by consciously seeking to be a real professional who has mastered her craft. In guiding her first "trick" to bed (and so symbolically usurping a male prerogative), Maryann thinks: "Now it was all clear to her. It had taken a long time, but now she understood. It was for this life she had been born. Some girls were born to be wives, some secretaries, some clerks, some actresses. But she had been born to be a whore."[9] In spite of her candor, Maryann remains devoted to: " 'Love. A home. Family. Security. Marriage. I'm no different than any other girl.' "[10] She does urge, however, that her trade requires as much commitment and skill as any other; and, thus, she emphasizes those qualities attributed to prostitutes by popular culture. According to this set of beliefs, whores possess hearts of gold (which can be reached *only* by the right man) and psychological shrewdness in their manipulation of their clientele. Such intuition and guile turns ladies of the evening into truly "lay" psychologists.

Sex in *79 Park Avenue* is presented in the customarily indirect and euphemistic ways that operate in 1950s' bestsellers; and Robbins' descriptions, as is to be expected, leave the imaginative burden to the reader. In an early scene between Maryann and Ross, the daring subjects of birth control and masturbation are presented; and, as a result, a degree of sordid reality intrudes. At fifteen, the protagonist already knows that pregnancy is her ultimate problem for, in a culture controlled by the sexual double standard, such a condition would bring shame to the girl while being dismissed as a natural "sowing of wild oats" by the boy. Confronted by this dualism, Maryann pragmatically knows she must fend for herself. When Ross, who has not been dismayed by being kneed earlier, tries to get her to go "all the way," Maryann sagely answers his demands.

> She stood quietly in his arms for a moment, her eyes looking into his. When she spoke her voice was gentle. "Even if I do, Ross, there's nothing I can do about it. I'm a girl, an' if I give in, I wind up in trouble. An' that's no good."
> "But there are things—"
> She interrupted him. "They don't always work."[11]

Maryann has already become a "consoling" analyst, for she comforts Ross (and thus retains mastery in this situation) while exhibiting more practical hygiene than her would-be seducer who is supposedly "street-wise." The girl's psychological dominance is further established when she offers to do " 'anything you want to make you happy Ross' " (except intercourse). In an exquisitely ambiguous phrase Maryann urges: " 'I'll help you, Ross, baby. Lie still.' "[12] While every reader will supply his own conclusion, Maryann's choice of "baby" describes Ross' dependence and reveals her command in an area conventionally assigned to the male.

Maryann loses her virginity to a cruel stepfather who rapes her to the accompanying cries of her infant brother. Peter not only slaps Maryann into semi-consciousness but catches hold of her hair and throws her around by the mane. Maryann is so delirious that she can only hallucinate as Peter succeeds.

Quick tiny flashes of pain all over her body as his hand became a blur in the dim light. Her body felt heavy, as if there was a great weight upon it. Then the last, most exquisite pain of all burst in her groin and she began to slide almost gratefully into the night that was closing fast around her bed.[13]

While no reader expects Maryann to enjoy this assault, her stepfather's attack points up the protagonist's essentially middle-class psychology for, in spite of frequent and supposedly lively intimacies, Maryann never seems physically moved by sex itself. She remains aloof and professional, and so proves by her actions (which the audience naturally believe speak louder than her words) that romantic love is more important than sex. For Maryann, her mind rather than her clitoris is the most important sex organ.

While Maryann goes out with Ross because he has money, cars and beach houses, she only truly feels love when Mike, working as an elevator operator where Ross' parents live, kisses her. After Maryann has spent considerable time with Ross, Mike asks for a date and they embrace.

She knew a lot of boys, and they never bothered her like this. She was always sure of how she felt about them. But this was different. It was another kind of feeling. A kind of weakness inside.

... Even the kiss was different.... This wasn't the game that it had been with others. This was her very own. The way she felt. The beginning of desire.[14]

Thus, Maryann finds the only man she will ever love; and, even though she will spend years away from Mike and become a prostitute, he is indelibly Mr. Right, the "one and only."

The novel arrives at its emotional climax when Maryann returns to Mike during World War II. By this time Robbins' protagonist has become one of New York's most efficient hookers, yet Maryann conceals this from Mike. In a scene perfected by Hollywood, Maryann waits for Mike to get off a train, and her nervousness about what he will think reverses customary roles (movie heroines—most notably Jennifer Jones in *Since You Went Away* (1944)—generally emoted in the steam of departure). Maryann is not in control because love precludes the mastery she has always attained with other men. After apparently missing him (Mike has failed to notice her and, of course, has lost weight due to the rigors of combat), Maryann runs after his retreating figure. For the first time in her life she actively seeks another person and, after she asks if she can carry his bag:

The cigarette hanging from his lips began to fall. It tumbled crazily across his lapel and dropped to the sidewalk between them. She stood trembling, waiting for him to speak.

His lips moved, but no sound came out.... She put out a hand to steady him. Then it was as if there were a fire between them, for she was in his arms and kissing his mouth and the salt of someone's tears was on their lips.[15]

This scene would bring the conventional Hollywood product to a close, for such a tearful and wordless reunion offers the climax adored by a sentimental, female audience. The characters are now so in love that words fail them and only tears (happy ones, of course) and caresses satisfy. Later, in a hotel room, Mike chivalrously offers to sleep on the couch, but Maryann seduces him into bed; and then, as they are only hugging, she experiences the most emotionally satisfying moment of her life.[16] Robbins wisely does not try to describe further intimacies, for there is really nothing the lovers can do for an encore.

79 Park Avenue's emphasis on children further underscores the middle-class values of its characters. Even Ross, whose life consists largely of momentary calculations of pain and pleasure, acquiesces when Maryann reveals she is pregnant with Mike's child; and, while the acceptance of another man's baby dramatizes Ross' utter dependence on Maryann, the hoodlum's attitude accords with the values of normal people. While Ross can snarl and abuse Maryann when she reveals her condition and its source (a knowledge that seems perplexing, even if prostitutes are experts in birth control and not subject to the same whimsicalities of chance as the general population), he agrees that she must have the baby. The birth of this daughter—a love child, if there ever was one—supplies the means for the novel's overly emotional ending. Mike is outraged when he discovers that Maryann has concealed the child's paternity (" 'The one thing you never should have done was cheat me of my child.' "[17]); however, the little girl's hand in his assures the audience that Maryann will find compassion and love when her "stretch" in "stir" is over. Thus, their child binds up the past and brings Maryann and Mike into the future.

* * *

A Stone for Danny Fisher opens with a device to delight movie buffs: just as the dead William Holden, floating face down in a pool, narrated his own demise in *Sunset Boulevard* (1950), so does Robbins' main character tell his own story from beyond the grave. Since the reader knows that Danny Fisher dies young and leaves a wife and son, the question becomes how did the narrator-protagonist reach his end. In presenting Danny moving from lower-middle-class respectability to lower-class grubbiness, juvenile delinquency, marriage and, finally, renewed middle-class respectability, Robbins presents his episodic plot with a prosy solemnity that founders on the rocks of overstatement. The protagonist constantly faces the "greatest" crisis in his life; and the reader, recalling the little boy who cried wolf, soon grows weary of such verbal overkill. Danny's shortsightedness about Sam Gottkin, his one-time employer and subsequent brother-in-law, epitomizes the difficulties of growing up in New York for an individual "on the make" and subject to the natural mistakes of youth. Danny's wish to pass on wisdom to his own son reflects the character's innately middle-class outlook: experience may be the great teacher but education (the vicarious transfer of information) fosters the constant hope that the future will be better than the past.

Unfortunately, the lesson of Danny's life gets obscured because the protagonist's innumerable difficulties never desist long enough for any perspective to be gained. While every incident leads to a major catastrophe, logic insists that there are, ultimately, no crises; thus, by living in unending tension, Danny discounts the tribulations which attend his setbacks by always undergoing a new experience. When his dog dies after the family moves to a tougher neighborhood, and because Danny has been challenged by some local boys, been kicked in the teeth and dropped "Rexie's" leash, the protagonist confronts his father. The old man, who has endured losing his business, now realizes he cannot provide any security for Danny: "His hand was on my shoulder, his eyes looking into mine. 'I'm sorry, Danny,' he said, his voice filled with sympathy. His eyes were dark with understanding, but it didn't matter—nothing mattered any more."[18] While Danny shrugs off his father's gesture as mere guilt, the protagonist's overstatement is never corrected by any more matured outlook. In reminiscing about his life, Danny never exhibits wisdom; indeed, he recounts individual incidents as though they were contemporary events. One misses any sense that Danny grows to be compassionate; instead, the Fishers quarrel and reconcile without ever voicing these changes in mood. Such lack of insight accords with the overstated rhetoric Danny consistently uses: for those who do not reflect, every successive moment looms as the sole boundary of experience.

Nellie, the love of Danny's life, introduces further logical difficulties for she often causes the protagonist to argue in solipsisms. She loses Danny when he flees to avoid trouble with the "mob" (a complication that arises when the protagonist becomes a prize fighter, must take the proverbial dive and, naturally, refuses) only to have him return clandestinely to the city and find her. When Danny says he must once more go "on the lam," Nellie swears that she will not leave his side: " 'You said that last time, Danny. Remember what you said? "No matter what happens, remember I love you." And then you didn't come back. But I remembered and remembered.' The tears were flooding down her cheeks. Her arms held me desperately. Her voice was heavy with a pain I could not know."[19] Danny thus records an unknowable sensation—the pain of one individual that another individual can never similarly experience—as a profound argument. Unfortunately, because it stresses the unique qualities of any person's feelings, this argument also precludes real communication between people—an aspect that never disturbs an uncritical mind like Danny's. As a further paradox, the romance of Danny and Nellie implies the exact opposite of what is urged here, for they get along because they do empathize. Like so many other heroes, Robbins' protagonist believes that women have finer (or deeper) feelings than men and so he attributes a greater sensitivity to Nellie than to himself.

As a prizefighter, Danny rises to the top of the Golden Gloves only to be seduced by the money and the easy women that accompany life at that level. This section of the novel, in which the elder Mr. Fisher constantly complains that boxing is no profession for a decent boy, reads like Clifford Odets' *Golden Boy* (1937), albeit, without that drama's happy ending. Since Danny has offended his parents by dating Nellie, who represents a "shiksa whore" to them, it is small wonder that the protagonist should ignore his father's advice about the ring. The money which Danny makes serves as a further wedge, for the boy continuously gives his parents funds to rub salt in his father's pride. After Danny agrees to throw a fight, a decision precipitated by a brief fling with an expensive call girl, Ronnie, the protagonist realizes: "Today was the day. Tomorrow it would be over and I would go back to the normal. Back to being a nobody."[20] Danny thus foreshadows that poignant moment when Terry Malloy (Marlon Brando) tells his brother Charlie (Rod Steiger) that he could (and should) have been a "contender" in *On the Waterfront* (1954). In both instances identity is measured by success, and the loss of face which results from "going in the tank" creates a crisis of self for the individual. This theme even provides an obvious background for *Rocky* (1977), a film in which a seemingly washed-up club fighter reemerges because he refuses to abandon his dream.

For Danny Fisher and Terry Malloy, living in a supposedly happier era, there is no question of a comeback in the ring. Since Sam Gottkin loses money when Danny throws the fight, their relationship ruptures only to be healed years later when the protagonist reminds his erstwhile benefactor that the sacrifice was not all on one side. Just as Budd Schulberg's Terry made his brother aware of mutual responsibility ("You shoulda' looked out for me, Charlie."), Robbins' leading man shifts the burden of guilt.

He sneered. "I sunk five grand once't on your word. Yuh think I'm a sucker for that again?"

I could feel my eyes grow cold. "That was a kid you bought, Sam. That wasn't me, that was your grab outta a hat for glory. I never saw any of it. The only payoff in it for me would have been a punchin' around."[21]

While the movie reaches more eloquent heights of feeling and dialog (Terry makes the same point by speaking of getting a "one-way ticket to palookaville"), Robbins uses this situation two years before the film's appearance. Writers and filmmakers have exploited this dramatic configuration because its elements reveal certain basic truths about American society; indeed, the prize fighter epitomizes the struggle for existence which a capitalistic ethos has elevated into a permanent and pervasive philosophical belief. The prize fighter, whether in *Golden Boy, Champion* (1949) or *Requiem for a Heavyweight* (1957), constitutes an American fictional type whose mores and struggles are as ritualized as the Western hero's.

Sexual daring was undoubtedly central to the sales success of *A Stone for Danny Fisher*, although the novel is never as overt or detailed as later efforts. Marjorie Ann Conlon, a local girl who has "developed" more rapidly than her peers, torments Danny by leaving her shades up at night. Robbins, protagonist even notes that his sister, Mimi, "wasn't all out of proportion around the breasts"[22] the way Marjorie is. Robbins thus manages to combine the 1950s' fixation about the female bosom with a suggestion of incest; and, while the latter motive remains veiled and dormant, Marjorie, after giving Danny the "steamiest" kiss he has ever received in a game of post office, asks if she can send in his sister. Incest as a fact of life crops up later when Marjorie, who has stayed home from a movie to entice Danny, tells the protagonist:

> "You're funny, Danny. . . . You're not like the other boys."
> I dragged at the cigarette. "How?" I asked.
> "You never try to feel me or anything."
> I looked down at the butt in my hand. "Why should I?"
> "All the other boys do," she said matter-of-factly, "even my brother, Fred." She began to laugh. "You know what?" she asked.
> I shook my head silently. I didn't trust my voice anymore.
> "He even tried to do more, but I wouldn't let him."[23]

Marjorie's aggressiveness foreshadows the female characters of Metalious and many another later 1950s' novel. When Danny inevitably takes Marjorie, he feels nausea rather than ecstasy. Even though the girl sagely insists that Danny will "never stop" now that he has been initiated into sex, the protagonist feels "drained and empty" and ends up crying over a wash basin. Marjorie is obviously not his dream girl, for her sexual demands have depressed Danny: the American male must not allow a woman to usurp his commanding place in such intimate moments. Marjorie thus emerges as a vampire draining vital energy from her victim, and Danny exorcises this contact (by punching himself to relish the pain in a bit of overworked symbolism).

Danny's next sexual encounter, with Miss Schindler, a school teacher having an affair with Sam, comes about when the woman arrives at a lodge Sam manages during the summer, only to discover that her lover is away on business. Although Miss Schindler seduces Danny, he, as befits his emerging manhood, carries her into a bedroom. Male supremacy is further asserted when she begs: " 'No more, Danny. No more, please.' "[24] Robbins' hero has thus reduced Miss Schindler to a bundle of sensations which can stand no further manipulating; and so, reassuringly, male stamina has again triumphed over female desire and anxiety. Danny must be told to stop for, once aroused, there is seemingly no end to his male vigor. Robbins, of course, traffics in ideal values so that his novels contain females who want to be dominated and endowed studs who surround them. The significance of being with Miss Schindler only becomes clear when, too restless to remain in bed, Danny takes a walk and thinks: "This was the joy of discovery. This was what I had been created for, this was why I was here in this world."[25] Clearly, Robbins' young man has found a calling that requires only a "willingness to learn."

Since a man needs love more than just physical intimacy, Danny gradually subjugates his delights in the flesh to that of the spirit. While Nellie becomes the object of such idealistic yearnings, Ronnie, a call girl "owned" by a gambler, initiates the main character into such a value system. In a bit of plotting that echoes medieval legend and grand opera (i.e. Wagner's "Lohengrin") one's name becomes a talisman for one's personality, so that Ronnie, who has been given to Danny as a reward for cooperating with a fight promoter, finally reveals that her name is Sarah Dorfman. Ronnie wants to be honest for she has fallen in love with Danny while realizing that, as a tainted woman, she can never expect to have her feelings reciprocated. Her real name is the only part of Ronnie Mr. Fields doesn't own and, by telling it to Danny, she creates a greater intimacy between them: "Her arms went up around my neck and pulled me down to her. I felt her lips moving against my ear. 'What I have to give you, Danny, is something he could never buy—no matter how much he is willing to pay.' "[26] Since this speech is followed immediately by metaphors about a "caldron of heat," Ronnie shows that, since her heart is in it, lovemaking with Danny is more intense and rewarding than "rutting" with a client.

Ronnie dramatizes a further male wish-fulfillment when, knowing that Danny loves Nellie, she still throws herself at the protagonist because one night in his arms will assuage the loneliness of a lifetime. Later, Ronnie urges that Danny has made her realize what she has lost through becoming a prostitute. Robbins' protagonist is apparently so good as a lover that he converts a whore from her basically loveless life. Because of one night with the main character Ronnie realizes she has cheated herself in substituting physical expertise for emotional comfort: " 'That's the way it was until the night you stayed because I asked you.... Never for love, always for money. Never for myself. Always for money. Until that night. Then suddenly I realized what I had traded away.' "[27] In spite of such an insight, Ronnie remains content with an occasional fling with Danny. Even though she knows Nellie will inevitably replace her, Ronnie gladly offers her emotions and her body to the protagonist—a process in which Danny comes to see himself as the means of the girl's redemption.

> "For once I want it to be different, for once I want it to be for me. For what I want, not for what I'm paid."
>
> I pressed my mouth gently to her lips. "It will be as you want it to be, Sarah," I said softly....
>
> Sarah had to find a way to repay herself for many things, and I was it.[28]

In this reversal of roles, Danny, as the object of desire, offers emotional comfort to Sarah. Symbolically, the girl washes away her sins not through abstinence but by having relations with a good man. Once she has undergone this purgation, Sarah can abandon her old life to become a member of normal society.

Danny attains real love only with Nellie who, in keeping with the sexual double standard, waits patiently and virginally for her true love. Nellie is so benevolent that she insists on Danny's going to see his family, even though his parents are bitterly opposed to their marriage. After this call, which leads to further bad feelings between parents and son, Danny returns downtrodden and depressed. While he wants to cut all ties with his family, Nellie counsels forgetting life's "hurts" and concentrating instead on its happier moments; and (fortunately) she includes immediate physical relations as a coating for this polyannish pill. Since she is wiser, Nellie brings Danny through his bout of depression.

> "I'll make you forget the hurt. I'll make you remember only the good."
> My eyes had widened. "How can anyone do that?"
> "I can and will," she whispered, looking up at me, her eyes deep and earnest. "I have so much love for you, my husband, that you will never need for affection from anyone."[29]

Since Robbins ends this section here, each reader is left to guess how Nellie accomplishes her very large promise.

Although *A Stone for Danny Fisher* traces the life of a character who, because of the Depression, loses status and then, by will power, re-establishes himself in the middle class, the novel abounds in bourgeois values. A middle-class emphasis on individual initiative with its concomitant refusal to accept charity makes Robbins' protagonist work out of trouble while refusing handouts from others, however well-meaning. Even when he, Nellie, and their daughter, Vickie, suffer privation, Danny retains this abiding distrust of "welfare." When Nellie suggests that taking relief can't be all bad, the protagonist insists: " 'Those people jus' don't wanna work. You can get a job if you want to bad enough. I want to work. I'll get a job.' "[30] Danny's self-confidence proves shortsighted, however, for the Fishers soon find themselves on the dole, having to answer the intrusive questions of welfare workers. Their distress culminates with the death of their baby, an event that causes Danny again to put pride before well-being. In a social class which places such great value on children as embodiments of the future, custom decrees that the family must nurture its offspring; and even though Danny has been unable to provide food, it remains a point of pride that he bury his own child without the state's help.

However, because he spends seventy dollars on Vickie's funeral, Danny falls foul of the welfare department and gets thrown off the relief rolls. As he notes, in explaining his dilemma: "That's where the buggers had you. You had to answer their questions or they'd cut you off. Still I couldn't bring myself to tell them where I got the dough. That was something personal between Vickie and us."[31] The welfare worker, who becomes so incensed by Danny's refusal that he leaves sputtering, is comparable to many another 1950s' fictional official. Just as psychiatrists, federal agents and psychological testers emerge as myopic bumblers (in *The Bad Seed*, *The Manchurian Candidate* and *No Time for Sergeants*), this official exhibits the same unfeeling, bureaucratic outlook one associates with an institutionalized society. Danny's refusal represents the individual asserting his will against the system. The protagonist's defiance soon gives way, however, to dreams of greater success once Danny has gotten back on his feet, a process which coincides with the new prosperity bred by World War II. Even though Danny enjoys economic security, he remains dissatisfied with working for his brother-in-law. Such unrest leads Danny to try selling his enthusiasm for coin-operated machines to Sam, who remains skeptical. Danny's immaturity surfaces as a result and precipitates the final crisis that produces his death.

The protagonist's earliest trauma arises from the loss of the family house and the subsequent removal to an inferior neighborhood. Danny's later career as a gang leader and a prize fighter grows out of this disappointment. It is only when he finds prosperity after the Depression that Danny can return to his old neighborhood to purchase his family's old house. While such behavior clearly dates the novel (for such an aspiration would seem foolish today when suburbia has replaced the older, central portions of nearly all major American cities), Robbins' central character is attempting to re-establish himself in his own past. This search for identity causes Danny finally to realize he has been too harsh with his father. Once again, however, Robbins presents a rapid volte face for Danny invites his parents over to see their old home and then realizes that his father's "voice was the voice of the house. It had never really been my house at all, it had belonged to him. When I told the house of my love, I was speaking to him, and when the house spoke to me, he was speaking to me. It would never be my house until he gave it to me, no matter how much I paid for it."[32] This mystical pronouncement suggests that Danny at last has arrived at a sense of compassion for his fellow men.

Unfortunately, by this time, Danny has also set in motion a scheme to remove Sam, and only checks his ambition when his brother-in-law does something dramatic for him. When Nellie suffers complications during her second pregnancy (the beginning of a miscarriage) a transfusion is needed to save the lives of mother and child; but, in familiar melodramatic fashion, the " 'type we need is one that only one donor in a thousand might have.' "[33] While everyone sweats, prays and grimaces, Sam turns out to have this blood type so that he restores Nellie to health and creates tremendous guilt feelings in Danny whose subsequent efforts to stop the murder he had set up lead to his own death. While the protagonist perishes in a flaming car after being raked by a machine gun volley, he is secure in the knowledge that his efforts have thwarted the hired killers. Thus, Robbins' aspirant middle-class hero lays down his life to preserve the ultimate source of bourgeois comfort and meaning—the family.

A Stone for Danny Fisher, which is written as a posthumous letter from Danny to his unborn son, thus presents a commentary on the average man's role in history. Danny arrives at genuine understanding by dying to prevent unjustified suffering, and his self-sacrifice epitomizes the role a civilized man should play. The novel, which initially portrayed Danny reclaiming a stray dog (Rexie) from a construction ditch in which the animal was trapped, ends by implying that human society exists because of the sacrifices of small (i.e. anonymous) men. In the same way that the dog's struggle with hopeless odds moved him to compassion, Danny rescues Sam and provides a worthwhile legacy to his own child. *A Stone for Danny Fisher* ends by pulling out all the emotional stops, for the protagonist, now speaking from beyond the grave in a most sonorous, movie-narrator tone, urges:

> ...I am the man who will live forever in the thousands of years yet to come. For I am the man who will reap the few benefits and pay for the many errors that are created by the great.
> And the great are but my servants, for...all who weep for their loved ones also weep for me....
> To live in the hearts we leave behind is not to die.[34]

While history may be about the "great" who do things but excite no emotionally deep feelings, its real workings are governed by the common man who suffers because of the actions of the "great" and finds solace in the loves of wife, children and family. Given a choice between accomplishment and domestic affection, the reasonable man (i.e. the one tempered by experience) will chose love and suffering over deeds. Thus, *A Stone of Danny Fisher* implies that the life of a family man is more valuable than that of a ruler—an argument which accords with what ordinary readers wanted to believe all along.

* * *

Around the World with Auntie Mame offers a classic example of media reciprocity. While its predecessor, *Auntie Mame* (1955), spawned a stage play and film, this sequel sold better because the audience had been alerted to Dennis' delightfully eccentric adventuress. As Hollywood's and television's formula productions so abundantly show, a sequel usually represents good business. In Auntie Mame's world comic eccentrics and parasites abound, yet she, although constantly assailed, survives and prospers. In retaining her fundamental innocence despite the most compromising of situations, Mame shares the comic otherworldliness one associates with Charlie Chaplin, Laurel and Hardy and Don Quixote, a capacity to survive as one's self through rising above circumstances. In this novel, Mame and her nephew, Patrick, travel through pre-World War II Europe to defeat various scoundrels, hypocrites and moochers who bestrew their path. Dennis' episodic narrative begins when the mature and now married Patrick commiserates with his wife over the two-and-a-half year "vacation" Mame has been taking with their seven-year-old son. Parental anxiety leads Patrick to recall his earlier trip so as to reassure his wife that Michael (who must now be ten) will survive. *Around the World with Auntie Mame* opens on a nostalgic note that is sustained throughout; for, when the narrator urges that women " 'Looked much better in 1937 then they do this year,' "[35] he implies that the past was more lively than the present.

Those earlier times were special because Auntie Mame loomed so large in Patrick's life. As his patroness and travelling companion, she treated him like an adult at a time when peers and parents insisted he was a child. The complaints of Patrick's wife, who insists that unless her son returns soon she will never be a den mother,[36] are laid to rest when Mame and the boy appear at the novel's conclusion. While Auntie Mame wonders about where to put some totem poles she has acquired on their travels (and Patrick implies that he could suggest a wonderful place for them), Dennis' central character naturally hasn't got time to listen to any suggestions (however vulgar). In her typical style, Mame can only deposit Michael and rush to a lecture she has promised to deliver. Her timing, generally of the just-in-the-nick-of variety, remains excellent for, on the earlier trip, Mame saved her nephew and friends, especially Vera Charles, from such potential catastrophes as being unable to perform at the Folies Beregère and mangy money grubbers. Mame functions as the novel's deus ex machina in extricating everyone from disaster. At one point, after Amadeo Armadillo, a Spanish playboy, descends on Vera and persuades her to marry, Mame confides to Patrick that Vera " 'came mincing idiotically into my room, like some Barrie character, and said that she was going to marry that snake. *Nothing* I've been able to say can shake her. She's out ordering her trousseau now—and *he's* out ordering *his*.' "[37] Mame's description, which equates Vera' conduct to a scene from *Peter Pan*, and her pride in her own power of persuasion are comic traits that disguise her good heart. She is actually distraught over Vera's choice and proceeds to seduce Amadeo into believing she will marry him instead, gets him to run away with her, and then locks him in the toilet of a chartered plane to escape his greasy charm.

In less exalted circumstances Mame takes Vera's place in a Folies Bergère review. While Patrick can describe this famous haunt as a "kind of Radio City Music Hall with bosoms," Mame's appearance in a dreadful pantomime about Catherine the Great is punctuated by scenes of backstage chaos in which Vera coaches her friend. When the last processional scene is to take place, Mame discovers that she must appear all-but-nude leading six Russian wolfhounds.

"Vera," Auntie Mame gasped, "what *is* this? An *animal* act."

"No, Mame," Vera said apologetically, "they're part of your props. You go with them in the big love scene."

"Vera! That's *sodomy*! I won't. . . .

"Oh, nothing like that, de-ah. See, they *like* you."[38]

This episode reaches its appropriate climax when Mame, after enduring thunderous applause and a heckler who keeps insisting that she "take it off," loses control of the dogs and lands in the lap of Mr. Babcock, an earlier dinner companion who had kept insisting that the Folies was fit only for lechers. Thus, hypocrisy is comically corrected by ridicule—a process which reaffirms the heroine's view of the world. Dennis' penchant for satirizing theatrical excess works again when Patrick attends an opera in

Vienna. After summarizing a plot in which a prince and a princess run away to avoid contracted marriages, only to meet and fall in love in an Alpine village, Patrick notes:

> The first act drew to a thundering finale with a sweet duet between the two stars—whose combined ages was just over a hundred and whose combined weight was just under five hundred—that established their love pretty firmly. Although considering their years, sizes, and corseting, I couldn't imagine how they'd ever be able to consummate it.[39]

For anyone familiar with opera, Patrick's description epitomizes what is apt to be a literal reaction to such an occasion.

Characters who attempt to live off Auntie Mame under false pretenses suffer even more biting comic fates. When Mame becomes obsessed with appearing at Court in England, she hires Lady Gravell-Pitt, an alleged confidante of royalty, to advise her. At an expensive party Mame gives, which is attended by supposed aristocrats who devour the hors d'ouevres and champagne, Patrick observes:

> None of them was a minute under sixty and they were all related to Lady Gravell-Pitt. The women were given to whiskers and the men to rheumatism. They were all dressed like something out of a rummage sale, and if *they* were the cream of Court circles, I felt awfully sorry for King George and Queen Elizabeth—[40]

Lady Gravell-Pitt influences Mame for a time, but when she charges her patroness one hundred guineas for a bedraggled costume that Patrick is to wear at a garden party, her greed becomes too apparent. The outdoor fete turns into a complete fiasco when a torrential rain drives the participants to cover and brings Mame to her senses. Ever the skeptic, Patrick dismisses the whole undertaking even before the shower: "the only difference I could see between the Royal Garden Party and a giant rally at Yankee Stadium is that Yankee Stadium has rest rooms and it's easier to get refreshments."[41]

Mame sends Lady Gravell-Pitt packing in the same abrupt way she later uses to dispatch her boorish brother-in-law, Elmore Jefferson Davis Burnside. While she genuinely loved her husband, Beauregard Jackson Pickett Burnside (and one notes that their Confederate "given" names are an attempt to cancel out their Yankee surname), Mame only endures Elmore, who descends on her in Venice when she's drunk. Since Elmore has come seeking her hand, and Mame has been sufficiently inebriated to appear acquiescent, Patrick worries that his beloved Aunt will marry this boisterous loudmouth. At dinner Elmore offers a typical bit of nudge-in-the-ribs, sophomoric humor.

> "Shoot mah shoes, what's tha-yut?"
> "It's fish balls," I hissed.
> "Best part of the fish! Ha *ha* ha *ha* ha *ha*!" I'd heard that witticism every Friday at school for seven years, and Auntie Mame had probably heard it seventeen years before that. Even so, she was helpless with laughter and choked on her wine.[42]

Elmore makes a further ass of himself at an exclusive party that Mame and a cafe society friend give; and, once again, the comic protagonist is enabled to elude a rapacious and boorish individual.

A more extended infatuation takes place between Mame and Baron von Hodenlohern ("Putzi"), an Austrian noble turned Nazi who wants to use the heroine's money to acquire arms for the Anschluss. Mame buys Putzi's castle near the village of Stinkenback-in-Tirol, but, upon discovering his real intentions, she destroys the whole place along with his cache of arms. In doing so, Mame triumphs over both her would-be suitor and Nazi Germany, for, by burning the castle she thwarts Putzi and subsequently collects from the largest insurance company in Hitler's Germany. Sailing to the Orient, Mame later saves Patrick from an infatuation with an apparent minister's daughter (who turns out to be the man's accomplice in a gun-running expedition to Shanghai). Before he begins to pine, Patrick describes the meals aboard their Greek tramp steamer.

> Of course we sat at the captain's table, because there wasn't any other. Its tablecloth was covered with wine spots, encrusted with old bits of gravy, ketchup and rancid olive oil. There was a smart centerpiece of salt, pepper, oil, vinegar, ketchup, A-1 sauce, and toothpicks. Everything jiggled and jingled to the vibrations of the engine. A vase of dusty artificial carnations and a large tinted photograph of Pola Negri completed the *decor* of the officer's mess.[43]

When Patrick's enchantress turns out to be a cockney moll named Rosy, the young man has learned that shortsightedness is a common human failing; and Auntie Mame, who never interfered in her nephew's infatuation, survives with her spirit intact. The power of Dennis' character is reconfirmed when she deposits Michael and runs to her lecture; in effect, she has enabled two generations to grow up.

*   *   *

The Catcher in the Rye is the most academically celebrated bestselling American novel from the 1950s and has been widely hailed as a classic account of the anxieties and frustrations of adolescence. While Salinger's novel has been banned from many a public bookshelf, it is neither pornographic nor prurient. If anything, Holden Caulfield's experiences exhibit life's disarming qualities, for he encounters characters and situations that are never completely explicable, so that readers experience a sense, finally, that existence contains more complexities than simplicities. Because of its character drawing, *The Catcher in the Rye* shows that man must struggle against the apparent meaninglessness and hypocrisy which surround him. Such a struggle does not always lead to success or happiness for the enigmas which beset Holden are largely unresolved at the end of the book. Thus, Salinger finally represents life as a mystery and a condition rather than a set of problems with solutions. Holden's character is such that any resolution, any tying together of disparate plot strands or sudden change on his part would ring untrue.

The novel's theme is appropriately stated as a question. After leaving the prep school he found hypocritical and from which he was about to be expelled, Holden meets numerous characters in New York. At one point, he meets Old Luce, a former schoolmate whom Holden remembers for his nightly "sex talks" to groups of awestruck underclassmen. Luce now attends Columbia and bridles when Holden treats him like an equal (by asking him about his love life). Finally, Luce asks, " 'When in *hell* are you going to grow up?' "[44] as a way of bringing the conversation to an end. Luce, as a spokesman for the adult, established world that Holden regards as phony, epitomizes those who have forgotten (or repressed) what adolescence was like and made virtues out of the necessities of adjustment and making a living. Holden, despite his self-indulgence and flight from responsibility, tries to preserve some sense of childhood while living in a society which looks askance at nostalgia. Because he sees hypocrisy in his elders, the question in Holden's mind is why grow up if one must become a phony to do so. The protagonist also recognizes the hypocrisy and viciousness of his peers and, finally, in those younger than himself, so that his adventures become an education which teaches Holden that, to preserve his innocence, he must struggle alone.

His frequent references to feeling alone and to loneliness symbolize the dawning awareness of Salinger's protagonist. As a corollary, Holden also realizes that communicating with others is nearly impossible: the people he meets consistently talk to him out of their own self-preoccupations, so that conversation becomes a process of talking *at* rather than talking *to*. Holden's dismay at this inability to "connect" surfaces in a nightclub when he asks a waiter to take a message to a singer: "I told him to ask old Valencia if she'd care to join me for a drink. He said he would, but he probably didn't even give her my message. People never give your message to anybody."[45] Holden's defense against the impersonality, play-acting and neglect in the world around him is humor-making fun of the surrounding absurdity is the only way to survive and to retain one's idealistic preconceptions. Thus, the protagonist has chosen laughter and ridicule as the means for enduring in the world.

Holden's awareness of the role-playing inherent in modern life captures our attention from the novel's onset. His favorite word, applied to teachers, students, relatives and celebrities, is "phony." While hypocrisy presents a continuous charge of youth against age, Holden makes a more precise accusation when he tells Phoebe:

"Lawyers are all right, I guess—but it doesn't appeal to me.... I mean they're all right, if they go around saving innocent guys' lives all the time, and like that, but you don't *do* that kind of stuff if you're a lawyer. All you do is make a lot of dough and play golf and play bridge and buy cars and drink Martinis and look like a hot- shot."[46]

In essence, Salinger's protagonist insists that society rewards only those members who socialize well, do not seriously question its values, and affirm the virtue of "getting along." While Holden's plight may be the dilemma of every young person at some point, American society with its emphases on adjustment, winning friends and influencing people, hardly represents the ideal environment for such difficult thoughts.

When Holden goes out with Sally, a girl whose inane conversation drives him onto the defensive, he pursues a "what if" discussion about getting married. According to Sally, there would be "oodles" of things to do after they were married, but Holden, whose anger has been slowly rising, lashes out.

> "I said no, there wouldn't be marvelous places to go to after I went to college and all. Open your ears... I'd be working in some office, making a lot of dough...and playing bridge all the time, and going to movies and seeing a lot of stupid shorts and coming attractions and newsreels. Newsreels. Christ almighty. There's always a dumb horse race, and some dame breaking a bottle over a ship, and some chimpanzee riding a goddam bicycle with pants on. It wouldn't be the same at all. You don't see what I mean at all!"[47]

The girl wants to reduce existence to a series of predictably repetitive actions and does not understand that such regularity would destroy life's spontaneity. Holden, on the other hand, wants to be aware of possibilities rather than just watch the same actions repeated mindlessly by different people. The newsreel symbolizes the triteness Holden sees in so much human effort; indeed, it serves as a tranquilizer to reduce existence to a series of familiar images which reassure the viewer that he already "knows" about life. As television has loomed ever larger in American life, Holden's perception has become even more striking. The maxim "the more things change, they more they remain the same" epitomizes this process by which Johnny Carson and *Charlie's Angels* replace Churchill Downs and Mrs. Truman.

Holden's only strong academic subject is English for, despite flunking everything else, he gladly writes a composition for a roommate whom he dislikes. The protagonist's acute sense of language carries over into perceptions of professional writers, many of whom he believes are as corny as the newsreels he fears having to watch for the rest of his life. On the train from school to New York, the protagonist is so distraught he cannot read the magazine stories he normally peruses.

> If I'm on a train at night, I can usually even read one of those dumb stories in a magazine without puking. You know. One of those stories with a lot of phony, lean-jawed guys named David in it, and a lot of phony girls named Linda or Marcia that are always lighting all the goddam Davids' pipes for them.[48]

Salinger's gift for parody enables Holden to demolish such productions; indeed, once one appreciates that all movie newsreels are the same and that magazine fiction is full of characters like those the narrator describes, such forms can never be taken as seriously again. While causing us to laugh, Holden also comes to appreciate that innocence does not lie in naivete but is, rather, a condition one attains only through contact with the world. To remain innocent (i.e. true to one's self) requires constant effort; and, by dismissing the corrupt portions of his world, Holden clears his vision so as to concentrate on those things and people which still retain their innocence.

Holden's attitude toward "corny" fiction extends to those who practice arts deceitfully and to those who praise such deceptions. Just as Hemingway drew a distinction between mere spectators and those with real understanding (at the bullfight in *The Sun Also Rises*), Salinger's protagonist delineates the gulf between real artistry and its derivative forms. After calling Sally Hayes for a date, Holden recalls his error in thinking the girl was smart because she knows a lot about literature and the theatre; indeed, the main character realizes: "If somebody knows quite a lot about those things, it takes you quite a while to find out whether they're really stupid or not."[49] The protagonist recognizes that the trappings of education—a knowledge of books, or performers in Sally's case—do not insure wisdom, for only the depth of one's feelings can do that. Sally confuses an ability to discuss anything glibly with true understanding, while Holden, because he lacks such certainties, may achieve wisdom through genuinely feeling the insights he gains.

When the main character listens to a piano player named Ernie, he is embarrassed by the performer's flamboyance. Ominously, Ernie plays in front of a large mirror which allows the audience to see his reactions to the music, but not his fingers, as Holden notes: thus, the pianist naturally assumes the audience prizes him more than the music. Ernie acts like a celebrity—someone whose personality supposedly transcends his accomplishments—and Salinger's insights are again strikingly apt for our time when celebrities are created and forgotten overnight. Ernie's failure is compounded because, while he is a snob, he plays at being humble when the audience applauds. Holden feels nauseated by both the performance and the spectators.

I'm not too sure what the name of the song was that he was playing when I came in, but whatever it was, he was really stinking it up. He was putting all those dumb, show-offy ripples in the high notes, and a lot of other tricky stuff that gives me a pain in the ass. You should've heard the crowd, though, when he was finished. You would've puked. They went mad. They were exactly the same morons that laugh like hyenas in the movies at stuff that isn't funny.[50]

Ernie substitutes flash for substance, technique for content, and inspiration for meaning: he has corrupted the relationship between an artist and his art by making the rendering of a work more important than the work itself; and, in so doing, makes the music illuminate him rather than the reverse.

Such elaborate showing off is matched, for Holden, by the Lunts whom he sees with Sally. After noting that the play seemed to consist of little more than tea pouring and drinking, Holden says:

Alfred Lunt and Lynne Fontaine were the old couple, and they were very good, but I didn't like them very much.... They didn't act like people and they didn't act like actors. It's hard to explain. I mean they were good. but they were *too* good.... They acted a little bit the way old Ernie, down in the Village, plays the piano. If you do something *too* good, then, after a while, if you don't watch it, you start showing off.[51]

The Lunts have become adept at playing what their public wants; in presenting the audience with a ritual, they have merged their stage and real personalities so completely that the seams don't show. At the supposedly more exalted level of the "legitimate" stage, they are simply giving the customers what the customers demand. Thus, P. T. Barnum, the movie newsreel and the Lunts all illuminate the common belief that the customer is always right. The Lunts are simply parts of a pandering, huckster society which Holden believes lacks any real substance.

Holden constantly criticizes the movies, a medium toward which he has adopted a love-hate attitude. He finds films despicable yet great sources for satiric material. When Holden has a brief liaison with a prostitute in a hotel (an adventure that ends when he gives the girl money without consummating the relationship), a misunderstanding between the young man and her bellhop-pimp causes Salinger's protagonist to get a bloody nose. After being knocked to the floor, Holden philosophizes: "I don't remember if he knocked me out or not, but I don't think so. It's pretty hard to knock a guy out, except in the goddam movies."[52] Thus, films are a further source of illusion—another means by which society's wishes are revealed and fulfilled. Throughout *The Catcher in the Rye* Holden experiences situations that remind him of movie clichés or which he can parody in terms of stock film devices. It is as though the world had become a B movie, as though life were not simply imitating art but had actually become a stock set of bromides. In an extended fantasy Holden imagines wreaking revenge on Maurice, the bellhop, in scenes that could have come out of *Murder My Sweet* (1944) or *The Big Sleep* (1946). After imagining himself as a wounded detective who has rid the world of a sadistic pimp, Holden comes abruptly back to reality and notes: "The goddam movies. They can ruin you. I'm not kidding."[53]

Hollywood is also suspect in Holden's eyes because his older brother, D.B., has abandoned writing stories and gone there to be a screenwriter. At the club where Ernie plays the piano, Holden meets one of his brother's old girlfriends, Lillian Simmons, whose only claim to attention is her "very big knockers." After Lillian exclaims how wonderful it is that D. B. has gone to Hollywood, the protagonist thinks: "I didn't feel like discussing it. You could tell she thought it was a big deal, his being in Hollywood. Almost everybody does. Mostly people who have never read any of his stories. It drives me crazy, though."[54] D. B. has "sold out" because screenwriting impresses the wrong people and reinforces the play-acting Holden sees nearly everywhere he goes. Later, when Holden pays a midnight visit to his sister, Phoebe, D. B. comes up in their conversation.

"D. B. coming home for Christmas?" I asked her.

"He may and he may not, Mother said. It all depends. He may have to stay in Hollywood and write a picture about Annapolis."

"Annapolis, for God's sake!"

"It's a love story and everything. Guess who's going to be in it! What movie star. Guess!"

"I'm not interested. An *na* polis, for God's sake. What's D. B. know about An *na* polis, for God's sake? What's that got to do with the kind of stories he writes?"[55]

While Holden is dismayed and mystified by what Hollywood seems to be doing to his brother, it is only a matter of time before he realizes that D. B. and also Phoebe have chosen less heroic lives of compromise.

The surrender Holden subconsciously perceives in his brother and sister becomes more obvious when Salinger's protagonist notes how ordinary people behave at the movies. While waiting for Sally on Broadway, Holden notices the surging Sunday crowds, is dismayed by their senseless bustling, yet:

...the worst part was that you could tell they all *wanted* to go to the movies. I couldn't stand looking at them. I can understand somebody going to the movies because there's nothing else to do, but when somebody really *wants* to go, and even walks fast so as to get there quicker, then it depresses hell out of me.[56]

In another passage Holden remembers going to the movies and watching a lady who alternated between crying over the maudlin screen characters and reprimanding her small, bored child. Such hypocrisy causes the protagonist to urge that the woman was "about as kindhearted as a goddam wolf. You take somebody that cries their goddam eyes out over phony stuff in the movies, and nine times out of ten they're mean bastards at heart. I'm not kidding."[57] Holden believes the play-acting mentality of the woman represses the child's more natural impulses; in effect, she is training the youngster to acquiesce to the second-rate fare she adores. While such conduct indicates the woman's bad taste, her actions ultimately force her child to learn to distrust his own feelings and perceptions. For Holden, this woman epitomizes a society which prizes those who repress their feelings and direct their emotions into stereotyped channels.

Unlike the movie audience, which doesn't bother perceiving a single performance too sharply, Holden believes life is a series of unique moments. He refuses to treat other people as though they were no more (and no less) than film characters (i.e. figures to be intensely concerned about briefly and then rapidly forgotten). What he cannot endure is that people act as though being an acquaintance were as close as one could ever hope to get to another person. Holden was all but despondent at the time of the death of his brother, Allie; however, now that that event is safely in the past, only he seems to still remember his dead brother. He recalls that on the night of Allie's funeral he slept in the garage and, eventually, broke all the windows there "just for the hell of it." As a result, Holden injured his hand and his parents considered having him psychoanalyzed; although he can no longer make a fist, Holden doesn't care much because, "I mean I'm not going to be a goddam surgeon or a violinist or anything *any* way."[58] Obviously, Holden's remarks are his ironic way of telling the audience that he cared desperately. His dismay at the funeral is even more pronounced, for he notices that the cars of the mourners easily slide away from the grave site and carry their occupants to nice meals and warm houses. His parents' desire to have him analyzed symbolizes Holden's lack of rapport with them. They are, in effect, too repressed to appreciate that grief might drive someone to such emotional excesses and they want to have Holden treated by experts so they can avoid dealing with him personally. By buying their son professional help, whether doctors or teachers, they can continue to believe they are good parents. The protagonist, rather then being hostile toward his parents, merely avoids them after he leaves prep school and later when he pays his midnight visit to Phoebe. Appropriately enough, the parents are then at a party so that Holden and his sister get to be alone; however, when the parents return and the mother steps into Phoebe's room, Holden hides to avoid her.

Holden wants desperately to intervene for those younger than himself, to save them from the pitfalls of life and so, symbolically, to keep them within the confines of childhood. This aspiration is voiced in the much quoted passage which "explains" the novel's title. Holden's speech answers Luce's question that each individual grow up, find a career, and define himself. Holden refuses to fit into a pigeon hole by which others can classify (and so dismiss) him.

> "Anyway, I keep picturing all these little kids playing some game in the big field of rye.... And I'm standing on the edge of some crazy cliff. What I have to do, I have to catch everybody if they start to go over the cliff—I mean if they're running and they don't look where they're going I have to come out from somewhere and *catch* them. That's all I'd do all day. I'd just be the catcher in the rye and all."[59]

Holden's idealism flies in the face of conventional wisdom and makes him akin to another inspired literary madman, Prince Myshkin of Dostoyevsky's *The Idiot*. While the Russian novelist raises the issue of who's mad—the individual or his society—Salinger's protagonist poises the most thoughtful literary critique of American society in the 1950s. Holden's withdrawal leads him to the spirituality of Jesus rather than to the rebelliousness of Lenin. In trying to preserve innocence in himself and others, and in failing to be a success in any terms society would recognize, Holden retains his individuality as a consolation.

As a character who has been exposed to the world's corruption and rejected its supposed pleasures, Holden prizes imagination and compassion above deeds and acquisitions. He reacts strongly at Phoebe's school, a place he used to attend and where he goes to waylay her so they can talk before she goes home. While waiting for her, Holden notices:

> ...something that drove me crazy. Somebody'd written "Fuck you" on the wall. It drove me damn near crazy. I thought how Phoebe and all the other little kids would see it, and how they'd wonder what the hell it meant, and then finally some dirty kid would tell them—all cockeyed naturally—what it meant, and how they'd all *think* about it and may even *worry* about it for a couple of days. I kept wanting to kill whoever'd written it.... But I knew, too, I wouldn't have the guts to do it. I knew that. That made me even more depressed.[60]

Although he rubs out the offensive expression partly out of a fear that he will be accused of having put it there, Holden's disgust measures his innocence and his desire to preserve that feeling among the children. As the "catcher in the rye," Holden would not shield the youngsters from all the danger but only prevent their running amok. Thus, his dismay centers on the garbled explanation that the world, in the form of the dirty kid, would provide and how such "knowledge" would disturb the school children. In effect, there is nothing wrong with knowing what "fuck you" means, the danger lies instead in receiving such information from a corrupt society which equates sex with conquest and accomplishment (i.e. "scoring") rather than love.

Holden's concern with sexual relations embodies idealistic qualities the world lacks. Although he would like to "get laid," Salinger's protagonist can never divorce intercourse from feeling. When he stops kidding a girl in a dance joint called the Lavender Room, we see that Holden places compassion above passion. After deciding to dance with three ugly girls, and while with Marty, the poorest dancer, Holden teases her.

> I told her I just saw Gary Cooper, the movie star, on the other side of the floor.
> "*Where?*" she asked me—excited as hell. "*Where?*"
> "Aw you just missed him. He went out. Why didn't you look when I told you?"
> "...Oh shoot!" she said. I'd just about broken her heart—I really had. I was sorry as hell I'd kidded her. Some people you shouldn't kid, even if they deserve it.[61]

Thus, wisdom resides not merely in comprehending the world and those around one, but in transcending one's personal awareness of others' duplicity and stupidity. Holden's compassion implies that laughing at others is an inadequate response: in realizing that even sensitive individuals suffer the same human shortcomings, Salinger's protagonist attains an informed innocence which is conditioned by his actions. He stops teasing Marty about Gary Cooper because he can derive no human pleasure from it. By referring to a movie star and calling up the associations the novel makes about that medium, Holden discerns that his behavior has become momentarily amusing but quickly rendered superficial, just like a movie.

Because he respects even this obtuse girl's individuality, Holden can refrain from asserting his will upon others, a point made clearer when he discusses his exploits as a teenage lover. After noting that whenever a girl insists he "stop" he always complies, Holden describes a one-time seduction attempt that turned into a comedy of errors: "Take this girl that I just missed having sexual intercourse with, that I told you about. It took me about an *hour* to just get her goddam brassiere off. By the time I did get it off, she was about to spit in my eye."[62] Holden's belittling of his savoir faire accords with Salinger's perception that people are more likely to have fumbling encounters than to experience the romantic and gymnastic shennanigans one so often finds in bestsellers. The protagonist's naivete is further reflected by his complying with the protests of the various girls whom Holden believes are always speaking the truth. Holden never questions that these young ladies could be attempting to save "face" by acting in "acceptable" ways; and so, his restraint represents a need to act on his own feelings and perceptions. It is finally more important for Holden to continue to believe people express their real feelings than to succeed in seducing someone.

Holden's closest friend is Phoebe whom he describes as a person "with sense and all."[63] Their relationship is tinged with pathos because Phoebe, although wanting to comfort her brother, is growing away from Holden. In her interest about who would star in D. B.'s screenplay, Phoebe shows that she is abandoning the emotional world of the protagonist. Salinger even has Phoebe mention that in her school pageant (which she believes "stinks") she symbolically is playing Benedict Arnold. The girl's dawning adulthood is further dramatized by her reaction to Holden's leaving school. He tells her of an old alumnus who spent his last visit to Pencey going from bathroom to bathroom to see where he had carved his initials; and Holden has already established that such signs (e.g. the "fuck you" at Phoebe's school) represent individual decadence and the loss of innocence. While the alumnus, clearly a man of the world, embodies values diametrically opposed to Holden's, the protagonist is unable to make his sister see this distinction.

> "Boy did he depress me! I don't mean he was a bad guy—he wasn't. But you don't have to be a bad guy to depress somebody—you can be a *good* guy and do it. All you have to do to depress somebody is give them a lot of phony advice while you're looking for your initials in some can door—that's all you have to do... he kept telling Stradlater and I to get all we could out of Pency. God, Phoebe!..."
>
> Old Phoebe said something then, but I couldn't hear her....
>
> "What?" I said. "Take your mouth away. I can't hear you with your mouth that way."
>
> "You don't like *any* thing that's happening."
>
> It made me even more depressed when she said that.[64]

Phoebe lacks empathy because she belongs to the popular world controlled by movies and by signs that reduce language to "shocking" slogans and thought to catch phrases. If *The Catcher in the Rye* shows its hero striving for his identity, this scene with Phoebe represents Holden's final step, for in it he realizes the extent of his isolation.

The novel's final pages convey an overwhelming sense of the power and absurdity of those forces Holden now resists. Although he is reconciled with Phoebe when she wears his red Sherlock Holmes winter hat to school, their relationship has been redefined in his mind. When Holden notices another obscenity scratched on a wall at Phoebe's school, he realizes: "It wouldn't come off. It's hopeless anyway."[65] In walking Phoebe to school, Holden notices a carousel which has played the same tune since he was a child and asks Phoebe if she'd like a ride. Although initially reluctant because she feels too grown up, Phoebe quickly gets caught up in grabbing for the brass ring. Holden watches her and feels that his ambition to be the "catcher in the rye" was foolish: "The thing with kids is, if they want to grab for the gold ring, you have to let them do it, and not say anything to them."[66] Thus, Salinger's protagonist has discovered that to have compassion for others, one must allow them to lead their own lives. Holden cannot be the moral guardian of childhood in others, for it will take all his energy to resist the world's inevitable inroads upon his own personality. The protagonist concludes the novel by noting that telling his story has made him sad, for he misses everyone he has mentioned, even his snobbish schoolmates. Although he can dismiss other people as "phony," Holden must still live with the pain of such dismissals. Salinger's character has learned that an individual must live with his emotional wounds either through becoming resigned or through becoming a "phony."

The Bad Seed
Evil as Permanent Mystery
(Deu Books)

Chapter 10

"If you stop and think about it, it scares you."

Popular 1950s' novels concerned with psychology are shortsighted or suspicious about this discipline. While the insights and theories of Freud, Jung and others had penetrated critical and intellectual circles, psychology was still regarded suspiciously by the mass audience. Thus, the comic dismissals of psychological theories and practitioners in *Rally Round the Flag, Boys!* and *No Time for Sergeants* find more serious counterparts in Frances Parkinson Keyes' *The Royal Box* (1954), William March's *The Bad Seed* (1954) and Meyer Levin's *Compulsion* (1957). Indeed, these three novels present psychology as a more or less inhumane undertaking.

The Royal Box, an attempt at a Sherlock Holmes style whodunit, relies on psychology to "explain" its murderer's behavior. Unfortunately, Keyes' psychology and psychologists, in adhering to the atmosphere and mores of a woman's novel, emerge as characteristic defenders of feminine, middle-class virtues. The killer's "maladjustment," which leads him to plan his mother's death and kill his real father by accident, can be discerned in his youthful malcontent and his subconsciously incestuous pursuit of his mother. Keye's misguided killer also embodies the figure of the "mad" artist, a being whose creative-neurotic personality is congenial to readers. This unfortunate figure, who needs a good woman to manage him but does not find one, must be retired to the pleasures of therapeutic crafts and plays.

March and Levin are more pessimistic for some of their most offensive characters are eager proponents of psychology's powers. *The Bad Seed* is dominated by a sense that men are bound by character and circumstance so that psychological expertise provides neither insight into nor defense against life's accidents. *Compulsion* treats the science more enigmatically and symbolically. Willie Weiss, a devoted student of Freud, is an "objective" observer whose "disinterest" is easily seen as inhuman: he prefers diagnoses and "studies" to understanding and compassion. Levin also suggests that his cold-blooded killers, lacking emotional maturity, are ironically devoid of compulsion. Indeed, most of the characters in *Compulsion* must learn the need for emotional release within a civilized framework, a lesson that implies the need for compassion (equal human culpability) rather than pity.

* * *

The Royal Box uses murder and suspense as backgrounds to a traditional woman's novel. Its mildly clever mystery substitutes conversation and psychology for elaborate detection and exhibits hardly any violence save the emotional tensions the characters experience. Considered only as a mystery, the novel would not seriously detain one; however, *The Royal Box* exhibits thematic concerns which typify popular American thought, the ideological climate of the 1950s, and the feminine psyche. Keyes plays (if only slightly) with the international theme—the American versus the European—that so marks Henry James. The American need for reassurance in the face of a Cold War also surfaces as an appropriate anxiety. The feminine mind seems apparent in the characters' concerns about appropriate manners, good marriages, and pleasing appearances.

In *The Royal Box*, Gradie Kirtland, a Scotland Yard Inspector, solves the murder of Baldwin Castle, an American millionaire who is the ambassador-designate to the oil-rich Middle Eastern nation of Aristan. Kirtland resembles Sherlock Holmes in thinking rather than gumshoeing his way to a solution. Kirtland knows when witnesses are lying because of his acute psychological understanding and he can piece relationships together because of his cerebral powers. Although he is not the main character, the Inspector dominates the novel's central section in which he interrogates and then reinterrogates the other characters. Kirtland functions as a deus ex machina to reveal that the novel's figures have more coherence as a group than one initially suspects and to bring the culprit to justice. Kirtland's formula—he looks for "moment, method and motive"—reduces the horror of the crime to manageable (i.e. reasonable) limits. An opposing type of fictional detective can be seen in Jake Gittes (Jack Nicholson) in *Chinatown* (1975). Gittes not only lacks Kirtland's mental capacities but also moves in an environment that cannot be understood reasonably. The film detective has to scramble about to solve his case, while Kirtland, in one morning with tired and lying witnesses, can unravel Castle's death. Kirtland's personality is dramatized when an anonymous assistant asks, " 'Was there anything you wanted?' " and the Inspector laconically responds, " 'No, just to go on thinking.' "[1]

Keyes overworks coincidence in *The Royal Box* to the extent that a theatre group brought together on the spur of the moment contains: (a) the American ambassador to Aristan who had once proposed marriage to a haughty English woman and later had an illegitimate son (unbeknown to him) with the leading lady in the play he is attending; (b) the haughty English woman now living in genteel poverty but still sufficiently well-connected to obtain the royal box for an evening; (c) the woman's daughter who must choose between a modestly well-off young American and a rich Frenchman; (d) the Frenchman who has political reasons for wanting Castle not to arrive in Aristan, and who possesses the pharmaceutical knowledge (a formula for coating aspirins) that would conceal a poisoning; (e) the leading lady who is now trying to adjust to her illegitimate son's awareness of his real father and his mother's refusal to take advantage of that fact; (f) the diplomat's present wife who has alcoholism, an unacknowledged child, and two previous marriages to hide; (g) the Aristan ambassador to

Great Britain who has some nefarious (but blessedly vague) plans about future Aristan-American relations; (h) the illegitimate son who is now the leading lady's leading man. In addition, a young diplomat, a newspaperman and his wife, the wife and mother-in-law of the Aristan ambassador, and the leading lady's husband-manager are in the entourage. Since many of these characters have apparent motives—rage, jealousy, political expediency—for murdering the ambassador, this diverse group represents a standard arrangement for a whodunit. Indeed, the interrelationships are reminiscent of the novels of Charles Dickens in which nearly everyone possesses intimate ties with everyone else. Such interconnectedness, which flies in the face of the impersonality and anonymity of modern urban life, reduces the individual reader's sense of being alone.

Kirtland exhibits another traditional gambit by resuming the case, a device which enables the reader to follow the plot (and so recognizes that only the rare individual will peruse the novel at a single sitting). While one expects characters to lie in a mystery, Keyes' figures often prevaricate to protect their vanity. Lady Laura Whitford, the penniless but snobbish English matron, reveals her previous relationship with the deceased but does not immediately (or ever completely) tell what that relationship was like. Lady Laura never mentions having written to Castle for money after her husband's death, nor that she received a mocking refusal in reply. Lady Laura never openly recounts her passionate feelings for Castle since such an admission would hardly accord with her sense of decorum; the reader only obtains such information when Lady Laura reminisces about her youth. In rounding out her characters, Keyes reveals that her thematic interests are only partially satisfied by the whodunit form. Given the structure of the novel, with its long introductory and concluding sections that lie outside the detection process, it becomes readily apparent that *The Royal Box* is only incidentally a mystery.

Keyes places a comparable emphasis on the undercurrent of Anglo-American rivalry which has Old English traditionalism looking askance, if not down on, American egalitarianism. Lady Laura's brief infatuation with Baldwin Castle grows out of his characteristic American forwardness, and when Lady Laura meets her future husband she quickly dismisses Castle because such brashness insults her sense of propriety. Mrs. Whitford's animosity later extends to her daughter Althea's love for Hilary Thorpe, an administrative aide at the American embassy. While Lady Laura's dislike is misplaced, the Castles emerge as archetypal American tourists whose wealth and political connections do not amend their public gaucheries. Mrs. Castle appears drunk and (all but) disorderly at the entre-act supper during the play; and, if this weren't enough, she even demands that Janice Lester, the star of *Gold of Pleasure*, joint this repast. Such a faux pas can only be expected from an American whose sense of privilege makes her oblivious to an older society where established ranks prevail. As a young man, Baldwin Castle's go-getter nature is reflected in Lady Laura's anecdote about a soiree at which Castle was described by an Arabian diplomat.

"That brash young American is going far," and I said, "Yes, to Aristan." The diplomat laughed and said, "I didn't mean far in that sense; I meant he'd make his mark in the world...he's got a good foundation.... It's evident he's absorbed a good deal...."[2]

When she hears this evaluation, Lady Laura is shaken because her sense of values—which has social etiquette as its keystone—seems misplaced. She must reconcile the dilemma of Castle's bad manners, which should mark him for social extinction, and his abilities, which suggest he will be successful.

Lady Laura gradually emerges as a snob and a deluded old woman, so that her constant laments over her loss of status since her husband's death (" 'It's gall and wormwood to know that I can hardly afford to live in the basement of my own house.' "[3]) are offset by her ironic fate in which the older woman is restored to a respectable social position by her son-in-law's American father who readily sees through Lady Laura and gladly provides her with a house and an annuity so that she will leave the newlyweds alone. An obvious thread of male chauvinism colors this section of the plot for the older woman is treated as incapable of handling serious affairs, and Hilary's father only supplies Lady Laura with a house on the condition that the property be in his daughter-in-law's name. This discrimination is appropriate because Lady Laura lacks any idealism about love and marriage; for her they are avenues to a comfortable existence, one devoted to problems such as who shall pour tea or who should ride with whom to the theatre. The older woman's snobbery makes her push Althea to marry Jacques de Valcourt, a titled military attaché to the French embassy in London, for Lady Laura realizes that her daughter:

...would then become the Marquise de Valcourt; not only exalted rank but immense wealth would be assured her and her mother would share in the benefits and pleasures of them. After years of penny-pinching and pretense, of humiliations and hurts, she would be lapped with luxury, treated with deference, able to condescend or to avenge as best suited her mood and her purpose.[4]

By presenting Lady Laura as a grasping hypocrite who places her child's welfare second to her own, Keyes uses popular American biases—the dislike of nobility, the distrust of pampered laziness, and the dismissal of romance—to defuse the Anglo-American theme.

Keyes' portrayal of the Castles who, despite embodying many undesirable American traits, are given more sympathetic fates, restores the balance somewhat. One can dismiss Baldwin Castle's rejection of Lady Laura's request for financial help because, after all, she was the major unrequited love of his life. In addition, Castle elicits sympathy because he stayed with his first wife out of a sense of duty (interestingly, the possibility that such an arrangement might have been as devastating to the first wife is not considered). The current Mrs. Castle's redemption from being an ugly American takes a long time to come about. At a cocktail party before the play Mrs. Castle "now well into a second glass of bourbon on the rocks, having tossed off the contents of one in record time... had managed to corral Jacques de Valcourt...and her remarks to him, delivered in a high strident voice, were clearly audible in the dining room."[5] Later, Lady Laura notes that Mrs. Castle shows too much bosom and too much jewelry (alas, one thinks of Mae West)—propensities that could ruin Baldwin Castle's career. While the notion that behind every successful man there must be at least a decorous wife is implied, Mrs. Castle commits more blunders at the theatre when she mocks her surroundings. Since she cannot see the value of old things, Mrs. Castle reflects the American distrust of history as a lived experience. At best, she sees the trappings of the past as quaint and amusing decorations.

"Why even the john—" She threw open the door which had been left so discreetly ajar and laughed aloud. "Say I haven't seen one of those, I mean one of *that kind*, since I was a kid. Talk about antiques! Just the same, it sort of adds to the Victorian atmosphere, doesn't it?"[6]

The clash between national values is caught by the juxtaposition of "john" (with its connotation of American servicemen) and the "discreetly ajar" door (with its suggestion of British reserve). Mrs. Castle, who looks so foolish at this point, is hardly redeemed when Kirtland subsequently dismisses her as a "vulgar, disheveled woman who was obviously the most ignorant among the suspects he had questioned, who, indeed, could not claim even the rudiments of refinement and culture which formed an integral part in the very birthright of all the others."[7]

Baldwin Castle has the supposed culture his wife lacks, yet this narrow egotist can be a cutting companion. While he suffers from the insecurities of a May-September relationship, Baldwin's interest in women is repeatedly shown to be proprietary and exhibitionistic rather than passionate or loving. Like Lady Laura, the woman against whom he harbored a grudge for more than twenty years, Castle concentrates on appearances and on doing the correct thing socially. He is at pains to convey the right impression with Jevad Ahani, the pushy Aristan ambassador, and even consults with Hilary Thorpe about what is proper etiquette. Castle's propriety naturally extends to his wife and reveals his contradictory nature; while Baldwin is supposed to be madly in love, his often cutting remarks do not accord with such a picture of infatuation. After she has a couple of pre- theatre drinks, Baldwin ironically chides her:

"And look here! I thought you didn't drink, and I just saw you gulp down one bourbon on the rocks after another. What's the idea? If you suddenly start going in for that sort of thing, one of these days you'll come out of a fog wondering whether what you vaguely recall doing after four highballs was or was not murder."[8]

While Baldwin Castle is hailed as the potential restorer of American prestige in Aristan, his possessive and sadistic streak in dealing with women marks him as a hero with clay feet. It is only poetic justice that, while secretly visiting Janice Lester, Baldwin drinks the poisoned ice water meant for her. Castle's demise punishes the illegitimacy he visited upon Evan and seems highly appropriate.

Keyes' treatment of psychology centers on Evan Neville, Castle's murderer. As a bastard, Evan lacks a strong masculine figure to imitate so that he becomes a whiner and finally makes a direct romantic approach to his own mother! While the latter blunder happens in part because Evan does not know about his parentage (Janice and Hugo Alban, her husband-manager have adopted Evan), no "normal" person would act in such a fashion. Evan has become a leading man in the theatre because of his mother's influence; and his emotional instability toward Janice hinges on his profession. As Janice tells it:

"In *Gold of Pleasure*, Evan plays the part of my stepson—a grown stepson with a young stepmother. He falls in love with her—in the play, I mean. He plays it wonderfully, so wonderfully that it doesn't seem like acting. It seems real. I mean, it seems real to the audience. It has from the beginning. And finally, it began to seem real to him. I mean, he began to imagine he was in love with me."[9]

These events have led Janice to reveal that she is Evan's mother; and they show Keyes employing a psychological determinism comforting in its rigidity. Evan cannot accept that his mother never used Castle to further their son's education. In embodying such qualities Evan, by definition, renders himself unsympathetic to an American audience. Keyes' use of the play-within-a-play scheme, which inevitably suggests Hamlet's trick to catch Claudius, also echoes Ronald Colman in *A Double Life* (1947), and, again, points to Evan Neville's shortcomings. While the Colman character confused his real life with Othello's (and strangled poor Shelly Winters as a result), Evan reacts to Janice's rebuff by struggling in vain to meld his two personalities. In both instances, a fear of the artist—the notion that the man who "performs" is neither quite a man nor completely sane—is played upon; and a popular American tendency to equate sensitivity with abnormality is used to underline Evan's characterization.

Neville's crime is sanitized by the psychological conditions which trigger it and he emerges as a victim rather than a victimizer. The court finds him "guilty but insane" and sends him to an asylum so that Evan can undergo corrective therapy to find his real (sociable) self and return to society. This therapeutic optimism, which has become a dominant belief in twentieth-century America, makes Evan's crime and state of mind problems which can be solved rather than conditions which must be endured. In the asylum Evan gradually drifts into play acting as an appropriate therapy and, when he directs the inmates' annual production, we are to assume he will recover. Since Keyes seems totally lacking in irony, her description of Evan's partial recovery abounds in unwittingly sinister undertones.

"It's not a new one," said Dr. Goring, speaking rather apologetically.... "However, I understand this was a great success when it was produced in New York about twenty-five years ago. It was first used as a starring vehicle for the well-known actress Maryse Verlaine, who later married a French nobleman. The name of the play is *Dusk in December*."[10]

Dr. Goring, Evan's psychiatrist, makes this speech to Janice and Hugo, unaware that this play was her first starring vehicle. While this new situation would suggest that mother really knows what's best, more paradoxical possibilities arise. Although Janice and Hugo are sufficiently relieved to return to their life in the theatre, a more skeptical (and admittedly 1970s-toned) reading would see Evan's choice as a clever continuation of his assault on Janice. In effect, by re-enacting her life, Evan hardly cuts himself loose from the emotional problems which drove him to murder. It is more likely that such plotting reveals something of Keyes' popularity: in essence, Evan's choice subconsciously flatters all those wise women who faithfully and tactfully support their men, for every American male, an Ozzie Nelson of one sort or another, needs a Harriet to keep him from running amok.

The Cold War serves as another background to *The Royal Box*. Baldwin Castle has been chosen to restore order in Aristan and so to further American interests, so that, in keeping with American foreign policy since 1945, his mission is to reestablish a tottering order. He has been selected because "American presidents seem to have a way of choosing gems in that category for their representatives; and sometimes these do surprisingly well in foreign posts."[11] Such a verdict implies that businessmen make the best diplomats (a defense of Eisenhower?) since diplomacy can be mastered by any competent administrator. While such a view shows Keyes' rudimentary notions of world politics, the purpose of Castle's mission reflects power politics as we know them. Hilary Thrope describes Castle as a man chosen to manage a crisis: " 'But it's my guess the President put it to him as a patriotic duty, to pull another rabbit out of the Aristanian turban for the United States and for the free world, as he did in the twenties.... I think he might have done it too.' "[12] Such diplomacy clearly shows the United States engaged in an ideological war which requires careful diplomacy (the same message as in *The Ugly American*) to prevent defections. Castle's goal is a stop-gap measure and, to Keyes' credit, after the ambassador's death a revolution in Aristan topples the present regime. Thus, at the last, realpolitik emerges as the busybody Ahani hurries back home in fear of his life, while de Valcourt, after failing with Althea, goes back to active military duty and dies in a parachute jump in Indochina, perhaps the first victim of the quagmire to appear in American fiction.

It is, however, as a woman's novel that *The Royal Box* works best. While handkerchief movies ("weepies") and soap operas are customarily dismissed as second-rate, the values they reflect are assumptions commonly held by their audiences. The woman's novel incorporates many of the psychological motifs that distinguish hardcore pornography, for concerns with dominance and power appear uppermost in both forms with the only major difference being the audience which is flattered. While *Deep Throat* (1972) panders to male fantasies about the sexual availability of women and the ways they can be satisfied by men, women's novels reverse the process by showing men living solely to satisfy feminine whims. Linda Lovelace, the archetypal female of male pornographic power fantasy, suggests that women are as sexually preoccupied as men: the numerous male leads in daytime TV soap operas live to listen to the various heroines' trials and tribulations—and, by so doing, imply that men are as preoccupied with etiquette, marriage and gossip as women are. While *The Royal Box* is hardly risqué, its depiction of sexual relations relies on the same daydreams of dominance that motivate more lurid productions.

In an extensive description of Althea Whitford's physique Keyes devotes great attention to the girl's hair which is meticulously coiffed yet still naturally beautiful. Althea's bosom (and that is always the word) is "youthful" and "showed promise of great beauty," euphemisms which might be rendered as "firm" and "stacked" for a different audience. Keyes here presents female sexuality in a way that her readers wish it to be delineated. Such wish-fulfillment (that hair is more important than figure, that no woman should be threateningly endowed—every man likes Marilyn Monroe but no nice man wants to marry her) goes a step further when Lady Laura is described:

> Like her daughter, she had beautiful golden hair; like her daughter, she had an exquisite complexion; like her daughter, she had an almost faultless figure. But she was by far the more soignee of the two. Her hair was carefully, even elaborately and becomingly, arranged; her skin had the almost petallike quality that comes not only from natural softness but from constant care....[13]

In linking mother and daughter Keyes flatters her audience's preoccupation with youthful looks and is at some pains to lessen her readers' anxieties about aging. Upon seeing Janice Lester, Joe Racina, a newspaper reporter and an old friend, notes that she was "infinitely more beautiful in her rich maturity than she had been in her untried youth."[14] Thus, youthful good looks do not provide the delights that maturity brings; and Keyes insinuates, in tried and true Horatio Alger, you-can-get-ahead-if-you-only-try fashion that happiness is controlled by effort and not by chance. Any woman can hone her personality and looks so as to overcome the advantages that youth and/or individual endowment have bestowed on others.

The figure of the queen bee—the female surrounded by undemanding worshippers—is best embodied by Janice Lester who so infatuated Baldwin Castle years before that he took whole days out of his hectic schedule to go shopping with her. The sinister side of such conduct—that Castle dresses Janice in a way he prefers, and thus treats her like a child or a piece of property—is ignored. The degree of Castle's attentiveness and his assumption of a traditional female role (i.e. the shopper) suggest how the character has been "neutered." Later, in another example of role reversal, Hugo Alban marries Janice without any assurance of future sexual relations, only to fall more deeply in love when he sees how Janice treats the baby (Evan) they have adopted. Thus, the male is all but castrated by having his sexual drive replaced by a love of children; Hugo has become a woman psychologically and can even say: " 'I didn't bother you, even if sometimes I wanted to rip out a piece of the wall between our rooms with my bare hands.' "[15] It is thoroughly appropriate that their marriage is finally consummated in New England against a Hollywood background of crashing surf and pounding waves.

Marriage is, of course, the principal social relationship in *The Royal Box*. Every girl must get married if only to become eligible for the group we see at the theatre. Once the marriage has taken place, a more profound relationship develops because "the fortunes of a devoted married couple were essentially interwoven."[16] In Keyes' fiction there is never any hint that monogamy doesn't work as a system: individuals may not enjoy their partners, and men may seek out physical companionship when they are widowers, but devotion and chastity are simply assumed inside marriage. A woman can, however, ruin her husband's career by failing in etiquette; thus, Mrs. Castle's plunging neckline and forward manner cause raised eyebrows. There is never any serious doubt that a wife's task is to enhance her husband (the values associated with corporate wives in William Whyte's *The Organization Man* loom large here) or any serious realization that rich people can be as gauche as they please. Unlike Charlie, Willy Loman's neighbor in Arthur Miller's *Death of a Salesman* who knew that J. P. Morgan's wallet "made" J. P. Morgan, the characters in *The Royal Box* believe that being well-liked is a key to social distinction. Women achieve this status by augmenting their husbands' careers, so that the first Mrs. Castle disappointed her spouse because, when it came to entertaining his business associates, "she wasn't so hot."[17] One might have excused this woman's being "dowdy" but the lack of such social grace is unforgivable.

The Royal Box also implies that every woman has only one true love, even though she may give her heart (and other sundries) elsewhere. Cornelia Castle, who has been divorced twice before marrying Baldwin, epitomizes this value for, after Castle's murder, she goes back to the husband and child she initially deserted. Since she is now rich, she can return to Iowa ostensibly to help her son, Barney, but she and Sam are soon remarried. This process of reuniting the true lovers centers on children—Barney brings Cornelia and Sam together and the baby she conceived with Castle serves as the bond that will tie them together in the future. In conventional woman's novel fashion, Sam readily accepts the prospect of another man's child and puts the welfare of the unborn above his own ego. The one and only notion becomes even more pronounced in a conversation between Janice Lester and Joe Racina. Janice, in describing her liaison with Baldwin, generalizes that for any woman, " 'perhaps the first man himself means more to her than any other, whatever he gives her or even if he never gives her anything.' "[18] Joe, when subsequently questioned by Kirtland about the possibility of Janice's having had an affair, reaffirms the monogamous ideal even more strongly.

"Yes, it's conceivable...but...I don't believe for a moment she'd have an affair with a man unless it really was a *love* affair.... I can't imagine anything like that happening unless she thought marriage *was* in the picture.... And it goes without saying that there never would have been but one such love affair. There couldn't have been."[19]

This earnest defense is another instance where Keyes gently emasculates a male character. In her fiction readers want to believe in the one true love—the Tristan for every Isolde (without any of the social complications that attended that mystical relationship)—as the sine qua non. Keyes' heroines bring troubles on themselves after they have found Mr. Right, so that the basic democratic belief that one's life can be created by individual will remains inviolate.

Love, which is more than physical passion, must be prized above wealth or ego. Althea's choice of Hilary Thorpe illustrates that money cannot substitute for feeling; however, since Thorpe has a "sweet little house in Devonshire Mews and a Cadillac car,"[20] this system of values is slightly ameliorated, if not entirely lost. Such an essentially pseudo- situation reveals that Keyes' readers do not want to consider choosing between real wealth and real poverty, at least in fiction. It is, of course, consistent with popular daydreams to choose between rich suitors; and the freedom to exercise such a choice represents another instance of the pornographic impulse at work. The value of love is underscored when Janice Lester, knowing that Castle is her first love, cannot convince him that their careers will not interfere with their feelings. Castle believes that neither can be sufficiently supportive of the other (i.e. that she cannot devote herself to him) and casts Janice aside, even though he " 'didn't know I'd rather have been Mrs. Baldwin Castle than a second Sarah Bernhardt.' "[21] Thus, Castle never placed enough value on a woman's love (the most precious gift) and, like Evan, became warped and twisted into a man who could not love (and *that* for Keyes and her readers is a fate truly worse than death).

Love also motivates the growing away from one's parents necessary to becoming an individual, a theme illustrated by Lady Laura and Althea. The shallowness of the mother appears again when she summarizes her reasons for rejecting Castle and accepting Guy Whitford. Although she loved him, Whitford:

"...didn't excite me, the way Baldwin Castle had excited me, but then I didn't want a life of excitement. I wanted a life of leisure and comfort, with a well-bred, considerate husband who would always treat me very tenderly, and who would realize that women adore romance and wouldn't be afraid of seeming quixotic by catering to this taste."[22]

The materialistic aims of the mother, which set in motion the whole chain of circumstances culminating in Castle's death, sharply contrast with Althea's idealistic motives with Thorpe. While the daughter chooses her American suitor and begins a symbolic healing process, her choice also sets the younger woman free from her parent's traditional world. Keyes signals this transformation of values by having Althea realize what Hilary Thorpe means to her during an interrogation with Kirtland. When Althea and the detective learn that Lady Laura has lied about her relationship with Castle, the younger woman feels that telling the truth:

...was what Hilary would count on her to do, even if she were frightened; and Hilary meant more to her than anyone else in the world, more even than her mother. She had just realized this; and with the realization had come the consciousness that she need not be frightened any more.[23]

Thus, love triumphs over material desires and mental satisfactions, for Althea has pledged her future to Hilary so thoroughly that she lives vicariously through him. Unlike her mother, Althea wants love that is not simply a contractual exchange of economic and psychological benefits.

The younger woman's rejection of the less romantic values of her mother's society for the more emotional drives of American society reemphasizes the international theme in *The Royal Box* while pointing up another feminine concern. Keyes, like most other bestselling novelists, does not question conventional lifestyles or long-established values; rather, she praises and reinforces these traditional ethical assumptions (which are often so deeply held as to be nearly inarticulate). Thus, what could be more natural than that a young woman find a husband, cast her life in his shadow, and be liberated by the experience? While the whole process may seem demeaning to present-day women's activists, it was the accepted social gospel of the 1950s (and probably more prevalent today than many would care to admit). If one is tempted to bemoan the lost potentials in Althea Whitford's life, it is perhaps only reasonable to observe that her dependence on Hilary Thorpe represents a clinging that might ultimately be as traumatic for him as her "surrender" might be to her. If absolute power corrupts absolutely, can a calculated frailty be nearly as damaging over a sufficient length of time?

* * *

The central character of *The Bad Seed*, Rhoda Penmark, foreshadows a preoccupation of the 1960s and 1970s—the malevolent or demonic child, as seen in *Rosemary's Baby* (1967) and *The Exorcist* (1971). While "bad seed" has become a cultural cliché, larger ironies mark *The Bad Seed* for William March urges the permanence of evil and the inadequacy of modern prescriptions, particularly psychological ones, to explain this aspect of man. Despite the sacrifices and sufferings of good people, the malevolent Rhoda endures and prospers to suggest that her story has only begun, as it were. To our more cynical eyes, Rhoda's motives seem too apparent and pronounced, so that one can become exasperated by the obtuseness of the adult characters around her who consistently acquiesce to her pleas of self-pity. While less popular suspense novels from the 1950s, such as Ira Levin's *A Kiss Before Dying* (1954), retain their capacity to startle through clever plotting, *The Bad Seed* often lumbers predictably, a measure of the extent to which March felt he could be "daring."

One of the most obvious ironies in *The Bad Seed* centers on the relationship between past and present. While the story takes place shortly after World War II, any tendency to urge the recovery of pre-1939 innocence in the present quickly collapses. The spinster Fern sisters, who run the private school Rhoda attends, give a year-end picnic at the opening of the novel, an occasion on which Rhoda murders a classmate, Claude Daigle, to gain a penmanship medal while the picnic's sponsors make innocuous remarks to the assembled parents. Ironically, Miss Octavia Fern, in a short outburst that stresses her family's economic decline, chooses to emphasize how sweet life used to be: " 'There was no dissension in those days; a quarrel was unknown in the society of the well-bred, a cross word never exchanged between ladies and gentlemen. My sisters and I remember those days with love and great longing.' "[24] Her wistful note sharpens the later events that mock it so that Miss Octavia's words counterpoint the author's more somber views. As Mrs. Penmark, Rhoda's horrified mother, gradually discovers there may be a genetic link between the girl and her maternal grandmother, a famed mass murderess names Bessie Denker, one realizes that the past hardly resembled the idyll Miss Octavia recalls. The spirit of Bessie Denker, whom Mrs. Penmark also slowly realizes was her own mother, suggests any lack of moral difference between past and present; thus, Bessie and Rhoda testify to man's producing the same difficulties and problems for himself in all ages.

March's characters consistently illustrate the shortsightedness of purely intellectual people. This point, which denies the optimistic nostrum that intelligence or knowledge is power, emerges clearly when Emory Breedlove, a bachelor who lives upstairs from the Penmarks, and Reginald Tasker, a murder mystery writer, discuss the times in which they live.

"If anybody asks me, I'd say the age we live in is an age of violence. It looks to me like violence is in everybody's mind these days. It looks like we're just going to keep on until there's nothing left to ruin. If you stop and think about it, it scares you."

"Well, maybe we live in an age of anxiety *and* violence."

"Now, that sounds more like it. Come to think about it, I guess that's what our age is really like."[25]

These remarks take on additional weight because Emory, who wants to aid Mrs. Penmark, remains oblivious to Rhoda; and Reginald, who unwittingly provides the evidence for Mrs. Penmark to discover her paternity, makes no connection between this distraught woman and what he has told her. March's point is that even with the best intentions men misunderstand each other: putting oneself in another's place is too difficult for his supposedly intellectual characters.

An even more outspoken individual, Monica Breedlove, Emory's sister and housekeeper, makes the same point more forcefully. Monica has been psychoanalyzed in Vienna before 1939 and constantly mouths analytical terms, yet the grim aspect of Freudian thought, with its emphasis on the powers of the irrational mind even in children, has not seriously penetrated her understanding. Thus, she can talk of penis envy as though it were a commonplace theory and a perfectly good after-dinner topic, while consistently failing to see any evil in Rhoda. The older woman's constant verbal concern about Mrs. Penmark finally indicts Monica and the psychology she preaches; because she conceptualizes all problems as self-induced and therefore correctable, Monica fails to understand that there can be permanent evil. While her penchant for analytical theories constitutes a defense mechanism which allows Monica to dismiss evil as merely personal caprice, her advice leads Mrs. Penmark to follow a course that ends in suicide. Despite Rhoda's calculating behavior and her overt envy toward Claude because of his award, Monica Breedlove can declare: " 'A child's mind is so wonderfully innocent. So lacking in guile or deceit.' "[26] Her myopia is matched by Mrs. Forsyth, another elderly woman who frequently babysits Rhoda. When Leroy, the janitor, burns to death, Mrs. Penmark sees the event and goes into hysterics because Rhoda has committed another murder; however, in a devastating bit of irony, Mrs. Forsyth subsequently urges, while bathing Mrs. Penmark's brow with cool water, " 'You must take Rhoda as an example. Rhoda isn't upset at all. She's behaving like a seasoned little trooper.' "[27] Rhoda's calm arises from her lack of deep feelings (save those surrounding her ego) and her enjoyment of Leroy's death.

The obtuseness of these individuals supports an equally gloomy view of society. Mrs. Penmark's faith in education, her hope that time and exposure will cure Rhoda, is compromised and then destroyed by events. The mother's optimism that a highly disciplined school, such as the Ferns', will improve her daughter founders because Rhoda imposes her will on the school. If anything, the girl utilizes a greater sense of discipline in concealing her murder of Claude, so that education simply makes Rhoda more acute in manipulating others. After the Fern sisters refuse to accept Rhoda for the next semester because of her evasiveness about Claude's death, Mrs. Penmark decides she must educate her daughter. The distraught mother accepts the premise: "It was only through knowledge that she could help her child, could guide her with both understanding and intelligence to more acceptable attitudes, toward more conventional goals."[28] Unfortunately, this hope leads Mrs. Penmark to seek Tasker's help in finding out the truth about Bessie Denker and so leads to self-destruction. Mrs. Penmark thus reverses the customary pattern by which a character gains wisdom and an enhanced identity through suffering, for in her case her bullet-riddled corpse and a slowly recovering Rhoda are the end results of the pursuit of knowledge. Mrs. Penmark becomes so distraught that her suicide-murder scheme, in which she drugs Rhoda and shoots herself, backfires. The girl's survival, revealed by Mrs. Forsyth's ironic reminder to the grieving Kenneth Penmark (who has been traveling on business throughout the summer) that he still has a daughter to comfort him, represents the ultimate comment on Mrs. Penmark's faith in education and knowledge.

A more symbolic dismissal of the therapeutic benefits of self-awareness arises when Mrs. Penmark, suspicious of Rhoda's involvement in Claude's death, visits the Ferns' country place. Miss Octavia, in showing the grounds, casually mentions an abortive scheme her father tried to implement.

"Once, when I was a little girl like Rhoda, my father had the idea of building a pen out into the water, so we could put crabs there and fatten them up to eat when they weren't plentiful at all; but it was an impractical as most of my father's ideas. You see, the crabs, when they were penned together, ate one another before we could eat them."[29]

This vision, which is echoed in Tennessee William's *Suddenly Last Summer* (1958), foreshadows Rhoda's amorality for the crab pen represents the school in which Rhoda (being intellectually "fattened up") finally "ate" Claude, and her classmate's drowning because of repeated blows from Rhoda's shoe makes this connection even clearer. While Miss Octavia's concluding line implies society's predatory nature, this gloomy extreme never becomes dominant in *The Bad Seed*.

Mrs. Penmark represents the classic victim of such a society, for she consistently blames herself for Rhoda's shortcomings. While no great love exists between mother and child, Mrs. Penmark punishes herself because of the subconscious perception that she has failed as a mother. On the conscious level, she can hold her guilt feelings in check by reason; however, her suicide reveals the depth of Mrs. Penmark's self-loathing. While some of her excesses are plot contrivances, the letters she writes and never sends to her husband (which chronicle Rhoda's wrongdoings) dramatize her hypersensitivity to public opinion and decorum. Her persuading Rhoda to take sleeping pills and then shooting herself follow her destruction of those letters, so that Rhoda remains undetected when the novel closes. Mrs. Penmark epitomizes the archetypal "permissive" parent when she wonders about Rhoda.

She looked back, reviewing the little girl's life from its beginning, in an effort to see how she had gone wrong in training or affection, to find the mistakes she had made—for it was plain, now, that she had made many mistakes—eager to blame herself, in this moment of self-abasement, for any omission, any error in judgement, no matter how tiny, no matter how innocently done; but she could find nothing of any true importance.[30]

Such a predisposition summarizes the popular American attitude that each individual causes his own problems and can only solve them through self-effort.

Mrs. Penmark thus operates in terms of values enshrined by Horatio Alger and Benjamin Franklin which rest on the assumption that success arises from solitary effort; however Rhoda represents a more serious issue. While some difficulties can be labelled as "problems" (and thus subconsciously linked to the notion of "solution") to be seen as tractable, those seen as "conditions" (and thus only capable of being "endured") underlie a much more sober view of life. In effect, *The Bad Seed* treats human evil as a condition, insists on the permanence of depravity, and destroys or ridicules those characters who resist this fatalistic perception. Mrs. Penmark's finding consolation in a belief that Rhoda only possesses some "quirks" poignantly symbolizes her love for the child and her own guilt feelings. When she learns about her own descent from Bessie Denker,

Mrs. Penmark subsequently rationalizes that she has transmitted the "bad seed" to a new generation, and so exonerates Rhoda as a victim of genetic circumstance. While one pities Mrs. Penmark, the harsher lesson of personal responsibility, which seems lost on her and the other characters, tempers such distress.

Leroy, the janitor, suffers from envy about a world he never made and in which he is never going to make it. Incapable of holding any job for long, he delights in petty torments, such as squirting water on the tenants' shoes and then acting innocent about it. While he constantly taunts Rhoda, Leroy does not possess the same degree of malevolence as the little girl. A terrible irony arises when Leroy unwittingly works out how Rhoda killed Claude, a process that climaxes when he guesses the last detail, uses it to tease Rhoda, and then, when confronted by her genuine savagery, decides not to torment her anymore. The next time we see Leroy he is encased in flames mutely appealing to his executioner, Rhoda, before dying. Thus, Leroy represents the perfect foil for, since he isn't respectable enough to be believed by other adults, his insights into Rhoda never reach the apartment's dwellers. His fate dramatizes another ironic facet of human nature, for evil can apparently only be denounced by an individual who exhibits what society labels as "normal" (i.e. decorous) behavior himself: being insightful by itself is not enough.

The janitor understands Rhoda because he shares some of her personality traits, albeit he tempers such aspects by fear and laziness. His constant reflections on Mrs. Penmark emphasize how stupid he thinks she is (i.e. he sees Rhoda has her mother completely fooled) while indulging daydreams of lust with a woman whose husband is away. Leroy despises Mrs. Penmark as "one of the ones that was eat up with kindness," a woman to whom, "You could do...a dirty trick, but instead of hitting back, or hating the hell out of you, she'd feel guilty, instead, thinking she must be the one that was wrong."[31] Leroy dislikes Mrs. Penmark because she is what she is and his feelings cannot be explained away as abhorrent or abnormal problems created by society or external circumstances. In his vibrant fantasy life, a trait that accords with his physical and social unattractiveness, Leroy indulges in elaborate sexual reveries which degrade Mrs. Penmark in more obvious ways.

Now that dizzy blonde—that trough-fed Christine Penmark— was something else again. He'd like to get her down in the basement some day. He'd let her have it, all right...He'd put it to her all the ways there were in the book, and he'd think up some extra ways besides... And when he got done with her, she'd follow him about like a begging bitch. He'd make her cry and beg him for it again, that's what.[32]

Leroy's fantasy of sexual power, however rooted in infantile notions and sadistic feelings, marks him as more human than Rhoda, for it shows that he has some feelings about others.

The girl, on the other hand, embodies a lack of empathy that has become an increasingly dominant note in American culture. Christine and the Fern sisters mark Rhoda's self-sufficiency and, more ominously, her lack of affection at the picnic. The little girl's calculating nature enables her to play on her mother's emotions and, because she has no need for love, Rhoda becomes a master at such tactics for she can dispassionately observe others. When Christine confronts Rhoda with evidence of her involvement in Claude's death, the girl quickly externalizes her guilt. She blames the boy for causing the murder because of being too stubborn to let her wear his medal; and, while such an excuse echoes the joke about the mugger telling his victims to "get your throat off my knife," this defense mechanism resembles Christine's explaining Rhoda's depravity in terms of genes. There are, unfortunately, times when every word Rhoda utters is a dead giveaway about her crimes, so that she appears without the perplexities and varying motives that characterize more rounded fiction creations.

As a symbolic production, however, March's little murderess embodies traits that link psychology to current events, for she slowly emerges as a representative twentieth-century figure. When Reginald Tasker describes the general character profile of mass murderers, he presents a set of values that accord well with the horrors of concentration camps.

> They never killed for those reasons that so often sway warm but foolish humans. They never killed for passion, since they seemed incapable of feeling it, or jealousy, or thwarted love, or even revenge. There seemed to be no element of sexual cruelty in them. They killed for two reasons only—for profit, since they all had an unconquerable desire for possessions, and for the elimination of danger when their safety was threatened.[33]

Material gain and self-preservation motivate the murders Rhoda commits for, while she kills Claude for his medal (after earlier pushing an old lady down a flight of steps to gain a necklace), Rhoda dispatches Leroy because she fears that he knows about her classmate's death. Like Eichmann, and numerous other Nazi death camp "mechanics," Rhoda suggests the everyday nature of evil: her lack of emotion and calculating nature would accord well with the extermination of people for ideological reasons. Indeed, it is finally harder to understand the mentality which delights in creating more efficient means of mass extermination than to comprehend a murder committed as act of passion. It is not simply the magnitude of the twentieth-century's "crimes against humanity," but the spirit in which such acts have been undertaken that poses so many distressing moral dilemmas. While Rhoda resembles man's moral sense as it might have existed before the dawn of history, the girl also incorporates traits that are all-too-familiar to our century of total war.

William March's analysis of psychology (a science whose prominence has blossomed even more since 1954) reflects not simply a comic annoyance at that discipline's more bizarre aspects. Octavia Fern implies that being analyzed is, finally, a source of false optimism when she tells Christine: " 'Monica thinks man's mind can be changed through lying on a couch and talking endlessly to another man who is often as lost as the patient. Really, Monica is far more trusting and romantic than I.' "[34] *The Bad Seed* shows us that only the foolish and the dead are on the side of the "trusting and romantic"; for Rhoda's very ordinariness underscores her permanence, so that March, like the more celebrated Alfred Hitchcock, portrays evil as banal and, as a result, not easily detected. History and psychology suggest that depravity is likely to appear as extremely ordinary, and Tasker makes the same point about mass murderers in presenting the novel's principal theme.

> In the first place, good people are rarely suspicious. They cannot imagine others doing the things they themselves are incapable of doing; usually they accept the undramatic solution as the correct one, and let matters rest there. Then, too, the normal are inclined to visualize the multiple killer as one who's as monstrous in appearance as he is in mind, which is about as far from the truth as one could well get.[35]

Thus, *The Bad Seed* has an open ending, for Rhoda's recovery implies that the human struggle with evil will continue as long as man does.

* * *

Compulsion, based on the Leopold-Loeb murder trial, brings together a suspenseful plot and insightful passages of social criticism. The novel's first-person narrator, Sid, who worked as a cub reporter on the case and knew the principals, recollects the killing of Paulie Kessler (Bobby Franks) by Judd Steiner (Leopold) and Artie Strauss (Loeb) thirty years later. These events, through which Sid became an established newspaperman, take on a more symbolic weight against the background of World War II. Indeed, this initially sensational crime comes to look commonplace to Sid's seasoned eyes; and the Kessler murder only remains the "crime of the century" because it dramatizes the violence of the entire age. As he gets older, Sid realizes he shares some of the same psychological desires that drove the murderers; and, because his editor wants a feature on the trial, Sid finally confronts the knowledge that morality represents a slender thread which opportunity and compassion often prevent from snapping. Levin's narrator remains obsessed throughout with making sense of the crime his peers committed, and his dawning awareness that he is not so very different from Judd and Artie serves as the novel's ultimate lesson. There are no rationally satisfactory explanations, for any formal diagnoses or theories supplied to account for Judd's and Artie's actions reduce themselves to ritualistic hocus-pocus whose main purpose is to insure professional credibility to their proponents. Only Sid, who remains curious about himself and about what happened, and does not arrive at fixed answers, comes close to understanding.

In dealing with events that are thoroughly documented, Levin risks being dismissed because of omitting or altering any single important detail from the Leopold-Loeb case. In anticipating such literal-minded criticism which does not recognize the fictional concerns of a novel, Levin has Sid note: " 'In some instances, the question will arise: Is this true, did this actually happen? And my answer is that it needed to happen in the way I tell it or in some similar way, or else nothing can be explained.' "[36]

Clearly, the novelist who would recount the recent past must strive to make moral sense out of its events; and, while it may be possible to write history from morally neutral grounds, such a treatment in fiction would be quickly dismissed as merely a recitation of names and events with no unifying purpose. Levin's narrator supplies this requisite moral meaning by linking the story of Judd and Artie to his own reactions.

Sid possesses an acute sense of how ordinary people conceptualize and then transmit the past by shaping and rounding off its disparate events so as to supply a greater coherence to their lives than was frequently present when they were actually living past events. At one point, in a small and unimpressive club where he meets Ruth, his fiancée, and some other friends, Sid notes: "I could not have known that in years to come jazz enthusiasts would look back reverently to this dim cellar as the birthplace of the Chicago style."[37] For anyone who has directly experienced what historians later treat formally Sid's reaction should be familiar, for what seemed insignificant and fleeting at the time now returns in more ceremonial garb. While the past needs to be rewritten because man's conception of himself keeps changing, such recasting must include not only polite laughter at customs and costumes now out of fashion but a more serious obligation to maintain the moral importance of what happened, according to Levin's narrator. Because Jonathan Wilk, the novel's Clarence Darrow, prevents the execution of Judd and Artie by arguing that men "are largely what their ideas make them,"[38] Sid recognizes that the intellectual aspects of life are more important than its material ones. His narrative thus attempts to present the ideas of each of the principals as of equal immediate validity: thus, each character has coherent reasons for believing and acting as he does and no one exhibits motivations that seem melodramatic or merely convenient.

The murderers, while distinctly different personalities, exhibit motives based on emotional grounds so that, even though their ideas are discredited, they remain characters who suggest the enigmas of human individuality. At the novel's end, when Sid faces a similar urge to murder an innocent and essentially anonymous individual, Judd and Artie's arguments become something more than just juvenile rationalizations. While Levin's killers show certain outward traits of genius beloved by testers (e.g. retention of textbook facts), their lack of feeling makes them figures to be pitied rather than despised. Judd, who finds love briefly with Ruth after the murder, experiences overwhelming guilt when he realizes that rational calculations cannot be the sole guide to conduct. Although caught in a homosexual liaison in which Artie has dominated him, Judd comes to love Ruth and to suffer the realization that such feelings reflect his true self.

> . . . he experiences a frightful sense of something wasted, the murder as a false and wasted act. He has to make an effort to confirm the murder experience as part of his own being. And then it has returned into him, with even a more terrible sense of doom and error, because if the newer self is the real one, he has in previous dark error forsworn it.[39]

Sid's use of the present tense supplies plausible motives to Judd by developing thoughts as though they were occurring in the character's mind. Judd elicits sympathy because, when he is with the girl, he moves from a reverie about Artie watching them to an unsettling awareness:

> To experience everything, to experience every possibility of life—why, that included not only the unusual, the bizarre, the depths of evil, but it should have included the other side too; the other range of experience should have come first. How could he now? How could he ever experience the most everyday common feelings, love and truth, with a girl like this?[40]

Thus, the character goes beyond his youthful and overly intellectual infatuation with Oscar Wilde and Nietzsche to an understanding of the necessity for mundane sentiment; in effect, he becomes aware that there are other valid states of being besides his own version of life.

Artie, on the other hand, remains stuck in his own animosity against the world so that revenge constantly serves as his prime motive. Sexual impotence causes Artie to be aggressive and he continually prods Judd and, when their scheme unravels, takes delight in tormenting his erstwhile ally. Artie uses his superabundant intellect to probe for others' weaknesses and prefers manipulating people to the pursuit of ideas; indeed, he kills Paulie Kessler to see the crime's effect on others, especially his own parents. While Judd shares Artie's desire to shock, his participation also arises from a belief in the Nietzschean Superman, the individual who may do as he will because he has risen above common morality through his greater capacities for understanding. Lacking this philosophical rationalization, Artie remains trapped in an infantile dream of raping the world (i.e. making it submit to his will and thus his manhood). In remembering how a workman once showed him a chisel and joked that such a hard, lengthy object "would really knock them dead," Artie combines that scene with a recollection of his own sexual failure in a brothel with his fraternity brothers.

> ...the fellows stood around in a circle, close. The raucous laughter...there was his broad all spread out and waiting, and he couldn't, he couldn't—hell, many times when he was alone, it did—but now, "little mousey," she said, and they all roared, the bastards, the stinking sonsabitches. They doubled over, laughing at his trying—he could kill every last sonofabitch...hell, he'd get it so hard he'd crack their skulls with it. Laughing at him— he'd knock them dead with it.[41]

In killing Paulie Kessler, by a blow to the head (as well as strangulation), Artie symbolically takes revenge on those who laughed at him. The little rich boy is but a younger version of the fraternity brothers—a son of the upper class bound inevitably for college and a career; and by striking him on the head Artie knocks someone "dead" literally.

Like many other popular culture figures from the 1950s—Marlon Brando in the *The Wild One*, James Dean in *Rebel without a Cause* and Elvis Presley—Judd and Artie feel an abiding alienation from their parents. While the 1950s combined an infatuation with youth for its own sake with a belief that the older generation was simply shortsighted and hypocritical, Judd and Artie react in a more perplexing way. Even though psychological health may require the individual to cast off parental influence, these young men go a step further in daydreaming about getting even with their forebears. At one point, they even consider murdering Artie's younger brother so they can more severely degrade the Strauss family. Although this scheme never gets beyond the talking stages, Artie significantly says: " 'My old man would give a hundred thousand simoleons and say 'Keep the punk!' ''; and Levin later adds: "Artie had kidded. And he had pictured where he would send his old man to pick up messages. His dignified pater. A message in a ladies' toilet! That had convulsed him."[42] In a novel saturated with psychology, Artie's fantasy reveals his own ambivalent feelings toward his father; and, while the "punk" might well be himself at a subconscious level, Artie's desire to humiliate his parent reveals the extent of his "abnormality."

The similarities between men as moral beings—a view which implies all generations are cut from the same cloth—colors Sid's description of Judd's and Artie's parents, once they are involved in the murder trial. At a press conference, where the two fathers explain how they will provide for their sons' defense, Sid feels compassion for these distraught men because he knows Judd and Artie are guilty. "The press crowded around them, these men of millions who had come, we felt sure, to take their sons out of the hands of the law. And I looked at the two fathers with a dazed sense of my own power... Had they known so little of their sons! And what did my own father know of me?"[43] Sid's more mature view suggests that believing in the imperfections of one's children is as difficult as discovering one's own shortcomings. Thus, Levin's narrator realizes that he embodies the same human fallibilities that his father, and every other man, does.

This awareness of a common humanity arises in Judd but remains forever beyond Artie's comprehension. During the trial Judd and Artie are analyzed by numerous psychiatrists; and, while much of their contradictory testimony only reveals the state of their psychological art, one analyst profoundly insists that the murderers simply lacked adult emotions. His testimony stresses the disparity between their intelligence and their feelings: "In both boys there was shown a clear lack of development in the affective, or emotional life, in the facilities of judgment. He would place them emotionally at a nine-year-old level, perhaps even at a younger stage, while intellectually they rated as mature."[44] American society has seemingly bred a whole generation of Judds and Arties, individuals who have acquaintances rather then friends and practice serial monogamy rather than marriage— conditions which nurture excessive self-concern and social anomie. According to such a diagnosis, Judd and Artie have compartmentalized their lives so thoroughly that their affections never interfere with their rational and cunning desires. Levin's murderers have divided their personalities into roles which can be played at the most appropriate moments. Judd and Artie are finally inhuman because they do not exhibit the emotional compulsions of normal people who trust other human beings despite intuiting that men are always fallible. Ironically, Judd and Artie lack the very depth of feeling that leads to involuntary behavior and are the least compulsive characters in *Compulsion.*

Sid's perspective, conditioned by his own post-World War II consciousness, colors the entire narrative. In an early interview with Judd, who has just been questioned by the police because his glasses were found near the location of the murdered boy's body, Sid believes Steiner must be innocent because he can offer plausible reasons for what has happened and, more important, because Sid feels he can read character in another's face.

Eagerly Judd replied, "Why on earth should anyone imagine I would kidnap someone for ransom? I get all the money I want from my father, and besides, I teach three classes in bird lore and get paid for it." He seemed to be speaking directly to me. And in that moment I was sure he was innocent.... Confronting him, I found the whole idea impossible to believe, and from that moment, I suppose, there had to grow for me the mistrust of human confrontation that is so deep a mark upon our time. What could you truly know of anyone by looking into his face, his eyes? How can you be certain of anything among human beings?[45]

Sid's resigned outlook denies that conventional wisdom, perhaps best epitomized by the political debate, according to which character is revealed by direct confrontation, a popular view thoroughly in tune with a jury trial. Sid's view questions such assumptions, while his confrontation with Judd raises the larger issue of the nature of evil. Levin's narrator has arrived at the same unsettling realization that colors so many of the films of Alfred Hitchcock: evil appears most often not in extraordinary guise but in the most ordinary trappings. Just as Otto Kruger in *Saboteur* (1942), Joseph Cotten in *Shadow of a Doubt* (1943) and Ray Milland in *Dial M for Murder* (1954) initially appear as respectable and then prove heinous, so Judd's hypocrisy temporarily conceals his crime. The equally disturbing corollary, which Levin's narrator implies and Hitchcock dramatically illustrates, is that ostensibly good characters can be seriously, if not quite fatally, compromised by their contacts with evil and their own desires. Farley Granger in *Strangers on a Train* (1951), James Stewart in *Vertigo* (1958) and Paul Newman in *Torn Curtain* (1966) play compulsive protagonists not above committing violence or repression when dealing with others. These cinematic leading men embody the same uneasy duality that Sid does in *Compulsion*; as a group, they are the 1950s' forerunners of the more deeply divided "anti-heroes" of the 1960s and 1970s.

In observing Judd and Artie, Sid, who shares their intellectual precocity and finds himself in graduate school with them at age 19, learns about the wishes and desires that lead men to madness. Levin's narrator is only redeemed (as Hitchcock's figures never are) by a critical intelligence unflinchingly directed at himself. Sid knows that he makes mistakes, a lesson Judd and Artie only learn when their plot unravels. Willie Weiss, another casual friend of the killers who obtains a position on the prosecutor's staff to study them up close, remains shortsighted for another reason. Willie epitomizes the academic investigator reducing human beings to data and so dismays Sid, who wants desperately to understand and not merely to diagnose. Weiss' preoccupation with psychology has become an ideology substituting for thought. After Sid tells Willie about a list of potential victims Judd and Artie drew up, the would-be psychiatrist rhapsodizes about the latent meanings in their choices and how such revelations obtained from an in-depth study would be:

"Fascinating. What an opportunity! Now that they're isolated. What an opportunity for a great study!"

At that moment I felt I knew why Willie had been the third member of their luncheon parties. Surely he fitted in, if he could now think of his friends only in terms of what a study they would make. I was reminded of Judd's remark about impaling a butterfly.[46]

Willie embodies a lack of feeling similar to the murderers'; and, in turning human beings into grist for his own intellectual mill, he foreshadows the detached cruelty of Auschwitz and Buchenwald. It is a chilling paradox that educated people can be as deficient in humanity as anyone else; for professional training (and its favored twentieth-century discipline, psychology) offers no guaranteed means to achieve a civilized outlook. Thus, Levin's narrator does not merely chide the obvious excesses of those in control (e.g. *No Time for Sergeants*) or demonstrate that psychology is not a predictive science (*The Bad Seed*) or present how psychological testimony can be manipulated in court (e.g. *The Caine Mutiny, Anatomy of a Murder*).

The narrator's compassion extends to his reflections on love when he belatedly realizes that Ruth, his first love, was the best woman in his life. Their relationship ultimately foundered not because of Judd Steiner but because of their own sophistication. Sid and Ruth confused sex with love and, as supposedly "mature" young adults, destroyed their affection by reducing it to mechanical terms.

Ruth was my girl at that time...whenever I think of her, and now as I write of her, the aura of that young love comes back, and I realize that what we then felt was indeed love. We were in love and afraid to know it, and nobody told us it was the true thing. Everybody, all the kids of our time, had endless doubts; we used to analyze ourselves and decide it was only sex attraction, and we didn't quite have the nerve to test that out either.[47]

In lacking sufficient idealism the lovers suffer from an absence of compulsion. They destroy genuine sentiments by rationalizing their feelings, and this shortcoming is underscored by Ruth's brief emotional attachment to Judd. While she never loves Steiner, Ruth senses the emotional depths which lurk beneath his intellectualized exterior. Judd's attempt to seduce Ruth (he awkwardly grapples with her during an ornithological walk) unsettles him because she offers him compassion as a result. Ruth causes Judd to recognize the essential, paradoxical question of romantic love, as opposed to sexual attraction: why is one so strongly drawn to a single individual and not by all presentable members of the opposite sex? Unwittingly, Ruth fosters love in Judd while she only encourages hostility and misunderstanding in Sid.

As members of a disenchanted century, none of Levin's characters achieves romantic satisfaction or fulfillment. Judd goes to prison while Sid and Ruth drift into lives of quiet regret. Myra, a cousin of Artie's, who reveals the depth of her feelings for young Strauss and her dismay at the nonfulfillment of that love, echoes their dissappointment. " 'Oh, Sid, I wish I were honest and decent like a whore. Do you think if I had given myself to him...oh, we're all such frauds—we pretend we're so emancipated. Sid, if I had, if I had, then maybe he wouldn't have got all tangled up with that awful Judd. That's what got him into it.' "[48] While this encounter takes place after the Kessler murder, Myra's optimism about love demonstrates that she is vulnerable enough to be human now that she has realized emotions count for more than intellectual sophistication. Sid, on the other hand, remains obtuse when trying to understand what Ruth tells him about Judd. The narrator's later experiences in World War II finally reveal the deeper truth his fiancée perceived; indeed, when Ruth argues that everyone shares a responsibility for what Judd has done, Sid dismisses such a sentiment as hogwash—a stance he cannot assume after the events of 1939-1945. Ruth wants to help Judd who is now on trial.

"Oh tell me what to do," she begged. "I would do anything to help him."

"There's nothing you can do," I said. "You're not mixed up in it."

"I am, I am. Everybody who knew him is. Everybody who let him come to a thing like that."[49]

Man's responsibility for his fellow man, a grim lesson that foreshadows the world's attempt to come to grips with the horror of the Nazi extermination of the Jews, clearly underlies Ruth's appeal.

By the very nature of their crime, and Wilk's choice to plead "insanity" as their defense, the murderers in *Compulsion* are surrounded by an atmosphere redolent with psychological questions and theories. Levin's narrator voices doubts about the new science, even though its growing awareness that the individual may not be in control of his mind may represent an accurate portrait of twentieth-century man. Sid agrees when Jonathan Wilk urges that the value of psychology lies only in what it can say after the fact; and, while contemptuous of psychology's predictive inability, Sid remains even more convinced that the problem-solving mentality encouraged by this discipline represents a catastrophe for the modern age. At the trial, as he tries to appreciate the motives of Judd and Artie, a chasm gradually opens beneath Sid's feet for he cannot remain content with uttering a verbal formula. In postulating that killing had become an abstraction for Judd and Artie, Sid goes on to reflect that there might be a "killing impulse in humanity,"[50] an insight which describes much of subsequent world history.

Sid, who gains a keener awareness of humanity's darker side during the trial, gradually realizes that he shares Judd's and Artie's impulses at some level. In the courtroom Sid desperately seeks for a reasonable explanation of the Kessler murder only to realize that he is looking for moral comfort rather than the truth.

> ...it was clear that what all hoped for was to hear an excuse, an explanation. This could only be, I suppose, a reflection of some guilt that is in all of us, a fear that in the deepest unknown of ourselves there exist capacities for doing what the boys had done. And from the psychiatrists, from the sages of our time, we hope for—what? Reassurance?[51]

While he can condemn psychiatrists as intellectual pacifiers, because he remains a child of this century Sid must recognize man's irrationality as pervasive and enduring. Jonathan Wilk gradually convinces the jury to show mercy to his disturbed clients and Sid finds himself in a dilemma, for the lawyer's argument implies an amoral universe: "It was the deeper kind of plea, for which we had waited from Wilk, the plea for compassion, yet delicately balanced, because if you carried it too far you would be saying what you really meant, that no one was responsible for any crime."[52] Wilk's plea suggests a difference in degree rather than in kind between his clients and their judges; and, for Sid, this delicate balancing act finally dramatizes the task of every civilized man who must live with evil and yet dismiss its means (e.g. capital punishment). Just as Joseph Conrad's Marlow had to come to terms with inhumanity and still remain human in *Heart of Darkness*, Sid must discover that morality is a continuous quest and not a state of being. The narrator has finally grown up when he stops seeking for expert opinions that will restore his lost sense of security.

Judd and Artie's trial becomes a rock concert or a "happening" as idle crowds mill about to glimpse the newest celebrities that the media have created. While these idlers must go on to ever new titillations, Sid ends up meditating on the meaning of what he sees in the crowd on the trial's opening day.

> There were women, mostly, and among them a very high proportion of young girls— excited flappers, their mouths flaming in their loudest lipstick, many with ill-applied spots of rouge in dollar-size patches on their cheeks, like the girls in more recent years who besieged the stage doors, waiting to waylay a favorite crooner. But there were also middle-aged women in clusters, like the ranks that were to appear at Rudolf Valentino's funeral.[53]

The pervasiveness of this spectator impulse is stressed again when Sid describes how Artie reacts to the crowd's attention.

> Certainly Artie evoked a hysterical tenderness in women. We heard it now in the corridor, a curious feminine shrieking and gasping, as the boys were pulled through the corridor crowd; we glimpsed bare arms, hands reaching above him, heard a few piercing girls' voices above the others—"Artie!" "Artie, honey!"—and we later described how pieces of his clothing were torn from him, for souvenirs.[54]

This carnival atmosphere resembles the same pageantry one associates with crowds whether surrounding Adolf Hitler or Elvis Presley. The irony here derives from Artie's impotence and the frustration which would quickly cause his admirers to shy away from more intimate moments with such a "dreamboat."

Although it dismays him, Sid records his father's reaction to the Kessler murder: " 'One thing is lucky in this terrible affair, Sid. It's lucky it was a Jewish boy they picked.' My father, with his own yardstick. What will it do to the Jews?"[55] Sid's irritation seems reasonable, yet the later spectacle of the Nazi extermination camps suggests that his narrow—minded father knew more of human nature than his educated son did. In keeping with such historical foreshadowing, Sid notes quite early that the Kessler murder was symptomatic of the entire century in that its victim was "chosen at random." The anonymity of modern warfare, in which technology wreaks havoc on the population at large, turns everyone who happens to be in the wrong place at the wrong time into a Paulie Kessler. Much later, when the trial starts to wind down, Sid reacts when an analyst argues that Judd and Artie had committed *folie a deux*, an act of madness whose participants are so emotionally intertwined that their desires feed on a similar source. After this psychiatrist notes the rarity of such a phenomenon, Sid wonders: "Wouldn't the needed personalities somehow attract each other, to come together? And since then, of course, we have seen other crimes out of such conjoinings."[56] The human heart, if history offers any evidence, cannot be swayed by the pronouncements of psychiatrists or analysts; indeed, as Sid comes to appreciate, human irrationality precludes any real understanding, save the most superficial.

Levin's narrator finally understands the most personal applications of Judd and Artie's crime at the very end of World War II when, as a combat correspondent in Germany, he and a friend take a jeep into unoccupied but safe territory. When they happen upon a young girl and Sid's companion urges that they rape and kill her—an act of violence that has been feeding their imaginations for months—Levin's narrator refuses and brings them back to their senses. The similarities between such a desire and Judd and Artie's crime are, of course, strikingly obvious; for, while Sid and his friend could exercise their violent fantasy as somehow being an act of patriotism, the same mentality which turns an anonymous individual into a murdered victim is clearly at work. For Sid, Jonathan Wilk's closing remarks at the trial epitomize the lessons he learns in Germany in 1945. Speaking in the aftermath of an earlier world war, Wilk urges that mercy be shown to Judd and Artie because man had spilled too much blood.

"...we have not only seen it shed in bucketsful, we have seen it shed in rivers, lakes, and oceans, and we have delighted in it; we have preached it, we have worked for it, we have advised it, we have taught it to the young, until the world has been drenched in blood and it has left stains upon every human heart and upon every human mind, and has almost stifled the feelings of pity and charity that have their natural home in the human breast."[57]

Thus, murder, which might be justified by passion, has come to be a social norm, and Judd Steiner and Artie Strauss in their lack of compulsion represent the all too common experience of the twentieth century. *Compulsion* finally argues that civilized conduct must come from the heart *and* the head, and never simply from one or the other. Its intellectual criminal (Judd) and its passionate criminal (Artie) represent extremes that reasonable men must avoid to preserve self, society and civilization.

Mandingo
A racist nightmare in an antebellum setting (Crest)

Chapter 11

"Well, that's him."

The 1950s saw the beginnings of the Civil Rights "explosion" of the 1960s. While the earlier decade witnessed a decline of black income in relation to white, judicial and social developments indicated the emergence of a new consciousness about racial discrimination. The Supreme Court's 1954 decision in *Brown v Board of Education* established the injustice of the "separate but equal" doctrine in public schools and set off two decades of turmoil, while the Montgomery bus boycott (1955-1956) brought Martin Luther King and his method of "non-violent resistance" to national prominence. By the end of this period Dr. King had organized the Southern Christian Leadership Conference and sit-ins were becoming a common form of black protest. Two weak Civil Rights Acts, dealing with voting rights and passed during the Eisenhower years (1957 and 1960), stand in marked contrast to the murder of Emmett Till in Mississippi (1955), the expulsion of Autherine Lucy from the University of Alabama (1956), and the Little Rock school crisis (1957). These events forced the federal government to become more active in implementing the Supreme Court's decisions; and, while he moved with great personal reluctance, President Eisenhower's actions foreshadowed the course his Democratic successors would take in the 1960s.

Kyle Onstott's *Mandingo* (1957), a runaway bestseller, and Ralph Ellison's *Invisible Man* (1952), a profoundly disturbing work, present many of the stereotyped qualities attributed to blacks by white society. However, the former encourages racist flights of fancy in its descriptions of the slaves at Falconhurst plantation who, seemingly live only to fight, feed and fornicate. Ellison's nameless protagonist, beset by images imposed by a majority which does not figuratively see him, reacts against these attributed roles with human anguish. This character's suffering gradually leads him to adopt a strategy of waiting for an inevitably more auspicious time. The two novels thus counterpoint each other for, while they both present familiar racist stereotypes of stupidity and sexual prowess, *Mandingo* aims to titillate while *Invisible Man* seeks to unsettle.

* * *

Mandingo strikingly illustrates the pitfalls of badly executed historical fiction. The work, a veritable racist nightmare complete with sexual, psychological and social fantasies that optimists would like to believe are outmoded, provides some local color; but its protracted plot and consistent obsessions with sex and violence override any factual acumen. In its portrayal of the antebellum South, the novel reduces men to avaricious monsters; and, while one may doubt that all plantation owners were as benevolent as Margaret Mitchell's O'Hara and Wilkes families in *Gone with the Wind*, the absence of any redeeming qualities in the Maxwells of Falconhurst equally denies human reality. Thus, *Mandingo*, despite all its author's avowed intentions and its publisher's avowals about historical accuracy, fails because of its overly narrow view of human nature.

While the novel abounds with historical allusions (as any six- hundred page "authorized uncensored abridgement" would) Onstott's use of such materials serves a saliciousness of mind rather than attempts to understand the American past. In presenting a highly stratified antebellum Southern society, Onstott even allows characters to meditate on their relative positions. Thus, the elder Maxwell, when confronted by the slave trader Brownlee, considers their differing statuses. The old man, who has come from lower-class origins to own a large plantation dedicated to breeding slaves, realizes: "his own rung of the social hierarchy was not that of a gentleman—not a fine gentleman at least, merely a gentleman by courtesy, far, far above a dealer but not quite a gentleman."[1] Such discrimination reflects the character's being a self-made man in a traditional society; in effect, Maxwell recognizes his marginal status but clings to privilege when confronted by someone with even less prestige. Given that thousands of Southerners who owned no slaves died in a struggle seemingly to preserve the psychological satisfaction of regarding blacks as inferiors, such a passage may offer a discerning understanding of the white Southern mentality at the time of the Civil War. Maxwell's son, Hammond, more certain of his standing, worries over performance and character. He even enjoys his crippled leg for it checks his pride.

A gentleman must live up to his heritage, accept its prerequisites and immunities, but the man proud of being a gentleman was something less than a gentleman, just as the man who aspired to be believed a gentleman, by so much, failed of his aspiration. Perhaps his own crippled leg, by curbing his pride, saved his gentility. Possibly this was its purpose, to chasten him.[2]

While suffering and wisdom are equated here in the formation of character, Hammond's insistence on having to suffer also accords with the character's psychological quirks; indeed, Hammond's stratified society gradually emerges as a sado-masochistic haven.

When Hammond courts Blanche Butler, a distant cousin, Onstott uses the girl, who has committed incest with her brother, to symbolize the South's moral decline. Blanche and her family are grasping parasites whose decorum conceals sexual repression and psychological excess: their hypocrisy ultimately threatens Hammond and his father with disease and insanity.

After listening to Dr. Wilson, a local physician who only wants to marry a rich widow and breed " 'superior niggers,' " expound on the physical degeneracy incest creates in the slave population, one knows that Blanche is anathema. Indeed, she is but the living representative of a crumbling house, a place even Hammond sees as a "bubble about to burst."[3] The young man marries Blanche to provide a legitimate heir for Falconhurst and, since his heart belongs to Ellen, a slave bedmate who welcomes his natural urges (and thus spares Blanche from too much "pestering"), he can be brutally honest about his white wife. Upon returning from an extended slave selling trip, Hammond despairs at again being a physical companion to Blanche.

He had neglected his marital duties, which were not entirely pleasant, what with the pallor of the soft white flesh, which he was not forced to see but of which he imagined the color under the heavy nightgown. Its very smell, though less heavy, was more offensive than Negro musk. The tang of fresh musk, if attenuated, was zestful, but the blonde effluvium connoted corruption.[4]

Thus, the weakness of the old-line aristocracy, whose wastrel sons dissipate themselves in gambling and "gaming," extends to its daughters who are no physical match for the more natural Negroes. In effect, Onstott's novel becomes a parable in which a crippled young hero, after suffering at the hands of a decadent aristocratic lady, must leave his father's home to regain his equilibrium. Unfortunately, such an arrangement reduces historical movements to moralistic terms (i.e. a society which produces deceitful, weak and self-indulgent members will destroy itself) and so denies such unsettling contingencies as technological change or simple chance.

Onstott's Blanche (whose very name underscores her whiteness and weakness) epitomizes the psychological and sexual preoccupations of a novel which abounds with scenes of sadism and masochism. At one point, Meg, a young house servant who has homosexual longings for Hammond, eagerly agrees to help his master whip another slave because, to his inflamed imagination, a beating resembles lovemaking. When Ellen becomes Hammond's bedmate, the jealous Meg does everything possible to get whipped, even begging for it and asking that pimentade, an ointment that accentuates the pain of the lashes, be rubbed on " 'my ass.' "[5] The boy's fantasy comes up short however when he sees that his twin brother, Mem, has not been personally whipped by Hammond: "Meg...thought of the ecstatic pain of the impact of the paddle in Hammond's own hands. He had, indeed, aspired to such a martyrdom, but had not envisioned that his master might delegate the task to another slave. It sobered him."[6] Hammond never whips slaves for pleasure because such sadism would link him to the decadent society around him. Charles Butler, Blanche's brother, delights in whipping Katy, a slave provided for his pleasure, much to Hammond's amazement. Later, when the Mandingo slave, Mede, who Hammond acquires to be a "fighting nigger," is seduced by Blanche, sadism is again linked to decadence. Hammond has brought identical earrings for Blanche and Ellen—and when his wife finds out, she forces Mede to wear the earrings Hammond bought for her. Since he cannot imagine Blanche and the slave as lovers, Hammond dismisses his wife's conduct as adolescent jealousy; however, violence and spiritual demise are plainly coupled for, in examining Mede, Hammond notices that the slave's ear has been pierced and asks:

> "Who punch that big hole, and whut he do it with? Wasn't no call to make that hole so big."
> "Mist'ess, suh. She do it with a eatin' fork," the Negro explained, flinching.
> When the master turned to the other ear, he found it inflamed, swollen, and festered. "This one sore, like," he said. "Jes' about rotted off. Whyn't you do somethin', take it out or somethin'?"
> "Mist'ess say wear'em, suh, Masta, please. I asted her to please take 'em out, but she wouldn't. She say to wear 'em."
> "I hopin' that ear ain't a-goin' to rot."
> ... The jewels were now useless. Having been in a Negro's ears, no white woman could ever be asked to wear them.[7]

Blanche's viciousness titillates the popular audience's stereotypes of women with too much leisure and black men as big, stupid oafs. Although the sadistic nature of slavery has been a popular motif in American literature since *Uncle Tom's Cabin,* the cruelty of Onstott's characters seems intended to shock rather then to enlighten.

Another aspect that further demeans Negroes is the novel's many descriptions of stripping and fondling that accompany its slave-trading scenes. Dealers like Brownlee not only examine the biceps and teeth but also fondle the genitals and ogle the physiques of potential purchases. As human cattle, the slaves at Falconhurst must submit to such physical pawings; however, their welcoming such attentions strains credibility. Typically, Big Pearl, the "plantation showpiece...delighted in being stripped and paraded and handled and bargained for, confident that the tremendous offers for her would be declined."[8] Homosexuality also underscores such simplistic views of man; indeed, like the more celebrated *Peyton Place, Mandingo* presents a world where everyone is "by sex obsessed." Onstott thus reduces human history to a single motive so that the past—a complex process containing the wishes, desires and plans of millions of individuals—becomes monochromatic and too easily comprehended. Onstott's outlook ironically makes *Mandingo* profoundly anti-historical; however, in keeping with his vision, homosexuality (a 1950s' phobia as seen in Spillane and elsewhere) offers another symptom of the South's social decay. Readers are flattered in two ways by being treated to the saliciousness of such passages and encouraged to dismiss the past as merely the present "in different clothes." Meg's fawning on Hammond is matched by Madison Church, a light-headed young plantation owner, whose instability crops up most dramatically when he urges his great devotion to Hammond: " 'I don' care, I don' care, I don' care. I ruther stay with you than have all the plantations an' niggers in the whole world. I wouldn't care was I a nigger on my own se'f, an' if I could be yourn an'work fer you.' "[9] Like Meg, Madison wants to be degraded, dominated and so reduced to a love object by Hammond. This constant equation of homosexuality, masochism and social decline suggests that a slave society based on cruelty can only contain people who inflict pain and who submit to it. The antebellum South is once more symbolized by the jaded Roche who buys Meg and Mem to enjoy them sexually. When he caresses these boys and lays his cheek against their bellies, history has been reduced to a moralistic and melodramatic spectacle.

While Falconhurst is a breeding farm where every able-bodied black female's duty is to get impregnated so that sexuality is "good business," the characters' desires far outrun mere commercial considerations. Hammond has a succession of black paramours, for when one becomes pregnant she is succeeded by another; in effect, the plot finally hinges on the young master's becoming so attached to Ellen that he forgets his own obligation to keep his "stock" breeding. Before Hammond becomes infatuated with Ellen, he sees sex as a duty. Big Pearl wants him desperately and, despite her physical opulence, Hammond only reluctantly agrees to "service" her, a guilt feeling reflective of male anxieties about one's own sexual prowess and an association of promiscuity with lower-class behavior. Like numerous nineteenth-century physicians and pornographers, Hammond believes that a man's sexual capacity is finite, a quality that drains away as time goes on. He expresses this concern when he chides Big Pearl, who has become Mede's lover, with wearing out the fighting Mandingo: " 'Big Pearl wear that Mede out, dreen his stren'th that I wants to fight with' "[10] Although it threatens male energy and potency, intercourse is a constant necessity for the female; thus, Big Pearl becomes happier after she has Hammond (and especially after she has had Mede) and Blanche blossoms as a result of "good" loving. Although he naively attributes her mood to other causes, even Hammond notices that Blanche was "more genial and generous, amiable and kind than he had come to expect of her"[11] after she has seduced Mede. In these instances good sex is violent sex, so that Mede and Blanche enact a rape and Big Pearl is so insatiable that her men must struggle to avoid being devoured. That antebellum plantations were sexual hothouses has, of course, long been a staple in the popular mind; while the sexual stereotype that women want to be raped hardly presents a novel perception of either humanity or the past.

A similar fantasy the novel encourages is that the superbly endowed male represents the answer to every woman's sexual prayers. While the equation of size and performance implies that familiar bromide that quantity is quality, Onstott's use of this popular superstition represents another instance in which folk "wisdom" is pandered to in a bestseller. Moreover, because Mede is a penile giant, a more blatantly racist nightmare comes into play. Mede, the super-sexed Negro, threatens and tempts all women so that Blanche's seduction of him dramatizes the deeper fear of the white male—that the white woman secretly longs to be raped by the more physically endowed black male. When Hammond buys Mede he discusses the Mandingo's sexual proportions with his former owner, who insists:

"He's got plenty of sap, as you say, probably too much; but he is too big...I had Ben call in the biggest, most experienced, old wench on the place...and turned this young Mede in to her. She was pleased as he was, although she was beyond child bearing, but he was so big, and hurt her so much, and she screamed so loud, that I pulled the boy right off of her, afraid he would tear her and ruin her.... I fear he will live a virgin all of his life unless I can get him a cow elephant."[12]

When Hammond mates Mede and Big Pearl (an inevitable match) he learns that, if anything, Big Pearl can wear out the Mandingo. Lucretia Borgia, Big Pearl's mother, recounts this to Hammond because she has been a witness at this titanic coupling. The older woman's description not only adds voyeurism to the novel but implies female sexual insatiability, for Lucretia Borgia describes Mede as a " 'reg'lar jackass' " and begs to use him. After Hammond discovers his wife's infidelity and kills both her and the Mandingo, Lucretia Borgia declares: " 'That Mede he right temptatious to a woman. You-all done seen him nekkid.' "[13] Such psychology clearly resembles that found in male pornography, for Lucretia worships the male organ. Obviously masochism —being impaled by the giant Mede—and racism—the saliciousness of Lucretia—dominate in much of the novel.

While one can excuse some of its racial slurs as technically necessary (how else would white Southerners of the period talk?), *Mandingo* becomes excessive in this vein. Since William Styron's *The Confessions of Nat Turner* (1967) elicited howls of outrage because of it supposed racism, one wonders how *Mandingo* escaped such a sociological and academic barrage. The patent irony here, however, is that Onstott's novel, however weak as literature, has reached a larger audience and so has probably been a more influential book. One encounters patent slurs and stereotypes from the opening page of *Mandingo*, for blacks are consistently presented as shiftless, lazy beasts whose natural smell is overwhelmingly offensive. Their equation with animals even extends to sexuality, for the elder Maxwell, speaking reflectively, opines: " 'They all lusty-like.... Made that way. I ain't a-blamin' 'em. It the baboon in 'em—half baboon. Ain't no call to behave, savin' you make 'em.' "[14] Certainly this view flatters those racists who would insist upon the lack of historical accomplishment among the dark races— a perception that myopically elevates western technology to the position of be-all and end-all of human effort.

The elderly Maxwell's opinions reduce blacks to creatures who only respond to simple stimuli. In an argument with Gasaway, a slave owner who wants to teach his Negroes Christianity, Maxwell urges: " 'All the wench care about is for a buck to pester her an' for a sucker to milk her tits.' "[15] This reduction of women to baby-making machines whose only feelings are for concupiescence, birth and nurturing hardly requires a Gloria Steinem to condemn it. While Maxwell goes on to insist, " 'so long as a nigger kin breed, he don't think nothin' about going' to heaven,' "[16] his narrow view ultimately applies to all people, for he declares: " 'Eatin' and fornication', about all a nigger got to live for—or a human either, so fur as that concerns.' "[17] The old man rejoices when Mede sires a boy with Big Pearl because that birth guarantees the Mandingo bloodline's future; and, when Blanche and Hammond have a child, the elderly Maxwell personally oversees the baby's care and feeding. Since Blanche does not want to "lose" her figure, she refuses to nurse and Big Pearl is chosen to suckle the offspring. This duty only falls on Big Pearl after Maxwell tests her.

> He handled the full breast and when he squeezed the nipple, a stream of milk squirted from it. He opened her dress further and withdrew her other breast and squeezed it. "Show papa," he said.
>
> The girl crawled on her knees toward the older man, who stroked the black breasts with approval, leaned forward and sucked a mouthful of milk and savored it. He nodded to his son.[18]

While such saliciousness is typical, the novel gradually assumes a more sinister tone. Maxwell's conduct foreshadows the genetic experiments of Nazi Germany and the physical horrors of its concentration camps. Indeed, since the old man can impose himself at will on all his slaves, a psychological ambience like that of a prison camp, where the inmates live at the whim of their master-guardians, quickly emerges.

A more "explosive" aspect of *Mandingo* concerns sexual relationships between blacks and whites. Hammond exhibits the familiar double standard by sleeping regularly with Ellen, even after he has married Blanche, and then becoming enraged when his wife seduces Mede. Blanche, in turn, finds herself caught between decorum—which insists she must act as though on a pedestal and her own lust for revenge. As a paragon of Southern womanhood, she has been taught to suffer sex as a duty and not to seek it as a pleasure; while Hammond has been warned that the girl must be treated kindly or, to put it more bluntly, that he must not "pester" her too much. Blanche's mother blisters Hammond, after her daughter has conceived with Mede, about his excessive lust and her hysterics emphasize that man is always and everywhere driven by sexual need. By urging that there " 'Ain't no end of whut men does to women,' "[19] she underscores the view of the white married woman as weak and dependent, a more exalted slave to be victimized by a master whom society has sanctified by a marriage ceremony rather than a bill of sale. Blanche, in remaining jealous of Hammond's attentions to Ellen, seeks out other lovers. Her initial effort with the doctor who attends her first pregnancy comes off badly; for, while she resists an urge to bare her breasts as too "forward," the young man subsequently exhibits more interest in a black servant girl whom he afflicts with venereal disease. Thus, Blanche is again linked to decadence since she lacks the wisdom to avoid corruption and, as an inferior vessel, needs the same guidance Hammond provides for the slaves.

While majority opinion in the United States has always frowned on black-white romances, the underside to such a strongly-held value finds release in fiction like *Mandingo*. While Meg is revolted by the sight of Hammond in bed with Ellen, such disapproval arises from jealousy rather than racial antipathy. Hammond, in turn, registers repulsion when he sees a genuine physical passion between Charles Butler and Katy, for he cannot conceive that such a relationship can be based on more than lust or convenience.

> Ham's disturbance... was disgust, bordering upon nausea, that a white man should assume an amatory equality with a Negro wench. It was beneath the dignity of his race—somehow bestial. A wench was an object for a white man's use when he should need her, not a goal of his affections, to be commanded and not wheedled ...."[20]

Later, Hammond falls in love with Ellen and moves away from the stereotyped thinking he here exhibits; indeed, when Ellen, who has been brought to serve as the master's "pestering wench," apologizes for her appearance and throws herself on his mercy, Hammond shows compassion. Such tenderness forces him to see through a stereotype and deal with a distinct human being.

Onstott's protagonist cannot, however, entertain the other possibility in black-white relations and, thus, show compassion to Blance and Mede. On an earlier trading expedition, Hammond encounters a licentious widow who buys male slaves to satisfy her lust. Despite her sexual remarks " 'Put away that one...I knowin' now why you named him Leddle 'Un.' "[20] Hammond cannot convince himself that the woman will really go to bed with a slave. When the other traders joke about it, Hammond becomes upset for, although he can internally acknowledge such a probability, he still must insist outwardly that it cannot be so: " 'You gen'lemen wrong.... She white, an' ain't no white lady goin' to pester with no nigger buck. You wrong.' The idea of sexual congress of a white female with a Negro male was too horrendous to credit, yet it was obvious to discern.' "[21] In the novel's "blistering" climax, Hammond, who realizes he has been cuckolded when Blanche delivers a black baby, destroys any trace of the perfidy he has experienced. After poisoning Blanche, he boils Mede alive in a cauldron until only his bones remain. Then, after burying Blanche and her dead black child in a section of the family plot set aside for slaves, Hammond symbolically dumps Mede's remains over the recently disturbed earth.

> When Hammond emptied the final bucketful over the now well-soaked grave, he noticed a piece of flesh not yet disintegrated. Two turkey buzzards wheeled in the sky and he knew that the flesh would not long remain.
>
> "Well, that's him," he said, standing erect. "Her a-wantin' him so bad, I reckon she got him now. He'll kind of sink and trickle down to her."[22]

The gothic exaggeration of this scene almost belies the savage wish-fulfillment it portrays. In effect, Hammond exorcises the Negro male—the bogeyman in white Southern racial and sexual fantasies—by reducing Mede to a pulp; and, in joining Mede and Blanche in death (impotence), he can stand "erect" (potence). Earlier, when puzzled by his attraction to Ellen and his distaste for Blanche, Hammond rationalized his feelings as purely physical: "He believed it to be the skin color and the odor of white bodies that he did not like, whereas in fact it was a need to possess, to command, to order, his sexual object, in a manner he was unable to do with a woman free and white."[23] In destroying Blanche and her victim-lover, Hammond finally gains control over a "woman free and white," albeit, he still fails to gain control over himself.

In the novel's final scene Hammond decides he must leave Falconhurst to seek revenge on anyone who knew of Blanche's indiscretion (and his "dishonor"). Meg and Mem, who had used Blanche's infidelity to blackmail her into bestowing sexual favors on them, are two figures Hammond vows to pursue and kill because through such an act he can restore himself and "clear" his head. Before he leaves on his quest, Hammond punishes Tense, Blanche's personal maid, for her complicity in her mistress's infidelity by demoting the girl to a field hand and finding: " 'the bigges', blackes', uglies' buck we got on this plantation an' I goin' to give him you. Reckoned we'd raise house niggers out'n you, but ain't goin' to raise fiel' niggers, big, black, greasy, dirty fiel' niggers.' "[24] While such a punishment exhibits the kind of sadistic wish-fulfillment racism always seems to inspire, Onstott notes that Tense was "not appalled at her promised fate."[25] If Tense's punishment ironically plays stereotypes against each other, the final action of the elder Maxwell represents a more consistent and familiar set of motives. In *Mandingo*, as in *Gone with the Wind*, the soil nurtures when people fail so that, like Scarlett O'Hara, the aged Maxwell rises from his chair and takes charge when Hammond leaves. His cry— " 'I got to throw to one side this rheumatiz, I reckon, an' take aholt' "[26]—reaffirms that land is the only wealth.

While social and sexual double standards abound in *Mandingo*, Onstott occasionally raises an ironic question in the narrative. One can recognize such obvious inconsistencies as Hammond's rationalization when deciding to murder Blanche, or Mede's urge to satisfy himself without consulting his paramours' needs or wishes; indeed, Blanche can even wonder why sexual standards must be different for men and women. However, the most perceptive criticism of the double standard occurs when Hammond initially meets the lusty widow who wants to buy some "studs." The young planter's dismay at this woman's failure to match his preconditioned standards leads to a fine piece of irony; for, after he has casually looked this woman up and down, Hammond is taken aback when he realizes that she, in turn, has appraised him "as if he were a slave on the auction block."[27] There, if only for a moment, *Mandingo* becomes a serious historical novel, one capable of presenting diverse and self-centered characters and suggesting that slaves and masters are both victims of the same social system. This long novel only reaches such a plateau once: to have reached it more often *Mandingo* would have had to be conceived by a more sophisticated and gentler intelligence.

* * *

As a harbinger of social change Ralph Ellison's *Invisible Man* may well be the 1950s' most prophetic novel; and, for many, it remains the fictional presentation of what it means to be black in contemporary America.

Ellison's protagonist, who remains unnamed and thus without an obvious identity, dramatizes the second-class status of his race. *Invisible Man* examines many of the same psychological stereotypes of the Negro as one finds in *Mandingo*, and after reading Onstott, it provides a sense of fresh air penetrating a stuffy room. Ellison's symbolic characters and situations attack the clichés in the more popular historical novel; indeed, every experience puts the narrator-protagonist further behind the social eight ball and, since the story begins with this character already at the point of furthest retreat, it only remains to see how he gets there. Ellison's indictment goes beyond merely blaming "whitey" for his novel emphasizes the endurance of racial prejudice and the desire for power at all levels and in all races. In his odyssey from promising college student, to factory worker, to revolutionary and, finally, to hermit, the protagonist exhausts the possibilities of leading a reasonable life as both a black and a human being in America.

Invisible Man echoes Dostoyevsky in its opening description of the narrator's apartment building basement: like the Russian novelist's "underground man," the protagonist chooses to avoid the external world that seems mad. In explaining his invisibility, he elaborates the novel's major theme.

> I am invisible, understand, simply because people refuse to see me. Like the bodiless heads you see sometimes in circus sideshows, it is as though I have been surrounded by mirrors of hard, distorting glass. When they approach me they see only my surroundings, themselves, or figments of their imagination—indeed, everything and anything except me.[28]

In his adventures Ellison's spokesman encounters characters and situations that consistently reduce him to stereotyped limits. He remains figuratively invisible because other people refuse to see what he truly is; thus, the powers in society perceive a young and sensitive black to be a dissident, an inefficient worker, a revolutionary anarchist, or an insatiable stud and rapist, as the case may be. The central character can find no identity because others consistently project their stereotypes of what a black should be onto him. He, like the entire black race, is dismissed as a product of a bad environment, a dangerous individualist, or a "bogeyman." His final choice to remain "rent-free" in a sealed room (in which he has constructed an elaborate lighting system so that he can never be "invisible" there) represents a symbolically appropriate revenge on the "system."

The narrator's retreat into hibernation symbolizes waiting for the moment when he can return to society and implies that present social conditions are too stifling for blacks in America. While Ellison's main character desperately needs to discover who he is, his encounters with those in control (supposed philanthropists, college presidents, factory supervisors, revolutionaries, bored housewives), whether black or white, only thwart his quest. At one point, the character's rage leads him to assault a man with blonde hair and blue eyes; yet, when Ellison's narrator is about to kill this conspicuously white individual, he realizes again that he has not been seen.

...it occurred to me that the man had not *seen* me, actually; that he, as far as he knew, was in the midst of a walking nightmare!... He lay there, moaning on the asphalt; a man almost killed by a phantom.... I was like a drunken man myself, wavering about on weakened legs. Then I was amused. Something in this man's thick head had sprung out and beaten him within an inch of his life.... Would Death himself have freed him for wakeful living?[29]

The protagonist lives in a nightmare world which gives him all the individuality of a bug (a comparison that underlines the frequent cliché that all members of a different racial group look alike to those who stereotype them). The central character's references to a Louis Armstrong lyric ("What did I do/To be so black/And blue?") epitomize the condition of the American Negro and become a haunting question because of his experiences.

Witnessing the eviction of elderly blacks in Harlem, the protagonist launches into a tirade against those who dispossess the aged couple and, in his rage, captures the condition of the Negro in America: " 'That's a good word, "Dispossessed!" "Dispossessed," eighty-seven years and dispossessed of what? They ain't *got* nothing, they caint *get* nothing, they never *had* nothing. So who was dispossessed?' "[30] Ultimately, such anger goes beyond physical need and re-emphasizes the lack of identity the main character feels: he truly suffers from being "in" but not "of." The only method for dealing with these dehumanizing powers comes from his grandfather; and, while this advice seems initially strange, Ellison's narrator comes to appreciate how insightful the old "odd guy" was. After emphasizing that he has been a " 'spy in the enemy's country ever since I give up my gun back in the Reconstruction,' " the protagonist's grandfather advises: " 'Live with your head in the lion's mouth. I want you to overcome 'em with yeses, undermine 'em with grins, agree 'em to death and destruction, let 'em swoller you till they vomit or bust wide open.' "[31] This voice of pragmatism argues that becoming a Steppinfetchit represents the only way to survive and to triumph, advice which becomes dramatically explicit when the narrator goes underground to wait for the day when he can reappear as a man. Even though he lives in a northern ghetto with different mores than the rural South of his grandfather, the main character finally shares the older man's internalized alienation.

The society which casts such a pall upon Ellison's narrator and, by implication, upon any sensitive black, is a sadistic master which tempts as it jerks the reins to let its lesser members know they are still subordinate. Ellison symbolizes such contradiction and oppression in the novel's opening section when the protagonist is invited to a white stag party. Since he has just delivered his high-school class valedictory—a speech which stressed "humility" as the very essence of "progress"—the main character naively believes he has been asked there to repeat his comments before the leading white citizens as a sign of increasing racial rapport. Upon his arrival in the hotel banquet room, however, he is dressed in boxing trunks and forced into a ring with other frightened black youths. The boys are initially exposed to a naked blonde woman who dances sensuously to arouse them and amuse the drunken audience. While the Negroes are literally forced to watch this performance, when the woman is finished she disappears into the throng of white men who toss her above their heads. This woman symbolizes the promise and hypocrisy that white society shows in dealing with its black minority, as the narrator's reaction makes clear.

> I wanted at one and the same time to run from the room, to sink through the floor, or go to her and cover her from my eyes and the eyes of the others with my body; to feel the soft thighs, to caress and destroy her, to love her and murder her, to hide from her, and yet to stroke where below the small American flag tattooed upon her belly her thighs formed a capital V.[32]

The prostitute that he could love and kill carries the signs (a flag, V for victory) that epitomize the United States as a triumphant world power; and she suggests the irony that national success has been won at the expense of the country's minorities.

After her removal, the boys must fight each other and scramble for the money they have been promised, a sequence which turns an already bloody ring into a mass of clawing humanity. The money, thrown down by the drunken "pillars of the community," creates the disunity which a capitalist society inevitably imposes on its lower classes whose existence has been reduced to its barest essentials. It is only after he has been bloodied and shown to be just another "nigger" (since he scrambled around for coins with the rest) that the narrator is allowed to deliver his speech. Although he uses the phrase "social responsibility" (and thus arouses suspicions among his audience), the protagonist exhibits gratitude when he receives a brief case. His naivete is further underscored when he opens the bag to see its contents: "My fingers a-tremble, I complied, smelling the fresh leather and finding an official-looking document inside. It was a scholarship to the state college for Negroes. My eyes filled with tears and I ran awkwardly off the floor."[33] The dancing woman and the shortsighted youth are simply different manifestations of a milieu that, in the words of Tennessee Williams, contains only buyers and sellers. The same process is repeated when the central character serves as a guide and chauffeur to Mr. Norton, a wealthy white benefactor of the small Negro college he attends. In their time together, the protagonist allows Mr. Norton to meet Jim Trueblood, a sharecropper who has impregnated both his wife and his daughter. While the white man has subconsciously incestuous feelings about his own dead daughter, Norton's eagerness to meet Trueblood and hear his story reflects prejudice rather than sympathy. In giving the sharecropper money, Norton pays for the privilege of believing that blacks conform to his stereotyped preconceptions: true to his blood, the farmer was so sexually insatiable that he raped his own daughter. Norton's charity to the man and to the college represents a reward to those who know (and stay in) their places. Since Trueblood reaffirms Norton's preconceptions, he is rewarded, while the narrator, who is offended by the sharecropper's actions and by the white man's gift, is expelled.

Invisible Man chronicles the narrator's travels, both geographically and socially, from Southern lower-middle-class passivity to northern urban alienation. In suffering at the hands of other self-involved characters he learns about social realities. The first and perhaps the most striking of this rogues' gallery is Dr. Bledsoe, the president of the college, who punishes the main character for bringing Mr. Norton and Trueblood together. In Bledsoe's mind whites must be deluded and used so that power can remain with those who, like himself, keep the lid on for respectable society. In Bledsoe, Ellison provides a sharp portrait of anyone who values power above humanity; indeed, the famed administrator emerges as a pious hypocrite controlled by egocentricity. Bledsoe's very name seems ironic since his personal sufferings have been more than assuaged by his power to repress those who, like the narrator, might eventually supersede him. In a fashion that resembles Stalin presiding over Lenin's funeral (and so establishing himself as the symbolic successor) Bledsoe accompanies the coffin of the Leader, the man who founded the school. Like the men who threw the narrator into the prize ring, Bledsoe despises ideas, believing instead simply in power and so reducing society to a matter of who can coerce whom.

"And I'll tell you something your sociology teachers are afraid to tell you," he said. "If there weren't men like me running schools like this, there'd be no South. Nor North either. No, and there'd be no country—not as it is today. You think about that, son." He laughed. "With all your speechmaking and studying I thought you understood something."[34]

The 1960s, alas, proved Dr. Bledsoe a prophet in his notion of education as a babysitting service offering the diversionary pablum of ideas, while his extension of racial strife to the north was underscored by riots in Watts, Detroit and elsewhere. Bledsoe speaks the language of the academic business manager, the man who thinks in dollars and cents (quantities) and dismisses avowed intellectual intentions (qualities) as window dressing.

If Bledsoe has become an all-too-familiar type in our institutionalized society, his insistence on power at the expense of personality separates him from the protagonist. Bledsoe's advice dismisses ends (what am I to become?) in favor of means (what are the ways I can achieve my goals?); for him, the possession of power and the ability to enforce his will upon others represents identity: " 'You let the white folk worry about pride and dignity— you learn where you are and you get yourself power, influence, contacts with powerful and influential people—stay in the dark and use it.' "[35]

While Bledsoe retains the independence of the seemingly obedient servant, he has power only because he acquiesces in the deprivations white society imposes on blacks. When he sends the narrator to New York with a letter of reference, ostensibly because Bledsoe feels the wayward youth needs a semester away from school, the good Doctor further reveals his hypocrisy. In spite of all his tough talk, Bledsoe won't directly expel the protagonist; instead, the Doctor encourages the main character to seek out interviews in New York with contacts Bledsoe has supplied. The narrator endures this charade until he reads the letter from Bledsoe which he has been so

proudly presenting to employers and learns that he has been expelled and
supplied with a damning reference.

The central character's subsequent experiences in the city reveal that,
while there are different activities for a young black there, human nature
remains the same. He fails in a paint factory because of a lack of supervision
from a foreman who expects perfection (yet another symbolic rendering
of the Negro's dilemma in a society whose rules he doesn't make, never
formally receives, and yet must never contradict). In keeping with Ellison's
conspicuously literary tone, the error which leads to the protagonist's
downfall arises from using the wrong chemical mixture and producing
black instead of white paint. After being demoted to being an assistant
to Mr. Brockway, a crazed old black whose expertise with boiler-room engines
makes him irreplaceable, the main character falls into further trouble by
sympathizing with a move to unionize the company. The narrator's feeling
so infuriates Brockway that the two men fight and, as a result, the boilers
blow up. Naturally, the protagonist is blamed and finds himself on the
street once his burns have healed. Brockway, a less intelligent Bledsoe who
worships the power which uses him as though it were a benevolent father
looking out for his best interests, even tells the narrator that he thought
up the company's principal advertising slogan.

"Well you might not believe it, but I helped the Old Man make up that slogan. 'If
It's Optic White, It's the Right White,' " he quoted with an upraised finger, like a preacher
quoting holy writ. "I got me a three-hundred-dollar bonus for helping to think that up...."

" 'If It's Optic White, It's the Right White,' " I repeated and suddenly had to repress
a laugh as a childhood jingle rang though my mind:

" 'If you're white, you're right,' " I said.[36]

Once again, a Negro is rewarded for spiritually selling out and reaffirming
the prejudices of the ruling class. Indeed, Brockway's subconscious
transformation of a slogan from black folk wisdom into a means for selling
white paint to white customers epitomizes being an Uncle Tom.

The narrator's involvement in a radical revolutionary movement finds
him caught up in the group's organizational infighting and, thus,
dissipating his rage at society upon his cohorts. Brother Jack, the movement's
guiding spirit, distrusts independence in his subordinates; thus, his
movement is controlled by a mind as politically suspicious as Julius Caesar's
when looking at Cassius for the first time in Shakespeare's play. Instead
of a revolution which would establish new mores, Brother Jack only wants
to replace society's present masters with himself. The narrator does not
perceive this self-serving tendency as rapidly as does his friend, Tod Clifton,
who symbolically appears on the streets of Harlem, after he has deserted
the movement, selling mechanical dolls named Sambo. The protagonist's
description makes clear that, to Tod at least, the toys symbolize the condition
of black people in white American society.

A grinning doll or orange-and-black tissue paper with thin flat cardboard disks forming
its head and feet and which some mysterious mechanism was causing to move up and down

in a loose-jointed, shoulder-shaking, infuriatingly sensuous motion, a dance that was completely detached from the black, mask-like face.[37]

The handmade doll resembles a puppet guided by invisible forces so as to please its masters while avoiding the expression of any personal feelings. The nightmare of the novel becomes even more apparent as a large crowd surrounds Tod and his dolls and then a policeman breaks up this gathering and, after pressing Clifton for the necessary vendor's license, shoots and kills the ex-revolutionary. Inevitably, Brother Jack's Brotherhood seizes upon Clifton's funeral for political gain, but the narrator, who has been exposed to hypocrisy and madness (in the bizarre form of Ras the Destroyer who preaches anarchy and revels in the rioting which follows Tod's death) has become disenchanted. He even argues that Ras is more logical than the Brotherhood because: "Outside the Brotherhood we were outside history; inside of it they didn't see us. It was a hell of a state of affairs, we were nowhere."[38] Since he is constantly seeking his own identity, the protagonist cannot accept the self-denial involved in the Brotherhood. For him, history remains too abstract a basis for any sense of being while, at the same time, ideological goals and principles, such as those of Brother Jack, vary too greatly from the surrounding social reality.

Sexual relations between blacks and whites, an area in which the stereotypes of the libidinous black male with an insatiable craving for the white female, and the white female wanting to experience black vigor, become central when the narrator meets Sybil. While he only wants to feel warm and protective (i.e. human) love for her, the protagonist once again realizes that white people only project their racial fantasies upon him. After Sybil whispers her desires in his ear (a remark that makes him ask, "Had life suddenly become a Thurber cartoon?") and he has suggested that they walk in the park instead, the woman insists:

"But I need it," she said, uncrossing her thighs and sitting up eagerly. "You can do it, it'll be easy for *you*, beautiful. Threaten to kill me if I don't give in. You know, talk rough to me, beautiful. A friend of mine said the fellow said, 'Drop your drawers'...and—

"He said what!" I said.
"He really did." she said.
"...Go on," I said..."Then what happened?"
"Well...he called her a filthy name," she said, hesitating coyly... "A really filthy name... Oh, he was a brute, huge, with white teeth, what they call a 'buck.' And he said, 'Bitch, drop your drawers,' and then he did it. She's such a lovely girl too, really delicate with a complexion like strawberries and cream....
"But what happened, did they catch him?" I said.
"Oh, of course not, she only told two of us girls. She couldn't afford to let her husband hear of it. He...well, it's too long a story."[39]

Because she believes in numerous stereotypes, Sybil wants the narrator to "gently" rape her so she can discover her feelings; by insisting that such an act won't be difficult for him, the white woman belies her apparent lack of prejudice by denying the central character any humanity. Since the only relationship they can enjoy is one of black stud and vulnerable white woman, Sybil represents the final defeat of the protagonist's attempt to live as his heart and conscience dictate.

Ellison's character now moves to a more resigned belief in possibilities, or as James Joyce's Stephen Daedaelus puts it in *A Portait of the Artist as a Young Man*, a trust in "silence, exile and cunning." The shift is revealed by his attitude toward Rinehart, a figure who is spoken of but never actually seen in the novel. While he epitomizes the con man who can change professions in a twinkling and continue to prey on human gullibility , Rinehart gradually emerges as the wise man in society.

> Could he himself be both rind and heart? . . . But how could I doubt it? He was a broad man, a man of parts who got around. Rinehart the rounder. . . . His world was possibility and he knew it. He was years ahead of me and I was a fool. I must have been crazy and blind. The world in which we lived was without boundaries. A vast seething, hot world of fluidity, and Rine the rascal was at home. Perhaps *only* Rine the rascal was at home in it.[40]

In a world that denies basic individual identity, criminal rascality becomes the ultimate adjustment; indeed, Rinehart elevates the black man's dependence into a means to remain free and to invent oneself. The lesson the narrator learns, and which the entire novel conveys, is that life is possibility: prejudice and dominance are for those who want life to be predictable and repetitive. Thus, *Invisible Man* closes on an austere, if hopeful, note—the individual can save himself, even if he cannot transform society; for the protagonist's quest finally enables him to reach a position where he can forget the roles other people impose upon him and concentrate on finding out who he is and what he can be.

Chapter 12

"There's nothing else on earth I want to be."

The American Dream has been given differing literary formulations at different times. While some of our most celebrated contemporary works, such as F. Scott Fitzgerald's *The Great Gatsby* (1925) and Arthur Miller's *Death of a Salesman* (1948), have questioned this popular aspiration, Horatio Alger's nineteenth-century emphasis on hard work as the key to success has remained an attractive idea to the mass audience. This equation of advancement with diligence underlies numerous 1950s' bestsellers. Indeed, this value system was only slightly modified by the period's comparatively strong emphases on the degree to which an individual had to conform to the dictates of the group, the qualities that made one a professional, and the differences between work conceived as a job, a career or a calling.

Henry Morton Robinson's *The Cardinal* (1950), in chronicling the rise of its protagonist within the Roman Catholic hierarchy, emphasizes personal commitment and adjustment as the keys to success. Morton Thompson's *Not as a Stranger* (1954), in transforming its young doctor from a cold-blooded diagnostician to a caring human being, shows that individual adjustment must conform with one's calling. Ernest Gann's *The High and the Mighty* (1953), an account of a group's reactions to a possible airline disaster, emphasizes how the old pro works within the group to create that cohesion known as professionalism. Evan Hunter's *The Blackboard Jungle* (1954), which relates the trials of a first-year teacher in a New York vocational high school, implies that "arriving" in one's chosen profession is often beset by jealous superiors and underlings. Robert Traver's *Anatomy of a Murder* (1958), a witty account of a "crime of passion," suggests that success derives from appreciating the inherent beauties of one's craft. Sloan Wilson's *The Man in the Gray Flannel Suit* (1955), in exploring the anxieties that beset life at the top, argues that a successful career does not satisfy everyone capable of answering the demands of upper echelon life.

* * *

The Cardinal, the most popular Catholic novel of the 1950s, rambles through the young manhood and middle age of Stephen Fermoyle against various locales. As the son of lower-class, Boston-Irish parents, Stephen grows to seek a life within the Church and progresses from novice to monsignor by learning humility and patience. His personal struggles are resolved by faith so that, by story's end, when he returns to America and his new duties as a cardinal, the protagonist can find comfort during a storm through prayer. While *The Cardinal* is little more than a set of adventures tied together by the central character's presence, Stephen's movements and relationships are more dramatic than insightful. The lessons he learns reaffirm rather than raise doubts; indeed, his career, which brings him in contact with the Ku Klux Klan (by whom he is whipped), the Nazis (in Austria) and the Fascists (by whom his good friend Captain Orselli is murdered), links events and personalities of the twentieth century to the narrative. Thus, *The Cardinal* emerges as a potpourri of action, adventure, biography and faith, a mixture designed to delight an audience seeking respectable vicariousness and a solemn tone. Stephen's early sense of being called to the priesthood, his relations with Cardinal Glennon and Ned Halley, his promotion to Rome, and his return to America, represent a spiritual progress in which all actions are necessary to the creation of a good *Catholic*.

The earliest fundamental virtue presented in the novel is family life; indeed, the Fermoyles define themselves through their relations so that marriages and births are momentous events. When Stephen decides to become a priest, his choice must be ratified by his parents—a motif that reappears when Mona, his younger sister, despondent over her Jewish lover's refusal to convert to Catholicism, deserts the family to be seduced and abandoned by another lover. Stephen chooses a career that brings status to his parents within the community; however, he does not select the priesthood simply to flatter them for, as he tells his mother: " 'No, Mother, your wanting me to be a priest didn't make me one. I used to wonder about it when I was younger. But now I know I'm a priest because there's nothing else on earth that I want to be. It's as simple as that, and it will never change.' "[1] While events temper Stephen, he never loses his enthusiasm for his calling; indeed, his faith enables him to transform depressing conditions into ennobling ones for himself and others. While he experiences occasional anxiety about his priestly role, Stephen never doubts that function has validity. When he finds himself infatuated with Countess Ghislana Falerni and tempted to quit his calling, the protagonist goes into retreat, confesses and finally abandons all thoughts of the flesh. By exploring his feelings with an older monk, Stephen realizes that pride, and not passion, has been the source of his doubts. Robinson's hero has an essentially fixed nature so that his pure virtue can (and ultimately does) pall in this lengthy work.

Stephen meets several good men in his career. The earliest and least likely of these exemplars of virtue is Captain Orselli, an Italian merchant marine commander who meets his death at the hands of Mussolini's thugs. Orselli's faith is tempered by secular doubt; however, as a ship's captain, he defies superior forces (a British search party) and retains his legal rights on the high seas. Thus, Stephen believes that Orselli possesses the courage of his convictions, a trait the Captain shares with the protagonist's teacher in Rome, Quarenghi. As Stephen puts it, " 'somehow these two men so utterly different, resemble one another. I'll put it this way: Quarenghi—elegant, fascinating, unforgettable—is the spiritualized counterpart of our captain.' "[2] In a bit of deus ex machina plotting later, Orselli persuades Countess Falerni to marry him shortly after Stephen has nearly succumbed to her charms. In a work like *The Cardinal* such coincidences always seem contrived, and yet using a larger and more anonymous cast would lead to a series of even looser episodes. Orselli's death further binds Stephen for it shows that the Captain was another competent professional willing to die for his beliefs.

In Ned Halley and Lawrence Cardinal Glennon, Stephen encounters the spiritual and the pragmatic sides of the priestly calling. He emerges as a better churchman for experiencing both the asceticism of the unsuccessful, dying parish priest and the political sagacity of the Monsignor of Boston. This dialectic process ironically begins when Cardinal Glennon sends Stephen to Ned Halley. The Cardinal is convinced that Stephen, who wants to publish his translation of a treatise by Quarenghi, needs to be curbed by dealing with the Church's day-to-day affairs. Glennon has the hero's best interests at heart, for in Stonebury the young priest discovers that good can exist in the face of miserable surroundings and grinding poverty. Father Halley, a classmate of Glennon's, has never managed to create a large parish that contributes vast sums to the Church; indeed, he has been sent to Stonebury because there was no other place for him. In this region of French-speaking woodsmen, Halley cannot hurt the Church's well-being; yet this failed priest emerges as the most faithful and saintly member of the religion Stephen holds most dear. Halley's spirit overcomes the conditions which assail him and Stephen comes to see him as a true ascetic. Naturally, Halley is not long for this world and, when he is beset by an illness for which the parish cannot afford the simplest remedies, a crisis of conscience develops for the protagonist. As Stephen nurses Halley, they discuss the older man's ostensible failures.

"Larry sent me...always lower in his great favor until there was no more favor. Only disappointment and bitterness at my"—tears streamed down Ned Halley's cheeks like raindrops down a car window—"at my failures."

"They were not failures," said Stephen gently, wiping the old man's eyes and mouth. "Many in those parishes remember your goodness. And in his heart of hearts, the Cardinal knows you to be a just and holy priest."[3]

Stephen reassures the saintly Halley and, in a fashion reminiscent of *Going My Way* (1944) in which Bing Crosby arranged for Barry Fitzgerald to see his aged mother, finally enables Halley to see Glennon (from whom he wishes to receive absolution).

When Stephen pawns his ordination ring to buy medicine for Halley, the artifact comes into the hands of Cardinal Glennon (who is well connected with police and pawnshops in Boston) and the protagonist must explain his apparent desire for worldly gain. Once again, Robinson provides his hero with an opportunity to rise above the situation for, after refusing to reveal why he pawned the ring, the young man confesses to his real reasons when Glennon guesses what is wrong. The Cardinal springs into action after he hears that Halley is dying, and so proves the benevolence of authority, while Stephen, who has not had to beg a favor, can go on believing in elevated goodness. The absolution scene between the Cardinal and the parish priest marks a transition for Stephen who, after Halley's death, becomes a member of Glennon's immediate entourage. At the same time, the meeting between the two older men shows that Halley's spirituality represents an ideal even Glennon would like to embody; however, the Church must exist in a real world where secular power is needed to preserve even God's favorite institution. It is Glennon who finally asks for forgiveness and Ned Halley who, true to his saintly nature, easily gives it.

"Gentle Ned, you deserved more than I ever gave. I should have made you my confessor, and lighted my path by the shining circle above your head. Instead, I saddled you with the packhorse assignments, mortgages, broken parishes." The Cardinal buried his face in the torn quilt. "Forgive me, Ned."

"Forgiven, Larry . . . all . . . ."[4]

Halley's willingness to forgive suggests the spirit one associates with Christ.

Stephen now ascends the hierarchical ladder as Glennon's protege. During a frenzied voyage on Orselli's ship to reach a conclave to elect a new Pope (an attempt that fails when Glennon arrives a day late to find the College of Cardinals has proceeded without him), the older man reveals that beneath his crusty exterior he is really loveable. While Glennon inspires loyalty in Stephen, his prostration from being unable to participate in the Papal election suggests the character's political ambitions. In time Stephen becomes an aide to Quarenghi and other members of the Vatican, and his elevation to Cardinal precedes the Pope's death by only a short time, so that Robinson can present the pageantry associated with a conclave to elect Catholicism's new leader. In these deliberations Cardinal Glennon gains one vote (on the first ballot naturally), a gesture which sparks gratitude in the form of comic anger in the old man.

When Pius XII retired for the *immantatio*, Lawrence Glennon sought out Stephen. "Eminent rascal," he chided, "confess your wickedness. Why did you cast that vote for me on the first ballot?"

"I?" Stephen feigned innocence.

"Who else?" said Glennon tenderly. "Who else would pour such balm on an old man's soul? I won't live to return the compliment"—Number One tinged prophecy with affection—"but mark me, Steve, the others will."[5]

While one here perhaps encounters an opening gambit for a sequel (Robinson blessedly did not write one), Stephen's rise has been accomplished in the most conservative, button-down collar fashion. He never offends his elders (indeed, he seems older than they most of the time) and so *The Cardinal* presents its hero as conformist. For an age concerned with getting ahead by being agreeable, Stephen's success through his relationship with Cardinal Glennon testifies eloquently to the power of supporting the "establishment."

The most agonizing situation that confronts Stephen Fermoyle is
Mona's unwed pregnancy, for complications in the delivery room lead to
a terrible choice between his sister's life and that of her unborn child. Catholic
doctrine, which decrees the mother's life must be risked, answers this
dilemma and renders the sequence pathetic and melodramatic, for Stephen
can only do as his Church prescribes and, since Mona's seducer didn't stay
around, there is no one to question his decision. Mona dies willingly because,
despite running away to a life of nightclubs and easy love affairs, her early
training tells and she expires saying contrition so that her soul can be
saved.

> "Make a good act of contrition, darling," he whispered.
> Mona looked up at her brother, tried obediently to speak. Her lips moved without sound.
> "Trust me, Monny. I won't let you down. Try hard. Say it after me."
> The essential words came. "Most heartily...sorry...for having offended Thee," breathed
> Mona. Stephen was giving her absolution when Dr. Parks' stethoscope caught the last flutter
> of her exhausted heart.[6]

Stephen's courage lies in making his sister adhere to their faith; indeed,
his example breaks down Mona's initial resistance and enables her to die
so that another individual (her child) may know God's Catholic grace.
Mona goes willingly to her grave and Stephen sends her there with little
hesitation because their faith has taught them that there is a reward in
leaving this world.

When Stephen nearly lapses with Countess Falerni, a secular passion
that would destroy his attempt to love all mankind, Robinson's protagonist
needs a confessor. Just as children turn over insurmountable difficulties
to adults, so Stephen leans on Dom Arcibal, an aged ascetic who represents
an authority whom the hero trusts will show him the error of his ways.
After questioning his involvement with the Countess, Dom Arcibal points
out that Stephen has confused the appearance of a Catholic with the
substance of faith. Stephen admits he has always regarded himself as one
of God's "favorites," and the aged confessor adds:

> "As I remember...Lucifer cherished a similar illusion. How do you account for such
> a grotesque notion on your part?"
> "I never thought of it as grotesque. I saw that God had blessed me with special gifts
> and believed I must demonstrate His favor by the excellence of my performance."
> " 'Performance' is a word used by actors. Are you a strolling player or a priest?"[7]

Dom Arcibal argues that the protagonist chose a sin (desiring Countess
Falerni) which was unlikely to be consummated and so acted out of pride
and not out of passion. Stephen has indulged himself by chastising himself
for an act that he could not have performed anyway. While religion and
psychology both take what individuals say seriously, the greater glory of
Catholicism is that whole generations derive their values from each other's
actions.

The purpose of Stephen's life is dramatized when his mother, by now
an agreeable grandmother, comes to Rome and has an audience with the
Pope, arranged by her dutiful son of course. After reading of the Fermoyles'

financial sacrifices to make this dream of every good Catholic mother come true, one anticipates the moment when Celia Fermoyle speaks with the Pope. In answer to his question as to whether or not she has a favorite child, this wise woman, who has suffered enough to have character, sagely notes:

> "I am very proud of my oldest son, Your Holiness. He has brought me great joy and never caused me a moment's sorrow." She started to check a mother's garrulity, then let it slip again. "When Stephen was a little boy, he used to beg me to say that I loved him more than the others. I wanted to tell him then, and I wish I could tell Your Holiness now, that he always was first in my heart. But I can't say something that would be unfair to the others. A mother must make all her children feel that she loves them equally. Anything else would be displeasing to God."
>
> Of the many words Pius XI heard that year, Celia's moved him more poignantly than most.[8]

In Robinson's novel dramatic high points are usually resolved by sentimental pathos such as Celia's. The audience is thus encouraged to believe that what most of them endure is life's genuine business; in effect, even the notable men of the world are governed by familiar sentiments and ideas. Existence is thus simple enough to be grasped by an overworked mother who has experienced its customary trials. The very obviousness of *The Cardinal,* its essential thematic reassurances, made it popular for in bestselling fiction nothing succeeds as frequently as the expected rendered excessively.

*   *   *

Doctors are often revered in life and fiction, being accorded the aura earlier societies attached to priests and soothsayers. In popular literature such practitioners are generally idealists of the first order (*Main Street, Magnificent Obsession*), heroes defending man against disease and his own heinous desires by standing squarely against social or intellectual forces—abortion, euthanasia—that would shorten life. *Not as a Stranger,* the most popular medical novel of the 1950s, follows in such traditional footsteps; however, Thompson's work places a heavy emphasis on the individual's need to compromise, so that it emerges as a tribute not simply to medicine but to conformity as well. Lucas Marsh, the protagonist, must learn empathy for his patients (i.e. treat them not as strangers and, through such emotional involvement, perhaps die a little emotionally when they suffer). Once again, the protagonist of a popular novel has his initial shortcomings corrected by situations which prove that the suppression of feelings in the name of efficiency is neither effective nor enhancing. This long novel chronicles Lucas' quest for honesty in medicine and, finally, for humility in himself. The plot, which consistently supplies new grist for the reader's curiosity, and the presentation of the business of doctors to the uninitiated, combine to keep *Not as a Stranger* afloat; indeed, the novel contains enough characters and situations—particularly romantic dilemmas—to appeal to temperaments attracted by soap opera.

Lucas Marsh's parents are divided on nearly every important issue; thus, Thompson's hero suffers early psychological damage. Caught between a grasping mother, who uses him as a substitute lover (and thus foments Oedipal problems), and a mercenary father, who wants his son to enter the anachronistic blacksmith business, Lucas must seek a rational sanctuary elsewhere. Job's avariciousness has poisoned the home environment, for Ouida firmly believes she has been used as a physical convenience rather than prized for herself. The parents argue constantly about Lucas' future, particularly after the boy shows an interest in medicine by trailing after local doctors on their house calls; and the issue becomes a debate over their respective ways of looking at the world. Job chides Ouida for being a romantic and seeing things as they should be rather than as they are: she responds by stressing Job's sexual brutality: " 'So he can grow up like his father? And someday rip a decent girl like an animal on her wedding night?... So he can grow up an ignorant swine who can't live unless he lies and steals from decent people?' "[9] Job retorts that his business tactics have kept a roof over their heads and that the world is not a spiritual place, and so Thompson establishes the conflicting values of materialism and sentimentalism that Lucas will struggle with as an adult. Ironically, while Ouida defends her son's desire to study medicine, her romantic view of the world is initially rejected by Lucas who remains skeptical of people until the very end of the novel.

The struggle between his parents, which ends when Ouida dies because she fails to see a doctor soon enough, causes Lucas to perceive himself as cut off from the world. The generational split he feels echoes the 1950s' emphasis on youth culture and the shortsightedness of parents so that, even though he experiences such feelings in 1918, Lucas' thoughts could well have come out of *Rebel without a Cause.*

"Much of the time Lucas felt himself a stranger to his mother and father. They were so unlike. He could be like neither without feeling a traitor to the other. Beyond this problem there was life as he knew it, the things in living that were exciting and important. And these things were entirely different from the important things in the lives of his parents. They were so different that he knew reluctantly he could never explain himself to them.[10]

Not as a Stranger offers an extended commentary on this passage, for Lucas Marsh must learn that his desires are similar to those of Job and Ouida, and thus come to feel compassion rather than pity toward them. Lucas does learn that even Job merits consideration based on their mutual human shortcomings. In so doing, the protagonist discovers the Biblical lesson of forgiveness when he stops hating the man who, in selling their home, pulled all financial security out from under him.

While Lucas experiences this loss of financial support when still an undergraduate bent on medical school, his energetic transformation into a self-supporting student only heightens his feelings of alienation from his peers. Although he dismisses many of these acquaintances because of their values—particularly his roommate who wants to be a doctor in order to get rich—Lucas even finds himself isolated in the library among those who are dedicated to learning. He remains constantly aware that while:

> ...the population of the college presented to the outside world the appearance of a tribe there were little lonely islands in it. And these islands remained lonely and apart. And he knew forlornly that he was one of these islands. He was one of a few dozen such islands, a youth incapable of youth on the common terms of youth.[11]

Although Thompson's use of short, overlapping sentences enables one's mind to run in second gear, as it were, Lucas' isolation is designed to make his final reconciliation more poignant. American literature abounds with lonely males such as James Fenimore Cooper's Narry Bumpo, foreshadowing the strong, silent cowboy hero, Herman Melville's Ahab, nursing pride and a desire for revenge, Ernest Hemingway's Jake Barnes, living emotionally alone because of his war wound, and Joseph Heller's Yossarian, fleeing from the group to retain life and sanity. In these characters, isolation represents a choice which ultimately leads to identity; however, in keeping with the reaffirmative nature of most bestselling fiction, Thompson's central figure shortsightedly chooses separation. Thus, Lucas' being weaned back to normalcy represents a triumph for the middle-class value system of home, wife and children. No individual can be big enough or brilliant enough to dismiss the values of his community; and Lucas Marsh's pride in being separate must be shattered so that society can feel reassured about its day-to-day affairs.

When Thompson's hero retreats into loneliness, he allegedly wants to meditate but he ends up remembering, so that the reader sees the character has a subconscious desire to "relate" to others.

> It was healing to be alone, it was like a sedative. And the darkness was ineffably kind. It was possible to think in the darkness as it was possible under no other condition of man's living, to be able to see the darkness and to think.
> There was nothing to think about, either.
> It was all remembering.[12]

Since Thompson does not attribute a sense of subtlety to his audience, he emphasizes Lucas' shortsightedness and eccentricity (who wants to see the darkness?); however, because the hero has a faithful wife whose pregnancy insures a future for their family, it is obvious the protagonist will be saved from himself. Even though Lucas married Kristina to get money for medical school, and even though he periodically cheats on his doting (and slightly older) wife, their emotional economy again assures readers that they know more about the protagonist than he does about himself. Kristina emerges as too good a woman and Lucas has too much desire for her (when he's in the mood) for there to be any doubt that their marriage was meant to be. While Lucas feels isolated at home because he cannot refrain from labelling his wife's interests as stupid (yet another sign of his emotional and intellectual immaturity), his rebirth as a human being takes place in Kristina's arms.

Lucas' obsession with becoming a doctor carries him through medical school and into a small, rural practice without his ever learning that life must contain more than medicine (or profession). Lucas' roommate, Alfred, expresses a view of the medical profession which the hero despises.

"You think you're being sarcastic, but you're not. You're hitting the nail right on the head. I'm aiming for a Rolls-Royce every other year, and the yacht that goes with it. I'm aiming for every one of those wonderful real things. And I'm aiming for the position and the dignity and the honors that go to the doctor for the rich."[13]

Lucas' quarrel with his materialist colleague reveals priggishness rather than idealism for the hero fails to understand that one can be a doctor to rich people just as surely as one can be to poor ones. Lucas may dislike Alfred's views, but motive must take a back seat when expertise is to be judged. The central character must also learn to accept human fallibilities in the form of an incompetent colleague, Doctor Snider, who decides when a local hospital's aged indigents should be exposed to pneumonia so that the country's taxrolls won't be overly strained. Lucas discovers that a frontal assault on Snider will get him nowhere; in effect, he must labor to keep his elder colleague's practices within bounds and, at the same time, to use Snider in the most effective way (i.e. as a tool for routine functions). This lesson in practical management leads to larger conceptions about compassion and a doctor's role. Despite his villainy and incompetence, Snider has the insight to predict that Lucas is heading for a fall.

When the protagonist finds himself lost during a hunting trip with some patients, he discovers his need for emotional connections. This transformation appears symbolically through the juxtaposition of an early scene with the novel's final lines. In medical school Lucas becomes fond of a cadaver he dissects, so fond that he feels love for the inanimate body while experiencing little or nothing for the living beings around him. After his experience in the woods—an event that concludes when he makes love with Kristina as a symbolic repentance for all that has happened between them—Lucas realizes that the affection he had for "Zebedee" (the cadaver) is an essential part of being a doctor. As Kristina, who has returned to nursing to help out because of the Depression, waits capped and gowned at the door, Lucas finally understands.

The sick were waiting. The maimed and the dying, the stupid and the brilliant, the lucky and the blind and the world in which they lived in the shadow of their doom.

Ahead was the future.

Ahead was all a man could be.

He picked up his bag and went out in the world and began the practice of medicine.[14]

Readers with short patience will find such a conclusion, after nearly eight-hundred pages, dismayingly simplistic; however, the message that compassion (the recognition that every individual shares common human failings, weaknesses and needs) must replace pity (a display of sorrow or anguish because another human being seems less advantaged than the beholder) comes through clearly.

The protagonist's pride exhibits itself in his quest for perfection. While every doctor has an obligation to keep patients alive as long as possible, Lucas adopts excessive means to guarantee dying individuals a few more hours of convulsive existence. He is infuriated when he learns that Snider allows patients to contract pneumonia because euthanasia represents a sin to Lucas, as does abortion. Although he wants Snider hauled up before a review board and stripped of his medical license, Lucas also wishes to prove to the hospital staff that the older doctor's methods are unnecessary. In order to teach this object lesson, and win a victory that again shows his immaturity, the protagonist spends an entire night in a bedside vigil with an aged itinerant dying of pneumonia. While the man gains some more hours and Lucas' proves he's on the side of life, the practical cost of his effort seems dubious. In a subsequent discussion with Kristina about patients who are dying, Lucas idealistically insists:

"Nobody's a goner, Kris. Not ever. Not even when they're drawing their last breath. You never can tell. So long as you've got a country you go on fighting. No matter how bad it is you go on fighting. When it's hopeless you go on fighting. You don't ever stop. You never switch to the other side. Well, a doctor's country is life."[15]

Since pressing the doctor's obligation to act as if there were no end to life would present Lucas as too noble a figure to need changing, this absolutist view of medical ethics emerges as unreasonable and myopic. Lucas must finally understand that a doctor can only do what other humans are capable of, so that all-night vigils with dying pneumonia patients are monuments to ego and not reasonable actions.

Lucas goes even further into illogicality when he tells Avery, the only friend he made in college: " 'Adjust? I'll never adjust! I can't! I wouldn't know how! Adjust to murder, maybe? Because, by God, I've seen murder— not mistakes, not error in judgment, not bad luck! Plain unadulterated murder! By a doctor! A doctor of medicine!' "[16] Such purity is not of this world because it unconsciously assumes that its proponent will never make the same errors and thus reveals no sense of compassion. Lucas' chastisement becomes a foregone conclusion because such extreme statements of principle can be discounted as an excess of youth bred by its perennial daydream of how the world should be. The voice of reason curiously becomes Dr. Snider who, despite being insulted by Lucas, exhibits a genuine concern for his more talented younger colleague. As he watches Lucas work frantically to keep a patient alive, Snider rhetorically asks:

...don't you know about mistakes, yet, about the two worlds, the world so far as the patient's concerned and we walking around in it knowing what they don't, and the world of mistakes, the thing we share together, the world where a man stands with his foot in his own bucket, just like he was born to it, which he was, making the mistakes a man's got to make no matter who he is, big or little, as natural as breathing a thing he's bound to.[17]

Snider reflects the world in which error is a part of human nature and, although his blunderings exceed what normal compassion should have to forgive, his view emerges finally as more honest than the protagonist's. Snider's outlook assumes that life and medicine include accidents and contingencies, so that the imposition of idealistic or scientific regularity on what is essentially an emotional chaos must ultimately destroy those who would attempt it.

Thompson emphasizes how shortsighted Lucas is and how experience gradually imposes Snider's compromised views on him. Although the protagonist thinks of patients as merely embodiments of disease (and even plays a game of diagnosing restaurant patrons by their outward appearances), Lucas cannot help but be impressed by individuals whose personalities transcend their symptoms. That such a human potential remains alive in Lucas is a testimony to man's indomitable need for emotional life. Ominously, in his drive to be analytical and objective, Lucas becomes a rebel declaiming his own rules in defiance of the order society has provided for him. Thompson's hero combines this philosophical amoralism with a desire for Harriet Lang, a local artist; thus, Lucas' intellectual revolt is reduced to a shield for his desire to commit adultery. Given such a scheme, Thompson's audience can rest assured that ideas do not genuinely matter, that philosophy is more likely to be a disguise to rationalize the individual's desires than an intrinsic concern. Lucas voices the height of folly when he declaims his new freedom.

> He could work...without conscience and without pity, he was free, he was bound by nothing, now, nothing but his own life, his own rules for it, his own needs, his own desires.
> He thought of Harriet Lang...without guilt, freely, liberated, exhilarated by freedom. She was his and he would make her his.... He would do what he wanted. And he wanted her. And he would have her. As soon as could be. He wanted her. He wanted her badly.
> And the medicine he practiced would be his Medicine.
> He was full of anger. He fell asleep.[18]

Such a loosening of the libido hardly constitutes being free, since Lucas' "philosophy" is tied to gaining possession of Harriet.

The character's ego transforms medicine into a discipline that belongs exclusively to him; however, such excessive pride reaps its just reward when, after Harriet has left him for a better job, the protagonist finds himself lost and alone in the woods. At that moment Lucas realizes:

> A lost man was a dying man, he could not live without his fellows, there was a poison in it, a deadly sickness, the sickness of a newborn and the cord ripped, and the man lost, and he must die.
> He must die.
> "...My species," he said aloud, seeing himself. And it may not be the best species,...but it's the best species I've got.
> And my people.
> And they may not be the best people but they're the only people there are.[19]

This climax symbolizes what Lucas has learned after more than seven hundred pages. Unfortunately, in order to depict the protagonist's transformation, Thompson pulls out all his stylistic stops so that his basic pattern of short, declarative sentences that sound like Hemingway but which (oh so) often repeat the predicates of their predecessors becomes modified by run-ons and countless short statements beginning with "and" which resemble Biblical scripture. Thompson's monotone probably suggests more about the mentality of his characters than anything they say.

In becoming a member of the human race Lucas Ma.sh finally accepts that the medical profession does not air its dirty linen in public. Incompetence must be treated more confidentially so that when a local doctor kills a patient by cutting the jugular vein he took for a wart, Lucas can notify the erring man's partner and get the incompetent dismissed. Dr. Runkleman, who hires Lucas as his assistant, sees the young man's need for compromise but realizes that such knowledge will come hard to Lucas. As the protagonist drifts toward Harriet, Runkleman keeps insisting that Kristina has a "good head" on her shoulders. The older physician, to whom Lucas becomes deeply attached, understands the younger man's wish to see the world in black-and-white (melodramatic) terms but dismisses such idealism as unreal and unnecessary.

> He needed compromise badly. Time would give it to him, but not easily as to other men, it would have to beat him down, he would get it painfully. He would probably rebel against compromise all his days. Nevertheless he needed to learn it. He needed compromise.
> ...You couldn't cure anybody with it.
> It wouldn't make you richer or poorer.
> And knowing that was the essence of compromise.
> Not just saying it.
> Really—really knowing it.[20]

When Dr. Runkleman loses his life savings in the stock market crash, has a heart seizure caused by venereal disease, and still insists on travelling to Australia, he becomes a martyr to Lucas. His death ends Lucas' hero-worshipping period for the practice which Runkleman bequeaths him has fallen on hard times and Lucas no longer enjoys the comfort of a colleague. In the novel's crescendo ending, Runkleman's words come true as Kristina emerges to be both Lucas' professional and emotional helpmate.

Sexual relations in *Not as a Stranger* conform to the stylistic limits the 1950s observed; however the female sexual drive looms in such scenes and the need for mutual satisfaction becomes yet another way for Thompson to portray his hero's disorientation and reintegration. For the most part, the novel's lovemaking scenes are veiled in an obscurity that, like the proverbial Hollywood movie, leaves most (if not all) to the audience's imagination. In a typical situation, Lucas exhibits the same quick reflexes that his father possessed, by making love to a student nurse on the lawn.

> He stopped her mouth with a long kiss. Her arms tightened about him. She held her mouth on his. The night drifted slowly over them. He moved, he moved again. For an instant she wrenched her mouth away.

"No! No, don't! Don't Luke...Luke!" And then, "Oh!...Oh!...Aahh...That's good...That's—that's...."

Then she was silent.[21]

While nothing happens that can literally be taken as prurient (indeed, one can imagine a couple of comedians using the same dialog to change a leaking faucet), the audience naturally imagines all sorts of gymnastics occurring (after all, don't doctors and nurses know all sorts of things?). Interestingly, the girl acts as an aggressor and Lucas responds to her satisfaction; of course, such feminine sexuality is not given too great a prominence since the man's movements ultimately trigger the oohs and aahs.

More complicated sexual maneuvering attends some scenes between Lucas and Kristina. Although his motives for marrying her were hardly romantic, Lucas demands a sexual awareness and appetite from Kristina that she does not naturally feel. His guilt prompts Lucas to insist that Kristina experience sexual orgasm; thus, he conceives of himself as an instrument to provide pleasure and not as an individual in whom she can confide emotionally or spiritually. In one lovemaking scene, Lucas forces Kristina to enjoy intercourse (or, at least, to say she does) so his own ego can be salved.

"What's the matter?" she asked, dismayed.
"You don't feel a thing!"
"I do! I do! I feel what you do!"
"All right, tell me! Tell me what you feel!"
"Oh, Lucas—
"Tell me! He pushed her away. "Tell me what you feel!"
"Lucas, what do you want of me? What is it? I'm trying! I'm trying so hard—"
"I don't want your trying! I want—I want—" he looked at her helplessly.

After some gentle fondling (which is all Kristina wanted without the palaver):

"Now?"
"Now," she whispered. A flutter trembled through her muscles. And again. "Now," she whispered, and there was another flutter, and "now" she said again.
And this time, caught up involuntarily, his sense exploded, he cried out, he soared above her, transported beyond her whisper, her body and her being.[22]

While one can be thankful that Lucas finally gets into the swing of things (if only to stop Kristina saying "Now"), he clearly turns sex into work, a situation that any popular sexologist would recognize as the beginning of a deterioration in a marriage. After his transformation, Lucas makes love to Kristina in a less demanding and more natural way to symbolize their bliss.

By the time Lucas turns into a considerate (i.e. adult) lover, Harriet Lang has fled the scene; however, before her departure, she and the protagonist engage in a tryst which epitomizes innumerable movies and their euphemistic pictures of crashing waves. In a bit of campy voyeurism

Lucas and Harriet have their appetites triggered by watching a stallion mount a mare. Harriet's perversity is shown by her fascination and horror at the coupling of the animals.

> The mare dashed to escape. There was no escape. Again the stallion sank his teeth in her neck. She trembled.
> Instantly he reared. He plunged on her. His loins moved convulsively, his hips aimed, drew back suddenly.
> "Oh! Oh, my God! He'll kill her."
> She clung to Lucas, her body twitched, with each movement of the stallion she gave a little moan, Lucas gripped her tighter, the stallion screamed, driving the mare almost to her knees.
> ...Lucas...was half running with her toward the open door of the barn.
> "...Luke! For the love of God!"
> She beat at him.
> She felt the prick of hay on her bare body.
> She stiffened.
> She cried out suddenly.
> Then she moaned and was still.[23]

The popular beliefs in "therapeutic" rape and overwhelming masculine sexual power and size are here brewed into a deliciously overdone symbolic situation in which Thompson's humans have just enough instinct to follow the horses' lead. In keeping with convention, the novel can be more explicit about what the animals do so that the audience really sees two seductions for the price of one. The by-now familiar notion that a woman must be forced into sex is also central here, for Harriet enjoys the "chills" of physical assault (proving once again that women seek rape) and needs the orgasmic satisfaction that only Luke can provide.

Not as a Stranger also touches on communism and, in keeping with the fear and trembling aroused by that subject during the early 1950s, provides another feeble portrait of this doctrine's adherents. The town's communist sympathizer, Ben Cosgrove, continually tries to convert others and, after bothering Lucas a few times, is steered to Oscar Glaimer, a shoemaker dying of cancer, because the protagonist hopes that Cosgrove's attentions will prove beneficial. Cosgrove is furious when he learns the truth, but Lucas defends himself on humanitarian grounds and one feels that those who preach nonsense and blasphemy deserve only the dying as converts. Thompson even explains Cosgrove as a neurotic whose predilection for Marxism derives from his dislike of his neighbors and community; thus, following the party line allows Cosgrove to vent his hostilities.

> He was a communist now...because it was the exact opposite to the religions, governments, and systems of belief by which men lived, and because communism made his fellows uneasy or angry...he detested the world into which he was born with a hatred so implacable for what it had destroyed in him that he would give his life to smash it and exult in the ruins and then prepare to smash the next one too.[24]

In keeping with the novel's principal theme, Ben Cosgrove is more deeply alienated than Lucas and so the would-be Marxist shows what happens to an individual who turns his back on the human community. In dismissing Cosgrove, Lucas foreshadows his own redemption and reintegration. Their argument over the Marxist approach suggests the differences between those who think social difficulties are problems to be solved and those who believe life embodies conditions that the individual must struggle with as best he can. Cosgrove boasts that Glaimer now has the answer to all his problems.

> "Not communism."
> "Yes, my friend, my poor, blind friend, yes, communism."
> "The problem of man is life."
> "The problem of man is man."[25]

In stressing the more amorphous "life," Lucas stands for individual dignity in contrast to Cosgrove who, thorough-going totalitarian that he is, wants to manipulate others' lives.

When Lucas finally stumbles upon enlightenment, he equates human existence with a quest for truth which creates a transcendent possibility in the individual. Man struggles to find what is actual, to gain the "glory (that) is his birthright," and to realize that "to be better than man, to be not man, is the highest endeavor of which he can dream."[26] Since life includes death, the individual must pursue existence where it leads, and not simply indulge in maneuvering men whose appetites can be used against them. As the soon-to-be mother of his child, Kristina will fulfill the mystical role of bringing forth new life and so creating a tie that will bind Lucas in a more permanent and elevated relationship. While she has connived at becoming pregnant (by ignoring precautions which, as one would expect, are never explicitly discussed), Kristina's trick saves Lucas from himself. As she awaits his attentions after she has decided to conceive:

> Kristina licked her dry lips in anticipation and fright quivering with the secret knowledge that she had deliberately not prepared herself, that she was open, now, open to conception, now and every night thereafter. Until it happened. Until that happened which was to make them one.[27]

Thus, Lucas Marsh becomes a convert to home, children and family— solid, middle-class values that represent normalcy at its most obvious. The protagonist's willing choice at the end of *Not as a Stranger* demonstrates that a man's calling must be tempered by a heart which endorses his community's values.

*   *   *

The High and the Mighty exposes a group of characters to death to show their reactions under stress. Shortly past the point of no return (at which fuel supplies prohibit turning back) an airliner from Honolulu to San Francisco develops mechanical problems that make a crash seem certain. Gann's passengers subsequently experience marked personality transitions as a result of this crisis and the crew's desperate efforts to stay aloft. Suspense arises from the novel's continuous references to distances and dwindling fuel so that a race against time looms throughout. Given such a sure-fire plot (which can be seen over and over in the numerous *Airport* films of the 1970s), *The High and the Mighty* represents highly efficient escapist fare, an unpretentious fiction that is easily completed. Since Gann was a flier, he emphasizes what being a pilot means, the techniques, knowledge and courage such an individual needs to sustain himself and those around him. Because of the constant tensions besetting characters both in the air and on the ground, Gann's figures live on the surface of existence, where emotions and activities are conspicuously normal—with wedded bliss, or at least monogamy, essential for women and a stiff upper lip de rigeur for men.

Professionalism emerges as the major thematic value stressed in *The High and the Mighty*, for Gann carefully distinguishes between useful and demeaning conduct for individuals and for groups. Hobie Wheeler, a young relief pilot, exhibits the enthusiastic shortsightedness of one who has yet genuinely to understand what flying is all about. The youngster stands in sharp contrast to Captain Sullivan, the pilot, and Dan Roman, the veteran co-pilot who is Gann's hero. When Sullivan looks at Hobie, as they are preparing to leave Hawaii, he feels old but realizes: "Though he could manipulate the controls with assurance and ease, Hobie Wheeler had still to learn what it was like to fly."[28] This special knowledge only results from experience, so that only time will make the youngster his elder's equal, a clear suggestion that youth is not everything. Gann seems reactionary in pleading that only special men (i.e. professionals) can operate essentially autonomous machinery; indeed, his pilots represent a throwback to a more comforting time when an older generation could take assurance from its knowledge of the world. Because Sullivan and Roman have lost the desire for adventure, they can operate efficiently within the limits of human capacity. In a crisis, clearly:

> The burden in the end, fell upon men like Sullivan with his big sure hands, and Dan Roman with his always deeply troubled eyes. Their pride in their part of the endeavor, their total absorption in this little time before the take-off, was an unlikely mixture of emotion and cold concern with numerical facts. Hobie Wheeler could not as yet fully appreciate either the pleasure or the seriousness of their mood. He thought their reactions slow and overcautious.[29]

Gann's professionals, in knowing the potential dangers that await them, reflect a conscious heroism, one which takes into account the imperfections of their aircraft. While Hobie's impatience shows his unawareness of such dangers, his dismay reveals a naive overconfidence in man and machine. Thus, his courage derives from foolhardiness rather than bravery, and his elders are more heroic because they face known dangers while he faces only unknown ones.

Captain Sullivan, who suffers a loss of confidence during the flight, has reached a point at which the perils of flying have begun to erode his judgment. Overly conscious of the small details that can go wrong, at thirty-five he is beginning to find the ground more attractive than the air. He remains honest enough to know that such doubts can enfeeble his effectiveness and, in reflecting on this personal fear, Sullivan suggests that being a professional is a continuous process and not a fixed condition.

> Eventually, if the pilot was unable to conquer the disease, the destruction of his confidence would become more obvious—there would be abortive turn-arounds when there was no sound technical reason for returning to a point of departure, there would be missed approaches to airports during bad weather, and sometimes distress signals sent when there was actually no need for them.[30]

During the trip Sullivan realizes his worst fears because the ship's small disturbances bloom into a full-fledged crisis. He nearly cracks under the strain, but he is finally saved by the other professionals so that the team carries him through. In dealing with staying airborne, landing in bad weather (with no margin for error) and sending distress signals, Captain Sullivan alternates between depression and elation, although his exterior belies this emotional seething. He rationalizes doubt by plunging into the mechanics of flying, rendered acute by the plane's having lost an engine, and even believes: "he was a better man for the period of doubt because he would have conquered his instability with reason instead of bravado."[31]

Sullivan remains hampered by his fears until Dan Roman takes charge and forces the Captain to act like a professional. As the stricken plane approaches the California coast, and the possibility of landing arises, Sullivan loses his nerve and insists the aircraft must be ditched. In spite of his navigator who urges they can risk landing and so avoid the perils of the ocean, Sullivan hysterically orders the plane to be abandoned. At this point, Dan Roman usurps the pilot's prerogative by insisting they will make for the airport; and, to bring Sullivan back to his senses, Roman strikes his Captain and so dispels his loss of nerve. The older co-pilot's action symbolizes his professional commitment to use every chance to bring his ship home safely. After Dan briefly takes over the controls so that Sullivan can compose himself, the men talk over the difficult landing; and, in a passage that echoes, alas, all too many cinematic melodramas, Sullivan thanks Dan.

> "Dan...."
>
> "Yeah?" His face was like an ancient wind-beaten rock. He kept his eyes fixed on the instruments, sparing Sullivan only a glance.
>
> "Thanks...."
>
> Dan raised an eyebrow... "Thought I'd lost my temper long ago," he said finally. "Guess I didn't. I'm sorry."
>
> "You should have hit harder. Thanks for knocking some sense into my head."[32]

Thus, at the supreme moment of crisis, age and experience prove their worth. The professionalism engendered by numerous trials enables Dan Roman to bring his Captain through, and with the reinvigorated Sullivan back in control, there can be little doubt that a safe landing will result.

Dan Roman personifies the old pro literally and intellectually. He says little, whistles to relieve his tensions, and lives with the memory of a plane crash in which he, the pilot, was the only survivor and in which his wife and son were killed. After more than a half-century as a pilot, Roman has reached the age when most fliers retire; however, he has chosen to persist and been hired as a kindness to a "has been." Garfield, the airline's owner-manager, feels that Dan needs to get flying out of his system by realizing that flight has become too strenuous for one his age; of course, such rationality only underscores the irony that the plane survives because of the older man's presence. One might, indeed, see this aspect of *The High and the Mighty* as consistent with a period when Americans looked to older men (Truman, Eisenhower) for leadership. Roman has a limp, which came from the accident that took his family, and a weathered briefcase which: "had two million miles on it or better. It sagged a little here and there. It was covered with scars and weather wounds, but it still had value and durability. It was not to be thrown away any more than Dan Roman— not quite yet a relic."[33] Only the crisis of the flight convinces the other crew members that Roman is more than a "legend" from flying's distant past: like his briefcase, the aged pilot still has value.

When the ship gets into trouble, Dan's steadiness inspires the less-experienced crew members; even Leonard, the navigator, "wished that his own behavior could match Dan's, for he was ashamed."[34] On the approach to San Francisco, Roman manipulates the propellers to conserve fuel, a tactic that risks stalling the motors unless done perfectly. Sullivan believes this maneuver will destroy them and wants to change the propellers' pitch.

> Dan caught his arm and held it firmly.
> "Hang on, chum! We'll make it this way! You can do it, man! Just hang on. Fly, and let me pray!"
> "Are you tired of living? If we try an instrument approach at San Francisco we'll run out of gas right in the middle of it."
> "Maybe yes, maybe no. Nothing is for sure yet. Try it this way for thirty minutes, will you? Don't be so goddamned anxious to go for a swim!"
> "It's crazy! She's starting to shake again!"
> "Let her shake! The hell with it as long as she don't fall off on a wing. Let her mush down a little if you have to. Look at our gas consumption...only one-fifty per hour! Hang on and *fly*, man!"[35]

Such determination to use any tactic born of experience epitomizes professionalism: to get the aircraft through, if humanly possible, shortages of fuel or nerve must be overcome by rational courage—bravery that calculates the possibilities between foolhardiness (Wheeler) and fear (Sullivan). When Roman gets off the plane in San Francisco there are no reporters or friends to greet him, only Garfield who watches the veteran pilot walk away and realizes "the ancient pelican" has saved his plane. Roman's professionalism can only be recognized by the few (i.e. the initiated), for average men cannot readily believe that such an unlikely-appearing individual can be a hero.

The ethic that Roman embodies concentrates on the value of work. His insistence that Sullivan keep flying and stop worrying about larger possibilities clearly suggests that men's actions determine their fates. The love of a job and the desire to do it well are components of the courage necessary to conquer fear. The crew must function in the face of death (an attitude embodied constantly by Roman) and find solace from doing their duties. The navigator, who can normally pilot their course very rapidly, must now proceed cautiously because of the gravity of the situation and his own nervousness.

> ...now aware of the confusion in his mind, he thought more slowly, checking and rechecking his figures against the chance of error. And gradually he settled into the familiarity of his work. The trembling subsided as he drew a small triangle on the chart. He became confident of his sights as they agreed with his dead-reckoning calculations.[36]

Work's repetitive detail frees the individual from worry; thus, Leonard and Captain Sullivan become machines and so relieve the tension of the moment. (Interestingly, and in keeping with his heroic stature, Roman lacks a definite function in which he can lose himself, so he remains the others' moral guide). The stewardess, Spalding, initially envies the activity in the cockpit, for she feels the fliers' duties take their minds off dangerous possibilities. Then she realizes that though "they had something to do with their hands and their minds to help them through the waiting," she also has tasks that can ease tension—"even if the things to do are not so clearly defined." [37] Thus,   man overcomes a crisis by turning his attention to the small but necessary tasks which simple existence imposes. Bravery consists in doing one's duty in the face of overwhelming possibilities, of narrowing one's vision so that the next moment becomes central and the eventualities of the next hour are pushed aside.

Gann's passengers represent the kind of cross-section one expects: a drunk; tourists returning from their "dream" vacation; a kept woman whose protector has died; a dynamic businessman; a Korean girl on her way to American freedom; newlyweds; a dissatisfied rich couple whose alternate desires (he wants to leave the advertising business, she loves New York) belie their genuine affection; an immigrant whose naivete about practical matters obscures his good sense about what truly counts; and a jealous husband who wants to kill his wife's (supposed) paramour. This assemblage, so reminiscent of *Grand Hotel* (1932) or John Ford's *Stagecoach* (1939), will undergo character transformations so that their concerns when they board will seem minute when they leave. Humphrey Agnew, who believes his wife has had a romantic liaison with Ken Childs, tries to kill the latter in mid-air, is disarmed, and sits brooding thereafter. Gann shows Agnew stewing over the injustices he feels the world has heaped on him. Since he believes he has always been looked down on by more elegant types like Childs, Agnew's jealousy represents deep-seated envy rather than romantic agony. The self-made millionaire, who has misunderstood his wife's relation to Childs, emerges as a materialist tottering on the brink of total paranoia.

He was envied and approached by so called gentlemen who suggested partnership in their failing enterprises... Not a penny of Agnew's hard-earned money would go to save those elegant failures. Let the weaklings crawl—as you had done for so long a time. Crawl, you slimy bastards, with your handsome looks, and your friends, and your parties which you would never open to me...crawl right past the man who was socially unacceptable because he was clever enough to milk a few million Polynesians and Orientals. Crawl, and find out what it is like to be without money. Money, you would soon discover, is not an unmentionable disease. Money is the most important thing in the world.[38]

The plane's encounter with death ameliorates Agnew's extremism for, in San Francisco, he is last seen rushing for a phone booth to (presumably) make a repentant call to the little woman. His supposed rival, Childs, who handles Agnew adroitly on the plane, suffers a loss of nerve when the possibility of a crash looms. When Garfield sees his former business associate and rival get off the plane, he realizes that Childs has been humbled and, as a result, thinks Childs might now be worth knowing.

The most extended interaction among the passengers takes place between the Josephs, who have visited Hawaii to get away from the pressures of home and children only to find themselves in more hectic circumstances, and the Rices, who have tentatively agreed to a divorce because he doesn't want to run the advertising agency she bought for him. Howard Rice wants to go into mineral exploration in Canada because he resents being kept by his wife. In tune with American tradition, he wants to forge his own character and career; and, in trying to explain this desire to the skeptical Lydia, Howard argues:

"It was only because the war was just over and I was confused that I ever consented to run your advertising agency in the first place. It's not for me, Lydia, and it never will be. I want to get up in the morning with the feeling that whatever I accomplish that day is due to my own efforts...not because my wife happened to inherit a business—"[39]

Thus, the Horatio Alger dream remains uppermost; and, while roughing it in the wilderness may not be immediately appealing, Lydia, to remain the ideal American wife, must accept Howard's natural right to be himself. The threat of the crash and the example of the Josephs combine to bring Lydia back to the track of true love. While Mr. Joseph initially appears to be a gratuitous windbag, his lengthy description of the hometown Good Neighbor Club—a group which offers crying towels to members who present small problems, while giving real aid to those in truly serious straits— establishes the Josephs as normal people. Thus, their bedrock goodness offers an example from which the more sophisticated Rices can learn.

At one point, Gustave Pardee, the theatrical producer, asks the nearly hysterical Mrs. Joseph if she would change anything in her life. Gustave has already seen the errors of his ways (taking his wife for granted) and wants to reconfirm his reawakened faith in matrimonial bliss. Naturally, Mrs. Joseph, even when facing death, tells him: " 'Why...I don't believe I would *change anything*.' "[40]; and, in so doing, reaffirms that a life of children, noise, debts and worries, with its brief interludes of vacations beset by rain, hotel drunks and, finally sunburn, is the best existence anyone can have. The same bourgeois values are reaffirmed when Mrs. Rice, after seeing the newlyweds' groping attempts at intimacy in the midst of chaos, realizes that "oomph" has been missing from her own marriage. She gradually comes to understand that love supersedes friends or material comforts and decides that the north woods would be a nice place to be isolated with an ardent husband. Her memories of physical passion bring Lydia Rice back to marriage.

> Howard was two men, one during the day and another man in the enormous bed which had certainly never held anything like Howard before. How lusty could a man get? Oh Howard . .could you ever be like that again? Even exile in the North woods would be worth it.[41]

In San Francisco, Lydia quickly cancels her divorce plans and agrees to go anywhere her master decrees, apparently her need for "thrilling" sex disarms the possibility that she may well have to shiver for it.

The High and the Mighty implies that individuals have hidden capacities which only emerge as a result of a crisis. Just as the professional can draw on hidden resources so can the seemingly ordinary individual exhibit extraordinary traits when such a need arises. Gustave Pardee, who has devoted his life to being witty in cafe society, becomes a tower of emotional strength when confronted with the possibility that the aircraft may crash. As the tension approaches panic in the cabin, he can tell a joke to dispel such incipient hysteria.

> He was the first to find his voice and, when he did so, the dilettante quality had disappeared entirely.
> "I know nothing whatsoever about airplanes," he said easily, "...but this one acts like the Fourth of July. I told Mrs. Pardee we should take the boat." Then he smiled at the formation of frightened faces and said, "Amen."
> The effect of his words was magical. Everyone began to talk at once.[42]

Pardee exhibits a different personality—one that amazes his wife and makes her even more in love with him—as a response to a need; and so, crisis forces each member of a group to do his best so that, hopefully, all may survive.

The test, of course, brings changes to all who undergo it; and Garfield, an old pilot himself, now awaiting the return of his company's stricken plane, reflects on how this process works.

> They would change, Garfield thought. Each one of them would change in his own way. Certain things that seemed important before suddenly become valueless—because you had to stand very near to complete destruction before you could see anything clearly.[43]

Appropriately enough, in a novel that stresses the values of humility, Garfield's formula reiterates the customary notions that an individual develops by enduring tests and trials and that wisdom results from the buffetings which he assimilates. While the idea that suffering brings wisdom is venerable, Americans have too often transformed this notion into the simplistic precept that the more one experiences (or endures) the wiser he will become. Unfortunately, the assumption that more is better omits the qualities of the individual who does the experiencing and so the quantity of experience gets substituted for the qualities which the sufferer brings to any situation. A shortsighted man hardly gains from excessive privation and pain: he may develop armor for dealing with such catastrophes in the future, but genuine wisdom may still be beyond his grasp. Garfield flatters Gann's audience by suggesting the individual can survive a crisis and inevitably become a better person as a result.

* * *

Every adult generation creates its own image of teenagers and registers the fear that these youngsters will fatally wrench the fabric of society. The figure of the juvenile delinquent has emerged since the 1920s and, with each passing decade, taken on more sinister overtones. While Billy the Kid suggests that juvenile delinquency is hardly peculiar to the twentieth century, the maladjustments of youth have frequently been accorded apocalyptic status. In American literature, the pranks of Tom Sawyer and the gropings of Studs Lonigan become the ruthlessness of the Amboy Dukes and, in the 1950s, the antics of Artie West, the archvillain of Evan Hunter's *The Blackboard Jungle*. In this novel, the schoolroom, heretofore a boring interlude in any hoodlum's career, becomes the battleground on which adult society confronts the teen menace. Hunter provides many traditional bestseller "thrills"—rape, attempted seduction, traumas of birth—against the background of a New York vocational high school whose students illustrate incorrigible neglect at home and a constant struggle in the city's streets. Rick Dadier, an idealistic World War II veteran who has used the G. I. Bill to earn a teaching certificate, is initially naive enough to illuminate conditions at North Manual Trades High School. Because he lacks the experiences that would sour him on the students, Rick commits mistakes a less daring character would avoid. *The Blackboard Jungle* chronicles Rick's first year at the school, a time during which his struggles with various personal problems make him a solidly professional faculty member.

Hypocrisy surrounds Rick from his first day in the school and, as the months go by, he realizes a special kind of "make believe" supports the educational system. Rick, an English teacher (always a writer's favorite), is interviewed by Mr. Stanley, the head of the English department. During this conversation Stanley, who delights in appearing stern, tests Rick by attributing a Shakespearean speech to the wrong play and, only after the protagonist has (obligatorily) corrected him, offers him a position. This moment of sweetness and light is short-lived for Rick asks:

> "The discipline problem here. Is it. . . ."
> Stanley's eyes tightened. "There is no discipline problem here," he said quickly. "I'll look for you on Friday."[44]

Such a rapid and vehement denial indicates that Stanley is expressing a hope and not a reality. As the novel progresses, Mr. Small, the Principal, appears less as a harried administrator and more as a shortsighted bureaucrat. When Rick discusses such expressions as "wop," "spic" and "nigger" to make a point about language and prejudice, Mr. Small's close-mindedness comes to the surface. He reads Dadier the riot act and only grasps Rick's argument when the protagonist gets as angry and as visceral in his responses as the Principal has been in his charges. Echoing methods that would have warmed the heart of Senator McCarthy, Mr. Small refuses to tell Rick the reason for such inquiries. When Dadier suggests that a man should know the crime he has allegedly committed, Small launches into a tirade: " 'No, you may not ask what it is all about...I'll damn well tell you what it's all about when I'm good and ready, and besides you know damn well what it's all about.' "[45] While Small seems an unlikely head for a school where conditions render teaching there a peril to life (who would willingly stay and keep him company?), this confrontation strains credibility even more when the Principal refuses to reveal the sources of his information. Clearly Small, in keeping with his name, has no sense that bias occasionally governs human affairs. Ironically, Artie West, who has been waging a one-man vendetta against Dadier, is the youth whose innocence cannot be compromised.

Small's shortsightedness reflects the entire system's failure to confront the realities of its student population. Rick recalls that at Hunter College:

> ...he could not remember any emphasis being placed on the vocational school. Passing mention, yes. But emphasis, no. And perhaps passing mention was sufficient for the fellow who wound up teaching at Christopher Columbus (a college prep school) but it was definitely not sufficient for someone who now found himself in a vocational high school.... When Rick had been assigned to Machine and Metal Trades, even though he asked for an academic high school, he'd been none too pleased about it. He'd voiced his displeasure, and Kraal, a mild-mannered man who preferred discussing the nickel glass of beer to education, had shrugged and simply replied, "Someone's got to get the trade schools. It'll be good experience for you."[46]

Such sympathy epitomizes the lack of interest the educational establishment places in vocational schools, and Kraal ("crawl"), as an advisor, seems hardly likely to produce any teachers who can or will cope with such problems. Thus, educational specialists have little or no understanding of what Dadier faces in the classroom for, while Small fails through arrogance, Kraal falters because of disinterest. The "profession" consists of those with credentials who, in allegedly administering it, constitute barriers to achievement rather than sources of help. Only when Rick stops looking for benevolent authority figures does he begin to succeed as a teacher; indeed, he perseveres because he has been "called" to this profession in a deeper way than Small or Kraal can comprehend.

Sex scenes and innuendo abound in *The Blackboard Jungle*. Rick finds himself caught between his pregnant wife, Anne, who feels threatened, and Lois Hammond, another first-year teacher who throws herself at him. Anne's dilemma surfaces when, after learning Rick has got a job, she makes love:

"She had begun to curse her mountain of a belly because she had always enjoyed bed with Rick, and now it was rapidly becoming anything but a pleasure."[47] Anne constantly calls attention to her appearance and, as anonymous letters accusing Rick of adultery begin arriving, she tries to submerge her feelings even further. Ultimately, these poison pen notes, another spiteful act by Artie West, do bring about a premature birth and a dead baby. At one point, Hunter implies that a girl only becomes a woman by being pregnant for, after momentarily "studying the insistent bulge with fascination," Anne walks over to a mirror: "shrugged...and unbuttoned the top part of her gown. She cupped one breast and studied it in the mirror, amazed at the way the nipple had darkened, had become somehow more mature, had become a woman's nipple."[48] This description combines the closed atmosphere of a woman's private life with obvious self-stimulation and voyeurism; thus the reader learns about high school *and* pregnant women. Anne's equation of maturity with physical experience represents another sop to the audience, for it divests growing up of any mental component and dismisses the woman as a baby-making machine whose interests lie primarily in recording those physical sensations which accompany this biological process. Such stereotyping even extends to the jealousy Anne feels for, after Rick has rescued Lois Hammond from an attempted rape by one of the students (on the first day of school!), his wife voices the popular notion that any woman who is assaulted "asks for it."

Unfortunately, Hunter's portrayal of Miss Hammond does nothing to contradict this appraisal; indeed, while she can hardly be called a nymphomaniac, Lois constantly flashes her femininity. On the first day of school she appears in a clinging skirt and draws wolf whistles as she ascends the auditorium stage. She exhibits even more carelessness when she allows herself to be trapped alone in the school library after hours. While rescuing her from a student assailant, Rick notices Miss Hammond's bare breast—a voyeuristic aside that underscores the novel's consistent fascination with that aspect of the female anatomy. Miss Hammond's attempt to seduce Rick culminates during the preparation of the Christmas pageant, a spectacle whose supervision falls on the protagonist as the newest member of the faculty. After some remarks that sound like double entendre (Lois doesn't know what " 'got into' " her assailant; she's sure that her freshmen don't have sex on the brain because they're " 'just little boys, really' ") Lois: "shrugged her shoulders as if she honestly could not understand what had provoked lust. But, in shrugging, her breasts moved, and Rick wondered for the second time if she were being artful, exhibiting her femininity while denying it."[49] This same pattern occurs earlier when Rick offers to help Lois, who has become the faculty advisor to the student newspaper. They find themselves together in a small, locked room and, in an obvious bit of maneuvering, Lois takes off her suit jacket to show off the very considerable assets beneath her filmy blouse. For several "steamy" pages thereafter Rick alternately feels temptation and dismay; however, all of this "eyeballing" ends on a note of symbolic excess. Since their conversation has been concerned with type faces and headlines, Lois naturally holds up the first page of the newspaper for Rick's inspection.

And above the page she extended, holding it just below her breasts, holding it so that his eyes took in a panorama of mimeographed page and cotton bra, above the page was the soft shadow, and the rounded mounds of white flesh on either side of the shadow. His eyes strayed from the page, and Lois said, "Do you like it?"[50]

Had Hunter stopped here, the symbolic overtness of the scene would have been amusing; however, he goes on to explain that each character knows what the other is thinking and so reassures the reader about *the* meaning of this sequence.

While Miss Hammond clearly dramatizes a culture infatuated with the exhibition of mammary glands, her forwardness also reveals a more unsettling possibility. Since she cannot seduce Rick in the newspaper room, Lois offers to help sew the costumes for the Christmas play with the proviso that she and Rick will celebrate after the show. While the protagonist avoids this confrontation by informing the gym teacher (who constantly seeks "tail") about Lois, and by having to attend Anne who goes into labor on the night of the show, he must listen to Lois' pleas. Even though he wants to keep things professional between them, Rick endures Miss Hammond's lament about the school and her entire life.

"But tell me, Rick, doesn't this goddamned place sometimes bore you to tears?...I know you're not.... But will you mind if I'm bored?... Will you mind if I consider the first day of school the only true piece of excitement we've had since I've been here. Will you mind that?"

"You mean...."

"Yes, I mean. I mean the time that stupid slob tried to rape me, Rick. That's exactly what I mean. My God, sometimes I wish he'd succeeded."[51]

Lois reconfirms Anne's diagnosis for, in her desire to avoid boredom—a condition she cannot control by an act of will—she welcomes any masculine attention. The seriousness attributed to this outlook suggests the degree to which *The Blackboard Jungle* panders to popular taste, for it is obviously easier to believe in a woman who invites sexual assault than in a woman who can exist comfortably without men or marriage.

This sexual dichotomy, according to which women only function as corollaries to men, colors Rick's thoughts about teaching. While he believes women find their reasons for living in homes and children, he feels men must seek out occupations to express themselves: "Women, he had reflected, had no such problem. Creation had been given them as a gift, and a woman was self-sufficient within her own creative shell. A man needed more, which perhaps was one reason why a woman could never understand a man's concern for the job he had to do."[52] In order to attain this lofty goal, Rick doggedly maintains his faith that education can modify human conduct for the better. Even when he is surrounded by older and more cynical colleagues, the protagonist can only momentarily agree that such pessimism is justified or accurate. His own faith rests on an inability to believe "the system was sham"[53]; and this trust in the validity of teaching constitutes

Rick's identity—if his profession were hypocritical or worthless, then he would possess no stature in his own eyes.

> Why not fool the system and fool the kids and fool yourself in the bargain? Why not collect a teacher's salary, and tuck the good vacations into your hip pocket, and all the while be an employee of the DSC?
>
> And you could forget all about being a man in addition.[54]

Thus, teaching represents a calling, a profession which constitutes what he must do with his life in order to realize his own personality in work. Rick accepts hard knocks and a cruel environment because his own identity is at stake. The novel's last page shows Rick and his colleagues at the end of the school year, grousing as they have through the term. Some of the others comment on Rick's disarming of Artie West, which resulted in a knife wound and an arm in a sling for the protagonist. When one of these colleagues says it was a hero's action, another more cynical, but admiring voice adds: " 'That's Dadier's trouble. He's a professional hero.' " In response, Hunter's principal character sagely opines: " 'No,...I'm just a teacher.' "[55] Rick has earned the title, and his qualification of it nicely understates the suffering he has experienced to become such a professional. Hunter's protagonist has learned that crises are overcome alone, for a teacher can expect no help from administrators or colleagues who are sympathetic at best and indifferent at worst.

Hunter's hero shares his liberal idealism with Josh Edwards, even though Rick knows that such theories cannot be implemented in all surroundings. Josh confesses that teaching has always been his ambition and then, while bemoaning how conditions at North Manual Trades impede his performance, he touches on the students' character.

> "So why won't they let me teach?"
> "Cause they're bad guys," Rick said.
> "Oh no, don't say that."
> "Yes," Rick said, "they're bad guys."
> "No," Josh said with drunken dignity, "tha's a common error, fallacy. They ain't bad guys. They're jus' ignorant."
> "Same thing." Rick said.[56]

Rick, who survives the term, realizes that an individual's actions are more important than any theoretical explanation of them. Josh Edwards, who bends over backwards to be nice to the students, attempts to "relate" from a theoretical standpoint, while the protagonist, who has experienced some difficult times in the Navy, recognizes that "punks" cannot be won over by shows of kindness or admissions of weakness. While Josh wants to expose his students to the life of the mind, Rick knows that he can only go a short way on such a path, and then only if the students think they are leading. In keeping with the novel's connection of work and identity, Josh quits when he realizes he can only be a "fake" at teaching and seeks another career in which he can be a "real" man. However, before he makes this change, Edwards must suffer the indignity of being unable to prevent a rowdy class from destroying his prized jazz collection. As he scrambles around the floor trying to preserve some of his records, Josh trips over a boy's foot and falls forward "on his face, his glasses shattering on the bridge of his nose."[57] The broken glasses symbolize Josh's demise, for the destruction of this "badge" of the egghead represents the triumph of disorder over order.

Rick reverses this process by standing up to his students day after day and so winning them over on two levels. He succeeds in reaching them intellectually by reading an allegory for which they supply the meaning from incidents in their own lives; and, when faced with the knife-wielding Artie West, Hunter's protagonist triumphs emotionally. The feud with Artie, which has built up since Dadier initially tried to impose discipline on this loudmouth, provides the novel's climax, for as he circles the armed juvenile, Dadier realizes that the other boys are preventing any interference. Gregory Miller, the brightest student in the class, and a Negro who leads by example, has been an enigma to Dadier until this moment; for, while he has mistakenly blamed many of his troubles on Miller, the protagonist now hears the boy's voice rallying those who are seeing that Rick and West fight on even terms. When Artie has been overcome, Miller, who constantly downgrades his own capacities, suggests that Artie should not be taken to the Principal's office. Rick, however, insists on West's punishment; and, by so doing, proves to Miller and the others that education, even at North Manual Trades, is worth fighting for. Thus, he becomes their "teacher" because he uses physical courage to demonstrate what he believes is necessary for them to learn.

Rick finally overcomes the students' dislike of education in general and of him in particular by reversing their opinions of themselves and of their school. In a classic example of expectation theory (the way one preconceives a situation is likely to be the way the situation turns out), an older teacher tells Rick:

"This is the garbage can of the educational system. Every vocational school in the city. You put them all together, and you got one big, fat, overflowing garbage can. And you want to know what our job is? Our job is to sit on the lid of the garbage can and see that none of the filth overflows into the streets. That's our job."[58]

While such a diatribe implies that high school is designed to keep young people out of the work force and so to preserve a fragile capitalism, this view of the teacher as babysitter is one that Rick cannot accept. Hunter's protagonist discovers that the students are aware that they attend a bad school, and this perception festers in him until he has a private conversation with Gregory Miller. They are painting scenery for the Christmas production (and by this time Miller has volunteered to be in the show and, although Rick does not know it, already been "reached") when they discuss the student's future. Rick is enraged that Miller seems willing to settle for a second-rate life as an automobile mechanic because, given the color of his skin, to aspire higher would be foolhardy. Dadier's anger does not, unfortunately, lead to a powerful argument so that Miller persuades him rather than vice-versa; however, when Rick finds himself becoming unfeeling about the students, he realizes he has accepted this "give it up" mentality. The final confrontation with West, which shows Miller that evil cannot be tolerated anywhere, dramatizes the main character's overcoming his despair.

The protagonist also overcomes the defenses his fellow teachers have erected against their students: in order to survive, Rick's colleagues have adopted tactics that preserve order (and their jobs) without ever endangering anyone with knowledge. In categorizing their different approaches, Rick demonstrates that intelligence should lead to constructive action rather than resignation or apathy. He discerns four types of incomplete teachers: clobberers, who rule by brute force and beat order into their classes; slobberers, who try to become "brothers and pals" and appeal for the students' sympathy; slumberers, who treat discipline as though it were never a problem, talk to themselves and, when things get too chaotic, step outside to be sure the Principal isn't in the vicinity; and fumblers, who don't know what to do but keep experimenting in the hope of finding a solution. Rick Dadier has placed himself in the last category until he disarmed Artie West, an action that proves juvenile terror cannot ride roughshod over a determined elder generation. In classic American fashion—the fair fight, the eyeball to eyeball shootout in the street—the lone man beats the lone villain (in this case by hitting the knife-flashing antagonist with a desk), the protagonist of *The Blackboard Jungle* preserves traditional American individualism within a social underworld.

* * *

Anatomy of a Murder combines a courtroom trial with explicit language about rape and murder. Its initial readers thus enjoyed a familiar plot device (the legal contest) and a tone that seemed "mature" for the time. Indeed, the word "panties" (used in testimony) causes titters in the courtroom and reflects the veiled proprieties considered normal for the period. Traver's novel still works because of the ironies embodied by the Manions, both the Lieutenant, on trial for murdering Barney Quill, and Laura, his carefree wife in whose "defense" the crime was committed. The Lieutenant, who emerges as a cautious and calculating figure, fools the jury and Paul Biegler, Traver's protagonist: Manion never says enough to be incriminated and, when he is acquitted, he avoids paying Biegler for his services. The Lieutenant remains enigmatic because of what he doesn't do, or at least what his silence suggests he could do but carefully avoids doing. Laura, on the other hand, appears blatantly obvious about her wishes, so much so that Biegler carefully supervises such details as her wardrobe for court. Her claim that Barney Quill, the owner of a local bar, picked her up and then raped her tests everyone's credulity, for she seems like a careless blonde throwing herself at men without too much forethought. Traver provides her with enough individual quirks and idiosyncrasies finally to make her testimony ring true. Laura, as a divorcée remarried to her first husband's best friend, hardly resembles a frail flower, yet her revulsion at Quill's act seems genuine. That she can cover up for her husband's premeditated crime also rings consistent with her character, for she clearly lives for love, or at least for a companionship she can solemnify with that word. Her morally ambiguous nature and the mixed motives of its other characters make *Anatomy of a Murder* more intellectually challenging than many another 1950s' bestseller; however, Traver's plot ultimately relies too much on legal maneuverings so that thematic subtleties get absorbed into a sea of (admittedly often entertaining) detail.

Paul Biegler, the defense attorney, shares the same mixture of pragmatism and idealism that distinguishes the novel's other characters. The defeat of his larger ambitions, after several terms as the local district attorney, has caused him to let his practice take a backseat to fishing expeditions and occasional drinking bouts. The Quill murder case reinvigorates Biegler, even though he only becomes defense counsel because Lt. Manion's first choice cannot be available. For Traver's protagonist, the law represents the major ideal in his life; and, because it reawakens this faith, the trial is a success for Biegler even though he receives no money for his labors. His pride in his craft surfaces when the character receives praise from the trial judge for a set of instructions that he and his aide-partner, Parnell, have drawn up to retail the legal alternatives the jury must consider in the case of Lt. Manion. While Biegler sounds like a schoolboy ecstatic about getting an "A" from a tough professor, his juvenile tendencies are nicely balanced by his own awareness of this form of pride: "I hurried away to tell Parnell the compliment the Judge had paid our instructions and supporting brief. As I clattered down the acres of soiled marble stairs I felt very expansive and virtuous, like a boy scout who had just thrown a rope to a drowning Smoky Madigan."[59] Such self-deprecation keeps Biegler from being a prig or a con man: his devotion to the law is hidden beneath his tendency to belittle himself and constantly pose questions designed to puncture euphoria.

While groping with the difficulties of a defense based on insanity—always a difficult plea because of psychiatrists' conflicting interpretations—Biegler and Parnell discover the doctrine of irresistible impulse and develop it as their central argument. Their discovery occurs in a typical passage in which the protagonist's humor belies his enthusiasm.

> The world of science is said to be full of remarkable examples of independent researchers, unknown to each other and sometimes separated by whole continents, coming up with identical answers to the same puzzling questions at the very same time. At least this was once true—true before our Soviet cousins rewrote history cozily—reminding us that they had invariably got there first. In any case that night shortly before midnight Parnell and I—separated not by continents but only by Grandma Biegler's old dining room-table—had, more modestly perhaps, experienced much the same exhilarating thrill.[60]

Given his tone, Biegler seems like the embodiment of fixed rural standards of right and wrong. He can make himself and his associate appear slightly ridiculous through posing their mundane accomplishments against those of Newton and Leibniz while, at the same time, suggesting the sort of clear-cut patriotism one would find in Michigan's Upper Peninsula. As a small-town lawyer, Biegler believes the day's events are transient excitements in the light of the longer perspective of human history. After succeeding in having the Army send a psychiatrist to examine Manion, Biegler greets this individual by jokingly revealing more of his conservatism.

"Perhaps, Doctor...perhaps you would join my committee to bomb the new bridge over the Straits of Mackinac?... Otherwise I'm afraid that before long the highways will be one continuous neon-lit hot-dog stand, with serpent lines of cars locked exhaust to exhaust, like hound dogs following a bitch in heat.... For years the Straits stood as our English Channel against invasion from the south. And now this goddam bridge, which our gleeful chamber of commerce sturdies have now added to their nightly prayers."[61]

Thus, Biegler is caught between a love for the past, symbolized by the old house in which he lives and preserves (in dusty disarray) his ancestors' artifacts, and the imposition of the present and future, symbolized by the military base to which Manion is assigned and the increasing commercialization encroaching upon Thunder Bay.

Traver dramatizes the contradictions in his protagonist's character by having Biegler defend the rootless and outwardly sophisticated Manions (the Lieutenant smokes cigarettes while using an ornate holder—surely a sign of his decadent personality). His successful defense implies that the law, which is built on precedent, can still provide justice in the new world of neon. Biegler initially rationalizes his reasons for accepting Manion as a client; however, when he realizes that the Lieutenant and Laura have fled after the trial, such ostensibly good reasons as running for Congress (and thus defeating the local district attorney) or becoming the most respected defense attorney in the region give way to his true feelings. He dismisses suing the Manions as an unprofitable venture, while his new partner, Parnell, heretofore the town drunk but now restored by working on the case, states their faith in the law as a way of life.

"Let's to the future, lad, you and me together—maybe makin' a little money, surely havin' a barrel of fun, practicin' our profession together, occasionally helpin' bastards and angels alike, between whom, always remember, our Lady Justice has never distinguished."[62]

For Biegler and Parnell happiness consists of being allowed to practice their craft and not merely in reaping its financial rewards.

Traver's protagonist believes that the American legal system, whose use of the jury resembles a political election, embodies the closest approximation men are likely to make to justice. While lecturing Manion on legal ethics and niceties when they first confer, Biegler keeps insisting that he is an officer of the court but also clearly implies how his client should act and plead. Even though what Manion decides is all right as long as Biegler isn't made directly aware of any prevarications, the protagonist still sees the law as society's best hedge against anarchy. He reminds the Lieutenant that without prisons, police and courts, arguments would lead to vendettas; and he ends by insisting that the law provides Manion's only chance to defend his act on reasonable grounds.

"Mr. Bumble (a character in Dickens' *Oliver Twist* who proclaimed that the law is "a ass") was only partly right because, for all its lurching and shambling imbecilities, the law—and only the law—is what keeps our society from becoming a snarling jungle.... More precisely, Lieutenant, in your case the law is all that stops Barney Quill's relatives from charging in here and seeking out and shooting up every Manion in sight.

"...Why, just look, man—just look at Russia.... There the law has been replaced by a stoic joyless gang of lumpy characters in round hats and floppy pants and double-breasted overcoats, men who peremptorily crack down on their Lieutenant Manions and everyone, all in the name of the juggernaut state."[63]

The law constitutes each man's right to be treated as a distinct individual and, thus, American jurisprudence provides every man with the best chance to defend himself against society's claims. In the Manion trial, Claude Dancer, who has been sent from the Attorney General's office to be the guiding genius of the prosecution, makes Biegler fight even harder. Ultimately, the exchanges between these characters lead the protagonist to scorn his accomplished opponent as an opportunist and a technician, "someone for whom law and justice and freedom is merely a cynical game."[64]

Such a charge makes the issue clear: no one can be a true lawyer who operates only as a stylist in the law, for to do so one must separate oneself from the human emotions and suffering with which the profession has to deal. The aged Parnell, who is content that the presiding judge at the Manion trial possesses a "heart" as well as a "head," insists that understanding human emotions is what makes both lawyers and human beings. He argues that a lack of communication is society's principal flaw: " 'For lack of it our world seems to be running down and dying—we now seem fatally bent on communicating only with robot missiles loaded with cargoes of hate and ruin instead of the human heart and its pent cargo of love.' "[65] Parnell's rumination also touches ironically on the case for he and Biegler significantly misjudge the motives of Mary Pilant, Quill's business partner. While they initially treat her as a hostile witness, they are stunned when Miss Pilant provides the definitive evidence that Quill did, indeed, rape Mrs. Manion. By testifying that she found a pair of Laura's panties in their wash, Mary Pilant, despite her affection for Barney, rises above personal feeling to acquiesce in the larger demands of the law. Biegler and Parnell marvel at what has happened because they appreciate the emotional cost involved: Claude Dancer (whose name suggests his shiftiness) remains forever blind to this perception because he is all "head" and no "heart." To the clever lawyer from Lansing, Mary Pilant represents only a monkey wrench thrown into his beautifully constructed case.

Although *Anatomy of a Murder* contains numerous interrogation scenes between Biegler, his clients and the often hostile eyewitnesses to the shooting, the novel's plot establishes reasonable grounds for Lieutenant Manion's actions; indeed, Barney Quill's rape and the enraged husband's murderous act are both born of compulsive needs. The novel never loses its ironic bite because its characters do not markedly change due to their experiences. Traver's case seems more "real" than most fictional murder stories if only because its details are sordid and its concerns are ones not of identity (who done it?) but of legal motive (was there a reasonable doubt?). This quality even attaches to the conclusion of the novel when Lieutenant Manion, who has been acquitted because the jury accepted the argument that a man can know the moral consequences of an action and yet be compelled to act against his rational (better) judgment, makes the only payment to Biegler that he ever intends to. As the court clears, a bailiff returns the murder weapon to Manion, and:

The Lieutenant blinked his eyes and quickly drew back. "Give it to my lawyer," he said. "As a memento. . . I—I guess maybe he's earned it."

I found myself standing holding with two fingers the gun that had killed Barney Quill. "Thanks," I said uncertainly, gingerly dropping it in my brief case.[66]

While the symbolism seems fairly obvious in that Biegler has taken possession of the weapon because, as a lawyer with a heart, he is the only one with enough moral sense to be its guardian, the more apparent irony is that Manion has once more passed the buck. The gun, which seems worthless to the Lieutenant, represents the majesty of the law and makes it an appropriate reward for Traver's leading man.

* * *

In the 1950s businessmen were held in greater esteem than they are today. Eisenhower's Cabinet of 1953, "eight millionaires and a plumber," epitomized the reverence accorded to business, while films like *Executive Suite* (1954) and *Woman's World* (1954) and a popular television drama, Rod Serling's *Patterns* (1955), dramatized public interest in corporate boardrooms. While the movies melodramatically suggested that only the man backed by a good woman could rise to the top of the corporate ladder, Serling's play and Sloan Wilson's *The Man in the Gray Flannel Suit* offered more thoughtful views of business. Indeed, the novel provided an enduring phrase for the harried commuters who manned Manhattan's towers while insisting that a man's career must not be all-consuming. Tom Rath, the protagonist, must adjust to moving from a transient middle-class life and assimilate this alteration to the larger values of family and love. While he struggles within the corporate world, Tom's need to become ethical ultimately overshadows any desire he has to make as much money as possible. In making restitution for his past Wilson's protagonist forges an even stronger emotional link between himself and his wife, Betsy, by restoring his own pride and by bringing her out from the shadow of inordinate greed. To many later commentators Tom Rath has come to represent the 1950s' uneasy acceptance of conformity, evidence that all "organization men" were not cheerfully acquiescent in their pecking orders. Such an emphasis distorts Wilson's novel into an anti-business tirade when, if anything, it is staunchly reverent toward those at the top.

The plot of *The Man in the Gray Flannel Suit* revolves around Tom Rath's concern with success. As a speechwriter and subsequent personal assistant to Ralph Hopkins, the head of United Broadcasting, Rath operates at the pinnacle of corporate power; yet, he decides that such status, which has come to him almost involuntarily, does not represent what he most wants from life. Wilson's central character ultimately prefers working at a lower level and being a happy family man. As Tom tells Betsy, geniuses must be totally consumed by their work and Hopkins, the personification of the workaholic, possesses just such a fanatical drive. As this individual's personal assistant, Tom must be as dogged about business, and it is this obligation which the protagonist cannot accept.

"I like Hopkins—I admire him. But even if I could, I wouldn't want to be like him.

I don't want to get so wrapped up in a broadcasting business that I don't care about anything else. And I'm afraid that in asking me to be his personal assistant, he's trying to make me be like him, and I know that's foolish. I never could do it, and I don't want to."[67]

Tom Rath does not want the burdens of success, the unending toil of being a corporation head or the necessity to make his individuality and the company become synonymous. By this point the main character has seen enough of life at the top to realize its demands and, given the heyday of Eisenhower prosperity, he can afford to be choosy.

Tom's dilemma is that he can tell Betsy what he dares not tell Hopkins, since business etiquette demands that one not be ungrateful about a promotion. In time, however, the protagonist's anxiety gives way and he finally confronts Hopkins with his doubts. When the older man asks if Tom really wants to "learn" the business, after a late night meeting at Hopkins' apartment (a standard operating procedure for this tycoon who uses it to disarm others' resistance), Rath launches into a set speech that proclaims the novel's central theme.

"I don't think I do want to learn the business. I don't think I'm the kind of guy who should try to be a big executive.... I don't think I have the willingness to make the sacrifices. I don't want to give up the time.... I want the money.... But I'm just not the kind of guy who can work evenings and week ends and all the rest of it forever.... I'm not the kind of person who can get all wrapped up in a job—I can't get myself convinced that my work is the most important thing in the world. I've been through one war. Maybe another one's coming. If one is, I want to be able to look back and figure I spent the time between wars with my family, the way it should have been spent."[68]

The character's desires reveal his profound fear about the world and his deep-seated distrust of success; there is too much chance that his world will be blown to bits for him to devote any more time than is necessary to making a living. Tom Rath fears that the world has gone mad and that he must squeeze as much pleasure as possible out of it while there is still time. Ironically, Tom's wish to be a smaller cog still commits him to the psychology of a career and to the status (and hours) that go with being salaried.

Indeed, Wilson's protagonist wants the best of both worlds: a secure financial position with executive duties which still allow him to leave the job behind at (presumably) no later than 5 p.m. Tom Rath will trade money for time, status for an unencumbered weekend. He convinces Hopkins to offer him a less hectic position as director of the publicity campaign for mental health—the project that initially drew Tom away from his deadend job with a philanthropic foundation. While he persuades Hopkins on "practical" grounds, Tom soothes Betsy and restores an emotional closeness with his wife when he convinces her that he cannot play in the big leagues of business. To reestablish the harmony of their marriage Tom divulges the secret which has haunted him since the end of World War II. In telling of his Italian mistress and his illegitimate son, Tom's feelings of guilt for abandoning the child, receiving news of the mother's destitution, and not sending money overseas, come to the surface. Since he has inherited his grandmother's estate and intends to build a subdivision on it, he decides to make restitution; indeed, sending such money finally provides an almost spiritual aura for the protagonist.

Betsy's initial reaction sends her out alone in the family car (a clunker that breaks down) to think and salve her pride. When she returns she knows Tom is right and that they must support the unseen child. Thus, they can face the future confidently and happily; and, although Tom promises to tell Betsy eventually about what he did in the war (heretofore a matter he had always kept from her) because of their new intimacy, it is simply being together that he now savors.

> "I want you to be able to talk to me about the war. It might help us to understand each other. Did you really kill seventeen men?"
> "Yes."
> "Do you want to talk about it now?"
> "No. It's not that I want to and can't—it's just that I'd rather think about the future. About getting a new car and driving up to Vermont with you tomorrow."
> "That will be fun. It's not an insane world. At least, our part of it doesn't have to be."
> "Of course not."[69]

Tom has freed himself from the psychological burden of his past because having to choose between running for the top and accepting a less highly-charged position has precipitated a change in his emotional economy. For he and Betsy being happy now means going away in a new car. While Wilson's protagonist has suffered, the materialistic solution to such agony underlines Rath's adherence to community values. Like most of the audience, he wants to enjoy the creature comforts of an opulent time without constantly remembering either the historical or the personal costs of such an existence.

For Tom and Betsy Rath life's difficulties are problems whose solutions offer a release from having to ever contemplate them again. Their pervasive belief in justice—that society can and does restore a balance between individuals—enables them to dismiss more tragic possibilities. The novel ends with a ringing confirmation of such idealism when Tom and Betsy mutually arrange with a local judge for a trust fund for Tom's wartime offspring. Bernstein, who has already adjudicated a dispute over Tom's inheritance, and who suffers from ulcers whenever he confronts a difficult legal question, is initially taken aback by Tom's request. However, just as he was surprised earlier when the protagonist didn't prove to be a slick operator, Bernstein is again startled by the main character. When he discovers that Betsy knows what her husband is doing, the old judge nearly cries.

> "Betsy already knows all about it," Tom said. "She and I are doing this together."
> "You are?" Bernstein said, unable to preserve his professional air of detachment.
> "...I suppose that may be a little unconventional, but to us it seems like simple justice.... What will you charge me for handling the matter?"
> "Nothing," Bernstein said.
> "What?"
> "No charge."
> "Why not?"

Bernstein smiled. "I like what you call 'simple justice,' " he said. "The kind I generally deal with is so complex."

... Bernstein's stomach wasn't aching any more... He saw them bow gravely toward each other as she transferred the bundles to Tom's arms. Then Tom straightened up and apparently said something to her, for suddenly she smiled radiantly, Bernstein smiled too.[70]

This conclusion abounds in upbeat elements for, in addition to the easing of Bernstein's digestive track, the Raths perform symbolic actions that epitomize their new-found existence. The transferring of grocery parcels from Betsy to Tom symbolizes the protagonist's acceptance of responsibility, while his posture implies that he will face the future confidently.

The Raths' earlier conflicts establish the emotional groundwork that justifies this ending. They are initially symbolized by a crack in the living room of their first home, a place they detest after having spent seven years in an "upwardly mobile" subdivision. While the house's exterior denotes its lack of care (Tom apparently doesn't do lawns), the chipped plaster, which was caused when he threw a vase in the heat of argument, appropriately resembles a question mark. Tom must spend his evenings looking at this shape which constantly seems to ask "whither thou?" The Raths are clearly caught in a static situation which is slowly driving them mad. While their budget prevents them from fixing the wall so that the mark becomes a constant reminder of their economic impotence, they remain ambitious enough to want to escape.

"I don't know what's the matter with us," Betsy said one night. "Your job is plenty good enough. We've got three nice kids, and lots of people would be glad to have a house like this. We shouldn't be so *discontented* all the time."

"Of course we shouldn't!" Tom said.

Their words sounded hollow. It was curious to believe that that house with the crack in the form of a question mark on the wall and the ink stains of the wallpaper was probably the end of their personal road. It was impossible to believe. Somehow something would have to happen.[71]

Thus, these characters confront the question, "Is this all there is?", and, in a society where standing still seems disloyal, have nearly abandoned any hope in the future.

Betsy recognizes that such unease represents a goad to force them out of their "prison" into a more successful and, therefore, happier life. When Tom has doubts about developing his inheritance, she emerges as the archetypal capitalist constantly investing in one venture to be able to reinvest in a bigger one, and Tom's lack of enthusiasm infuriates her.

"In the end we might have a hundred thousand dollars and the pick of the new houses for ourselves."

"Dreams of glory," he said. "I've spent my whole life getting over them."

"Look, Tommy.... You know what you are? You're spoiled. You've spent most of your life feeling sorry for yourself... you're licked before you start... you're not really willing to go out and fight for what you want. You came back from the war, and you took an easy job, and we both bellyached all the time because you didn't get more money. And what's more, you're a coward. You're afraid to risk a goddamn thing!"[72]

Betsy's tirade represent an all-too-human response to the feeling that one has finally settled into a life that is little more than a waiting for death. Her positive outlook, which emphasizes that life's problems can be solved, eventually wins Tom away from his more passive view that the difficulties of existence are conditions to be endured.

This philosophic divergence provides the basis for the Raths' disagreements about money and success. Betsy initially drives Tom to seek a better paying job and, after he has made contact with United Broadcasting, Tom then assumes the energetic role. In Betsy's mind enthusiasm separates those who are capable from those who are outstanding; thus, she insists that a successful individual makes his own luck and berates Tom for not trying.

> "It's not just strength," she said. "It's something in you. When you really want something, I don't think anything in the world can stand in your way. That's why you were so damned good in the war."
> "It was luck," he said. "Whether you get out of a war or not is ninety per cent luck."
> "Maybe," she said, "but since you've gotten back, you haven't really wanted much. You've worked hard, but at heart you've never been really trying."[73]

The protagonist must realize that he can determine his own destiny if he will stop believing in fate. Success thus becomes a matter of appearance and motive, and the darker perception found in Arthur Miller's *Death of a Salesman* (1948) that ability and not simply being well-liked counts most in business never surfaces. Just as Willy Loman insisted that successful men "do not whistle in the elevator," so does Betsy berate Tom for being a "wisecracker."

> "I'll bet Hopkins doesn't go around making wisecracks!" she said. "Does he?"
> "No."
> "Nobody does who gets anywhere. You've got to be positive and enthusiastic."
> "How come you know so much all of a sudden about how to get ahead?"
> "I just *know*," she said. "I'm sick of being smart and broke."[74]

While Willy Loman's advice proved naive in Miller's play, Betsy's assault on wit and intellect is eventually vindicated by Tom's success when he quits being cynical. Her advice echoes the popular adage, "if you're so smart, why aren't you rich?", by urging that intelligence must be shaped to serve personal ends, to dissimulate, or, as she tells Tom, to be "naive" if necessary.

Betsy believes she is merely asking Tom to compromise his beliefs so that they can have a future; and Tom convinces himself she is right when he receives an offer from United Broadcasting. In thinking about Ralph Hopkins, the self-made tycoon who runs the media empire, Tom implicitly makes personality central to success.

What did a man have to be like to make so damn much money? It's never just luck that lets them make it, he thought, and it isn't just who they know—I won't let myself fall into the trap of thinking that. Hopkins has got something, something special, or he wouldn't be making two hundred thousand a year. What is it?[75]

While his subsequent exposure to Hopkins demonstrates that a high tolerance for work separates that figure from lesser men, Tom's perception elevates his boss above the vicissitudes of time and place. In typical American fashion, the protagonist wants to dismiss history and family connections in order to proclaim that the successful man manufactures his destiny independently of the forces which mark common men. Thus, in spite of his traumatic war experience, Tom still wants to believe that life centers on a principle more susceptible to human influence than chance.

When Tony Bugala, a young local contractor, proposes a partnership to develop Tom and Betsy's inheritance, Wilson's protagonist, now thinking like a sensible businessman because of the challenge of working at United Broadcasting, realizes: "If you wanted to become really tops in the business, you had to forget the small-time cleverness and play it straight."[76] As a working ethic, doing one's best all the time reflects Tom's idealism; obviously, the shoddiness of a bureaucratized society had not penetrated as deeply into popular consciousness in 1955 as it has in our time. Thus, Rath reflects a society which regards work in a more honorable light; indeed, the individual must seek out difficult tasks to develop his character to the fullest and not simply to "optimize" earnings or status. The therapeutic quality of work also emerges when Betsy plunges into selling their house so they can move away from the nagging question mark on the wall. While she experiences momentary doubts, Betsy feels that the anxieties which age inevitably brings cannot be overcome by the advice of others, such as psychiatrists, but must be faced independently.

The psychiatrist would have an explanation, Betsy thought, but I don't want to hear it. People rely too much on explanations these days, and not enough on courage and action. Why make such a complicated thing out of selling this house? We don't like Greentree Avenue, so we'll move. Tom has a good job, and he'll get his enthusiasm back, and be a success at it. Everything's going to be fine. It does no good to wallow in night thoughts. In God we trust, and that's that.[77]

Betsy's opinion about her individual capacity is hedged by this declaration that there are no panaceas by which to escape one's responsibilities. In effect, she insists that attempting to find hidden motives or complex explanations for existence wastes time and destroys nerve; thus, thought can be stultifying (as she has argued with Tom) while activity can be enervating.

Betsy's emphasis on the active life is shared by Ralph Hopkins, Tom's millionaire boss who is so impressed by a speech Rath writes about mental health that he hires the protagonist to be his personal assistant. Hopkins' public beneficence counterpoints his private life in which his wife lives in the country while he resides in town and his daughter finds existence boring because of not having to struggle for anything. Hopkins' zeal for work never appears as a character flaw, but is instead presented as a necessary attitude for one who is serving a veritable martyrdom to a higher calling, one in which he is doomed to be misunderstood by the less enlightened and less capable souls around him. As network head, Hopkins has his finger on the public pulse so that when his daughter becomes infatuated with a playwright whose work is "over" people's heads he can bring her down a peg or two. Like Betsy Rath, Ralph Hopkins does not subscribe to expert preconceptions about human conduct, and so he urges his daughter to tell her playwright lover: " 'to stop trying to give pat explanations of men and women.... If he had learned that, his play might not have closed down so quickly.' " When the girl objects that the play failed because the public lacks understanding, her pragmatic parent, as the voice of experience and wisdom, educates her about popular taste.

"If you want to know what the public wants, I'll tell you: great art on the extremely rare occasions when it's available, but no phony art—they'd rather have good honest blood and thunder. The public doesn't like fakers, and neither do I. If you want to meet some playwrights, tell me, and I'll get some good ones up here for you."[78]

For Hopkins, the public judges art properly—a potentially self-serving argument since, in the television business, one hardly knows whether people like what they watch or simply enjoy what is put before them. Hopkins obviously embodies enough of the merchant (e.g. the customer is always right) to defend such an aesthetic theory. Again, he is like Betsy Rath in arguing a position on the bases of motive and sincerity; and, also like her, he shows no awareness that his formula contains loose generalizations (how, for example, does one detect phony art?).

Tom Rath represents a wish-fulfillment on the older man's part, for Hopkins clearly wants an heir to whom he can leave the business. Since his own family has not supplied such a successor, Hopkins must seek him within the company; and he hires Tom in the hope that he has found the worthy man at last. Hopkins' concern about Tom's future and the benevolence he extends when the younger man finds that high-level corporate career is not for him mark the network head as a special person. In providing a more appropriate career for Rath with the corporation, Hopkins appears as a kindly figure who combines business sense with human feelings, but his monomaniacal nature surfaces too. There can be no doubt about Hopkins' zealous dedication when he tells Tom: " 'Somebody has to do the big jobs!... This world was built by men like me! To really do a job, you have to live it body and soul! You people who just give half your mind to your work are riding on our backs!' "[79] Since he quickly regains his composure and assures Tom that deciding not to endure life at the top is wise, Hopkins remains ultimately benevolent for he protects his wife, his daughter and the protagonist. While such largesse is offered voluntarily, the question as to why these individuals need Hopkins' guidance is never raised. Perhaps being a business success doesn't finally supply enough emotional sustenance so that a man can be satisfied as a husband and a father, nor enough attractive situations to sustain the interest of those with real ability (Tom Rath). In either event, Hopkins' views are not seriously challenged by the other characters so that his loneliness implies a monastic discipline rather than individual idiosyncrasy.

His gray flannel business suit symbolizes Tom Rath's position at the beginning of the novel for, like hordes of others, he is simply one small cog in an enormous machine, a face in the crowd. When he goes for an initial interview at United Broadcasting, the protagonist proclaims his clothing, which is duplicated by the man who greets him, to be the "uniform" of the times; thus, Tom has left one army only to ease himself (subconsciously, as it were) into another. As a further reflection of modern man, Wilson's main character perceives his life as composed of compartments that do not overlap. Although he feels that these separate compartments are unequal in value, Tom errs in thinking they do not influence each other; and so he must learn that achievement in one area (business) can enable him to bring other areas into a working harmony. Initially, however, Tom is adamant in believing:

> There were really four completely unrelated worlds in which he lived.... There was the crazy, ghost-ridden world of his grandmother and dead parents. There was the isolated, best-not-remembered world in which he had been a paratrooper. There was the matter-of-fact, opaque-glass-brick-partitioned world of places like the United Broadcasting Company.... And there was the entirely separate world populated by Betsy and Janey and Barbara and Pete, the only one of the four worlds worth a damn. There must be some way in which the four worlds were related, he thought, but it was easier to think to them as entirely divorced from one another.[80]

Such thinking foreshadows schizophrenia and, while Tom remains sane and sober, he must achieve a better integration of these realms if he is to enjoy any worthwhile happiness.

Another serious shortcoming that experience corrects is Tom's aversion to responsibility: his reticence about the land development scheme reflects how he has internalized his war experiences. Tom is uncertain when dealing with his grandmother's estate because past experiences have produced a rationalization that the birth of his illegitimate son and his constant reminiscing about Maria " 'really wasn't my fault.... It was no one's fault. I am not to blame.' "[81] This evasive tactic, which contradicts Tom's own recognition that the past constantly impinges on the present, must be overcome if the protagonist is to become a useful member of society. Tom needs to realize that the bliss he felt with Maria derived from his being fully engaged with existence. By clinging to the belief that contingencies made those days the happiest of his life, Tom shortchanges Betsy by regarding her as too naive to understand what he has experienced. He even thinks of her as someone whose views of the world are still what they were in 1939 and, in so doing, saves himself from the difficulties of telling her the truth. He maintains that a decision he made shortly after returning home must be sustained for the rest of his life for, when Betsy asked if he had much to tell about the war, Tom gladly lapsed into silence.

Betsy had never been insensitive. She had not pursued the matter, and with gratitude he had felt he would never have to tell her anything about the war, not about Maria. . .not about anything. It would be better that way, he had thought, far better for both of them.

She had not seemed to mind his reticence. . . . As he listened to her, he had gradually realized that here in this pretty girl sitting across the room from him in a pair of silk pajamas was himself as of 1939. Here was a kind of antique version of himself, unchanged.[82]

Tom's intellectual errors are that the past can be successfully buried and that individuals remain the same; indeed, such fixed entities and personalities represent a dream which belies the dynamic of life itself.

The lessons Tom learns from Hopkins' high-pressure world make him accept responsibility while celebrating the author's praise of business and its leaders. Hopkins advises Tom that a successful career always taxes the individual to his utmost: naturally, a delicate balance must be achieved, but ambition directs a man to confront constant challenges: " 'A young man has to get started right. The ideal thing is to find a job which always expects a little more than you can deliver, but not so much that you get snowed under. A job should always keep you straining at the limits of your abilities. That's the way men learn.' "[83] Hopkins' optimism, which implies that of the author, seems old-fashioned now when people subscribe more readily to the Peter Principle (one rises to the level of one's inefficiency) or Parkinson's Law (work expands so as to fill available time). The basis of the assembly line—that each man can be replaced easily because the work process has been simplified in the name of efficiency—dominates business and popular thinking far more than such dynamic individualism as that of Hopkins. While Tom Rath initially doubts that a man's character is shaped by his work, he gradually becomes convinced that business is where men find themselves. When writing the mental health speech, a process whose numerous rewrites become a nightmare to Tom, the protagonist wavers between being subservient and candid with Hopkins. Once again, Betsy snaps Tom out of a dilemma for, although she hates the subservient appearance, she still wants him to succeed as both a man and a wage earner.

"You looked disgusting! You looked just like the kind of guy you always used to hate. The guy with all the answers. The guy who has no respect for himself or for anyone else!"

"What do you want me to do?" he asked quietly. "Do you want me to go in there tomorrow and tell Hopkins I think his speech is a farce?"

"I don't care what you tell him, but I don't like the idea of your becoming a cheap cynical yes-man, and being so self-satisfied and analytical about it. You never used to be like that."[84]

Thus, Tom Rath must discover that his ideas are worth fighting for, whether they concern his marriage or his employer's speech; life is too short for the individual to wallow in cynicism or reticence.

Chapter 13

"Everybody decides for themself...
and always wrong."

James Jones has never been praised for his style, yet *From Here to Eternity* (1951) represents the most intellectually challenging novel in our survey. While Jones flatters the outward requirements of bestselling fiction by detailing much action and sex, his characters finally challenge the melodramatic assumptions—home, family, romantic love—which underlie most of the other works we have encountered. While *From Here to Eternity* is often conceded to be Jones' masterpiece, the work seemingly suffers from a kind of benign neglect, occupying a respectable but unread niche in American literary history (and thus consigned to what Leon Trotsky described, in an admittedly different context, as the "dustbin of history"). As an outstanding instance of a writer utilizing the formulas of popular fiction to question the central assumptions of his audience, Jones' novel subverts middle-class values not in a political or a doctrinal way but as a work of art. The novel's many characters blend to provide its final incidents—Prewitt's death, Warden's acceptance of his being a "lifer," the ironic conversation between Karen Holmes and Lorene on shipboard—with great symbolic weight. Its quality uggests that the 1950s, despite the supposed calm of Eisenhower prosperity, contained a more serious side, even in its bestsellers.

A grimly realistic tone dominates from the outset for, on one level, the novel reads like an "insider's" chronicle of the ennui that is day-to-day military life. The setting of Pearl Harbor inevitably calls up memories, for anyone who experienced the news of December 7, 1941, can generally recall what he was doing at that moment (as those in a later generation can recollect their activities when they heard that John F. Kennedy had been shot). At a time when most Americans still regarded World War II and the men who fought it as inspired by a sense of duty that transcended a sense of self, *From Here to Eternity* presented the Army as an institution which all but prevented victory. Jones' soldiers are but small cogs in a large machine (society itself) that is permanently at war with nonconformity and creativity at all levels. This struggle centers on Prewitt and, to a lesser degree, Warden because they still believe in individual dignity and rights in a world where such notions have become antiquated. Jones' protagonists find themselves in a time when their personalities no longer fit: they are the modern-day equivalents of the cowboy heroes who, like Jack Schaefer's Shane, render themselves anachronistic and so must either move or die. Prewitt and Warden struggle against such a fate and, in this naturally uncqual contest, their defeats prove their humanity. Jones' two leading characters operate out of idealistic motives—it is more important to go down fighting than to survive through losing one's sense of self. Neither character is naive however, for they would agree: " 'Life in time takes every maidenhead, even if it has to dry it up; it does not matter how the owner wants to keep it.' "[1] While growing older forces most individuals to acquiesce in the way things are, Jones' principals cannot cease struggling for their beliefs; indeed, like the mythical Sisyphus condemned to an absurd task for eternity, Prewitt and Warden rebel to prove that freedom still exists.

Jones uses geography to delineate social class and so the larger analogy, in which the Army represents humanity, is made clear. When Prewitt transfers to G Company he enrages Captain Holmes by refusing to box. Holmes then orders Prewitt to do a double-time stint with a full field pack in mid-afternoon; and, as he rises into the hills above the base, the beleaguered Prewitt looks down on the golf course to see officers' wives and the comparatively luxurious life they lead. Jones' heroes are not found on the golf course, a place of privilege, and this symbolic equation becomes even clearer when, after Pearl Harbor has been bombed and G Company ordered into shore defense, Prewitt, who has been AWOL for weeks, attempts to rejoin the outfit. Attired in a sports shirt, he tries to cross the golf course, now guarded by MPs who, naturally, kill him and so destroy a better soldier than most of them. Prewitt does not resist or cry out when the searchlights find him, for he accepts his fate as consistent with his own sense of military obligation. He has gambled and lost and willingly pays the price of dying ignominiously and silently in a sand trap while his pursuers wonder why he didn't give up or try to dodge their lights. In symbolic terms, the society which has repressed Prewitt because of his creative spirit has finally triumphed over him: its subordinates (the MPs) have destroyed the protagonist on the golf course (the appropriate environmental symbol of the ruling class). Jones' theme is that a society which creates excess and waste (by stymying those individuals whose capacities far outweigh any tasks they encounter) must destroy those creative spirits which do not conform.

The final meeting between Prewitt and Warden further reveals Jones' scheme of values. Warden has been agonizing over whether or not to become an officer, a career Karen Holmes wants him to pursue but one which repels him because he equates officers with incompetence. At the same time, the top sergeant must deal with Prewitt, who though AWOL, is still being carried as present on the Company roster. Warden has broken Army rules because he believes that Prewitt, like himself, is a real soldier; however, the Sergeant must now either convince the wayward soldier to return or end the charade. Prewitt, who murdered a sadistic stockade guard, Fatso Judson, and was injured in the process, finds himself torn between his love for Lorene and his commitment to duty. In their conversation, Warden talks tough because he cares for Prewitt.

"Don't kid yourself," Warden said viciously. "I wouldn't of done it for you. I wouldn't have carried you one single day. You were a fuckup when you got in this company and you're still one and you'll always be one. I don't know why the fuck I'm down here bothering to talk to you right now."

"Because yu're ashamed of being an officer," Prew grinned.

"I've never been ashamed of anything I ever did in my life," Warden snorted. "Includin that. Shame aint a spontaneous emotion; shame is an induced emotion. A man who knows his own mind dont know what shame is."

"What book did you read that in?"[2]

Prewitt represents Warden's conscience; for these men being a good soldier (and so having an identity) precludes joining the officer class, even if it means giving up a Karen Holmes. Thus, Jones' characters fulfill themselves not through love and marriage but through dedication to craft and loyalty to other true soldiers: professionalism does not center on doing good for others (e.g. family, as in *The Man in the Gray Flannel Suit*, or society, as in *Not as a Stranger* or *The Blackboard Jungle*) but in remaining true to one's self. Individuality can only be established by those who deny the entanglements—love, home, status—society provides; for Prewitt and Warden freedom resides in never become a willing cog in society's machine (as Warden seems in danger of becoming until Prewitt reminds the top sergeant of his real nature).

While Robert E. Lee Prewitt becomes briefly compromised because of Lorene, he never seriously doubts that he is a "thirty-year man." Prewitt loves the Army, while its institutional-minded operators hate him; indeed in his devotion to duty and craft one sees the courage and loyalty so conspicuously absent in most of the other troops and officers. Prewitt lives in a splendid isolation for, although surrounded by friends and lovers, he consistently reflects on the basic loneliness of existence. In cultivating such separateness the character emerges as the most individualistic American hero of the 1950s, for, unlike such popular alienated figures as those portrayed by James Dean and Marlon Brando in the movies, Jones' protagonist never doubts the validity of certain actions (the art of playing the bugle, the need to be a good soldier). Prewitt refuses to become a victim or to blame others for his troubles, implying that a man's fate arises from choice and not from luck. Despite the often sensational circumstances which surround him—whorehouses, the stockade, murder and, finally, his own violent death—Prewitt remains a moralist constantly questioning his own and others' conduct. He feels an occasional need to meditate and so, at one point, he sits beneath a tree "because there are times every man must be alone and in the squadroom there is no aloneness, only loneliness."[3] Prewitt's distinction here emphasizes the barren nature of the Army (and so society) by implying that one is always in a "lonely crowd" there.

On a busy night at the brothel, Prewitt listens to Lorene's entreaties that he finish quickly or "take a raincheck" and decides:

...this modern MAN with so much to be grateful for, with the heritage of the ages in his hands, could hear his shoes scraping scraping against the gilt-flaking bed frame like one of the higher-priced more accurate metronomes reminding him not to get the clean sheet muddy—this creature was not even HAPPY! Just because he could not get outside his plexiglass space suit, his sanitary all-purpose all-weather space suit, just because he was not *known*, just because he did *know*, just because he could not touch another human soul.[4]

The protagonist's awareness of the limits of human communication—the entire scene suggests that even romantic love is an illusion that the strong need to recognize as such—precludes Prewitt's ever being happy in any conventional way. His outlook, which is ironically juxtaposed to Lorene's bourgeois dream of comfortable respectability in her hometown after making enough money in Hawaii, rejects the familiar middle-class faith in Mr. Right, the "one and only." The central characters of *From Here to Eternity* are disappointed in love not because they lack emotions but because they cannot sustain its necessary illusions. Prewitt and Warden, while themselves hardly embodiments of perfection, recognize their own fallibilities.

> "A mans got to decide for himself what he has to do," Prew said.
> "Everybody decides for themself," Warden said. "And always wrong."[5]

These characters understand the paradox of any selection—whether of conduct, friend, lover—that such a choice imposes loss, so that one can never make the best choice but only muddle along guided by those compulsions one's personality imposes.

Prewitt's quest for moral clarity compels him to examine what situations imply about society and himself: he obviously refuses to lead what Socrates labelled as the life of a "swine." Prewitt can deplore being a catalyst for others, forcing them to make choices when they would be happy substituting custom for thought; yet, in spite of such regret, the character remains convinced: "it was always better to face things no matter what it cost anybody. He knew that. He believed it. Only in the bad spells did life frighten him with its unbelievable cruelty, its inconceivable injustice, its incredible pointlessness."[6] Existence remains dreadful whether one confronts it or buries it under social or institutional guises; and for Prewitt recognizing life's absurdity means the individual must define himself in ways that preclude evasion. The Army, with its tiresome details and petty intrigues, imposes a test on Jones' characters so that in the course of *From Here to Eternity* Prewitt goes through a kind of "pilgrim's progress" in which trials lead to salvation. Prewitt's lack of what society would label as success establishes that the United States is not the land of opportunity nor of justice, and certainly not, despite any rhetoric to the contrary, the land of individualism. Because he deplores society's hypocrisy, Prewitt fights for underdogs simply because they are more likely to be worthwhile: "This too-ingrained-to-be-forgotten philosophy of life of his had led him, a Southerner, to believe in fighting for the Negroes against the Whites everywhere, because the Negroes were nowhere near the top dog, at least as yet."[7] Prewitt opposes power and privilege no matter where he finds them. Thus, he shares the faith that Steinbeck's Tom Joad held for the oppressed in *The Grapes of Wrath*, albeit, without attributing essential goodness either to them or to himself. Jones' soldier never becomes simply a spokesman against social injustice, for there is more to Prewitt than being a political animal.

His austere nature surfaces early when he transfers out of a company in which he has been the lead bugler and into Company G, where he will only be an infantryman. While Prewitt's buddies cannot comprehend his abandoning such a soft position, the character believes that, despite his abiding love for the bugle, remaining in a position where he is indulged will ultimately corrupt him. Thus, he defines existence as a matter of continuously challenging oneself and so avoiding simply waiting for death. To retain his purity, both as an artist and a man, Prewitt must abandon the bugle for the trials of Company G. He refuses to imitate Red, who sees the Army in terms of easy duty and time to "goof off."

> The reason was, he wanted to be a bugler. Red could play a bugle well because Red was not a bugler. It was really very simple, so simple that he was surprised he had not seen it standing there before. He had to leave the Bugle Corps because he was a bugler. Red did not have to leave it. But he had to leave, because he wanted most of all to stay.[8]

Although he is part of an impersonal organization, Prewitt resists the institutional mentality which would label him a success in the eyes of the enlisted men (who strive for easy duty) or the officers (who see obedience and rewards as proper goals). To preserve his love for the purity of the art of the bugle he abandons his beloved instrument to avoid becoming a "professional" doing a job without any strong feelings about it. For Prewitt, success and happiness represent illusions which can only be attained and sustained by compromise: America will inevitably demand to be served by men like Red who manipulate the system and accept its rewards as obvious proofs of their contentment, while men like Prewitt, who believe that one's private life cannot be compromised, will be shunted aside or destroyed.

Prewitt does not adapt to others (even to Warden whom he respects) and in eschewing conventional conversation and personality becomes a pariah in Company G. His outspoken honesty about himself and others means that, like Dostoyevsky's Prince Myshkin in *The Idiot* who brought society's wrath down upon his head by always speaking the truth, Prewitt is doomed. When pressed to become a boxer, the protagonist avoids the easy way out (merely delaying his decision would have precluded any confrontation for months) because: "He was not honest enough to dupe them, when he himself refused to be their dupe. He had not the makings of that honest man to whom success comes naturally."[9] Irony only makes the point clearer, for like many another misunderstood figure, Prewitt suffers at the hands of those whom his conduct unsettles and, finally, infuriates. The character's inability to adjust recurs time after time. When he breaks up with Violet, the girl he spends all his weekends with while a bugler (for enlisted men's wisdom has it that a "shack job" is superior to going to a brothel), Prewitt reflects on the nature of love. As he leaves the girl, he feels more affection for her than ever before; yet Prewitt's honesty prevents him from rushing back.

But thats not love, he thought, thats not what she wants, nor what any of them want, they do not want you to find yourself in them, they want instead that you should lose yourself in them....

And it seemed to him then that every human was always looking for himself, in bars, in railway trains, in offices, in mirrors, in love, especially in love, for the self of him that is there, someplace, in every other human. Love was not to give oneself, but find oneself, describe oneself.[10]

Prewitt sees love as a means to explore the self, while conventional wisdom has it that this emotion consists of giving and taking so that different psychological drives are brokered (as, for example, in the novels of Francis Parkinson Keyes in which females submit to male wishes so as to enjoy domesticity and respectability). The novel comes full circle when Maylon Stark, Company G's chief cook who sees doing one's duty well as an imperative, tries to advise Prewitt. Stark wants the young soldier to be a permanent part of his staff and ultimately berates Prewitt for turning down such an offer.

"And, now, when I'm offering you a good angle, one that will get you back onto safe ground, you're turnin it down. It just aint smart, it aint even sensible, because thats the only way anybody can get along in this world."

"I guess I just aint sensible," Prew said. "But I hate to believe that thats the only way a man can get along. Because if it is, then what a man is dont mean anything at all. A man himself is nothing."[11]

Prewitt clings to his belief in merit and quality, while Stark urges that conformity is the only way to survive; thus, to Jones' hero, getting along must ultimately take a back seat to his longings for justice and more genuine people. Prewitt would rather struggle to make his self-perception actual than compromise and have to agree that life is only "getting along."

While only a handful of men ever discipline themselves sufficiently to attain real understanding of a craft (as Prewitt does with the bugle), the people and things an individual loves are weaknesses that finally compromise him. Preem, who has been replaced by Stark as mess Sergeant, urges this paradox about strength being weakness when he tells his successor:

"But whenever a man likes somethin, he caint take cover.... If you love the kitchen like I love the kitchen, than you ought to get out of it and do straight duty.... That way you're safe, you'll be a success then, you'll get the ratings and you'll keep them, because you wont have no weak spot where they can hurt you."[12]

While these remarks amplify Prewitt's decision to transfer, Preem's advice suggests that if survival requires accepting what one hates then, inevitably, the individual will come to hate himself (a theme Jones repeats with Corporal Bloom, a boxer in Company G who commits suicide because of the empty existence he has chosen in order to "get along"). Stark resembles Prewitt and Warden in his love of work and his desire that things not merely get done but be resolved in the most efficient ways. Just as Prewitt plays the bugle as it is meant to be played (without any of the showy gestures designed to awe the audience) and Warden runs Company G so that a minimum of friction is produced between those who are needed (Prewitt) and those who command (Holmes), so does Stark exhibit his mastery in the kitchen. When Prewitt is assigned there, Stark protects him from a bullying assistant cook and then helps him with the dirtiest job. Thus, Stark proves to be a genuine leader, one who guides by example rather than by words, and his conduct brings about a shock of recognition in Prewitt. When Stark grabs "the spatula and began to scrape one of the worst ones with the deftness and economy of a great kitchen stylist.... Prew could only watch admiringly, feeling warmer inside now than he had felt for a long time."[13] This capacity to recognize genuine talent represents the only worthwhile tribute one good man can pay to another; yet, in a society that dismisses individual qualities and lauds group impersonality, such recognitions are anathema. Neither Prewitt nor Stark demonstrates any envy, unlike their society which is run by "second-raters" (Holmes and his cronies) who fear competent men like the ex-bugler and the cook.

Prewitt's belief in giving one's best to one's calling emerges in a conversation with two homosexuals from whom Angelo Maggio is hoping to wheedle money. When one of these characters, Tommy, tells Prewitt that he never puts his own name on the books he writes (for that would be beneath his sense of serious literature) Jones's protagonist is mystified. After suggesting that Tommy probably never gets drunk (an implication that the character never truly engages with life), Prewitt declares:

"I wouldnt play a bugle call unless I was proud of it.... Thats one thing I got, see? If I did do it, it would never be the same again. I'd never have it any more."

"Oh," Tommy smiled. "A bugler. We've got an artist in our midst, Hal."

"No," Prew said. "Only a bugler. But I don't even bugle any more. And you'll never write no book. You only want to talk about it."[14]

While Jones shares the popular 1950s' aversion to homosexuals in his portrayal of Hal and Tommy as cowards easily manipulated by Angelo and Prewitt, a particular intellectual affectation is his real target here. Prewitt believes that art consists in the doing and not in the telling, so that being false to one's craft (as Tommy is by supposedly writing junk) besmirches one's identity or soul. Thus, a man defines himself by what he does, how well he does it, and how willingly he gives it up when it brings him the corruption of success; and all these attitudes are contradicted by Tommy who has accepted giving the public "what it wants."

While most men never find anything to be passionate about save perhaps the bitch-goddess success, Prewitt has found his spiritual home in the Army, not in the institution that victimizes him but in those men within it who exhibit competence and courage (Stark, Warden). On the novel's opening page Prewitt looks out over a quadrangle and reflects: "Somewhere along the line...these things have become your heritage. You are multiplied by each sound that you hear. And you cannot deny them, without denying with them the purpose of your existence. Yet now, he told himself, you are denying them, by renouncing the place that they have given you."[15] Prewitt believes that his past has imposed a loyalty to the present, even though his momentary doubts about transferring are quickly made real by the treatment he receives from Holmes and from sycophants like Ike Gavrilovitch, an inarticulate drillmaster to whom the Captain's words are law, and to whom Prewitt is an object to be worn down. Although the Army "allowed" the protagonist to play "Taps" at Arlington, he must obey his own urge to be more human than its institutionalism (whether playing the bugle or boxing for Company G) will permit. His own feelings about military duty are best expressed when, after hearing about the December 7 bombing, he tells Lorene he must go back to his outfit. The girl combines outrage and distress at what she perceives to be sheer folly.

> "What do you want to go back to the Army for?" she cried, getting her breath. "What did the Army ever do for you? besides beat you up, and treat you like scum, and throw you in jail like a criminal? What do you want to go back to that for?"
> "What do I want to go back for?" Prewitt said wonderingly. "I'm a soldier."[16]

The protagonist realizes a duty to himself which must be performed; indeed, if he were to follow Lorene's arguments, Prewitt would become merely another "success" carefully calculating the profit or advantage to be derived from each and every situation. His own self-image is at stake here for if he fails to go back, then he is simply another hypocrite with values as rhetorical as Tommy's affected statements about writing.

Since he is determined to prove his spirit cannot be contained by anyone or anything, Prewitt deliberately takes reckless chances to attain what he hopes will be greater pleasures. As he prepares to go on leave and resume his budding romance with Lorene, Jones' hero decides he needs more money to buy all of his prostitute girlfriend's available time. In the gambling tents, where many another enlisted man tries to acquire the brass ring of temporary riches, Prewitt's natural excitement prevents his operating rationally.

> He didn't need to win the next one. What he had from the first was plenty. But he had promised himself two hands, not one, so he stayed in. But he did not win the second hand, Warden won it, and he had dropped $40 which left him only about a hundred and now he felt he needed the second win before he dropped out so he stayed in. But he did not win the third hand either, or the fourth, nor did he win the fifth. He dropped clear down to less than $50, before he finally won another one.[17]

Such recklessness (he soon loses all his money) demonstrates the extent to which the protagonist will go to remain free; even though he desperately wants to be with Lorene, he falls victim to trying to win one more big hand because he cannot calculate on the level of tiny pleasures. By operating in such an either/or fashion Prewitt is again at odds with sober, middle-class temperaments; indeed, his conduct emerges as heroic by virtue of its very excesses for he is struggling to be something more than another bourgeois in a culture which prizes security and success. Prewitt finally, like Dostoyevsky's famous underground man, acts irrationally simply to prove that society's "explanations" cannot circumscribe the human personality.

In the stockade Prewitt comes to hate Fatso Judson, the sadistic bully who, in doing whatever his superiors command, never shows any regrets about the systematic beatings he delivers. Prewitt feels Judson has sold out to become, as the tormentor of Maggio and countless others, the epitome of success, security and corruption. Prewitt cannot excuse the guard as just another cog in the machine, just another individual doing what social necessity imposes, and so he pledges to kill Judson because another convict, Berry, has been beaten to death. In the hero's moral philosophy, every man is solely responsible for what he does or agrees to do, and there can be no excuse that the individual (e.g. Judson), in acquiescing to society's wishes, has somehow been absolved of his actions. "But he could not blame the system, because the system was not anything, it was only a kind of accumulation of everybody, and you could not blame everybody, not unless you wanted the blame to become diluted into a meaningless term, a just nothing."[18] In our century, with its Nazi officials pleading duty above conscience, Prewitt exemplifies an older, clearer morality which insists men must judge personally the actions performed by individuals and not by abstract forces, so that the need for corrective redress still exists. Because Prewitt feels that a causeless cause is absurd, he cannot easily attribute someone like Judson to the "system." That American intellectuals and academics flocked to French existentialism in the 1950s and dismissed Jones and his obviously alienated though moral hero would suggest that prophets are often ignored elsewhere than in Mecca (a condition which is, perhaps, further reflected in Jones' fifteen-year exile in Paris 1958-1973 after the critical reception of *Some Came Running* in 1957). In killing Fatso Judson, Prewitt proves that he will not subscribe to the equivocal doctrine that "no one is to blame."

Milt Warden has learned to barter his efficiency for a secure place in the Army's hierarchy. He takes great, if not excessive, pride in running Company G's day-to-day affairs to suit himself. At thirty-four, he has achieved a precarious equilibrium between his hatred of officers and his need to dominate the enlisted ranks. Warden sees his superiors and his subordinates as equally capable of "fucking up"; however, those in command cause problems due to social biases while those who take orders make mistakes out of human weakness. Thus, Warden can despise but obey Captain Holmes, while admiring but chastising Prewitt. Falling in love with Karen Holmes and considering becoming an officer forces Warden to be even more confounded than he is normally. The sergeant despises traditional American middle-class values and, as he tells Karen, choosing to become "brass" would be selling out.

"All my life, from the time my goddam brother became a priest, I've fought their beef-eating middle-class assurance. I fought everything it stood for. I've made myself stand for everything they were against.

"Who do you think it was put Hitler up? The workers? No, it was the same middleclass.

Who do you think gave the Communists Russia? The peasants? No, the Commissars....
I've stood up for me Milt Warden as a man, and I've made a place for myself in it, by
myself, where I can be myself, without brownnosing any man, and I've made them like it."[19]

Unfortunately, the sergeant has nowhere—be it a place or a profession—
to which he can permanently escape and so he remains vulnerable and
incapable of lasting happiness. The best Warden can achieve is control
of Company G's inner workings, a condition that derives partly from Captain
Holmes' disinterest and so can shift radically despite anything Warden does.
In proclaiming his independence, Warden occupies a place in a long line
of isolated American heroes from Cooper's Natty Bumpo to the innumerable
heroes of Western movies. The major difference is that Warden has no
avenue of action to express his character; indeed, like the very society he
castigates, the sergeant proves better at hating than at creating better
conditions.

Warden lacks Prewitt's tough-minded honesty, for the older man
believes illusions are necessary to sustain life. In a drunken moment he
begins to analyze the "disease" of romantic love but soon realizes that such
conjecture is worse than useless. Warden's divided spirit comes clearly to
the surface when, while anguishing about becoming an officer or giving
up Karen, he bitterly reflects: " 'If a man could just hang onto one illusion
he could still love. The main trouble with being an honest man was that
it lost you all your illusions.' "[20] Once again, the cost of making a choice
looms prominently for, since deep wounds do not heal permanently, Warden
must endure the pain of refusing Karen for the rest of his life. Jones does
not prescribe answers that would lead to happy endings: the individual
either compromises with society (and perhaps reaps its material rewards
at the cost of his own identity) or resists it (and is obliterated like Prewitt
or turned skeptical like Warden). As the top sergeant said earlier, the
individual's choice is "always wrong" because no selection can bring
happiness to a man who wants to preserve his own individuality. In believing
that a man must demonstrate his freedom in order to be truly alive, Warden
initially tries to seduce Karen Holmes because he sees her as the symbolic
paragon of the ruling group and as a means to establish that he is not
completely bound by social rules and fears. Even after he learns that Karen
has been the plaything of numerous enlisted men in order to alleviate her
own boredom, Warden still decides to pursue her because:

Yet above all that he still knew that he would do it, not as vengeance or even retribution,
but as an expression of himself, to regain the individuality that Holmes and all the rest
of them, unknowing, had taken from him. And he understood suddenly why a man who
has lived his whole life working for a corporation might commit suicide simply to express
himself, would foolishly destroy himself because it was the only way to prove his own existence.[21]

The individual proves his identity through passionate (i.e. irrational) acts
that establish his difference from a hypocritical society. Thus, in the world
of Company G, Warden's desire for his commanding officer's wife represents
an acceptable drive. The larger irony, which sustains the novel's sense of

humanity, lies in Warden's finding real love with Karen (and she with him); indeed, even those who know choose badly.

In a jeep with Prewitt, Warden, who has been getting slowly drunk, upbraids Weary, his PFC driver, about the difference between successful soldiers and good ones. Since Prewitt is asleep, he does not hear Warden urge that the ex-bugler is worth several of Weary, who has risen through conforming rather than through ability.

> "Cmere," Warden said and grabbed him by his arm. "Dont you know we got to look out for this man, Weary?" he whispered. "He's the best fuckin soljer in the Compny." He paused thoughtfully. "The *ony* fuckin soljer in the Compny," he amended.
> "What is this?" Weary said. "A mutual backslapping society I stumbled into?"
> "We got to take care of him while we can, see?" The Warden told him urgently. "This man may not be with us for long, and we got to take caref this man."[22]

Warden functions not only as a beneficent authority figure (in keeping with his surname) but also to foreshadow Prewitt's demise for in his recognition that the private will not last long, the top sergeant reemphasizes the opposition between a conformist society and the isolated individual. After Prewitt kills Judson and flees to Lorene's home in the hills, Warden, after an extended and traumatic vacation with Karen, returns and decides he will protect the deserter because he believes Prewitt to be a natural thirty-year man who "couldn't" quit. While the passage of time erodes this deception, Warden is ultimately vindicated when Prewitt tries to rejoin Company G. After identifying Prewitt's body for the MPs, the top sergeant pronounces a valedictory on his dead comrade: " 'I think he was nuts. He loved the Army. Anybody who loves the Army is nuts. I think he was crazy enough to have made a good paratrooper, if he wasn't so small, or commando. He loved the Army the way most men love their wives. Anybody who loves the Army that much is nuts.' "[23] One needs only to compare this speech with the farewell address of General Douglas MacArthur (delivered before a joint session of Congress in the same year—1951) to see how Jones' characters embody values at odds with those officially sanctioned by American society. While " 'old soldiers never die... they simply fade away' " has become a rhetorical staple in American history, the more contemporary disdain of all military sentiments is also missing from the sergeant's speech. Warden does not hate the Army, for to do so would be to deny himself; rather, his emotional ambivalence bespeaks the sophistication of his character and the tragic sense of *From Here to Eternity*.

There are obviously two armies in the novel: one which contains Prewitt all the time and Warden most of the time, and the other which is the bailiwick of Holmes, other officers and their sycophants. The mentality of the second group is epitomized when Holmes, who fails to see that Prewitt's refusal to box is genuine, orders the protagonist to walk several punishment tours because he is convinced straight duty will change any soldier's mind.

> "Oh by the way, how is this new man Prewitt making out with straight duty now?"

"Doing fine. That boy is a good soldier."

"I know he is," Holmes said. "Thats what I'm counting on. I never saw a good soldier who liked to do straight duty as a private. I'm expecting to see him out for Company smokers this summer."[24]

Holmes underestimates Prewitt and the attractions of straight duty because he belongs to the officer class and sees the Army as a career leading to prestige and status rather than a calling in which to find himself. As Chief Choate, an indian sergeant and one of the Company's leading "jocks," tells Prewitt, the Army belongs to the false soldiers like Holmes: " 'A man knows where he belongs is lucky way I see it... Warden's a good man, but he just don't belong in the Army. Pete Karelsen's a good man, but he don't belong in the Army neither. Dynamite belongs in the Army.' "[25] Appropriately, Pete Karelsen, an aging non-com, must resign before December 7 because of pressure from the brass whose solicitude creates yet another symbol of society's wastefulness. If Karelsen's dismissal is a vicious irony, the honorific title ("Dynamite") the men have bestowed on Holmes mocks his stationary nature. In either event, Holmes continues up the corporate ladder with even greater prospects in store once the war has begun, while capable men like Karelsen are shunted aside.

Prewitt describes the real army as the embodiment of history, an endless shifting of power in which ruling classes create crises that are rectified by the sacrifices of anonymous (good) men.

The clerks, the kings, the thinkers; they talked, and with their talking ran the world. The truckdrivers, the pyramid builders, the straight duty men; the ones who could not talk, they built the world out of their very tonguelessness—so the talkers could talk about how to run it, and the ones who built it. And when they had destroyed it with their talking the truckdriver and the straight duty man would build it up again, simply because they were hunting for some way to speak.[26]

Such a view of history echoes that of Tolstoy in *War and Peace* for, just as Pierre had to learn the life of a peasant could be as important as that of a Napoleon, so Prewitt believes in the importance of humble men. The real army includes those men who perform its work (even the menial aspects of straight duty) rather than those who talk about getting things done. It is only fitting that Prewitt should find the real Army most abundantly represented in the stockade; for the incorrigible prisoners, those who refuse to surrender to sadists like Judson, and who acquire extra time as a result, are the elite corps which Prewitt comes to equate with real soldiers. Only in Stockade Number Ten does Prewitt feel he has finally become a real soldier, a member of a group whose sense of duty outweighs any commitment to merely "getting along." Perhaps the ultimate irony is that the "establishment" would be saved by the very elements it oppresses, a process that is dramatically symbolized by Prewitt's death and Holmes' promotion and return to the United States.

Love and war are equated throughout *From Here to Eternity* not only in obvious metaphoric comparisons between physical intimacy and combat but in its presentation of relationships between men and women as permanently strained. Even in the best circumstances, men and women bring different aims into love so that individuals are generically conditioned to maintain roles at the expense of each other's desires. Prewitt emphasizes the loneliness human beings experience in love when he says goodbye to Violet. Later, in the stockade, Prewitt worries about Lorene's remaining faithful: because he has asked Warden to explain to the girl about his being imprisoned, the distraught protagonist contemplates the top sergeant taking advantage of the situation. Prewitt jealously reflects that women are susceptible to male importunings about loneliness—it is their nature to want to assuage such sentiments.

> He remembered how easily she had sucked in his loneliness spiel. The fact that his had been true did not make any difference. They were all true. Nobody ever lied about being lonely. But they were all lies too, he knew from himself, because as soon as you started to talk to a woman about your loneliness you werent alone any more, you were like the playwright believing in the hero of his own play, the novelist trying to live his own novels. As soon as you saw the audience was affected you knew you had something to gain and you started to act, to make the truth more convincing. And then the truth wasnt there any more, it got lost in the shuffle.[27]

To the tender-minded such a passage will represent the most unsettling insight in Jones' novel; for, while Prewitt's reflection may be dismissed as the overdrawn sentiment of a slightly maladjusted individual, the impossibility of communicating in love looms as a more haunting possibility. To a culture which was (and still is) devoted to romantic love as an emotional and individual panacea, Prewitt's thoughts resemble day-old beer; indeed, everything that has been lauded by novelists as diverse as Frances Parkinson Keyes and Grace Metalious about the wonders of romantic intimacy comes under a cloud here. There can be no salvation in love and marriage if the individual must play a role because his very means of expression (words and personality) preclude his retaining any individual identity in such a relationship.

The love between Milt Warden and Karen Holmes enables them to transcend, if only for a time, the social and generic barriers between men and women. While the earlier scenes between them develop central themes through sexual action, it is the later moments in their relationship which reveal the quality of their feelings. The ambivalent nature of their love is briefly described when, in a meeting that has been arranged with great difficulty, the lovers urge:

> "I've never been so miserable in my life as I have since I met you," Warden said.
> "Neither have I," Karen said.
> "I wouldn't trade a minute of it," Warden said.
> "Neither would I," Karen said.[28]

Jones' older couple represents another bitter irony for, as Karen makes abundantly clear, they have come together because of love—an emotion she believes conventional America distrusts as a diversion from proper goals. According to Karen, American husbands cannot understand being deserted for love, and American wives, who have acquiesced to their spouses' materialism, recognize they have sold out but despise those females who cling to romantic idealism. Jones thus implies that traditional American beliefs in romantic marriage represent desperate concealments of personal despair. In *From Here to Eternity* true love only comes to those who are honest enough or naive enough to experience it, and it only lasts for a short time since people's basic drives (even good people's) are incompatible. Both Warden and Karen have a need to be individuals and so their love affair founders when an adjustment to reality—the possibility of their marrying—comes into view. While Karen presses Warden to become an officer, her real wishes are better served when the top sergeant decides not to sacrifice for her. Jones' characters illustrate the paradox that genuine feeling precludes wanting to change the other party (an insight which often escapes more decorous writers whose heroines frequently prattle about having to train a husband after marrying him). Karen loves Warden for what he is, so that her disappointment at his refusal is tempered.

> "I couldnt help it. I couldnt do anything else. I tried, but I couldnt."
>
> "I know you couldnt," she said soothingly.
>
> "And you knew all the time," he said inexpressively, "even when I called you."
>
> "I've known a lot longer than that. I think I've known for a long time. Only I just wouldnt let myself admit it. I think thats maybe why I love you, because I knew all along you couldnt."
>
> "Maybe we love only the things we cannot have. Maybe thats all love is."[29]

In becoming an officer, Warden would cease to be Warden and Karen would lose the man she loves. Thus, Jones conveys the emotional ambiguity of love—its volatile combination of hate, jealousy and affection—while implying that tranquility probably lies in never being granted one's deepest wishes. Since Warden knows all choices exact a cost, he is not surprised by the emotional devastation which accompanies his losing Karen Holmes. During their last evening together, despite refusing to have sexual relations with Karen, in her embrace Warden arrives at the most emotionally satisfying moment in his life. The mystery of love has been most nearly approached in 1950s' best-selling fiction by Jones' couple for it is only with them that a reader feels any genuine sense of passionate intimacy.

On the surface Lorene suggests a recurrent American male daydream— the hooker with the heart of gold—and when Prewitt becomes her lover and, later, when she shields him from the MPs, Lorene fulfills that role. Her actions imply the right man has finally come along and saved her from a life of degradation; unfortunately, despite her feelings for Prewitt (which constitute a mental monogamy), Lorene continues working at Mrs. Kipfer's brothel. Prewitt's initial jealousy (at one point he even nags one of her customers) gradually eases so that he becomes reconciled to her occupation while staying at Lorene's home. During his time in hiding, Prewitt comes to regard the girl as a mother figure rather than a lover; indeed, his professional conscience subconsciously nags him so that Lorene fades because of being in conflict with his commitment to the Army. The prostitute's values are, ultimately, far too conventional for Prewitt ever to live happily with her. Jones uses one of their early meetings to establish the temperamental similarity between soldiers and hookers.

"And lots who re-enlist," Prew said. "Lots who end up thirty year men."

"Not necessarily. There are some, but not nearly as many as you think. Lots of them, like me, figure it all out beforehand. Get in one hitch and clean up and then get out. Lots of them do that."

"Is that what you aim to do?"

"You dont think I mean to do this all my life? For fun? In another year I'll be back home, with a pile of bills big enough to choke a steer. And then I will be all set, for life."[30]

Lorene's essential naivete, that being financially secure will insure happiness, clearly contradicts Prewitt's beliefs that "home" and "wealth" are dreams at best; and his gradual disengagement from her reiterates his disillusionment with bourgeois values. When Lorene insists she will go home to find the "proper" man with the position who will want to have "proper" children and make her happy, Prewitt can only wonder whether such a Mr. Right will ever love Lorene as he does. While hoping she can achieve all this, Jones' protagonist remains inwardly appalled by the girl's ordinary wishes. After trying to discover some sense of daring in Lorene and never succeeding, Prewitt, in a fit of frantic despair, buys a night with Georgette, Lorene's prostitute roommate, simply to prove his freedom from middle-class convention.

The final irony of their relationship emerges through a comparison of Prewitt's initial feelings for Lorene with the novel's concluding shipboard scene when the girl and Karen Holmes exchange brief remarks. In keeping with Warden's comment about wrong choices, Prewitt first sees Lorene as possessed of a great tranquility.

Suffering doesnt make whores beautiful, it makes them ugly. But thats because they do not understand the suffering. But she understands it. Such poised serenity as this, the poised serenity I've always hunted after for myself and never found, comes only from great wisdom, the wisdom of the understanding of suffering, the wisdom I've never been able to acquire, the wisdom that I need, that maybe all men need, he thought profoundly, and that you never guessed would turn up in a whorehouse.[31]

Unfortunately, Lorene only appears to embody such depths of understanding for her persistent emphases on acquiring wealth and going home clearly show she has sublimated and repressed her emotional life. Prewitt's equation of wisdom and suffering suggests that he sees life as a set of conditions the individual grapples with as best he can, while Lorene's bourgeois goals imply that she sees reality as a number of problems with natural solutions. The survival of Lorene and the destruction of Prewitt counterpoint the irony in the protagonist's initial correlation of beauty and suffering which underscores the familiar American trait of associating looks with profundity. Jones thus suggests that, unlike the movies, life often couples emotional shallowness with pretty faces and heroic courage with ungainly countenances.

Captain Holmes embodies the bureaucratic mentality which invents itself and then invests itself with importance. He consistently sublimates his personal wishes to his superiors' whims and sincerely believes that his intelligence keeps things going in Company G. Warden sees the entire officer class embodied in Holmes; indeed, the top sergeant realizes why he hates his commanding officer shortly after they discuss Prewitt's experience with straight duty.

> It was because he had always feared him, not him personally not his physique or mind, but what he stood for. Dynamite would make a good general someday, if he got the breaks. Good generals ran to a certain type, and Dynamite was it. Good generals had to have the type of mind that saw all men as masses. . .that could be added and subtracted and understood on paper.[32]

In his cold-bloodedness Holmes resembles Lorene, albeit, he lacks her romantic daydreams as humanizing traits. The Captain has imposed his middle-class values on his relationship with Karen, while the deterioration of their love is symbolically rendered by the ugly hysterectomy scars she carries, the results of a bout with venereal disease she contracted from her husband. While she blames him for her resultant sterility, Karen suffers more from Holmes' insistence on outward decorum and convention, values which trap her in a loveless marriage in which she goes through the motions for the children (in this case, a son who disconcertingly echoes his father's mentality at age ten). Holmes' dismay at discovering Karen's affair with Warden reveals the accuracy of his wife's earlier observation that the Captain always seeks to impose guilt feelings on her because status and security mean more to him than love.

> "Why do you think I've done all I have? All this," Holmes said contentedly. He spread his arms.
> "Done all what."
> "Why worked my ass off with this goddamned miserable boxing squad that I've hated. Brownnosed with Col Delbert and Gen Slater. Degraded myself. Had my nose rubbed in it."
> "I dont know. Why."
> "Why; for you, that's why. Because you're my wife, and I love you. For you and our son and our home, thats why."
> "I always thought you did it because you wanted to get ahead," Karen said.[33]

Since he believes he has sacrificed himself to provide middle-class stability, Holmes demands loyalty from Karen because he has played society's game by society's rules and expects her to follow them as well. Ironically, Holmes argues that society would crumble if all women acted as Karen has, a further paradox since the reader has already seen Holmes in less savory circumstances.

As an officer Holmes represents a bureaucratized elite which makes lots of noise about theories but becomes useless in a crisis. It is typical that, on the morning of December 7, an anonymous colonel orders a bugler to play throughout the raid; and, when the beleaguered Warden questions this man, the classic reply of "only following orders" is invoked. Holmes also represents a philosophy of history directly opposed to that of Prewitt. General Sam Slater impresses the necessity for a ruling elite on the sycophantic Holmes at a stag party. Slater insists society has arrived at a time when repression in the form of a master class that keeps the neurotic masses under control is essential. Clearly, this character speaks for totalitarianism, a system naturally suspicious of individualism like that of Prewitt and Warden. In discussing John Dillinger, who served in Hawaii and was incarcerated in the same stockade in which Prewitt ends up, Slater insists that any man can be broken. Dillinger's subsequent resolution to get even with the United States is dismissed when General Slater declares that the criminal's death demonstrates his thesis. While death hardly seems a very useful way to control people (one is reminded of Tacitus' admonition about the Romans making a "desert and calling it peace"), Slater emphasizes that individualism must be suppressed: " 'But the important thing is they did kill him, like they always kill them. The only thing wrong with Dillinger was he was an individualist, and you can't understand that,... But thats why they had to kill him. Crime never pays, see?' "[34] Obviously, individualism is a crime society must never allow and, in keeping with this view, Slater, who has tempted Holmes with the prospect of a staff appointment, insists that the Captain must exact obedience from Prewitt as a precondition to any promotion.

Prewitt's time in the stockade firms up the humanistic values he had intuitively followed until then because he meets Jack Malloy, the spokesman for the hardened convicts who reside in Stockade Number Ten. The older man, who has joined the Army after being a labor agitator, preaches non-violence and has even convinced Angelo Maggio, Prewitt's best friend in Company G, of the value of that doctrine. When Maggio finally persuades the authorities that he is mentally disturbed (only after several beatings from Fatso Judson), Prewitt is drawn even closer to Jack Malloy. The older man insists that each man has a right to commit suicide: " 'In our world, citizens... theres only one way a man can have freedom, and that is to die for it, and after he's died for it it dont do him any good. Thats the whole problem, citizens. In a nutshell.' "[35] Malloy thus articulates the code of freedom and irrationality which Jones' principal characters have acted upon subconsciously; and, in dismissing the traditional middle-class connection of freedom with responsibility, the veteran convict emphasizes that freedom is a state of mind whose dictates prevent individuals from surrendering to any abstract social entity. Unlike Holmes who sacrifices his identity to gain status, the free man wants to find out who and what he is; or, to adopt terminology that accords more readily with the 1950s, the free man is "inner directed" while the conventional man is "outer directed." [36] At a time when conformity was viewed unfavorably, Jones' characters transcend the often superficial and bourgeois preoccupation with adaptation. Far from asking whether or not the individual must conform, Prewitt and Malloy do not even consider such a question. Malloy, rather, reinforces Warden's insight about life's consisting of inevitably wrong choices when he urges that what he learned as a socialist was that social action was self-defeating. Not only did propaganda fail to better the workers' lot but the very assumption of goals led to defeat, because: " 'In the end, the end will not only justify the means, it will not even be achieved by them; you cant divide the mass by a common factor that will give you a norm to work by, because while it may be mathematically correct it is false when applied to the individual member.' "[37] Thus, Malloy rejects the totalitarian schemes of Fascism, Communism and General Slater; and his dismissal of all social science implies that those who would impose order on a phenomenon as irrational and free as man must be resisted. After the older convict finally escapes from Stockade Number Ten (a feat not even Dillinger achieved) Prewitt, because of his love for the Army, finds himself alone in a terrible dilemma. After being discharged from there, Jones' protagonist wreaks vengeance on Judson, even though in fleeing to Lorene he loses his reason for being. There is obviously no sanctuary for Prewitt for the girl's bungalow offers none of those restorative qualities which earlier heroes in American fiction found in the woods or on the range.

Prewitt's desire to kill Judson again displays the ex-bugler's inability to accommodate himself to the modern, corporate, "organizational" world. Prewitt remains temperamentally a man of an earlier time; indeed, in his emphasis on individual responsibility, he emerges as the tight-lipped man of action one inevitably associates with Gary Cooper in *High Noon* (which appeared initially in 1952 and was directed by Fred Zinneman who also did the 1953 film version of Jones' novel). When Prewitt discusses his desire for revenge with Malloy, the younger man shows that he cannot accept the passive resistance preached by the older man. Prewitt unlike Malloy, believes that no corporate means exist by which an individual like Judson can be brought up short; if anything, the officer class which represents society's wishes in the Army, uses the stockade Sergeant as its tool so that official channels have no interest in removing Judson. Malloy, despite being chagrined over the younger man's refusal to use passive resistance, makes the point that Prewitt is not simply attacking an isolated figure when he moves against Judson.

"Well, Fatso is as much a part of the Army you love as your 1st/Sgt, Warden, that you're always talking about. One as much as the other. Without the Fatsos you couldnt have the Wardens."

"Someday we will."

"No. You never will. Because when that day comes you wont have any Armies, and there will be no more Wardens. You cant have the Wardens without the Fatsos, either."

"You don't mind if I go on thinking we will?"

"No. You ought to think that. But what you want cant be achieved by killing off all the Fatsos. When you kill your enemy Fatso, you are killing your friend Warden."

"Maybe so. I still cant help what I got to do."[38]

Prewitt, like the veritable Western hero, must live with himself first so that Malloy's advice, while an accurate description of the bureaucratic realities of Army life, does not speak to the protagonist's sense of values. If anything, Malloy only represents another version of the argument that the system cannot be resisted, and Prewitt refuses to become so compromised or cynical that he must believe that. While continuously beset by doubts about his own view of reality, Prewitt clings to a faith that he has found subtlety and profundity within himself and can attribute it to others (even though he appreciates how difficult it is to get through to them); thus, to accept Malloy's vision of the Army would be to abandon this fondest hope. While he can accept his ill treatment in Company G, Prewitt remains convinced that being a real soldier demands conduct which most soldiers lack. Common sense quickly convinces us that Prewitt is naive in such beliefs (and characters like Fatso Judson and Ike Gavrilovitch confirm our suspicions); however, the protagonist's decision to resist demonstrates that to be human one must be capable of being foolish.

From Here to Eternity implies that society's laws and its professed desire for justice are often at odds. In a nation where lawyers have all but replaced ministers, one needs only to notice the ease with which Americans go to trial and the often ambiguous ethical nature of some American lawyers (e.g. the Watergate defendants) to see that justice is often buried by legal procedure. Jones' novel stresses the disparity which arises from rank and privilege, so that his outranked good soldiers must do the bidding of unjust superiors. As Chief Choate reminds Maggio, when the latter laments that he cannot stand seeing someone being abused: " 'You might as well get use to it.... You probably be seein it often before you die.' "[39] The legal mentality, which puts constant emphasis on form and process at the expense of results, emerges when Warden becomes enraged at the simple inefficiency it breeds. When he catches one of his orderlies reading a comic book, the top sergeant raises the paradox of law enforcement: " 'What're you reading?... The story of J. Edgar and Mel Purvis and the Stool Pigeon in Red? Dont tell me you want to grow up to be a G Man too? If the whole next generation becomes G Men who are they going to find to arrest?' "[40] Warden's dislike of constituted authority takes on a more urgent air when one recalls that Jones' novel appeared at a time when official "witch hunting" (in the form of Joseph McCarthy) was considered essential to the nation's best interests. Some of Warden's animus derives, of course, from his own hatred of compromise, a process which has brought him rank in a group that is at least as highly organized as the F.B.I.

The novel's concern with the theme of human waste, a motif that Alfred Kazin finds dominant,[41] is implicit in Jones' plot which shows incompetence consistently rewarded (Holmes) and efficiency merely holding its own (Warden) or being penalized (Prewitt). While Warden is tolerated because his efficiency is the minimum need to keep things running, the top sergeant rests uneasily with the power he has acquired by appearing to be outwardly loyal. It is, however, Warden's extension of the idea of inefficiency and waste not only to society but to the very biological foundation of life itself that gives Jones' top sergeant stature as a truly unsettling critic. Karen Holmes epitomizes the uneasiness which such a perception breeds in anyone capable of appreciating it; as a mother, and the wife of a rising career officer, she should be happy so that her doubts assail all the values traditionally imposed on women by American society.

> There must be more, there must be, something told her, someplace, somewhere, there must be another reason, above, beyond, somewhere another reason, above, beyond, somewhere another Equation beside this virgin, marriage, motherhood, grandmotherhood-honor, justification, death. There must be another language, forgotten unheard unspoken, than the owning of an American Homey Kitchen complete with dinette, breakfast nook, and fluorescent lighting.[42]

The idea of conspicuous consumption and Thoreau's adage about ordinary people leading "lives of quiet desperation" are at the depths of Karen's unease. Unlike such conventional heroines as those of Frances Parkinson Keyes, Karen Holmes feels that domesticity cannot constitute life's final goal; and while lacking any interest in religion, she implies that the integrity of an individual's soul clearly outweighs any socially-approved lifestyle. Her ennui leads her to Warden and the pain their unresolvable love affair brings on; yet, her discomfort and anguish constitute more and better human feelings than her dismay at the novel's beginning. In her affair with the top sergeant, Mrs. Holmes realizes that life has greater emotional possibilities than kitchen utensils, albeit, she must break with Warden to gain this insight—a bit of plotting that, again, sets off Jones' novel from others in this survey.

Sexual relations are treated openly in *From Here to Eternity*, although not as physically explicit as one finds in fiction after the Supreme Court's 1959 decision concerning the publication of the uncensored version of *Lady Chatterley's Lover*. If anything, physical intimacy, at least initially, is an overwhelmingly fleshy experience: copulation, rather than the loss of self in romantic illusion, comes first for Jones' characters. Warden and Prewitt seek out Karen and Lorene because of physical pressure and not for companionship; however, in yet another ironic reversal, their lust brings them to love. In the first, and most extended, seduction scene between Warden and Karen, the woman establishes herself as a personality rather than just a body. As Warden elaborates on his belief that there are no mortal sins, Karen interrupts to ask:

> "Then I take it you dont believe in sin at all?"
> ... Warden sighed. "I believe the only sin is a conscious waste of energy. I believe all conscious dishonesty, such as religion, politics and the real estate business, are a conscious waste of energy. I believe that at a remarkable cost in energy people agree to pretend to believe each other's lies so they can prove to themselves their own lies are the truth...."[43]

While we expect this from the top Sergeant, Karen's response elevates her from the level of melodramatic female so often encountered elsewhere. She does not turn mushy because Warden has been honest; instead, throughout this scene, Karen accepts his advances in a reluctant and bored fashion. She symbolically tears up the orders which Warden brought with him (as a possible cover) in a gesture which indicates she thinks of herself as a whore receiving payment.

Karen's chiding of Warden, in which she belittles his attempts to approach her intellectually or spiritually, only ceases after his comment about waste. She poses a conundrum after he has finished: " 'Well.... He's smart as well as virile. Lucky little female, to be allowed to enclose the erect pride of such virility. But since you believe the conscious waste of energy is a sin, dont you believe the loss of semen is a sin? unless accompanied by impregnation?' "[44] Warden fences with her objection as best he can, yet his remarks fail to obscure the seriousness of her question. Biology presents the spectacle of waste in the very creation of life, so how can the individual hope to oppose this primary condition of nature? Karen's remark underlines the absurdist quality of existence with which the principal characters in *From Here to Eternity* grapple; indeed, it is the quality of the characters' mental lives which separates Jones' novel from the rest of our list. In them we encounter figures whose thoughts resemble some of the discomforts real people feel; moreover, Jones' characters do not find the soothing solutions—either in marriage or career—that characters in other bestsellers do. Prewitt, Warden and Karen Holmes remain too honest and too human to accept any panaceas, and their nonconformity serves as the most thoughtful protest against the "problem solving" mentality illustrated so abundantly elsewhere in American life and fiction in the 1950s. Jones attains genuinely tragic dimensions with these figures who find themselves torn between life as they wish it would be and as it is. While it is easy to reduce *From Here to Eternity* to a tract in which an evil society persecutes a moral individual, closer scrutiny suggests that Jones' characters confront the dilemma that being ethical often places one in opposition to society rather than aligning one with it, as melodrama suggests.

The immediate popularity of Jones' novel seemingly derives from its open approach to sex and vulgarity. While Norman Mailer's soldiers had to coin a neologism ("fug") for their favorite four letter profanity in *The Naked and the Dead* in 1948, Jones' characters use "fuck" constantly and continuously. In the same vein, the novel is extremely realistic about physical passion, an activity constantly presented as a biological drive which centers in specific parts of the male and female anatomy. No exhilarating loss of self accompanies intercourse, so that, even though Jones observes contemporary standards of fictional decorum, his lovers emerge as lusty and satiated rather than as transformed. In its portrayal of this transient sexual atmosphere, the novel catches the tone of regular Army life with its rhythms of long stretches of routine duty interrupted by brief instances of intense pleasure (the work week and the Saturday night pass). When Warden and Karen make love for the first time the reader interested in prurience is offered Jones' most shocking (by 1951 standards) scene, one that startles even now, despite its implied notion that the top sergeant will somehow find his identity within the relationship. Once more, Karen Holmes supplies the difference for her candor and intelligence again surface, as does her reluctance to be emotionally caught by Warden. After she has stripped for him, she urges:

"There.... That is what you want. Thats what all the talk's about. Thats what all you virile men, you intellectual men, always want. Isnt it? You big strong male men who are so virile and intelligent, but who are as helpless as babies without a fragile female body to root around on."[45]

While many a later feminist might applaud such sentiments, Karen's challenge represents a lover's test rather than an anti-masculine tirade. Like Warden, Karen must find her way to genuine emotional union by overcoming the importance of the body. While she remains convinced that the physical unattractiveness of her hysterectomy renders her unworthy of love, as Warden embraces her, the dualism of romantic feelings (the combination of physical and mental attachment) begins to surface.

The juxtaposition of Karen's fears and Warden's lust gives the ensuing passage (for all its overwritten qualities) an honesty we have missed elsewhere.

Warden found himself staring at the twisted navel and the ridge of scar-tissue that ran down from it, disappearing in the hairy mattress, and that was so old now as to almost be a shadow.

"Pretty isn't it?" she said. "And its a symbol, too. A symbol of the waste of energy."

Warden set his glass down carefully. He moved toward her on the chair, seeing the nipples wrinkle tightly like flowers closed for the night, seeing the feminine grossness that he loved, that was always there, that he always knew was there, hidden maybe behind perfume, unmentioned, unacknowledged, even denied, but still always there, existing, the beautiful lovely grossness of the lioness and the honest bitch dog, that no matter how much, shrinking, they tried to say it wasnt so, in the end always had to be admitted.[46]

The top sergeant echoes the always popular notion that women are every bit as sexually preoccupied as men, an insight that is spelled out more overtly here than in the novels of Mickey Spillane where female sensuality was approached in a more psychologically protective fashion. Mike Hammer's confrontations with various femme fatales lead to his eventual extermination of these nymphomaniacal threats to his own male identity; Milt Warden, in responding to Karen's flawed physicality by falling in love with her, creates the depths of that emotion for both of them. While the skeptical reader can easily dismiss both Spillane's and Jones' openly sexual women as simply contrivances by which prurient interest are pandered to, the points of contrast between Mike Hammer and the bizarre villainnesses he encounters and the relationship of Warden and Karen clearly demonstrate the intellectual depths and the unsettling insights contained in *From Here to Eternity*.

While individuals ordinarily transform their pasts into memories which stress pleasant and exciting features, Jones' principal characters do not adopt this tactic. If anything, Prewitt's sense of the past embodies a running criticism of what he sees in the present. Jones' protagonist, in being critical of what he loves, discusses the merits and demerits of several Hollywood Western stars. The relationship between the early screen cowboys and the American frontier is dimly grasped by Prewitt, who argues more convincingly that the newcomers (in 1941) represent a degradation of an art form consistent with the end of a historical epoch. In dismissing Gene

Autry and Roy Rogers as dismaying imitations of earlier celluloid heroes, Prewitt urges:

> "All the regular cowboys got to be musicians now. . . . Musicians first and cowboys second. Because they're not Westerns anymore, they're Musicals," he said, suddenly surprisedly realizing that he had watched and been a part of a phase of America that was dying just as surely as the Plains Indian Wars that gave it birth had died. . . .[47]

Prewitt's temperament is symbolized through such a reflection for, unlike the bourgeois outlook which insists on progress, he perceives that change always embodies loss as well as gain. This sense of balance gives him a tragic dimension: even in the stockade's privations Prewitt never condemns entire groups or becomes close-minded. He even perceives that Jack Malloy's leadership implies a larger truth about American society: "We have become a nation of cop haters, he thought sadly, we have taken for our hero a Robin Hood myth that never existed except in our history books, and then only 500 years after, when it was safe to print it. It must be hard on a man, being a cop. I'm glad I'm not a cop."[48] Prewitt's subsequent decision about Judson is consistent with such a view for, while there are bad cops, no individual is compromised by being a cop. The character's refusal to adopt demagogic generalizations, whether those of Holmes or of Malloy, enables him to be the embodiment of a genuine individualism. Jones' sense of irony is once more apparent because, in a culture which pays lip service to individualism, his protagonist demonstrates the cost exacted when someone seriously follows it.

The novel ends on a sustained ironic note when, on board a ship to the mainland, Karen Holmes sees a beautiful ("Madonna-face") girl and speaks to her. After the pensive girl explains that her fiancée died on December 7 trying to taxi a plane to cover, Karen experiences a sense of uplift from these young lovers' sacrifice. Her exultation is shortlived however, for the girl then tells how her lover's posthumous Silver Star was sent to his mother and reveals:

> "They're very fine people," the girl smiled tremulously. "He comes from an old Virginia family, The Prewitts. They've lived there since before the Revolution. His great grandfather was a General under Lee in the Civil War. Thats who he was named after: Robert E. Lee Prewitt."
>
> "Who?" Karen said numbly.
>
> "Robert E. Lee Prewitt," the girl said tremulously on the verge of tears. "Isn't that a silly old name?"
>
> "No," Karen said. "I think its a fine name."
>
> "Oh, Bob," the girl said quiveringly out across the water. "Bob, Bob, Bob."
>
> "Now; now," Karen said, feeling all the grief that had been in her boiling over into a wild desire to laugh out loud. She put her arm around the girl. "Try to get hold of yourself."[49]

Karen knows the truth because of her relationship with Warden, and we share her desire to laugh; yet, the equivocal nature of Jones' ending, with its suggestions that middle-class pretense (Lorene has obviously adapted her experience with Prewitt to accord with such mores) and the austere honesty that the novel's outcasts embody (Karen has survived as a witness to the truth) seems thoroughly appropriate. Having worked so diligently to present the bewildering nature of human existence, Jones remains true to the tenor of *From Here to Eternity* by implying there can be no definitive resolution for his characters (or, by extension, for us). Karen Holmes does not laugh out loud because she understands that no individual is ever so secure as to be able to judge another's conduct. In the same way that Warden, after having separated from her, reflects that he will always love her and hurt because of what could not be, Karen realizes that integrity lies in continuing to choose badly because not to choose at all constitutes death.

From Here to Eternity
Maintaining individuality in an institutionalized world (Signet)

Chapter 14

Conclusion

Popular values, which often represent wish-fulfillments and daydreams as well as consciously held ideas, permeate the artistic media of any society. For the United States in the 1950s such widespread social and personal beliefs and ideals are clearly reflected by that period's bestselling novels. Indeed, given their sales success, such works are obviously "in tune" with many, if not all, of their contemporaries' underlying views of the world about them. Throughout our century the bulk of American bestselling fiction has reaffirmed the basically absolutist—morally black and white—views of the mass audience. In so doing, such fictions have underscored a dichotomy between the melodramatic and the tragic ways of perceiving existence which appears to be basic to American cultural and intellectual life.

Most bestsellers reaffirm the social and moral values found among their consumers. Such works serve as intellectual rituals by which the individual consciously or subconsciously reaffirms his ideas about himself, his society and the world. Thus, for the most part, such works are "necessary" because they create and sustain their audience's basic beliefs. Except for the rare instance (e.g. *From Here to Eternity*), such works do not directly or consistently challenge the underlying assumptions of their readers. They do, however, gradually alter these values by slowly changing the "rules" of the standard literary forms and situations they utilize. In the same way that genre films embody changing popular perceptions (the moralizing tone and posture of *The Public Enemy*, 1931, gives way to the cynicism of *The Godfather*, 1972-1974,) over time, so does bestselling fiction reflect and partially create its audience's value systems.

Within the bestselling fictions of the 1950s, the most striking contrast lies between the attitudes I have labelled melodrama and tragedy, and which are most overtly embodied by Mickey Spillane and James Jones, respectively. The political jingoism and sexual chauvinism of Mike Hammer are thrown into the sharpest relief by the actions and attitudes of Prewitt, Warden and Karen Holmes. The certain choices of conduct made by Spillane's protagonist, who is driven by a psychic need for vengeance, throw the muddled and perplexing choices which face Jones' cast, who struggle with finding their identities, into the highest contrast.

This same assurance/questioning pattern, which might be thought of in 1950s' terms as "conformity" versus "non-conformity," is repeated in various ways in the chapters of this study. Thus, the self-confident world of *Battle Cry* is offset by the more melancholy tone of *The Revolt of Mamie Stover*; the patriotic idealism of *The Bridges at Toko-ri* is contrasted by the comic exaggerations and excesses of *The Manchurian Candidate*; and the idealism about society found in *Exodus* gives way to the extreme individualism and irony of *The Damned*.

While this same kind of design, moving from most certain to most questioning in the treatment of individual novels, has guided the organization of each separate chapter, chapters 6 and 7 illustrate an additional, larger contrast. The sexual mores embodied by the characters of Grace Metalious and Frances Parkinson Keyes dramatically point up this difference. The overtly physical and ultimately testing sexual and romantic world of *Peyton Place* reflects an ethos where popular male psychology seems dominant. The openly sentimental and finally emotionally-fulfilling world of *Joy Street* reflects an ethos where popular female psychology seems dominant. The disparate sexual "philosophies" in these works do not, however, challenge the 1950s' basic adherence to family life (chapter 8), as best seen, again, in Frances Parkinson Keyes (*Steamboat Gothic*).

Chapters 9 through 11 illustrate more problematic popular concerns and more widely divergent views between novelists. In effect, these difficulties—juvenile delinquency, psychology, Blacks—are either exorcised or brooded upon. The actions of Danny Fisher ultimately reassured the 1950s more than did the sarcasms of Holden Caulfield, while the logically inconsistent kind of psychotherapy found in *The Royal Box* probably soothed more readers than did the perplexities of *Compulsion*. The quality of difference between the opposing visions is nowhere more pronounced than in *Mandingo* and *Invisible Man*, for the racial stereotypes of the former seem ludicrous and vicious when compared to the anguish found in Ellison's nameless protagonist. The difficulties of personal and career adjustment, an implicit motif in the novels of chapters 9 through 11, are treated more elaborately in chapter 12. Hopefully, one finds a calling either within oneself (*The Cardinal*) or through experience (*The Blackboard Jungle*); however, Tom Rath's moderation in *The Man in the Gray Flannel Suit* represents an ideal middle-class compromise between the demands of job and family.

It would, of course, be convenient to insist that popular American thinking in the 1950s was simply dichotomous (or, to be more catchy, "schizophrenic"). Alas, such an argument would be as overdrawn as seeing the decade as a time of either extreme suspicion (with Senator McCarthy as the prime symbolic figure) or unbridled euphoria (with television's Ozzie and Harriet as an appropriate iconographic pair). If we would arrive at more rounded interpretations or explanations of the cultural life of this period, we must avoid looking only at those works which later generations have sanctified as "classics." Because public libraries, for reasons partly economic and partly social, often do not contain the most immediately influential of printed materials, we frequently practice an unwitting critical myopia when treating the literary/social scene of the past.

In this light it is finally useful to remember that, in 1952, Mickey Spillane's *Kiss Me, Deadly* had, if not a greater, at least as great an immediate popular effect as did Ernest Hemingway's *The Old Man and the Sea*. While many would simply dismiss such a fact as yet another lamentable testimony to the lack of popular taste in America, a better understanding of the literary and social landscape can only emerge when such "aesthetic" evaluations are set aside. Just as the best critical reading of a literary work is one that explains and illuminates the greatest number of individual details within that work, the most insightful historical/ literary thesis about a particular period will be one that incorporates as many individual works and levels of excellence as possible.

932

Mickey Spillane

The Long Wait

The New Thriller by the author of THE BIG KILL

A SIGNET BOOK
Complete and Unabridged

The Long Wait
Truth through punishment (Signet)

Notes

Chapter 1: Introduction.

[1]See Appendix I: The Bestsellers (pp. 391-393). Titles 1-37 in that list are arranged in order of total sales.

[2]Appendix I, Nos. 38, 39, 45, 47, 48 and 49.

[3]Appendix I, Nos. 40, 43 and 44.

[4]Appendix I, Nos. 41 and 46.

[5]Appendix I, Nos. 42 and 50.

Chapter 2: "Why couldn't they act like men and fight with me."

[1]Quoted in Christine Nasso, ed., *Contemporary Authors*, Volumes 25-28 (First Revision), (Detroit: Gale Research Company, 1974), p. 684.

[2]Gore Vidal, *Matters of Fact and Fiction* (New York: Random House, 1977), p. 5.

[3]Stuart M. Kaminsky, *American Film Genres: Approaches to a Critical Theory of Popular Film* (New York: Dell Publishing Co., Inc., 1977 (1974)), p. 72.

[4]Mickey Spillane, *My Gun is Quick* (New York: E. P. Dutton & Co., Inc., 1950), p. 143. (Hereafter MG)

[5]MG, p. 5.

[6]MG, p. 5.

[7]MG, p. 20.

[8]Mickey Spillane, *The Long Wait* (New York: E.P. Dutton & Co., Inc. 1951), p. 51. (Hereafter LW)

[9]Mickey Spillane, *Kiss Me, Deadly* (New York: E.P. Dutton & Co., Inc., 1952), p. 154 (Hereafter KMD)

[10]MG, p. 92.

[11]KMD, p. 94.

[12]Mickey Spillane, *The Big Kill* (New York: E.P. Dutton & Co., Inc., 1951), p. 78. (Hereafter BK)

[13]MG, p. 9.

[14]KMD, p. 36.

[15]KMD, p. 38.

[16]Mickey Spillane, *One Lonely Night* (New York: E.P. Dutton & Co., Inc. 1951), p. 29. (Hereafter OLN)

[17]BK, p. 61.

[18]KMD, p. 33.

[19]Mickey Spillane, *Vengeance Is Mine* (New York: E.P. Dutton & Co., Inc., 1950), pp. 117-118. (Hereafter VIM)

[20]OLN, 24.

[21]KMD, 68.

[22]OLN, 34-35.

[23]OLN, 35.

[24]OLN, 38.

[25]OLN, 171-172.

[26]LW, 71-72.

[27]LW, 46.

[28]VIM, 169.

[29]KMD, 169.

[30]OLN, 166.

[31]OLN, 176.

[32]BK, 175.

[33]MG, 170.

[34]MG, 171.

[35]KMD, 176.

[36]KMD, 46.

[37]OLN, 157.

[38]BK, 6.

[39]OLN, 139.

[40]BK, 143.

[41]KMD, 148.

[42]Quoted in Charles Higham, *The Art of the American Film* (Garden City: Anchor Books, 1974), p. 223.

[43]VIM, 131.

[44]VIM, 172.

[45]OLN, 160.

[46]BK, 41-42.

[47]BK, 161.

[48]OLN, 16.

[49]LW, 40.

[50]BK, 154.

[51]MG, 84.

[52]Russell Nye, *The Unembarrassed Muse: The Popular Arts in America* (New York: The Dial Press, 1970), p. 42.

[53]LW, 100.

[54]KMD, 30.

[55]VIM, 18.

[56]KMD, 21.

[57]BK, 49.

[58]BK, 73.

[59]VIM, 32.

[60]OLN, 15.

[61]MG, 85.

[62]MG, 146.

[63]OLN, 90.

[64]VIM, 41.

[65]LW, 113.

[66]OLN, 164-165.

Chapter 3: "I can't leave my outfit."

[1]Leon Uris, *Battle Cry* (New York: G. P. Putnam's Sons, 1953), pp. 120-121.

[2]254.   [3]434.   [4]490.[5]72.   [6]19-20.   [7]503.   [8]272.   [9]26.   [10]93.   [11]341.   [12]399.

[13]Howard Koch, *Casblanca: Script and Legend* (Woodstock, N.Y.: The Overlook Press, 1973), p. 175.

[14]475. [15]446. [16]351. [17]114. [18]144-145. [19]380. [20]485.

[21]Herman Wouk, *The Caine Mutiny* (Garden City: Doubleday & Company, Inc., 1951), p. 223.

[22]60. [23]115. [24]477. [25]364. [26]317. [27]192-193. [28]379. [29]498. [30]109. [31]243. [32]463. [33]102-103. [34]127. [35]129. [36]193. [37]164. [38]217. [39]437-438. [40]90. [41]97. [42]457. [43]354. [44]357-358. [45]447. [46]387. [47]388.

[48]William Bradford Huie, *The Revolt of Mamie Stover* (New York: Signet Books, 1951), p. 5 .

[49]136-137. [50]6 [51]75-76 [52]109 [53]18 [54]105 [55]113 [56]23 [57]126 [58] 110 [59]111 [60]119 [61]144.

Chapter 4: "Perhaps we'd stabilize at the Mississippi?"

[1]William Manchester, *The Glory and the Dream* (Boston: Little, Brown & Company, 1973, 1974), pp. 561-565.

[2]James Michener, *The Bridges at Toko-ri* (New York: Random House, 1953), p. 127.

[3]36. [4]42. [5]99. [6]146-147. [7]39-40. [8]57. [9]63-64. [10]83-84 [11]145-146. [12]93. [13]142. [14]43-44.

[15]Eugene Lederer and Eugene Burdick, *The Ugly American* (New York: W. W. Norton & Company, Inc., 1958) p. 24.

[16]145. [17]39. [18]261. [19]82.

[20]The best discussion of these bright young men can, of course, be found in David Halberstam, *The Best and the Brightest* (New York: Random House, 1972).

[21]73. [22]149. [23]224. [24]238.

[25]Allen Drury, *Advise and Consent* (Garden City: Doubleday & Company, Inc., 1959) p. 17.

[26]641. [27]770. [28]30. [29]411. [30]577. [31]36. [32]483. [33]63. [34]384. [35]166. [36]161. [37]249. [38]193. [39]439. [40]283. [41]331. [42]390. [43]426. [44]454-455. [45]122. [46]210.

[47]Particularly enlightening here is David Halberstam, *The Powers That Be* (New York: Alfred A. Knopf, 1979), especially those sections which deal with the Los Angeles *Times'* treatment of congressional candidate Richard Nixon in 1946.

[48]503. [49]462. [50]267. [51]594. [52]615.

[53]Richard Condon, *The Manchurian Candidate* (New York: New American Library, 1959), p. 158.

[54]51. [55]63. [56]65. [57]11. [58]256. [59]213. [60]71. [61]351. [62]MC, 190. [63]224. [64]171. [65]290. [66]95. [67]247. [68]306. [69]344-345. [70]303. [71]212. [72]161. [73]77. [74]9. [75]145. [76]252. [77]269.

Chapter 5: "The on-going thing that she had started.........was now more powerful than she."

[1]Leon Uris, *Exodus* (New York: Bantam Books, 1959), p. 33.

[2]114-115. [3]328. [4]253. [5]275. [6]571. [7]572. [8]315. [9]554. [10]341. [11]597. [12]184. [13]45. [14]35. [15]394-395. [16]444. [17]579. [18]589. [19]599.

[20]James Michener, *Hawaii* (New York: Bantam Books, 1961), p. 653.

[21]John Steinbeck, *East of Eden* (New York: Bantam Books, 1955), pp. 150-151.

[22]Michener, p. 745.

[23]899. [24]789. [25]810. [26]4. [27]14. [28]65. [29]313. [30]105. [31]784. [32]900. [33]503. [34]152. [35]209. [36]327. [37]379. [38]406

[39]Hamilton Basso, *The View from Pompey's Head* (New York: Popular Library, 1964), p. 85.

[40]11. [41]250-251. [42]38-39. [43]78. [44]157. [45]15. [46]271-272. [47]384. [48]184. [49]290. [50]324. [51]236.

[52]332. [53]355

[54]Max Shulman, *Rally Round the Flag, Boys!* (New York: Bantam Books, 1958), pp. 20-21.

[55]129. [56]30. [57]35. [58]3-4. [59]204. [60]226. [61]46. [62]8-59. [63]67-68. [64]114.

[65]Mac Hyman, *No Time for Sergeants* (New York: New American Library, 1956), p. 73.

[66]93. [67]95. [68]98

[69]John D. MacDonald, *The Damned* (New York: Fawcett Gold Medal Books, 1952), pp. 160-161.

[70]122. [71]24. [72]82. [73]20. [74]152-153. [75]78. [76]121. [77]124. [78]91. [79]15. [80]113. [81]142. [82]259. [83]69. [84]123.

Chapter 6: "He felt her body arch crazily against him and saw red lights behind his eyes."

[1]Thirty-five of the novels have scenes describing intercourse; Drury (homosexuality), Robinson (illegitimacy), Traver (rape), March (lechery), Shulman (seduction) and Dennis (burlesque) utilize sexual elements in their plots; Keyes (in *Joy Street*), Wilson, L'Amour, Stone and Michener (in the *Bridges at Toko-ri*) feature domestic relations prominently enough so that sex is constantly, if decorously, implied in their narratives; only Lederer and Burdick, Hyman and Gann fail to center some major portion of their plots on human sexuality.

[2]Harold Robbins, *Never Leave Me* (New York: Avon Books, 1954), p. 6.

[3]193. [4]217. [5]58. [6]74. [7]26. [8]8. [9]6-7. [10]47. [11]210. [12]110. [13]111. [14]172. [15]9. [16]202. [17]31. [18]199.

[19]Charles Mergendahl, *The Bramble Bush* (New York: Bantam Books, 1959), p. 269.

[20]284 [21]26. [22]160-161 [23]300-301. [24]35. [25]210-211. [26]212-213. [27]181. [28]273. [29]47-48. [30]89. [31]111 [32]136. [33]310. [34]459. [35]67. [36]279. [37]305.

[38]Frank Yerby, *Floodtide* (New York: Dell-Publishing Company, 1967), p. 23.

[39]108. [40]303-304. [41]129. [42]55. [43]59. [44]243. [45]266. [46]314. [47]91. [48]219. [49]163. [50]171. [51]263. [52]194. [53]262.

[54]Kinsey interviewed a thousand couples in which the wife remained virginal a year after marriage because of ignorance about the reproductive process.

[55]Nathaniel Cooper, a liberal member of the Board of Trustees for the town of Cooper Station in *The Tight White Collar* (1960), Metalious' third novel, hopes that a new Board member will allow the town library to have something more daring in it than "the limp mutterings of Frances Parkinson Keyes."

[56]Grace Metalious, *The Tight White Collar* (New York: Pocket Books, 1960), p. 92.

[57]Grace Metalious, *Peyton Place* (New York: Dell Publishing, Inc., 1957). p. 53. (Hereafter PP.)

[58]Tight, 11.

[59]Grace Metalious, *Return to Peyton Place* (New York: Dell Publishing Co., Inc., 1960), p. 103. (Hereafter Return).

[60]Return, 99. [61]193. [62]255.

[63]PP, 378.

[64]Return, 63. [65]67.

[66]PP, 287. [67]142. [68]302-303. [69]238-239.

[70]Return, 25

[71]PP, 29. [72]210-211. [73]383-384. [74]385.

[75]Return, 121. [76]132. [77]153. [78]218. [79]243.

[80]PP, 91. [81]427-428. [82]85. [83]503.

[84]Return, 14. [85]162

Chapter 7: "But you care in another way and it's a good way."

[1]Frances Parkinson Keyes, *Joy Street* (New York: Pocket Books, 1974) p. 221.
[2]351. [3]363. [4]578. [5]160-161. [6]595. [7]60. [8]621

[9]John Cawelti, *Adventure, Mystery and Romance: Formula Stories as Art and Popular Culture* (Chicago: The University of Chicago Press, 1976), pp. 44-45.

[10]Frances Parkinson Keyes, *Steamboat Gothic* (New York: Pocket Books, 1974), p. 186.

[11]544. [12]685-686. [13]257. [14]298. [15]403. [16]216. [17]446. [18]23. [19]321. [20]307. [21]65. [22]66. [23]190. [24]347. [25]641. [26]720.

[27]Irving Stone, *Love is Eternal* (New York: New American Library, 1969), p. 29.

[28]434-435. [29]487. [30]20. [31]345. [32]114-115. [33]405. [34]55. [35]68. [36]183. [37]392-393. [38]478. [39]25. [40]267. [41]244-245. [42]257. [43]429. [44]499. [45]502. [46]505.

[47]Anya Seton, *The Winthrop Woman* (New York: Fawcett Crest Books, 1958), p. 134.

[48]199. [49]593. [50]46. [51]108. [52]396. [53]635. [54]137. [55]512. [56]534. [57]635. [58]297. [59]604. [60]279. [61]219. [62]610

[63]Rona Jaffe, *The Best of Everything* (New York: Avon Books, 1976), pp. 48-49.

[64]253. [65]190. [66]279. [67]222. [68]51. [69]413. [70]371-372. [71]401. [72]419. [73]60. [74]131. [75]11. [76]59-60. [77]101. [78]105. [79]368. [80]117.[81]418. [82]279.

Chapter 8: "A man without a woman, without a home, and without a child was not a man at all."

[1]Louis L'Amour, *Hondo* (New York: Fawcett Publications, Inc., 1953), p. 65.
[2]87. [3]113. [4]166. [5]69. [6]116-117. [7]117. [8]157. [9]121. [10]122. [11]16. [12]137. [13]25. [14]39. [15]41. [16]122

[17]John Steinbeck, *East of Eden* (New York: Bantam Books, 1955), p. 36.
[18]21. [19]86. [20]108. [21]142-143. [22]30. [23]367. [24]355. [25]598. [26]190. [27]414. [28]567. [29]212. [30]151. [31]151. [32]475. [33]477.

[34]James Gould Cozzens, *By Love Possessed* (Greenwich: Fawcett Crest Books, 1957), p. 305.
[35]7. [36]14. [37]544. [38]10. [39]82. [40]143. [41]430. [42]126. [43]396. [44]398. [45]256. [46]13. [47]216. [48]528. [49]524. [50]537-538

[51]John O'Hara, *Ten North Frederick* (New York: Bantam Books, 1957), p. 408.
[52]230. [53]246. [54]345-346. [55]105. [56]54. [57]74. [58]110-111. [59]76-77. [60]229-270. [61]119 [62]278. [63]162-163. [64]44. [65]164-165. [66]27. [67]220. [68]358. [69]385. [70]387. [71]385. [72]393.

[73]Jack Kerouac, *On the Road* (New York: New American Library, 1958), p. 244.
[74]119. [75]130. [76]31. [77]122. [78]224. [79]228. [80]54. [81]173. [82]201. [83]48. [84]48. [85]48-49. [86]200. [87]8. [88]106. [89]10. [90]148-149.[91]253-254.

Chapter 9:"When in *Hell* are you going to grow up?"

[1]Harold Robbins, *79 Park Avenue* (New York: Pocket Books, 1956), p. 129.
[2]130. [3]223. [4]254. [5]275-276. [6]16. [7]32. [8]98. [9]165. [10]205. [11]69-70. [12]70. [13]115. [14]76. [15]217. [16]219. [17]273.
[18]Harold Robbins, *A Stone for Danny Fisher* (New York: Pocket Books, 1953), p. 106.
[19]276. [20]200. [21]347. [22]23. [23]53. [24]85. [25]86. [26]189. [27]227. [28]232. [29]291-292. [30]304. [31]329. [32]411. [33]415. [34]430-431
[35]Patrick Dennis, *Around the World with Auntie Mame* (New York: New American Library, 1959), p. 19.
[36]10. [37]777. [38]27-28. [39]124. [40]46. [41]53. [42]102-103. [43]204.
[44]J. D. Salinger, *The Catcher in the Rye* (New York: Bantam Books, 1964), p. 146.
[45]149. [46]172. [47]133. [48]53. [49]105. [50]84. [51]126. [52]45. [53]104. [54]86. [55]164. [56]116. [57]140. [58]39. [59]173. [60]201. [61]74. [62]93. [63]66. [64]169. [65]202. [66]211.

Chapter 10: "If you stop and think about it, it scares you."

[1]Frances Parkinson Keyes, *The Royal Box* (New York: Fawcett Crest Books, 1952), p. 234.
[2]107. [3]17. [4]51. [5]39. [6]56. [7]168. [8]47. [9]239. [10]300. [11]50. [12]93. [13]19. [14]70. [15]190. [16]190. [17]162. [18]176. [19]204. [20]21. [21]179. [22]115. [23]214.
[24]William March, *The Bad Seed* (New York: Dell Publishing Co., Inc., 1972), p. 6.
[25]33. [26]27. [27]201. [28]127. [29]117. [30]88. [31]20. [32]36. [33]129. [34]121-122. [35]165.
[36]Meyer Levin, *Compulsion* (New York: Pocket Books, 1958), p. 3.
[37]139. [38]481. [39]165. [40]200. [41]357. [42]31. [43]263. [44]363. [45]241. [46]317-318. [47]772. [48]320. [49]344. [50]272. [51]409. [52]403. [53]388. [54]389. [55]326. [56]413. [57]485-486.

Chapter 11: "Well, that's him."

[1]Kyle Onstott, *Mandingo* (Greenwich: Fawcett Publications, Inc., 1958), p. 16.
[2]276. [3]143. [4]372. [5]48. [6]125. [7]585. [8]52. [9]569. [10]229. [11]581. [12]168. [13]632. [14]628. [15]260. [16]54. [17]728. [18]537. [19]603. [20]152. [21]479. [22]636. [23]440. [24]634. [25]635. [26]639. [27]476.
[28]Ralph Ellison, *Invisible Man* (New York: New American Library, 1952), p. 7.
[29]8. [30]242. [31]19-20. [32]22. [33]34. [34]127. [35]129. [36]190. [37]372-373. [38]432. [39]448-449. [40]430.

Chapter 12: "There's nothing else on earth I want to be."

[1]Henry Morton Robinson, *The Cardinal* (New York: Pocket Books, Inc., 1952), p. 53.
[2]9. [3]204. [4]217. [5]630-631. [6]321. [7]414. [8]433-434.
[9]Morton Thompson, *Not as a Stranger* (New York: New American Library, 1956), p. 69.
[10]50. [11]112. [12]447. [13]216. [14]790. [15]428. [16]451. [17]562. [18]497. [19]776. [20]522. [21]179. [22]285-286. [23]633. [24]531. [25]700. [26]789. [27]587-588.
[28]Ernest Gann, *The High and the Mighty* (New York: Bantam Books, 1968), p. 19.
[29]44-45. [30]101. [31]193. [32]266. [33]9. [34]144. [35]246. [36]146. [37]198. [38]225. [39]106. [40]253. [41]205. [42]152. [43]247-248.
[44]Evan Hunter, *The Blackboard Jungle* (New York: Dell Publishing Co., Inc., 1966), p. 18.

[45]221. [46]139. [47]25. [48]185. [49]105. [50]194-195. [51]264-265. [52]144. [53]141. [54]217. [55]319. [56]116. [57]180. [58]66-67

[59]Robert Traver, *Anatomy of a Murder* (New York: Dell Publishing Co., Inc., 1959), p. 294

[60]237-238. [61]395. [62]511. [63]77. [64]474. [65]371. [66]505.

[67]Sloan Wilson, *The Man in the Gray Flannel Suit* (New York: Arbor House, 1983), p. 227.

[68]251. [69]272. [70]276. [71]3. [72]63-64. [73]64. [74]107. [75]38. [76]147. [77]112-113. [78]207-208. [79]252. [80]22. [81]77. [82]173. [83]224. [84]186.

Chapter 13: "Everybody decides for themself...and always wrong."

[1]James Jones, *From Here to Eternity* (New York: Avon Books, 1975), p. 23.

[2]701. [3]97. [4]349. [5]701. [6]395. [7]267. [8]14. [9]27. [10]96. [11]206. [12]180. [13]189. [14]375. [15]9. [16]743-744. [17]287. [18]529. [19]594. [20]672. [21]107. [22]461. [23]768. [24]104. [25]480-481. [26]130. [27]502. [28]593. [29]785. [30]250. [31]225. [32]105. [33]793. [34]336. [35]561.

[36]David Riesman, Nathan Glazer and Reuel Denney, *The Lonely Crowd* (Garden City: Doubleday & Company, Inc., 1950), pp. 17-53; 133-188.

[37]Jones, 614.

[38]630. [39]257. [40]495.

[41]Alfred Kazin, *Bright Book of Life: American Novelists and Storytellers from Hemingway to Mailer* (Boston: Little, Brown and Company, 1973), pp. 77-81.

[42]Jones, 69. [43]117-118. [44]118. [45]118. [46]118-119. [47]194. [48]521. [49]815.

Appendix I:
The Bestsellers

The following list includes original publishing information for each of the fifty novels in this study as well as authors' birthdates and death dates (where applicable). Titles 1-37 are listed according to sales figures provided in Alice Hackett Payne's *80 Years of Bestsellers, 1895-1975*, while titles 38-50 are listed in a random fashion. This list is meant to be used in conjunction with the text of Chapter One.

1. Grace Metalious (1924-1964), *Peyton Place* (New York: Julian Messner, Inc., 1956).
2. J. D. Salinger (1919-   ), *The Catcher in the Rye* (Boston: Little, Brown and Company, Inc., 1951).
3. Mickey Spillane (1917-   ), *The Big Kill* (New York: E.P. Dutton & Company, Inc., 1951).
4. Leon Uris (1924-   ), *Exodus* (New York: Doubleday & Company, Inc., 1958),
5. Mickey Spillane (1917-   ), *My Gun is Quick* (New York: E.P. Dutton & Company, Inc. 1950).
6. Mickey Spillane (1917-   ), *One Lonely Night* (New York: E.P. Dutton & Company, Inc. 1951).
7. Mickey Spillane (1917-   ), *The Long Wait* (New York: E.P. Dutton & Company, 1951).
8. Mickey Spillane (1917-   ), *Vengence is Mine* (New York: E.P. Dutton & Company, 1950).
9. Mickey Spillane (1917-   ), *Kiss Me, Deadly* (New York: E.P. Dutton & Company, 1952).
10. Kyle Onstott (1887-   ), *Mandingo* (New York: William Denlinger, 1958).
11. William Lederer (1912-   ) and Eugene Burdick (1922-1965), *The Ugly American* (New York: W.W. Norton & Company, Inc., 1958).
12. Grace Metalious (1924-1964), *Return to Peyton Place* (New York: Julian Messner, Inc., 1959).
13. Harold Robbins (1912-   ), *79 Park Avenue* (New York: Alfred A. Knopf, 1955).
14. Anya Seton (1916-   ), *The Winthrop Woman* (Boston: Houghton Mifflin Company, 1958).
15. James Michener (1906-   ), *Hawaii* (New York: Random House Inc., 1959).
16. James Jones (1921-1978), *From Here to Eternity* (New York: Charles Scribner's Sons, 1951).
17. Harold Robbins (1912-   ), *A Stone for Danny Fisher* (New York: Alfred A. Knopf, 1952).
18. Francis Parkinson Keyes (1885-1970), *The Royal Box* (New York: Julian Messner, Inc. 1954).
19. Robert Traver [John D. Voelker] (1903-   ), *Anatomy of a Murder* (New York: St. Martin's Press, 1958).
20. Henry Morton Robinson (1898-1961), *The Cardinal* (New York: Simon and Schuster, 1950).

21. Harold Robbins (1912-   ), *Never Leave Me* (New York: Alfred A. Knopf, 1954).
22. Rona Jaffe (1932-   ), *The Best of Everything* (New York: Simon and Schuster, 1958).
23. Patrick Dennis (1925-   ), *Around the World with Auntie Mame* (New York: Harcourt, Brace and Company, Inc., 1958).
24. Morton Thompson (?-1954), *Not as a Stranger* (New York: Charles Scribner's Sons, 1954).
25. Leon Uris (1924-   ), *Battle Cry* (New York: G.P. Putnam's Sons, 1953).
26. Allen Drury (1917-   ), *Advise and Consent* (New York: Doubleday & Company, Inc., 1959).
27. Mac Hyman (1923-1963), *No Time for Sergeants* (New York: Random House, Inc., 1956).
28. John D. MacDonald (1916-1986), *The Damned* (New York: Fawcett Gold Medal Books, 1952).
29. William Bradford Huie (1910-1986), *The Revolt of Mamie Stover* (New York: Duell, Sloan and Pearce., 1951).
30. Max Shulman (1919-   ), *Rally Round the Flag, Boys!* (New York: Doubleday & Company, Inc. 1957).
31. Herman Wouk (1915-   ), *The Caine Mutiny* (New York: Doubleday & Company, 1951).
32. Charles Mergendahl (1919-   ), *The Bramble Bush* (New York: G.P. Putnam's Sons, 1958).
33. Frances Parkinson Keyes (1885-1970), *Joy Street* (New York: Julian Messner, Inc., 1950).
34. Frances Parkinson Keyes (1885-1970), *Steamboat Gothic* (New York: Julian Messner, 1952).
35. Irving Stone (1903-   ), *Love is Eternal* (New York: Doubleday & Company, Inc., 1954).
36. Frank Yerby (1916-   ), *Floodtide* (New York: The Dial Press, 1950).
37. Hamilton Basso (1904-1964), *The View From Pompey's Head* (New York: Doubleday & Company, Inc., 1954).
38. James Gould Cozzens (1903-1978), *By Love Possessed* (New York: Harcourt Brace and World, 1957).
39. Sloan Wilson (1920-   ), *The Man in the Gray Flannel Suit* (New York: Simon and Schuster, 1955).
40. Louis L'Amour (1908-   ), *Hondo* (New York: Fawcett Publications, Inc., 1953).
41. Richard Condon (1915-   ), *The Manchurian Candidate* (New York: McGraw-Hill Book Company, 1959).
42. Ralph Ellison (1913-   ), *Invisible Man* (New York: Random House, Inc., 1952).
43. Ernest Gann (1910-   ), *The High and the Mighty* (New York: William Morrow and Company., 1953).
44. Evan Hunter (1922-   ), *The Blackboard Jungle* (New York: Simon and Schuster, 1954).
45. John Steinbeck (1902-1968) *East of Eden* (New York: The Viking Press, Inc., 1952).
46. William March (1893-1954), *The Bad Seed* (New York: Holt, Rinehard and Winston, Inc., 1954).
47. John O'Hara (1905-1970), *Ten North Frederick* (New York: Random House, Inc., 1955).
48. Meyer Levin (1905-1981), *Compulsion* (New York: Simon and Schuster, 1956).
49. James Michener (1906-   ), *The Bridges at Toko-ri* (New York: Random House, Inc., 1953).

50. Jack Kerouac (1922-1969), *On the Road* (New York: The Viking Press, Inc., 1957).

Appendix II:
Bibliography of Secondary Sources

The following list presents a selective group of secondary sources on the history and arts of the 1950s. Serious students will, of course, consult the more extensive bibliographies in Goldman, Manchester, Parmet and others.

1. Brode, Douglas. *The Films of the Fifties*. Secaucus: The Citadel Press, 1976.
2. Cawelti, John G. *Adventure, Mystery, and Romance: Formula Stories as Art and Popular Culture*. Chicago: The University of Chicago Press, 1976.
3. Chapelle, Steve and Reebee Garofalo. *Rock 'n Roll Is Here to Pay: The History and Politics of the Music Industry*. Chicago: Nelson-Hall, 1977.
4. Davis, Kenneth C. *Two Bit Culture: The Paperbacking of America*. Boston: Houghton Mifflin Company, 1984.
5. Dowdy, Andrew. *The Films of the Fifties: The American State of Mind*. New York: William Morrow and Company, 1973.
6. Fiedler, Leslie. *Waiting for the End*. New York: Stein & Day, 1964.
7. Hackett, Alice Payne and James Henry Burke. *80 Years of Bestsellers, 1895-1975*. New York: R. R. Bowker, 1977.
8. Halberstam, David. *The Best and the Brightest*. New York: Random House, 1972.
9. Halberstam, David. *The Powers That Be*. New York: Alfred A. Knopf, 1979.
10. Hart, James D. *The Popular Book: A History of American's Literary Taste*. New York: Oxford University Press, 1950.
11. Hart, Jeffrey. *When the Going was Good!: American Life in the Fifties*. New York: Crown Publishers, Inc., 1982.
12. Hassan, Ihab. *Radical Innocence: Studies in the Contemporary American Novel*. New York: Harper & Row Publishers, 1961.
13. Higham, Charles. *The Art of American Film*. Garden City: Anchor Press, 1973.
14. Hofstadter, Richard. *Anti-Intellectualism in American Life*. New York: Vintage, 1963.
15. Jahn, Mike. *Rock from Elvis Presley to the Rolling Stones*. New York: Quadrangle, 1973.
16. Kaminsky, Stuart. *American Film Genres*. New York: CEBCO/Standard Publishing, 1974.
17. Karl, Frederick R. *American Fictions 1940-1980*. New York: Harper & Row, Publishers, 1983.
18. Kazin, Alfred. *Bright Book of Life: American Novelists and Storytellers from Hemingway to Mailer*. Boston: Little, Brown and Company, 1973.
19. Koch, Howard. *Casablanca: Script and Legend*. Woodstock, New York: The Overlook Press, 1973.
20. Lloyd, Ann, ed. *Movies of the Fifties*. London: Orbis Publishing, 1982.
21. Manchester, William, *The Glory and the Dream: A Narrative History of America, 1932-1972*. Boston: Little, Brown and Company, 1974.
22. Miller, Douglas T. & Marion Nowak. *The Fifties The Way We Really Were*. Garden City: Doubleday & Company, Inc., 1977.

23. Mott, Frank Luther. *Golden Multitudes: The Story of Best Sellers in the United States.* New York: The Macmillan Company, 1947.

24. Nye, Russell. *The Unembarrassed Muse: The Popular Arts in America,*New York: The Dial Press, 1970.

25. Parmet, Herbert. *Eisenhower and the American Crusades.* New York: The Macmillan Company, 1972.

26. Riesman, David. *The Lonely Crowd.* New Haven: Yale University Press, 1950.

27. Schreuders, Piet. *Paperbacks, U. S. A.: A Graphic History*, trans. Josh Pachter. San Diego: Blue Dolphin Enterprises, Inc., 1981.

28. Stone, I. F. *The Haunted Fifties.* New York: Random House, 1963.

29. Stone, I. F. *The Truman Era.* New York: Random House, 1953.

30. Time-Life, Editors of *This Fabulous Century: Volume VI: 1950-1960.* New York: Time-Life Books, 1970.

31. Time-Life, Editors of, *Time Capsule/1950.* New York: Time Incorporated, 1967.

32. Time-Life, Editors of, *Time Capsule/1959.* New York: Time-Life Incorporated, 1968.

33. Vidal, Gore. *Matters of Fact and Fiction: Essays 1973-1976.* New York: Random House, 1977.

34. Warshow, Robert. *The Immediate Experience: Movies, Comics, Theatre & Other Aspects of Popular Culture.* Garden City: Doubleday & Company, Inc., 1952.

35. Whyte, William H., Jr. *The Organization Man.* New York: Anchor Books, 1956.

36. Wood, Michael. *America in the Movies or "Santa Maria, It Had Slipped My Mind."* New York: Basic Books, 1975.

Appendix III:
A Chronology of Other Notable American Novels from the 1950s

This selective list presents the more notable novels from 1950-1959 which are not treated in the text. As such, it does not pretend to be an exhaustive compilation; indeed, many notable genre writers with numerous productions to their credit during the 1950s have been omitted for reasons of space. Among these writers are: detective and mystery writers such as Rex Stout, Ellery Queen and Erle Stanley Gardner; Western novelists like Luke Short and Louis L'Amour; science fiction authors like Isaac Asimov and Robert Heinlein; and such prolific writers as Pearl S. Buck, Frank G. Slaughter and, of course, John D. MacDonald (who published thirty titles during the decade).

1950:

Gwen Bristow, *Jubilee Trail*
Erskine Caldwell, *A Swell Looking Girl*
Ernest Hemingway, *Across the River and into the Trees*
John Hersey, *The Wall*
Jack Kerouac, *The Town and the City*
Sinclair Lewis, *World So Wide*
Ross MacDonald, *The Drowning Pool*

Conrad Richter, *The Town*
Budd Schulberg, *The Disenchanted*
Max Shulman, *Sleep Till Noon*
Gore Vidal, *A Search for the King*
Robert Penn Warren, *World Enough and Time*
Tennessee Williams, *The Roman Spring of Mrs. Stone*
Kathlyn Winsor, *Star Money*

1951:

William Barrett, *The Left Hand of God*
John Dos Passos, *Chosen Country*
Howard Fast, *Spartacus*
William Faulkner, *Requiem for a Nun*
Mary McCarthy, *The Groves of Academe*
Norman Mailer, *The Barbary Shore*
John P. Marquand, *Melville Goodwin USA*
Edison Marshall, *The Viking*
Willard Motley, *We Fished All Night*
William O'Connor, *The Oracle*
John O'Hara, *The Farmer's Hotel*
Irwin Shaw, *The Troubled Air*
Vern Sneider, *The Teahouse of the August Moon*
Cardinal Spellman, *The Foundling*
Irving Stone, *The President's Lady*
William Styron, *Lie Down in Darkness*
Agnes Sligh Turnbull, *Gown of Glory*
Frank Yerby, *A Woman Called Fancy*

1952:

Louis Auchincloss, *Sybil*
John Dos Passos, *District of Columbia*
Edna Ferber, *Giant*
Cameron Hawley, *Executive Suite*
Ernest Hemingway, *The Old Man and the Sea*
Tom Lea, *The Wonderful Country*
Bernard Malamud, *The Natural*
Frank O'Connor, *Wise Blood*
William Styron, *The Long March*
Gore Vidal, *The Judgment of Paris*
Kurt Vonnegut, *Player Piano*
Philip Wylie, *The Disappearance*
Frank Yerby, *The Saracen Blade*

1953:

Saul Bellow, *The Adventures of Augie March*
Niven Busch, *The Hate Merchant*
Raymond Chandler, *The Long Goodbye*
Davis Grubb, *The Night of the Hunter*
Mark Harris, *The Southpaw*

Ira Levin, *A Kiss before Dying*
Tom Wicker, *The Kingpin*
Ben Ames Williams, *The Unconquered*
Richard Wright, *The Outsider*

1954:

Vance Bourjaily, *The Hound of Earth*
Taylor Caldwell, *Never Victorious, Never Defeated*
John Dos Passos, *Most Likely to Succeed*
William Faulkner, *A Fable*
Ernest Gann, *Soldier of Fortune*
Michael Hayes, *The Desperate Hours*
Randall Jarrel, *Pictures from an Institution*
Alan Lemay, *The Searchers*
William McGivern, *Rogue Cop*
James Michener, *Sayonara*
William Shirer, *Stranger Come Home*
John Steinbeck, *Sweet Thursday*
Gore Vidal, *Messiah*
Philip Wylie, *Tomorrow*

1955:

Erskine Caldwell, *Gretta*
Patrick Dennis, *Auntie Mame*
William Gaddis, *The Recognitions*
Davis Grubb, *A Dream of Kings*
Cameron Hawley, *Cash McCall*
William Heath, *Violent Saturday*
MacKinley Kantor, *Andersonville*
Mary McCarthy, *A Charmed Life*
Norman Mailer, *The Deer Park*
John P. Marquand, *Sincerely, Willis Wade*
Kenneth Roberts, *Boon Island*
Robert Ruark, *Something of Value*
Leon Uris, *The Angry Hills*
Robert Penn Warren, *Band of Angels*
Herman Wouk, *Marjorie Morningstar*

1956:

Nelson Algren, *A Walk on the Wild Side*
James Baldwin, *Giovanni's Room*
     Go Tell it on the Mountain
John Barth, *The Floating Opera*
Saul Bellow, *Seize the Day*
William Brinkley, *Don't Go Near the Water*
Eugene Burdick, *The Ninth Wave*
Peter DeVries, *Comfort Me with Apples*
Ernest Gann, *Twilight for the Gods*
Mark Harris, *Bang the Drum Slowly*

John Hersey, *A Single Pebble*
William O'Connor, *The Last Hurrah*
John O'Hara, *A Family Party*
Robert Powell, *The Philadelphian*
Theodore White, *The Mountain Road*

1957:

James Agee, *A Death in the Family*
John Cheever, *The Wapshot Chronicle*
William Faulkner, *The Town*
Gerald Green, *The Last Angry Man*
James Jones, *Some Came Running*
Frances Parkinson Keyes, *Blue Camellia*
Alan Lemay, *The Unforgiven*
Bernard Malamud, *The Assistant*
John P. Marquand, *Stopover Tokyo*
Richard Mason, *The World of Susie Wong*
Wright Morris, *Love Among the Cannibals*
Ayn Rand, *Atlas Shrugged*
Conrad Richter, *The Lady*
John Steinbeck, *The Short Reign of Pippin IV*
Jerome Weidman, *The Enemy Camp*

1958:

Louis Auchincloss, *Venus in Sparta*
John Barth, *The End of the Road*
Vance Bourjaily, *The Violated*
Raymond Chandler, *Playback*
Edna Ferber, *Ice Palace*
Ernest Gann, *The Trouble with Lazy Ethel*
Francis Gwallney, *The Violaters*
William Humphreys, *Home from the Hill*
Evan Hunter, *Strangers When We Meet*
James Jones, *The Pistol*
Jack Kerouac, *The Dharma Bums*
      The Subterraneans
Frances Parkinson Keyes, *Victorine*
Helen MacInness, *North from Rome*
John P. Marquand, *Women and Thomas Harrow*
Willard Motley, *Let No Man Write My Epitaph*
John O'Hara, *From the Terrace*
Glendon Swarthout, *They Came to Cordura*
Robert Traver, *Small Town D.A.*
John Updike, *The Poorhouse Fair*
Sloan Wilson, *A Summer Place*

1959:

Hamilton Basso, *The Light Infantry Ball*
Saul Bellow, *Henderson the Rain King*

Robert Bloch, *Psycho*
Niven Busch, *California Street*
Taylor Caldwell, *Dear and Glorious Physician*
John Farris, *Harrison High*
William Faulkner, *The Mansion*
Gerald Frank, *Alas, Babylon*
Paul Gallico, *Mrs. Arris Goes to Paris*
Gerald Green, *The Lotus Easters*
Arthur Hailey, *The Final Disaster*
John Hersey, *The War Lover*
William Bradford Huie, *The Americanization of Emily*
John Knowles, *A Separate Peace*
Bernard Malamud, *The Magic Barrel*
Leo Rosten, *The Return of H*Y*M*A*N*K*A*P*L*A*N*
Robert Ruark, *Poor No More*
Max Shulman, *I Was a Teenage Dwarf*
Dariel Telfer, *The Caretakers*
Kurt Vonnegut, *The Sirens of Titan*

Appendix IV:
The Movie Versions of the Novels

The following list presents the studios, years of release, directors, screenwriters and performers of those roles mentioned most prominently in the discussions of the novels in this study for the film versions that emerged or were based on these works. It is, perhaps, worth noting the release dates of these productions for the time lag between their appearance in print and on celluloid represents a significant measure of what Hollywood considered would be accepted by its supposedly more conservative audiences. While a two to three years lapse would represent the normal average, in some cases (e.g. *Peyton Place*) that interval was shorter while in others (e.g. *Mandingo*) it was considerably longer.

A more detailed study of these particular films would reveal the kinds of changes that at least two of the cinema versions, those of *The Best of Everything* and *From Here to Eternity*, demonstrate. Not only does the first film version omit the seamier sexual aspects of Jaffe's novel but it "tacks on" a decidedly upbeat ending in which the heroine (Caroline Bender) literally walks off into the sunset with the reformed editor (Mike Rice). Jones' story is streamlined by omitting many of the novel's characters and telescoping others into single figures (the movie's Maggio dies while the novel's Maggio is dishonorably discharged) and miscasting others (the conspicuously middle-aged Philip Ober as Captain Holmes) to simplify the conflicts of the original material.

1. *Advise and Consent*
Columbia (1962)
Otto Preminger
Wendell Mayes
Charles Laughton (Seab Cooley), Don Murray (Brigham Anderson), Walter Pidgeon

(Bob Munson), Franchot Tone (The President), Henry Fonda (Leffingwell), Lew Ayres (Arly Richardson), Burgess Meredith (Herbert Gelman), George Grizzard (Fred Van Ackerman)

2. *Anatomy of a Murder*
Columbia (1959)
Otto Preminger
Wendell Mayes
James Stewart (Paul Biegler), Ben Gazzara (Lieutenant Manion), Lee Remick (Laura Manion), Arthur O'Connell (Parnell), George C. Scott (Claude Dancer), Kathryn Grant (Mary Pilant)

3. *The Bad Seed*
Warner Brothers (1956)
Mervin LeRoy
John Lee Mahin
Nancy Kelly (Christine Penmark), Patty McCormack (Rhoda Penmark), Henry Jones (Leroy), Evelyn Jarden (Monica Breedlove)

4. *Battle Cry*
Warner Brothers (1955)
Raoul Walsh
Leon Uris
Van Heflin (Major Huxley), Aldo Ray (Andy), Mona Freeman (Kathy), Nancy Olson (Pat), James Whitemore (Mac), Tab Hunter (Danny)

5. *The Best of Everything*
Twentieth-Century Fox (1959)
Jean Negulesco
Edith Sommers & Mann Rubin
Joan Crawford (Amanda Farrow), Hope Lange (Caroline Bender), Stephen Boyd (Mike Rice), Suzy Parker (Gregg Adams), Louis Jourdan (David Wilder Savage), Diane Baker (April Morrison), Robert Evans (Dexter)

6. *The Blackboard Jungle*
Meto-Goldwyn-Mayer (1955)
Richard Brooks
Richard Brooks
Glenn Ford (Richard Dadier), Anne Francis (Anne Dadier), Maggie Hayes (Lois Hammond), Richard Kiley (Josh Edwards), John Hoyt (Mr. Small), Sidney Poitier (Gregory Miller), Vic Morrow (Artie West)

7. *The Bramble Bush*
Warner Brothers (1960)
Daniel Petrie
Michael Sperling & Philip Yordan
Richard Burton (Guy Montford), Barbara Rush (Margreth McFie), Tom Drake (Larry McFie), Jack Carson (Bert Mosley), Angie Dickinson (Fran Walker)

8. *The Bridges at Toko-Ri*
Paramount (1953)

Mark Robson
Valentine Davies
William Holden (Brubaker), Grace Kelley (Nancy Brubaker), Fredrich March (Admiral Tarrant), Mickey Rooney (Mike Forney), Earl Holliman (Nestor Gammidge), Charles McGraw (Cag).

9. *By Love Possessed*
United Artists (1961)
John Sturges
John Dennis
Lana Turner (Marjorie Penrose), Efrem Zimbalist, Jr. (Arthur Winner), Jason Robards, Jr. (Julian Penrose), Barbara Bel Geddes (Clarissa), Thomas Mitchell (Noah Tuttle), Susan Kohner (Helen Detweiler)

10. *The Caine Mutiny*
Columbia (1954)
Edward Dmytrk
Stanley Roberts
Humphrey Bogart (Captain Queeq), Jose Ferrer (Barney Greenwald), Van Johnson (Merrick), Fred MacMurray (Tom Keefer), Robert Francis (Willie Keith), May Wynn (May Wynn), Tom Tully (Captain DeVriess)

11. *The Cardinal*
United Artists (1963)
Otto Preminger
Robert Dozier
Tom Tryon (Stephen Fermoyle), Carol Lynley (Mona Fermoyle), John Huston (Cardinal Glennon), Burgess Meredith (Ned Halley), Romy Schneider (Countess Falerni)

12. *Compulsion*
Twentieth-Century Fox
Richard Fleischer
Richard Murphy
Orson Welles (Jonathan Wilk), Bradford Dillman (Artie Strauss), Dean Stockwell (Judd Steiner), Martin Milner (Sid), Diane Varsi (Ruth)

13. *East of Eden*
Warner Brothers (1955)
Elia Kazan
Paul Osborn
James Dean (Cal Trask), Julie Harris (Abra), Raymond Massey (Adam Trask), Jo Van Fleet (Cathy Ames), Richard Davalos (Aaron Trask)

14. *Exodus*
United Artists
Otto Preminger
Dalton Trumbo
Paul Newman (Ari Ben Canaan), Eva Marie Saint (Kitty Fremont), Lee J. Cobb (Barak Ben Canaan), Ralph Richardson (Bruce Sutherland), Sal Mineo (Dov Landau), Jill Haworth (Karen).

15. *From Here to Eternity*
Columbia (1953)
Fred Zinneman
Daniel Taradash
Burt Lancaster (Sergeant Warden), Montgomery Clift (Prewitt), Deborah Kerr (Karen Holmes), Frank Sinatra (Maggio), Donna Reed (Lorene), Philip Ober (Captain Holmes), Ernest Borgnine (Fatso Judson)

16. *Hawaii*
United Artists (1966)
George Roy Hill
Daniel Taradash & Dalton Trumbo
Max Von Sydow (Abner Hale), Julie Andrews (Jerusha Hale), Richard Harris (Rafer Hoxworth)

17. *The High and the Mighty*
Warner Brothers (1954)
William Wellman
Ernest Gann
John Wayne (Dan Roman), Robert Stack (Captain Sullivan), Wally Brown (Leonard), William Campbell (Hobie Wheeler), Doe Avedon (Spalding), Laraine Day (Lyia Rice), John Howard (Howard Rice), Robert Newton (Gustave Pardee), David Brian (Ken Childs), Sidney Blackmer (Humphrey Agnew), Phil Harris (Mr. Joseph)

18. *Hondo*
Warner Brothers (1955)
John Farrow
James Edward Grant
John Wayne (Hondo Lane), Geraldine Page (Angie Lowe), Lee Aaker (Johnny Lowe), Leo Gordon (Ed Lowe), Ward Bond (Buffalo), Michael Pate (Vittorio) Rodolfo Acosta (Silva)

19. *King Creole* (Based on *A Stone for Danny Fisher*)
Paramount (1958)
Michael Curtiz
Herbert Baker & Michael V. Gazzo
Elvis Presley (Danny Fisher), Dolores Hart (Nellie Fisher), Dean Jagger (Mr. Fisher)

20. *Kiss Me, Deadly*
United Artists (1954)
Robert Aldrich
A.I. Bezzerides
Ralph Meeker (Mike Hammer)

21. *The Long Wait*
United Artists (1954)
Victor Saville
Alan Green & Lesser Samuels
Anthony Quinn (Johnny McBride)

22. *The Man in the Gray Flannel Suit*
Twentieth-Century Fox (1956)

Nunally Johnson
Nunally Johnson
Gregory Peck (Tom Rath), Jennifer Jones (Betsy Rath), Frederich March (Hopkins), Lee J. Cobb (Bernstein)

23. *The Manchurian Candidate*
United Artists (1962)
John Frankenheimer
George Axelrod
Frank Sinatra (Ben Marco), Laurence Harvey (Raymond Shaw), Janet Leigh (Rosie), Angela Lansbury (Mrs. Iselin), James Gregory (John Iselin), Knigh Dhiegh (Yen Lo)

24. *Mandingo*
Paramount (1975)
Richard Fleischer
Norman Wexler
James Mason (Maxwell), Susan George (Blanche), Perry King (Hammond Maxwell), Ken Norton (Mede)

25. *My Gun is Quick*
United Artists (1957)
George White & Phil Herbert
Richard Collins & Richard Powell
Robert Bray (Mike Hammer)

26. *No Time for Sergeants*
Warner Brothers
Mervin LeRoy
John Lee Mahin
Andy Griffith (Will Stockdale), Murray Hamilton (Irvin), Nick Adams (Ben), Myron McCormick (Sergeant King), Don Knotts (Tester)

27. *Not as a Stranger*
United Artists (1955)
Stanley Kramer
Edward and Edna Anhalt
Olivia De Havilland (Kristina), Robert Mitchum (Lucas Marsh), Frank Sinatra (Alfred), Gloria Grahame (Harriet Lang), Charles Bickford (Dr. Runkelman), Myron McCormick (Dr. Snider)

28. *Peyton Place*
Twentieth-Century Fox (1957)
Mark Robson
John Michael Hayes
Lana Turner (Constance Mackenzie), Hope Lange (Selena Cross), Lee Philips (Michael Rossi), Diane Varsi (Allison Mackenzie), Russ Tamblyn (Norman Page), David Nelson (Ted Carter), Leon Ames (Leslie Harrington)

29. *Rally Round the Flag, Boys!*
Twentieth-Century Fox (1958)
Leo McCarey

Leo McCarey
Claude Binyon & Leo McCarey
Paul Newman (Harry Bannerman), Joanne Woodward (Grace Bannerman), Joan Collins (Angela Wexler), Jack Carson (Oscar Wexler), Tuesday Weld (Comfort Goodpasture)

30. *Return to Peyton Place*
Twentieth-Century Fox (1961)
Jose Ferrer
Ronald Alexander
Carol Lynley (Allison Mackenzie), Jeff Chandler (Lewis Jackman), Eleanor Parker (Constance Mackenzie)

31. *The Revolt of Mamie Stover*
Twentieth-Century Fox
Raoul Walsh
Sidney Boehm
Jane Russell (Mamie Stover), Richard Egan (Jim, the Narrator), Joan Leslie (Annalee)

32. *Ten North Frederick*
Twentieth-Century Fox (1958)
Philip Dunne
Philip Dunne
Gary Cooper (Joe Chapin), Geraldine Fitzgerald (Edith Chapin), Diane Varsi (Ann Chapin), Suzy Parker (Kate Drummond)

33. *The Ugly American*
Universal International (1963)
George England
Steward Stern
Marlon Brando, (Gilbert MacWhite), Eiji Okada (Deong), Pat Hingle (Homer Atkins)

34. *The View from Pompey's Head*
Twentieth-Century Fox (1955)
Philip Dunne
Philip Dunne
Richard Egan (Anson Page), Dana Wynter (Dinah Blackford), Cameron Mitchell (Micah Blackford), Sidney Blackmer (Garvin Wales)

Index

References for the fifty novels treated in the text can be found under author's name.